CLUB I   wiley.com/college/turban

www.wiley.com/college/turban Club IT, is a simulated downtown music venue which presents live shows and DJs. Look for the Club IT box at the end of each chapter for more information on the assignments. Students are "hired" as consultants for the club and asked to work on such projects as:

- **Data Management:** Helping the Club IT owners manage inventory by tracking food and beverages on spreadsheets.

- **Data Mining:** Mining web resources to predict music/nightclub trends.

- **Wireless:** Advertising through mobile devices; SMS-ing at Club IT; streaming DJ's shows onto the internet.

- **E-commerce:** Making epayments to beverage suppliers; selling tickets to shows online.

- **Ethics:** Making sure DJs pay royalties on music that is played in the club; discussing the ethics of profiling customers to get marketing information.

INTRODUCTION TO INFORMATION TECHNOLOGY

Third Edition

EFRAIM TURBAN
University of Hawaii at Manoa

R. KELLY RAINER, JR.
Auburn University

RICHARD E. POTTER
University of Illinois, Chicago

JOHN WILEY & SONS, INC.

PROJECT EDITOR	Lorraina Raccuia
MEDIA EDITOR	Allison Keim
ACQUISITIONS EDITOR	Beth Lang Golub
DEVELOPMENT EDITOR	Ann Torbert
EDITORIAL ASSISTANT	Ame Esterline
MARKETING MANAGER	David Woodbury
SENIOR PRODUCTION EDITOR	Norine M. Pigliucci
COVER DESIGN	Harry Nolan
ILLUSTRATION EDITOR	Anna Melhorn
PHOTO EDITOR	Lisa Gee
PRODUCTION MANAGEMENT SERVICES	Suzanne Ingrao/Ingrao Associates
COVER PHOTOGRAPH	© SGM/age fotostock America

This book was set in Times Ten by GGS Book Services, Atlantic Highlands and printed and bound by Von Hoffmann Corporation. The cover was printed by Von Hoffmann Corporation.

This book is printed on acid-free paper. ∞

Library of Congress Cataloging-in-Publication Data

Turban, Efraim.
    Introduction to information technology / Efraim Turban, R. Kelly Rainer, Jr., Richard E. Potter — 3rd ed.
        p. cm.
    Includes bibliographical references and index.
    ISBN 0-471-34780-9 (cloth)
        1. Information technology. 2. Management information systems. I. Rainer, R. Kelly (Rex Kelly) II. Potter, Richard E. III. Title

    T58.5.T87 2004
    658'.05—dc22

                                                                            2004042229

    ISBN 0-471-34780-9
    WIE ISBN 0-471-66136-8

Printed in the United States of America

10 9 8 7 6 5 4 3 2 1

Efraim Turban (right in photo) is currently a Visiting Scholar with the Pacific Institute for Information Systems Management College of Business University of Hawaii at Manoa. He obtained his MBA and Ph.D. degrees from the University of California, Berkeley. His industry experience includes eight years as an industrial engineer, three of which were spent at General Electric Transformers Plant. He also has extensive consulting experience to small and large corporations as well as to foreign governments. In his 30 years of teaching, Dr. Turban has served as Distinguished Professor at Eastern Illinois University, and as Visiting Professor at UCLA, City University of Hong Kong, Nanyang Technological University in Singapore, Hong Kong University of Science and Technology, and University of Miami. He has also taught at UCLA, USC, Simon Fraser University, and California State University, Long Beach and has held permanent positions with Lehigh University, Simon Fraser University, and Florida International University. Dr. Turban was a co-recipient of the 1984/85 National Management Science Award (Artificial Intelligence in Management). In 1997 he received the Distinguished Faculty Scholarly and Creative Achievement Award at California State University, Long Beach. He was the co-chair of the 1999 International Conference of Electronic Commerce. Dr. Turban has published over 100 articles in leading journals. He has also published 21 books, including *Electronic Commerce 2004: A Managerial Perspective.*

R. Kelly Rainer, Jr. (center in photo) is George Phillips Privett Professor of Management Information Systems at Auburn University, Auburn, Alabama. He received his BS degree in Mathematics from Auburn and his Doctor of Dental Medicine (DMD) from the University of Alabama in Birmingham. After practicing dentistry for ten years, Professor Rainer returned to school and received his Ph.D. at the University of Georgia. He has published numerous articles in leading journals. His current research interests include health care informatics and information technology security.

Richard E. Potter (left in photo) is Assistant Professor of Information and Decision Sciences in the College of Business Administration at the University of Illinois

at Chicago. He received a bachelors degree in psychology from California State University–Hayward, and an MS in Management degree and Ph.D. degree in Management and Management Information Systems from the University of Arizona. Dr. Potter was a Postdoctoral Fellow at the University of Michigan's School of Public Health and Visiting Scholar and Adjunct Professor of MIS at the University of Arizona's Keller School of Management. He also served Mexico's ITESM system as Director of Research and Doctoral Programs at their Mexico City Graduate School of Business.

Dr. Potter's current research interest is cognition and behavior in the electronic environment, with emphasis on performance assessment and intervention with electronically supported groups, and cultural effects on collaborative technology use. He has published in a number of leading scientific journals, has authored numerous book chapters, and has presented his work in academic conferences around the world.

PREFACE

As the digital revolution continues to transform the business landscape, successful organizations must sustain their profits in a rapidly changing, intensely competitive global marketplace, while surviving upheavals in world politics that change their markets and labor sources. For an organization to thrive in today's economy, managers and functional specialists in all areas—accounting, finance, marketing, production and operations management, and human resources management—must perform their jobs even more effectively and efficiently. Information technology provides the tools that enable all organizational personnel to solve increasingly complex problems and to capitalize on opportunities that contribute to the success, or even the survival, of the organization.

This book is based on the fundamental premise that the major role of information technology (IT) is to support organizational personnel, regardless of their functional area or level in the organization. IT supports business processes that enable companies to operate in the digital era by quickly and properly reacting to changes. In many cases, IT is the basis for aggressive proactive strategies that can radically alter the competitive landscape of an industry. We aim here to teach all business majors, especially undergraduate ones, how to use IT to master their current or future jobs and to help ensure the success of their organization. Our focus is not on merely *learning* the concepts of information technology but rather on *applying* those concepts to facilitate business processes.

KEY FEATURES

We have been guided by the following goals that we believe will enhance the teaching and learning experience.

Active Learning. We recognize the need to actively involve students in problem solving, creative thinking, and capitalizing on opportunities. Every chapter includes a variety of hands-on exercises, activities, and mini-cases, including exercises that ask students to use software application tools. Through these activities and an interactive Web site, we enable students to actually do something with the concepts they learn, such as how to improve a business through IT, to configure products, and to use spreadsheets to facilitate problem solving.

Cross-functional Approach. We show why IT is important by calling attention in each chapter to how that chapter's IT topic relates to students in each major. Icons guide the reader to relevant issues for their specific functional area—accounting (ACC), finance (FIN), marketing (MKT), production operations management (POM), and human resources management (HRM). In addition, chapters end with a summary of how the concepts relate to each functional area ("What's in IT for Me?").

Diversified and Unique Examples from Different Industries. Extensive use of vivid examples from large corporations, small businesses, and government and not-for-profit organizations helps to enliven concepts by showing students the capabilities of IT, its cost and justification, and innovative ways that real corporations are using IT in their operations. Each chapter constantly highlights the integral connection between IT and business. This is especially evident in the "IT's about Business" boxes. In addition to the icons noted above, other icons highlight government (GOV) and service-company (SVC) examples.

Successes and Failures. Like other textbooks, we present many examples of IT success. But, we also provide numerous examples of IT failures, in the context of lessons that can be learned from such failures. Misuse of IT can be very expensive, as we illustrate.

Innovation and Creativity. In today's rapidly changing environment, creativity and innovation are necessary for a business to operate effectively and profitably. Throughout the book we show how these concepts are facilitated by IT.

 Global Focus. Since an understanding of global competition, partnerships, and trading is essential to success in business, we provide a broad selection of international cases and examples. We discuss how IT facilitates export and import, the management of multinational companies, and electronic trading around the globe. These global examples are highlighted with the global icon.

Cutting Edge Information on Wireless Technologies, e-Commerce, and Web Services. Mobile and Internet technologies have created a paradigm shift in the way that the world does business. We offer a comprehensive chapter on wireless technologies (Chapter 6) and a chapter on electronic commerce (Chapter 5). In addition, we offer extensive examples of Web Services, including how companies use Web Services to improve the supply chain.

WHAT'S NEW IN THE THIRD EDITION

New Organization Including Technology Guides

Recognizing the challenges of teaching an introductory MIS course to students of varied backgrounds and interests, and responding to today's trends in outsourcing systems development projects, we have reorganized the textbook. The body of the textbook focuses on how organizations use IT to be more profitable and efficient. The Technology Guides, at the end of the book, give in-depth descriptions of the technologies themselves that comprise the term *information technology*. These Technology Guides can be taught separately or in combination with the textbook chapters, or students and professors may choose simply to refer to them throughout the course. We feel that this new organization strengthens the text's focus on business and provides instructors and students with the appropriate flexibility for this course.

Chapter 6 on Mobile, Wireless, and Pervasive Computing

We've devoted Chapter 6 to looking at how mobile and wireless computing technologies are transforming organizations and the way we conduct business. The ability to communicate and collaborate any time and from anywhere provides organizations with strategic advantage by increasing productivity, speed, and customer service and by enabling mobile commerce. Additionally, mobile and wireless computing are creating the foundations of the futuristic computing environment called pervasive computing. Chapter 6 explores various topics related to mobile, wireless, and pervasive computing, including Wi-Fi, location-based commerce, RFID, and the possibility of an "Internet of things."

Chapter 8 on Enterprise Systems

This new chapter consolidates material that appeared in several chapters in the second edition. It presents, in one place, information on enterprise-wide systems, which have become more important for modern organizations. Included in this chapter is discussion of supply chains, their problems and solutions for dealing with those problems, enterprise resource planning (ERP), and customer relationship management (CRM).

Chapter 9 on Interorganizational and Global Information Systems

The Internet and e-commerce have made it both possible and desirable for the information systems of two or more organizations to be connected. This new chapter expands into a full chapter the coverage of interorganizational systems from the second edition. Included in this chapter are interorganizational information systems (IOSs), global information systems, B2B exchanges, virtual corporations, EDI/Internet, XML, and Web Services.

Chapter 11 on Acquiring ITs Applications and Infrastructure

Based on Chapter 14 of the second edition, this heavily revised chapter describes the process of IT resource acquisition from a managerial perspective. This chapter gives special attention to the available options, including outsourcing and how to evaluate those options. The chapter also takes a close look at planning and justifying the need for information systems.

The related technological issues, starting with an examination of traditional systems development life cycle—the "how" involved in constructing information systems—are described in Technology Guide 6. By moving the technology aspects to Technology Guide 6, we were able to concentrate Chapter 11 on managerial issues such as evaluating options for systems acquisitions, outsourcing development, and using utility computing. Separating the managerial view of IT acquisition from the more technical view allows instructors to omit the technical view if they would like to focus on managerial issues in their course, or to assign it for those classes interested in the development methodologies, such as the life cycle, prototyping, and CASE tools.

Focus on Ethics

With corporate scandals in the headlines and news daily, ethics and ethical questions have come to the forefront of business people's minds. In addition to a chapter that concentrates on ethics and security (Chapter 12), we have included examples and cases that focus on business ethics throughout the chapters. These examples are highlighted with the ethics icon.

New Pedagogical Features

- *Chapter Roadmaps.* These enhanced figures provide a visual overview of the processes and topics covered in the chapters.
- *Lessons from IT Failures.* A special "Lessons from IT Failures" icon highlights the cases and examples that focus on what went wrong in IT projects. We've included more coverage of IT failures in order to provide a realistic view of IT projects and allow students to sharpen their problem-solving skills.

- *Marginal Glossary.* This study tool highlights the importance of the vocabulary within the chapters and makes chapter review easier. In the index, the page number on which a term is defined is shown in boldface type.
- *Interactive Learning Sessions.* The book's Student Web Site contains engaging activities for each chapter, including interactive drag-and-drop exercises and simulations, as well as animations that help students visualize IT processes. For example, students are asked to answer questions about a simulation of a UPS order tracking system. The Web site allows students to print their work and submit it to their instructor. The "Interactivities" are accessed on the Web with a password included in new copies of the book.
- *Virtual Company.* The new Web-based Virtual Company case at the end of each chapter gives students the opportunity to develop IT solutions for a simulated music venue called Club IT, which presents live music and DJs. Students are "hired" as consultants for the club and asked to work on such projects as helping

the club owners manage inventory by tracking food and beverages on spreadsheets, mining Web resources to predict music/nightclub trends, advertising through mobile devices, and streaming the DJ's shows onto the Internet. These assignments also ask students to apply their software applications skills by creating presentations in Microsoft PowerPoint and databases in Microsoft Excel and Access.

PEDAGOGICAL STRUCTURE

Other pedagogical features provide a structured learning system that reinforces the concepts through features such as chapter-opening organizers, section reviews, frequent applications, and hands-on exercises and activities.

Chapter Opening organizers include the following pedagogical features:

- The *Chapter Preview* gives an overview of the concepts and topics covered in the chapter.
- The *Chapter Outline* lists the major concepts covered in the chapter.
- *Learning objectives* tell what students can expect to learn in the chapter.
- A *real-world opening case* identifies a business problem faced by an actual company, describes the IT solution applied to the business problem, presents the results of the IT solution, and summarizes what students can learn from the case.

Study Aids are provided throughout each chapter. These include the following:

- *IT's about Business* boxes provide real-world applications, with questions that relate to concepts covered in the text. Icons relate these sections to the specific functional areas.
- Highlighted *Examples* interspersed throughout the text show the use (and misuse) of IT by real-world organizations and help illustrate the conceptual discussion.
- *Managers' Checklists* review the advantages/benefits and disadvantages/limitations of important systems and processes.
- *Tables* list key points or summarize different concepts.
- End of section reviews (*Before You Go On . . .*) prompt students to pause and test their understanding of concepts before moving on to the next section.

End-of-Chapter Study Aids provide extensive opportunity for the reader to review and actually "do something" with the concepts they have just studied:

- *What's in IT for Me?* is a unique chapter summary section that shows the relevance of topics for different functional areas (accounting, finance, marketing, production/operations management, and human resources management).
- The *Chapter Summary*, keyed to learning objectives that were listed at the beginning of the chapter, enables students to review the major concepts covered in the chapter.
- The *Interactive Learning Session* refers students to the book's Web site, where they will find interactive, animated exercises and cases to apply the concepts they have learned.
- *Discussion Questions, Problem-Solving Activities, Internet Activities*, and *Team Assignments* provide practice through active learning. These exercises are hands-on opportunities to use the concepts discussed in the chapter.
- A *Real-World Case* presents a case organized around a business problem and shows how IT helped to solve it; questions at the end of the case relate it to concepts discussed in the chapter.
- *Club IT*, as described earlier, gives the student an assignment as an intern for virtual-company Club IT. Students are referred to the Wiley Web Site for support information.

SUPPLEMENTS

This book also facilitates the teaching of an Introduction to IT course by providing extensive support materials for instructors and students. Go to *wiley.com/college/turban* to access the Student and Instructor Web Sites.

Software Skills Lab Manuals   Discovering Microsoft Office XP (0-471-47029-5), a lab manual by Ed Martin, can be packaged with the text. For further information on lab manual packaging options, please ask your Wiley representative. To find your Wiley representative, go to *wiley.com/college/rep*.

Instructors Manual   The *Instructor's Manual* includes a chapter overview, teaching tips and strategies, answers to all end-of-chapter questions, supplemental mini-cases with essay questions and answers, experiential exercises that relate to particular topics, and "war stories" for each chapter. This manual also includes within each chapter a feature called "What's Next," which provides a glimpse of what is to come in the next chapter. Finally, also included are a Video Guide with three to five viewing questions that relate to chapter topics, relevant Web links wherever possible, and a case correlation guide that provides a correlation of each case the text authors have provided with the related chapters from the text.

Test Bank.   Prepared by Kelly Rainer, the *Test Bank* is a comprehensive resource for test questions. It contains approximately 125 questions per chapter consisting of multiple choice, true/false, fill-in-the blank, matching, and short answer questions.

PowerPoint Presentations.   The *PowerPoint Presentations* consist of a series of slides for each chapter of the text that are designed around the text content, incorporating key points from the text and all text illustrations as appropriate.

Image Library.   All textbook figures are available for download from the Web Site. These figures can easily be added to PowerPoint presentations.

BusinessExtra Select   This feature allows instructors to package the text with software applications, lab manuals, cases, articles, and other real-world content from sources such as INSEAD, Ivey and Harvard Business School cases, *Fortune, The Economist, The Wall Street Journal*, and much more. You can combine the Third Edition with the content you choose to create a fully customized textbook. For additional information, go to *www.wiley.com/college/bxs*.

On-line Quizzes.   These practice tests for students to help prepare for class tests are provided as an online resource within the text Web site. Once students have completed a particular quiz, they can submit it electronically and receive feedback regarding any incorrect responses.

Nightly Business Report Videos.   This comprehensive video compilation offers selections from the highly respected business news program, Nightly Business Report (NBR). The segments within this video package tie directly to the core topics of the text and bring real-world examples of information technology in practice to life. Each segment is approximately 3 to 7 minutes long and can be used to introduce topics to the students, enhance lecture material, and provide real-world context for related concepts.

Course Management.   New WebCT and Blackboard courses are available with this text. WebCT and Blackboard are tools that facilitate the organization and delivery of course materials via the Web. It provides powerful communication, loaded content, easy and flexible course administration, sophisticated online self-tests and diagnostic systems, and ease of use for both students and instructors.

Acknowledgments

Creating, developing, and producing a new text for the introduction to information technology course is a formidable undertaking. Along the way, we were fortunate to receive continuous evaluation, criticism, and direction from many colleagues who regularly teach this course. We would like to acknowledge the contributions made by the following individuals.

We are very grateful to Christy Cheung of City University of Hong Kong for her contributions to Chapters 8 and 11, and to Robert Davison of City University of Hong Kong for the ethics and professional issues scenarios in Online Appendix W12.1.

Third Edition Reviewers: Lawrence Andrew, *Western Illinois University*; Bay Arinze, *Drexel University*; Kakoli Bandyopadhyay, *Lamar University*; Jack Becker, *University of North Texas*; James Borden, *Villanova University*; Kuan Chen, *Purdue University Calumet*; Dan Davidson, *Miami University*; Thomas Dillon, *James Madison University*; Ely Dorsey, *Bridgewater State College*; Bonnie Glassberg, *Miami University*; Dale Gust, *Central Michigan University*; Veronica Hinton-Hudson, *University of Louisville*; Wayne Huang, *Ohio University*; Doug Isanhart, *University of Central Arkansas*; Brian Janz, *The University of Memphis*; Kapil Ladha, *Drexel University*; Rebecca Lawson, *Lansing Community College*; Robert Lawton, *Western Illinois University*; Dwight Leonard, *Ryerson University*; Scott Lloyd, *University of Rhode Island*; Wenhong Luo, *Villanova University*; Roger Mchaney, *Kansas State University*; Fiona Nah, *University of Nebraska, Lincoln*; M. O'Hara, *East Carolina University*; Thomas C. Padgett, *State University of West Georgia*; Ravi Paul, *East Carolina University*; Gail Rein, *State University of New York Brockport*; George Schneller, *Baruch College—CUNY*; David K. Smith, *Cameron University*; Therese Viscelli, *Georgia State University*; Bruce White, *Quinnipiac University*; Bill Wittman, *East Carolina University*; Zachery Wong, *Sonoma State University*; and Marie Wright, *Western Connecticut State University*.

Third Edition Survey Respondents: Ihssan Alkadi, *University of Louisiana Lafayette*; Russell Baker, *University of Tampa*; David Chou, *Eastern Michigan University*; Megan Conklin, *Elon University*; Neelima Bhatnager, *University of Pittsburgh*; Mohammad Dadashzadeh, *Wichita State University*; Bernie Esposito, *Notre Dame College, Maryland*; Bassam Hasan, *University of Toledo*; Jan Kwasniewski, *Fanshawe College*; Lawrence Jacowitz, *West Virginia University*; Vinod Lall, *Minnesota State University*; Alireza Lari, *Fayetteville State University*; Susan Lippert, *Drexel University*; Makoto Nakayama, *CTI DePaul*; John Pearson, *Southern Illinois University Carbondale*; Roger Pick, *University of Missouri Kansas City*; David K. Smith, *Cameron University*; Sandy Staples, *Queens University, Canada*; Virginia Wilch, *Suffolk Community College*; and Marie Wright, *Western Connecticut University*.

Second Edition Reviewers: Omar Benli, *California State University–Long Beach*; Warren Boe, *University of Iowa*; Russell Casey, *Delaware State University*; Debra Chapman, *University of Southern Alabama*; Eli Cohen, *Kozminski Academy of Entrepreneurship and Management*; Mohamad Dadashzadeh, *Witchita State University*; Tony Kendall, *Naval Postgraduate School*; Brian Kovar, *Kansas State University*; Patricia Logan, *Weber State University*; Rajiv Sabherwal, *University of Missouri, St. Louis*; Linda Salchenberger, *Loyola University–Chicago*; David Schaefer, *California State University–Sacramento*; Rod Sink, *Northern Illinois University*; Cheri Speier, *Michigan State University*; Zachary Wong, *Sonoma State University*; Haw Jan Wu, *Whittier College*; and Marie Wright, *Western Connecticut State University*.

First Edition Reviewers: Murugan Anandarajan, *Drexel University*; Bay Arinze, *Drexel University*; Boris Baran, *Concordia University–Montreal*; Jack Becker, *University of North Texas*; Bill Bistline, *St. John's University*; Alan Brandyberry, *University of Minnesota–Duluth*; Dan Davis, *Rowan University*; Lauren Eder, *Rider University*; Vipul Gupta, *St. Joseph's University*; Dale Gust, *Central Michigan State University*; Joan Hoopes, *Marist College*; Chang-Tseh Hsieh, *University of South Mississippi*; Edward Kaplan, *Bentley College*; Donald Kaufman, *Maryville University–St. Louis*; Dennis Kira, *Concordia University–Montreal*; Douglas Lavery, *Sir Sandford Fleming College*; Douglas

Leif, *Bemidji State University*; James Linderman, *Bentley College*; Pat Logan, *Weber State University*; Jane Mackay, *Texas Christian University*; Jack Marchewka, *Northern Illinois University*; Anne Massey, *Indiana University*; Suzanne McClure, *Bowling Green State University*; Gordon McCray, *Wake Forest University*; Enrique Mu, *University of Pittsburgh*; Barin Nag, *Towson State University*; Maggie O'Hara, *Eastern Carolina University*; Sasan Rahmatian, *California State University–Fresno*; Stephanie Robbins, *University of North Carolina–Charlotte*; Linda Salchenberger, *Loyola University of Chicago*; Tom Seymour, *Minot State University*; Jae P. Shim, *Mississippi State University*; Cheri Speier, *Michigan State University*; Amita Suhrid, *Keller Graduate School*; Jack Van Deventer, *Washington State University*; Marie Wright, *Western Connecticut State University*; Vincent Yen, *Wright State University*; and Dale Young, *Miami University* (*Ohio*).

Supplements Authors: We are especially grateful to Vinod Lall of Moorhead State University, who developed the Interactive Learning Sessions Website that accompanies this book; and to Dolly Samson of Hawaii Pacific University, who created the Virtual Company case that is on the book's Web Site. In addition, we thank Roberta Roth of the University of Northern Iowa, who prepared the Instructor's Manual, and Alireza Lari, who prepared the PowerPoint slides.

Efraim Turban
Kelly Rainer
Richard Potter

BRIEF CONTENTS

CONTENTS

The IT-Based Organization in the Digital Economy

Chapter Preview

This chapter discusses how business is done at the beginning of the twenty-first century and the fundamental and powerful roles that information technologies play in helping businesses survive and prosper in today's dynamic, competitive, global environment. We describe how various types of pressures, particularly new technologies, are forcing businesses to transition from the Old Economy to the New Economy. We show you how any information system, properly used, can be *strategic*, meaning that the information system can provide a competitive advantage. We also describe information systems that have failed, often at great cost to the enterprise. We finish up the chapter with an explanation of why you should learn about information technology.

Chapter Outline

Learning Objectives

1. Describe the characteristics of the digital economy and e-business.
2. Discuss the relationships among business pressures, organizational responses, and information systems.
3. Describe strategic information systems (SISs) and explain their advantages.
4. Describe Porter's competitive forces model and how information technology helps companies improve their competitive positions.
5. Describe 12 strategies that companies can use to achieve competitive advantage in their industries.

DELTA AIR LINES' DIGITAL NERVOUS SYSTEM

A major hub-and-spoke airline like Delta (*delta.com*) has costs that can be 150 percent higher than those of "no-frills" carriers. AirTran, JetBlue, and Southwest are squeezing all the major network carriers, but Delta is feeling it the most. The Atlanta-based company, which lost $1.3 billion in 2002, estimates that 40 percent of its customers can choose service from low-cost carriers—more than any other major carrier. In 2002, in key New York–to–Florida markets, JetBlue grabbed 80 percent of the market from Delta.

Delta's business problems fall into two major areas. First, the company must cut costs across every area of its operations, including: ticketing, baggage handling, customer service, and maintenance. Second, the company is starting two new businesses: a new, low-cost airline called Song (a $75 million venture) and a new business that provides maintenance services to other airlines.

Over the past five years, Delta spent $1.5 billion to develop a new information technology infrastructure, which it named the Delta Nervous System (DNS). The DNS cuts inefficiencies out of virtually every area of Delta's operations. The DNS links some 30 to 40 customer and flight databases that track everything from reservations and ticketing, to check-in and baggage handling, to flight and crew operations. Linked through the DNS, individual systems report changes—a new ticket reservation, a flight delay, a gate change—in real time. Messaging software carries each change to any system that needs it. A ticket reservation, for example, will be recorded in Delta's financial systems, its frequent-flier database, and its boarding and flight records, among other systems.

Delta is using its DNS to push ticket purchasing away from travel agents and toward its Web site (*delta.com*). A ticket booked through a travel agent costs an airline more than $20 in fees. A reservation handled live by the carrier's own call center can cost $15, but it costs only about $6 to handle the reservation online. In 2002, Delta sold 13 percent of all its tickets over its Web site, a savings of $57 million in ticket costs and $25 million in call center costs. Delta's goal is to sell at least half of its tickets online.

Delta is also using its DNS to computerize baggage-processing. Delta bag handlers attach scannable tags to bags, and the bags' destinations show up on screens on the airfield carts that the handlers drive, allowing them to figure out the fastest route to distribute a load of bags to various aircraft. It costs Delta $150 to track a lost bag. In 2002, use of the DNS in baggage-handling resulted in a savings of $8.7 million in bags that did not go astray.

The DNS also improves customer service. At each gate, huge flat-screen plasma displays list passengers by name for the flight's standby list; give the times various rows will be called to board the plane; show scheduled departure times; and update the weather in the destination city. These gate displays are a big part of how Delta is using its system to streamline check-in and boarding procedures. Self-service kiosks are another key component. The DNS has enabled Delta to reduce the number of agents at each gate. Potential savings range from $300 to $450 million per year.

The DNS also allows Delta to automate its aircraft maintenance, repair, and overhaul (MRO) unit. While labor is an airline's highest cost, aircraft maintenance is second—usually about 25 percent of an airline's costs. Delta is offering its maintenance and repair facility to other airlines. To accomplish this, the company must accurately track people and parts. The company uses specialized software to calculate fleet airtime, aircraft types, upgrade schedules, and other factors in order to determine which parts are going to be needed when. In 2002, savings in maintenance expense totaled $90 million. In addition, Delta has signed long-term service and maintenance contracts with World Airways and Miami Air, and two major contracts with Boeing to maintain a fleet of military and executive jets. Delta is generating $150 million in new revenue from its for-profit maintenance operation.

Delta's Digital Nervous System has provided the airline with a competitive advantage over its rivals. And Delta's lead is likely to grow, considering the financial condition of competitors like United Airlines and American Airlines.

Source: D. Gage and J. McCormick, "Delta's Last Stand" (2003), *Baseline Magazine*, April 1, 2003.

WHAT WE LEARNED FROM THIS CASE

This case illustrates how a company can achieve competitive advantage in the digital age through the use of information technology. Delta's Digital Nervous System illustrates the following points: It is sometimes necessary to change business models and strategies to succeed in the digital economy. Web-based IT enables companies to gain competitive advantage and to survive in the face of serious corporate threat. IT may require a large investment over a long period of time. Extensive networked computing infrastructure is necessary to support a large global organization. And Web-based applications can be used to provide superb customer service.

We see that fierce competition drives even large corporations in mature industries such as the airlines to find ways to reduce costs, increase productivity, and improve customer service. These efforts are best achieved by using Web-based systems, which are the major enablers in the transformation to an e-business in the digital economy.

In this chapter, we describe the extremely competitive business environment in which companies operate today, the business pressures under which they operate, and what companies are doing to counter these pressures.

1.1 DOING BUSINESS IN THE DIGITAL ECONOMY

Conducting business in the digital economy means using Web-based systems on the Internet and other electronic networks. First, we will consider the concept of networked computing and then we will look at the impact it has made on how companies do business.

Networked Computing

As described in the opening case, Delta Airlines was an established "old-economy" operation that saw the need to transform into a "new-economy" business, performing various functions electronically in order to enhance its operations. Delta's Digital Nervous System is a good example of networked computing that facilitates electronic commerce. Delta uses its DNS to cut costs (e.g., selling tickets on its Web site and computerizing baggage-handling to minimize lost bags) and to start a new line of business (its for-profit aircraft maintenance operation).

Any organization that performs business functions (e.g., buying and selling goods and services, servicing customers, collaborating with business partners) electronically, in order to enhance its operations, is considered to be doing e-business or e-commerce. The infrastructure for e-business is *networked computing*, which connects computers and other electronic devices via telecommunication networks. Such connections allow users to access information stored in many places and to communicate and collaborate with others, all from their desktop or mobile computers. These computers may be connected to the global networked environment, known as the *Internet*, or to its counterpart within organizations, called an *intranet*. In addition, many companies link their intranets to those of their business partners over networks called *extranets*. These connections typically are done via wireline systems; since 2000, though, more and more communication and collaboration are done via wireless systems.

e-business / e-commerce *The conducting of business functions (e.g., buying and selling goods and services, servicing customers, collaborating with business partners) electronically, in order to enhance an organization's operations.*

In general, the collection of computing systems used by an organization is termed information technology (IT), which is the focus of this book. Almost all organizations, private and public, in most industries use information technologies to support their operations. The reason for this widespread IT use is that IT has become the major facilitator of business activities in the world today. IT is also a catalyst of fundamental changes in the structure, operations, and management of organizations, due to the

information technology *The collection of computing systems used by an organization.*

Table 1.1   Major Capabilities of Information Systems

- Perform high-speed, high-volume, numerical computations.
- Provide fast, accurate, and inexpensive communication within and between organizations.
- Automate both semiautomatic business processes and manual tasks.
- Store huge amounts of information in an easy-to-access, yet small space.
- Allow quick and inexpensive access to vast amounts of information, worldwide.
- Facilitate the interpretation of vast amounts of data.
- Enable communication and collaboration anywhere, any time.
- Increase the effectiveness and efficiency of people working in groups in one place or in several locations, anywhere.
- Facilitate work in hazardous environments.

capabilities shown in Table 1.1. These capabilities support the five general business objectives of improving productivity, reducing costs, improving decision making, enhancing customer relationships, and developing new strategic applications.

What Is the Digital Economy?

digital economy *An economy based on digital technologies, including communications networks (the Internet, intranets, and extranets), computers, software, and other related technologies; also sometimes called the* Internet economy, *the* new economy, *or the* Web economy.

All organizations—for-profit, nonprofit, private sector, public sector—in the twenty-first century operate in the **digital economy**, which is an economy based on digital technologies, including digital communications networks (the Internet, intranets, private *value-added networks* or VANs, and extranets), computers, software, and other related information technologies. The digital economy is also sometimes called the *Internet economy*, the *new economy*, or the *Web economy*.

In this new economy, digital networking and communications infrastructures provide a global platform over which people and organizations interact, communicate, collaborate, and search for information. This platform includes, for example (Choi and Whinston, 2000):

- A vast array of digitizable products (products that can be converted to digital format)—databases, news and information, books, magazines, TV and radio programming, movies, electronic games, musical CDs, and software—which are delivered over the digital infrastructure any time, anywhere in the world
- Consumers and firms conducting financial transactions digitally—through digital currencies or financial tokens carried via networked computers and mobile devices
- Physical goods such as home appliances and automobiles that are embedded with microprocessors and networking capabilities

The term *digital economy* also refers to the convergence of computing and communications technologies on the Internet and other networks, and the resulting flow of information and technology that is stimulating electronic commerce and vast organizational change. This convergence enables all types of information (data, audio, video, images) to be stored, processed, and transmitted over networks to many destinations worldwide. The digital economy has helped create an economic revolution, which was evidenced by unprecedented economic performance and a long period of continuous economic expansion (from 1991 until 2000).

The New Economy versus the Old Economy

The changes brought by the digital economy are significant. Computer-based information systems of all kinds have been enhancing business competitiveness and creating strategic advantage on their own or in conjunction with e-commerce applications (see Carr, 2001). Here are a few examples that illustrate differences between doing business in the new economy and the old economy.

Example #1: Buying and Selling Textbooks

Old Economy.   You go to the local bookstore and buy your textbooks, either new or used. After your semester ends, you go back to the bookstore to sell your books at a reduced price. The bookstore is your only alternative for buying and selling your books.

New Economy.   You go online to the Web site of the textbooks' publishers, where you can buy the books direct and have them shipped to your residence. Or, you go online to *amazon.com*, *half.com*, *buy.com*, *bestwebbuys.com*, or *eBay.com*, where you buy or sell your books and can negotiate the prices. The Internet provides you with additional outlets and information to improve your buying or selling positions. The next step will be all-digital books, to be downloaded at your convenience from a publisher.

Note to readers: Web site addresses (technically known as Uniform Resource Locators, or URLs) are set in italics throughout the book. To get to a site, you generally can type the URL immediately after "http://" on your Internet browser. In some cases, you will need to add "www." between "http://" and the URL in order to access the site. Be aware that content on the Internet is in flux, so some sites referenced in this textbook may have become unavailable since publication of the book.

Example #2: Registering for Classes

Old Economy (the way your parents' generation registered).   To register for classes, you walk around the campus to each department that offers the course you want. At that department, you pick up a computer punchcard with the course information on it. After picking up the cards for all the courses you want, you go to the Registrar's Office, where you wait in long lines to turn in your cards, manually fill out your registration, and have it approved by a clerk.

New Economy.   To register for classes, you access your campus Web site, log into the registration site, and electronically register for classes without leaving your room. The registration Web site automatically checks for prerequisites, overloads, full classes, or other constraints.

Example #3: Photography

Old Economy.   You buy film at the store, insert it into your camera, and take pictures. Once you complete the roll of film, you take it to the store for processing. You get the photos back and examine them to see which you like. You go back to the store and pay for enlargements and duplications. You mail some of the photos to family and friends. Of course, if you want to take moving pictures, you need a second, different camera.

New Economy.   In first-generation digital photography, you followed the old-economy process up to the point of getting the pictures back from the photo lab. But when you had the pictures, you scanned the ones you liked, and then made reprints, enlarged them, or sent them to your family and friends via e-mail.

In the second generation of digital photography, you use a *digital camera*, which can also take videos. No film is needed, and no processing is required. You can see the results immediately, and you can enlarge photos and position and print them quickly. In minutes, you can send the pictures to your family and friends. They can view the pictures on their personal computer, personal digital assistant (PDA), or cell phone. You can print pictures, or use them in a multimedia presentation.

In the third generation of digital photography, your digital camera can be small enough to be installed in your cell phone, a palmtop computer, or a pair of binoculars. You are traveling, and you see interesting scenery or an athletic event. You take pictures with your tiny digital camera, and within a few seconds they are sent to any destination on the Internet for viewing or reprints. Cameras of this type are already in use (e.g., by the paparazzi who sell pictures of celebrities to tabloids).

Example #4: Paying for Gasoline

Old Economy.   You drive up to the pump at a gas station, fill up your car, and then go inside to stand in line to pay for your gas, using either cash or a credit card.

New Economy.   Using the first generation of "pay-at-the-pump" systems, you drive up to the pump, insert your credit card in the card-swipe slot on the pump, receive authorization for the charge, pump your gas, receive your receipt, and drive away.

The Exxon Mobil (*exxonmobil.com*) Speedpass is an example of the second generation of pay-at-the-pump systems. The Speedpass token, usually carried on a key ring, allows customers to fill their tanks with a wave of the token at a gas-pump sensor. The Speedpass stores customer details on a small chip. When waved over the sensor, a short-range wireless link starts an automatic activation and authorization process, and the total purchase is then charged to a preapproved credit card. The pump recognizes you electronically, so there is no waiting for credit authorization and pump activation, and no buttons to push. You never have to take your credit cards or cash out of your car. (You can enroll online to get your Speedpass at *mobil.com/speedpass.*)

Example #5: Paying for Transportation in New York City

Old Economy. At first, travelers had to pay cash to a cashier for public transportation. Long delays caused mass transit to turn to metal tokens. For over 50 years, New Yorkers have used tokens to pay for transportation on buses and subways. The tokens save time and are easy for travelers to use. However, it costs $6 million a year to manufacture replacement tokens and to collect the tokens out of turnstiles and fare boxes ("New York City Transit Tokens. . . ," 2003). New York needs this money for other services.

New Economy. The new-economy solution has been to switch to MetroCards. By 2002, only 9 percent of all commuters were still using tokens. Despite the fact that they have to occasionally swipe the MetroCard through the card reader several times, travelers generally like the new cards. (A new generation of contactless cards does not have this problem.) MetroCards are offered at discounts, which riders like.

Other cities have made the transition to electronic cards as well. Chicago's transit system moved to cards in 1999, replacing the century-old tokens. Washington, D.C., Paris, and London also use transit cards. In Hong Kong, millions use a contactless card not only for transportation but also to pay for telephone, Internet access, food in vending machines, and much more.

The next generation of public transport payment will use wireless devices, perhaps carried on a key chain. Commuters will simply walk past a reader, and their credit cards, debit cards, or bank accounts will be debited automatically.

Example #6: Paying for Goods: The Checkout Experience

Old Economy. In the "old-old" economy, when you visit stores that sell any type of retail product (e.g., groceries, office supplies), you place your items in a shopping cart and proceed to checkout. At the checkout counter, you stand in line while a clerk punches in the price of each item on a manual adding machine. After the clerk adds up all your items, you pay for them in cash. Note here that no information is gathered about the item itself, other than the price.

Using the next generation of checkout technology, you take your items to a clerk, who swipes the barcode of each item over a "reader." The reader captures data on the price and description of each item and automatically enters that data into the organization's database. (This is an example of *source-data automation*, where human intervention in data input is minimized.) You receive an itemized account of your purchases and the total price.

New Economy. In the new economy, you take your items to a self-service kiosk, where you swipe the barcode of each item over a reader. After you have swiped all your items, the kiosk gives your directions about how to pay (cash, credit card, or debit card). Your wait in line is minimized.

In the next generation of checkout technology, all items will have wireless radio frequency identification tags either attached to or embedded in them. After you have finished shopping, you will simply walk your cart with all its items through a device similar to an airport security scanner. This device will "read" the wireless signals from each item, generate an itemized account of all your purchases, total up the price, and automatically debit your debit card or credit card. You will not wait in line at all, but walk from the store to your car.

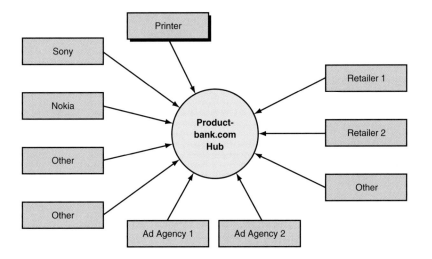

Figure 1.1 *Changing a linear supply chain to a hub.*

Example #7: Supplying Commercial Photos

Old Economy.   Thousands of companies around the world provide photos of their products to retailers who advertise products in newspapers, in paper catalogs, or on-line. In the old economy, the retailer sends the manufacturer a request for a picture of the item to be advertised, say a Sony TV set. Sony then sends to a designated ad agency, by courier, alternative pictures that the agency can use. The agency selects a picture, designs the ad, gets an approval from the retailer, and sends the approved picture by courier to the printer. There it is rephotographed and entered into production for the catalog. An improvement in the old-economy process, introduced several years ago, allows the ad agency to send the picture to a scanning house. There, a digital image is made, and that image is moved to the printer.

In both of the old-economy processes, both the retailer and the ad agency may be involved in a quality check at various times, further slowing the process. The cycle time per picture can be four to six weeks. The total processing cost per picture is about $80.

The New Economy.   Orbis Inc., a very small Australian company, changed the old-economy linear supply chain to a hub-like supply chain, as shown in Figure 1.1. In the new process, the manufacturer (e.g., Sony) sends many digitized pictures to Orbis (at *productbank.com.au*), and Orbis organizes the pictures in a database. When a retailer needs a picture, it enters the database and selects a picture (or several alternatives). The choice is e-mailed with the picture's ID number to the ad agency. The agency enters the database, views the digitized pictures, and works on them. The final digitized pictures are e-mailed to the printer. The entire process takes less than a week at a cost of about $50 per picture.

In each of the examples above, we can see the advantage of the new economy over the old economy in terms of at least one of the following: cost, quality, speed, innovation, and customer service. Information technology can also transform universities. As we see in IT's about Business 1.1 (page 8), Dartmouth College is using wireless technology to enable students and faculty to communicate in new ways to enhance learning and teaching.

The new economy brings not only digitization, but also the opportunity to use new business models. In the next section, we discuss business models of the digital economy, all of which are enabled by Web-based information technology.

Business Models in the Digital Economy

The Internet is revolutionizing the economic, societal, and technological foundations of the old economy. Organizations are developing new models for business, the economy, and government.

IT's ABOUT BUSINESS

1.1: Dartmouth College Goes Wireless

Dartmouth College (*dartmouth.edu*), one of the oldest in the United States (founded in 1769), was one of the first to embrace the wireless revolution. Operating and maintaining a campuswide information system with wires is very difficult, since there are 161 buildings with more than 1,000 rooms on campus. In the year 2000 the campus introduced a campuswide wireless network that includes more than 500 Wi-Fi (wireless fidelity) systems (see Chapter 6). By the end of 2002 the entire campus became a fully wireless, always-connected community—a microcosm that provides a peek at what neighborhood and organizational life may look like for the general population in just a few years.

As a pioneer in campuswide wireless, Dartmouth has made many innovative uses of the system, some of which are the following:

- Students are developing new applications for the Wi-Fi. For example, one student has applied for a patent on a personal-security device that pinpoints the location of campus emergency services to one's mobile device.
- Students no longer have to remember campus phone numbers, as their mobile devices contain all the numbers and can be accessed anywhere on campus.
- Students primarily use laptop computers on the network. However, an increasing number of Internet-enabled PDAs and cell phones are used as well. The use of regular cell phones is declining on campus.
- Students are making extensive use of SMS (short message service), sending messages to each other. Messages reach the recipients in a split second, any time, anywhere, as long as they are sent and received within the network's coverage area.

- Students can submit their class work via the network, as well as watch streaming video and listen to Internet radio.
- Professors are using wireless-based teaching methods. For example, students armed with Handspring Visor PDAs, equipped with Internet access cards, can evaluate material presented in class and can vote on multiple-choice questions relating to the presented material. Tabulated results are shown in seconds, promoting discussions. According to faculty, the system significantly increases participation.
- In the fall of 2003, Dartmouth moved into the world of voice-over IP (VoIP) via its wireless network. Students entering the class of 2007 were given the option of downloading VoIP software onto their computers. Using the software together with a headset, the students can make local or long-distance calls free. Each student is assigned a traditional seven-digit telephone number.

Sources: K. Hafner, "A New Kind of Revolution in the Dorms of Dartmouth," *New York Times*, September 23, 2003; and *dartmouth.edu*.

QUESTIONS

1. In what ways is the Wi-Fi technology changing the life of Dartmouth students?
2. Is the wireless system at Dartmouth contributing to improved learning, or just adding entertainment that may reduce the time available for studying? Debate your point of view with students who may hold a different opinion.
3. What are the major benefits of the wireless system over the previous wireline system? Do you think wireline systems will disappear from campuses one day? (Do some research on this topic.)

---

business model *A method of doing business by which a company can generate revenue to sustain itself; spells out how the company adds value to its products or services.*

A **business model** is a method of doing business by which a company can generate revenue to sustain itself. The model spells out how the company adds value that consumers are willing to pay for, in terms of the goods and/or services the company produces in the course of its operations.

Five Representative Business Models of the Digital Age. Here we present five business models that have arisen in response to business pressures. Further discussion of new business models will be found throughout this book and at *digitalenterprise.org*.

Name-Your-Own-Price. Pioneered by Priceline (*priceline.com*), the *name-your-own-price* model allows the buyer to state a price he or she is willing to pay for a specific product or service. Using information in its database, Priceline will try to match the buyer's request with a supplier willing to sell on these terms. Customers may have to submit several bids before they find a price match for the product they want. Price-line's major area of operation is travel (airline tickets, hotels).

Bidding Using Reverse Auctions.   Big buyers typically employ the *bidding using reverse auctions model*. Via a *request for quote (RFQ)*, the buyer indicates a desire to receive bids on a particular item, and would-be sellers bid on the job. Pioneered by General Electric Corporation (*gxs.com*), bidding systems are popular. In fact, several government entities are mandating electronic bidding as the only way to sell to them.

Affiliate Marketing.   *Affiliate marketing* is an arrangement in which marketing partners place a banner ad for a company on their Web site. Every time a customer clicks on the banner, moves to the advertiser's Web site, and makes a purchase there, the advertiser pays a 3 to 15 percent commission to the host site. In this way, businesses can turn other businesses into their *virtual commissioned sales force*. Pioneered by CDNow (now *amazon.com*), the concept is now widespread.

Group Purchasing.   Typically, companies pay less per unit when buying more units. Using the concept of *group purchasing*, where the purchase orders of many buyers are aggregated, a small business, or even an individual, can get a discount. This method can be facilitated by making contacts online. *Electronic aggregators* (e.g., *etrana.com* and *usa-llc.com*) find individuals or small/medium enterprises that want to buy the same product, aggregate their small orders, and then negotiate (or conduct a bid) for the best deal.

E-Marketplaces.   **E-marketplaces** are markets in which buyers and sellers negotiate online. They introduce operating efficiencies to trading, and if well managed, can provide benefits to both buyers and sellers. Of special interest are *vertical e-marketplaces*, which concentrate on one industry (e.g., *chemconnect.com* in the chemical industry and *covisint.com* in the automotive industry). Chapter 5 will explore e-marketplaces in more detail.

e-marketplaces   *Markets in which buyers and sellers negotiate online.*

Now that we have considered some aspects of doing business in the digital economy, we turn our attention to the business pressures that companies face in the new, digital economy and some responses to those pressures.

Before you go on . . .

1. What are the major differences between the old economy and the new economy?
2. What are some other examples of the new economy versus the old economy?
3. Which new economy business model is most applicable for you as a student? (Hint: Think about your textbooks.)

1.2 BUSINESS PRESSURES, ORGANIZATIONAL RESPONSES, AND IT SUPPORT

Modern digital organizations must compete in a challenging marketplace—one that is rapidly changing, unpredictable, complex, global, hypercompetitive, and customer-focused. Companies must rapidly react to problems and opportunities arising from this dynamic environment.

Business Pressures

The *business environment* is the combination of social, legal, economic, physical, and political factors that affect business activities. Significant changes in any of these

Figure 1.2 *IT support for organizational responses.*

factors are likely to create business pressures on organizations. Organizations typically respond to these pressures with activities supported by IT. Figure 1.2 shows the relationships among business pressures, organizational responses, and IT. We will focus on three types of business pressures that organizations face—market, technology, and societal pressures. We first discuss the market pressures.

Market Pressures. Market pressures come from the global economy and strong competition, the changing nature of the workforce, and powerful customers.

Global Economy and Strong Competition. The move to a global economy has been facilitated by advanced telecommunications networks and particularly by the Internet. Regional agreements such as the North American Free Trade Agreement (United States, Canada, and Mexico) and the creation of a unified European market with a single currency, the euro, have contributed to increased world trade.

Low labor costs make Chinese firms attractive as partners in joint manufacturing ventures.

One important pressure that exists for businesses in a global market is the cost of labor, which varies widely among countries. In general, labor costs are higher in developed countries than in developing countries. Also, developed countries usually pay high fringe benefits to employees, which makes the cost of doing business even higher. Therefore, many labor-intensive industries have moved their operations to countries with low labor costs. These moves are greatly facilitated with IT (see Chapter 5).

Changing Nature of the Workforce. The workforce, particularly in developed countries, is becoming more diversified, as increasing numbers of women, single parents, minorities, and persons with disabilities work in all types of positions. Information technology is easing the integration of this wide variety of employees into the traditional workforce. IT is also allowing people to work from home (telecommute). (See Chapter 4.)

Powerful Customers. Consumer sophistication and expectations increase as customers become more knowledgeable about the availability and quality of products and services. On the Internet, customers can now easily find detailed information about products and services, compare prices, and buy at electronic auctions.

Customers today want customized products and services, with high quality and low prices. For example, Nike will let you design your own sneakers online and will make and ship them to your home in two weeks (*nike.com*). Also, automakers are selling build-to-order cars whose configuration is done on the Internet (see *jaguar.com*).

The importance of customers has forced organizations to increase efforts to acquire and retain customers. An enterprisewide effort to do just that is called **customer relationship management (CRM)**. (We address this topic in detail in Chapter 8.)

customer relationship management (CRM) *An enterprisewide effort to acquire and retain customers, often supported by IT.*

Technology Pressures. The second category of business pressures consists of those pressures related to technology. Two major pressures here are technological innovation and information overload.

Technological Innovation and Obsolescence.   New and improved technologies rapidly create or support substitutes for products, alternative service options, and superb quality. As a result, today's state-of-the-art products may be obsolete tomorrow. The technology that contributes the most to this pressure is Web-based information technology.

Information Overload.   The amount of information available on the Internet more than doubles every year, and much of it is free. The Internet and other telecommunications networks are bringing a flood of information to managers. Therefore, the accessibility, navigation, and management of data, information, and knowledge, which are necessary for managerial decision making, are critical. The only effective solutions are provided by information technology (e.g., search engines, intelligent databases, data mining).

"Every two years the speed doubles and the size decreases. They'll soon be infinitely fast, but so tiny we won't be able to use them."

Societal Pressures.   The third category of business pressures consists of those pressures related to society. These pressures include social responsibility, government regulation/deregulation, spending for social programs, spending to protect against terrorism, and ethics.

Social Responsibility.   Social issues that affect businesses range from the state of the physical environment to companies' contributions to education (e.g., by allowing interns to work in companies). Some corporations are willing to spend time and/or money on solving various social problems. These various activities are known as *organizational social responsibility*.

One social problem is the *digital divide*, which means that between countries and between different groups of people within countries, there is a wide division between those who have access to information and communications technology and are using it effectively, and those who do not. In the following example, IBM responds to this problem.

EXAMPLE   ***IBM Helps Bridge the Digital Divide.*** Boys & Girls Clubs of America (*bgca.org*) comprises a national network of more than 3,300 neighborhood-based facilities annually serving some 3.6 million young people, primarily from disadvantaged circumstances. IBM has provided wireless computing environments, known as Wi-Fi, for more than 600 Boys & Girls Clubs across the United States, providing Internet access for more than 200,000 children. For many of these children, it is the first time they have had the opportunity to use a computer or access the Internet after school.

The use of Wi-Fi allows the Clubs to bridge the digital divide, while reducing expenses for hardware, software, and installation by more than 50 percent. Wi-Fi has turned each Club into a digital center where up to 10 children can simultaneously access the Internet, using 6,400 IBM desktop PCs equipped with wireless cards. The children are learning skills that will be essential in the job market. (*Source: ibm.com.*)

Government Regulations and Deregulation.   Other business pressures are related to government regulations regarding health, safety, environmental control, and equal opportunity. Government regulations are usually viewed as expensive constraints on businesses. In general, government deregulation intensifies competition.

Protection Against Terrorist Attacks.   Since September 11, 2001, organizations have been under increased pressure to protect themselves against terrorist attacks. In addition, employees in the military reserves may be called up for active duty, creating personnel problems.

Information technology can contribute in the area of protection, by providing security systems and possibly identifying patterns of behavior that will help to prevent terrorist attacks (including cyberattacks) against organizations. One weapon in the global attack on terrorism is facial-recognition software, as the next example illustrates.

EXAMPLE   *Facial-Recognition Software Helps Fight Terrorism.* For a fleeting moment, Mohamed Atta appeared on an airport security camera minutes before he boarded one of the planes that crashed into the World Trade Center on September 11, 2001. Was there any way the camera or its operator would have been able to identify Atta as a suspect before he hijacked and flew the first of two planes into the twin towers? A new technology might answer this question.

This new technology for recognizing faces scans and maps the human face as a three-dimensional surface, by measuring the distances between a number of points on that surface. The advantage of the system is its ability to compare facial structures as they appear in different poses, light conditions, or facial expressions. The system could be employed at airports or border crossings where 3-D security cameras could scan faces and compare them with a database of 3-D pictures of suspected criminals or terrorists. Facial signatures could also be embedded in credit cards. People withdrawing money from an ATM or seeking access to a secure facility could have their identity verified by an on-site camera. (*Source: cnn.com.*)

ethics *Standards of right and wrong.*

Ethical Issues.   Ethics relates to standards of right and wrong, and *information ethics* relates to standards of right and wrong in information-processing practices. Ethical issues are very important because, if handled poorly, they have the power to damage the image of an organization and to destroy the morale of employees.

The use of information technology raises many ethical issues, ranging from monitoring e-mail to potential invasion of privacy of millions of customers whose data are stored in private and public databases. Chapter 12 covers ethical issues in detail.

The pressures on organizations are increasing, mandating that organizations be prepared to take responsive actions if they are to succeed. These organizational responses are described next.

Organizational Responses

Traditional organizational responses may not be effective with new types of business pressures. Therefore, many old solutions need to be modified, supplemented, or eliminated. Organizations' major responses are divided here into seven categories: strategic systems, customer focus, continuous improvement, restructuring, make-to-order and mass customization, business alliances, and e-business. The Delta case at the beginning of the chapter provides an example of all seven categories of business responses.

Strategic Systems.   Strategic systems provide organizations with advantages that enable them to increase their market share and/or profits, to better negotiate with suppliers, or to prevent competitors from entering their markets. We discuss strategic systems in detail in the next section of this chapter.

Customer Focus.   Organizational attempts to provide superb customer service can make the difference between attracting and keeping customers, or losing them to competitors. Numerous IT tools and business processes are designed to keep customers happy (see Chapter 8).

Superb customer service is a necessity in the healthcare industry, which is a huge business in the United States ($1.4 *trillion* spent in 2002). As IT's about Business 1.2 demonstrates, Medco Health Solutions uses Web-enabled technologies to take excellent care of its subscribers, many of whom are elderly, while increasing efficiency and cutting costs.

Continuous Improvement.   Many companies conduct programs that continuously attempt to improve their productivity and quality, and these programs are facilitated by IT. Examples of such programs are total quality management (TQM), Six Sigma, and just-in-time (JIT) processing. The underlying purpose of IT support in

1.2: Web-Enabled Business Operations at Medco

In 2002, Medco Health Solutions amassed more than $1.4 billion in sales through its Web site (*medco-health.com*), a 51 percent increase over 2001. The Web site fills 260,000 prescriptions every week. It takes a sophisticated infrastructure to handle all these transactions. Medco's Internet business is not a standalone operation, but a component linked to the company's retail and mail-order businesses. With over 64 million subscribers, Medco manages prescription drug plans for some of the nation's largest enterprises, including insurance companies and HMOs. Although some members order drugs directly from Medco, others purchase from one of the 58,000 retail pharmacies that use Medco to process and adjudicate benefits claims.

The Web site customizes the customer experience, displaying all the patients' options—retail, mail-order, and Internet—along with prices. The site suggests low-cost generic alternatives. The advantage to patients is seeing the options. The advantage to Medco: If a patient does not need a medication immediately, steering patients from retail pharmacies to Medco's home-delivery channels reduces the cost of filling prescriptions. Also, when a patient places an order, the Web site automatically checks the patient's history from all channels to see whether he or she had previously ordered medication that might adversely interact with the new prescription.

One challenge has been to make the site accessible for older users. Prescription drug use tends to increase with age. The average age of a Medco mail-order customer is about 65. So, the site is designed for accessibility. Buttons and tabs are large, and users can navigate with keyboards—handy for those lacking the dexterity to use a mouse.

Source: A. Cohen, "Online Prescriptions," *PC Magazine*, August 19, 2003.

QUESTIONS

1. Electronic commerce can be conducted by virtual companies that exist only as an organized network of order-filling suppliers and a Web-based transaction entity—almost no "brick-and-mortar" infrastructure. Are the values of brand names more or less important to such companies compared to traditional companies?
2. What are the various functions provided by Medco's Web site? Can you think of others the company might add?

---

continuous improvement is to monitor and analyze performance and productivity and to gather, share, and better use organizational knowledge.

Restructuring Business Processes.   To achieve dramatic improvements, organizations initially used the *business process reengineering (BPR)* approach, where the company fundamentally and radically redesigned a particular business process (e.g., purchasing, accounts payable, or new product design) (Hammer and Champy, 1993). Such radical redesign causes a major innovation in an organization's structure and the way it conducts its business. If done on a scale smaller than corporatewide, the redesign process may be referred to as a *restructuring*. Information technology plays a major role in restructuring. IT provides automation; allows business to be conducted in different locations; provides flexibility in manufacturing; permits quicker delivery to customers; creates or facilitates new business models; and supports rapid and paperless transactions among suppliers, manufacturers, and retailers.

Make-to-Order and Mass Customization. **Build-to-order** is a strategy of producing customized products and services. The business problem is how to provide customization and do it efficiently and at a reasonably low cost. Part of the solution is to change manufacturing processes from mass production to mass customization. In mass production, a company produces a large quantity of identical items. In **mass customization**, items are produced in a large quantity but are customized to fit the desires of each customer. IT and electronic commerce are ideal facilitators of mass customization, for example, by enabling interactive communications between buyers and designers so that customers can quickly and correctly configure the products they want. Also, electronic ordering reaches the production facility in minutes.

build-to-order *The strategy of producing customized products and services.*

mass customization *Production process in which items are produced in a large quantity but are customized to fit the desires of each customer.*

For example, at this time the automakers are trying to move in the direction of mass customization, but it is extremely difficult to build cars to order and still keep costs at a reasonable level. A startup company, though, called Build-To-Order Inc. (*btogroup.com*), plans to build highly customized vehicles (starting at a price of $35,000) by outsourcing just about all aspects of the cars' construction to suppliers and consolidating final construction at the factory. BTO will publish specifications for all parts of the car on the Web to encourage suppliers to build components to standard sizes.

For additional information on the build-to-order production model, see Appendix W1.1 on the book's Web site.

wiley.com/college/turban

Business Alliances. Many companies realize that alliances with other companies, even competitors, can be very beneficial. For example, Lockheed Martin and Northrop Grumman are working together on the next-generation Joint Strike Fighter for the U.S. Air Force (see *lmaeronautics.com* and *northgrum.com*).

virtual corporation *A business that operates through telecommunications networks, usually without a permanent headquarters, to produce a product or service.*

One of the most interesting types of business alliance is the **virtual corporation**, in which business partners operate through telecommunications networks, usually without a permanent headquarters, to produce a product or a service. Rather than forming virtual corporations with business partners, some individual companies *operate virtually*, as the example of Trend Micro (*trendmicro.com*) shows.

> **EXAMPLE** *Quicker Responses to Virus Attacks.* When the first reports surfaced at 12:17 P.M. Pacific Time on August 11, 2003, that the Blaster computer virus was spreading, researchers at antivirus-software company Trend Micro Inc. scrambled to come up with a fix. Meanwhile, the company's five global alert commanders began sizing up Blaster via cell-phone calls and e-mails. At 1:55 P.M., the commander based in Japan declared a global alert, signaling that this virus was nasty enough to require all the company's resources. Just 51 minutes later, a cure was ready.
>
> The company routinely is among the first responders to viruses, often delivering fixes 30 minutes before market leader Symantec Corp. (*symantec.com*), according to GEGA IT-Solutions (*gega-it.de*) in Germany, a response tester. Trend Micro is able to respond so quickly partly because it is not organized like most companies. It has spread its top executives, engineers, and support staff around the world to improve its response to new virus threats. The main virus response center is in the Philippines. (*Source:* Hamm, 2003.)

Trend Micro is among a new type of high-tech companies (called *transnationals*) aiming to transcend nationality altogether. The company represents what has been identified as the fourth stage of globalization. In the first stage, companies operate in one country and sell into others. Second-stage multinationals set up foreign subsidiaries to handle one country's sales. The third stage involves operating an entire line of business in another country. In the fourth stage, the executive suite is virtual. Companies place their top executives and core corporate functions in different countries to gain a competitive edge through the availability of talent or capital, low costs, or proximity to their most important customers. This dispersal of key corporate functions is made possible by information technologies, especially the Internet.

Other companies are also using geodiversity to great advantage. Logitech (*logitech. com*), with dual headquarters in Switzerland and Silicon Valley, has placed its manufacturing headquarters in Taiwan to capitalize on low-cost Asian manufacturing. Meanwhile, its business-development headquarters in Europe has lined up strategic partnerships that have kept the company at the cutting edge of peripherals design, particularly for optical pens and mice. Wipro Ltd. (*wipro.com*), the global IT outsourcing and consulting firm, has its vice-chairman in the Silicon Valley to be close to the huge U.S. market. At the same time, the company can underprice Western rivals because 17,000 of its 20,000 software engineers and consultants are in India, where the annual cost per employee is less than one-fifth that of Silicon Valley.

Electronic Business and E-Commerce.   As seen in the opening case, companies are transforming part or all of their operations into e-businesses. Doing business electronically is the newest and perhaps most promising strategy that many companies can pursue. Chapter 5 will focus extensively on this topic, and e-commerce applications are introduced throughout the book.

We have described the pressures that affect companies in today's business environment and the responses that organizations take to manage these pressures. To plan for the most effective responses, companies formulate strategies. In the new digital economy, these strategies are often enabled by information technology, specifically strategic information systems. In the next section, we discuss corporate strategy and strategic information systems.

> ## Before you go on . . .
>
> 1. Describe some of the pressures that characterize the modern global business environment.
> 2. What are some of the organizational responses to these pressures? Are any of the responses specific to a pressure? If so, which ones?

1.3 COMPETITIVE ADVANTAGE AND STRATEGIC INFORMATION SYSTEMS

A competitive strategy is a broad-based formula for how a business is going to compete, what its goals should be, and what plans and policies will be required to carry out those goals (Porter, 1985). Through its competitive strategy an organization seeks a **competitive advantage** in an industry—an advantage over competitors in some measure such as cost, quality, or speed. Competitive advantage leads to control of a market and to larger-than-average profits.

Competitive advantage in the digital economy is even more important than in the old economy, as we demonstrate throughout our book. In most cases, the digital economy has not changed the *core business* of companies. That is, Internet technologies simply offer the tools that can increase organizations' success through their traditional sources of competitive advantage—such as low cost, excellent customer service, or superior supply chain management. For most organizations, the first step to competitive advantage in the digital economy is to answer this question, "Where, given my industry and position, does my competitive advantage come from?" Then, the second step is to answer the follow-up question, "How can IT, especially the Internet, help my business?" The answer often involves strategic information systems.

Strategic information systems (SISs) are systems that help an organization gain a competitive advantage through their contribution to the strategic goals of an organization and/or their ability to significantly increase performance and productivity. An SIS is characterized by its ability to *significantly* change the manner in which business is conducted, in order to give the firm strategic advantage. Any information system that changes the goals, processes, products, or environmental relationships to help an organization gain a competitive advantage *or* reduce a competitive disadvantage is a strategic information system.

competitive advantage *An advantage over competitors in some measure such as cost, quality, or speed; leads to control of a market and to larger-than-average profits.*

strategic information systems (SISs) *Systems that help an organization gain a competitive advantage through their contribution to the strategic goals of an organization and/or their ability to significantly increase performance and productivity.*

Porter's Competitive Forces Model

The most well-known framework for analyzing competitiveness is Michael Porter's **competitive forces model** (Porter, 1985). It is used to develop strategies for companies to increase their competitive edge. It also demonstrates how IT can enhance the competitiveness of corporations.

The model recognizes five major forces that could endanger a company's position in a given industry (see Figure 1.3, page 16). However, the Internet has changed the nature of competition, and Porter (2001) concludes that the *overall* impact of the

competitive forces model *A business framework, devised by Michael Porter, for analyzing competitiveness by recognizing five major forces that could endanger a company's position.*

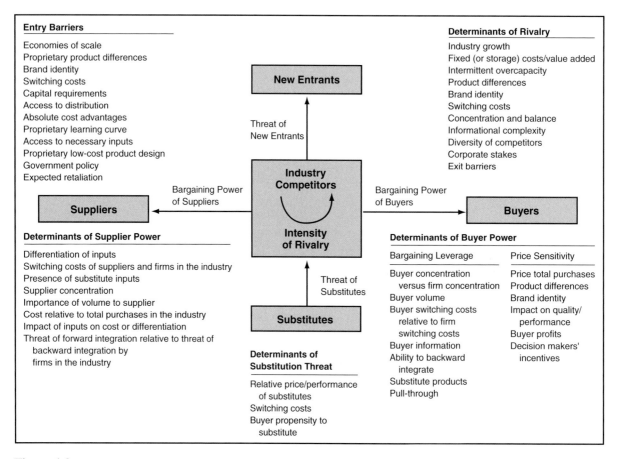

Figure 1.3 *Porter's five forces model, including the major determinants of each force. (Source: Adapted with permission of the Free Press, a division of Simon & Schuster, Inc., from Michael Porter,* Competitive Advantage: Creating and Sustaining Superior Performance, *p. 6. © 1985, 1998 by Michael Porter.)*

Internet is to increase competition, which negatively impacts profitability. The five forces and the way that the Internet influences them can be generalized as follows:

1. ***The threat of entry of new competitors.*** For most firms, the Internet *increases* the threat of new competitors. First, the Internet sharply reduces traditional barriers to entry, such as the need for a sales force or a physical storefront to sell goods and services. Competitors need only set up a Web site. This threat is particularly acute in industries that perform an intermediation role (e.g., stock brokers and travel agents) as well as in industries where the primary product or service is digital (e.g., the music industry). Second, the geographical reach of the Internet enables distant competitors to compete more directly with an existing firm.

2. ***The bargaining power of suppliers.*** The Internet's impact on suppliers is mixed. On one hand, buyers can find alternative suppliers and compare prices more easily, reducing the supplier's bargaining power. On the other hand, as companies use the Internet to integrate their supply chain and join digital exchanges, participating suppliers will prosper by locking in customers and increasing switching costs.

3. ***The bargaining power of customers (buyers).*** The Web greatly increases a buyer's access to information about products and suppliers. Internet technologies can reduce customer switching costs (the costs, in money and time, of a decision to buy elsewhere), and buyers can more easily buy from other suppliers. These factors mean that the Internet greatly increases customers' bargaining power.

4. ***The threat of substitute products or services.*** Information-based industries are in the greatest danger from substitutes. Any industry in which digitalized information can replace material goods (e.g., music, books, software) must view the Internet as a threat.

5. ***The rivalry among existing firms in the industry.*** The visibility of Internet applications on the Web makes proprietary systems more difficult to keep secret, reducing differences among competitors. (That is, when I see my competitor's great new sys-

tem online, I am likely to have to match its features to remain competitive.) In most industries, the tendency for the Internet to lower variable costs relative to fixed costs encourages price discounting. Both these forces encourage destructive price competition in an industry.

In many other ways Web-based systems are changing the nature of competition and even industry structure. For example, bookseller Barnes & Noble, hardware company The Home Depot, and other companies have created independent online divisions, which are competing against the parent companies physical stores. Companies that have both online and offline sales operations are termed "click-and-mortar" firms, because they combine both "brick-and-mortar" and e-commerce operations.

Another way in which Web-based systems are changing industry structure is that some competitors are getting together and becoming more willing to share information. Examples include the vertical exchanges owned by industry leaders. The "Big Three" automobile manufacturers, for example, created the auto exchange *covisint.com*. Similar exchanges exist in the paper, chemical, and many other industries.

Finally, competition is being affected by the fact that the variable cost of digital products is almost zero. Therefore, if large quantities are sold, the product's price can be so low that it might be given away for free. For example, some analysts predict that commissions for online stock trading will approach zero for this reason. That is, consumers have the information available now via the Internet to be able to make their own decisions regarding buying and selling stocks. Consumers do not need brokers to give them the information that they can obtain themselves, virtually for free.

Strategies for Competitive Advantage

Organizations continually try to develop strategies aimed at establishing a profitable and sustainable position against Porter's five forces. Porter and others have proposed various strategies to gain competitive advantage; we discuss 12 of those strategies here.

1. *Cost leadership strategy*—produce products and/or services at the lowest cost in the industry. As IT's about Business 1.3 illustrates, Staples uses software to examine the costs of its products in order to provide pricing that will please customers while generating profits. Another example is Wal-Mart's automatic inventory

---

IT's ABOUT BUSINESS   ACC FIN

1.3: Staples Redesigns the Showroom Floor

Executives at the $11.6 billion office-supply retailer Staples (*staples.com*) needed to measure corporate performance and product profitability. Their goal was to achieve "one version of the truth" and to track key performance indicators. Staples decided to use business intelligence (BI) software, which allows users to do sophisticated data analysis themselves. Using BI software from Hyperion (*hyperion.com*), Staples built product profitability models, which help managers determine the optimal mix of products and the best strategies for presenting them. The system provides graphical representations of high-level data—for example, revenues and costs for a line of products from a particular vendor. From their desktops, executives can drill down to more detailed levels—for example, checking the costs of marketing, distribution, and rent attributed to a particular stock-keeping unit.

For example, furniture is a product category that at first seemed to be a top performer, because it tends to produce large gross margins. After Staples' managers factored in the costs of storage, distribution, handling, damage, labor, and rent, the overall profitability of furniture turned out to be significantly lower than that for less space-intensive categories like basic office supplies. As a result, Staples reduced the floor space devoted to furniture and now devotes more room to categories for which the inventory turns over more often, such as chairs and filing cabinets.

Source: J. Caplan, "Applying a Little Business Intelligence," *CFO.com*, July 22, 2003.

QUESTIONS

1. Identify the benefits of the new software to Staples.
2. What does it mean when Staples executives say they want "one version of the truth"?

replenishment system, which enables Wal-Mart to reduce inventory storage requirements. As a result, Wal-Mart stores use floor space to sell products, not store them, thereby reducing inventory costs.

2. *Differentiation strategy*—offer different products, services, or product features. Southwest Airlines, for example, has differentiated itself as a low-cost, short-haul, express airline, and that has proven to be a winning strategy for competing in the highly competitive airline industry. Also, Dell has differentiated itself in the personal computer market through its mass-customization strategy.

3. *Niche strategy*—select a narrow-scope segment (niche market) and be the best in quality, speed, or cost in that market. Some of the best-selling products on the Internet are niche products. For example, *dogtoys.com* and *cattoys.com* offer a large variety of pet toys that no other pet toy retailer offers.

4. *Growth strategy*—increase market share, acquire more customers, or sell more products. Web-based selling can facilitate growth by creating new marketing channels, such as electronic auctions. An example is Dell Computer (*dellauction.com*), which auctions both new and used computers mainly to individuals and small businesses.

5. *Innovation strategy*—introduce new products and services, put new features in existing products and services, or develop new ways to produce them. A classic example is the introduction of automated teller machines (ATMs) by Citibank. The convenience and cost-cutting features of this innovation gave Citibank a huge advantage over its competitors. Like many innovative products, the ATM changed the nature of competition in the banking industry so that now an ATM is a competitive *necessity* for any bank. Eight ways that IT can introduce technological innovation for competitive advantage are listed in Table 1.2.

6. *Alliance strategy*—work with business partners in partnerships, alliances, joint ventures, or virtual companies. This strategy creates synergy, allows companies to concentrate on their core business, and provides opportunities for growth. Alliances are particularly popular in e-commerce ventures. For example, in August 2000, Amazon.com and Toysrus.com launched a co-branded Web site to sell toys, capitalizing on each other's strengths. In the spring of 2001, they created a similar baby-products venture. Of special interest are alliances with suppliers, some of

Table 1.2 Ways for IT to Introduce Technological Innovation

Innovation	Advantage
New business models	Jump ahead of competitors by being first to establish a new model. The Web enables innovative business models. *Example*: Priceline's "name-your-own-price," Auto-by-Tel's infomediary model.
New markets, global reach	Find new customers in new markets. *Example*: Via the Web, Amazon.com sells books in over 200 countries.
New products	Constantly innovate with new products and services. *Examples*: Electronic Art Inc. introduced CD-ROM-based video games; MP3 Inc. enabled downloading of music from its Web site.
Extended products	Leverage old products with new extensions. *Example*: a Korean company introduced "fuzzy logic" in its washing machines, and sales went up 50 percent in a few months.
Differentiated products	Offer unique products or added value. *Example*: Compaq gained PC market share by providing self-diagnostic disks with its computers.
Supersystems	Erect competitive barriers that cannot be easily duplicated. *Examples*: American Airlines' reservation system, SABRE, Delta's Digital Nervous System; and Caterpillar's equipment maintenance system.
Interorganizational systems	Link two organizational information systems to lock out the competition. *Example*: American Hospital Supply installed supply-reordering systems in hospitals.
Computer-aided sales	Provide computer support to marketing and sales. *Example*: Equip salespeople with wireless handheld computers that allow them to provide price quotations at the customer's location.

whom monitor inventory levels electronically and replenish inventory when it falls below a certain level (e.g., Wal-Mart and Procter & Gamble).

Alliances can also be made among competitors in a strategy known as "co-opetition" (cooperation + competition). For example, airlines in global alliances such as OneWorld (*oneworldalliance.com*) and the Star Alliance (*star-alliance.com*) compete for ticket sales on some routes, but once the ticket is sold they may cooperate by flying passengers on competitor's planes to avoid half-full planes.

7. **Operational effectiveness strategy**—improve the manner in which internal business processes are executed so that a firm performs similar activities better than rivals. Such improvements increase employee and customer satisfaction, quality, and productivity, while decreasing time to market. For example, improvements in Delta's baggage handling process saved the airline millions of dollars.

8. **Customer-orientation strategy**—concentrate on making customers happy. Strong competition and the realization of the importance of the customer are the basis of this strategy. Amazon.com, for example, excels at this strategy. Web-based systems are particularly effective in this area because they can provide a personalized, one-to-one relationship with each customer. The major entertainment networks are particularly interested in increasing the number of customers in their fantasy sports leagues, as IT's About Business 1.4 demonstrates.

IT's ABOUT BUSINESS [MKT]

1.4: Are You Ready for Some Football?

Millions of people are playing fantasy football, a booming entertainment and business phenomenon. Participants create leagues, draft players, set lineups, make trades, and see their teams win or lose based on the performance of real players week after week. The fantasy football champ is CBS SportsLine (*cbs.sportsline.com*), which has over two million players and also operates the fantasy football games on AOL, CNNSI.com, and NFL.com. SportsLine has introduced new technology to bring more realism to fantasy-league play.

SportsLine's Football Commissioner technology lets groups of up to 12 players create a league on SportsLine's servers at a cost of $139.95, divided among the players. SportsLine allows each league to create its own scoring rules before the season starts. For example, if a running back scores a touchdown, he can be awarded six points. But he can also get two points for every 25 yards he rushes or two points for every pass he catches—whatever the league decides. Leagues can also opt for a default set of scoring rules, provided by SportsLine. Once the participants set rules and draft players (this process is done either via the site or offline), each "owner" logs on to his or her own Web page to set lineups, make trades, and drop or add players.

The challenge for SportsLine is to rapidly crunch the numbers according to each league's unique set of rules. Each Sunday during the regular season, SportsLine will get more than 100 million unique page views on its fantasy football Web site, as fantasy team owners check to see how player performance in the real games affects the fantasy games.

At each stadium, a data-entry specialist keys in the results of each "live" play—yardage and players involved—and sends these stats to SportsLine's data center, where 300 Intel-based servers running Red Hat Linux process the data according to each league's set of scoring rules. The updated stats and scores are then sent to each team owner's Web page, a personalized page where owners see their team rosters side by side with those of opponents. The whole process—from the actual play in the stadium to the fantasy player's on-screen updates—can take as little as 6 seconds. When the real games end on Monday night, SportsLine tallies each team's fantasy points and adjusts the standings accordingly.

Source: A. Cohen, "Fantasy Football: CBS SportsLine," *PC Magazine*, December 24, 2002.

QUESTIONS

1. What is so important about updating players' Web pages so rapidly?
2. How might CBS use information technology to improve the fantasy football experience for players?

9. *Time strategy*—treat time as a resource, then manage it and use it to the firm's advantage. One of the driving forces behind time as a competitive strategy is the need for firms to be immediately responsive to customers, markets, and changing market conditions. A second factor is the time-to-market race. Often, most of the economic value of a product is realized early in its life.

10. *Entry-barriers strategy*—create barriers to entry for new competitors. For example, Priceline.com received U.S. patent 5,794,207 on its name-your-own-price business model. Cisco's Dynamic Configuration Tool (*cisco.com/appcontent/Apollo/configureHomeGuest.html*) allows prospective buyers to complete an online configuration of a Cisco product and receive intelligent feedback about compatibility and ordering. Service levels such as this make it difficult for new competitors to compete against Cisco.

11. *Lock in customers or suppliers strategy*—encourage customers or suppliers to stay with you rather than going to competitors. A classic example is frequent-flyer and similar buyer-loyalty programs in the airline, hospitality, and retail industries. A business-to-business example in the car industry is the e-procurement system Covisint, which locks in car manufacturers as customers and parts manufacturers as suppliers.

12. *Increase switching costs strategy*—discourage customers or suppliers from going to competitors for economic reasons. For example, Master Builders builds in switching costs with a concrete additive tank-monitoring system that notifies Master Builders to resupply customers' tanks on a just-in-time basis. The customer benefits from an assured supply of product, less capital tied up in inventory, and reduced inventory management time and processing.

Before you go on . . .

1. What are strategic information systems?

2. What are the five forces that Porter says could endanger a firm's position in its industry or marketplaces?

3. What strategies might companies use to gain competitive advantage?

1.4 STRATEGIC INFORMATION SYSTEMS: EXAMPLES

As we noted, any information system, properly used, can provide a competitive advantage. Therefore, there are millions of examples of strategic information systems. We provide several examples here, along with the strategies that each example supports. Note that each strategic information system can provide support for multiple organizational strategies.

POM

EXAMPLE *The Los Angeles Lakers Gain an Edge.* Chris Bodaken, the video coordinator for the Los Angeles Lakers (*nba.com/lakers/*), sleeps in the office during April. He "slices and dices" hours of video footage in myriad ways to help the team prepare for its usual appearance in the playoffs. Back when he had to manually create tapes using side-by-side VCRs, he averaged one hour of sleep per night. But he now uses a digital video-editing software package from Pinnacle Systems (*pinnaclesys.com*). The system integrates video effects and statistical analysis on the same screen, so that Bodaken can quickly and easily assign a data tag to each play or even insert a tag each time a certain player touches the ball. The system also lets him sift through archived footage of the Lakers against various opponents for the past several years. For example, the team can look at all of Shaquille O'Neal's post-ups on the left side of the key against Sacramento during the season. This information gives coach Phil Jackson a powerful tool to plot strategy for dealing with Chris Webber and Mike Bibby in a probable playoff clash with the Sacramento Kings. (*Source*: Salkever, 2003.)

Strategies supported: operational effectiveness, differentiation, innovation, time.

EXAMPLE   *Burlington Northern Railroad Improves Effi-* `POM` *ciency.* About 40 percent of all freight shipping is done by rail. Yet the railroads bring in only about 10 percent as much revenue as the $300 billion trucking industry. Industry profits have fallen about one-third since 1996. Burlington Northern (*bnsf.com*), the nation's second largest railroad, is now using remote-controlled loco-motives, satellite-based mapping, and sophisticated software for trip planning and monitoring, to keep trains running on time, to lower fuel and labor costs, and to take market share away from trucks.

In a mile-long three-locomotive train, when the engineer nudges the throttle, a computer wirelessly adjusts and blends the three engines' outputs for maximum effi-ciency and fuel conservation. Every railcar has a radio-frequency identification tag similar to those used by automobiles at tollbooths. Managers can track the progress of any train in the system on the company's Web site. A train's location is updated each time it passes one of the tag readers scattered along the line.

Every engine is connected to a digital event recorder similar to a black box on an airplane. It records speed, power, throttle positions, braking, air pressure, and other performance measures. This information is sent via Wi-Fi base stations along rail lines to the network operations center at company headquarters, where it is analyzed. The railroad's chief engineer uses the analysis to constantly monitor his engineers' perfor-mance. If they are making mistakes, they come into headquarters for additional train-ing on a simulator. Burlington Northern uses a GPS map of all 32,500 miles of its rail lines in its simulator software. Engineers are now tested on a simulation of the exact conditions they will encounter on the line.

Burlington Northern, with its scheduling software, has the ability to meet timeta-bles accurately enough to guarantee arrival times for trucking customers. The railroad is saving hundreds of millions of dollars a year through lower fuel consumption and better asset utilization. Productivity is up: Ton-miles per employee, the railroads' standard productivity gauge, has increased 22 percent since 1998. (*Source*: Schonfeld, 2003.)

Strategies supported: operational effectiveness, increase switching costs.

EXAMPLE   *Music Retailers Fight Back with Web-Based* `FIN` `POM` *Alliance.* The rise of music piracy is such a severe threat that six of the largest music retailers—Best Buy (*bestbuy.com*), Tower Records (*towerrecords.com*), Virgin Entertainment Group (*virgin.com/us/entertainment*), Wherehouse Entertainment (*wherehouse.com*), Hastings Entertainment (*gohastings.com*), and TransWorld Enter-tainment (*twec.com*)—have joined into an alliance called Echo (*echo.com*) in an effort to address the two-year decline in CD sales. Wherehouse, for example, recently filed for bankruptcy protection, and Best Buy has closed 107 stores, both as a result of poor CD sales.

Echo is obtaining licenses from the recording companies to distribute their music through their member retailer's own Web sites. The new firm is following the lead of companies like Universal Music Group, which distributes more than 60,000 songs through sites such as Best Buy and Circuit City for 99 cents per song or $9.99 per album.

Under Echo's plan, once the group receives the necessary licenses, the partners would market their services both together and separately. Efforts might include pro-motions like "Buy a CD, get a free download." The retailers could also enable cus-tomers to download music in stores using portable devices like the Apple iPod. Some analysts suggest, however, that even alliance strategies like Echo's will not be effective. What has to happen, they say, is for CD prices, which now average $14.21, to come down to get pirates to move from free sites to legitimate ones. (*Source: echo.com.*)

Strategies supported: alliance, customer orientation, lock-in customers.

MKT   **EXAMPLE**   *Procter & Gamble Searches for New Products.* Procter & Gamble (*pg.com*) is a $40 billion consumer-products manufacturer. Creating new products and getting them quickly to market has been a weak spot for the company. To better leverage its research and development efforts, P&G created InnovationNet, an internal portal for P&G's scientists to share ideas and create new products.

However, the company still struggles to find enough big ideas to fill its pipeline. So, P&G created a "connect-and-develop" program, inviting outsiders onto its team. P&G gives access to Innocentive (*innocentive.com*), a network of research scientists, as well as about 150 individual entrepreneurs. P&G's goal is to look for more ideas like the Crest Spin Brush toothbrush, one of the company's biggest new products in recent years. With a new product idea, P&G uses the Web to test and market the product, largely replacing live focus groups for early-stage analysis. P&G uses virtual presentations that can demonstrate new concepts and allow for rapid prototyping of new features for current products. (*Source: pg.com.*)

Strategies supported: innovation, time, alliance, growth.

MKT   **EXAMPLE**   *Merrill Lynch Manages Information Flow for Analysts and Clients.* Merrill Lynch (*merrilllynch.com*) recently implemented a service that gathers, organizes, streamlines, and customizes real-time news from thousands of Web sites for 400 desktops in its equity-sales and trading groups. The firm previously had numerous sources for news and research, both internal and external, all coming in through different channels. Searching numerous diverse sources was costing time that could be spent focusing on more valuable activities. The customized service provides each user the ability to set up specific queries, profiles, and interest lists, in order to get the information most relevant for him or her. The system enables users to easily send relevant information to clients and colleagues with no more than a point and click. There is also a capability for users to add their own perspectives into the system in order for other users to view their commentary. (*Source: merrilllynch.com.*)

Strategies supported: operational effectiveness, customer orientation.

MKT   **EXAMPLE**   *MetLife Leads Online Policyholder Support.* Insurance company MetLife (*metlife.com*) recently launched its first password-protected policy administration site to the general public. The site provides auto and home policyholders access to a multitude of information online, ranging from policy information and billing detail through claims status. The launch is significant because MetLife is the largest issuer of group auto insurance, and its push into e-servicing reflects a trend by major insurers.

On its Web site, MetLife breaks out policy information in a manner that makes it easy for clients to comprehend coverages for multiple cars and multiple drivers. Premiums are displayed so that a policyholder can determine how much each coverage for each vehicle costs. In fact, individual dollar values are assigned to individual coverages and vehicles to give policyholders a detailed view of what makes up their overall premium. On the site, MetLife even notes discounts that policyholders are not currently taking advantage of—a rarity in the industry. (*Source: metlife.com.*)

Strategies supported: customer orientation, lock-in customers.

EXAMPLE   *Increasing Sales at National Geographic.* The National Geographic Society (NGS) (*nationalgeographic.com*) has 10 million striking digital images in its photographic archives. Now, some 10,000 of these images are commercially available from the e-commerce site that the nonprofit scientific and educational organization has launched at *ngsimages.com.* Corporations worldwide pay license fees to use the organization's images for advertising campaigns. Until recently, customers worked directly with the sales staff in the NGS Image Sales group, who would research the organization's photographic archives for them.

To increase customer ease-of-use, NGS created its searchable, business-to-business digital media e-commerce site. NGS global customers can log on at their convenience to research and buy from a portfolio of digitized images. This new sales channel has tripled NGS revenue from photographic sales, without having to increase its sales staff. NGS has also substantially cut its handling costs for licensing the images.

Once customers are ready to buy, they can add selected images to a virtual shopping cart and proceed to checkout. The NGS Web site offers customers a variable, usage-based pricing model and an easy-to-use pricing calculator. NGS also offers customers different payment options—credit card or purchase order—as well as the choice of downloading images or receiving a CD or slides. (*Source: ibm.com,* 2003.)

Strategies supported: cost leadership, customer orientation, operational effectiveness.

Information Systems Failures

So far, we have introduced you to many success stories. You many wonder, though, "Is IT all success?" The answer is, "Absolutely not." There are many failures, and we can learn from failures as much as from successes. We will show you examples of IT failures throughout the book. Our next example and the Real-World Case of Pepsi at the end of this chapter describe two IT failures.

EXAMPLE   *Bugs Ground Planes in Japan.* A software bug in a program running in an air traffic control computer grounded all flights across Japan on Saturday, March 2, 2003. The system, which handles the distribution of flight information to airports, failed at 7 A.M., resulting in the immediate halt of all departures from Japanese airports, said an official.

The fault was thought to have been caused by a bug in new software that was loaded onto the machine at 1 A.M. the same day, said the official. The software handles exchange of data between the control center's computer and a similar computer at the Defense Ministry.

The new software worked for the first six hours. However, it failed at exactly 7 A.M., coinciding with the running of a program that collects data on the previous day's air traffic. The ministry was looking into the possibility that an incompatibility between the two programs caused the problem.

The failure caused the cancellation of 192 flights and the delay of 1,342 flights for 30 minutes or more, said local media reports. The longest delay was more than six hours, and the problems inconvenienced an estimated 270,000 people, including 39,000 travelers who were forced to give up their travel plans. The ministry official said the new software was tested on a backup system for two weeks and no problems were observed. However, the official could not confirm whether data exchange with the new Defense Ministry system or the daily data-gathering software was part of the test. (*Source*: Williams, 2003.)

It is also possible that too much IT can be "too much of a good thing." In fact, Washington Federal Savings and Loan feels that less IT is better, as the following example demonstrates.

Lessons From
IT
IT Failures

FIN | **EXAMPLE** | *Less IT Proves Better for Savings and Loan.*
Washington Federal Savings and Loan Association (*washingtonfederal.com*) in Seattle, Washington, is one of the West's fastest-growing savings and loan institutions, with 119 branches in eight states and $7.4 billion in assets. Yet it owns no automated teller machines; it has no online banking, no voice mail, no "press 3" automated phone system. Typewriters still sit on desks at headquarters, and there are only five Internet-connected PCs. Yet the firm last year reported record earnings of $144 million, a 27 percent increase over fiscal 2001. At a time when some critics are questioning the value of IT, Washington Federal seems to be proving those contrarians right: In this case, less is more.

Washington Federal keeps its technology spending down to 1 percent of its annual operating expenses and has an IT department of seven. While other thrift institutions spend 45 cents to produce $1 of net revenue, Washington Federal spends 18 cents (including the one cent for IT) to earn a dollar. Washington Federal's CEO notes that the firm's customer base is older and wants "high-touch" levels of service that they cannot get at other institutions, which concentrate mainly on low costs. So Washington Federal employees answer their own phones. The company's Web site provides customer and investor information, with a single e-mail contact for inquiries. (*Source*: Winkler, 2003.)

Although there are many reasons for failure of an IT project, one of the most critical is our inability to predict the future of information technology with any accuracy. Information technology is evolving and continuously changing in a rapid fashion, as we discuss in Chapter 2.

Before you go on . . .

1. Why do strategic information systems support many corporate strategies?
2. What are other reasons that IT projects might fail?

1.5 WHY SHOULD YOU LEARN ABOUT INFORMATION TECHNOLOGY?

We have demonstrated in this chapter that we live in a digital economy and that the ways we live and do business are changing dramatically. The organizational impacts of IT are growing rapidly, especially with the introduction of the Internet and e-commerce. We are becoming more and more dependent on information systems. Here we consider several characteristics of IT that answer the question, "Why should I learn about IT?"

IT Facilitates Work in Organizations

A major role of IT is being a facilitator of organizational activities and processes. That role will become more important as time passes. Therefore, it is necessary that every manager and professional staff member learn about IT not only in his or her specialized field, but also in the entire organization and in interorganizational settings as well.

You will be more effective in your chosen career if you understand how successful information systems are built, used, and managed. You also will be more effective if you know how to recognize and avoid unsuccessful systems and failures. Also, in many ways, having a comfort level with information technology will enable you, at work and at home, to take advantage of new IT products and systems as they are developed. For help gaining this comfort level, see *howstuffworks.com*. Finally, you should learn about IT because being knowledgeable about information technology can also increase employment opportunities. Even though computerization eliminates some jobs, it creates many more.

IT Is Used by All Departments

Information technology is vital for every functional area of an organization, and IT systems are integral to every functional area. In *finance* and *accounting*, for example, managers use such systems to forecast revenues and business activity, determine the best sources and uses of funds, manage cash and other financial resources, analyze investments, and perform audits to ensure that the organization is fundamentally sound and that all financial reports and documents are accurate.

In *sales* and *marketing*, managers use information technology to develop new goods and services (product analysis), determine the best location for production and distribution facilities (site analysis), determine the best advertising and sales total revenues (promotion analysis), and set product prices to get the highest total revenues (price analysis). Marketing managers also use IT to manage the customer relationship.

In *manufacturing*, managers use IT to process customer orders, develop production schedules, control inventory levels, and monitor product quality. In addition, these managers use IT to design products (computer-assisted design or CAD) and to manufacture items (computer-assisted manufacturing or CAM).

Managers in *human resources* use IT to screen job applicants, administer performance tests to employees, and monitor employee productivity. These managers also use legal IT to analyze product liability and warranties and to develop important legal documents and reports. IT's about Business 1.5 shows how information technology helps manage human resources at DaimlerChrysler.

These are just a few examples of the roles of information technology in the various functional areas of an organization. We think it is important for students from the different functional areas to see the value of the information systems in their fields. To help do this, we have included at the end of every chapter a section called "What's in IT for Me?" that discusses the chapter's relevance to the various business functions.

IT's ABOUT BUSINESS   HRM

1.5: Worldwide Human Resources Management at DaimlerChrysler

DaimlerChrysler (*daimlerchrysler.com*), one of the world's largest automakers, has manufacturing facilities in 37 countries and over 370,000 employees. The company's strategy, based on global presence, strong brands, broad product range, and technology leadership, means that the firm must find ways to work more efficiently, reduce costs, and enable easy access to information. To meet these goals, the company needed to (1) establish common HR business processes around the world; (2) reduce administrative costs through workforce self-service; and (3) streamline recruitment to better compete for talent in Germany and the United States.

DaimlerChrysler implemented PeopleSoft's HRMS, which provided employees with easy access to information across the enterprise. The company now has a centralized source for global workforce information, delivered through the Internet. The software also provides collaboration tools for employees to use while working on projects.

The software also provides self-service for employees. They can use the applications to change their home address or view a paycheck through any browser—whether they are at work, at home, in an Internet café, or using a kiosk in the break room of a factory. Self-service helps DaimlerChrysler decrease its administrative costs while providing better service for the workforce.

DaimlerChrysler is also concerned with attracting and retaining the most talented people. Headquartered in Germany and the United States, the company is faced with aging workforces, meaning that there is going to be more competition for a smaller pool of workers. Using PeopleSoft's eRecruit, the company has eliminated much of the paperwork and delays from its recruiting process. Applicants now can apply for jobs online, in real time. With integrated workflow applications, the company is now able to respond to applicants much more quickly.

Sources: peoplesoft.com and daimlerchrysler.com.

---

1. What are the reasons that DaimlerChrysler needed a human resources information system?
2. What advantages did the company gain from its HR information system?

WHAT'S IN IT FOR ME?

FOR ALL BUSINESS MAJORS

Regardless of the functional area, managers use information technology as a competitive weapon. Interestingly, due to the magnitude of many strategic decisions, all the functional areas often work together to provide input to a decision.

`ACC`

FOR THE ACCOUNTING MAJOR

Consider opening a new factory in another country, clearly a strategic decision. Financial and accounting managers use IT to calculate and analyze the investment, forecast revenues and business activity, determine the best sources and uses of funds (e.g., currency exchange rates), manage cash and other financial resources, and perform ongoing audits to ensure that the concept is fundamentally sound and that all financial reports and documents are accurate.

`MKT`

FOR THE MARKETING MAJOR

Marketing managers use IT to perform the site analysis (determine the best location for the facility), determine the best advertising channels in that country, and set product prices. Marketing managers also manage the customer relationship, which entails an in-depth knowledge of the local language and culture.

`POM`

FOR THE PRODUCTION/ OPERATIONS MANAGEMENT MAJOR

Production/operations managers use IT to process customer orders, develop production schedules, control inventory levels, and monitor product quality. These managers are responsible for designing the new plant and its products, and then for the actual manufacturing operations (computer-aided design, computer-assisted manufacturing, computer-integrated manufacturing—CAD/CAM/CIM). In addition, they utilize IT to manage the supply chain, which will be a more complex operation because it is international.

`HRM`

FOR THE HUMAN RESOURCES MANAGEMENT MAJOR

Human resources managers use IT to screen job applicants, administer performance tests to employees, and monitor employee productivity. These managers also use legal IT to analyze product liability and warranties and to develop important legal documents and reports.

IT Offers Career Opportunities

The demand for traditional information technology staff—such as programmers, systems analysts, and designers—is substantial. In addition, many well-paid opportunities exist in emerging areas such as the Internet and e-commerce, mobile commerce, network security, object-oriented programming, telecommunications, and multimedia design. For details about careers in IT, see *techjourney.com* and also "Career resources" and "Technology careers" at *wageweb.com*. In addition, Table 1.3 provides a list of IT jobs with a description of each type of job.

Before you go on . . .

1. What are the major reasons why it is important to know about information technology?

2. Why is it important to know about information technology when you are not working as an IT employee?

Table 1.3 Information Technology Jobs

Position	Job Description
Chief information officer (CIO)	Highest-ranking IS manager; responsible for strategic planning in the organization.
IS director	Responsible for managing all systems throughout the organization and day-to-day operations of the entire IS organization.
Information center manager	Manages IS services such as help desks, hot lines, training, and consulting.
Applications development manager	Coordinates and manages new systems development projects.
Project manager	Manages a particular new systems development project.
Systems manager	Manages a particular existing system.
Operations manager	Supervises the day-to-day operations of the data and/or computer center.
Programming manager	Coordinates all applications programming efforts.
Systems analyst	Interfaces between users and programmers; determines information requirements and technical specifications for new applications.
Systems programmer	Writes the computer code for developing new applications or maintaining existing applications.
Emerging technologies manager	Forecasts technology trends and evaluates and experiments with new technologies.
Network manager	Coordinates and manages the organization's voice and data network.
Database administrator	Manages the organization's databases and database management software usage.
Auditing or computer security manager	Manages ethical and legal use of information systems.
Webmaster	Manages the organization's World Wide Web site.
Web designer	Creates World Wide Web sites and pages.

SUMMARY

1. **Describe the characteristics of the digital economy and e-business.** Conducting e-business in the digital economy means using Web-based systems on the Internet and other electronic networks. The digital economy is based on digital technologies, including digital communications networks (the Internet, intranets, extranets, and others), computers, software, and other related information technologies. Digital networking infrastructures enable the digital economy by providing a global platform over which people and organizations interact, communicate, collaborate, and search for information.

2. **Discuss the relationships among business pressures, organizational responses, and information systems.** The business environment is the combination of social, legal, economic, physical, and political factors that affect business activities. Significant changes in any of these factors are likely to create business pressures on organizations. Organizations typically respond to these pressures with activities supported by IT. These responses are grouped into seven categories: strategic systems, customer focus, continuous improvement, restructuring, make-to-order and mass customization, business alliances, and e-business.

3. **Describe strategic information systems (SISs) and explain their advantages.** Strategic information systems are systems that support or shape a business unit's competitive strategy. An SIS is characterized by its ability to significantly change the manner in which business is conducted, in order for the firm to gain a competitive advantage or reduce a competitive disadvantage.

4. **Describe Porter's competitive forces model and how information technology helps companies improve their competitive positions.** Porter's competitive forces model is used to develop strategies for companies to gain competitive advantage. It also demonstrates how IT can enhance the competitiveness of corporations. The model recognizes five major forces that could endanger a company's position in a given industry: the threat of entry of new competitors, the bargaining power of suppliers, the bargaining power of customers (buyers), the threat of substitute products or services, and the rivalry among existing firms in the industry. However, the Internet has changed the nature of competition; Porter concludes that the *overall* impact of the Internet is to increase competition, which negatively impacts profitability.

5. **Describe 12 strategies that companies can use to achieve competitive advantage in their industries.** The 12 strategies are as follows: (1) *cost leadership strategy*—produce products and/or services at the lowest cost in the industry; (2) *differentiation strategy*—offer different products, services, or product features; (3) *niche strategy*—select a narrow-scope segment (niche market) and be the best in quality, speed, or cost

in that market; (4) *growth strategy*—increase market share, acquire more customers, or sell more products; (5) *innovation strategy*—introduce new products and services, put new features in existing products and services, or develop new ways to produce them; (6) *alliance strategy*—work with business partners in partnerships, alliances, joint ventures, or virtual companies; (7) *operational effectiveness strategy*—improve the manner in which internal business processes are executed so that a firm performs similar activities better than rivals; (8) *customer-orientation strategy*—concentrate on making customers happy; (9) *time strategy*—treat time as a resource, then manage it and use it to the firm's advantage; (10) *entry-barriers strategy*—create barriers to entry for new competitors; (11) *lock in customers or suppliers strategy*—encourage customers or suppliers to stay with you rather than going to competitors; (12) *increase switching costs strategy*—discourage customers or suppliers from going to competitors for economic reasons.

INTERACTIVE / LEARNING

Instructions for accessing the Interactivities on the Student Web Site:

1. Go to
   wiley.com/college/turban
2. Select Turban Rainer Potter's *Introduction to Information Technology, Third Edition*
3. Click on Student Resources Site, in the toolbar on the left
4. Click on Interactivities Web Site
5. Click on Interactivities Web Site and use your password to enter the site (your password card is located in the inside cover of your textbook)

How Does UPS Track Its Orders?

Go to the Interactivities section on the Student Web Site and access Chapter 1: The IT-Based Organization in the Digital Economy. There you will find an animated simulation of the UPS Tracking system, as well as some hands-on activities that visually explain business concepts in this chapter.

More Resources

More resources and study tools are located on the Student Web Site. You'll find additional chapter materials and links to organizations, people, and technologies for each chapter. In addition, self-quizzes that provide individualized feedback are available for each chapter.

DISCUSSION QUESTIONS

1. What has been the impact of the digital economy on competition?
2. Review the examples of the new versus old economy cases. In what way did IT make the difference in each case?
3. Is IT a strategic weapon or a survival tool? Discuss.
4. Why might it be difficult to justify a strategic information system?
5. List eight ways that IT can support corporate strategy.
6. Describe the five forces in Porter's competitive forces model and how the Internet has affected each one.
7. Why is the Internet said to be the creator of new business models?
8. Discuss the idea that an information system by itself can rarely provide a sustainable competitive advantage.
9. Discuss why some information systems fail.

PROBLEM-SOLVING ACTIVITIES

1. Visit some Web sites that offer employment opportunities in IT (such as *execunet.com* and *monster.com*). Compare the IT salaries to salaries offered to accountants, marketing personnel, financial personnel, operations personnel, and human resource personnel. For other information on IT salaries, check *Computerworld*'s annual salary survey and *techjourney.com*.
2. Prepare a short report on the role of information technology in government. Start with *whitehouse.gov/omb/egov/, estrategy.gov, ctg.albany.edu, e-government*.

govt.nz, and *worldbank.org/publicsector/egov*. Find e-government plans in Hong Kong and in Singapore (*info. gov.hk/digital21/e-gov/eng/index.htm* and *egov.gov.sg*).

3. The market for optical copiers is shrinking rapidly. It is expected that by 2005, as much as 85 percent of all duplicated documents will be done on computer printers. Can a company such as Xerox survive?
   a. Read about the problems of Xerox in 2002–2003 at *fortune.com*, *findarticles.com*, and *google.com*.
   b. Identify the business pressures on Xerox.
   c. Find some of Xerox's response strategies (see *xerox.com*, *fortune.com*, and *forbes.com*).
   d. Identify the role of IT as a contributor to the business technology pressures.
   e. Identify the role of IT as a facilitator of Xerox's responses.

INTERNET ACTIVITIES

1. Access the Web site of Federal Express (*fedex.com*).
   a. Find out what information is available to customers before they send a package.
   b. Find out about the "package tracking" system; be specific.
   c. Compute the cost of delivering a 15″ × 20″ × 10″ box, weighing 35 pounds, from your hometown to Honolulu, Hawaii. Compare the fastest delivery against the least cost.
2. Surf the Internet (use *google.com*, *brint.com*, or a similar search engine) to find information about:
   a. International virtual corporations (at least two examples).
   b. Virtual corporations in general.
3. Access *digitalenterprise.org*. Prepare a report regarding the latest EC developments in the digital age.
4. Access *x-home.com* and find information about the easy life of the future.
5. Experience customization by designing your own shoes at *nike.com*, your car at *jaguar.com*, your CD at *musicmaker.com*, and your business card at *iprint.com*. Summarize your experiences.

TEAM ASSIGNMENTS

1. Review the *Wall Street Journal*, *Fortune*, *Business Week*, and local newspapers of the last three months to find stories about the use of Web-based technologies in organizations. Each team will prepare a report describing five applications. The reports should emphasize the role of the Web and its benefit to the organizations. Cover issues such as productivity, quality, cycle time, and globalization. One of the groups should concentrate on mobile commerce (e-commerce transactions conducted in a wireless environment) and another on electronic marketplaces. Present and discuss your work.

2. Assign group members to each of the major car rental companies. Find out their latest strategies regarding customer service. Visit their Web sites, and compare the findings. Have each group prepare a presentation on why its company should get the title of "best customer service provider." Also, each group should use Porter's competitive forces model to help make its case.
3. Assign group members to UPS, FedEx, DHL, and the U.S. Postal Service. Have each group study the e-commerce strategies of one organization. Then have members present the organization, explaining why it is the best.

REAL-WORLD CASE

INFORMATION TECHNOLOGY PROBLEMS AT PEPSICO

THE BUSINESS PROBLEM With annual sales of $25 billion, PepsiCo (*pepsico.com*) is one of the most successful consumer products firms in the world. PepsiCo controls 55 brands of food and drink through its five business units, Frito-Lay, Pepsi-Cola, Tropicana, Quaker Foods, and Pepsi bottlers.

PepsiCo's corporate culture is to allow its business units autonomy. PepsiCo's CEO notes that the company has "big brands and big businesses" and cannot be run in a centralized fashion. As long as business units meet growth and profit targets, management does not want to interfere. However, the company's gross margin of profit is shrinking, and Pepsi-Cola is losing momentum to Coca-Cola in the beverage business. In the snack business, private-label competitors are undercutting Frito-Lays' pricing, which is squeezing margins. Therefore, PepsiCo is looking to cut costs wherever possible.

Information technology would seem to be a logical solution for cost-cutting, but PepsiCo has problems with its IT as well. The company has no central, unified IT infrastructure, IT architecture, nor IT services. As a result, the business units have different IT infrastructures, enterprise software, databases, human resources systems, financial applications, distribution hardware, and distribution software.

For example, drivers for PepsiCo's three major bottlers each use different handheld appliances to track the products they deliver. All the handhelds can send information over Bluetooth, Wi-Fi, and wireless area networks, but all use different software. Frito-Lay runs Oracle software for financials and human resources and i2 Technologies software for managing its supply chain. But Quaker had to recently stop an SAP software project and revert to older custom-built applications while preparing to move to Oracle applications.

In another example, PepsiCo has always wanted to have its products delivered to customers on one or two trucks. Frito-Lay chips, Quaker granola bars, Tropicana juices, Aquafina water, and Pepsi-Cola could be packed together to arrive at a supermarket. But today, four or more trucks with items from the different business units drive up to stores' loading docks on different schedules. Indeed, the company operates separate distribution centers for the business units, even though they all deliver to the same grocery and convenience stores.

THE IT SOLUTION To address these problems, PepsiCo set up a central information technology group (called its Business Solutions Group) to adopt software for human resources, finance, procurement, and sales and marketing, for use across all business units. Its goals are to create a central data warehouse; set IT infrastructure standards (e.g., network infrastructure); develop a set of IT services to be shared across the business units; and manage the corporate data center.

THE RESULTS In fact, PepsiCo's Business Solutions Group has not been able to successfully unify information systems across PepsiCo's businesses. When PepsiCo created the Business Solutions Group, it did not dismantle the technology management group in each of the business units. Unit managers are compensated and rewarded for meeting financial goals of their divisions, not for how well they cooperate with each other or with the Business Solutions Group.

The idea of a central IT group was a good one, but failed, largely because it required major cultural changes at PepsiCo. The idea required that business unit executives give up authority, and none of them embraced that idea. If PepsiCo had been able to achieve a unified, centralized IT strategy, analysts estimate that the company would have saved $1.7 billion a year.

Source: K. S. Nash and M. Duvall, "PepsiCo: No Deposit, No Return," *Baseline Magazine*, May 1, 2003.

QUESTIONS

1. Do PepsiCo's problems lie with information technology, with the structure of the company itself, or both? Support your answer by discussing the problems of the company with IT and with corporate structure.
2. Why did PepsiCo's proposed IT solution fail?
3. How might PepsiCo have ensured that its proposed IT solution had a better chance for survival?

CLUB IT — wiley.com/college/turban

WELCOME TO YOUR INTERNSHIP AT CLUB IT!

Club IT is a downtown music venue managed and owned by Ruben Keys and Lisa Tejada. They both graduated with Business Administration degrees in 1998 and decided to follow their dream to open a nightclub. During college, they supported themselves by working as musicians, Lisa playing bass and Ruben playing drums, so they learned quite a bit about nightclub operations from experience. In addition, they learned business principles from their studies. Lisa and Ruben have just completed extensive remodeling of the interior of Club IT and are pleased with the results. Its high ceilings and colorful lighting creates a hip, fun atmosphere. They hire live bands on Fridays and Saturdays and have a live DJ Mondays through Thursdays (closed on Sundays). The DJ uses a collection of MP3's, playing hip-hop, techno, and electronic music with some pop thrown in.

Lisa and Ruben run the office and maintain all financial and business-related records. They realize that while the resources they spent on remodeling are paying off well, their information management is lagging behind. They hired you to analyze their information needs.

To prepare for your first day of work, you and a few friends decide to spend a Friday night at Club IT. Your visit is a lot of fun—you meet some interesting people and enjoy hearing a new band. Reporting to work on Monday afternoon, you wonder how much information technology a nightclub can possibly need, and if there will be enough information and technology analysis opportunities to justify your internship.

Sitting in the empty club a few hours before opening, you have your initial meeting with Ruben and Lisa. They give you background on the club and tell you about their need to boost their information technology, data management, and decision-making capabilities. Your first task is to get acquainted with the club and its operations, so Lisa has you log in to their Web site from her desk in their tiny back office.

ASSIGNMENT

1. Visit the Club IT Web site, and answer the following questions:

   a. What is Club IT's mission?
   b. Who is Club IT's primary clientele?
   c. What are the current employment opportunities at Club IT?
   d. What is your boss' e-mail address?
   e. What information is available to employees only (password is "clubit")

2. Find another nightclub on the Web and describe the information it provides via its Web site.

Go to wiley.com/college/turban to access the CLUB IT Web Site on the Student Web Site

Information Technologies: Concepts and Management

Chapter Preview

Now you are acquainted with how business is done in the digital age and the supporting role of IT in helping businesses survive and gain competitive advantage. In Chapter 2 we turn our attention to the basic concepts of information systems in organizations.

The two major determinants of IT support are organizational structure and the functions that employees perform within organizations. As this chapter shows, information systems tend to follow the structure of organizations, and they are based on the needs of individuals and groups.

Information systems are located everywhere inside organizations, as well as between organizations. Such diversity of information systems creates difficulty in managing them. This chapter looks at the types of support that information systems provide to organizational employees and briefly at how IT systems are managed in organizations.

Learning Objectives

1. Differentiate between information technology infrastructure and information technology architecture.
2. Describe the components of computer-based information systems.
3. Describe various information systems and their evolution.
4. Identify the major internal support systems for each organizational level.
5. Compare mainframe-based legacy systems, client/server architecture, and peer-to-peer architecture.
6. Describe the major types of Web-based information systems and understand their functionalities.
7. Describe the emerging computing environments.
8. Describe how information resources are managed and the roles of the information systems department and the end users.

LAND O'LAKES COLLABORATES WITH COMPETITORS

Land O'Lakes, Inc. (*landolakesinc.com*) is a $6 billion food and agricultural cooperative serving family farmers nationwide. The company is owned by and serves more than 7,000 producer-members and approximately 1,300 local community cooperatives. It is the nation's third-largest seller of branded dairy foods.

Land O'Lakes ran into trouble in 2002 in every major area of operations. Sales fell $712 million from the previous year, to $5.8 billion, partly due to smaller markets for branded dairy products as a result of the slow economy. Land O'Lakes is also burdened with debt from its 2001 acquisition of Purina Mills.

Another factor is Wal-Mart, which is moving further into the grocery business. Wal-Mart's renowned distribution system includes superefficient regional distribution centers across the country, where trucks bringing goods in and taking them out can simply "cross-dock" without having to keep large amounts of inventory in a holding area. Land O'Lakes and its competitors, therefore, must be able to accommodate Wal-Mart's demanding schedules by having trucks show up exactly when they are due.

Land O'Lakes also has to compete for space in supermarkets' refrigerated sections with huge competitors such as Dean Foods (*deanfoods.com*) and Kraft Foods (*kraft.com*). These giants use their size, clout, and relationships with supermarket retailers, paying slotting allowances (up-front payments that a food manufacturer must pay to a supermarket for access to its shelves) and engaging in other practices that make the fight for grocery-store space extremely competitive.

THE IT SOLUTION

These pressures are forcing Land O'Lakes to find ways to become more efficient, in order to reduce costs. In the packaged foods industry, delivery trucks are empty about 25 percent of the time. Just two years ago, Land O'Lakes truckers—some 50 different carriers—spent much of their time shuttling empty trucks down slow-moving highways, wasting several million dollars annually. To address these inefficiencies, Land O'Lakes is using Web-based collaborative logistics. The company turned to Nistevo (*nistevo.com*), a hosted software service that enables manufacturers, retailers, and carriers to plan and execute their inbound and outbound logistics.

Nistevo's Web site continuously updates and consolidates information about routes, loads, and schedules from members' in-house logistics scheduling systems. Only Nistevo sees the whole picture. For example, if General Mills and Land O'Lakes are sharing a route, Land O'Lakes' routes are not shown to General Mills, and vice versa. Nistevo scans the millions of possible route configurations and route-load combinations to look for empty trucks and less-than-truckload product amounts. When finding these situations, Nistevo can merge loads from different companies bound for the same destination, or destinations along the way.

THE RESULTS

To join Nistevo's network, Land O'Lakes paid an initial subscription fee of $250,000, and the co-op incurred another $250,000 in related startup costs, such as training its 10-person logistics staff to use the Web site. However, the company says that savings from its logistics strategy covered those fees within the first six months of use. In fact, the new logistics strategy is cutting freight costs by 15 percent annually, for an annual savings of over $2 million.

Now, thanks to the Web, the company can identify the empty trucks and the best carriers, and find the fastest routes—and can piggyback onto dozens of General Mills' and Georgia-Pacific Corp.'s routes to gain savings.

Source: Compiled from D. Buss, "Land O'Lakes Shares the Load," *CIO Insight*, May 9, 2003.

In the digital economy, how well companies transform themselves from traditional modes of operation to e-business will depend on how well they can adapt their structure and business processes to take advantage of emerging technologies. Land O'Lakes has created for itself an entirely new business process, collaboration with competitors, by using Web-based logistics systems, thereby increasing operational efficiency and saving money. The case also shows the role of outsourcing (to Nistevo), which frees companies to concentrate on their core business. In this chapter we describe how information systems of different kinds are structured, organized, and managed so that they can support businesses in the twenty-first century.

2.1 INFORMATION SYSTEMS: CONCEPTS AND DEFINITIONS

Before we focus on the details of information technology (IT) and its management, we describe the major concepts of information systems.

Information Technology Architecture

An organization's **information technology architecture** is a high-level map or plan of the information assets in an organization. It is a guide for current operations and a blueprint for future directions. It assures managers that the organization's IT structure will meet its strategic business needs. Therefore, the IT architecture must integrate the information requirements of the organization and all users, the IT infrastructure (discussed next), and all applications.

The IT architecture is analogous to the architecture of a house. The architecture of a house, shown through blueprints, describes how the house is to be constructed, including the integration of the components of the house, such as the plumbing system, the electrical system, and so forth. In preparing the IT architecture, the designer needs similar information, which can be divided into two parts:

information technology architecture *A high-level map or plan of the information assets in an organization, which guides current operations and is a blueprint for future directions.*

1. The business needs for information—that is, the organizational objectives and problems, and the contribution that IT can make. Potential users of IT must play a critical role in this part of the design process.
2. The existing and planned IT infrastructure and applications of the organization. This information includes how the planned IT resources can be integrated among themselves or with present (and potential future) resources to support the organization's information needs.

The IT architecture of an e-business (travel agency) is shown in Figure 2.1. The important thing to remember about IT architecture is that it provides the plan for all the organization's computer-based information systems.

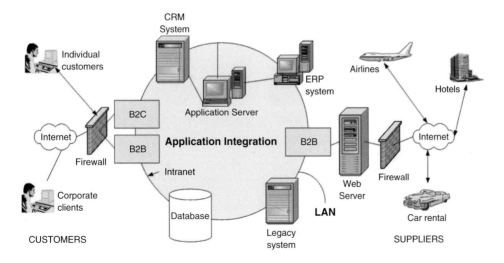

Figure 2.1 *Architecture of an online travel agency.*

Information Technology Infrastructure

information technology infrastructure *The physical facilities, IT components, IT services, and IT management that support an entire organization.*

An organization's **information technology infrastructure** consists of the physical facilities, IT components, IT services, and IT management that support the entire organization (see Figure 2.2). *IT components* are the computer hardware (see Technology Guide 1), software (Technology Guide 2), and communications technologies (Technology Guides 3 and 4) that are used by IT personnel to produce IT services. *IT services* include data management (Chapter 3), systems development (Chapter 11), and security concerns (Chapter 12). IT infrastructures include these resources as well as their integration, operation, documentation, maintenance, and management. The IT infrastructure also tells us how specific computing resources are arranged, operated, and managed. IT's about Business 2.1 shows how Mythic Entertainment uses information technology infrastructure to create virtual worlds for online gamers.

information technology (IT) *Broadly, an organization's collection of information resources, their users, and the management that oversees them; includes the IT infrastructure and all other information systems in an organization.*

The term **information technology (IT)** is sometimes confusing. In this book we use the term IT in its broadest sense—to describe an organization's collection of information resources, their users, and the management that oversees them. That is, information technology includes the IT infrastructure and all other information systems in the organization. Typically, though, the term *information technology* is used interchangeably with *information system*. The purpose of this book is to acquaint you with all aspects of information systems/information technology.

information system (IS) *A process that collects, processes, stores, analyzes, and disseminates information for a specific purpose; most ISs are computerized.*

Computer-Based Information Systems

computer-based information system (CBIS) *An information system that uses computer technology to perform some or all of its intended tasks.*

An **information system (IS)** collects, processes, stores, analyzes, and disseminates information for a specific purpose. An information system is not necessarily computerized, although most of them are.

A **computer-based information system (CBIS)** is an information system that uses computer technology to perform some or all of its intended tasks. (Note that the term

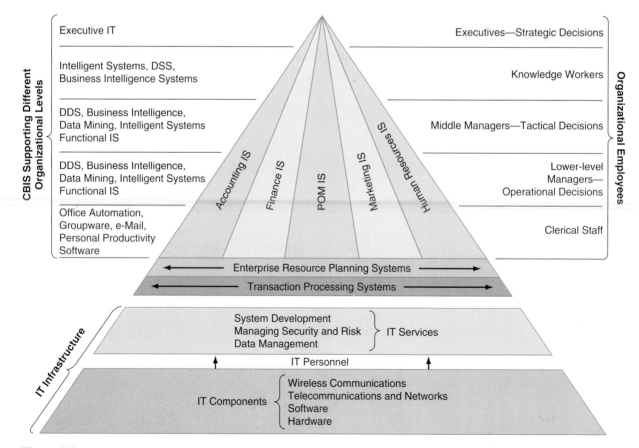

Figure 2.2 *Information technology inside your organization.*

IT'S ABOUT BUSINESS   MKT

2.1: Keeping Online Gamers Happy

Online gamers are an obsessive group, often racking up dozens of hours each week doing battle with other players. The most elaborate adventures—known as massively multiplayer online role-playing games—require monthly fees and huge time commitments from players. For developers, that means constant pressure to keep games interesting and growing. The developers must create a compelling story but also must set up a technological infrastructure that can accommodate different styles of play, minimize time lags, maximize customer support, and handle frequent updates to content and graphics. All of these elements are essential to keeping players happy and paying.

Mythic Entertainment's (*mythicentertainment.com*) Dark Age of Camelot entertains over 225,000 players who each pay from $11 to $13 per month to inhabit a world based on Arthurian legends. At company headquarters, there are 120 dual-processor Pentium servers (see Technology Guide 1) running the Linux operating system (Technology Guide 2). Each group of six servers runs a gamespace—a virtual world inhabited by thousands of players. The idea is to create different gamespaces for different types of players. One player may prefer to stay in character at all times, keeping character names true to the Arthurian era. Another may want a more action-oriented game, where players can more easily do battle against each other.

While each gamespace could conceivably handle 20,000 simultaneous players, Mythic limits them to about 4,000 players each, adding new gamespaces when necessary instead of increasing the load on the ones already running. Mythic says, "If you have too many people, the worlds get too crowded."

Mythic also puts much of the game program itself on the servers, which handle the artificial intelligence, combat calculations, and character data. The client software on each player's PC is essentially a graphics shell that draws the visuals. As subscribers join, transforming combat from 100-player clashes to 400-player battles, the messaging system must be continually refined. Because the messaging program resides on the servers, site developers can update it on the fly without having to send fixes to players.

Mythic devotes another 30 servers to support activities, such as archiving player data and handling the game's "appeals" process. When a player gets stuck, he or she can confer with a customer support representative, who will appear as an avatar (human-like figure) on the screen.

Source: Compiled from A. Cohen, "Inside the Dark Age of Camelot," *PC Magazine*, July 1, 2003.

QUESTIONS

1. Describe the information technology infrastructure of the Dark Age of Camelot game.
2. Why does Mythic use 120 Pentium servers instead of one large mainframe?
3. Look over the Emerging Computing Environments section in this chapter (Section 2.7). Which emerging computing environments would you recommend to Mythic? Why?

---

information system is typically used synonymously with the term computer-based information system.) Such a system can include as little as a personal computer and software. Or it may include several thousand computers of various sizes with hundreds of printers, plotters, and other devices, as well as databases and communication networks (wireline and wireless). In most cases an information system also includes people. The basic components of information systems are listed below. Not every system includes all these components.

- **Hardware** is a set of devices such as the processor, monitor, keyboard, and printer. Together, these devices accept data and information, process them, and display them.

- **Software** is a set of programs that enable the hardware to process data.

- A **database** is a collection of related files, tables, relations, and so on that stores data and the associations among them.

- A **network** is a connecting system (wireline or wireless) that permits the sharing of resources by different computers.

- **Procedures** are the set of instructions about how to combine the above components in order to process information and generate the desired output.

- *People* are those individuals who work with the information system, interface with it, or use its output.

hardware *A set of devices (e.g., processor, monitor, keyboard, printer) that together accept data and information, process them, and display them.*

software *A set of programs that enable the hardware to process data.*

database *A collection of related files, tables, relations, and so on, that stores data and the associations among them.*

network *A connecting system (wireline or wireless) that permits the sharing of resources by different computers.*

procedures *The set of instructions about how to combine information systems components in order to process information and generate the desired output.*

Application Programs

application program *A computer program designed to support a specific task, a business process, or another application program.*

An **application program** is a computer program designed to support a specific task or a business process (such as execute the payroll) or in some cases another application program. There are dozens of applications in each functional area. For instance, in managing human resources, it is possible to find one application for screening job applicants and another for monitoring employee turnover.

Some applications in a functional area might be completely independent of each other, whereas others are interrelated. The collection of application programs in a single department is usually considered a *departmental information system*. For example, the collection of application programs in the human resources area is called the *human resources information system* (*HRIS*).

Data, Information, and Knowledge

Information systems are built to attain several goals. One of the primary goals is to economically process data into information or knowledge. Let us define these concepts:

data items *An elementary description of things, events, activities, and transactions that are recorded, classified, and stored, but are not organized to convey any specific meaning.*

Data items refer to an elementary description of things, events, activities, and transactions that are recorded, classified, and stored, but are not organized to convey any specific meaning. Data items can be numeric, alphanumeric, figures, sounds, or images. A student grade in a class is a data item, and so is the number of hours an employee worked in a certain week. A *database* consists of stored data items organized for retrieval.

information *Data that have been organized so that they have meaning and value to the recipient.*

Information is data that have been organized so that they have meaning and value to the recipient. For example, a grade point average is data, but a student's name coupled with his or her grade point average is information. The recipient interprets the meaning and draws conclusions and implications from the data.

knowledge *Data and/or information that have been organized and processed to convey understanding, experience, accumulated learning, and expertise as they apply to a current problem or activity.*

Finally, **knowledge** consists of data and/or information that have been organized and processed to convey understanding, experience, accumulated learning, and expertise as they apply to a current problem or activity. Data that are processed to extract critical implications and to reflect past experiences and expertise provide the recipient with *organizational knowledge*, which has a very high potential value. Currently, *knowledge management* is one of the hottest topics in the IT field (see Chapter 3).

Before you go on. . .

1. What is the difference between applications and computer-based information systems?

2. Provide other examples of data, information, and knowledge.

2.2 EVOLUTION OF INFORMATION SYSTEMS

The first business applications of computers (in the mid-1950s) performed repetitive, high-volume, transaction-computing tasks. The computers "crunched numbers," summarizing and organizing transactions and data in the accounting, finance, and human resources areas. Such systems are generally called *transaction processing systems* (*TPSs*).

As the cost of computing decreased and computers' capabilities increased, *management information systems* (*MISs*) were developed. These systems accessed, organized, summarized, and displayed information for supporting routine decision making in the functional areas. *Office automation systems* (*OASs*), such as word processing systems, were developed to support office and clerical workers. Computers were also introduced in the manufacturing environment, with applications ranging from robotics to computer-aided design and manufacturing (CAD/CAM).

Decision support systems were developed to provide computer-based support for complex, nonroutine decisions. The microcomputer revolution, which started around 1980, began the era of end-user computing, in which the principal users of a system's output—such as analysts, managers, and many other professionals—can build and use systems on their own desktop computers. Decision support expanded in two directions: first, toward executives and then managers (*executive support systems*), and second, to people working in groups (*group support systems*).

Eventually, interest in programming computers to perform intelligent problem solving led to commercial applications known as *intelligent support systems* (*ISSs*). These systems include *expert systems*, which provide the stored knowledge of experts to nonexperts, and a new type of intelligent systems with *machine-learning capabilities* that can learn from historical cases.

As our economy has become more focused on knowledge work, *knowledge management systems* have been developed specifically to support the creating, gathering, organizing, integrating, and disseminating of an organization's knowledge. Included in this category are software for word processing, document management, and desktop publishing.

A major innovation in the evolution of information systems has been the development of *data warehousing*. A data warehouse is a database designed to support DSS, ESS, and other analytical and end-user activities. The use of data warehouses is a part of *business intelligence*, the gathering and use of large amounts of data for query and analysis by DSS, ESS, and intelligent systems.

The latest support system in organizations is mobile computing. Mobile computing supports mobile employees, those who are working with customers or business partners outside the physical boundaries of their companies. Mobile employees carry portable devices, including PDAs (personal digital assistants such as Palm Pilots) and cell phones, which can access the Internet. These devices enable communications with organizations and other individuals via wireline or wireless networks.

The information systems described so far were designed mostly to support the activities inside organizations. However, companies discovered that their external activities could also be improved with information systems. The first type of information system that was developed in the 1980s to improve communications with business partners was electronic data interchange (EDI), which involved computer-to-computer direct communication of standard business documents (such as orders and order confirmations) between business partners. These systems became the basis for *electronic markets*, which later developed into *electronic commerce*. These systems expanded later to improve *collaboration* of planning and other business activities among business partners. Still later, systems intended to support customers were developed, grouped under the umbrella term, *customer relationship management* (*CRM*).

Web-based systems, which began appearing in the mid-1990s, deliver business applications via the Internet. As we will show throughout the text, today many—and probably most—of the innovative and strategic systems in medium and large organizations are Web-based. Using their browsers, people in these organizations communicate, collaborate, access vast amounts of information, and run most of the organization's tasks and processes by means of Web-based systems.

As we have seen, there are a wide variety of information systems available to organizations today. Online File W2.1 on the book's Web site lists and describes these systems, along with the types of employees they support (which we discuss in the next section). IT's about Business 2.2 (page 40) provides an example of many of these diverse systems in the Dallas Mavericks basketball team.

We now turn our attention to classifying information systems. The two classifications we describe will help you understand how information systems support organizations and their employees.

end-user computing   *The use or development of information systems by the principal users of the systems' outputs, such as analysts, managers, and other professionals.*

"We digitized our copy, we digitized our pictures, and now we're beginning to digitize our staff." (Cartoon by Sidney Harris.)

mobile computing   *Information systems that support employees who are working with customers or business partners outside the physical boundaries of their companies; can be done over wireline or wireless networks.*

electronic   data   interchange (EDI)   *Computer-to-computer direct communication of standard business documents between business partners.*

wiley.com/college/turban

IT'S ABOUT BUSINESS

MKT

2.2: The Dallas Mavericks: Using IT for a Successful Business

Mark Cuban, the owner of the Dallas Mavericks, spent $280 million to buy a half-interest in the team and its new arena in 2000. He expects the franchise to perform as a business. He wants to fill every seat at every game and to maximize sales from concessions and souvenir sales.

Cuban's strategy to reach his business goals is to give fans the best possible experience, with a high-quality team on the floor and excellent service at arena bars, barbecue stands, and souvenir shops. In the 2002 season, the Mavs filled the 19,200-seat American Airlines Center to 103.7 percent capacity, bringing in folding chairs to handle the overflow demand for tickets. Dallas was named the best NBA city by *The Sporting News*.

Filling seats is critical. To track attendance, the Mavs became the first NBA team to put barcodes on tickets, in part to find out if group sales and community-organization giveaways were putting bodies in seats or just wasting tickets. By enabling improved forecasting for particular games, the system has helped reduce beverage inventories by 50 percent.

Each of the 144 luxury suites in the Center is equipped with PCs that handle orders for merchandise, food, and beverages. Wireless access from all seats in the arena is being developed so that fans can place orders directly from their seats. All 840 registers at concession stands, restaurants, stores, and bars use a sophisticated point-of-sale system. In the big retail store on the ground floor, salespeople wielding handheld computing devices ring up credit-card purchases when lines get too long. The system allows the Mavs to process credit-card transactions in only three seconds, because there is an always-on Internet connection to the processing facility. And, during a game managers can see which concession stands are busy and which ones can be closed early to cut labor costs.

Technology also supports the Mavs on court. The team has 10 assistant coaches (other NBA teams have three or four), and each has a laptop and handheld. Game film is streamed over the Web for coaches to view on the road or at home. A digital content management system developed in-house matches game footage with the precise, to-the-minute statistics provided for every play of every game by the NBA. The searchable database allows coaches to analyze the effectiveness of particular plays and combinations of players in different game situations.

In 2002, the Mavs started using handheld computers to track the performance of each referee in every one of their games. The coaches can look at trends—for example, to see which referee favors a given team or which one calls more three-second violations—and they can tell the team. Another program logs different offensive and defensive schemes used against the Mavs. This system will let coaches make adjustments on the floor based on statistics from previous games.

Source: Compiled from E. Cone, "Dallas Mavericks," *Baseline Magazine*, October 1, 2003.

QUESTIONS

1. Do these information systems give the Dallas Mavericks an unfair on-court advantage in games?
2. Should the NBA regulate these systems?
3. What would you do if you were other NBA teams?

Before you go on. . .

1. Why were "number-crunching" information systems developed first?
2. Why are most of the strategic systems today Web-based?

2.3 CLASSIFICATION OF INFORMATION SYSTEMS

It is useful to classify information systems into groups that share similar characteristics. Such classifications may help in identifying systems, analyzing them, planning new systems, planning integration of systems, and making decisions such as the possible outsourcing of particular systems. We discuss the two most common classifications next: classification by breadth of support and classification by organizational levels.

Classification by Breadth of Support

Organizations are made up of components such as divisions, departments, and work units, most typically organized in hierarchical levels. Typical information systems that follow the hierarchical organizational structure are *functional (departmental), enterprisewide*, and *interorganizational*. As was seen in Figure 2.2, a departmental system supports the functional areas in each company. At a higher level, the enterprisewide system supports the entire company, and interorganizational systems connect different companies. Figures 2.3 (below) and 2.4 (page 42) show these relationships.

Functional (Departmental) Information Systems.
The major functional information systems are organized around the traditional departments—functions—in an organization: manufacturing (production/operations), accounting, finance, marketing, and human resources. Functional informational systems are briefly described later in this chapter and discussed in detail in Chapter 7.

Enterprise Information Systems.
While a departmental information system is usually related to a functional area, other information systems serve several departments or the entire enterprise. These information systems, together with the departmental systems, comprise the **enterprisewide information system**. Enterprisewide systems enable people to communicate with each other and access information throughout the organization (see Figure 2.2).

enterprisewide information system
An information system that encompasses an entire organization, including both departmental systems and those of the entire enterprise.

One of the most popular enterprise applications is *enterprise resource planning* (*ERP*), which enables companies to plan and manage the resources of an entire enterprise (see Chapter 8). Another type of enterprise information system is the *transaction processing system*, which is briefly described later in the chapter and discussed in detail in Chapter 7.

Interorganizational Systems.
Information systems that connect two or more organizations are referred to as **interorganizational information systems (IOSs)**. IOSs support many interorganizational operations, of which supply chain management is the best known.

interorganizational information systems (IOSs) *Information systems that connect two or more organizations and support many interorganizational operations.*

An organization's **supply chain** describes the flow of materials, information, money, and services from raw material suppliers through factories and warehouses to the end customers. The supply chain shown in Figure 2.4 is linear and fairly simple. As we show in Chapter 9, supply chains can be much more complex. Note that the supply chain in Figure 2.4 shows both physical flows and the flow of information.

supply chain *The flow of materials, information, money, and services from raw material suppliers through factories and warehouses to the end customers.*

IT provides two major types of software solutions for managing supply chain activities. First, *enterprise resource planning* (*ERP*) software, mentioned above as an enterprisewide system, has expanded from integrating only the internal functions of an organization to managing external relationships with business partners (see Chapter 8). Therefore, ERP can be both an enterprisewide system and an interorganizational system. Second, *supply chain management* (*SCM*) software helps in decision making

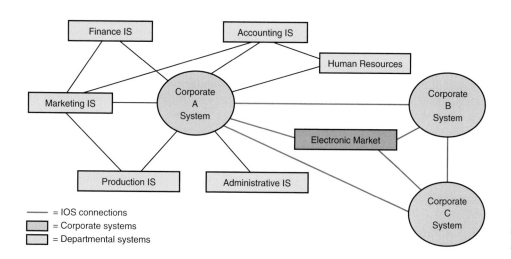

= IOS connections
= Corporate systems
= Departmental systems

Figure 2.3 *Departmental, corporate, and interorganizational information systems.*

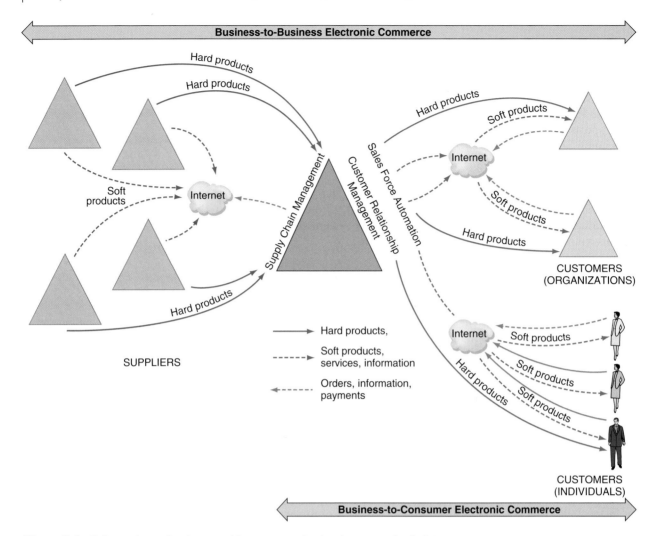

Figure 2.4 *Information technology outside your organization (your supply chain).*

related both to internal segments of the chain and to their relationship with external segments of the supply chain (see Chapter 9).

The next section discusses how information systems support employees in different levels of the organization. We see that there are a wide variety of such systems, including functional information systems. Notice that the next section discusses information systems *inside* the organization, as opposed to interorganizational systems.

Classification by Organizational Levels

Another way to classify information systems is according to the type of support they provide to employees in each organizational level. As we saw in Figure 2.2, the typical enterprise is organized hierarchically, from the clerical and office worker layer, to the operational layer, the managerial layer, the knowledge worker layer, and finally the strategic layer. The triangular shape of the figure also illustrates the quantity of employees involved in the various types of activities and the decisions relating to those activities. Top managers are few, and they are located at the apex of the triangle.

For each level, we first discuss the employees in that level, their work, and the decisions they make. Then we briefly discuss the support that information systems provide for each level. There will be some crossover, as several types of information systems may provide support for a particular organizational level.

The Clerical Level. Clerical workers constitute a large class of employees who support managers at all levels of the company. Among clerical workers, those who use, manipulate, or disseminate information are referred to as *data workers*. These employees include bookkeepers, secretaries who work with word processors, electronic file clerks, and insurance claim processors.

Information Systems Support.   Clerical workers are supported by office automation and communication systems including document management, workflow, e-mail, and coordination software. These workers may also be supported by transaction processing systems, management information systems, and mobile systems, though usually not in a decision-making capacity.

The Operational Level.   Operational, or first-line, managers deal with the day-to-day operations of the organization, making routine decisions such as assigning employees to tasks and recording the number of hours they work, or placing a purchase order. Operational activities are structured and short-term in nature.

Information Systems Support.   Transaction processing systems provide the major support for operational managers. These managers are also supported by management information systems and mobile systems.

A **transaction processing system (TPS)** supports the monitoring, collection, storage, processing, and dissemination of data from the organization's basic business transactions, each of which generates data. The TPS collects data continuously, typically in *real time* (that is, as soon as they are generated), and provides the input data for the corporate databases. The TPSs are considered critical to the success of any enterprise because they support core operations, such as purchasing of materials, billing customers, preparing a payroll, shipping goods to customers, and many others. Table 2.1 presents examples of routine business transactions in a manufacturing company. We discuss transaction processing systems in detail in Chapter 7.

transaction processing system *An information system that supports the collection, processing, and dissemination of data from the organization's basic business transactions.*

The Managerial Level.   Middle-level managers make tactical decisions, which deal in general with activities such as short-term planning, organizing, and control.

Information Systems Support.   The functional area management information systems (often called simply MISs) provide the major support for these managers. **Functional MISs** are designed to summarize data and prepare reports for the functional areas, such as accounting or marketing. Middle managers can also obtain answers to queries from MISs as the need arises. Middle-level managers are also supported by the transaction processing systems.

Functional management information systems are put in place to ensure that business strategies come to fruition in an efficient manner. Typically, a functional MIS provides periodic information about such topics as operational efficiency, effectiveness,

functional MISs *Information systems designed to summarize data and prepare reports for functional areas, such as accounting or marketing.*

Table 2.1   Routine Business Transactions in a Manufacturing Company

Payroll
Employee time cards
Employee pay and deductions
Payroll checks

Purchasing
Purchase orders
Deliveries
Payments (accounts payable)

Finance and Accounting
Financial statements
Tax records
Expense accounts

Sales
Sales records
Invoices and billings
Accounts receivable
Sales returns
Shipping

Production
Production reports
Quality-control reports

Inventory Management
Material usage
Inventory levels

Table 2.2 Support Provided by MISs for Managerial Activities

Task	MIS Support
Statistical summaries	Summaries of new data (e.g., daily production by item, monthly electricity usage).
Exception reports	Comparison of actual performances to standards (or target). Highlight only deviations from a threshold (e.g., above or below 5 percent).
Periodic reports	Generated at predetermined intervals.
Ad-hoc reports	Generated as needed, on demand. These can be routine reports or special ones.
Comparative analysis and early detection of problems	Comparison of performance to metrics or standards. Includes analysis such as trends and early detection of changes.
Projections	Projection of future sales, cash flows, market share, etc.
Automation of routine decisions	Standard modeling techniques applied to routine decisions such as when and how much to order or how to schedule work.
Connection and collaboration	Internal and external Web-based messaging systems, e-mail, voice mail, and groupware (see Chapter 4).

and productivity by extracting information from databases and processing it according to the needs of the user. Table 2.2 shows examples of the types of support that MISs provide for managers.

Management information systems are also used for planning, monitoring, and control. For example, a sales forecast by region is shown in Figure 2.5. Such a report can help the marketing manager make better decisions regarding advertising and pricing of products. Another example is that of a human resources information system, which provides a manager with a daily report of the percentage of employees who were on vacation or called in sick, as compared to forecast figures.

The Knowledge-Work Level. As you could see in Figure 2.2, an additional level of staff support has been introduced between top and middle management. These are professional employees, such as financial and marketing analysts, engineers, production planners, lawyers, and accountants, to mention just a few. They act as advisors and assistants to both top and middle management and are often subject-area experts in a particular area. Many of these professional workers are classified as **knowledge workers**, people who create information and knowledge as part of their work and integrate it into the business. Knowledge workers are responsible for finding or developing new knowledge for the organization and integrating it with existing knowledge. Therefore, they must keep abreast of all development and events related to their professions.

knowledge workers *Professional workers who create information and knowledge as part of their work and integrate it into the business.*

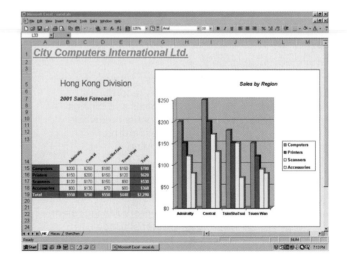

Figure 2.5 *Sales forecast by region, generated by marketing MIS.*

Information Systems Support.   Information systems that support knowledge workers range from Internet search engines (which help knowledge workers find information) and expert systems (which support information interpretation) to decision support systems and business intelligence systems (for user-driven data analysis). Knowledge workers are the major users of the Internet for business purposes.

The Strategic Level.   Top-level or strategic managers (the executives) make decisions that deal with situations that may significantly change the manner in which business is done. Introducing a new product line, expanding the business by acquiring supporting businesses, and moving operations to a foreign country are prime examples of strategic activities. Traditionally, strategic decisions had a long-range time horizon (three to five years). However, in the digital economy, the time horizon has been dramatically reduced to one to two years, or perhaps even months.

Information Systems Support.   Executives are supported mainly by executive support systems and to a lesser extent by decision support systems and business intelligence systems.

Before you go on. . .

1. Describe information systems support for knowledge workers. Are middle-level managers knowledge workers?

2. As we move up the organization's hierarchy, from clerical workers to executives, how does the support provided by information systems change?

2.4 EXAMPLES OF INFORMATION SYSTEMS

Millions of different information systems are in use throughout the world. The following examples show the diversity of applications and the benefits provided.

EXAMPLE   *IT Infrastructure Helps Worldspan Survive.* In 1996, the management of Worldspan (*worldspan.com*) faced a critical decision. Of the big three U.S.-based computerized travel reservations companies, Worldspan was the third. Market-leader Sabre had just launched Travelocity (*travelocity.com*), and there was a great deal of pressure on Worldspan to copy Sabre's e-commerce move.

However, the management team felt that Worldspan did not, like Sabre, want to compete with its travel-agent customers. Instead, in addition to offering reservations and bookings to traditional travel agents, the company would develop interactive reservations services and start to target its products and services to the growing number of online travel agencies, such as Expedia (*expedia.com*). Therefore, Worldspan decided to use information technology to change strategic directions and move successfully into new areas of business.

Worldspan uses its Global Distribution System (GDS) to take orders from travel agents, book the reservations, issue tickets, and charge the hospitality and transportation companies fees for each transaction. The GDSs of Worldspan and its chief rivals, Sabre, Galileo, and Amadeus, are essentially the same: large mainframes running a 40-year-old operating system and doing everything from holding airline ticket inventories to handling transactions.

Worldspan, however, moved its fare and pricing applications to faster, less-expensive servers. Now, when a fare request comes into Worldspan, its system asks whether the transaction is best executed through a server, which can quickly handle simple requests such as a round-trip from New York to Los Angeles, or on a mainframe, which has the processing power to handle complicated trips, such as an international flight with multiple stops.

In an effort to find the absolute lowest fare, clients used to send Worldspan multiple requests. For example, one request would be for an everyday low fare and the other request for the lowest negotiated fare (one with an additional discount). Worldspan would have to analyze both requests, send both results back to the client, and the client would choose between them. For greater efficiency, Worldspan created its "combo entry," which lets clients send in just one request for a fare. Worldspan analyzes the request, performing a search for the negotiated fare on the mainframe and scouting out other low fares on its servers. Worldspan then sends just one message showing the best possible fare, back to its clients.

From 2000 to 2003, Worldspan has increased its market share in terms of overall bookings. Much of the growth is coming from online travel. Worldspan has used its streamlined reservations system to attract online travel agents and now has four of the five largest travel Web sites as customers: Expedia, Priceline.com, Orbitz, and Hotwire. Worldspan now handles 100 online travel agencies and 10 times the number of requests as before the IT change. (*Sources:* McCormick, 2003; *worldspan.com.*)

POM   **EXAMPLE**   *Wal-Mart Pushes RFID Adoption.* Wal-Mart (*wal-mart.com*) has told its top 100 suppliers that they will need to have radio-frequency identification (RFID) systems in place for tracking pallets of goods through the supply chain by January 25, 2005. RFID systems consist of RFID tags on pallets and RFID readers. The RFID tags are small, wireless devices that transmit information (much more information than barcodes provide) about the pallets to the reader. RFID has several advantages over barcodes, foremost of which is that it can be read without a line-of-sight to an item, making it easier to obtain automated reads and to do so in large quantities instead of one by one. The overall goal of using RFID is to gain visibility into and accuracy throughout Wal-Mart's supply chain.

Industry analysts predict that RFID will be adopted more quickly than barcode readers were in the late 1970s and early 1980s. One reason is that Wal-Mart is not the only large company supporting it. In addition to many other businesses, the U.S. government is supporting RFID development because it sees applications for homeland security (Malaysia already uses RFID tags in its passports) as well as for the military. Second, for many high-value items, RFID costs are reasonable today, and are expected to fall in cost, making their use possible for lower-value items in the future. Third, other retailers are planning on being fast followers because they fear that Wal-Mart will gain a significant cost advantage. For example, Gillette plans to deploy RFID tags to help the company keep its products on the shelves when and where customers want them. In the United States, nearly $70 billion is lost in the retail sector due to products not being found on shelves or lost in the supply chain.

RFID also offers the advantage of automatically collecting far more data than is possible today—not just product information, but even temperature, humidity, and shocks to products in the course of shipment. However, there are disadvantages: RFID readers do not currently come in wide enough variety for different types of pallets; wireless networks in the stores interfere with RFID readers; readers are not fast enough; and there are problems with integration, reading errors, and even forklift drivers knocking out readers. (*Sources:* Murphy, 2003; and Lundquist, 2003).

ACC   **EXAMPLE**   *Managing Accounting Information across Asia.*

Le Saunda Holding Company (Hong Kong) manages 32 subsidiaries in four Asian countries, mostly in the manufacture, import, and sale of shoes (*lesaunda.com.hk*). Managing the financing and cash flow is a complex process. All accounting information flows to headquarters electronically. Also, sales data are electronically collected at point-of-sale terminals. The sales data, together with inventory data (which are updated automatically when each sale occurs), are transferred to headquarters. Other relevant data, such as advertising and sales promotion, names and addresses of merchants who buy the company's products, and cash flow, are also transmitted electronically and collected in a centralized database for storage and processing.

To cope with the rapid growth of the company, a sophisticated accounting software package was installed. The result was a radical improvement in accounting procedures. For example, it now takes less than 10 minutes, rather than an entire day, to produce a complex ad-hoc report (a report prepared in response to a special request). The company's accountants can generate reports as they are needed, helping functional managers make quicker and better decisions. The system is also much more reliable, and internal and external auditing is easier. Headquarters knows what is going on almost as soon as it occurs. All these improvements have led to a substantial growth in revenue and profits for the firm. (*Source: lesaunda.com.hk.*)

EXAMPLE   *Wide Area Network Empowers Hot Topic Employees.* **HRM** Hot Topic (*hottopic.com*) is a retailer of music-influenced apparel for young people, with an emphasis on alternative styles. The company has over 500 stores and prides itself on its receptivity to employee suggestions.

Hot Topic recently implemented a wide-area network linking all 500 of its stores. The biggest benefit of the new network has been faster connections between store employees and marketing and other managers at company headquarters. The company has always encouraged suggestions from the field. By longstanding policy, Hot Topic translates its "All About the Music" slogan into action by reimbursing store employees for concert tickets if they write up a report on the fashions they saw at the show. The idea is for the employees and the company to stay in close touch with rapidly changing customer tastes. Hot Topic expects its employees to be able to talk knowledgeably with customers about current music and the related fashions.

Prior to the new network, employees did not make much use of e-mail to transmit their suggestions because messages could only be sent at the beginning or end of the day, when the modem lines were no longer needed for credit-card transactions. In addition, the credit-card authorization process took 30 seconds per customer, leading to longer checkout lines, the potential for customers being impatient and simply walking out of the store without making a purchase, and employee frustration.

Using the wide-area network, employees can now share style tips and suggestions by dashing off a quick e-mail from the same personal computer that powers the cash register. Alternatively, they can use an Internet protocol phone and make a toll-free call to headquarters to tip off buyers for the chain on a trend that might be forming. As for credit cards, authorization now takes 2 to 3 seconds, and multiple transactions can go through simultaneously. This speed makes a big difference during busy seasons such as back-to-school and Christmas. In 2002, Hot Topic reported sales per square foot of store of $619, higher than any other youth-apparel retailer. (*Source:* Carr, 2003.)

EXAMPLE   *Abbey National Moves to E-Banking.* When the **FIN** Abbey National Group (*abbeynational.com*), one of the UK's leading retail banks, decided to enter the fast-moving e-banking arena, they knew that their success would be contingent on their agility. Central to Abbey's strategy was the creation of an entirely new bank, Cahoot (*cahoot.com*), which would be located within the Abbey National Group but would be positioned and branded to appeal to a new customer base.

Cahoot wanted to carve out a significant proportion of the online banking market in the United Kingdom, and it set itself the target of opening 200,000 accounts within its first 12 months of operations. Cahoot is a very lean business. While Abbey employs 300,000 staff, Cahoot has only 50 employees. As a result, Cahoot is heavily dependent on its information technology systems.

Cahoot and IBM developed the entire e-business solution in less than a year, and the new banking venture proceeded to reach its goals. Cahoot's interactive service allows customers to access current banking information, including the latest stock market and interest rate data, whenever and wherever they like, even from mobile devices. Both the bank's financial advisors and its customers can access general and personalized stock market and account information, transfer money, request loans, buy and sell stocks and bonds, and pay bills. This move into mobile e-banking is Abbey's key first step in a strategy to exploit the potential of e-business, while extending the bank's brand reach. (*Source: www-1.ibm.com/industries/financialservices/ doc/content/casestudy/277262103.html.*)

Before you go on. . .

1. How can Wal-Mart dictate to its suppliers that they must use RFID tags by a certain date?

2. Was Cahoot a high-risk venture for Abbey National Group? Did information technology reduce or increase this risk?

2.5 THE MODERN COMPUTING ENVIRONMENT

computing environment *The way in which an organization's information technologies (hardware, software, and communications technology) are organized and integrated for optimal efficiency and effectiveness.*

legacy systems *Older systems, typically those that process an organization's high-volume transactions, that are central to the operations of a business.*

The wide variety of information systems function within a computing environment. A **computing environment** is the way in which an organization's information technologies (hardware, software, and communications technology) are organized and integrated for optimal efficiency and effectiveness.

The dominant computing environment until the mid-1980s was the *mainframe environment.* In this environment, one or more mainframe computers performed the processing. Users worked with passive (so-called "dumb") terminals, which were used to enter or change data and access information from the mainframe and were controlled by it.

Legacy systems are older systems that are central to the operations of a business; typically they process an organization's high-volume transactions. Legacy systems that exist today typically were developed from the late 1950s through the 1980s and are closely related to the mainframe environment. These systems are still, in some cases, part of the backbone of the overall IT architecture of an organization. Today, they are usually part of a distributed system in which the mainframe plays the major role.

As a result of communications networks and especially the Internet and intranets, distributed computing has become the dominant environment of almost all organizations. We first discuss the distributed computing environment and then the two major types of distributed computing—client/server and peer-to-peer architectures.

Distributed Computing

distributed computing *Computing architecture that divides the processing work between two or more computers, using a network for connection; also called* distributed processing.

Distributed computing (*distributed processing*) divides the processing work between two or more computers, using a network for connection. The participating computers are a combination of all different types (e.g., mainframes, midrange computers, and personal computers). (See Technology Guide 1.) They can be in one location or in several. Distributed computing allows intra- and interorganizational cooperation in computing; accessibility to vast amounts of data, information, and knowledge; and high efficiency in the use of computing resources.

Today, software applications are based on the *distributed computing model*, where applications collaborate to provide services and provide functionality to each other. As a result, the primary role of many new software programs is to support information exchange (through Web servers and browsers), collaboration (through e-mail and instant messaging), and individual expression (through Weblogs, discussed in Chapter 4). IT's about Business 2.3 demonstrates the power of collaboration made possible by the distributed computing model.

The most important configuration of distributed processing is the *client/server architecture*, where several computers share resources and are able to communicate with many other computers via networks. The Internet, intranets, and extranets are all based on the client/server model of distributed computing.

IT's ABOUT BUSINESS

MKT   POM

2.3: Collaboration Creates a Swarm

At Lowe & Partners Worldwide (*loweworldwide.com*), a large advertising agency, when an account executive in Hong Kong receives a request for a proposal from a prospective client, he opens up a collaboration space on his PC and invites in subject-area experts, planners, and other creative people from India to England. Each can invite others from his or her personal network, whether inside or outside the company. In minutes, a "swarm" of creative talent is exploiting the opportunity. Artists post relevant images; content experts surf the Web in unison to find useful sites; researchers drop in pertinent files; copywriters type or edit documents together in real time.

Swarming is a type of collaboration in which large numbers of geographically dispersed people quickly self-organize in a peer-to-peer network to deal with a problem or opportunity. It is a fluid, shifting network with no central control. A swarm can be as complex as a global business network or as simple as a "cell-phone posse" (a group, or swarm, of people holding an impromptu teleconference on their cell phones). Swarming lets organizations do more, quickly, with the same resources, and it enables more agile, rapidly assembled, ad-hoc collaborations of all kinds.

Lowe, a large multinational organization (180 offices in over 80 countries), had to match the agility of smaller competitors and turned to software called Groove, from Groove Networks (*groove.net*), to facilitate the swarming approach. Lowe's prospective clients have asked to see how the team space works, and they have been invited to come in by downloading free trial software from the Web. As a result, the clients have become collaborators.

For Lowe, swarming has saved on expenses such as international couriers, travel, and faxing. But the swarming technology really saved Lowe when the SARS virus brought commerce in Hong Kong to a virtual halt in 2003. Real-time collaboration spaces linked clients in Hong Kong, subcontractors in India and Taiwan, and headquarters executives in London.

Source: Compiled from K. Melymuka, "Meeting of the Minds," *Computerworld*, July 28, 2003.

QUESTIONS

1. Is there any control over the swarm at Lowe? If not, should there be? If needed, how would you implement control over a swarm?
2. Would a lack of control over a swarm cause the swarm to be less effective?
3. What other applications can you think of for swarms?

Client/Server Architecture.   **Client/server architecture** divides distributed computing units into two major categories, *clients* and *servers*, connected by a network. A **client** is a computer (such as a PC attached to a network) that is used to access shared network resources. A **server** is a computer that is attached to this same network and provides clients with a variety of services. The purpose of client/server architecture is to maximize the use of computer resources. This architecture provides a way for different computing devices to work together, each doing the job for which it is best suited.

There are several models of client/server architecture. In the most traditional model, the mainframe acts as the database server, providing data for analysis done by the PC clients using spreadsheets, database management systems, and application software.

When client/server architecture is used throughout the organization, it is called **enterprisewide computing**; it is a cohesive, flexible, and powerful computing environment. This architecture is the core of Web-based systems, which we discuss in Section 2.6. An enterprisewide client/server architecture provides total integration of departmental and corporate IS resources. It thereby allows for an additional class of applications that spans the enterprise and benefits both corporate central management (providing controls) and end-user systems (providing empowerment). It also provides better control and security over data in a distributed environment. By implementing enterprisewide computing, organizations can maximize the value of information by increasing its availability.

Peer-to-Peer Architecture.   **Peer-to-peer (P2P) architecture** is a type of distributed computing network in which each client computer shares files or computer resources (such as processing power) *directly* with others *but not through a central server*

client/server architecture *A type of distributed architecture that divides distributed computing units into two major categories,* clients *and* **servers**, *connected by a network.*

client *A computer (such as a PC attached to a network) that is used to access shared network resources.*

server *A computer that is attached to a client/server network and provides clients with a variety of services.*

enterprisewide computing *Computing environment in which client/server architecture is used throughout an organization.*

peer-to-peer (P2P) architecture *A distributed computing network in which each client computer shares files or computer resources directly* with others *but not through a central server (as in traditional client/server architecture).*

as in the traditional client/server architecture. The technology is more productive than traditional client/server because it enables direct connections among computers, vastly reducing (or even eliminating) the cost of setting up and maintaining servers.

The main benefit of P2P is that it can enormously expand the amount of information accessible from a personal computer or a mobile device. Other advantages over traditional client/server architecture are that there is no need for a network administrator, the network is fast and inexpensive to set up and maintain, and each PC can make a backup copy of its data to other PCs for improved security.

P2P architecture is the basis on which companies such as KaZaA, Morpheus, and Gnutella operate. We discuss these companies in greater detail in Chapters 4 and 12.

Before you go on...

1. Why are legacy systems still in operation?
2. What is the difference between client/server architecture and P2P architecture?

2.6 WEB-BASED SYSTEMS

Web-based systems *Applications or services that are resident on a server that is accessible using a Web browser and is therefore accessible from anywhere via the Internet.*

A type of client/server computing, Web-based systems are those applications or services that are resident on a server that is accessible using a Web browser and is therefore accessible from anywhere in the world via the Internet. The only client-side software needed to access and execute Web-based applications is a Web browser environment, and the applications must conform to the Internet protocols.

The rapid development of Web-based systems, as well as the introduction of new concepts such as utility computing and software services (presented in Section 2.7), are changing the way companies are organizing their computing resources. Therefore, as is shown throughout this book and especially in Chapters 4 and 5, the Internet, intranets, and sometimes extranets are becoming an indispensable part of most IT architectures. New Web-based architectures may replace old architectures, or may integrate legacy systems into their structure.

The Internet

Internet ("the Net") *A worldwide system of computer networks—a network of networks; a public, cooperative, and self-sustaining facility accessible to hundreds of millions of people worldwide.*

Sometimes called simply "the Net," the Internet is a worldwide system of computer networks—a network of networks. Today, the Internet is a public, cooperative, and self-sustaining facility accessible to hundreds of millions of people worldwide.

The wireless devices that access the Internet and the integration of television and computers will allow the Internet to reach every home, business, school, and other organization. Then the Information Superhighway will be complete. This "superhighway" is a national fiber-optic-based network and wireless infrastructure that will connect all Internet users in a country. Singapore is likely to be the first country to have such a national information superhighway completely installed. Maui, Hawaii, is the first community to have a wireless Internet all over the island.

Information Superhighway *A national fiber-optic-based network and wireless infrastructure that will connect all Internet users in a country.*

Physically, the Internet uses a portion of the total resources of the currently existing public telecommunications networks. Technically, what distinguishes the Internet is its use of a set of protocols, called TCP/IP (for Transmission Control Protocol/Internet Protocol). Internet applications and technology are discussed in more detail in Technology Guide 4. Two adaptations of Internet technology, intranets and extranets, also make use of the TCP/IP protocol.

World Wide Web *An application that uses the transport functions of the Internet; has universally accepted standards for storing, retrieving, formatting, and displaying information via a client/server architecture.*

Let us briefly explain the relationship of the Internet to the World Wide Web. The Internet functions as the transport mechanism, and the World Wide Web (also called the Web, WWW, or W3) is an *application* that uses those transport functions. The Web is a system with universally accepted standards for storing, retrieving, formatting, and displaying information via a client/server architecture. For more on the Internet and the Web, see Technology Guide 5.

Intranets

An **intranet** is the use of Web technologies to create a private network, usually within one enterprise (see Technology Guide 4). A security gateway such as a firewall is used to segregate the intranet from the Internet and to selectively allow access from outside the intranet.

intranet *A private network, usually within one enterprise, that uses Web technologies, such as browsers and Internet protocols; separated from the Internet by a security gateway such as a firewall.*

Intranets have a variety of uses, as we show throughout the book and especially in Chapters 4 and 5. They allow for the secure online distribution of many forms of internal company information. Intranets are used for workgroup activities and the distributed sharing of projects within the enterprise.

Extranets

Extranets connect several intranets via the Internet, by adding to the Internet a security mechanism. They form a larger virtual network that allows remote users (such as business partners or mobile employees) to securely connect over the Internet to the enterprise's main intranet. Extranets allow two or more enterprises to communicate and collaborate in a controlled fashion, and therefore they play a major role in the development of business-to-business electronic commerce (see Chapter 5 for details).

extranet *A secured network that connects several intranets via the Internet; allows two or more enterprises to communicate and collaborate in a controlled fashion.*

Corporate Portals

Corporate portals are Web sites that provide the gateway to corporate information from a single point of access. Intranets are usually combined with and accessed via a corporate portal. Portals aggregate information from many places (e.g., internal databases, external databases, data warehouses, news, etc.) and present it to the user. The function of corporate portals is often described as "corecasting," because they support decisions central to particular goals of the enterprise. Corporate portals also help to personalize information for employees and customers. IT's about Business 2.4 shows an application of a corporate portal. For further discussion of corporate portals, see Chapter 4.

corporate portal *Web site that provides the gateway to corporate information from a single point of access.*

IT's ABOUT BUSINESS [POM]

2.4: The Enterprise Information Portal at Covance

The time and money involved in bringing a new drug to market is staggering—it can take over 10 years and cost over one billion dollars. As a result, pharmaceutical companies are using IT to streamline workflows, make clinical information more accessible, and help reduce time to market.

Covance (*covance.com*), an $800 million pharmaceutical company, launched its enterprise information portal to streamline data review and data management. The corporate portal cuts at least two weeks from each of the 200 or so clinical trials that Covance has in the pipeline at any given time. The portal enables everyone who is working on a clinical drug trial to have access to the same updated information and forecasts. Two weeks might not sound like much for a decade-long project, but every extra day it takes to bring a drug to market can cost a pharmaceutical company up to $3 million in projected sales.

The biggest savings should occur during the testing phase of a clinical drug trial. This phase consists of setting up dozens of test sites, which are used by physicians with patients who volunteer to test the ef-

fects of a drug before it has been approved by the U.S. Food and Drug Administration. During these trials, Covance collects and evaluates information on how patients at different sites are reacting to a drug. Using the portal to gather, collate, and analyze the data, project managers determine whether a change in the frequency or size of a drug's dosage is needed. They gather and analyze this data faster by using the portal than when they pored over paper-based forms and entered data into spreadsheets. Covance plans to provide physicians involved in the clinical trials with external connections to Covance's portal.

Source: Compiled from T. Hoffman, "Speedy Cures," *Computerworld*, December 23, 2002.

QUESTIONS

1. What are the ways that Covance's portal helps speed drugs to market?
2. How does Covance's portal relate to the phrase "Don't reinvent the wheel"?
3. In what other ways could Covance use its portal?

Web-Based Electronic Commerce Systems

Most e-commerce applications run on the Internet, intranet, and extranets, using Web-based features. Therefore, Web-based systems are the engines of e-commerce. They enable business transactions to be conducted seamlessly 24 hours a day, seven days a week. A central property of the Web and e-commerce is that you can instantly reach millions of people, anywhere, any time. The major components of Web-based electronic commerce are electronic storefronts, electronic markets, mobile commerce, and the Enterprise Web.

electronic storefront *The Web-equivalent of a showroom or a physical store through which an e-business can display and/or sell its products.*

Electronic Storefronts.   An **electronic storefront** is the Web-equivalent of a showroom or a physical store. Through the electronic storefront, an e-business can display and/or sell its products. The storefront may include electronic catalogs that contain descriptions, graphics, and possibly product reviews. Most electronic storefronts have the following common features and functions: an e-catalog, a shopping cart, a checkout mechanism (for shipments), payment processing, and an order-fulfillment system (see Chapter 5).

electronic market *A network of interactions and relationships over which information, products, services, and payments are exchanged.*

electronic exchange *A Web-based public electronic market in which many buyers and many sellers interact electronically.*

mobile commerce (m-commerce) *The buying and selling of goods and services in a wireless environment.*

location-based commerce (l-commerce) *M-commerce transactions targeted to customers in specific locations at specific times.*

Electronic Markets.   Web-accessed electronic markets are rapidly emerging as a vehicle for conducting e-commerce. An **electronic market** is a network of interactions and relationships over which information, products, services, and payments are exchanged. The means of interconnection vary among parties and can change from event to event, even between the same parties.

When the marketplace is electronic, the business center is not a physical building but a Web-based location where business interactions occur. In electronic markets, the principal participants—transaction handlers, buyers, brokers, and sellers—not only are at different locations but seldom even know one another. Electronic markets that reside in one company are referred to as *private marketplaces* (see Chapter 5). Electronic markets outside any one organization are known as *public marketplaces* or *exchanges.*

Electronic Exchanges.   A form of electronic markets is **electronic exchanges**, which are Web-based public marketplaces where many buyers and many sellers interact dynamically. They were originally set as trading places for commodities. A variety of exchanges have since emerged for all kinds of products and services (see Chapter 5).

Mobile computing helps businesses provide strategic advantage.

Mobile Computing and Mobile Commerce.   As indicated earlier in the chapter, *mobile computing* is designed for mobile employees and others who wish to have a real-time connection between a mobile device and other computing environments. **Mobile commerce** or **m-commerce** (see Chapter 6) is buying and selling of goods and services in a wireless environment, such as through wireless devices like cellular telephones and PDAs. For example, m-commerce can offer customers the location information of a product they want to purchase. This feature is important for merchants, because it allows customers to act instantly on any shopping impulse. This application, in which customers are targeted at specific times based on their specific locations, is referred to as **location-based commerce**, or **l-commerce**. (For details, see Chapter 6.)

Enterprise Web *An open environment for managing and delivering Web applications, by combining services from different vendors in a technology layer that spans platforms and business systems.*

Enterprise Web.   The **Enterprise Web** is an open environment for managing and delivering Web applications. The Enterprise Web combines services from different vendors in a technology layer that spans rival platforms and business systems, creating a foundation for building applications at lower cost. This foundation consists of the services most commonly used by Web applications, including business integration, collaboration, content management, identity management, and search, which all work together via integrating technologies such as middleware (see Technology Guide 2), component-based development (Chapter 11), and Web services (Chapter 11).

The Enterprise Web environment spans the entire enterprise and is available to all audiences. It offers several benefits: Providing a common foundation for Web applications built on any platform lowers infrastructure and development costs. Integrating resources from different systems into Web applications increases the return on those systems. Finally, creating a common user experience for audiences across the enterprise to work together drives enterprise productivity and increases profits. Enterprise Web environments are available from all major software vendors (e.g., Microsoft, IBM, SAP, Oracle, BEA, Peoplesoft, and more).

Before you go on. . .

1. As more users connect to the Internet every day and additional content is added, will the Information Superhighway ever catch up with the increased load? Do you see a solution?

2. Would a portal be of any use at your university? In your College of Business?

3. What is the Enterprise Web?

2.7 EMERGING COMPUTING ENVIRONMENTS

During the last decade several new computing environments have emerged, some of which are based on Web technologies. These systems are in the early stages of use, and some are still under development, but they may reshape the IT field. In this section we provide several examples of these new initiatives. The following are representative initiatives of emerging computing environments.

Utility Computing

Utility computing is computing that is as available, reliable, and secure as electricity, water services, and telephony. The vision behind utility computing is to have computing resources flow like electricity on demand from virtual utilities around the globe—always on and highly available, secure, efficiently metered, priced on a pay-as-you-go basis, dynamically scaled, and easy to manage. If (or when) it becomes successful, utility computing will change the way software is sold, delivered, and used in the world.

utility computing *Unlimited computing power and storage capacity that, like electricity and water services, can be obtained on demand from virtual utilities around the globe.*

> **EXAMPLE**   *Having Computing Services Flow like Beer.*
> Beer-maker Guinness (*guinness.com*) recently signed a utility-computing deal with IBM. Under a seven-year contract, IBM is providing Guinness with a range of computing services, including the management of its data center and server operations. Guinness will pay a variable rate for the amount of its processing requirements over the term of the contract. (*Source:* McDougall, 2003.)

Subscription Computing

Subscription computing, a variety of utility computing, puts the pieces of a computing platform together as services, rather than as a collection of separately purchased components. Users can obtain programs, information, or storage over the Internet (usually protected by virtual networks; see Technology Guide 4).

subscription computing *A type of utility computing that puts the pieces of a computing platform together as services, rather than as a collection of separately purchased components.*

Grid Computing

In **grid computing**, the unused processing cycles of various computers can be harnessed into a network in order to create powerful computing capabilities. Grid-computing applications, already in limited use, are typically in areas that formerly would have required supercomputers (see Technology Guide 1). The grid does the computing at a much lower cost.

grid computing *The use of networks to harness unused processing cycles of various computers in order to create powerful computing capabilities.*

A well-known grid-computing project is the *SETI@Home* project (Search for Extraterrestrial Intelligence), located at *setiathome.ssl.berkeley.edu*. In this project, PC users worldwide donate unused processor cycles to help the search for signs of extraterrestrial life by analyzing signals coming from outer space. In other examples, United Devices (*ud.com*) has one grid-computing project to perform smallpox research and used to have another called the PatriotGrid to conduct global bioterrorism research.

EXAMPLE *Speeding Drugs to Market May Improve Your Health.* Entelos (*entelos.com*), a biotechnology firm, uses computer software to simulate the behavior of the human body and predict its response to various drugs. Pharmaceutical companies approach Entelos with ideas for new drugs, and Entelos simulates the drug's effect on hundreds of "patients" who take the medication in hundreds of different circumstances. Each trial can involve up to 13,000 simulations. To handle this processing load, Entelos uses grid computing to use processing power from 145 different machines spread across its offices. Simulations that used to take two years on a mainframe now take one month on the grid. (*Source:* Metz, 2003.)

Pervasive Computing

pervasive computing *Invisible, everywhere computing that is embedded in the objects around us.*

With **pervasive computing**, we envision a future in which computation becomes part of the environment. Computation will be embedded in things, not only in computers. Relentless progress in semiconductor technology, low-power designs, and wireless technology will make embedded computation less and less obtrusive. Pervasive computing is closely related with IT support systems, especially intelligent systems and decision support systems. For more details about pervasive computing, see Chapter 6.

Web Services

Web services *Universal, prefabricated business process software modules, delivered over the Internet, that users can select and combine through almost any device, enabling disparate systems to share data and services.*

By using universal prefabricated business process software modules called **Web services**, computer users soon will be able to integrate applications, business processes, databases, and more into all kinds of applications, and do so rapidly and inexpensively. By using a set of shared protocols and standards for Web services, developers can create a truly open computing environment independent of any vendor or product. Web services, illustrated in Chapters 4 and 12, provide for inexpensive and rapid solutions for application integration, access to information, and application development.

Commercial Efforts in New Computing Environments

Three software companies currently are developing major products in the emerging computer environments. All will incorporate utility computing, pervasive computing, and Web services sometime in the future. Microsoft is launching a major research effort, known as Microsoft.net (*Microsoft.com/net/default.asp*). IBM is developing its WebSphere platform (*ibm.com/software/websphere*). And Sun Microsystems is building a new system architecture in its N1 Project (*sun.com/software/solutions/n1/index.html*).

Whether an organization uses mainframe-based legacy systems or cutting-edge Web-based systems, its information resources are extremely important organizational assets that need to be protected and managed. This topic is presented in Section 2.8.

Before you go on. . .

1. How might subscription computing affect the major software vendors, such as Microsoft?

2. How might grid computing affect the major hardware vendors, such as IBM?

2.8 MANAGING INFORMATION RESOURCES

A modern organization possesses many information resources. In addition to the computing resources, numerous applications exist, and new ones are continuously being developed. Applications have enormous strategic value. Firms rely on them so heavily that, in some cases, when they are not working (even for a short time), an organization cannot function. Furthermore, the acquisition, operation, security, and maintenance of these systems may cost a considerable amount of money. Therefore, it is essential to manage these information systems properly. The planning, organizing, implementing, operating, and controlling of the computing resources and the organization's portfolio of applications must be done with great skill.

Which IT Resources Are Managed and By Whom

The responsibility for the management of information resources is divided between two organizational entities: the *information systems department* (*ISD*), which is a corporate entity, and the *end users*, who are located throughout the organization. This division of responsibility raises important questions such as: Which resources are managed by whom? What is the role of the ISD, its structure, and its place in the organization? What are the relationships between the ISD and the end users? Brief answers to these questions are provided in this section.

There are many types of information systems resources, and their components may come from multiple vendors and be of different brands. The major categories of such resources are *hardware* (all types of computers, servers, and other devices), *software* (development tools, languages, and applications), *databases*, *networks* (local, wide, Internet, intranets and extranets, and supporting devices), *procedures*, *security facilities*, and *physical buildings*. The resources are scattered throughout the organization, and some of them change frequently. Therefore, it may be rather difficult to manage IS resources.

There is no standard menu for the division of responsibility for the development and maintenance of IS resources between the ISD and end users. That division depends on many things: the size and nature of the organization, the amount and type of IT resources, the organization's attitudes toward computing, the attitudes of top management toward computing, the maturity level of the technology, the amount and nature of outsourced IT work, and even the country in which the company operates. Generally speaking, the ISD is responsible for corporate-level and *shared resources*, while the end users are responsible for departmental resources.

Because of interdependencies of information resources, it is important that the ISD and the end users work closely together and cooperate regardless of who is doing what. We discuss the ISD's role in the organization below.

Information resources typically are divided between the information systems department (ISD), which is a corporate entity, and the end users, who are located throughout the organization.

The Role of the IS Department

As Manager's Checklist 2.1 shows, the role of the ISD is changing from purely technical to more managerial and strategic. As a result of this changing role, the position of the ISD within the organization has been elevated from a unit reporting to a functional department (such as accounting) to a unit reporting to a senior vice president of administration or even to the CEO. In this new role, the ISD must be able to work closely with external organizations such as vendors, business partners, consultants,

MANAGER'S CHECKLIST 2.1

The Changing Role of the Information Systems Department

Traditional Major IS Functions
❏ Managing systems development and systems project management
❏ Managing computer operations, including the computer center
❏ Staffing, training and developing IS skills
❏ Providing technical services

New (Additional) Major IS Functions
❏ Initiating and designing specific strategic information systems
❏ Infrastructure planning, development, and control
❏ Incorporating the Internet and electronic commerce into the business
❏ Managing system integration including the Internet, intranets, and extranets
❏ Educating the non-IS managers about IT
❏ Educating the IS staff about the business
❏ Supporting end-user computing
❏ Partnering with the executive level that runs the business
❏ Managing outsourcing
❏ Proactively using business and technical knowledge to "seed" innovative ideas about IT
❏ Creating business alliances with vendors and IS departments in other organizations

research institutions, and universities. In addition, the ISD and the end-user units must be close partners. The mechanisms that build the required cooperation are described in Chapter 11.

The role of the director of the ISD is also changing, from a technical manager to a senior executive, sometimes referred to as the **chief information officer (CIO)** or the *chief technology officer* (*CTO*). Details are provided in Chapter 11.

chief information officer (CIO)
The director of the IS department.

Before you go on. . .

1. How important are end users to the management of the organization's information resources?
2. Where do you think the IT staff should be located? Decentralized in the functional areas? Centralized at corporate level? A combination?

2.9 THE PLAN OF THIS BOOK

A major objective of this book is to bring you to the point where you will understand the roles of information technologies in today's digital organizations. Another objective is to prepare you to think strategically about information systems—to be able look into the future and see how these tools can help you, your organization, and your world. A third objective is to demonstrate how information technology supports all of the functional areas of the organization.

This textbook is divided into four parts. The content of each part is as follows.

Part I: The Organization in the Digital Economy

To survive and thrive in the new digital economy requires effective use of information technologies. Chapter 1 discussed how information technology can help organizations gain competitive advantage in today's modern business environment. Chapter 2 has introduced basic concepts relating to information systems, the various configurations of information systems, current and emerging computing environments, and management of information resources.

Part II: Foundations of Business Transactions and Processes

The technologies that form the information technology infrastructure and provide the foundation for business transactions and processes are introduced in the next four chapters and in Technology Guides 1 through 5 (at the end of the book). The chapters include: data and knowledge management (Chapter 3); network computing (Chapter 4); electronic commerce (Chapter 5); and wireless technologies (Chapter 6). Technology Guides 1 through 5 include computer hardware, computer software, data management, telecommunications and network basics, and Internet basics.

Part III: Applying Information Technology for Competitive Advantage

Technologies and systems do not solve problems or give competitive advantage until people understand how to apply them. This part of the book shows information technologies and systems in action, solving organizational problems and creating competitive advantage. Chapters 7, 8, and 9 follow the three tiers of information systems from functional systems (e.g., accounting information systems, marketing information systems, etc.), to enterprise information systems (e.g., enterprise resource planning systems, customer relationship management systems, etc.), to interorganizational information systems (e.g., supply chain management systems).

Part IV: Acquiring and Implementing Information Systems

Dynamic business environments force organizations to implement new information systems quickly and effectively. Chapter 11 focuses on how organizations acquire their information systems. Further, as the world becomes increasingly "connected," information systems are having greater impacts on businesses on the one hand, while businesses are becoming more vulnerable to their information systems on the other hand. Chapter 12 addresses the issues of IT impacts and security, as well as ethical considerations brought about by new technologies.

WHAT'S IN IT FOR ME?

Data and information are the lifeblood of the accounting function. Transaction processing systems, now Web-based, capture, organize, analyze, and disseminate data and information throughout organizations, often through corporate intranets. The Internet has vastly increased the number of transactions (especially global) in modern businesses. Transactions such as billing customers, preparing payrolls, and purchasing and paying for materials provide data that the accounting department must record and track. These transactions, particularly with customers and suppliers, are now usually online, through extranets. In addition, accounting information systems must integrate with other information systems in other parts of a large organization, so that transactional information from a sales or marketing information system becomes input for the accounting system.

ACC

FOR THE ACCOUNTING MAJOR

The modern financial world turns on speed, volume, and accuracy of information flow, all facilitated by information systems and networks. Finance departments use information systems to monitor world financial markets and to provide quantitative analyses (for cash flow projections and forecasting, for example). They use decision support systems to support financial decision making (for portfolio management, for example). Financial managers now use business intelligence software to analyze information in data

FIN

FOR THE FINANCE MAJOR

warehouses. Enterprisewide information systems (e.g., enterprise resource planning packages) also tightly integrate finance with all other functional areas.

MKT

FOR THE MARKETING MAJOR

Marketing now uses customer databases, decision support systems, sales automation, data warehouses, and business intelligence software to perform its functions. The Internet has created an entirely new global channel for marketing from business-to-business and business-to-consumer. The Internet has dramatically increased the amount of information available to customers, allowing rapid and thorough product and price comparisons and increasing the sophistication of customers. As a result, marketing managers must work harder to acquire and retain customers and are now using customer relationship management software for these purposes. The Internet helps here, because it provides for much closer contact between the customer and the supplier.

POM

FOR THE PRODUCTION/ OPERATIONS MANAGEMENT MAJOR

Organizations are competing on price, quality, time (speed), and customer service—all of which are concerns of productions and operations management. Every process in a company's operations that adds value to a product or service (e.g., purchasing inventory, quality control, and inbound and outbound logistics) can be enhanced by the use of Web-based information systems. Further, information systems have enabled the production and operations function to extend beyond the organization to other organizations in the firm's supply chain. From computer-aided design and computer-aided manufacturing, through Web-based ordering systems, information systems support the production and operations function.

HRM

FOR THE HUMAN RESOURCES MANAGEMENT MAJOR

Human resources management is well supported by information systems. Record keeping is greatly improved in terms of speed, convenience, and accuracy. Dissemination of HR information throughout the company via intranets means that employees receive consistent information and can handle much of their personal business (configuring their benefits, for example) themselves, without help from HR personnel. The Internet makes a tremendous amount of information available to the job seeker, increasing the fluidity of the labor market. Finally, information systems skills are necessary in many careers. HR professionals must have an understanding of these systems and skills to best support hiring, training, and retention.

SUMMARY

1. **Differentiate between information technology infrastructure and information technology architecture.** An organization's information technology *architecture* is a high-level map or plan of the information assets in an organization. The IT architecture integrates the information requirements of the organization and all users, the IT infrastructure, and all applications. An organization's information technology *infrastructure* consists of the physical facilities, IT components, IT services, and IT management that support the entire organization.

2. **Describe the components of computer-based information systems.** A *computer-based information system (CBIS)* is an information system that uses computer technology to perform some or all of its intended tasks. The basic components of CBISs are hardware, software, database(s), telecommunications networks, procedures, and people. Hardware is a set of devices (e.g., the processor, monitor, keyboard, and printer) that accept data and information, process them, and display them. Software is a set of programs that enable the hardware to process data. A database is a collection of related files, tables, relations, and so on, that stores data and the associations among them. A network is a connecting system (wireline or wireless) that permits the sharing of resources by different computers. Procedures are the set of instructions about how to combine the above components in order to process information and generate the desired output. People are those individuals who work with the information system, interface with it, or use its output.

3. **Describe various information systems and their evolution.** *Transaction processing systems* summarize and organize data from business transactions. *Management information systems* access, organize, summarize, and display information for supporting routine decision making in the functional areas. *Of-*

fice automation systems support office and clerical workers. *CAD/CAM systems* support the manufacturing environment. *Decision support systems* provide computer-based support for complex, nonroutine decisions, and *executive support systems* provide structured support for top managers. *Group support systems* support people working in groups.

Expert systems provide the stored knowledge of experts to nonexperts. *Knowledge management systems* support the creating, gathering, organizing, integrating, and disseminating of an organization's knowledge. A *data warehouse* is a database designed to support DSS, ESS, and other analytical and end-user activities. *Business intelligence systems* gather and use large amounts of data for query and analysis by DSS, ESS, and other intelligent systems. *Mobile computing* supports mobile employees working outside the physical boundaries of their companies. *Electronic data interchange* involves computer-to-computer direct communication of standard business documents between business partners. Systems intended to support customers are grouped under the umbrella term, *customer relationship management.* *Web-based systems* deliver business applications via the Internet.

4. **Identify the major internal support systems for each organizational level.** At the *clerical-worker level,* employees are supported by office automation and communication systems and may also be supported by transaction processing systems, management information systems, and mobile systems. At the *operational level,* transaction processing systems provide the major support. Operational managers are also supported by management information systems and mobile systems. At the *managerial level,* functional area management information systems (often called simply MISs) provide the major support. Middle managers are also supported by the transaction processing systems. At the *knowledge-worker level,* Internet search engines, expert systems, decision support systems, and business intelligence systems (for user-driven data analysis) support knowledge workers. At the *strategic level,* executives are supported mainly by executive support systems and to a lesser extent by decision support systems and business intelligence systems.

5. **Compare mainframe-based legacy systems, client/server architecture, and peer-to-peer architecture.** In the *mainframe* environment, one or more mainframe computers perform the processing. Users work with passive ("dumb") terminals, which enter or change data and access information from the mainframe, and are controlled by it. Legacy systems are older systems that are central to the operations of a business; typically they process an organization's high-volume transactions. Legacy systems are closely related to the mainframe environment. *Client/server architecture* divides distributed computing units into two major categories, *clients* and *servers,* connected by a network. This architecture provides a way for different computing devices to work together, each doing the job for which it is best suited. *Peer-to-peer (P2P) architecture* is a type of network in which each client computer shares files or computer resources *directly* with others *but not through a central server* as in the traditional client/server architecture.

6. **Describe the major types of Web-based information systems and understand their functionalities.** The *Internet* is a public, cooperative, self-sustaining worldwide system of computer networks—a network of networks. An *intranet* is the use of Web technologies to create a private network, usually within one enterprise. *Extranets* form a larger virtual network that allows remote users to securely connect over the Internet to the enterprise's main intranet. *Corporate portals* are Web sites that provide the gateway to corporate information from a single point of access. An *electronic storefront* is the Web-equivalent of a showroom or a physical store. An *electronic market* is a network of interactions and relationships over which information, products, services, and payments are exchanged. A form of electronic markets is *electronic exchanges,* which are Web-based public marketplaces where many buyers and many sellers interact dynamically. *Mobile commerce* is the buying and selling of goods and services in a wireless environment (through wireless devices). The *Enterprise Web* is an open environment for managing and delivering Web applications.

7. **Describe the emerging computing environments.** *Utility computing* enables computing resources to flow like electricity on demand from virtual utilities around the globe. *Subscription computing,* a variety of utility computing, puts the pieces of a computing platform together as services, rather than as a collection of separately purchased components. In *grid computing,* the unused processing cycles of all computers in a given network can be harnessed to create powerful computing capabilities. With *pervasive computing,* computation will be embedded in things, not only in computers. *Web services* are universal prefabricated business process software modules, enabling computer users to integrate applications, business processes, and databases, and do so rapidly and inexpensively.

8. **Describe how information resources are managed and the roles of the information systems department and the end users.** The responsibility for the management of information resources is divided between two organizational entities: the *information systems department (ISD),* which is a corporate entity, and the *end users,* who are located throughout the organization. Generally speaking, the ISD is responsible for corporate-level and *shared resources,* while the end users are responsible for departmental resources.

INTERACTIVE / LEARNING

Instructions for accessing the Interactivities on the Student Web Site:

1. Go to
   wiley.com/college/turban
2. Select Turban Rainer Potter's *Introduction to Information Technology, Third Edition*
3. Click on Student Resources Site, in the toolbar on the left
4. Click on Interactivities Web Site
5. Click on Interactivities Web Site and use your password to enter the site (your password card is located in the inside cover of your textbook)

How Does IT Keep the Dallas Mavericks on Top of Their Game?

Go to the Interactivities section on the Student Web Site and access Chapter 2: Information Technologies: Concepts and Management. There you will find an animated simulation of the technologies used to maximize profits at Dallas Maverick games, as well as some hands-on activities that visually explain business concepts in this chapter.

More Resources

More resources and study tools are located on the Student Web Site. You'll find additional chapter materials and links to organizations, people, and technologies for each chapter. In addition, self-quizzes that provide individualized feedback are available for each chapter.

DISCUSSION QUESTIONS

1. Discuss the logic of building information systems in accordance with the organizational hierarchical structure.
2. Describe how IT architecture and information infrastructure are interrelated.
3. Discuss the following concepts: distributed processing, client/server, and enterprisewide computing.
4. Discuss the capabilities of P2P architecture.
5. Is the Internet an infrastructure, architecture, or an application program? Why? If none of the above, then what is it?

6. There is wide speculation that m-commerce will surpass "wireline" e-commerce (e-commerce that takes place over wired networks) as the method of choice for digital commerce transactions. What industries or application areas do you think will be most affected by m-commerce?
7. Some speculate that utility computing will be the dominating option of the future. Do you agree? Discuss why or why not.

PROBLEM-SOLVING ACTIVITIES

1. Characterize each of the following systems as one (or more) of the IT support systems:
   a. A student registration system in a university.
   b. A system that advises farmers about which fertilizers to use.
   c. A hospital patient-admission system.
   d. A system that provides a marketing manager with demand reports regarding the sales volume of specific products.
   e. A robotic system that paints cars in a factory.
2. Select two companies you are familiar with and find their mission statement and current goals (plans). Explain how these goals are related to operational, managerial, and strategic activities on a one-to-one basis. Then explain how information systems (by type) can support the activities (be specific).

3. Review the systems of the following companies, presented in this chapter, and identify the support provided by IT:
   - The Dallas Mavericks
   - Guinness
   - Mythic Entertainment
   - Lowe and Partners
   - Covance
   - Worldspan
   - Hot Topic
   - Abbey National Banking Group
   - Le Saunda
   - Cigna (see Real-World Case)

INTERNET ACTIVITIES

1. Enter the site of Federal Express (*fedex.com*) and find the current information systems used by the company or offered to FedEx's customers. Explain how the systems' innovations contribute to the success of FedEx.
2. Surf the Internet for information about airport security regarding bomb and weapon-detecting devices. Examine the available products, and comment on the IT techniques used.
3. Enter the Web site of Hershey Foods (*hersheys.com*). Examine the information about the company and its products and markets. Explain how an intranet can help such a company compete in the global market.
4. Investigate the status of utility computing by visiting *infoworld.com/forums/utility*, *aspnews.com* (discussion forum), *google.com*, *ibm.com*, *oracle.com*, and *cio.com*. Prepare a report that will highlight the progress today and the current inhibitors.
5. Enter *argus-acia.com* and learn about new developments in the field of information architecture. Also, view the tutorials at *hotwired.com/webmonkey* on this topic. Summarize major new trends.
6. Enter *cio.com* and find recent information on the changing role of the CIO and the ISD. Prepare a report.

TEAM ASSIGNMENTS

1. Observe a supermarket checkout counter that uses a scanner. Find some material that describes how the scanned code is translated into the price that the customers pay.
   a. Identify the following components of the system: inputs, processes, and outputs.
   b. What kind of a system is the scanner (TPS, DSS, ESS, ES, etc.)? Why did you classify it as you did?
   c. Having the information electronically in the system may provide opportunities for additional managerial uses of that information. Identify such uses.
   d. Checkout systems are now being replaced by self-service checkout kiosks and scanners. Compare the two.
2. Divide the class into teams. Each team will select a small business to start (a restaurant, dry cleaning business, small travel agency, etc.). Assume the business wants to become an e-business. Each team will plan the architecture for the business's information systems, possibly in consultation with Microsoft or another vendor. Make a class presentation.

REAL-WORLD CASE

INFORMATION TECHNOLOGY PROBLEMS AT CIGNA

THE BUSINESS PROBLEM Philadelphia-based Cigna (*cigna.com*) is the nation's fourth-largest insurance company. It was formed by the merger of the Insurance Company of North America and the Connecticut General Life Insurance Company in 1982. Increased competition in the insurance industry contributed to a $500 million net loss for Cigna in 2002 and a 40 percent decrease in the company's stock price. Cigna was under other pressures as well.

First, the company, along with other national insurers such as Aetna and Humana, was being sued by thousands of doctors nationwide who were furious about delays in payment for patient care. The doctors accused the insurers of deliberately delaying payment and improperly rejecting claims in order to save money.

Second, Cigna's sales team, in order to win large employer accounts in an increasingly competitive environment, had promised that Cigna would be developing new information technology systems to provide improved customer service. However, the systems had not yet been developed.

Third, Cigna's management was under pressure to cut costs after posting disappointing earnings. Executives were anxious for the new systems' promised cost reductions and productivity gains.

THE IT SOLUTION Cigna developed an ambitious plan to consolidate and upgrade its antiquated IT systems, some of which dated back to the 1982 merger. The idea was to have an integrated system for enrollment, eligibility, and claims processing so that customers would receive one bill, medical claims could be processed faster and more efficiently, and customer service representatives would have a single, unified view of customers (called "members").

To accomplish these goals, Cigna would have to consolidate its many back-end systems for claims processing and billing (these were the company's old legacy transaction processing systems), and integrate them with new customer-facing applications. Therefore, Cigna would have to develop and integrate two systems, one for claims eligibility that customers can use, and the other for billing. Cigna's IT group had to build an entire information infrastructure from scratch that could support the two main systems (or platforms). To do all this, the IT group had to completely reengineer its legacy back-end systems.

Cigna did most of the work in house, but the company did hire Cap Gemini Ernst & Young (CGEY) to help implement the change management and business processes involved. Cigna also worked with CGEY to develop and implement the new customer-facing applications that would allow members to enroll, check the status of their claims and benefits, and choose from different health-plan offerings—all online. Those applications would also give customer service representatives the promised single unified view of members' accounts, so that when a member called with problems or questions, the representatives would have a full history of the member's interaction with the company.

THE RESULTS   In January 2002, Cigna's $1 billion IT overhaul and customer relationship management initiative went live in a big way, with 3.5 million members moved from 15 legacy systems to the two new platforms in a matter of minutes. The migration to the new systems did not go smoothly. In fact, there were glitches in customer service so severe that millions of dissatisfied customers walked away, causing Cigna to lose 6 percent of its health-care membership in 2002.

Members suddenly had trouble obtaining health coverage. Cigna's systems could not confirm health coverage for some new members for several weeks. Workers at one company effectively lost coverage when their membership information would not load properly into the new systems. Cigna issued member ID cards with incorrect identifiers and cards missing prescription icons, which meant that members could not get their prescriptions filled at their local drugstores.

Cigna's customer service center was, predictably, inundated with calls. However, in anticipation of increased productivity from the new systems, the company had laid off some of its customer service representatives. Now there were not enough reps to handle the call load. In addition, representatives still with Cigna had not been adequately trained in how to work with the new systems.

There were also problems with data migration from the old legacy systems to the new applications. Converting back-end data to customer-facing applications is tricky, as the data have to be cleaned and filtered in order to be understandable to customer service reps taking calls and to members seeking information online.

After six months of hard work, Cigna succeeded in fixing the problems with the new systems, and successfully migrated another 700,000 members. The company also launched MyCigna.com, an online portal where Cigna members can look up their benefits, choose from an array of health plans, check on the status of their claims, retrieve health information, and talk to nurses online.

Source: Compiled from A. Bass, "Cigna's Self-Inflicted Wounds," *CIO Magazine,* March 15, 2003.

QUESTIONS

1. What were the major reasons why Cigna felt it had to do an IT overhaul?

2. What were the major reasons for the initial failure of Cigna's IT overhaul?

3. What could Cigna have done to increase its chances of success with its IT project?

IDENTIFYING INFORMATION AT CLUB IT

Most of the computer business information systems at Club IT have been developed as needed by Lisa and Ruben. For example, they keep their food and beverage inventory on a spreadsheet, one worksheet per month; employee payroll is done with QuickBooks; the advance ticket sales for Friday and Saturday night bands are handled manually using tickets created with a word processor. Club IT also has a members' program where frequent guests are rewarded with free beverages and cover discounts. Ruben asks you to do preliminary research and propose some ways to better automate these and other information systems at Club IT.

ASSIGNMENT

1. Can Club IT do a better job managing their food and beverage inventory? Do a Web search for au-

tomated systems. (Hint: Food, beverage, information, and systems are good keywords.) Describe a particularly useful system you find, the data it tracks, and the kinds of reports it produces. How would it benefit Club IT?

2. Lisa and Ruben want to know more about the club's members and their preferences. Build a small database, using Microsoft Access, that could serve as a prototype members' database for Club IT. Use data items that would provide useful profiles of the members.

3. Review the job categories for Club IT on its Web site. Who would be the end users of different information systems in this chapter?

Go to wiley.com/college/turban to access the CLUB IT Web Site on the Student Web Site

Data and Knowledge Management

Chapter Preview

Chapters 1 and 2 and Technology Guides 1 and 2 introduced you to information systems and organizational topics as well as insights into how IT hardware and software function. These technologies and systems support organizations through their ability to handle—acquire, store, access, analyze, and transmit—electronic data. Properly managed, these data become *information* and then *knowledge*, highly valuable organizational resources and the basis of much competitive advantage.

Data warehousing represents a new concept of data management—to put data in a form easily understandable (intuitive) to managers and analysts, so that they can access it themselves and analyze it according to their needs with a variety of tools, producing information. They can then apply their experience to place this information in the context of a business problem, producing knowledge. Knowledge management, enabled by information technology, captures and stores knowledge in forms that all organizational employees can access and apply, creating the flexible, powerful "learning organization."

Chapter Outline

3.1 Data Management: A Critical Success Factor
3.2 Data Warehousing
3.3 Information and Knowledge Discovery with Business Intelligence
3.4 Data Mining Concepts and Applications
3.5 Data Visualization Technologies
3.6 Web-Based Data Management Systems
3.7 Introduction to Knowledge Management
3.8 Information Technology in Knowledge Management

Learning Objectives

1. Recognize the importance of data, their managerial issues, and their life cycle.
2. Describe the sources of data and their collection.
3. Describe document management systems.
4. Explain the operation of data warehousing and its role in decision support.
5. Describe information and knowledge discovery and business intelligence.
6. Understand the power and benefits of data mining.
7. Describe data presentation methods, and explain geographical information systems, visual simulations, and virtual reality as decision support tools.
8. Recognize the role of the Web in data management.
9. Define knowledge and describe the different types of knowledge.
10. Describe the technologies that can be utilized in a knowledge management system.

FINDING DIAMONDS BY DATA MINING AT HARRAH'S

Harrah's Entertainment (*harrahs.com*) is a very profitable casino chain. With 26 casinos in 13 states, it had $4 billion sales in 2002 and net income of $235 million. Harrah's business problem is very simple: how to attract visitors to come and spend money in your casino, and do it again and again.

Most casino operators use intuition to plan inducements for customers. Almost all have loyalty cards, provide free rooms to customers who visit frequently, give them free shows, and more. The problem is that there is very little differentiation among the casinos. Casinos believe they must give those incentives to survive, but do the incentives help casinos to excel? Harrah's is doing better than most competing casinos by effectively leveraging information technology.

Harrah's strategy is based on IT-enabled customer relationship management (CRM) and the use of customer database marketing to test promotions. This combination enables the company to fine-tune marketing efforts and service-delivery strategies that keep customers coming back. Noting that 82.7 percent of its revenue comes from slot machines, Harrah's started by giving each player a loyalty smart card. A smart-card reader on each slot machine in all 26 of its casinos records each customer's activities. (Readers are also available in Harrah's restaurants, gift shops, etc., to record any spending.)

Logging players' activities, Harrah's gives credits, as in other loyalty programs, that can be used for free hotel rooms, dinners, and so forth. Such programs are run by most competitors, but Harrah's goes a step further: It uses a 300-gigabyte data warehouse to analyze the data recorded by the card readers. By tracking millions of individual transactions, Harrah's IT systems assemble a vast amount of data on customer habits and preferences. These data are fed into the enterprise data warehouse, which contains not only millions of transactional data points about customers (such as name, address, age, gender) but also details about their gambling, spending, and preferences.

This data warehouse has become a very rich repository of customer information, and it is mined for decision support. For example, analysis discovered that the company's best customers were middle-aged and senior adults with discretionary time and income, who enjoyed playing slot machines. These customers did not typically stay in a hotel, but visited a casino on the way home from work or on a weekend night out. These customers responded better to an offer of $60 of casino chips than to a free room, two steak meals, and $30 worth of chips, because they enjoyed the anticipation and excitement of gambling itself (rather than seeing the trip as a vacation getaway). As in other casinos with loyalty programs, Harrah's segregates players into three tiers, and the biggest spenders get priorities in waiting lines and in awards. Every experience in Harrah's casinos was redesigned to drive customers to want to earn a higher-level card.

This strategy offered a way to differentiate Harrah's brand. Understanding the lifetime value of the customers became critical to the company's marketing strategy. The company began to focus on customers' total spending over a long time. And, by gathering increasingly specific information about customer preferences, running experiments and analyses on the newly collected data, and determining ways of appealing to players' interests, the company was able to increase the amount of money customers spent by appealing to their individual preferences. For example, the casino knows which specific customers were playing at particular slot machines and at what time. Using data mining techniques, Harrah's can discover what specific machines appealed to specific customers. This knowledge enabled Harrah's to configure the casino floor with a mix of slot machines that benefited both the customers and the company.

In addition, by measuring employee performance and analyzing these results with data mining, the company is able to provide its customers with better experiences as well as earn more money for the employees. Harrah's implemented a bonus plan to reward hourly workers with extra cash for achieving improved customer satisfaction scores. (Bonuses totaling $43 million were paid over three years.) The bonus program worked because the reward depends on everyone's performance. The general manager of a lower-scoring property might visit a colleague at a higher-scoring casino to find out what he could do to improve his casino's scores.

THE RESULTS

Harrah's experience has shown that the better the experience a guest has and the more attentive the casino can be to him or her, the more money the casino will make. For Harrah's, good customer service is a daily routine. Harrah's continues to enhance benefits to its Total Rewards program, improves customer loyalty through customer service supported by the data mining, and of course makes lots of money.

Sources: Compiled from M. Levinson, "Jackpot! Harrah's Entertainment," *CIO*, February 1, 2001; and G. Loveman, "Diamonds in the Data," *Harvard Business Review*, May 2003.

WHAT WE LEARNED FROM THIS CASE

The opening case about Harrah's illustrates the importance of data to a large entertainment company. It shows that it is necessary to collect vast amounts of data, organize and store the data items properly in one place, and then analyze the data and use the results to make better marketing and other corporate decisions. The case shows us that new data go through a process in stages: Data are collected, processed, and stored in a data warehouse. Then, data are processed by analytical tools such as data mining and decision modeling. The findings of the data analyses direct promotional and other decisions. Finally, continuous collection and analysis of fresh data provide management with feedback regarding the success of management strategies. Further, analyzing this feedback adds value to a company's information. This process produces knowledge, which is information in action and in context.

In this chapter we explain how this process is executed with the help of IT. We will also deal with some additional topics that typically supplement the data management process. The chapter concludes with a look at knowledge management and how it is supported by IT.

3.1 DATA MANAGEMENT: A CRITICAL SUCCESS FACTOR

As illustrated throughout this textbook, IT applications cannot be done without using data. Data should be high-quality, meaning that it should be accurate, complete, timely, consistent, accessible, relevant, and concise. However, there are increasing difficulties in acquiring, keeping, and managing data. For a technical overview of data management, see Technology Guide 3.

The Difficulties of Managing Data

Since data are processed in several stages and possibly places, they may be subject to some problems and difficulties. Managing data in organizations is difficult for various reasons:

- The amount of data increases exponentially with time. Much past data must be kept for a long time, and new data are added rapidly.
- Data are scattered throughout organizations and are collected by many individuals using several methods and devices. Data are frequently stored in several servers and locations and in different computing systems, databases, formats, and human and computer languages.
- An ever-increasing amount of external data needs to be considered in making organizational decisions.
- Data security, quality, and integrity are critical, yet are easily jeopardized. In addition, legal requirements relating to data differ among countries and industries and change frequently.

critical success factors (CSFs) *Those few things that must go right in order to ensure an organization's survival and success.*

Critical success factors (CSFs) are those few things that must go right in order to ensure an organization's survival and success. Increasingly, organizations are viewing data management as a critical success factor. The recognition of data as a critical organizational asset and the difficulties with data have caused organizations to search for efficient and effective data management solutions. A starting point for understanding these solutions is the data life cycle.

The Data Life Cycle

Businesses run on data that have been processed into information and knowledge, which managers apply to businesses problems and opportunities. As seen in the Harrah's case, *knowledge* fuels solutions. However, because of the difficulties of managing data, listed earlier, deriving knowledge from accumulated data may not be simple or easy.

Transformation of data into knowledge and solutions is accomplished in several ways. In general, it resembles the process shown in Figure 3.1. It starts with new data collection from various sources. These data are stored in a database(s). Then the data are preprocessed to fit the format of a data warehouse or data mart, where they are stored. Users then access needed data in the warehouse or data mart for analysis. The analysis is done with data analysis and mining tools which look for patterns, and with intelligent systems, which support data interpretation.

The result of these activities is the generation of decision support and knowledge. Both the data (at various times during the process) and the knowledge (derived at the end of the process) must be presented to users. The presentation can be accomplished by using different visualization tools. Additionally, the created knowledge may be stored in an organizational knowledge base (as we will see later in this chapter) and used, together with decision support tools, to provide solutions to organizational problems. The elements and the process shown in Figure 3.1 are discussed in the remaining sections of this chapter.

Data Sources

The data life cycle begins with the acquisition of data from data sources. Data sources can be classified as internal, personal, and external (particularly the Internet).

Internal Data Sources.　An organization's internal data are about people, products, services, and processes. Such data are usually located in corporate databases and are usually accessible via an organization's intranet.

Personal Data.　IS users or other corporate employees may document their own expertise by creating personal data. These data are not necessarily just facts, but may include concepts, thoughts, and opinions. These data can reside on the user's PC or be placed on corporate databases or on corporate knowledge bases.

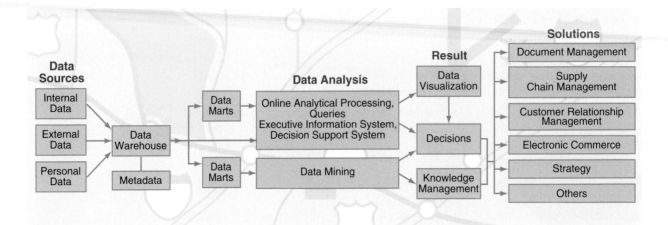

Figure 3.1　*Roadmap: data life cycle.*

External Data Sources.   There are many sources for external data, ranging from commercial databases to sensors and satellites. Government reports constitute a major source of external data. Data are available on CD-ROMs and memory chips, on Internet servers, as films, and as sound or voices. Pictures, diagrams, atlases, and television are other sources of external data. Hundreds of thousands of organizations worldwide place publicly accessible data on their Web servers, flooding us with data. Most external data are irrelevant to any single application. Yet, external data must be monitored and captured to ensure that important data are not overlooked.

The Internet and Commercial Database Services.   Many thousands of databases all over the world are accessible through the Internet. Much external data are free; other data are available from commercial database services.

A commercial *online database publisher* sells access to specialized databases, newspapers, magazines, bibliographies, and reports. Such a service can provide external data to users in a timely manner and at a reasonable cost. Many commercial database publishers will customize the data for each user. Several thousand services are currently available, most of which are accessible via the Internet. Many consulting companies (e.g., *aberdeen.com*) sell reports online. For an interesting look at a commercial multimedia database, see Online File W3.1.

The different types of data and the sheer volume of data can create data-quality problems. Therefore, data must be validated. The classic expression that sums up the "data situation" in organizations is "garbage in, garbage out" (GIGO). Online File W3.2 discusses data quality and data integrity.

wiley.com/college/turban

wiley.com/college/turban

Document Management

There are several major problems with paper documents, which include version control, update frequency, security, distribution, and storage. As IT's about Business 3.1 illustrates, even when employees know the problems with paper documents, they still may find it difficult to give up paper.

One of the earliest IT-enabled tools of data management is called *document management*. **Document management** is the automated control of electronic documents,

document management   *The automated control of electronic documents, page images, spreadsheets, word processing documents, and other complex documents through their entire life cycle within an organization.*

IT'S ABOUT BUSINESS   FIN ACC

3.1: Give Up Paper? No Way!

When the 8,000 employees at Huntington Bancshares (*huntington.com*) heard that their paper report—called the balance sheet income report—was going to be transformed into a Web-based database, they were not happy about it. Complaints came flooding in. But Huntington, a $28 billion regional bank holding company, had good reasons for replacing the paper reports. The reports amounted to 200,000 pages sent to hundreds of offices every month. That is 2.4 million pages per year. The reports had to be mailed via an interoffice distribution system to 2,500 locations for a diverse user group ranging from operations clerks to financial controllers.

In place of all that paper, the bank chose to load the financial data into an Oracle database. The bank also purchased a Web-based system for reporting, analysis, and information delivery. The results were clear. First, the bank is now saving $30,000 per year

in paper costs alone. Second, cost center managers can now see the balance sheet income reports immediately online. Third, managers can easily see and resolve exceptions, which are items in an account balance that do not match the credits. Fourth, Huntington now has a standard set of metrics on a single online report that each branch manager can use to determine the "health" of his or her branch.

Source: Compiled from L. Mearian, "Breaking the Paper Habit," *Computerworld,* August 4, 2003.

QUESTIONS

1. Why did Huntington's employees initially resist the move away from paper reports?

2. In the Information Age, are we using more or less paper? Why?

page images, spreadsheets, word processing documents, and other complex documents through their entire life cycle within an organization, from initial creation to final archiving. Document management offers various benefits: It allows organizations to exert greater control over production, storage, and distribution of documents. It yields greater efficiency in the reuse of information, the control of a document through a workflow process, and the reduction of product cycle times. One way to manage documents is to image them, as Online File W3.3 demonstrates.

Document management systems (DMSs) provide information in an electronic format to decision makers. The full range of functions that a document management system may perform includes document identification, storage, and retrieval; tracking; version control; workflow management; and presentation. The major tools of document management systems are workflow software, authoring tools, scanners, imaging systems, and databases (object-oriented mixed with relational, known as *object-relational database management systems;* see Technology Guide 3). One of the major vendors of document management software is Lotus Development Corporation. Its document databases and their replication property provide many advantages for group work and information sharing (see *lotus.com*). For further discussion see *imrgold.com* and *docuvantage.com*.

Here are some examples of how companies use document management systems to manage data and documents.

wiley.com/college/turban

document management systems (DMSs) *Computer systems that identify, store, retrieve, track, and present information in an electronic format to decision makers.*

POM

EXAMPLE *Electronic Medical Records Provide Information Quickly, Accurately.* The Surgery Center of Baltimore stores all of its medical records electronically, providing instant patient information to doctors and nurses anywhere and any time. The system also routes charts to the billing department, whose employees can scan and e-mail any related information to insurance providers and patients. The DMS also helps maintain an audit trail, including providing records for legal purposes or action. Business processes have been expedited by more than 50 percent, the cost of such processes is significantly lower, and morale of office employees in the center is up. (*Source: laserfiche.com/newsroom/baltimore.html.*)

HRM

EXAMPLE *Digitized Records Simplify Personnel Administration.* The University of Cincinnati, a state university in Ohio, is required to provide authorized access to the personnel files of 12,000 active employees and tens of thousand of retirees. There are over 75,000 queries about the personnel records every year, and answers need to be found among 2.5 million records. Finding answers with the antiquated microfilm system took days. The solution was a DMS that digitized all paper and microfilm documents, making them available via the Internet and the intranet. An authorized employee can now use a browser and access a document in seconds. (*Source: imrgold.com/en/case_studies/edu_Univ_of_Cin.asp.*)

POM

EXAMPLE *Knowledge Base Created from Document Management System.* The European Court of Human Rights (44 countries in Europe) created a Web-based document and KM system that was originally stored on an intranet and now is stored in a separate organizational knowledge base. The DMS has had over 20 million hits in 2002. Millions of euros are saved each year just on printing and mailing documents. (*Source: echr.coe.int.*)

POM

EXAMPLE *Eliminating Paper and Saving Money.* McDonnell-Douglas (now part of Boeing Company) distributed aircraft service bulletins to its customers around the world using the Internet. The company used to distribute a staggering volume of bulletins to over 200 airlines, using over 4 million pages of documentation every year. Now it is all on the Web, saving money and time both for the company and for its customers. (*Source: boeing.com.*)

Before you go on . . .

1. What are some of the difficulties in managing data?
2. Describe the data life cycle.
3. What are the various sources for data?

3.2 DATA WAREHOUSING

Many large and even medium-size companies are using data warehousing to make it easy and faster to process, analyze, and query data.

Transactional versus Analytical Processing

Data processing in organizations can be viewed either as *transactional* or *analytical*. The data in transaction processing systems (TPSs) are organized mainly in a *hierarchical structure* (see Technology Guide 3) and centrally processed for fast and efficient processing of routine, repetitive data.

Today, however, the most successful companies are those that can respond quickly and flexibly to market changes and opportunities, and the key to this response is the effective and efficient use of data and information, as shown in the Harrah's case. This is done not only via transaction processing, but also through a supplementary activity, called **analytical processing**, which involves analysis of accumulated data, frequently by end users. Analytical processing, also referred to as *business intelligence*, includes data mining, decision support systems (DSSs), enterprise information systems, Web applications, querying, and other end-user activities. Placing strategic information in the hands of decision makers aids productivity and empowers users to make better decisions, leading to greater competitive advantage.

Data warehouses, which provide for improved analytical processing, are the subject of the next section.

analytical processing *Analysis of accumulated data, frequently by end users; also referred to as* business intelligence.

Describing the Data Warehouse

A **data warehouse** is a repository of subject-oriented historical data that are organized to be accessible in a form readily acceptable for analytical processing activities (such as data mining, decision support, querying, and other applications). Characteristics of a data warehouse include:

- *Organization.* Data are organized by subject (e.g., by customer, vendor, product, price level, and region), and contain information relevant for decision support only.
- *Consistency.* Data in different operational databases may be encoded differently. For example, gender data may be encoded 0 and 1 in one operational system and "m" and "f" in another. In the data warehouse, though, they will be coded in a consistent manner.
- *Time variant.* The data are kept for many years so that they can be used for trends, forecasting, and comparisons over time.
- *Nonvolatile.* Data are not updated once entered into the warehouse.
- *Multidimensional.* Typically the data warehouse uses a multidimensional structure.
- *Web-based.* Today's data warehouses are designed to provide an efficient computing environment for Web-based applications.

data warehouse *A repository of subject-oriented historical data that are organized to be accessible in a form readily acceptable for analytical processing.*

Some successful data warehouse applications are summarized in Table 3.1. Hundreds of other successful applications are reported. For example, see client success stories and case studies at Web sites of vendors such as Hyperion (*hyperion.com*), Business Objects (*businessobjects.com*), Cognos Corp. (*cognos.com*), Information

Table 3.1   Summary of Strategic Uses of Data Warehousing

Industry	Functional Areas of Use	Strategic Use
Airline	Operations and Marketing	Crew assignment, aircraft deployment, mix of fares, analysis of route profitability, frequent-flyer program promotions
Apparel	Distribution and Marketing	Merchandising, and inventory replenishment
Banking	Product Development, Operations, and Marketing	Customer service, trend analysis, product and service promotions, reduction of IS expenses
Credit Card	Product Development and Marketing	Customer service, new information service for a fee, fraud detection
Health Care	Operations	Reduction of operational expenses
Investment and Insurance	Product Development, Operations, and Marketing	Risk management, market movements analysis, customer tendencies analysis, portfolio management
Personal Care Products	Distribution and Marketing	Distribution decisions, product promotions, sales decisions, pricing policy
Public Sector	Operations	Intelligence gathering
Retail Chain	Distribution and Marketing	Trend analysis, buying pattern analysis, pricing policy, inventory control, sales promotions, optimal distribution channel decisions
Steel	Manufacturing	Pattern analysis (quality control)
Telecommunications	Product Development, Operations, and Marketing	New product and service promotions, reduction of IS budget, profitability analysis

Source: Y. T. Park, "Strategic Uses of Data Warehouses," *Journal of Data Warehousing*, April, 1997, p. 19, Table 2.

Builders (*informationbuilders.com*), NCR Corp. (*ncr.com*), Oracle (*oracle.com*), Computer Associates (*ca.com*), and Pilot Software (*pilotsoftware.com*). For further discussion visit the Data Warehouse Institute (*dw-institute.org*).

As Table 3.1 suggests, thousands of companies have profited from the benefits of data warehousing. The Harrah's case illustrates some of the benefits of data warehousing, which include:

- End users can access needed data quickly and easily via Web browsers because they are located in one place.
- End users can conduct extensive analysis with data in ways that may not have been possible before.
- End users can have a consolidated view of organizational data.

These benefits can improve business knowledge, provide competitive advantage, enhance customer service and satisfaction, facilitate decision making, and help in streamlining business processes. IT's about Business 3.2 demonstrates the benefits of data warehousing at Ben and Jerry's ice cream factory.

Data warehouses do have problems. Their cost can be very high, both to build and to maintain. Furthermore, it may difficult and expensive to incorporate data from obsolete legacy systems. Finally, there may be a lack of incentive to share data with other departments within an organization.

Building a Data Warehouse

The process of building and using a data warehouse is shown in Figure 3.2. The organization's data are stored in operational systems (left side of the figure). Using special software called ETL (extraction, transformation, load), the system processes data and then stores the processed data in a data warehouse. Not all data are necessarily transferred to the data warehouse. Frequently only a summary of the data is transferred. The data that are transferred are organized within the warehouse in a form that is

IT'S ABOUT BUSINESS

3.2: Ben & Jerry's Keeps Track of Their Pints

At the Ben & Jerry's (*benjerry.com*) factory in Waterbury, Vermont, huge pipes pump out 190,000 pints of ice cream each day. Throughout the day, refrigerated tractor trailers pull up, pick up the pints, and deliver them to depots. From there, the ice cream is shipped out to 50,000 grocery stores in the United States and 12 other countries. There, the ice cream is placed on the freezer shelves.

At the company's headquarters, the life of each pint of ice cream—from ingredients to sale—is tracked. Once the pint is stamped and sent out, Ben & Jerry's stores its tracking number in an Oracle data warehouse and later analyzes the data. Using business intelligence software, the sales team can check to see if Chocolate Chip Cookie Dough is gaining ground on Cherry Garcia for the coveted Number 1 sales position. The marketing department checks to see whether company promotions and advertising are leading to increased sales. The finance people use the tracking number in their analyses to show the profit generated from each type of ice cream. Since the company started using the software, the accounting department has sharply reduced the amount of time it takes to close the monthly books. And probably most important to a company focused on customer loyalty, the consumer affairs staff matches up each pint with the 225 calls and e-mails received each week, checking to see if there were any complaints.

Source: Compiled from J. Schlosser, "Looking for Intelligence in Ice Cream," *Fortune*, March 17, 2003.

QUESTIONS

1. What other analyses can Ben & Jerry's do with their business intelligence software? For example, can the company use the software for human resources management?
2. What is the role of Ben & Jerry's information technology department?

easy for end users to access. The data are standardized and organized by subjects (called *business dimensions*), such as functional area, vendor, or product.

Relational and Multidimensional Databases. To make data more accessible, detail-level operational data must be transformed to a *relational* or *multidimensional* form, which makes them more amenable to analytical processing. As shown

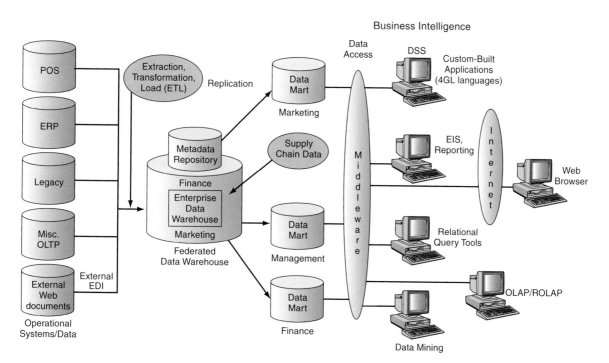

Figure 3.2 *Data warehouse framework and views.*

(a) 2001

Product	Region	Sales
Nuts	East	50
Nuts	West	60
Nuts	Central	100
Screws	East	40
Screws	West	70
Screws	Central	80
Bolts	East	90
Bolts	West	120
Bolts	Central	140
Washers	East	20
Washers	West	10
Washers	Central	30

(b) 2002

Product	Region	Sales
Nuts	East	60
Nuts	West	70
Nuts	Central	110
Screws	East	50
Screws	West	80
Screws	Central	90
Bolts	East	100
Bolts	West	130
Bolts	Central	150
Washers	East	30
Washers	West	20
Washers	Central	40

(c) 2003

Product	Region	Sales
Nuts	East	70
Nuts	West	80
Nuts	Central	120
Screws	East	60
Screws	West	90
Screws	Central	100
Bolts	East	110
Bolts	West	140
Bolts	Central	160
Washers	East	40
Washers	West	30
Washers	Central	50

Figure 3.3   *Relational databases.*

multidimensional database *A database that is organized and can be analyzed by different views or perspectives, which are called dimensions.*

in Technology Guide 3, relational databases store data in two-dimensional tables. Multidimensional databases typically store data in arrays, which consist of at least three business dimensions.

In a **multidimensional database**, the data can be viewed and analyzed from different views or perspectives, which are called *business dimensions*. These dimensions form a *data cube*. The business dimensions are the edges of the cube, and represent the primary views of the business data. Multidimensional databases are often the core of data warehouses.

To differentiate between relational and multidimensional databases, suppose your company has four products (nuts, screws, bolts, and washers), which have been sold in three territories (East, West, and Central) for the previous three years (2001, 2002, and 2003). In a relational database, these sales data would look like Figures 3.3a, b, and c. In a multidimensional database, these data would be represented by a three-dimensional matrix, as shown in Figure 3.4. We would say that this matrix represents sales *dimensioned by* products and regions and year. Notice that in Figure 3.4a we can see only sales for 2001. Therefore, sales for 2002 and 2003 are shown in Figures 3.4b and 3.4c. Figure 3.5 shows the equivalence between these relational and multidimensional databases.

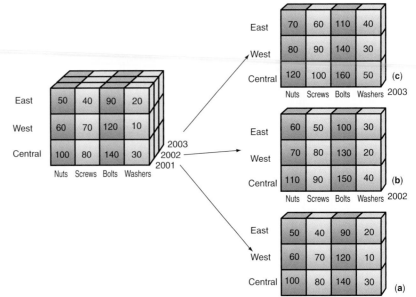

Figure 3.4   *Multidimensional database.*

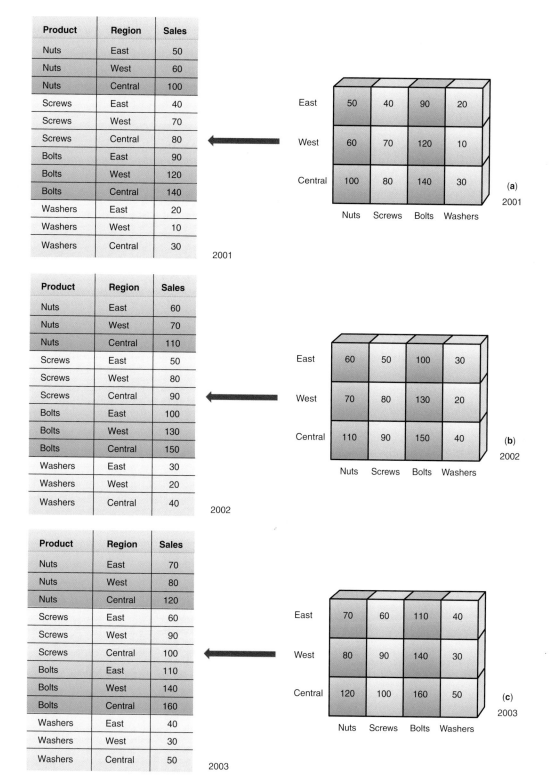

Figure 3.5 *Equivalence between relational and multidimensional databases.*

Data Marts

The high cost of data warehouses confines their use to large companies. An alternative used by many other firms is creation of a lower cost, scaled-down version of a data warehouse called a data mart. A **data mart** is a small data warehouse designed for a strategic business unit (SBU) or a department.

The advantages of data marts include: low cost (prices under $100,000 versus $1 million or more for data warehouses); significantly shorter lead time for implementation,

data mart *A small data warehouse designed for a strategic business unit (SBU) or a department.*

often less than 90 days; local rather than central control, conferring power on the using group. Also, because they contain less information than the data warehouse, they have more rapid response and are more easily understood and navigated than an enterprisewide data warehouse. Finally, they allow a business unit to build its own decision support systems without relying on a centralized IS department.

Before you go on . . .

1. What is a data warehouse, and what are its characteristics?

2. What is the multidimensional database model?

3. What is a data mart, and how is it different from a data warehouse?

3.3 INFORMATION AND KNOWLEDGE DISCOVERY WITH BUSINESS INTELLIGENCE

Business Intelligence

business intelligence (BI) *A broad category of applications and techniques for gathering, storing, analyzing, and providing access to data to help enterprise users make better business and strategic decisions.*

Once the data are in the data warehouse and/or data marts they can be accessed by managers, analysts, and other end users. Users can then conduct several activities. These activities are frequently referred to as analytical processing or more commonly business intelligence. **Business intelligence (BI)** is a broad category of applications and techniques for gathering, storing, analyzing, and providing access to data to help enterprise users make better business and strategic decisions (Oguz, 2003). The process of BI usually, but not necessarily, involves the use of a data warehouse, as seen in Figure 3.6.

How Business Intelligence Works. Operational raw data are usually kept in corporate databases. For example, a national retail chain that sells everything from grills

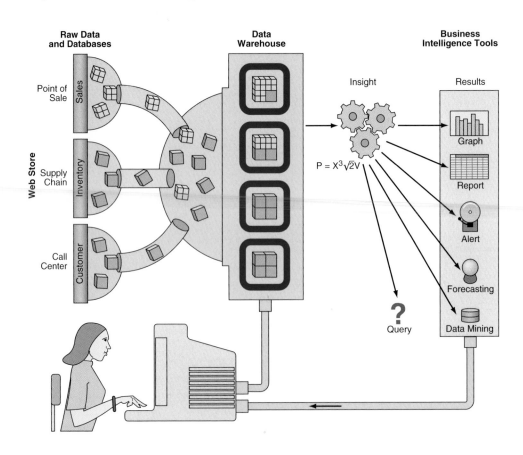

Figure 3.6 *How business intelligence works.*

and patio furniture to plastic utensils has data about inventory, customer information, data about past promotions, and sales numbers in various databases. Though all this information may be scattered across multiple systems—and may seem unrelated—a data warehouse can bring it together. Using business intelligence software the user can post queries, request ad-hoc reports, or conduct any other analyses. The results of requests and analyses can be reports, predictions, alerts, and/or graphical presentations.

The Tools and Techniques of Business Intelligence.   BI employs a large number of tools and techniques. The major applications include the activities of query and reporting, online analytical processing (OLAP) (discussed in the next section), decision support (discussed in Chapter 10), data mining (discussed in the next section), forecasting, and statistical analysis. A major BI vendor is SAS (*sas.com*). Other vendors include Microstrategy, Cognos, SPSS, and Business Objects.

We can divide BI tools into two major categories: (1) *information and knowledge discovery* and (2) *decision support and intelligent analysis*. In each category there are several tools and techniques, as shown in Figure 3.7. In this chapter we will describe the information and knowledge discovery category; Chapter 10 is dedicated to decision support and intelligent systems.

The Tools and Techniques of Information and Knowledge Discovery

Information and knowledge discovery differs from decision support in its main objective: *discovery*. Once discovery is done, the results can be used for decision support. Let's first distinguish between information discovery and knowledge discovery.

The Evolution of Information and Knowledge Discovery.   *Information discovery* started in the late 1960s with data collection techniques. It was basically simple data collection, and it answered queries that involved one set of historical data. This analysis was extended with tools such as SQL and relational database management systems (see Table 3.2, page 76, for the evolutionary stages). During the 1990s, better tools to manage the ever-increasing amount of data were needed, resulting in the creation of the data warehouse and the appearance of OLAP and multidimensional databases. When the amount of data to be analyzed exploded in the mid-1990s, *knowledge discovery* emerged as an important analytical tool. Online File W3.4 discusses Web-based information discovery tools.

wiley.com/college/turban

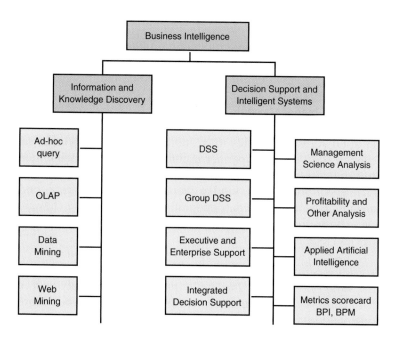

Figure 3.7 *Categories of business intelligence.*

Table 3.2 Stages in the Evolution of Information and Knowledge Discovery

Evolutionary Stage	Business Question	Enabling Technologies	Characteristics
Data collection (1960s)	What was my total revenue in the last five years?	Computers, tapes, disks	Retrospective, static data delivery
Data access (1980s)	What were unit sales in New England last March?	Relational databases (RDBMS), structured query language (SQL)	Retrospective, dynamic data delivery at record level
Data warehousing and decision support (early 1990s)	What were the sales in region A, by product, by salesperson?	OLAP, multidimensional databases, data warehouses	Retrospective, dynamic data delivery at multiple levels
Intelligent data mining (late 1990s)	What's likely to happen to the Boston unit's sales next month? Why?	Advanced algorithms, multiprocessor computers, massive databases	Prospective, proactive information delivery
Advanced intelligent systems; complete integration (2000–2004)	What is the best plan to follow? How did we perform compared to metrics?	Neural computing, advanced AI models, complex optimization, Web services	Proactive, integrative; multiple business partners

Sources: Based on material from *accure.com* (Accure Software).

knowledge discovery (KD) *The process of extracting knowledge from volumes of data; includes data mining.*

The process of extracting useful knowledge from volumes of data is known as **knowledge discovery (KD)**. KD's major objective is to identify valid, novel, potentially useful, and ultimately understandable patterns in data. KD is useful because it is supported by three technologies that are now sufficiently mature: massive data collection, powerful multiprocessor computers, and data mining and other algorithms. In this section we will describe two tools of information discovery: ad-hoc queries and OLAP.

Ad-Hoc Queries and Reporting. *Ad-hoc queries* allow users to request, in real time, information from the computer that is not available in periodic reports. Such answers are needed to expedite decision making. Simple ad-hoc query systems are often based on menus. More sophisticated systems use structured query language (SQL), described in Technology Guide 3. The most sophisticated systems are based on natural language processing (Chapter 10), and some can communicate with users using voice recognition. Later on we will describe the use of Web tools to facilitate queries.

online analytical processing (OLAP) *The analytical processing of data as soon as transactions occur.*

Online Analytical Processing. The term **online analytical processing (OLAP)** describes the analytical processing of data as soon as transactions occur. OLAP tools can analyze data to reflect actual business needs. Assume that a business might organize its sales force by regions—say the Eastern, Western, and Central (see Figures 3.3, 3.4, and 3.5). These three regions might then be broken down into states. The VP of sales could use OLAP with the firm's multidimensional database to see the sales figures for each region (e.g., the sales of nuts, screws, bolts, and washers). The VP might then want to see the Eastern region broken down by state so that the performance of individual state sales managers could be evaluated. Note that the business organization is reflected in the data structure.

The power of OLAP is in its ability to create these business structures (sales regions, product categories, fiscal calendar, partner channels, etc.) and combine them in such a way as to allow users to quickly answer business questions. "How many bolts were sold in the Eastern region in 2002?" is the kind of question that OLAP is very good at answering. Users can interactively slice the data and drill down to the details they are interested in. In addition to answering users' queries, OLAP may analyze the relationships among data categories and look for patterns, trends, and exceptions. For example: "What is the trend in sales of washers in the Western region over that past three years?"

Today's software permits access, usually with a browser, to very large amounts of data, such as several years of sales data; it also makes possible analysis of the relationships between many types of business elements, such as sales, products, regions, and channels. It enables users to process aggregated data, such as sales volumes, budgeted dollars, and dollars spent, to compare aggregated data over time and to present data in different perspectives, such as sales by region versus sales by product or by product within each region. Today's software also enables complex calculations between data elements, such as expected profit as calculated as a function of sales revenue for each type of sales channel in a particular region. It responds quickly to user requests so that users can pursue an analytical thought process without being stymied by the system. For more information, products, and vendors visit *olapreport.com* and *olap.com*.

Although OLAP and ad-hoc queries are very useful in many cases, they are retrospective in nature and cannot provide the automated and prospective knowledge discovery that is done by advanced data mining techniques, which we discuss next.

Before you go on . . .

1. What is business intelligence?
2. What is online analytical processing, and how does it relate to business intelligence?

3.4 DATA MINING CONCEPTS AND APPLICATIONS

Data mining is becoming a major tool for analyzing large amounts of data, usually in a data warehouse. **Data mining** derives its name from searching for valuable business information in a large database, data warehouse, or data mart. (See the Harrah's case at the start of the chapter.)

data mining *The process of searching for valuable business information in a large database, data warehouse, or data mart.*

Capabilities of Data Mining

Given databases or data warehouses of sufficient size and quality, data mining technology can generate new business opportunities by providing these capabilities:

* *Automated prediction of trends and behaviors.* Data mining automates the process of finding predictive information in large databases. Questions that traditionally required extensive hands-on analysis can now be answered directly and quickly from the data. A typical example of a predictive problem is *targeted marketing*. Data mining can use data from past promotional mailings to identify the targets most likely to respond favorably to future mailings. Other predictive examples include forecasting bankruptcy and other forms of default, and identifying segments of a population likely to respond similarly to given events.

* *Automated discovery of previously unknown patterns.* Data mining tools identify previously hidden patterns in one step. An example of pattern discovery is the analysis of retail sales data to identify seemingly unrelated products that are often purchased together, such as baby diapers and beer. Other pattern-discovery problems include detecting fraudulent credit card transactions.

Data mining can be conducted by end users with little or no programming skill to ask ad-hoc questions and get answers quickly. Data mining tools can be combined with spreadsheets and other end-user software development tools, making it relatively easy to analyze and process the mined data. "Striking it rich" in data mining often involves finding unexpected, valuable results.

Many commerical products are available for conducting data mining (e.g., *dbminer.com*, *data-miner.com*, and *spss.com*). For a directory, see *kdnuggets.com/software*.

Data Mining Applications

Large numbers of applications exist in data mining both in business and other fields (Apte et al., 2002). According to a GartnerGroup report (*gartnergroup.com*), more than half of all the Fortune 1000 companies worldwide are using data mining technology, as illustrated by the representative examples that follow. Note that the intent of most of these examples is to identify a business opportunity in order to create a sustainable competitive advantage.

- *Retailing and sales.* Predicting sales, and determining correct inventory levels and distribution schedules among outlets and loss prevention. For example, retailers such as AAFES (stores on military bases) use data mining to combat fraud by employees in their 1,400 stores, using Fraud Watch solution from a Canadian company, Triversity.

- *Banking.* Forecasting levels of bad loans and fraudulent credit card use, credit card spending by new customers, and which kinds of customers will best respond to (and qualify for) new loan offers.

- *Manufacturing and production.* Predicting machinery failures, and finding key factors that control optimization of manufacturing capacity.

- *Insurance.* Forecasting claim amounts and medical coverage costs; classifying the most important elements that affect medical coverage; predicting which customers will buy new insurance policies.

- *Policework.* Tracking crime patterns, locations, and criminal behavior; identifying attributes to assist in solving criminal cases.

- *Health care.* Correlating demographics of patients with critical illnesses; developing better insights on symptoms and their causes and how to provide proper treatments.

- *Marketing.* Classifying customer demographics that can be used to predict which customers will respond to a mailing or buy a particular product. Additional examples of how companies use data mining to support marketing are shown in Online File W3.5.

wiley.com/college/turban

Text Mining and Web Mining

text mining *The application of data mining to nonstructured or less-structured text files.*

Text Mining. Text mining is the application of data mining to nonstructured or less-structured text files (see Berry, 2002). Documents rarely have strong internal infrastructure, and when they do, it is frequently focused on document format rather than document content. Text mining helps organizations to do the following: (1) find the "hidden" content of documents, including additional useful relationships and (2) group documents by common themes (e.g., identify all the customers of an insurance firm who have similar complaints).

Web mining *The application of data mining techniques to discover actionable and meaningful patterns, profiles, and trends from Web resources.*

Web Mining. Web mining is the application of data mining techniques to discover actionable and meaningful patterns, profiles, and trends from Web resources. Web mining is used in the following areas: information filtering (e-mails, magazines, and newspapers); surveillance (of competitors, patents, technological development); mining of Web-access logs for analyzing usage (clickstream analysis); assisted browsing; and services that fight crime on the Internet.

In e-commerce, Web mining is especially critical, due to the large number of visitors to e-commerce sites. For example, when you look for a certain book on *Amazon.com*, the site will also provide you with a lot of books purchased by the customers who have purchased the specific book you are looking for. By providing such mined information, the *Amazon.com* site minimizes the need for additional search and provides customers with a valuable service.

Web mining can perform the following functions:

"With over 400 million pages on the Web, just be happy you find anything."

- *Resource discovery.* Locating unfamiliar documents and services on the Web.

- *Information extraction.* Automatically extracting specific information from newly discovered Web resources.

- *Generalization.* Uncovering general patterns at individual Web sites and across multiple sites.

Miner3D (*miner3d.com*) is a suite of visual data analysis tools including a Web-mining tool that displays hundreds and even thousands of search hits on a single screen. The actual search for Web pages is performed through any major search engine, and this add-on tool presents the resulting search in the form of a 3-D graphic instead of displaying links to the first few pages. For details on a number of Web mining products see *Kdnuggets.com/software/web.html.* Also see *spss.com* and *bayesia.com* (free downloads).

Before you go on . . .

1. Describe the capabilities of data mining.
2. What are the differences among data mining, text mining, and Web mining?

3.5 DATA VISUALIZATION TECHNOLOGIES

Once data have been processed, they can be presented to users as text, graphics, tables, and so on, via several data visualization technologies. A variety of visualization methods and software packages are available to support decision making.

Data Visualization

Visual technologies make pictures worth a thousand numbers and make IT applications more attractive and understandable to users. **Data visualization** refers to visual presentation of data by technologies such as digital images, geographical information systems, graphical user interfaces, multidimensional tables and graphs, virtual reality, three-dimensional presentations, videos and animation, and any other multimedia formats. Visualization is becoming more and more popular on the Web not only for entertainment but also for decision support (see *spss.com, microstrategy.com*). Visualization software packages offer users capabilities for self-guided exploration and visual analysis of large amounts of data, as demonstrated in IT's about Business 3.3 (page 80).

data visualization *Visual presentation of data by technologies such as graphics, multidimensional tables and graphs, videos and animation, and other multimedia formats.*

   Data visualization is easier to implement when the necessary data are in a data warehouse. Our discussion here will focus mainly on the data visualization techniques of multidimensionality, geographical information systems, visual interactive modeling, and virtual reality. Related topics, such as multimedia (see *informatica.com*) and hypermedia, are presented in Technology Guide 2.

Geographical Information Systems

A **geographical information system (GIS)** is a computer-based system for capturing, storing, checking, integrating, manipulating, and displaying data using digitized maps. Its most distinguishing characteristic is that every record or digital object has an identified geographical location. By integrating maps with spatially oriented databases and other databases (called *geocoding*), users can generate information for planning, problem solving, and decision making, increasing their productivity and the quality of their decisions. GISs provide a large amount of extremely useful information that can be analyzed and utilized in decision making. The graphical format makes it easy for managers to visualize the data.

geographical information system (GIS) *A computer-based system for capturing, storing, checking, integrating, manipulating, and displaying data using digitized maps.*

   GIS software varies in its capabilities, from simple computerized mapping systems to enterprisewide tools for decision support data analysis. Since the 1990s, however, the cost of GIS software and its required hardware have dropped dramatically. Now relatively inexpensive, fully functional PC-based GIS packages are readily available. Representative GIS software vendors are ESRI (*esri.com*), Intergraph (*intergraph.com*), and Mapinfo (*mapinfo.com*).

   GIS data are available from a wide variety of sources. Government sources (via the Internet and CD-ROM) provide some data, while vendors provide diversified commercial data as well. Some are free (see CD-ROMs from Mapinfo, and downloadable material from *esri.com* and *data.geocomm.com*).

IT'S ABOUT BUSINESS   MKT POM HRM

3.3: Danskin's Virtual Showroom

Danskin (*danskin.com*), a manufacturer of women's activewear and dancewear, needed an easier way to communicate with the company's more than 3,000 specialty store accounts. Danskin has an external sales force of 15 people for the specialty store market, but at most, the company's reps can meet or deal extensively with a total of only 150 to 250 accounts during each selling season. The remaining stores primarily receive a Danskin catalog and are asked to communicate via phone and fax with a special team of customer service reps.

Traditionally, store buyers travel to New York City four to six times a year to preview upcoming collections of apparel, accessories, and shoes. Faxes and phone calls were (and sometimes still are) the main communications channel between retailers (e.g., the specialty stores) and suppliers like Danskin. This process is very inefficient for both the retailers and suppliers. To improve the process, Danskin established a virtual online showroom where specialty store buyers can view products, read descriptions, check inventory availability, place orders, and keep abreast of changes in Danskin's product lines.

To create this visual business-to-business Web presence, Danskin formed a partnership with 7thOnline (*7thonline.com*), a company that provides visual merchandising and assortment planning technology to the global fashion industry. The 7thOnline platform streamlines the merchandising and communica-

tions process between manufacturers and retailers by offering a visual, online product catalog. 7thOnline also provides electronic data interchange integration, which enables retailers to transmit product purchase orders over the Internet.

While some "touch and feel" elements cannot be replaced by the virtual showroom, it can help decrease potential human errors and the high travel and operating costs associated with the manual buying routine. Buyers from the specialty stores now have earlier and more convenient access to product information, giving them time to plan, so that they come to market better equipped to make final purchasing decisions. Essentially, the 7thOnline system provides for much closer collaboration between Danskin and specialty stores.

And the external Danskin reps? They can now concentrate on the company's biggest, most profitable accounts as well as developing new accounts.

Source: Compiled from D. Buss, "Danskin Launches Virtual Showroom for Retail Clients," *Stores*, March 2003.

QUESTIONS

1. Why is a visual B2B solution so important for the fashion industry? Would a visual solution be as important in other industries? Provide some examples.
2. If you were a Danskin external sales rep, how would you feel about the 7thOnline system?

There are countless applications of GISs to improve decision making in the public or private sector. Examples include the following.

POM   **EXAMPLE**   ***Routing Commercial Drivers.*** Sears makes 20 million household visits a year to deliver packages or service. Using GIS to plan the most efficient routes, the retailer not only reduced its costs by $50 million, but is now able to promise its customers an arrival time within a two-hour window.

MKT   **EXAMPLE**   ***Finding Locations for New Restaurants.*** McDonald's uses a GIS system to overlay all kinds of demographic information on maps to help decide exactly where to put new restaurants.

GOV   **EXAMPLE**   ***A One-Stop GIS Portal.*** The federal government opened the Geospatial One-Stop portal, which will ultimately bring together all kinds of federal, state, county, and local databases that can be mapped in any combination onto any part of a high-resolution map of the United States. Go to *geodata.gov* and click on the Launch Map link in the upper left. You will be able to navigate through a map of the United States and overlay various kinds of information, from streams and water bodies to elevations and highway names. (*Source: geodata.gov.*)

EXAMPLE   *Even Natives Get Lost in Tokyo.* When a Tokyo computer programmer lost the remote to his car's navigation system, he called in sick to work because he was afraid of getting lost. Japanese cities, famous for their incomprehensible street systems, have driven the adoption of, and drivers' dependence on, GPS technology. Japan's street nomenclature works like this: 2–14–12 is area 2, block 14, building 12. And, buildings are numbered according to when they were built. So, building 23 could be between building 3 and building 12. One Japanese GPS system uses voice recognition to enable drivers to input their destination, and the system recites directions. (*Source: Red Herring,* March 2003.)

Additional examples of successful GIS applications are summarized in Online File W3.6 on the book's Web site.

wiley.com/college/turban

GIS and The Internet or Intranets.   Most major GIS software vendors are providing Web access, such as embedded browsers, or a Web/Internet/intranet server that hooks directly into their software. Thus, users can access dynamic maps and data via the Internet or a corporate intranet.

A number of firms are deploying GISs on the Internet for internal use or for use by their customers. For example, Visa Plus, which operates a network of automated teller machines, has developed a GIS application that lets Internet users call up a locator map for any of the company's 300,000 ATM machines worldwide. A common application on the Internet is a store locator. Not only do you get an address near you, but you may also be told how to get there in the shortest way (e.g., try *homedepot.com* and use the Store Finder).

Emerging GIS Applications.   The integration of GISs and global positioning systems (GPSs) has the potential to help restructure and redesign the aviation, transportation, and shipping industries. It enables vehicles or aircraft equipped with a GPS receiver to pinpoint their locations as they move. Emerging applications of GPSs include personal automobile mapping systems, vehicle tracking, and earth-moving equipment tracking (Terry and Kolb, 2003).

Visual Interactive Models and Simulation

Visual interactive modeling (VIM) uses computer graphic displays to represent the impact of different management or operational decisions on goals such as profit or market share. A VIM can be used both for supporting decisions and for training.

visual interactive modeling (VIM) *The use of computer graphic displays to represent the impact of different management or operational decisions on goals such as profit or market share.*

One of the most developed areas in VIM is **visual interactive simulation (VIS)**, a method in which the end user watches the progress of the simulation model in an animated form, using graphics terminals. The user may interact with the simulation and try different decision strategies. VIS is an approach that has, at its core, the ability to allow decision makers to learn about their own subjective values and about their mistakes. Therefore, VIS can be used for training, as in the case of flight simulators, as well as for games.

visual interactive simulation (VIS) *A visual interactive modeling method in which the end user watches the progress of the simulation model in an animated form, using graphics terminals.*

Animation systems that produce realistic graphics are available from many simulation software vendors (e.g., see *sas.com* and *vissim.com*). The latest visual simulation technology is tied in with the concept of virtual reality, where an artificial world is created for a number of purposes—from training to entertainment to viewing data in an artificial landscape.

Virtual Reality

There is no standard definition of virtual reality. The most common definitions usually imply that **virtual reality (VR)** is interactive, computer-generated, three-dimensional graphics delivered to the user through a head-mounted display. In VR, a person "believes" that what he or she is doing is real even though it is artificially created.

virtual reality (VR) *Interactive, computer-generated, three-dimensional graphics delivered to the user through a head-mounted display.*

More than one person and even a large group can share and interact in the same artificial environment. VR thus can be a powerful medium for communication,

Table 3.3   Examples of Virtual Reality Applications

Applications in Manufacturing

Training

Design testing and interpretation of results

Safety analysis

Virtual prototyping

Engineering analysis

Ergonomic analysis

Virtual simulation of assembly, production, and maintenance

Applications in Medicine

Training surgeons (with simulators)

Interpretation of medical data

Planning surgeries

Physical therapy

Applications in Amusement

Virtual museums

Three-dimensional racecar games (on PCs)

Air combat simulation (on PCs)

Virtual reality arcades and parks

Ski simulator

Applications in Business

Real estate presentation and evaluation

Advertising

Presentation in e-commerce

Presentation of financial data

Applications in Research and Education

Virtual physics lab

Representation of complex mathematics

Galaxy configurations

Applications in Architecture

Design of building and other structures

---

entertainment, and learning. Instead of looking at a flat computer screen, the VR user interacts with a three-dimensional computer-generated environment. To see and hear the environment, the user wears stereo goggles and a headset. To interact with the environment, control objects in it, or move around within it, the user wears a computerized display and hand position sensors (gloves). Virtual reality displays achieve the illusion of a surrounding medium by updating the display in real time. The user can grasp and move virtual objects.

Virtual Reality and The Web.   A platform-independent standard for VR called *virtual reality markup language (VRML)* makes navigation through online supermarkets, museums, and stores as easy as interacting with textual information (see *vrmlsite.com*). VRML allows objects to be rendered as an Internet user "walks" through a virtual room. Virtual malls, which can be delivered even on a PC (*synthonics.com*), are designed to give the user a feeling of walking into a shopping mall.

Extensive use of virtual reality is expected in e-commerce marketing. For example, Tower Records offers a virtual music store on the Internet where customers can "meet" each other in front of the store, go inside, and preview CDs and videos. They select and purchase their choices electronically and interactively from a sales associate. Applications of virtual reality in other areas are shown in Table 3.3.

Before you go on . . .

1. Why is data visualization important?

2. What is a geographical information system?

3. What is virtual reality, and how does it contribute to data visualization?

3.6 WEB-BASED DATA MANAGEMENT SYSTEMS

Data management and business intelligence activities—from data acquisition, through warehousing, to mining—are often performed with Web tools or are interrelated with Web technologies and e-business. Users with browsers can log onto a system, make inquiries, and get reports in a real-time setting. This is done through intranets and, for outsiders, via extranets (see *remedy.com*).

E-commerce software vendors are providing Web tools that connect the data warehouse with EC ordering and cataloging systems. For example, Hitachi's EC tool suite, Tradelink (at *hitachi.com*), combines EC activities such as catalog management, payment applications, mass customization, and order management with data warehouses, data marts, and ERP systems.

Data warehousing and decision support vendors are connecting their products with Web technologies and EC. For example, IBM's Decision Edge makes OLAP capabilities available on the intranet from anywhere in an organization using browsers, search engines, and other Web technologies. MicroStrategy offers DSS Agent and DSS Web for help in drilling down for detailed information, providing graphical views, and pushing information to users' desktops. Oracle's Financial Analyzer and Sales Analyzer and Hummingbird's BI/Web and BI/Analyze, among others, bring interactive querying, reporting, and other OLAP tasks to many users (both company employees and business partners) via the Web.

The systems described in the previous sections of this chapter can be integrated on Web-based platforms, such as the one shown in Figure 3.8. The Web-based system is accessed via a portal, and it connects the following parts: the business intelligence (BI) services, the data warehouse and marts, the corporate applications, and the data infrastructure. A security system protects the corporate proprietary data. All of these components can work together via the corporate portal.

Enterprise BI Suites and Corporate Portals

Enterprise BI suites (EBISs) integrate query, reporting, OLAP, and other tools. They are scalable, and offered by many vendors (e.g., IBM, Microsoft, Hyperion Solutions, and Sagent Technology). EBISs are offered usually via corporate portals.

In Chapter 4 we introduced the concept of corporate portals as a Web-based gateway to data, information, and knowledge. As seen in Figure 3.8, the portal integrates data from many sources. It provides end users with a single Web-based point of personalized access to BI and other applications. Likewise, it provides IT with a single

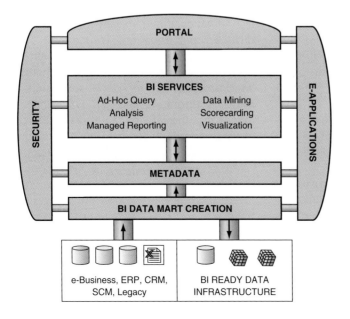

Figure 3.8 *Web-based data management system. (Source: Cognos.com, Platform for Enterprise Business Intelligence. (© Cognos Inc., 2001.)*

point of delivery and management of this content. Users are empowered to access, create, and share valuable information.

Clickstream Data Warehouse

clickstream data *Data collected about user behavior and browsing patterns by monitoring users' activities when they visit a Web site.*

Organizations can collect huge amounts of data about consumers, products, and so on that they can use in selling to consumers. Such data come from several sources: internal data (e.g., sales data, payroll data, etc.), external data (e.g., government and industry reports), and clickstream data. **Clickstream data** are those that occur inside the Web environment, when customers visit a Web site. They provide a trail of the users' activities in the Web site, including user behavior and browsing patterns. By looking at clickstream data, an e-tailer can find out such things as which promotions are effective and which population segments are interested in specific products. IT's about Business 3.4 shows how Victoria's Secret integrates clickstream data with other data streams in the company's data warehouse.

IT's ABOUT BUSINESS [ACC] [FIN] [POM] [MKT]

3.4: Victoria's Secret's Data Warehouse

For direct-to-consumer merchants, the "death of an order" can occur at any time during the transaction. The "death of an order" means that customers change their minds at some point during the ordering process. By using an enterprise data warehouse to capture customer information and decision-support tools to analyze shopping patterns, however, Victoria's Secret (*victoriassecret.com*) is keeping orders alive and working to provide a better shopping experience.

Unlike a bricks-and-mortar purchase, the direct sale of products through electronic storefronts provides vast amounts of unique and diverse data elements at all stages of an order's life. To turn collected data into actionable information, the company uses a data warehouse solution from Teradata (a division of NCR). The retailer monitors all customer touches and shopping patterns with its data warehouse.

The data warehouse holds data collected from several data streams:

- The first data source is the customer. Besides having access to all customer names and addresses, the company also differentiates buyers from product recipients, based on storing each different shipping address.
- The company also stores customer payment information. Victoria's Secret uses the payment data to monitor the purchasing habits of the company's shoppers.
- The third data stream comes from direct customer contacts via the firm's direct-mail operations. For example, the company has more than 50 domestic and international catalog mailings (300 million catalogs per year).
- The retailer's call center provides another data stream. Each day hundreds of fashion consultants field thousands of calls ranging from orders and

"up-sell" opportunities (opportunities to sell customers more expensive items) to complaints and resolutions about merchandise.
- The company's online channel produces a huge amount of customer data, as it accepts thousands of orders daily for both online and catalog merchandise. Each customer's activities on the Web site are stored in the data warehouse.

Victoria's Secret puts all of these data into action in many ways. The company creates targeted e-mail messages, adding up to 150 million outbound e-mail messages each year. These messages include offers, merchandise specials, invitations, announcements, and other calls to action.

The company analyzes the status of every individual product by customer, by day, for each order. The data warehouse is enabling Victoria's Secret to improve predictions of customer behavior. The data warehouse also enables the company to stay abreast of each order's profit equation. To measure the revenue of each order, Victoria's Secret starts with the merchandise price and subtracts shipping, handling, and related taxes, as well as special service charges, such as shipping upgrades and gift wrapping. This process means that the retailer can measure the profitability of every customer, order, catalog, and product.

Source: Compiled from D. Amato-McCoy, "Victoria's Secret Works to Keep Orders Alive," *Stores*, January 2003.

QUESTIONS

1. What does Victoria's Secret mean by "keeping an order alive?" Would this phrase apply to other businesses? Why or why not? Give examples.
2. Describe the various data streams that feed Victoria's Secret's data warehouse.

The Web is an incredibly rich source of business intelligence, and many enterprises are scrambling to build data warehouses that capture the knowledge contained in the clickstream data from their Web sites. By analyzing the user behavior patterns contained in these clickstream data warehouses, savvy businesses can expand their markets, improve customer relationships, reduce costs, streamline operations, strengthen their Web sites, and hone their business strategies.

Before you go on . . .

1. What is an enterprise business intelligence suite?
2. What are clickstream data?

3.7 INTRODUCTION TO KNOWLEDGE MANAGEMENT

As we have discussed in this chapter, data and information are critically important organizational assets. Organizations have realized that knowledge is an important asset as well, and many have created the position of **chief knowledge officer (CKO)** at the executive level. The CKO's objectives are to maximize the firm's knowledge assets, design and implement knowledge management strategies, and effectively exchange knowledge assets internally and externally.

Another objective of the CKO is to encourage the growth of communities of practice (COPs). A **community of practice** is a group of people in an organization with a common professional interest. Ideally, all knowledge management system users should each be in at least one COP.

We now describe the basic concepts of knowledge and knowledge management.

Concepts and Definitions

Successful managers have always used intellectual assets and recognized their value. But these efforts were not systematic, nor did they ensure that knowledge gained was shared and dispersed appropriately for maximum organizational benefit. Moreover, industry analysts estimate that 85 percent of a company's knowledge assets are not housed in relational databases, but are dispersed in e-mail, Word documents, spreadsheets, and presentations on individual computers (Ziff-Davis, 2002).

Knowledge management (KM) is a process that helps organizations identify, select, organize, disseminate, transfer, and apply important information and expertise that are part of the organization's memory and that typically reside within the organization in an unstructured manner. For organizational success, *knowledge, as a form of capital, must be exchangeable among persons, and it must be able to grow.* IT's about Business 3.5 (page 86) demonstrates how valuable knowledge management can be for an organization.

Knowledge.   In the information technology context, knowledge is very distinct from data and information. Figure 3.9 (page 86) shows the relationships among data, information, and knowledge. Data are a collection of facts, measurements, and statistics; information is organized or processed data that are timely (i.e., inferences from the data are drawn within the time frame of applicability) and accurate (i.e., with regard to the original data). As discussed in Chapter 2, **knowledge** is information that is *contextual*, *relevant*, and *actionable*. Simply put, knowledge is *information in action* (O'Dell et al., 2003). **Intellectual capital** (or **intellectual assets**) is another term often used for knowledge (Edvinsson, 2003).

To illustrate with an example, a bulletin listing all the courses offered by your university during one semester could be considered data. When you register, you process the data from the bulletin to create your schedule for the semester. Your schedule would be considered information. Awareness of your work schedule, your

chief knowledge officer (CKO) *Executive whose objectives are to maximize the firm's knowledge assets, design and implement knowledge management strategies, and effectively exchange knowledge assets internally and externally.*

community of practice   *A group of people in an organization with a common professional interest.*

knowledge management (KM)   *A process that helps organizations identify, select, organize, disseminate, transfer, and apply information and expertise that are part of the organization's memory and that typically reside within the organization in an unstructured manner.*

knowledge   *Information that is contextual, relevant, and actionable.*

intellectual capital (intellectual assets)   *Other terms for knowledge.*

IT's ABOUT BUSINESS

3.5: Knowledge Management at Commerce Bank

Commerce Bank (*commerceonline.com*), a $15.4 billion financial institution, has a network of 214 branches and ambitious plans for more growth. The company empowers each branch to make business decisions in an effort to better meet the needs of its customers.

While undergoing explosive growth, Commerce Bank encouraged its associates to learn all about the bank's customers and the right ways to service them. To support this initiative, the bank needed to tap into its employees' knowledge and find a way to train employees consistently and conveniently across the entire branch network.

The first step for new employees is Commerce University, a boot camp where they are instilled with the fundamentals of customer service. But the program covers only a few of the issues that an associate might encounter. Knowing that boot camp would not give answers for every scenario, the bank needed a tool that could help its employees find any answer to any topic at any time.

Commerce used IBM's Lotus Notes to develop a workflow-based knowledge management system called the "Wow Answer Guide." The guide provides a central repository of knowledge about all bank transactions and helps employees learn a process and respond to customer inquiries. The guide con-

tains more than 400 applications, and Commerce plans to add a customer relationship management application very soon. The guide streamlines internal knowledge sharing and routes data and information to appropriate employees within the organization. "Wow" therefore dramatically reduces the completion time for approval transactions, improves the bank's capacity, and minimizes labor costs. Commerce also deployed another version of "Wow" that empowered the bank's online customers.

Knowledge management at Commerce has saved the bank over $1 million per year. In fact, the bank achieved a return on its investment within one month of launching the appropriately named "Wow."

Source: Compiled from D. Amato-McCoy, "Commerce Bank Manages Knowledge Profitably," *Bank Systems and Technology*, January 2003.

QUESTIONS

1. In what ways does the "Wow" knowledge management system benefit Commerce Bank?
2. How do you think Commerce calculated its savings from "Wow"? Would it be difficult to quantify the benefits from a knowledge management system? Why?

major, your desired social schedule, and characteristics of different faculty members could be construed as knowledge, because it can affect the way you build your schedule. We see that this awareness is contextual and relevant (to developing an optimal schedule of classes), as well as actionable (can lead to changes in your schedule). The implication is that knowledge has strong experiential and reflective elements that distinguish it from information in a given context. Having knowledge implies that it can be exercised to solve a problem, whereas having information does not carry the same connotation.

explicit knowledge *The more objective, rational, and technical types of* knowledge.

Tacit and Explicit Knowledge. **Explicit knowledge** deals with more objective, rational, and technical knowledge. In an organization, explicit knowledge consist of the policies, procedural guides, white papers, reports, designs, products, strategies, goals, mission, and core competencies of the enterprise and the information technology infrastructure. It is the knowledge that has been codified (documented) in a form that can be distributed to others or transformed into a process or strategy. For exam-

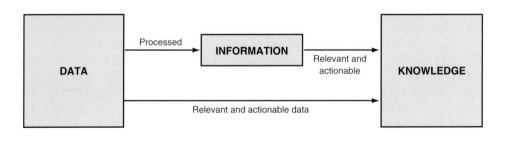

Figure 3.9 *Data, information, and knowledge.*

ple, a description of how to process a job application would be documented in a firm's human resources policy manual.

Tacit knowledge is the cumulative store of subjective or experiential learning. In an organization, tacit knowledge is the cumulative store of the experiences, insights, expertise, know-how, trade secrets, skill sets, understanding, and learning that an organization has. It also includes the organizational culture that has embedded in it the past and present experiences of the organization's people, processes, and values. Tacit knowledge is generally slow and costly to transfer and can be plagued by ambiguity. It is highly personal, and because it is unstructured, without tangible form, it is therefore difficult to formalize or codify.

tacit knowledge *The cumulative store of subjective or experiential learning; it is highly personal and hard to formalize.*

The Need for Knowledge Management Systems

The goal of knowledge management is for an organization to be aware of individual and collective knowledge so that it may make the most effective use of the knowledge it has. Historically, management information systems have focused on capturing, storing, managing, and reporting explicit knowledge. Organizations now recognize the need to integrate both explicit and tacit knowledge in formal information systems. **Knowledge management systems (KMSs)** refer to the use of modern information technologies (e.g., the Internet, intranets, extranets, LotusNotes, software filters, software agents, data warehouses) to systematize, enhance, and expedite intra- and interfirm knowledge management. KMSs are intended to help an organization cope with turnover, rapid change, and downsizing by making the expertise of the organization's human capital widely accessible.

knowledge management systems (KMSs) *Information technologies used to systematize, enhance, and expedite intra- and interfirm knowledge management.*

The Knowledge Management System Cycle

A functioning knowledge management system follows six steps in a cycle (see Figure 3.10). The reason the system is cyclical is that knowledge is dynamically refined over time. The knowledge in a good KM system is never finished because the environment changes, over time, and the knowledge must be updated to reflect the changes. The cycle works as follows:

1. ***Create knowledge.*** Knowledge is created as people determine new ways of doing things or develop know-how. Sometimes external knowledge is brought in.

2. ***Capture knowledge.*** New knowledge must be identified as valuable and be represented in a reasonable way.

3. ***Refine knowledge.*** New knowledge must be placed in context so that it is actionable. This is where human insights (tacit qualities) must be captured along with explicit facts.

4. ***Store knowledge.*** Useful knowledge must then be stored in a reasonable format in a knowledge repository so that others in the organization can access it.

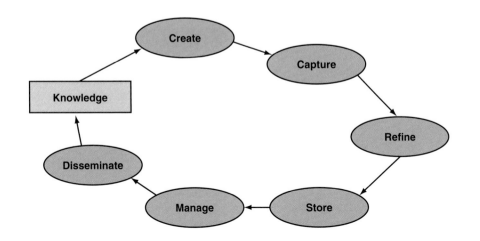

Figure 3.10 *The knowledge management cycle.*

5. *Manage knowledge.* Like a library, the knowledge must be kept current. It must be reviewed to verify that it is relevant and accurate.

6. *Disseminate knowledge.* Knowledge must be made available in a useful format to anyone in the organization who needs it, anywhere and any time.

Before you go on . . .

1. What is knowledge management?
2. What is the difference between tacit knowledge and explicit knowledge?
3. Describe the knowledge management system cycle.

3.8 INFORMATION TECHNOLOGY IN KNOWLEDGE MANAGEMENT

Knowledge management is more a methodology applied to business practices than a technology or product. Nevertheless, information technology is *crucial* to the success of every knowledge management system. Information technology enables KM by providing the enterprise architecture on which it is built.

Knowledge management systems are developed using three sets of technologies: *communication*, *collaboration*, and *storage and retrieval*.

1. *Communication technologies* allow users to access needed knowledge, and to communicate with each other—especially with experts. E-mail, the Internet, corporate intranets, and other Web-based tools provide communication capabilities.

2. *Collaboration technologies* provide the means to perform group work. Collaborative computing capabilities such as electronic brainstorming enhance group work, especially for knowledge contribution.

3. *Storage and retrieval technologies* originally meant using a database management system to store and manage explicit knowledge. Electronic document management systems and specialized storage systems that are part of collaborative computing systems are the tools used to capture, store, and manage tacit knowledge.

Technologies Supporting Knowledge Management

Several technologies have contributed to significant advances in knowledge management tools. Artificial intelligence, intelligent agents, and knowledge discovery in databases are examples of technologies that enable advanced modern knowledge management systems. These technologies form the basis for future innovations in the KM field.

Artificial Intelligence. *Artificial intelligence (AI)* is the study of human thought processes and the representation of those processes in machines (e.g., computers, robots, etc.). AI methods can assist in identifying expertise, eliciting knowledge automatically and semiautomatically, interfacing through natural language processing, and performing intelligent search by means of intelligent agents. AI methods (notably expert systems, neural networks, fuzzy logic, and intelligent agents) are used in knowledge management systems to perform various functions: They assist in and enhance searching knowledge (e.g., intelligent agents in Web searches), including scanning e-mail, documents, and databases and helping establish knowledge profiles of individuals and groups. They identify patterns in data (usually through neural networks), induce rules for expert systems, and provide advice directly from knowledge by using neural networks or expert systems.

intelligent agents *Software systems that learn how users work and provide assistance in their daily tasks.*

Intelligent Agents. **Intelligent agents** are software systems that learn how users work and provide assistance in their daily tasks. Intelligent agents of various kinds are discussed in Chapter 12.

Intelligent agents can help in knowledge management systems in a number of ways. Typically they are used to elicit and identify knowledge. Examples are:

- IBM (*ibm.com*) offers an intelligent data mining family, including Intelligent Decision Server (IDS), for finding and analyzing massive amounts of enterprise data.
- Gentia (Planning Sciences International, *gentia.com*) uses intelligent agents to facilitate data mining with Web access and data warehouse facilities.
- Convectis (HNC Software Inc.) searches text data and images in order to discern the meaning of documents for an intelligent agent. This tool is used by InfoSeek, an Internet search engine, to speed up the creation of hierarchical directories of Web topics.

Knowledge Discovery in Databases.   **Knowledge discovery in databases (KDD)** is a process used to search for and extract useful information from volumes of documents and data. Data are often buried deep within very large databases, data warehouses, text documents, or knowledge repositories, all of which may contain data, information, and knowledge gathered over many years.

knowledge discovery in databases (KDD)   *A process used to search for and extract useful information from volumes of documents and data, often buried deep within very large databases, data warehouses, or other knowledge repositories.*

Knowledge Management Products and Vendors

Technology tools that support knowledge management are called **knowware**. Most knowledge management software packages include one or more of the following seven tools: collaborative computing tools, knowledge servers, enterprise knowledge portals, electronic document management systems, knowledge harvesting tools, search engines, and knowledge management suites. Brief descriptions of these tools and sample products are shown in Table 3.4, Online File W3.7 provides additional examples of these tools and more products/vendors.

knowware   *Technology tools that support knowledge management.*

wiley.com/college/turban

Table 3.4   Seven Knowledge Management Tools

Tool	Description	Vendor/Product Examples
Collaborative computing	Groupware products; used to enhance tacit knowledge transfer within an organization	GroupSystems; Lotus Notes/Domino
Knowledge server	Contains the main knowledge management software, including the knowledge repository; provides access to other knowledge, information, and data.	Hummingbird Knowledge Server; Autonomy's Intelligent Data Operating Layter (IDOL)
Enterprise knowledge portal	Presents a single access point into a knowledge management system; organizes the sources of unstructured information in an organization.	Plumtree; Hyperwave
Electronic document management	Allows users to access needed documents over a corporate intranet; allows electronic collaboration on document creation and revision.	DocShare; Lotus Notes
Knowledge-harvesting tools	Capture organizational knowledge unobtrusively; may be embedded in a knowledge management system.	KnowledgeMail; ActiveKnowledge
Search engines	Locate and retrieve documents from vast collections in corporate repositories.	Google; Verity; Inktomi
Knowledge management suites	Integrate communications, collaboration, and storage technologies in one complete, out-of-the-box solution.	WebSphere; KnowledgeX

> **Before you go on . . .**
>
> **1.** Describe the three technologies that are the basis for knowledge management systems.
>
> **2.** Discuss the technologies that support knowledge management.

WHAT'S IN [IT] FOR ME?

ACC

FOR THE ACCOUNTING MAJOR

The accounting function is intimately concerned with keeping track of the transactions and internal controls of an organization. In particular, the Sarbanes-Oxley Act of 2002 placed strict requirements on the accounting function in the matters of disclosure and the certification of the effectiveness of internal controls. Modern data warehouses and data mining enable accountants to perform these functions more effectively. Data warehouses help accountants manage the flood of data in today's organizations so that they can keep their firms in compliance with the new standards.

Accountants also play a role in cost-justifying the creation of a knowledge base and its auditing. In addition, if you work for a large CPA company that provides management services or sells knowledge, you will most likely use some of your company's best practices that are stored in a knowledge base.

FIN

FOR THE FINANCE MAJOR

Financial managers make extensive use of computerized databases external to the organization, such as CompuStat or Dow Jones, to obtain financial data on organizations in their industry. They can use this data to determine if their organization meets industry benchmarks in return on investment, cash management, or other financial ratios.

Modern data mining techniques are effective in finance, particularly for the automated discovery of relationships in securities and portfolio management. Financial managers, who produce the organization's financial status reports, are also closely involved with the Sarbanes-Oxley Act. Data warehouses will help these managers stay in compliance with the new standards.

The finance department is responsible for cost-justifying major investments such as an organizational knowledge base and enterprise systems. In addition, DSS applications such as what-if and goal-seeking analyses are found largely in financial management and analysis.

MKT

FOR THE MARKETING MAJOR

Marketing personnel access data from the organization's marketing transactions (e.g., customer purchases) to plan targeted marketing campaigns and to evaluate the success of previous campaigns. They also link this information to geographic databases to determine where certain products will sell the best.

Data warehouses and data mining helps marketing managers uncover many unanticipated relationships between some aspect of the buyer's "profile," the product, and the marketing and advertising campaigns that, when identified and exploited, can increase sales substantially. In fact, marketing research is one of the most common applications of data mining.

Knowledge about customers can make the difference between success and failure. In many data warehouses and knowledge bases, the vast majority of information and knowledge is about customers, products, sales, and marketing. Marketing managers will certainly use an organization's knowledge base and will probably participate in its creation. Numerous DSS models are used in topics ranging from allocating advertising budgets to evaluating alternative routings of salespersons.

Production/operations personnel access organizational data to determine optimum inventory levels for parts in a production process. Past production data enable POM personnel to determine the optimum configuration for assembly lines. Firms also keep quality data that inform them not only about the quality of finished products, but also about quality issues with incoming raw materials, production irregularities, shipping and logistics, and after-sale use and maintenance of the product.

Data warehousing and data mining automate discovery of previously undetected production, logistics, or other issues. These issues might be within the organization or along the supply chain.

Knowledge management is extremely important for running complex operations. The accumulated knowledge regarding scheduling, logistics, maintenance, and other functions is very valuable. Innovative ideas are necessary for improving operations and can be supported by knowledge management. Complex production and operations decisions, in areas ranging from inventory to production planning, are supported by decision support systems.

POM

FOR THE PRODUCTION/ OPERATIONS MANAGEMENT MAJOR

Organizations keep extensive data on employees, including gender, age, race, current and past job descriptions, and performance evaluations. Human resources personnel access these data to provide reports for government agencies regarding compliance with federal Equal Opportunity guidelines. HR managers also use these data to evaluate hiring practices in the organization, evaluate salary structures, and manage any discrimination grievances or lawsuits brought against the firm.

Data warehouses and data mining can help the HR professional investigate relationships in the data that bear upon the health, safety, productivity, and retention of valuable human resources. Data warehouses can help HR managers provide assistance to all employees as more and more decisions about their health care and retirement planning are turned over to the employees themselves. The employees can use the data warehouses for help in selecting the optimal mix among these critical choices.

Human resource managers need to use a knowledge base frequently to find out how past cases were handled. Consistency in how employees are treated is important and is a protection against legal actions. Also, training for building, maintaining, and using the knowledge system could be the responsibility of the HR department. Finally, the HR department might resolve the issue of compensating employees for contributing their knowledge.

HRM

FOR THE HUMAN RESOURCES MANAGEMENT MAJOR

SUMMARY

1. **Recognize the importance of data, their managerial issues, and their life cycle.** IT applications cannot be done without using data. Data should be accurate, complete, timely, consistent, accessible, relevant, and concise. Managing data in organizations is difficult for various reasons: The amount of data increases with time; data are stored in various systems, databases, formats, and languages; and data security, quality, and integrity are often compromised.

   The data life cycle starts with data collection. The data are stored in a database(s) and then preprocessed to fit the format of a data warehouse or data marts. Users then access data from the warehouse or data mart for analysis. Data analysis and mining tools look for patterns, and intelligent systems support data interpretation. The result of all these activities is the generation of decision support and knowledge.

2. **Describe the sources of data and their collection.** Data sources can be internal, personal, and external (particularly the Internet). Internal data are usually located in corporate databases and are usually accessible via an organization's intranet. IS users create personal data by documenting their own expertise. These data can reside on the user's PC or be placed on corporate databases or on corporate knowledge bases. Sources of external data range from commercial databases to sensors and satellites. Government reports constitute a major source for external data. Many thousands of databases all over the world are accessible

through the Internet. Much external data are free; other data are available from commercial database services.

3. **Describe document management systems.** Document management systems provide information in an electronic format to decision makers. The functions of DMSs include document identification, storage, and retrieval; tracking; version control; workflow management; and presentation. The major tools of document management are workflow software, authoring tools, scanners, imaging systems, and databases.

4. **Explain the operation of data warehousing and its role in decision support.** A data warehouse is a repository of subject-oriented historical data that are organized to be accessible in a form readily acceptable for analytical processing activities. End users can access needed data in a data warehouse quickly and easily via Web browsers. They can conduct extensive analysis with data and can have a consolidated view of organizational data. These benefits can improve business knowledge, provide competitive advantage, enhance customer service and satisfaction, facilitate decision making, and help in streamlining business processes.

5. **Describe information and knowledge discovery and business intelligence.** Information discovery started with simple data collection and answered queries that involved one set of historical data. This analysis was extended with tools such as SQL and relational database management systems. Better tools to manage the ever-increasing amount of data were needed, resulting in the creation of the data warehouse and the appearance of OLAP and multidimensional databases. When the amount of data to be analyzed exploded in the mid-1990s, knowledge discovery emerged as an important analytical tool. The process of extracting useful knowledge from volumes of data is known as *knowledge discovery*. Knowledge discovery's major objective is to identify valid, novel, potentially useful, and ultimately understandable patterns in data.

6. **Understand the power and benefits of data mining.** Data mining is a major tool for analyzing large amounts of data, usually in a data warehouse. Given databases or data warehouses of sufficient size and quality, data mining technology can generate new business opportunities by providing automated prediction of trends and behaviors and automated discovery of previously unknown patterns.

7. **Describe data presentation methods, and explain geographical information systems, visual simulations, and virtual reality as decision support tools.** Data visualization involves presentation of data by technologies such as digital images, geographical information systems, three-dimensional presentations, videos and animation, virtual reality, and other multimedia. A geographical information system (GIS) is a computer-based system for manipulating and displaying data using digitized maps. Visual interactive modeling uses computer graphic displays to represent the impact of different management or operational decisions. Visual interactive simulation is a method in which the end user watches the progress of the simulation model in an animated form. Virtual reality is interactive, computer-generated, three-dimensional graphics delivered to the user through a head-mounted display.

8. **Recognize the role of the Web in data management.** Data management and business intelligence activities are often performed with Web tools or are interrelated with Web technologies and e-business. E-commerce software vendors are providing Web tools that connect the data warehouse with EC ordering and cataloging systems. Data warehousing and decision support vendors are connecting their products with Web technologies and EC. The Web-based system is accessed via a portal, and it connects the following parts: the business intelligence (BI) services, the data warehouse and marts, the corporate applications, and the data infrastructure. Enterprise BI suites (EBISs) integrate query, reporting, OLAP, and other tools. Clickstream data occur inside the Web environment, when customers visit a Web site. They provide a trail of the users' activities in the Web site, including user behavior and browsing patterns.

9. **Define knowledge and describe the different types of knowledge.** Knowledge is information that is contextual, relevant, and actionable. Explicit knowledge deals with more objective, rational, and technical knowledge. Tacit knowledge is usually in the domain of subjective, cognitive, and experiential learning; it is highly personal and difficult to formalize.

10. **Describe the technologies that can be utilized in a knowledge management system.** Knowledge management systems are developed using three sets of technologies: communication, collaboration, and storage and retrieval. Communication technologies allow users to access needed knowledge, and to communicate with each other, especially with experts. E-mail, the Internet, corporate intranets, and other Web-based tools provide communication capabilities. Collaboration technologies provide the means to perform and enhance group work, especially for knowledge contribution. Storage and retrieval technologies originally meant using a database management system to store and manage explicit knowledge. Capturing, storing, and managing tacit knowledge usually requires electronic document management systems and specialized storage systems.

INTERACTIVE / LEARNING

Following Cherry Garcia: A Look at Tracking at Ben and Jerry's

Go to the Interactivities section on the Student Web Site and access Chapter 3: Data and Knowledge Management. There you will find an animated simulation of the technologies used to track the life of ice creams at Ben and Jerry's, as well as some hands-on activities that visually explain business concepts in this chapter.

More Resources

More resources and study tools are located on the Student Web Site. You'll find additional chapter materials and links to organizations, people, and technologies for each chapter. In addition, self-quizzes that provide individualized feedback are available for each chapter.

Instructions for accessing the Interactivities on the Student Web Site:

1. Go to **wiley.com/college/turban**
2. Select Turban Rainer Potter's *Introduction to Information Technology, Third Edition*
3. Click on Student Resources Site, in the toolbar on the left
4. Click on Interactivities Web Site
5. Click on Interactivities Web Site and use your password to enter the site (your password card is located in the inside cover of your textbook)

DISCUSSION QUESTIONS

1. Discuss the factors that make document management so valuable.
2. Describe the process of information and knowledge discovery, and discuss the roles of the data warehouse, data mining, and OLAP in this process.
3. Discuss the benefits of data warehousing to end users.
4. Distinguish between data warehouses and data marts.
5. Explain why it is important to capture and manage knowledge.
6. Compare and contrast tacit knowledge and explicit knowledge.

PROBLEM-SOLVING ACTIVITIES

1. Review the list of data management difficulties in Section 3.1. Explain how a combination of data warehousing and data mining can solve or reduce these difficulties. Be specific.
2. Ocean Spray Cranberries is a large cooperative of fruit growers and processors. Ocean Spray needed data to determine the effectiveness of its promotions and advertisements and to make itself able to respond strategically to competitors' promotions. The company also wanted to identify trends in consumer preferences for new products and to pinpoint marketing factors that might be causing changes in the selling levels of certain brands and markets. Ocean Spray buys marketing data from Information Resources Inc. (IRI) (*infores.com*), a company that collects data using barcode scanners in a sample of 32,500 stores nationwide, and from A.C. Nielsen. The data for each product include sales volume, market share, distribution, price information, and information about promotions (sales, advertisements).

   The amount of data provided to Ocean Spray on a daily basis is overwhelming (about 100 to 1,000 times more data items than Ocean Spray used to collect on its own). All the data are deposited in the corporate marketing data mart. To analyze this vast amount of data, the company developed a DSS based on an expert system–based data-mining process, which summarizes information in accordance with user preferences. The company can now identify trends, discover cause-and-effect relationships, present hundreds of displays, and provide any information required by the decision makers. This system alerts managers to key problems and opportunities.

   a. Find information about Ocean Spray by entering Ocean Spray's Web site (*oceanspray.com*).
   b. Ocean Spray has said that it cannot run the business without the system. Why?
   c. What data from the data mart are used by the DSS?

d. Enter *infores.com* and review the marketing decision support information.

e. How does IRI collect data? (Check the Custom Store Tracking product.)

3. Investigate the literature for information on the position of CKO. Find out what percentage of firms with KM initiatives have CKOs and what their responsibilities are.

4. Investigate the literature for new measures of success (metrics) for knowledge management and intellectual capital. Write a report on your findings.

INTERNET ACTIVITIES

1. Conduct a survey on document management tools and applications by visiting *opentext.com*, *documentum.com*, and *aiim.org*.

2. Access the Web sites of one or two of the major data management vendors, such as Oracle, Informix, and Sybase, and trace the capabilities of their latest products, including Web connections.

3. Access the Web sites of one or two of the major data warehouse vendors, such as NCR or SAS; find how their products are related to the Web.

4. Enter *teradatauniversitynetwork.com*. Prepare a summary on resources available there. Is it valuable to a student?

5. Enter *visualmining.com* and review the support they provide to business intelligence. Prepare a report.

6. Try the KPMG Knowledge Management Framework Assessment Exercise at *kmsurvey.londonweb.net* and assess how well your organization (university or company with which you are familiar) is doing with knowledge management. Are the results accurate? Why or why not?

TEAM ASSIGNMENTS

1. Several applications now combine GIS and GPS.
   a. Survey such applications by conducting literature and Internet searches and query GIS vendors.
   b. Prepare a list of five applications, including at least two in e-commerce (see Chapter 5).
   c. Describe the benefit of such integration.

2. Prepare a report on the topic of "data management and intranets." Specifically, pay attention to the role of the data warehouse, the use of browsers for query, and data mining. Also describe the role of extranets in support of business partner collaboration. Each student will visit one or two vendors' sites, read the white papers, and examine products (Oracle, Red Brick, Hyperion, NCR, SAS, and Information Advantage). Also, visit the Web site of the Data Warehouse Institute (*dw-institute.org*).

3. Compare and contrast the capabilities and features of electronic document management with those of collaborative computing and those of knowledge management systems. Each team represents one type of system. Present the ways in which these capabilities and features can create improvements for an organization.

4. Read the article by A. Genusa titled "Rx for Learning," available at *cio.com* (February 1, 2001), which describes Tufts University Medical School's experience with knowledge management. Determine how these concepts and such a system could be implemented and used at your college or university. Explain how each aspect would work; if they would not work, explain why not.

REAL-WORLD CASE

SIEMENS LEARNS WHAT IT KNOWS THROUGH KNOWLEDGE MANAGEMENT

THE BUSINESS PROBLEM Siemens AG (*siemens. com*), a $73 billion electronics and electrical-engineering conglomerate, produces everything from lightbulbs to x-ray machines, from power generation equipment to high-speed trains. During its 156-year history, Siemens developed into one of the world's largest and most successful corporations. Siemens is well known for the technical brilliance of its engineers. However, much of their knowledge was locked and unavailable to other employees. Facing competitive pressure, Siemens is trying to maximize the contributions of each business unit. One way to do so was to learn to leverage the knowledge and expertise of its 460,000 employees worldwide.

THE IT SOLUTION The roots of knowledge management (KM) at Siemens go back to 1996 when a number of people within the corporation with an interest in KM formed a "community of interest." They researched the subject, learned what was being done by other companies, and looked for ways that knowledge management could benefit Siemens. Without any suggestion or encouragement from senior executives, mid-level employees in Siemens business units began creating knowledge repositories, communities of practice, and informal techniques of sharing knowledge. By 1999, the senior management of Siemens AG confirmed the importance of knowledge management to the entire company by creating an organizational unit that would be responsible for the worldwide deployment of KM.

At the heart of Siemens' technical solution to knowledge management is a Web site called *ShareNet*, which combines elements of a database repository, a chat room, and a search engine. Online entry forms allow employees to store information they think might be useful to colleagues. Other Siemens employees are able to search the repository or browse by topic, and then contact the authors for more information using one of the available communication channels. In addition, the system lets employees post an alert when they have an urgent question.

Although KM implementation at Siemens involved establishing a network to collect, categorize, and share information using databases and intranets, Siemens realized that IT was only the tool that enabled knowledge management.

The movement toward knowledge management by Siemens has presented several challenges to the company, some of which are cultural. Siemens used a three-pronged effort to convince employees that it is important to participate in the exchange of ideas and experiences and to share what they know. It has assigned 100 internal KM "evangelists" around the world who are responsible for training, answering questions, and monitoring the system. Siemens' top management has shown its full support for the knowledge management projects. And the company is providing incentives to overcome employees' resistance to change. In exchange for employees posting documents to the system and for using the knowledge, Siemens rewards its employees with "shares," much like frequent-flyer miles. Once collected and accumulated, these shares can be exchanged for things like consumer electronics or discounted trips to other countries.

However, the real incentive of the system is much more basic. Commission-driven salespeople have already learned that knowledge and expertise of their colleagues available through ShareNet can be indispensable in winning lucrative contracts. Employees in marketing, service, R&D, and other departments are also willing to participate and contribute as long as they realize that the system provides them with useful information in a convenient way.

The *ShareNet* has undergone tremendous growth, which resulted in several challenges for Siemens. The company strives to maintain balance between global and local knowledge initiatives as well as between knowledge management efforts that support the entire company or individual business units. Furthermore, Siemens works to prevent *ShareNet* from becoming so overloaded with information that it becomes useless. It employs a group of people who monitor the system and remove trivial and irrelevant content.

THE RESULTS *ShareNet* has evolved into a state-of-the-art Web-based knowledge management system that stores and catalogues volumes of valuable knowledge, makes it available to every employee, and enhances global collaboration. Numerous companies, including Intel and Volkswagen, studied *ShareNet* before setting up their own knowledge management systems. Furthermore, Teleos, an independent knowledge management research company, acknowledged Siemens as being one of the Most Admired Knowledge Enterprises worldwide for five years in a row.

Siemens also has realized a variety of quantifiable benefits afforded by knowledge management. For example, in April 1999 the company developed a portion of ShareNet to support its Information & Communications Networks Group at the cost of $7.8 million. Within two years, the tool had helped to generate $122 million in additional sales.

Ultimately, knowledge management may be one of the major tools that will help Siemens prove that large diversified conglomerates can work and that being big might even be an advantage in the Information Age.

Sources: Compiled from G. S. Vasilash, "447,000 Heads Are Better Than One," *Automotive Design and Production*, June 2002; *The Economist* (2001) (*economist.com/displaystory.cfm?story_id=638605*).

QUESTIONS

1. What are various reasons why knowledge management is so important to Siemens? Do these reasons apply to other companies? Why or why not?
2. What challenges did Siemens face in implementing its knowledge management initiative?
3. What is the most valuable incentive offered by Siemens knowledge management initiative?

DATA AND KNOWLEDGE USED AT CLUB IT

To learn more about Club IT's operations, you stayed until the 2:00 A.M. closing this morning to see how everything was tallied and accounted for at the end of a business day. It was a little hard to get going this morning, but you now have a better picture of the daily business cycle at Club IT. You're energized when Lisa asks you for suggestions to use club and public resources to help keep Club IT's edge as the high-energy, high impact club it strives to be.

ASSIGNMENT

1. Search the Web for resources that can be mined to identify and predict nightclub trends. What are some resources? What data and knowledge do they provide?

2. Identify a nightclub trend, describe some data that could be used to validate that trend, and then create a scenario for the life cycle of these data.

3. Describe some examples of tacit knowledge and explicit knowledge that you think Lisa and Ruben use in running Club IT.

Go to wiley.com/college/turban to access the CLUB IT Web Site on the Student Web Site

Network Computing

Chapter Preview

Without networks, the computer on your desk would be merely another productivity enhancement tool, just like the typewriter once was. The power of networks, however, turns your computer into an amazingly effective tool for discovery, communication, and collaboration, vastly increasing your productivity and your organization's productivity. Regardless of the type of organization (profit/not-for-profit, large/small, global/local) or industry (manufacturing, financial services, healthcare), networks have transformed the way business is done.

Networks support new ways of doing business, from marketing, to supply chain management, to customer service, to human resources management. In particular, the Internet and its private organizational counterpart, intranets, have an enormous impact on our lives, both professionally and personally. In fact, for all organizations, having an Internet strategy is no longer just a source of competitive advantage; it is necessary for survival.

Chapter Outline

4.1 Network Computing—An Overview
4.2 Discovery
4.3 Communication
4.4 Collaboration
4.5 Collaboration-Enabling Tools: From Workflow to Groupware
4.6 E-Learning, Distance Learning, and Telecommuting

Learning Objectives

1. Understand the concepts of the Internet and the Web, their importance, and their capabilities.
2. Understand the role of intranets, extranets, and corporate portals for organizations.
3. Identify the various ways in which communication is executed over the Internet.
4. Describe how people collaborate over the Internet, intranets, and extranets using various supporting tools.
5. Describe groupware capabilities.
6. Describe and analyze the role of e-learning and distance learning.
7. Understand the advantages and disadvantages of telecommuting for both employers and employees.

NEW CARS IN 18 MONTHS: NETWORKS REVOLUTIONIZE PRODUCT DEVELOPMENT AT GM

THE BUSINESS PROBLEM

General Motors (GM, *gm.com*), the world's largest manufacturer of cars and trucks, has traditionally been slow-moving and bureaucratic, and was suffering from bloated cost structures, labor troubles, forgettable products, and intensifying global competition. The company's market share fell from nearly 60 percent in the 1960s to less than 30 percent in 2002.

The problems were worst in product development. The average time to introduce a new car (from concept to production) was four years, far behind industry averages. The time lag at GM produced dated, unappealing vehicle designs. Executives would often see just one design option for a prospective car or truck. If they recommended a change, it would take months to build a new physical model and receive approval from manufacturing that the updated version was buildable.

THE IT SOLUTION

General Motors used information technology to revamp its product development process. The company invested more than $1.7 billion in Internet applications, while eliminating 3,500 older, or legacy, information systems.

The company created its Advanced Design Studio and the Virtual Reality Lab. In the Advanced Design Studio, three 20-foot "power walls" wrap around one section of the room, displaying larger-than-life, three-dimensional projections of vehicles in progress, for everyone to examine and dissect. Engineers, designers, digital sculptors, and software programmers sit side by side, collaborating on various aspects of each vehicle appearing on the screens.

The vehicle model manager of the studio addresses the Smart Board, a 50-inch flat-panel computer display synchronized with the power wall. With the tip of his index finger, he maneuvers around the screen three dimensional sketches of upcoming GM vehicles (for example, views of the Chevy SSR, Super Sport Roadster, and the Hummer H2). Just a few years ago, all sketches were created by hand and stapled to a display board for review. Clay or hard Styrofoam models had to be sculpted for each new design. Now, designing and displaying vehicle models is done by software.

GM's Virtual Reality Lab is equipped with a wraparound, floor-to-ceiling display wall and special 3-D glasses that GM executives wear at design reviews. Here, the executives receive a virtual look at the new Chevy SSR from various distances and angles. Executives can occupy the virtual space of the driver's seat and get a sense of the interior. They can also "drive" the prospective vehicle through simulations of downtown Las Vegas or along a twisting highway. The lab is digitally linked to all 14 GM engineering centers overseas via a corporate intranet, allowing executives and designers to collaborate on product reviews with colleagues around the world and around the clock.

THE RESULTS

GM vehicles are now being created in 18 to 21 months from concept to production, and this once slow-moving company is introducing a new vehicle every 23 days. This shorter production cycle makes GM much more responsive to changes in consumer tastes. Designers can respond to data gathered directly from dealers and customers via the Internet. By monitoring buying preferences on GM Buy Power (*gmbuypower.com*), for example, designers and engineers develop a far better sense of what customers actually want. GM can also put the design concept for a vehicle on the Internet, and prospective customers can propose modifications.

The expensive physical processes of model building and crash testing have been streamlined by using digital simulation technology. Ten years ago, for example, 80 Chevy Caprice test cars had to be built and driven head-on into walls to ensure their crashworthiness and to meet federal regulations. Today, with digital simulation replacing physical testing, the number of test vehicles is down to fewer than 10, reducing time and costs tremendously. In order to support this simulation, GM has increased its supercomputing capacity (see Technology Guide 1) by 1,200 percent.

Major investments in networking and Internet technologies are allowing cross-functional sharing and collaboration at GM, thereby shortening the product development cycle. The result has been that GM is saving $1.5 billion annually. Also, 9,000 suppliers are now linked in real time to the company via GM Supply Power (*gmsupplypower.com*). All this is aimed at making GM a smaller, quicker, more agile organization. The payoff has been double-digit productivity gains in each of the past five years.

Source: Compiled from G. Rifkin, "GM's Internet Overhaul," *MIT Technology Review*, October 2002.

The opening case about General Motors illustrates three fundamental points about network computing. First, computers do not work in isolation in modern organizations. Rather, they constantly exchange data and/or applications. Second, this exchange of data—facilitated by telecommunications technologies—brings a number of very significant advantages to companies. Third, this exchange can be over any distance and over networks of any size. The networks in the GM case range from local area networks in one room (e.g., the Advanced Design Studio) to the Internet (global collaboration among executives and designers). We see that discovery, communications, and collaboration occur not only within GM, but also between suppliers, customers, and GM. Networks in general, and the Internet in particular, have fundamentally altered the way we do business and the way we live.

In this chapter we learn about the major capabilities of network computing to support discovery of information, communication, and collaboration activities in organizations. We also learn how organizations are exploiting network computing for e-learning and telecommuting.

WHAT WE LEARNED FROM THIS CASE

4.1 NETWORK COMPUTING—AN OVERVIEW

An Overview of the Internet and the Web

Many aspects of the way we work and live in the twenty-first century will be determined by the vast web of electronic networks, sometimes referred to generally as the *Information Superhighway* but usually called the *Internet*. As discussed in Chapter 2, the Internet is a *global network of computer networks*. It links the computing resources of businesses, government, and educational institutions using a common computer communication protocol, TCP/IP (described in Technology Guide 5). Recall, also from Chapter 2, that the World Wide Web (the Web) is an *application* that uses the transport functions of the Internet.

Future versions of the Internet will allow even larger volume and a more rapid flow of information. Eventually we may see several information superhighways. It is probable that the original concept of a scientific-educational system will be separated from the commercial one. For example, the Internet2 (*internet2.edu*) project (described in Technology Guide 5) offers advanced next-generation applications such as remote diagnosis, digital libraries, distance education, online simulation, and virtual laboratories that will enable people to collaborate and access information in ways not possible using today's Internet (Choi and Whinston, 2000).

The Evolution of Commercial Applications on the Internet. With the commercialization of the Internet in the early 1990s, we have seen an explosion of commercial applications. An interesting facet of these applications is that Internet technologies encourage entrepreneurs to start businesses. Here are four examples of entrepreneurs who have started successful businesses using the Internet and the World Wide Web.

SVC

EXAMPLE *Applying the Internet to a Social Problem.* Benetech (*benetech.org*) is a not-for-profit organization that applies information technology to social problems in order to help disadvantaged communities across the world. The company got its start by selling PC readers for the blind. Today, it operates BookShare, an Internet library with 14,000 books where blind, visually impaired, and learning-disabled people can legally store and share scanned publications. (*Source: benetech.org*, last accessed November 5, 2003.)

MKT

EXAMPLE *Internet Enables Entrepreneurs to Start on a Shoe-String.* Jim Holland and John Bresee, two self-described ski bums, started the Backcountry Store (*backcountrystore.com*) on $2,000. The company has been profitable for five straight years and is now the number-two online outdoor-gear seller, behind REI, offering products from Black Diamond, North Face, Oakley, Rossignol, and more than 150 other brands. The two entrepreneurs built the company without any outside investment and expect to ring up $15 million in sales in 2003. How did they do it?

They chose an open-source application (see Technology Guide 2) to process transactions and an open-source database for product and inventory records. Then, for about $200,000, they customized the software, saving the high costs of commercial products. Rather than advertising, they signed "affiliate marketers"—partners who refer customers to the store in exchange for a piece of any resulting transactions. The founders have replaced consultants and focus groups with online tools: Search requests and Web traffic logs provide better, cheaper data on what customers want. Finally, they persuaded fellow ski bums to become phone reps, and they reward them with free gear, not for making quotas but for spending nights in a tent or testing hiking boots. That way, Backcountry customers can talk to salespeople with firsthand knowledge of the products. (*Source:* McDonald, 2003.)

MKT

EXAMPLE *Chinese Entrepreneurs Want to Be like Amazon.* Dangdang.com (*dangdang.com*) is China's biggest online bookseller. Peggy Yu, the company's co-founder (with her husband), follows Amazon.com's successes and failures very closely. Although the company has experienced rapid growth, there are concerns about whether it can thrive in a country where the Internet and the exchange of free information remain subject to the whims of China's authorities and where people are still reluctant to order online. In general, Ms. Yu steers clear of offering books on politics, so as not to attract the scrutiny of China's authorities.

In a country where only 8 million out of 68 million Internet users have ever shopped online, Ms. Yu says that the learning curve has been steep. It has been equally difficult to convince customers to use credit cards over cash. So Dangdang uses 30 bicycle courier companies in 12 cities to deliver the products and collect the cash, which is then wired to Dangdang.

The company now handles up to 4,000 orders a day—about half books and the rest videos, CDs, computer games, and software. How-to books on business and parenting are hot; thrillers and diet books are not. (*Source:* Chen, 2003.)

MKT

EXAMPLE *College Student Founds Successful Business while Still in School.* Campusfood.com provides interactive menus to college students, using the Internet to enhance traditional telephone ordering of meals. Launched at the University of Pennsylvania, the company took thousands of orders for local restaurants, delivering pizza, hoagies, and wings to the Penn community.

Founder Michael Saunders, with the help of some friends, launched the site in 1998 and began building the company's customer base. This process involved registering other schools, generating a list of local restaurants from which students could order food to be delivered, and attracting student customers. By 2003, there were more than 200 participating schools and more than 1,000 participating restaurants.

Financed through private investors, friends, and family members, the site was built on an investment of less than $1 million. Campusfood.com's revenue is generated through transaction fees: The site takes a 5 percent commission on each order. (*Sources:* Prince, 2002, and *campusfood.com,* last accessed November 5, 2003.)

Commercial Internet applications evolve through four major phases: *presence, e-commerce, collaboration, and integration.* The major characteristics of each phase as they have evolved over time are illustrated in Figure 4.1. Specific applications in each phase are demonstrated throughout this book.

Another way to look at the applications of the Internet is via the generic categories that they support, as presented next.

Internet Application Categories.   The Internet supports applications in the following major categories:

- *Discovery.* Discovery involves browsing and information retrieval and provides customers the ability to view information in databases, download it, and/or process it. Discovery is facilitated by software agents since the amount of information on the Internet and intranets is growing rapidly. Discovery methods and issues are described in Section 4.2.

- *Communication.* The Internet provides fast and inexpensive communication channels that range from messages posted on online bulletin boards to complex information exchanges among many organizations. It also includes information transfer (among computers and via wireline and wireless) and information processing. E-mail, chat groups, and newsgroups (Internet chat groups focused on specific categories of interest) are examples of major communication media presented in Section 4.3 and in Technology Guide 5.

- *Collaboration.* Due to improved communication, electronic collaboration between individuals and/or groups and collaboration between organizations are increasing rapidly. Several tools can be used, ranging from screen sharing and teleconferencing to group support systems, as we illustrate in Section 4.4. Collaboration also includes resource-sharing services, which provide access to printers and specialized servers. Several collaboration software products, called groupware and workflow, can be used on the Internet and on other networks.

See Online Files W4.1 and W4.2 at the book's Web site for an overview of discovery, communication, and collaboration services.

wiley.com/college/turban

TIME			
	Presence	**E-Commerce**	**Collaboration and Interaction**	**Integration and Services**
Emphasis	Eyeballs (human review)	Review, expansion	profit	Capabilities, services
Type of transaction	No transaction	B2C, C2C, C2B, G2C, e-CRM	B2B, B2E, supply chain, c-commerce, G2B	Portals, e-learning, m-commerce, l-commerce
Nature	Publish information	Process transaction	Collaborate	Integrate, provide services
Target	Pages	Process transaction	Digital systems	Digital environments
Concentrate on	Web sites	Web-enabled existing systems, dot-coms	Business transformation consolidation	Internal and external integration
	1993-1994	1995-1999	2000-2001	2001-2005

Figure 4.1 *Roadmap: The evolution of the Internet over time.*

The Net is also used for education, entertainment, and work. People can access the content of newspapers, magazines, and books. They can download documents, and they can do research. They can correspond with friends and family, play games, listen to music, view movies and other cultural events, and even visit many major museums and galleries worldwide.

The Network Computing Infrastructure: Intranets and Extranets

In addition to the Internet and the Web there are two other major infrastructures of network computing: the intranet and the extranet.

The Intranet.   As discussed in Chapter 2, an *intranet* is a network designed to serve the internal informational needs of a company, using Internet concepts and tools. It is a network confined to an organization for its internal use. It provides easy and inexpensive browsing and search capabilities.

Intranets also support communication and collaboration. They are frequently connected to the Internet, enabling a company to conduct e-commerce activities. (Such activities are facilitated by *extranets*, as described later in this chapter and in Chapter 5.) Using screen sharing and other groupware tools, intranets facilitate the work of groups. Companies also publish newsletters and deliver news to their employers via their intranets. For extensive information about intranets, see *intranetjournal.com*.

Intranets have the power to change organizational structures and procedures and to help reengineer corporations. Intranets can be implemented using different types of local area network (LAN) technologies, including wireless LANs (see Technology Guide 4). IT's about Business 4.1 provides an example of an intranet that saves lives.

Extranets.   As discussed in Chapter 2, an *extranet* connects the intranets of different organizations and allows secure communications among business partners over the Internet (using VPN, see Technology Guide 4). It offers limited accessibility to the intranets of the participating companies, as well as the necessary interorganizational communications, using Internet tools.

IT's ABOUT BUSINESS   [SVC] [POM]

4.1: An Intranet Helps Premature Babies

Pediatrix (*pediatrix.com*) provides neonatal and maternal-fetal physician services through 200 natal intensive care units (NICUs) nationwide. Neonatal case records are kept in a clinical database accessible via the company's intranet. The database is designed to support research, improve the quality of baby care, and justify insurance claims (a significant task for a healthcare business). The database has now grown to over 50 gigabytes, with records on more than 192,000 babies.

In 2000, Pediatrix set out to improve weight gains for very small infants. Infants born prematurely have slower physical and mental development than those infants carried to full term. Researchers accessed the database via the intranet to identify the Pediatrix NICUs with the highest and lowest weight gain results. They visited the units at both extremes and found 16 significant differences in practices. They placed the information about these differences on the intranet and encouraged all NICUs to apply the

beneficial processes. One year later, Pediatrix found that 76 percent of the NICUs had improved their weight gain record.

The intranet is having a bottom-line impact as well, thanks to an application that uses data from the clinical record to suggest the standard insurance code to apply for each day of care. That is significant because disputes with insurers often revolve around the difference between codes for "evaluation and monitoring" and for "critical" care; the latter is reimbursed at a higher rate.

Source: Compiled from D. Carr, "Pediatrix," *Baseline*, October 1, 2003.

QUESTIONS

1. What is the relationship between the Pediatrix database and its intranet?
2. What are the advantages of the intranet at Pediatrix?

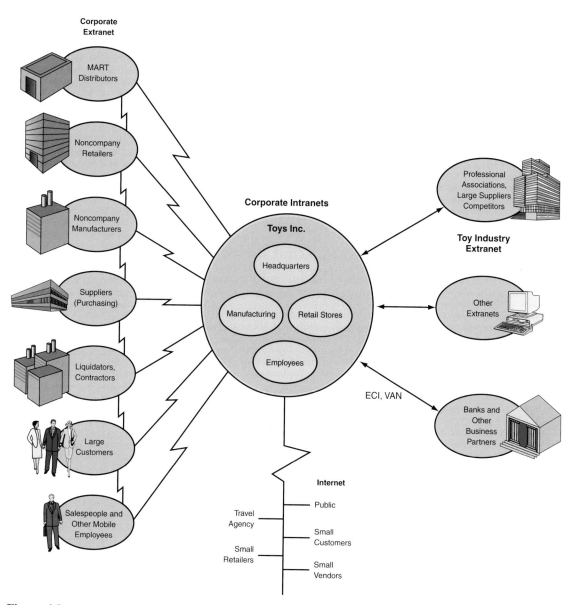

Figure 4.2 *How a company uses the Internet, intranet, and extranets.*

The use of extranets is rapidly increasing due to rapid decreases in communication costs. Extranets enable innovative applications of business-to-business (B2B) e-commerce (see Chapter 5). Finally, extranets are closely related to improved communications along the supply chain.

The Internet, intranets, and extranets can be used in various ways in a corporate environment in order to gain competitive advantage. Examples are provided throughout the book. An example of how a hypothetical company, Toys Inc., might use all network computing infrastructures is shown in Figure 4.2.

The discovery, communication, and collaboration capabilities available at low cost on the Internet, intranets, and extranets provide for a large number of useful applications. In the next four sections of this chapter, we discuss these capabilities.

Before you go on . . .

1. Describe the difference between the Internet and the World Wide Web.

2. What are the three major types of Internet applications?

4.2 DISCOVERY

The Internet permits users to access information located in databases all over the world. The discovery capability can facilitate education, government services, entertainment, and commerce. For example, one Web site, the Golf Handicap and Information Network (*ghin.com*), enables anyone to get the goods on any golfer: handicaps, most recent rounds played, home courses, and even scores. Golfers can check this site before they play to avoid losing money to "sandbaggers" (golfers who fudge their handicaps).

Discovery is done by *browsing* and *searching* data sources on the Web. The major problem of discovery is the huge amount of information available. The solution is to use different types of search and other software agents.

The Role of Internet Software Agents

A large number of Internet software agents can be used to automate and expedite discovery. **Software agents** are computer programs that carry out a set of routine computer tasks on behalf of the user and in so doing employ some sort of knowledge of the user's goals. We examine some of these agents in this section.

software agents *Computer programs that carry out a set of routine computer tasks on behalf of the user and in so doing employ some sort of knowledge of the user's goals.*

Search Engines, Directories, and Various Software Agents. The amount of information on the Web doubles approximately each year. This makes navigating through the Web and gaining access to necessary information more and more difficult. *Search engines* and *directories* are two fundamentally different types of search facilities available on the Web. A **search engine** (e.g., Altavista, Google, Mamma) is a computer program that can contact other network resources on the Internet, search for specific information by key words, and report the results. A search engine maintains an index of hundreds of millions of Web pages (over three billion pages in the case of Google) and uses that index to find pages that match a set of user-specified keywords. Such indexes are created and updated by software robots called **softbots**, which execute routine tasks for the benefit of their users. Search engines have brought much information and an ability to research an incredible number of topics to our fingertips. But there is a potential downside of search engines, as IT's about Business 4.2 illustrates.

search engine *A computer program that can contact other network resources on the Internet, search for specific information by key words, and report the results; an example is Google.*

softbots *Software robots that execute routine tasks (such as maintaining search engines) for the benefit of their users.*

Directories are a slightly different type of software agent, which some people confuse with search engines. A **directory** (e.g., Yahoo, About.com) is a hierarchically organized collection of links to Web pages. Directories are compiled manually, unlike search engine indexes, which are generated by computers.

directory *A hierarchically organized collection of links to Web pages, compiled manually; an example is Yahoo.*

Search engines and directories often present users with links to thousands or even millions of pages. It is quite difficult to find information of interest from such a large number of links. Therefore we can use additional tools to refine the search. Two of these tools are metasearch engines and intelligent agents. **Metasearch engines** search several engines at once and integrate the findings of the various search engines to answer queries posted by the users. Examples include MetaFind (*metafind.com*), Surfwax (*surfwax.com*), Metacrawler (*metacrawler.com*), Ungoogle (*ungoogle.com*), Ixquick (*ixquick.com*), and Dogpile (*dogpile.com*).

metasearch engine *A computer program that searches several engines at once and integrates the findings of the various search engines to answer queries posted by users.*

Software agents that exhibit intelligent behavior and learning are called *intelligent agents*. The topic of intelligent agents is discussed more fully in Chapter 10. Here we present only a few examples of Internet-based software agents, which appear under names such as *wizards*, *softbots*, and *knowbots*. Major types of agents available for help in browsing and searching include Web-browsing-assisting agents, FAQ agents, and indexing agents.

Web-Browsing-Assisting Agents. Some agents can facilitate browsing by offering the user a tour of the Internet. Known as *tour guides*, they work while the user browses. For example, NetCaptor (*netcaptor.com*) is a custom browser application (only with Internet Explorer) that makes browsing more pleasurable and productive.

IT'S ABOUT BUSINESS
`SVC` `MKT`

4.2: Are Web Search Results Objective?

Some 550 million Internet searches are performed every day. Many search engines are sprinkling growing numbers of paid corporate Web pages into the search results and accepting money each time one of these so-called "paid-inclusion links" is clicked. These paid inclusions are virtually invisible to average Web surfers. Google, the leading search engine, steers clear of paid inclusions, saying that they undermine confidence in the objectivity of search results. So, are Web searches objective?

Ask Rob Spooner, who runs a travel site called On-line Highways (*ohwy.com*), which provides informational pages about various small towns throughout the United States. Inktomi, a search engine that now belongs to Yahoo, contacted him about becoming a paid-inclusion participant. The proposal: Spooner would pay 10 cents for every visitor Inktomi passed along. Spooner declined the offer.

Then, things went downhill. Spooner's Web pages soon plunged in Inktomi's search rankings and disappeared from key sites like MSN, where Inktomi powers the search process. After Spooner demanded to know what happened, he learned from Inktomi that his site "contained editorial flaws" that hurt his ranking, and he would have to become a paid-inclusion customer to learn what these flaws were. All this occurred while his pages remained well ranked on Google.

Source: Compiled from B. Elgin, "Web Searches: The Fix Is In," *Business Week*, October 6, 2003.

QUESTIONS

1. Do you think search engines should include paid-inclusion sites? Why or why not?

2. Do you think that objectivity is important for search engine results? Why or why not?

NetCaptor opens a separate tab for each Web site visited by the user. Users can easily switch between different tabs. The CaptorGroup feature creates a group of links that are stored together so the user can get single-click access to multiple Web sites. The PopupCaptor feature automatically closes pop-up windows displayed during browsing. NetCaptor also includes a utility, called Flyswat, to turn certain words and phrases into hyperlinks. Clicking on these links opens a window with links to Web sites with relevant information. For more details on Web browsing assistants see *botspot.com*.

Frequently Asked Questions (FAQ) Agents. *FAQ agents* guide people to the answers to frequently asked questions. When searching for information, many people tend to ask the same or similar questions. In response, newsgroups, support staffs, vendors, and others have developed files of those FAQs and an appropriate answer to each. But there is a potential problem: When using natural language, people may ask the same questions in several different ways. The FAQ agent addresses this problem by indexing large numbers of FAQ files. Using the text of a question submitted in natural language, the software agent can locate the appropriate answer.

AskJeeves (*askjeeves.com*), a popular FAQ assistant, makes it easy to find answers on the Internet to questions asked in plain English. The system responds with one or more closely related questions to which the answers are available. Parts of such questions may contain drop-down menus for selecting from different options. After the user selects the question that is closest to the original question, the system presents a reply page containing different sources that can provide answers.

Intelligent Indexing Agents. Indexing agents (also called *Web robots*, *spiders*, and *wanderers*) can carry out a massive autonomous search of the Web on behalf of a user or, more commonly, of a *search engine* like Google, Mamma, or Altavista. First, they scan millions of documents and store an index of words found in document titles, key words, and texts. The user can then query the search engine to find documents containing certain key words.

IT's about Business 4.3 (page 106) provides an insight into a specific application of search and indexing technology.

indexing agents *Software agents that can carry out a massive autonomous search of the Web on behalf of a user or, more commonly, of a search engine.*

IT's ABOUT BUSINESS

4.3: Plagiarism and How to Catch It

A study by the Center for Academic Integrity showed that 80 percent of college students had admitted to cheating at least once (see *plagiarism.org*). Today, students are faced with an old temptation made much easier by the Internet: taking the work of others and passing it off as one's own. Internet plagiarism has become as simple as cut-and-paste. Students may not even have to cut-and-paste when they can go to "term-paper mills" on the Internet and purchase ready-made papers on all topics. For an interesting look at term-paper mills in general and by subject see Margaret Fain's lists (*coastal.edu/library/mills2.htm* and *coastal.edu/library/mills5.htm*).

At the same time, the Web has made it easier to catch plagiarists. A growing number of educators routinely use Web-based services for detecting uno-riginal work. Turnitin.com offers a simple method that allows teachers and students to submit papers to electronic scrutiny. The service compares the paper against a database of previous submissions and papers offered by term-paper mills. Turnitin.com then sends a report with the results to the teacher.

Sources: Compiled from plagiarism.org (accessed November 5, 2003); turnitin.com (accessed November 5, 2003).

QUESTIONS

1. Do you support the use of antiplagiarism technology to catch cases of cheating at school?
2. Are there other methods for catching plagiarism? What would they be?

Other Discovery Aids

There are numerous search engines and discovery aids available. Table 4.1 shows some examples of useful ones.

Toolbars

To get the most out of search engines, you may use add-on toolbars and special software. Some are attached to the popular search engines, others are independent. Most are free. Examples are: Google Toolbar (*toolbar.google.com*), Copernic Agent Basic (*copernic.com*), KartOO (*kartoo.com*), Yahoo Companion (*companion.yahoo.com*), and Grokker (*groxis.com*).

Table 4.1   Useful Search Engines and Discovery Aids

Site	Description
Webopedia.com	Directory of technology-related terms, arranged alphabetically; provides relevant Internet resources with links and key word search.
Whatis.com	Tool that provides information about IT, especially about the Internet and computers, as well as hyperlinked cross-references between definitions/topics and to other sites for further information.
eBizSearch	This engine searches the Web as well as (*gunther.smeal.psu.edu*) academic and commercial articles for various aspects of e-business.
Elibrary	This site (*ask.elibrary.com*) searches for books, articles, maps, pictures, and so on that you can have for a seven-day free trial. After that, you must pay for the files. Abstracts are free.
Howstuffworks.com	This entertaining site combines a search engine and a menu system; here, you can learn about thousands of products, things, concepts, etc.
Findarticles.com	This search engine specializes in finding articles, usually from trade magazines, on topics of your choice. Like library search engines, it is limited to certain magazines.

Discovery of Material in Foreign Languages

There is a huge amount of information on the Internet in languages that you may not know. What one needs to access this information is *automatic translation* of Web pages. Such translation is available, to and from all major languages, and its quality is improving with time.

Automatic translation of Web pages is an application offered by many vendors. Because the quality of automatic translation has not always been as good as human translation, many experts advocate use of the computer as a productivity booster, with human translation as a double-check.

Some major translation products are: Babel Fish Translation (*world.altavista.com*), *AutoTranslate* (offered in Netscape browser), "BETA" (*google.com/language_tools?hl=en*), and products and services available at *trados.com* and *translationzone.com*.

Portals

With the growing use of intranets and the Internet, many organizations encounter information overload. Information is scattered across numerous documents, e-mail messages, and databases at different locations and systems. Finding relevant and accurate information is often time-consuming and may require access to multiple systems.

One solution to this problem is to use portals. We discussed corporate portals in Chapter 2, and here we broaden the concept of portals to include other types. More broadly, a **portal** is a Web-based personalized gateway to information and knowledge that provides relevant information from disparate IT systems and the Internet using advanced search and indexing techniques. One way to differentiate portals is to look at their content, which can vary from narrow to broad, and their community or audience, which can also vary. We distinguish among seven types of portals below.

> **portal** *A Web-based personalized gateway to information and knowledge that provides information from disparate IT systems and the Internet, using advanced search and indexing techniques.*

1. **Commercial (public) portals** offer content for diverse communities and are the most popular portals on the Internet. Although they offer customization of the user interface, they are still intended for broad audiences and offer fairly routine content, some in real time (e.g., a stock ticker and news on a few preselected items). Examples are *yahoo.com*, *lycos.com*, and *msn.com*.

> **commercial (public) portal** *Web site that offers fairly routine content for diverse audiences; offers customization only at the user interface.*

2. **Publishing portals** are intended for communities with specific interests. These portals involve relatively little customization of content, but they provide extensive online search and some interactive capabilities. Examples are *techweb.com* and *zdnet.com*.

> **publishing portal** *Web site intended for communities with specific interests; offers little customization of content, but provides extensive online search and some interactive capabilities.*

3. **Personal portals** target specific filtered information for individuals. They offer relatively narrow content but are typically much more personalized, effectively having an audience of one.

> **personal portal** *Web site that targets specific filtered information for individuals; offers narrow content but is typically personalized for an audience of one.*

4. **Affinity portals** support communities such as hobby groups or a political party (Tedeschi, 2000). They offer a single point of entry to an entire community of affiliated interests.

> **affinity portal** *Web site that offers a single point of entry to an entire community of affiliated interests.*

5. **Mobile portals** are portals accessible from mobile devices. Although most of the other portals mentioned here are PC-based, increasing numbers of portals are accessible via mobile devices. One example is i-mode from DoCoMo in Japan.

> **mobile portal** *Web site that is accessible from mobile devices.*

6. **Voice portals** are Web portals with audio interfaces, which enables them to be accessed by a standard or cell phone. Companies such as tellme.com and i3mobile.com offer the software for such services. Voice portals use both speech recognition and text-to-speech technologies.

> **voice portal** *Web site with audio interface, enabling access by a standard or cell phone; uses both speech recognition and text-to-speech technologies.*

7. **Corporate portals** coordinate rich content within relatively narrow corporate and partners' communities. A corporate portal is a personalized, single point of access through a Web browser to critical business information located inside and outside of an organization. It is also known as an *enterprise portal*, *information portal*, or *enterprise information portal*.

> **corporate portal** *Web site that provides a single point of access to critical business information located inside and outside of an organization.*

Many large organizations have already implemented corporate portals to cut costs, free up time for busy executives and managers, and improve profitability. In addition,

IT'S ABOUT BUSINESS POM

4.4: Kaiser Permanente Uses Google to Build a Portal

Kaiser Permanente (*kaiserpermanente.org*), America's largest not-for-profit health maintenance organization (HMO), has almost nine million members. The amount of available medical knowledge doubles about every seven years, so keeping up with new knowledge is an important aspect of good caregiving. When Kaiser Permanente developed a clinical-knowledge corporate portal for its 50,000 doctors, nurses, and other caregivers, search was a key part of the plan. The Permanente Knowledge Connection, available from anywhere in the Kaiser wide-area network, gives medical staff access to diagnostic information, best practices, publications, educational material, and other clinical resources. The portal's resources are distributed across the entire United States. Putting the right information quickly and easily into caregivers' hands is essential to the clinical portal's success.

Kaiser turned to the Google Search Appliance, which enabled the HMO to index 150,000 documents distributed across the Kaiser network. Clinicians now search the site in situations that run the gamut from leisurely research to urgent care, from the exam room to the emergency room. Doctors and nurses use the Appliance to help them reach diagnoses and specify treatments, check the side effects of new medications, and consult clinical research studies and other medical publications. Google's spell checking is especially useful in the medical profession: Doctor's handwriting can be problematic, and pharmaceutical product names are difficult.

*Source: Compiled from *services.google.com/marketing/ links/banner_gsa03_eweek/casestudies* (last accessed November 6, 2003).*

QUESTIONS

1. Why did Kaiser Permanente need Google's Search Appliance?

2. What benefits did Kaiser Permanente gain from implementing Google's Search Appliance?

---

corporate portals offer customers and employees self-service opportunities (see, for example, CRM in Chapter 8). Top portal applications include providing knowledge bases and learning tools; business process support; and customer-facing sales, marketing, and support. Additional examples of corporate portals are presented in Online File W4.3 on the book's Web site. Also, Online Minicase W4.1 illustrates a business intelligence portal at the Amway Corporation.

IT's about Business 4.4 shows how Kaiser Permanente used Google's Search Appliance to build a corporate portal.

Industrywide Communication Networks (Portals). In addition to single-company portals, there are also portals for entire industries. An example is *chaindrugstore.net*, which links retailers and product manufacturers and provides product and industry news and recall and promotional information. The site has an offshoot for independent pharmacies (called *CommunityDrugStore.net*). The service reaches more than 130 retailers representing 32,000 stores. The service is free to the retailers; suppliers pay annual fees in exchange for being able to use the portal to communicate information to retailers (e.g., to advertise special deals, to notify retailers about price changes). The portal also provides industry news, and it can be personalized for individual retailers. The site has "Call Me" and "Send Me" buttons, so retailers can click and receive product information in seconds.

Figure 4.3 depicts a corporate portal framework that illustrates the features and capabilities required to support various organizational activities using internal and external information sources.

wiley.com/college/turban

Before you go on . . .

1. What are the major tools for discovery?

2. Describe the various kinds of portals.

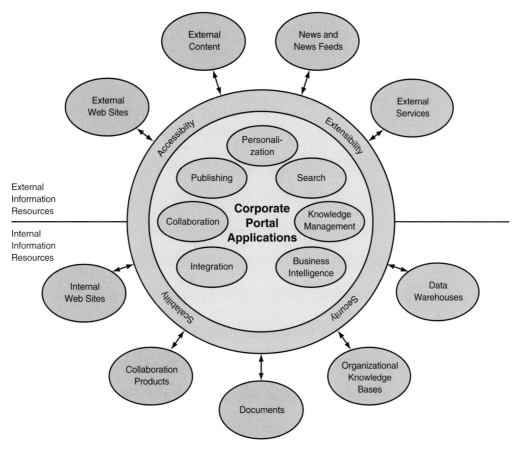

Figure 4.3   *A corporate portal framework. (Sources: Compiled from A. Aneja et al., "Corporate Portal Framework for Transforming Content Chaos on Intranets,"* Intel Technology Journal, *Q1, 2000, and from T. Kounandis, "How to Pick the Best Portal,"* e-Business Advisor, *August 2000.)*

4.3 COMMUNICATION

A wide variety of technologies support communications, and it is useful to classify these technologies as we study them. *Place* and *time* can be used to create a framework for classifying IT communication and collaboration support technologies. Considering place, sender(s) and receiver(s) can be in the same room, in different rooms at the same location, or at different locations. Considering time, messages can be sent at a certain time and received some time later, as occurs with e-mail and electronic bulletin boards. Such communications are termed **asynchronous**. On the other hand, messages can be sent at a certain time and received almost simultaneously. Such **synchronous (real-time)** communication is provided by telephones, instant messaging online, teleconferencing, and face-to-face meetings.

According to this time/place framework, IT communication is divided into four cells, as shown in Figure 4.4 (page 110), with a representative technology in each cell. The time/place cells are as follows:

1. ***Same-time/same-place.*** In this setting, participants meet face-to-face in one place and at the same time. An example is communication in a meeting room, which can be electronically supported by group systems (see *groupsystems.com* and Chapter 10). "Same time" is also known as "real time," and the tools to support it are known as *real-time collaboration* (RTC) tools (see section 4.5).

2. ***Same-time/different-place.*** This setting refers to a meeting whose participants are in different places but communicate at the same time. A telephone conference call, desktop videoconferencing, chat rooms, and instant messaging are examples of such situations.

asynchronous communication *Communication in which a message sent at a certain time is received some time later (e.g., e-mail).*

synchronous (real-time) communication *Communication in which a message is sent at a certain time and received almost simultaneously (e.g., telephone, instant messaging online).*

PLACE

		Same	Different
TIME	**Same**	A decision room GDSS (see Chapter 10) Management cockpit (see Chapter 10) Whiteboard RTC tools	RTC tools Videoconferencing Instant messenger Screen sharing Whiteboard Chat room Internet telephony
	Different	Multishift control center E-mail Workflow	E-mail Bulletin board Web-based call center Workflow GDSS Autoresponder (Chapter 7)

Figure 4.4 *A framework for IT communication support. (Source: G. DeSanctis and B. Gallupe, "A Foundation for the Study of Group Decision Support Systems,"* Management Science, *vol. 33, no. 5, 1987.)*

3. **Different-time/same-place.** This setting can materialize when people work in shifts. The first shift leaves electronic or voice messages for the second shift.

4. **Different-time/different-place.** Participants are in different places, and they send and/or receive messages (for example, via the Internet) at different times.

The Internet has become a major supporter of interactive communications. People are using a variety of Internet technologies—Internet phones, smart cell phones, Internet videoconferencing, Internet radio, whiteboards, chat rooms, and more—for communication. In Section 4.5 we will discuss some of the IT tools cited in connection with Figure 4.4. In this section, we will discuss four types of communications technologies.

Web-Based Call Centers

Effective personalized customer contact is becoming an important aspect of customer support through the Web. Such service is provided through *Web-based call centers* (also known as *customer care centers*). There are at least four categories of capabilities employed by Web-based call centers—e-mail, interactive text chat, callbacks, and simultaneous voice and Web sessions. For example, if you need to contact a software vendor for technical support, you will usually be communicating with the vendor's Web-based call center. If you have a simple problem, you may use e-mail or a telephone conversation (callback). A more difficult problem might require an interactive text chat or a simultaneous voice/Web session. Web-based call centers may be located in countries such as India. Such *outsourcing* has lately become an issue for U.S. companies. Nevertheless, enabling Web collaboration and simultaneous voice/Web contact can differentiate a company from its competitors. WebsiteAlive (*websitealive.com*), a Web-based call center support product, delivers live customer-service capabilities for any online company.

Electronic Chat Rooms

chat room *A virtual meeting place where groups of regulars come to "gab" electronically.*

Electronic chat refers to an arrangement whereby participants exchange conversational messages in real time. A **chat room** is a virtual meeting place where groups of regulars come to "gab." Chat programs allow you to send messages to people who are connected to the same channel of communication *at the same time.* Anyone can join in the online conversation. Messages are displayed on your screen as they arrive, even if you are in the middle of typing a message.

Chat rooms can be used to promote a commercial, political, or environmental cause, to support people with medical problems, or to let hobbyists share their interest. And since many customer–supplier relationships have to be sustained without face-to-face meetings, online communities are increasingly being used to serve business interests, including advertising (see *Parachat.com* and Technology Guide 5).

Two major types of chat programs exist: (a) Web-based chat programs, which allow you to send messages to Internet users using a Web browser and visiting a Web chat site (e.g., *chat.yahoo.com*), and (b) an e-mail-based (text only) program called *Internet Relay Chat (IRC)*. A business can use IRC to interact with customers, provide online experts' answers to questions, and so on.

Voice Communication

The most natural mode of communication is voice. When people need to communicate with each other from a distance, they use the telephone more frequently than any other communication device. Voice communication can now be done via the Internet using a microphone and a sound card (see *protocols.com*). You can also talk long distance on the Internet without paying the normal long-distance telephone charges. This is known as **Internet telephony (voice-over IP)**, and it is further described in Technology Guide 5. Voice communication enables workers, from forklift drivers to disabled employees to military pilots, to have portable, safe, and effective access to computer technology from their work areas. In addition, voice communication is faster than typing (about two and half times faster), and fewer errors in voice data entry are made compared to keyboard data entry. To connect from computers to regular telephones, try, for example, *dialpad.com*, which offers low-cost long-distance calls through the Internet to regular telephones in U.S. cities from anywhere in the world.

Internet telephony (voice-over IP) *The use of the Internet as the transmission medium for telephone calls.*

Weblogging (Blogging)

Blogs and blogging provide individuals with a way to do personal publishing. A **Weblog** (**blog** for short) is a personal Web site, open to the public, in which the site creator expresses his or her feelings or opinions. Bloggers (people who create and maintain blogs) write stories, tell news, and provide links to other articles and Web sites that are of interest to them.

To start blogging, the simplest method is to sign up with a blogging service provider, such as Blogger (*blogger.com*) or *pitas.com*. The free version of Blogger has only the basic features, such as text posting; the Pro version includes features such as spell checking, image posting, and e-mail submission. Another blogging service provider is LiveJournal (*livejournal.com*). Eventually you may need blogging software. Moveable Type (*moveabletype.org*) is a popular blogging tool. PHP-Nuke (*phpnuke.com*) is a full-fledged miniportal system that many experienced bloggers use, as it offers more features than typical blogs. With this service, bloggers are handed a fresh space on their Web site to write in each day. They can easily edit, add entries, and broadcast whatever they want by simply clicking on the send key.

Bloggers are creating their own rich terminology. For a blogger's dictionary, see *marketingterms.com/dictionary/blog* and *samizdata.net/blog/glossary.html*.

Many people find blogging an interesting activity that creates a sense of community and can result in two-way communication and collaboration. However, blogging can lead to trouble, as the following example shows.

Weblog (blog) *A personal Web site, open to the public, in which the site owner expresses his or her feelings or opinions.*

> **EXAMPLE** *Warning! Blogging Can Cause Discomfort.* Mr. Smith, a marketing consultant, keeps a Web log. After receiving some teasing from a friend who told him that blogging was a waste of time, he wrote in his blog that the friend "was fat and runs like a girl," adding that he was sure the friend would not be offended "because he doesn't read blogs." With the push of a button, the comment was published on Mr. Smith's site. A few days later, though, his friend became curious about blogs. He quickly found Mr. Smith's site and was "deeply aggrieved," according to Mr. Smith. Their friendship barely survived the episode.
>
> The proliferation of blogs has affected the social fabric among younger people. "It's like all your friends are reporters now," said one man, a blogger himself. Blogs can cause problems such as hurt feelings, newly wary friends and relatives, and the occasional inflamed employer. (*Source:* Compiled from W. St. John, "Dating a Blogger, Reading All About It." *New York Times*, May 18, 2003.)

4.4 COLLABORATION

collaboration *Mutual efforts by two or more individuals who perform activities in order to accomplish certain tasks.*

One of the abiding features of a modern organization is that people collaborate to perform work. **Collaboration** refers to mutual efforts by two or more individuals who perform activities in order to accomplish certain tasks. The individuals may represent themselves or organizations, or they may be members of a team or a group. Also, people work with customers, suppliers, and other business partners in an effort to improve productivity and competitiveness. Finally, group members participate in decision making. In all of the above cases they need to collaborate. Collaboration can be supported electronically by several technologies described later in this chapter.

workgroup *Two or more individuals who act together to perform some task, on either a permanent or temporary basis.*

virtual group (team) *A workgroup whose members are in different locations and who "meet" electronically.*

The term **work group** refers to two or more individuals who act together to perform some task. The group can be permanent or temporary. It can be in one location (face-to-face meetings) or in several. If group members are in different locations, we say we have a **virtual group (team)**, and they conduct *virtual meetings* (they "meet" electronically). Members can meet concurrently or at different times.

An interesting variation on collaboration is a *flash mob*—an organized, often big, sometimes loud, frequently fun, and peculiar gathering. It is a sudden grouping of people who carry out some generally odd ritual in unison and then, just as suddenly as they appeared, disperse. The happenings organize via sites like *FlockSmart.com* through which participants receive e-mail giving the locations and times. The movement has grown into a worldwide phenomenon with events in Berlin, London, and beyond.

Flash mobs are a cousin of *smart mobs*, which are coordinated groups of people using technology such as mobile phones and the Internet to organize and then act simultaneously. For example, the demonstrations at the World Trade Organization meetings in 1999 were carried out by smart mobs relying on this type of high-tech coordination. Flash mobs, however, seem more inclined to fun than to social change or disruption.

Virtual Collaboration

virtual collaboration *The use of digital technologies that enable organizations or individuals to collaboratively plan, design, develop, manage, and research products, services, and innovative IT and EC applications.*

collaborative commerce *Collaboration among business partners.*

Virtual collaboration (or *e-collaboration*) refers to the use of digital technologies that enable organizations or individuals to collaboratively plan, design, develop, manage, and research products, services, and innovative IT and EC applications. E-collaboration enables **collaborative commerce**—collaboration among business partners. Collaborative commerce implies communication, information sharing, and collaborative planning done electronically through tools such as groupware and specially designed EC collaboration tools. Major benefits of virtual collaboration and collaborative commerce cited are cost reduction, increased revenue, and improved customer retention.

There are several other varieties of virtual collaboration, ranging from joint design efforts to forecasting. Collaboration can be done both between and within organizations. The following are some types and examples of virtual collaboration.

Collaborative Networks. Traditionally, collaboration took place among supply chain members, frequently those that were close to each other (e.g., a manufacturer and its distributor, or a distributor and a retailer). Even if more partners are involved, the focus has been on the optimization of information and product flow between existing nodes in the traditional supply chain.

The traditional collaboration resulted in a vertically integrated supply chain. However, as discussed in earlier chapters, IT and Web technologies can *fundamentally change* the shape of the supply chain, as well as the number of players within it and their individual roles and collaboration patterns. The new supply chain can be a hub, or even a network. A comparison between the traditional supply chain collaboration and the collaborative network is shown in Figure 4.5. Notice that the traditional chain (part a, for the food industry) is basically linear. The collaborative network (part b) shows that partners at any point in the network can interact with each other, bypassing traditional partners. Interaction may occur among several manufacturers and/or distributors, as well as with new players such as software agents that act as aggregators,

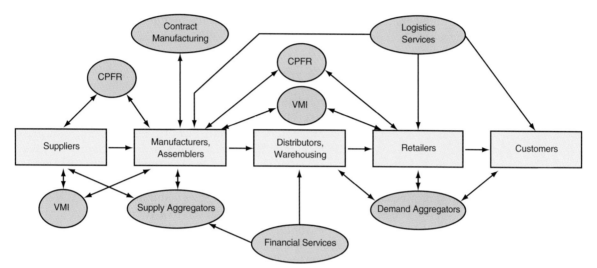

Part **(a)** Traditional collaboration. CPFR is collaborative planning, forecasting, and replenishment. VMI is vendor-managed inventory.

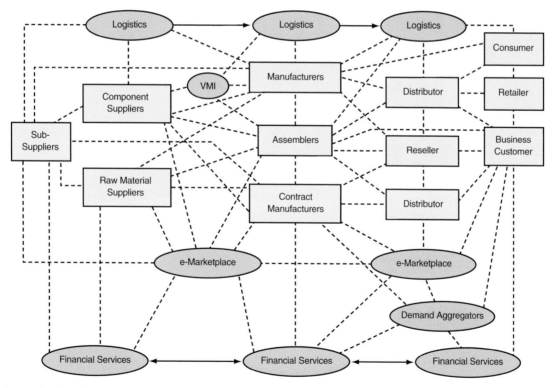

Part **(b)** Supply chains are evolving into collaborative networks.\

Figure 4.5   *Comparing traditional supply chain collaboration and collaborative networks. (Sources: Part (a): Based on B. Walton and M. Princi, "From Supply Chain to Collaborative Network," white paper, Gordon Andersen Consulting 2000 (see Walton.ASCET.com). Part (b): Based on C. C. Poirier, "Collaborative Commerce: Wave Two of the Cyber Revolutions,"* Computer Science Corporation Perspectives, *2001).*

wiley.com/college/turban

B2B e-marketplaces, or logistics providers. For additional explanation of Figure 4.5, see Online File W4.4.

Representative Examples of Virtual Collaboration.   Leading businesses are moving quickly to realize the benefits of e-collaboration. For example, the real estate franchiser RE/MAX uses an e-collaboration platform to improve communications and collaboration among its nationwide network of independently owned real estate franchises, sales associates, and suppliers. Similarly, Marriott International, the world's largest hospitality company, started with an online brochure and then developed a c-commerce system that links corporations, franchisees, partners, and suppliers, as well as customers, around the world. There are many examples of e-collaboration. Here we present some additional representative ones.

POM

> **EXAMPLE**   *Information Sharing between Retailers and Their Suppliers.* One of the most notable examples of information sharing is between Procter & Gamble (P&G) and Wal-Mart. Wal-Mart provides P&G access to sales information on every item Wal-Mart buys from P&G. The information is collected by P&G on a daily basis from every Wal-Mart store, and P&G uses the information to manage the inventory replenishment for Wal-Mart. By monitoring the inventory level of each P&G item in every Wal-Mart store, P&G knows when the inventories fall below the threshold that triggers a shipment. All this is done electronically. The benefit for P&G is that they can sell to a good customer, and the benefit to Wal-Mart is adequate inventory of its shelves. P&G has similar agreements with other major retailers. (*Source: pg.com*, accessed November 11, 2003, and *wal-mart.com,* accessed November 12, 2003.)

POM

> **EXAMPLE**   *Reduction of Product Development Time.* Caterpillar, Inc. (*caterpillar.com*) is a multinational heavy-machinery manufacturer. In the traditional mode of operation, cycle time along the supply chain was long because the process involved paper document transfers among managers, salespeople, and technical staff. To solve the problem, Caterpillar connected its engineering and manufacturing divisions with its active suppliers, distributors, overseas factories, and customers through an extranet-based global collaboration system. By means of the collaboration system, a request for a customized tractor component, for example, can be transmitted from a customer to a Caterpillar dealer and on to designers and suppliers, all in a very short time. Customers also can use the extranet to retrieve and modify detailed order information while the vehicle is still on the assembly line. Remote collaboration capabilities between the customer and product developers have decreased cycle time delays caused by rework time. Suppliers are also connected to the system, so they can deliver materials or parts directly to Caterpillar's repair shops or directly to the customer if appropriate. The system also is used for expediting maintenance and repairs. (*Source: caterpillar.com*, accessed November 5, 2003.)

The previous examples demonstrated corporate collaboration. In IT's about Business 4.5, we show how "darknets" enable individual collaboration as well as corporate collaboration.

Before you go on . . .

1. What is a virtual team?
2. What is virtual collaboration?

IT's ABOUT BUSINESS

POM

4.5: The Underground Internet

Darknets are "gated communities" or mininetworks that run on the Internet but are open only to those who belong to the private network. Darknets usually include 50 to 100 people because of technology limitations or security concerns.

Typically, people who want to build a darknet will start by installing specialized software on their computers, which they can buy or often download for free from the Internet. Then these individuals swap passwords or digital keys so their computers can communicate with each other. The data flowing between computers often are encrypted, a security feature similar to that used for online credit card transactions. This makes darknets more secure than typical corporate intranets, because companies usually do not encrypt data located inside corporate firewalls.

There are three major uses for darknets:

FREEDOM OF SPEECH. Independent developers are giving away Freenet (*freenet.sourceforge.net*) and invisibleNET (*invisiblenet.net*), software that allows dissidents in countries where censorship exists to get information from the outside world and to speak more freely among themselves. Freenet-China (*freenet-china.org*), a Mandarin-translation Web site, publishes news that the Chinese government would censor and allows dissidents to read banned sites, such as *CNN.com*. Freenet works by organizing a "bucket brigade" of computers that dedicate a portion of their hard drives to encrypted data and talk only to their nearest neighbor on the network. When a request for some information is made, each computer queries its neighbor to determine if it has the information. If not, the request is passed to another neighbor that the first computer does not know about.

CORPORATE SECURITY. File sharing software lets corporations create closed networks over the public Internet. GlaxoSmithKline is using a darknet so that chemists, biologists, and other scientists in-house and at some universities can share information for the development of an obesity drug. Hewlett-Packard and Siemens are using darknets to allow them to share sensitive data with outside partners while protecting the data from rivals.

COPYRIGHT INFRINGEMENT. Free peer-to-peer software can be used to bring together vetted, closed groups, often of no more than 50 people, who share music, movies, and software. One such product, named Waste, designed by America Online's Nullsoft division, caught on among pirated-music dealers. Although AOL quickly yanked the software off Nullsoft's site, programmers with copies downloaded from the Web are busily enhancing it.

BadBlue (*badblue.com*) and Groove Networks (*groove.net*) sell collaboration software that permits a company to safely share sensitive documents or financial information among partners. Since the Recording Industry Association of America (RIAA) started targeting individuals who are sharing music files, monthly revenues of BadBlue's software have increased by 50 percent.

Source: Compiled from H. Green, "The Underground Internet," *BusinessWeek*, September 15, 2003.

QUESTIONS

1. Do you feel that darknets should be regulated? What is the relationship between darknets and freedom of speech?
2. How do you think the music and motion picture industries feel about darknets?

4.5 COLLABORATION-ENABLING TOOLS: FROM WORKFLOW TO GROUPWARE

As mentioned earlier, corporate portals facilitate e-collaboration. Also available for this purpose are a large number of tools and methodologies. In this section we present workflow technologies, groupware, and other collaboration-enabling tools.

Workflow Technologies

Workflow is the movement of information as it flows through the sequence of steps that make up an organization's work procedures. **Workflow management** is the automation of workflows, so that documents, information, or tasks are passed from one participant to another in a way that is governed by the organization's rules or procedures. Workflow

workflow *The movement of information as it flows through the sequence of steps that make up an organization's work procedures.*

workflow management *The automation of workflows, so that documents, information, or tasks are passed from one participant to another through all of the steps in a business process.*

IT'S ABOUT BUSINESS

FIN

4.6: German Bank Uses Workflow System to Manage Currency Flows

Dresdner Bank (*dresdner-bank.com*), in Germany, has automated the way it handles the trading of currency orders. Whether they originate from within a single operation or across its trading rooms worldwide, the bank routes these orders using a workflow system called the Limit Order Application (LORA). This workflow system, built with Microsoft Exchange, replaced previous telephone and fax-based processes.

One of the main problems that Dresdner Bank sought to solve with the system was the allocation and uptake of orders between different trading rooms around the world. Being able to route orders would allow more efficient trading across different time zones—for instance, making it easier for traders to execute a Frankfurt order in New York after close of business in Germany.

Three types of bank staff personnel—traders, controllers, and administrators—use this system, which works as follows: When an order is received, it is placed into an electronic folder by the controller. All order folders are held in a "public" file and can be viewed by the relevant staff. Next, when a trader accepts an order, he or she is responsible for that order from that moment on. Although the order can still be canceled or reversed at this stage, the details of price and order quantity cannot be changed. The status of the order is displayed, and any order is locked when accessed, to prevent anyone from altering it. (Even small changes in the details of an order could result in huge profits or losses for the bank or its clients.) Fi-

nally, when the order is executed, or if it is canceled or reversed or it expires, then it is sent to a subfolder to be archived.

The bank dropped an initial plan to implement global common folders that could be accessed by any of its 1,000 traders in any location. It did so because of resistance from the traders, who did not like the idea of relinquishing local control and allowing other traders to process or execute their orders. Instead, the bank has implemented a system of local folders that reside within the branch of origin; these can be read by, but cannot be processed by, traders elsewhere.

With LORA, users can respond more quickly and accurately to customer queries, because they are able to access and view on the computer screen the precise status of orders. There is also improved control, with responsibility for any order always assigned to a specific staff member. The user interface was carefully designed to meet stringent requirements with respect to efficiency and ease of use.

Sources: Compiled from *microsoft.com/resources/ casestudies/CaseStudy.asp?CaseStudyID=13324* (accessed October 31, 2003) and from *dresdner-bank.com* (accessed November 8, 2003).

QUESTIONS

1. Identify the parties in the bank that need to collaborate with each other.
2. How does LORA facilitate collaboration?

---

workflow systems *Business process automation tools that place system controls in the hands of user departments.*

management involves all of the steps in a business process from start to finish, including all exception conditions. **Workflow systems** are business process automation tools that place system controls in the hands of user departments. They employ a set of software programs that automate almost any information-processing task.

The major workflow activities to be managed are job routing and monitoring, document imaging, document management, supply chain optimization, and control of work. These activities are done by workflow applications. IT's about Business 4.6 shows how the Dresdner Bank uses a workflow application. Since workflow management systems support more than one individual, they are considered by some to be a subset of groupware, our next topic.

Groupware

groupware *Software products that support groups of people who collaborate on a common task or goal and that provide a way for groups to share resources.*

Groupware refers to software products that support groups of people who share a common task or goal and who collaborate on its accomplishment. These products provide a way for groups to share resources and opinions. Groupware implies the use of networks to connect people, even if the people are in the same room. Many groupware products are available on the Internet or an intranet, enhancing the collaboration of a large number of people worldwide. There are many different approaches and technologies for the support of groups on the Internet. In this section we will describe some of the most common groupware products.

Electronic Meeting Systems.   An important area of virtual collaboration is electronic meetings. There have been numerous attempts to improve meetings by using information technologies. Web-based systems provide some of the best IT support for electronic **virtual meetings**, those whose members are in different locations, often in different countries.

virtual meetings *Meetings whose members are in different locations, often in different countries.*

Electronic Teleconferencing.   **Teleconferencing** is the use of electronic communication that allows two or more people at different locations to have a simultaneous conference. There are several types of teleconferencing. The oldest and simplest is a telephone conference call, where several people talk to each other from multiple locations. The biggest disadvantage is that it does not allow for face-to-face communication. Also, participants in one location cannot see graphs, charts, and pictures at other locations. One solution is *video teleconferencing*, in which participants can see each other as well as the documents.

teleconferencing *The use of electronic communication that allows two or more people at different locations to have a simultaneous conference.*

Video Teleconferencing.   In a **video teleconference** (or *videoconference*), participants in one location can see participants at other locations. With videoconferencing, participants can share data, voice, pictures, graphics, and animation by electronic means. Data can also be sent along with voice and video. Such **data conferencing** makes it possible to work on documents together and to exchange computer files during videoconferences. This allows geographically dispersed groups to work on the same project and to communicate by video simultaneously.

Videoconferencing offers various benefits. We have already mentioned two of them—providing the opportunity for face-to-face communication for individuals in different locations, and supporting several types of media during conferencing, including voice and radio.

Participating in a desktop videoconference.

video teleconference *Virtual meeting in which participants in one location can see and hear participants at other locations and can share data and graphics by electronic means.*

Web Conferencing.   **Web conferencing** is conducted on the Internet for as few as two and as many as thousands of people. Web conferencing is done *solely* on the Web. (Videoconferencing is usually done on regular telephone lines, although it may also be done on the Web.) However, Web conferencing is much cheaper than videoconferencing because it runs on the Internet.

The latest technological innovations permit both business-to-business and business-to-consumer applications of Web conferencing. For example, banks in Alaska use *video kiosks* in sparsely populated areas instead of building branches that will be underutilized. The video kiosks operate on the banks' intranet and provide videoconferencing equipment for eye-to-eye interactions. Some examples of other uses are to educate staff members about a new product line or technology, to amplify a meeting with investors, or to walk a prospective client though an introductory presentation.

data conferencing *Virtual meeting in which data, graphics, and computer files are sent electronically; allows geographically dispersed groups to work on the same project and to communicate simultaneously.*

Web conferencing *Video teleconferencing that is conducted solely on the Internet (not on telephone lines).*

Real-Time Collaboration Tools.   The Internet, intranets, and extranets offer tremendous potential for real-time and synchronous interaction of people working in groups. *Real-time collaboration (RTC)* tools help companies bridge time and space to make decisions and to collaborate on projects. RTC tools support synchronous communication of graphical and text-based information. These tools are being used in distance training, product demonstrations, customer support, and sales applications. Some examples of RTC tools follow.

Interactive Whiteboards.   Computer-based **whiteboards** work like "physical world" whiteboards with markers and erasers, with one difference: Instead of one person standing in front of a meeting room drawing on the whiteboard, all participants can join in. Throughout a meeting, each user can view and draw on a single document "pasted" onto the electronic whiteboard on a computer screen. Digital whiteboarding

whiteboard (electronic) *An area on a computer display screen on which multiple users can write or draw; multiple users can use a single document "pasted" onto the screen.*

sessions can also be saved for later reference or other use. Some whiteboarding products let users insert graphics files that can be annotated by the group.

Screen Sharing. In collaborative work, members are frequently in different locations. Using screen sharing software, group members can work on the same document, which is shown on the PC screen of each participant. This capability can expedite the design of products, the preparation of reports and bids, and the resolution of conflicts. A special screen sharing capability is offered by Groove Inc. (*groove.net*). Its product synchronizes people, computers, and information to enable the joint creation and/or editing of documents on your PC.

screen sharing software *Software that enables group members to work on the same document, which is shown on the PC screen of each participant.*

Groupware Suites. Groupware technologies are often integrated with other computer-based technologies to create *groupware suites*. (A *software suite* is created when several products are integrated into one system.) Integrating several technologies can save time and money for users. For example, PictureTel Corporation, in an alliance with software developer Lotus, developed an integrated desktop video teleconferencing product that uses Lotus Notes. (Polycom Inc., polycom.com, later acquired PictureTel.) Using this integrated system, publisher Reader's Digest has built several applications combined with videoconferencing capabilities. Lotus Notes/ Domino is one of the most popular groupware suites.

Lotus Notes/Domino. The *Lotus Notes/Domino* suite (*lotus.com*) provides online collaboration capabilities, workgroup e-mail, distributed databases, bulletin whiteboards, text editing, (electronic) document management, workflow capabilities, instant virtual meetings, application sharing, instant messaging, consensus building, voting, ranking, and various application development tools. All these capabilities are integrated into one environment with a graphic menu-based user interface.

Thanks to electronic networks, e-mail, and the ability to exchange or update data at any time and from any place, group members using Lotus Notes/Domino might store all their official memos, formal reports, and informal conversations related to particular projects in a shared, online database. Then, as individual members need to check on the contents, they can access the shared database to find the information they need.

Online Minicase W4.2 illustrates how the U.S. Marine Corps uses Lotus Notes/ Domino. In addition, other groupware suites are discussed in Online File W4.4 on the Web site.

wiley.com/college/turban

wiley.com/college/turban

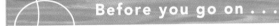

Before you go on . . .

1. What is groupware?
2. What is real-time collaboration, and what technologies support it?

4.6 E-LEARNING, DISTANCE LEARNING, AND TELECOMMUTING

Web-based systems enable many applications related to discovery, communication, and collaboration. Several important applications are presented in this section— e-learning, distance learning, and telecommuting.

E-Learning versus Distance Learning

e-learning *Learning supported by the Web; can be done inside traditional classrooms or in virtual classrooms.*

There can be some confusion between e-learning and distance learning since they overlap each other. Therefore we begin with brief definitions.

E-learning refers to learning supported by the Web. It can be done inside classrooms as a support to conventional teaching, such as when students work on the Web at home or in the classroom. It also can be done in *virtual classrooms*, in which all coursework is done online and classes do not meet face-to-face. Then it is a part of distance learning.

Distance learning (DL) refers to learning situations in which teachers and students do not meet face-to-face. It can be done in different ways. The oldest mode was correspondence, where all communication was done by mail. As early as the 1920s the radio was added to support DL. Then came voice cassettes, videotapes, and TV for delivering lectures. Students communicated with the professor by "snail mail," telephone, and faxes. A breakthrough occurred when the CD-ROM was introduced, because CD-ROMs are media rich and enable self-testing and feedback. Today, the Web provides a multimedia interactive environment for self-study.

In both cases, Web-enabled systems make knowledge accessible to those who need it, when they need it, any time, anywhere. E-learning and DL can be useful both as an environment for facilitating learning at schools and as an environment for efficient and effective corporate training. See Online Minicase W4.3 of e-learning at Cisco Systems.

distance learning (DL) *Learning situations in which teachers and students do not meet face-to-face.*

wiley.com/college/turban

The Benefits of E-Learning

In theory, there are many benefits to e-learning. Self-paced and self-initiated learning has been shown to increase content retention (Urdan and Weggen, 2000). Online materials offer the opportunity to deliver very current content, of high quality (created by content experts) and consistent (presented the same way every time). Students in e-learning situations have the flexibility of learning from any place, at any time, and at their own pace. In corporate training centers that use e-learning, learning time generally is shorter, and more people can be trained due to the faster training time. As a result, training costs can be reduced, and savings can be made on facility space as well.

Some drawbacks do exist that may offset the benefits of e-learning: Instructors may need training to be able to teach electronically, and the purchase of additional multimedia equipment may be necessary. Students must be computer literate and may miss the face-to-face interaction with instructors. Also, there are issues with assessing students' work, as instructors really do not know who completed assignments.

E-learning does not usually replace the classroom setting, but enhances it, taking advantage of new content and delivery technologies. Advanced e-learning support environments, such as Blackboard (*blackboard.com*) and WebCT (*webct.com*), add value to traditional learning in higher education.

Blackboard and WebCT, which are competing products, provide the Internet infrastructure software for e-learning in schools. The publisher places a book's content, teaching notes, quizzes, and so forth on Blackboard or WebCT in a standardized format. Instructors can access modules and transfer them into their own specific Blackboard or WebCT sites, which can by accessed by their students.

The competing products have slightly different visions and strategies: Blackboard offers a complete suite of enterprise software products and services that power a total "e-education infrastructure" for schools, colleges, universities, and other education providers. Of special interest are the discussion rooms that can be for everyone or for a restricted group. WebCT provides a similar set of tools, but it uses advanced pedagogical tools to help institutions of higher education make distance-learning courses possible. Such courses enable schools to expand campus boundaries, attract and retain students and faculty, and continually improve course and degree program quality.

Textbook publishers are embracing these tools by making their major textbooks Blackboard and/or WebCT enabled. Thus, your professor can easily incorporate this book's content into the software that is used by thousands of universities worldwide.

Virtual Universities

The concept of **virtual universities**—online universities from which students take classes from home or an off-site location, via the Internet—is expanding rapidly. Hundreds of thousands of students in dozens of countries, from Great Britain to Israel to Thailand, are studying via such institutions. A large number of existing universities,

virtual universities *Online universities from which students take classes from home or an off-site location, via the Internet.*

including Stanford University and other top-tier institutions, offer online education of some form. Some universities, such as University of Phoenix (*phoenix.edu*), California Virtual Campus (*cvc.edu*), and the University of Maryland (*umuc.edu/distance*), offer thousands of courses and dozens of degrees to students worldwide, all online. Other universities offer limited online courses and degrees but use innovative teaching methods and multimedia support in the traditional classroom.

The virtual university concept allows universities to offer classes worldwide. Moreover, we may soon see integrated degrees, where students can customize a degree that will best fit their needs by taking courses at different universities. Several all-virtual schools include *eschool-world.com, walden.com,* and *trainingzone.co.uk*. For information about specific e-learning programs, see *Petersons.com, ECollege.com, icdl.open.ac.uk,* and *usdla.org*.

Online Corporate Training

Like educational institutions, a large number of business organizations are using e-learning on a large scale. Web-based learning technologies allow organizations to keep their employees up-to-date, and training via the Web can run 24 hours per day, every day ("24/7"), at striking cost advantages.

Corporate training is often done via the intranet and corporate portals. However, in large corporations with multiple sites, and for training from home, the Internet is used to access the online material. Some companies, like Barclays Bank (*barclays.co.uk*) and Qantas Airways (*qantas.com.au*), offer online training in learning centers that they call "universities." Vendors of online training and educational materials can be found at *digitalthink.com, click2learn.com*, and *deitel.com*.

Virtual Work and Telecommuting

virtual work environments *Work environments in which the work teams are geographically distributed and sometimes are interorganizational teams.*

Virtual (or distributed) **work environments** refer to geographically distributed work teams, global project teams, interorganizational teams, and nontraditional work environments such as virtual organizations, satellite work centers, and telecommuting. Next we discuss one type of virtual work environment—telecommuting.

telecommuting *Arrangement whereby employees work at home, at the customer's premises, in special workplaces, or while traveling, usually using a computer linked to their place of employment.*

Telecommuting. **Telecommuting**, or *teleworking*, refers to an arrangement whereby employees can work at home, at the customer's premises, in special work places, or while traveling, usually using a computer linked to their place of employment. Regular and overnight mail, special messengers, and fax typically have been used to support telecommuting, but they are relatively slow and expensive, and the Internet is gradually replacing them. Almost all groupware technologies can be used to support telecommuting.

Telecommuting can be used on a temporary basis. For example, during the 1996 Summer Olympics, Atlanta employers anticipated that the 750,000 additional cars of spectators would create a traffic nightmare. So, many Atlanta companies set up temporary data transmission network lines and told employees to work at home. Vendors cooperated: Symantec and U.S. Robotics offered companies free software to provide remote access to corporate networks. The Olympics offered many employees and companies their first taste of telecommuting.

Telecommuting has a number of potential advantages for employees, employers, and society. For employees, there is less stress, improved family life, and employment opportunities for housebound people such as single parents and disabled persons. Telecommuting can provide the organization with increased productivity, the ability to retain skilled employees, and the ability to tap the remote labor pool.

However, telecommuting also has some potential disadvantages. The major disadvantages for the *employees* are increased feelings of isolation, possible loss of fringe benefits, lower pay (in some cases), no workplace visibility, the potential for slower promotions, and lack of socialization. The major disadvantages to *employers* are difficulties in supervising work, potential data security problems, training costs, and the high cost of equipping and maintaining telecommuters' homes.

The American Telecommuting Association (ATA) provides information, developments, ideas, and lists of equipment required for supporting teleworkers (*knowledgetree.com/ata.html*).

Before you go on . . .

1. What is the difference between e-learning and distance learning?
2. What are the benefits of e-learning?
3. What is telecommuting? Do you think you would like to telecommute?

WHAT'S IN IT FOR ME?

ACC

FOR THE ACCOUNTING MAJOR

Accounting personnel use corporate intranets and portals to consolidate transaction data from legacy systems to provide an overall view of internal projects. This view contains the current costs charged to each project, the number of hours spent on each project by individual employees, and how actual costs compare to projected costs. Internet access to government and professional Web sites for discovery keeps accounting personnel informed on legal and other changes affecting their profession.

FIN

FOR THE FINANCE MAJOR

Corporate intranets and portals can provide a risk-evaluation model so that financial analysts can evaluate the risk of a project or an investment. The analysts use two types of data in the model: historical transaction data from corporate databases via the intranet and industry data obtained via the Internet. The Web can also be a marketing and service provision channel for financial services firms.

MKT

FOR THE MARKETING MAJOR

Marketing managers use corporate intranets and portals to coordinate the activities of the sales force. Sales personnel access corporate portals via the intranet to discover updates on pricing, promotion, rebates, customer information, or for information about competitors. Sales staff can also download presentations and customize them for their customers. The Internet, particularly the Web, opens a completely new marketing channel for many industries. Just how advertising, purchasing, and information dispensation should occur appears to vary from industry to industry, product to product, service to service.

POM

FOR THE PRODUCTION/ OPERATIONS MANAGEMENT MAJOR

Companies are using intranets and portals to speed product development, by providing three-dimensional models and animation for the development team. All team members can access the models for faster exploration of ideas and enhanced feedback. Corporate portals, accessed via intranets, provide for close management of inventories and management of real-time production on assembly lines. Extranets are also proving valuable as communication formats for joint research and design efforts among companies. The Internet is also a great source of cutting-edge information for POM managers to discover.

HRM

FOR THE HUMAN RESOURCES MANAGEMENT MAJOR

Human resources personnel use portals and intranets to publish corporate policy manuals, job postings, company telephone directories, and training classes. Many companies deliver online training obtained from the Internet to employees through their intranets. Via intranets, human resources departments offer employees health care, savings, and benefit plans, as well as the opportunity to take competency tests online. The Internet supports worldwide recruiting efforts, and it can also be the communications platform for supporting geographically dispersed work teams.

SUMMARY

1. Understand the concepts of the Internet and the Web, their importance, and their capabilities. The Internet is a global network of computer networks, linking the computing resources of businesses, government, and educational institutions using a common computer communication protocol, TCP/IP. The World Wide Web is the most widely used application on the Internet. Commercial applications of the Internet have evolved through *presence, e-commerce, collaboration, and integration.* The Internet supports discovery, communications, and collaboration applications.

2. Understand the role of intranets, extranets, and corporate portals for organizations. An *intranet* is a network designed to serve the internal informational needs of a company, using Internet concepts and tools. It provides easy and inexpensive browsing and search capabilities. Intranets also support communication and collaboration.

An *extranet* connects the intranets of different organization and allows secure communications among business partners over the Internet. It offers limited accessibility to the intranets of the participating companies, as well as the necessary interorganizational communications, using Internet tools.

A *portal* is a Web-based personalized gateway to information and knowledge that provides relevant information from disparate IT systems and the Internet, using advanced search and indexing techniques.

3. Identify the various ways in which communication is executed over the Internet. Effective personalized customer contact is provided through Web-based call centers (customer care centers). These employ capabilities such as e-mail, interactive text chat, and simultaneous voice and Web sessions.

Electronic chat rooms are virtual meeting places where you can send messages to people who are connected to the same channel of communication at the same time. Two major types of chat programs exist: (a) Web-based chat programs, which allow you to send messages over the Internet using a Web browser and visiting a Web chat site, and (b) an e-mail-based (text only) program called Internet Relay Chat (IRC).

Voice communication can now be done on the Internet using a microphone and a sound card. This is known as Internet telephony (or voice-over IP).

Blogs and blogging provide individuals with a way to do personal publishing. A Weblog (blog for short) is a personal Web site, open to the public, in which the creator expresses his or her feelings or opinions.

4. Describe how people collaborate over the Internet, intranets, and extranets using various supporting tools. Workflow management is the automation of workflows, so that documents, information, or tasks are passed from one participant to another in the regular business process. Workflow systems place system controls in the hands of user departments. Groupware refers to software products that support groups of people who share a common task or goal and who collaborate on its accomplishment.

Web-based systems provide IT support for electronic virtual meetings. Teleconferencing allows two or more people at different locations to have a simultaneous conference. In a videoconference, participants in one location can see participants at other locations. Web conferencing is similar, but is done *solely* on the Web.

Real-time collaboration (RTC) tools support synchronous communication of graphical and text-based information. Computer-based whiteboards allow multiple users to view and draw on a single document "pasted" onto a computer screen. Using screen sharing software, group members can work on the same document, which is shown on the PC screen of each participant.

5. Describe groupware capabilities. Groupware products provide a way for groups to share resources and opinions. For example, the Lotus Notes/Domino suite provides online collaboration capabilities, workgroup e-mail, distributed databases, bulletin whiteboards, text editing, (electronic) document management, workflow capabilities, instant virtual meetings, application sharing, instant messaging, consensus building, voting, ranking, and various application development tools.

6. Describe and analyze the role of e-learning and distance learning. E-learning refers to learning supported by the Web. It can be done inside classrooms or as a support to conventional teaching. It also can be done in virtual classrooms, in which all coursework is done online, and then it is a part of distance learning. Distance learning refers to situations where teachers and students do not meet face-to-face. The Web now provides a multimedia interactive environment for self-study.

7. Understand the advantages and disadvantages of telecommuting for both employers and employees. For employees who telecommute, there is less stress, improved family life, and employment opportunities for housebound people. Telecommuting can provide the organization with increased productivity, the ability to retain skilled employees, and the ability to tap the remote labor pool.

The major disadvantages for the employees are increased feelings of isolation, possible loss of fringe benefits, lower pay (in some cases), no workplace visibility, the potential for slower promotions, and lack of socialization. The major disadvantages to employers are difficulties in supervising work, potential data security problems, training costs, and the high cost of equipping and maintaining telecommuters' homes.

INTERACTIVE / LEARNING

From Tokyo to Atlanta: How Does an International Bank Stay Connected?
Go to the Interactivities section on the Student Web Site and access Chapter 4: Network Computing. There you will find an animated simulation of the technologies used for communication between the headquarters and regional offices of an international bank, as well as some hands-on activities that visually explain business concepts in this chapter.

More Resources
More resources and study tools are located on the Student Web Site. You'll find additional chapter materials and links to organizations, people, and technologies for each chapter. In addition, self-quizzes that provide individualized feedback are available for each chapter.

> Instructions for accessing the Interactivities on the Student Web Site:
>
> 1. Go to
>   wiley.com/college/turban
> 2. Select Turban Rainer Potter's *Introduction to Information Technology, Third Edition*
> 3. Click on Student Resources Site, in the toolbar on the left
> 4. Click on Interactivities Web Site
> 5. Click on Interactivities Web Site and use your password to enter the site (your password card is located in the inside cover of your textbook)

DISCUSSION QUESTIONS

1. Identify some commercial tools that allow users to conduct browsing, communication, and collaboration simultaneously.
2. Describe how agents can help people find specific information quickly.
3. Explain the advantages of electronic mail over regular mail.
4. Discuss the role of Web-based call centers and their contribution to competitive advantage.
5. Explain why the topic of group work and its support is getting increased attention.
6. How can computers support a team whose members work at different times?
7. Based on what you know about Lotus Notes, can it support different-time/different-place work situations?

PROBLEM-SOLVING ACTIVITIES

1. From your own experience or from the vendor's information, list the major capabilities of Lotus Notes/Domino. Do the same for Microsoft Exchange. Compare and contrast the products. Explain how the products can be used to support knowledge workers and managers.
2. Visit *polycom.com* and sites of other companies that manufacture conferencing products for the Internet. Prepare a report. Why are conferencing products considered part of video commerce?
3. Marketel is a fast-growing (hypothetical) telemarketing company whose headquarters are in Colorado, but the majority of its business is in California. The company has eight divisions, including one in Chicago. The company has just started penetrating the Midwest market. Recently Marketel was approached by two large

telephone companies, one in Los Angeles and one in Denver, for discussions regarding a potential merger.

Nancy Miranda, the corporate CEO who was involved in the preliminary merger discussions, notified all division managers on the progress of the discussions. Both she and John Miner, the chief financial officer, felt that an immediate merger would be extremely beneficial. However, the vice presidents for marketing and operations thought the company should continue to be independent for at least two to three years. "We can get a much better deal if we first increase our market share," commented Sharon Gonzales, the vice president for marketing.

Nancy called each of the division managers and found that five of them were for the merger proposal and three objected to it. Furthermore, she found that the division managers from the West Coast strongly opposed discussions with the Colorado company, and the other managers were strongly against discussions with the Los Angeles company. Memos, telephone calls, and meetings of two or three people at a time resulted in frustration. It became apparent that a meeting of all concerned individuals was needed.

Nancy wanted to have the meeting as soon as possible in spite of the busy travel schedules of most division managers. She also wanted the meeting to be as short as possible. Nancy called Bob Kraut, the chief information officer, and asked for suggestions about how to conduct a conference electronically. The options he outlined are as follows.

(1) Use the corporate intranet. Collect opinions from all division managers and vice presidents, then disseminate them to all parties, get feedback, and repeat the process until a solution is achieved.

(2) Fly all division managers to corporate headquarters and have face-to-face meetings there until a solution is achieved.

(3) Use the Web for a meeting.

(4) Fly all division managers to corporate headquarters. Rent a decision room (a facility designed for electronic meetings) and a facilitator from the local university for $2,000 per day and conduct the meetings there.

(5) Conduct a videoconference. Unfortunately, appropriate facilities exist only at the headquarters and in two divisions. The other division managers can be flown to the nearest division that has equipment. Alternatively, videoconferencing facilities can be rented in all cities.

(6) Use a telephone conference call.

Answer the following questions:

a. Which of these options would you recommend to management and why?

b. Is there a technology not listed that might do a better job?

c. Is it possible to use more than one alternative in this case? If yes, which technologies would you combine, and how would you use them?

INTERNET ACTIVITIES

1. You plan to take a three-week vacation in Hawaii this December, visiting the big island of Hawaii. Using the Internet, find information that will help you plan the trip. Such information includes, *but is not limited to,* the following:
   a. Geographical location and weather conditions in December.
   b. Major tourist attractions and recreational facilities.
   c. Travel arrangements (airlines, approximate fares).
   d. Car rental; local tours.
   e. Alternatives for accommodation (within a moderate budget) and food.
   f. Estimated cost of the vacation (travel, lodging, food, recreation, shopping, . . .).
   g. State regulations regarding the entrance of your dog that you plan to take with you.
   h. Shopping (try to find an electronic mall).
2. Visit *cdt.org*. Find what technologies are available to track users' activities on the Internet.
3. You are assigned the task of buying desktop teleconferencing equipment for your company. Using the Internet:

   a. Identify three major vendors.
   b. Visit their Web sites and find information about their products and capabilities.
   c. Compare the least expensive products of two vendors.
   d. Find a newsgroup that has an interest in video teleconferencing. Post new questions regarding the products selected. (For example, what are the users' experiences with the products?)
   e. Prepare a report of your findings.
4. Both Microsoft Explorer and Netscape Navigator have the capability for Internet telephony; all you need is a sound card, microphone, and speakers on your PC. (If you do not have these browsers, access the VocalTec Web site at *vocaltec.com/*, and download and install its fully functional Internet long-distance telephone software.) Get a friend in another city to do the same. Contact each other via the Internet using your computer as a telephone. What are the advantages and disadvantages of using the Internet for telephone service? Compare your experience to that of making a standard telephone call.

TEAM ASSIGNMENTS

1. You are a member of a team working for a multinational finance corporation. Your team's project is to prepare a complex financing proposal for a client within one week. Two of the team members are in Singapore, one is in Seoul, South Korea, one is in London, and one is in Los Angeles. You cannot get the team members together in one place. Your team does not have all the required expertise, but other

corporate employees may have it. There are 8,000 employees worldwide; many of them travel. You do not know exactly who are the experts in your company.

Your company has never prepared such a proposal, but you know that certain parts of the proposal can be adapted from previous proposals. These proposals are filed electronically in various corporate databases, but you are not sure exactly where. (The company has over 80 databases, worldwide.) Finally, you will need a lot of external information, and you will need to communicate with your client in China, with investment groups in Japan and New York, and with your corporate headquarters in London.

If the client accepts your proposal, your company will make more than $5 million in profit. If the contract goes to a competitor, you may lose your job.

Your company has all the latest information and communication technologies.

   a. Prepare a list of tasks and activities that your team will need to go through in order to accomplish the mission.

   b. Describe what information technologies you would use to support the above tasks. Be specific, explaining how each technology can facilitate the execution of each task.

2. Assign each group member to an integrated group support tool kit (Lotus Notes, Exceloncorp.com, GroupWise, etc.). Have each member visit the Web site of the commercial developer and obtain information about this product. As a group, prepare a comparative table of the major similarities and differences among the kits.

3. Assign each team to a college collaborative tool such as Blackboard, WebCT, etc. Establish common evaluative criteria. Have each team evaluate the capabilities and limitations of its tool, and convince each team that its product is superior.

4. Have each team download a free copy of Groove from *groove.net*. Install the software on the members' PCs and arrange collaborative sessions. What can the free software do for you? What are its limitations?

REAL-WORLD CASE

MCDONALD'S GLOBAL NETWORKCOMES UP SHORT

THE BUSINESS PROBLEM Serving burgers is big business! McDonald's (*mcdonalds.com*), a $15.4 billion company, has more than 30,000 restaurants in 121 countries serving more than 46 million customers a day. However, the company had a number of problems.

First and foremost, McDonald's scores from the American Customer Satisfaction Index (ASCI) were lower than those of Wendy's, Burger King, Pizza Hut, and Kentucky Fried Chicken, its major competitors. Customer complaints centered on slow service and an "old, tired" menu. McDonald's wants to speed up service and develop a menu offering more "healthy" options. Second, data that was batch processed on the McDonald's proprietary mainframe system at headquarters every night did not offer the detail that executives needed, and it took as long as a week to be analyzed and distributed to managers. While McDonald's collects daily sales data, the company's decade-old financial reporting systems were not built with real-time business intelligence in mind. Third, unskilled workers and employee turnover mandate training new employees quickly and making the assembly-line method of food preparation extremely easy to understand.

THE PROPOSED IT SOLUTION McDonald's planned to spend $1 billion over five years to tie all its operations into an Internet-based, global, real-time digital network called Innovate, the most expensive and extensive information technology project in the company's history. Headquarters wanted to create a means of con-

trolling the key quality that makes a fast-food chain successful: consistency. Therefore, executives needed to know what was going on in stores.

Innovate was designed to be a Web-based network of computers and monitors connected to every key piece of equipment in every store. Information delivered instantly would have given executives the ability to monitor, and possibly to affect in real time, the company's ability to get a consistent product to customers as fast as possible. Innovate would also have given executives an overall view of the entire system at any minute of the day. McDonald's hoped that Innovate would let its executives see at any time of day how sales of any product at any store were proceeding, where backup supplies sat anywhere between its stores and its suppliers' plants, and manage its stores accordingly.

The hub of Innovate was to have been an Oracle enterprise resource planning system, which would replace the company's homegrown IBM mainframe general ledger accounting system and the company's finance, supply chain management, and human resources systems. The network would have linked all of the company's restaurants and all of its more than 300 vendors 24 hours a day, seven days a week, to the back-office system at its headquarters.

Innovate would simplify the scheduling of crew members because the system would tell managers, for example, exactly how many customers order Big Macs or Quarter Pounders between noon and 2 P.M. every day of the week. Innovate would also streamline the delivery of employee training and benefits data over the Web.

McDonald's hoped to use Innovate to make life easier for its franchisees by automatically generating historical temperature logs for food safety reports required by the Food and Drug Administration. It could also alert owner-operators in the event of an unusually large voided transaction at the drive-through window point-of-sale system (suggesting that a crew member might be pocketing money instead of putting it in the register).

THE RESULTS After just two years, though, McDonald's wrote off $170 million when the company discontinued Innovate. Though the company had shown little or no expertise in large-scale information systems implementations when Innovate was initiated, its executives thought they could completely revamp their entire core technology infrastructure.

McDonald's fell victim to classic pitfalls that befall corporations trying to implement and justify information systems projects of this size for the first time. The company had a lack of experience in this area as it had never been on the cutting edge of technology. Further, its executives did not understand technology and made it a low priority for the company.

Source: Compiled from L. Barrett, and S. Gallagher, "McBusted," *Baseline,* July 2, 2003.

QUESTIONS

1. What were the major problems that led to the failure of Innovate?
2. What discovery, communication, and collaboration functions/capabilities did McDonald's need to address its business problems?

CLUB IT   wiley.com/college/turban

TELECOMMUNICATIONS AT CLUB IT

The Internet research you have been doing for Lisa and Ruben has been eye-opening, but it's also exasperatingly slow on their dialup connection in their cramped back office. After reading Chapter 4, you have a lot of ideas for high-speed wireless networking inside Club IT. It would even make it easier for you to work if you could bring in your wireless notebook and use it at a table in the club, rather than inconvenience Lisa or Ruben by working at their desk. So, you take the initiative to prepare a proposal for them to consider as one step in expanding the club's information technology capabilities.

ASSIGNMENT

1. What basic networking capabilities would you recommend for Club IT? Consider, for example, daily business transactions where data and information is shared among employees and with external entities such as suppliers and guests. Describe several networking technologies and their vendors that would be useful and discuss the business case for adding these capabilities.

2. Most of Club IT's members and guests are in their 20's. What kinds of mobile communication devices are they likely to use? How could Club IT take advantage of these devices and communicate with members and guests in order to build more club loyalty? Describe some examples of SMS, MMS, and email applications that Club IT should consider using.

3. Listen to an Internet radio station (the Real Player streaming audio player has a radio guide, or look here: http://www.radiotower.com/). Then assess the feasibility of streaming the DJ's shows on the Internet for a small subscription fee (pcdj.com makes DJ streaming software, for example).

Go to wiley.com/college/turban **to access the**
CLUB IT Web Site on the Student Web Site

E-Business and E-Commerce

Chapter Preview

One of the most profound changes currently transpiring in the world of business is the introduction of electronic commerce, also known as e-business. The impact of electronic commerce on procurement, shopping, business collaboration, and customer services as well as on delivery of various services is so dramatic that almost every organization is affected. E-commerce (EC) is changing all business functional areas and their important tasks, ranging from advertising to paying bills. The nature of competition is also drastically changing, due to new online companies, new business models, and the diversity of EC-related products and services. E-commerce provides unparalleled opportunities for companies to expand worldwide at a small cost, to increase market share, and to reduce costs. In this chapter we will explain the major applications of e-business, the issues related to its successful implementation and to its failures, and what services are necessary for its support. We look at business-to-consumer e-commerce, business-to-business e-commerce, intrabusiness e-commerce, and e-government.

Chapter Outline

Learning Objectives

1. Describe electronic commerce, its scope, benefits, limitations, and types.
2. Understand the basics of how online auctions and bartering work.
3. Describe the major applications of business-to-consumer commerce, including service industries, and the major issues faced by e-tailers.
4. Discuss the importance and activities of online advertising.
5. Describe business-to-business applications.
6. Describe intrabusiness and B2E e-commerce.
7. Describe e-government activities and consumer-to-consumer e-commerce.
8. Describe the e-commerce support services, specifically payments and logistics.
9. Discuss some ethical and legal issues relating to e-commerce.
10. Describe EC failures and strategies for success.

E-COMMERCE IMPROVES INVENTORY CONTROL AT HI-LIFE CORPORATION

Hi-Life Corporation owns and operates 720 convenience retail stores in Taiwan, where the company sells over 3,000 different products. A major problem is keeping a proper level of inventory of each product in each store. Overstocking is expensive due to storage costs and tying up money to buy and maintain the inventory. Understocking reduces potential sales and could result in unhappy customers who may go to a competitor.

To calculate the appropriate level of inventory, it is necessary to know exactly how many units of each product are in stock at specific times. This is known as *stock count*. Periodic stock count is needed since the actual amount in stock frequently differs from the theoretical one (inventory = previous inventory − sales + new arrivals). The difference is due to "shrinkage" (e.g., theft, misplaced items, spoilage, etc.). Until 2002, stock counts at Hi-Life were done manually. Employees counted the quantity of each product and recorded it on data collection sheets on which the products' names were preprinted. Then, the data were painstakingly keyed into each store's PC. The process took over 21 person-hours, in each store, each time a count was needed, sometimes once a week. This process was expensive and frequently was delayed, causing problems along the entire supply chain due to delays in count and errors.

The first phase of improvement was introduced in spring 2002. Management introduced a Pocket PC (a handheld device) from Hewlett-Packard. The Pocket (called Jornada) enables employees to enter the inventory tallies directly into electronic forms using Chinese characters for additional notes. Once the Pocket PC is placed in its synchronized cradle (see Chapter 6), inventory information can be relayed instantly to Hi-Life's headquarters.

In the second phase of improvement, in summer 2003, a compact barcode scanner was added on in the Pocket PC's expansion slot. Employees can now scan the products' barcodes and then enter the quantity found on the shelf. This new feature expedites data entry and minimizes errors in product identification. The up-to-the second information enables headquarters to compute appropriate inventory levels in minutes, to better schedule shipments, and to plan purchasing strategies using decision-support system formulas. The stores use the Internet (with a secured feature known as VPN; see Technology Guide 4) to upload data to the intranet at headquarters.

The results have been astonishing. Inventory taking has been reduced from 21 to less than 4 hours per store, per count. Errors are down by more than 90 percent, order placing is simple and quick, and administrative paperwork has been eliminated. Furthermore, quicker and more precise inventory counts have resulted in lower inventory levels and in quicker response times for changes in demand. The entire product-management process has become more efficient, including stocking, price checks, and reticketing.

For the employees, the new system is very user friendly, both to learn and to operate. Hi-Life's employees now have more time to plan, manage, and chat with customers. More important, faster and better inventory and purchasing decisions are enabled at headquarters, contributing to greater competitiveness and profitability for Hi-Life.

Sources: Compiled from *hp.com/jornada* (May 2003) and from *microsoft.com/asia/mobile* (May 2003).

The output of an information system is only as good as the input data. When data are inaccurate and/or delayed, the decisions that use the data are not the best, as in Hi-Life's old system, which resulted in high inventories and low customer satisfaction. The e-commerce system described in this case expedited and improved the flow of information to the corporate headquarters. This case illustrates an *intrabusiness* application of e-commerce, involving employees, which is referred to as business-to-employees (B2E) e-commerce. There are several other types of e-commerce, all of which are discussed in this chapter.

5.1 OVERVIEW OF E-BUSINESS AND E-COMMERCE

Definitions and Concepts

Electronic commerce (EC or e-commerce) describes the process of buying, selling, transferring, or exchanging products, services, or information via computer networks, including the Internet. Some people view the term *commerce* as describing only *transactions* conducted between business partners. When this definition is used, some people find the term *electronic commerce* to be fairly narrow. Thus, many use the term *e-business* instead. **E-business** refers to a broader definition of EC, not just the buying and selling of goods and services, but also servicing customers, collaborating with business partners, conducting e-learning, and conducting electronic transactions within an organization. Others view e-business as the "other than buying and selling" activities on the Internet, such as collaboration and intrabusiness activities.

In this book we use the broadest meaning of electronic commerce, which is basically equivalent to e-business. The two terms *will be used interchangeably* throughout the chapter and the remainder of the text.

electronic commerce (e-commerce, EC) *The process of buying, selling, transferring, or exchanging products, services, or information via computer networks, including the Internet.*

e-business *A broader definition of EC, including buying and selling of goods and services, and also servicing customers, collaborating with business partners, conducting e-learning, and conducting electronic transactions within an organization.*

Pure versus Partial EC. Electronic commerce can take several forms depending on the *degree of digitization*—the transformation from physical to digital—involved. The degree of digitization can relate to: (1) the product (service) sold, (2) the process, or (3) the delivery agent (or intermediary).

Choi et al. (1997) created a framework that explains the possible configurations of these three dimensions. A product can be physical or digital, the process can be physical or digital, and the delivery agent can be physical or digital. In traditional commerce all three dimensions are physical. Purely physical organizations are referred to as **brick-and-mortar organizations**. In *pure EC* all dimensions are digital. All other combinations that include a mix of digital and physical dimensions are considered EC (but not pure EC).

If there is at least one digital dimension, we consider the situation *partial EC*. For example, buying a shirt at Wal-Mart Online or a book from Amazon.com is partial EC, because the merchandise is physically delivered by FedEx. However, buying an e-book from Amazon.com or a software product from Buy.com is *pure EC*, because the product, its delivery, payment, and transfer agent are all done online. In this book we use the term EC to denote either pure or partial EC.

brick-and-mortar organizations *Organizations in which the product, the process, and the delivery agent are all physical.*

EC Organizations. Companies that are engaged only in EC are considered **virtual** (or pure-play) **organizations**. **Click-and-mortar** (or click-and-brick) **organizations** are those that conduct some e-commerce activities, yet their primary business is done in the physical world. Gradually, many brick-and-mortar companies are changing to click-and-mortar ones (e.g., Wal-Mart Online). Indeed, in many ways e-commerce is now simply a part of traditional commerce, and like the addition of credit card payment capabilities a generation ago, many people expect companies to offer some form of e-commerce.

virtual organizations *Organizations in which the product, the process, and the delivery agent are all digital; also called* pure-play *organizations.*

click-and-mortar organizations *Organizations that do business in both the physical and digital dimensions.*

Types of E-Commerce Transactions

E-commerce transactions can be done between various parties. The common types of e-commerce transactions are described below.

- **Business-to-business (B2B):** In B2B transactions, both the sellers and the buyers are business organizations. The vast majority of EC volume is of this type.

business-to-business (B2B) *E-commerce in which both the sellers and the buyers are business organizations.*

collaborative commerce (c-commerce) *E-commerce in which business partners collaborate electronically.*

business-to-consumers (B2C) *E-commerce in which the sellers are organizations and the buyers are individuals; also known as e-tailing.*

consumer-to-consumer (C2C) *E-commerce in which an individual sells products or services to other individuals.*

consumers-to-businesses (C2B) *E-commerce in which consumers make known a particular need for a product or service, and suppliers compete to provide the product or service to consumers.*

intrabusiness (intraorganizational) commerce *E-commerce in which an organization uses EC internally to improve its operations.*

B2E (business to its employees) EC *A special case of intrabusiness e-commerce in which an organization delivers products or services to its employees.*

government-to-citizens (G2C) *E-commerce in which a government provides services to its citizens via EC technologies.*

government-to-business (G2B) *E-commerce in which a government does business with other governments as well as with businesses.*

mobile commerce (m-commerce) *E-commerce conducted in a wireless environment.*

business model *The method by which a company generates revenue to sustain itself.*

- **Collaborative commerce (c-commerce):** In c-commerce, business partners collaborate (rather than buy or sell) electronically. Such collaboration frequently occurs between and among business partners along the supply chain (see Chapter 8).

- **Business-to-consumers (B2C):** In B2C, the sellers are organizations, and the buyers are individuals. B2C is also known as *e-tailing*.

- **Consumer-to-consumer (C2C):** In C2C, an individual sells products or services to other individuals. (You also will see the term C2C used as "customer-to-customer." The terms are interchangeable, and both will be used in this book to describe individuals selling products and services to each other.)

- **Consumers-to-businesses (C2B):** In C2B, consumers make known a particular need for a product or service, and suppliers compete to provide the product or service to consumers. An example is Priceline.com, where the customer names a product and the desired price, and Priceline tries to find a supplier to fulfill the stated need.

- **Intrabusiness (intraorganizational) commerce:** In this case an organization uses EC internally to improve its operations. A special case of this is known as **B2E (business to-its-employees) EC**, which was illustrated in the opening case.

- **Government-to-citizens (G2C) and to others:** In this case a government entity (unit) provides services to its citizens via EC technologies. Government units can do business with other government units as well as with businesses (**G2B**).

- **Mobile commerce (m-commerce):** When e-commerce is done in a wireless environment, such as using cell phones to access the Internet and shop there, we call it m-commerce.

EC Business Models

Each of the above types of EC is executed in one or more **business models**, the method by which a company generates revenue to sustain itself. For example, in B2B one can sell from catalogs or in auctions. The major business models of EC are summarized in Manager's Checklist 5.1.

Brief History and Scope of EC

E-commerce applications began in the early 1970s with such innovations as electronic transfer of funds. However, the applications were limited to large corporations and a few daring small businesses. Then came electronic data interchange (EDI), which automated routine transaction processing and extended EC to all industries. (See Chapter 9 for details about EDI.)

In the early 1990s, EC applications expanded rapidly, following the commercialization of the Internet and the introduction of the Web. A major shakeout in EC activities began in 2000 and lasted about three years; hundreds of dot-com companies went out of business. Since 2003, EC has continued to show steady progress. Today, most medium and large organizations and many small ones are practicing some EC.

The Scope of EC. Figure 5.1 (page 132) describes the broad field of e-commerce. As can be seen in the figure, there are many EC applications (top of the figure); many of these are shown throughout the book. To execute these applications, companies need the right information, infrastructure, and support services. Figure 5.1 shows that the EC applications are supported by an infrastructure that includes hardware, software, and networks, ranging from browsers to multimedia, and also by the following five support areas:

1. *People:* They are the sellers, buyers, intermediaries, information systems specialists and other employees, and any other participants.

2. *Public policy:* There are legal and other policy and regulating issues, such as privacy protection and taxation, that are determined by the government.

EC Model	Description
Online direct marketing	Manufacturers or retailers sell directly to customers. Very efficient for digital products and services. Can allow for product or service customization.
Electronic tendering system	Businesses conduct online tendering, requesting quotes from suppliers. Uses B2B with a *reverse auction* mechanism (see Section 5.2).
Name-your-own-price	Customers decide how much they are willing to pay. An intermediary (e.g., Priceline.com) tries to match a provider.
Find-the-best-price	Customers specify a need; an intermediary (e.g., Hotwire.com) compares providers and shows the lowest price. Customers must accept the offer in a short time or may lose the deal.
Affiliate marketing	Vendors ask partners to place logos (or banners) on partner's site. If customers click on logo, go to vendor's site, and buy, then vendor pays commissions to partners.
Viral marketing	Receivers send information about your product to their friends. (Be on the watch for viruses.)
Group purchasing (e-co-ops)	Small buyers aggregate demand to get a large volume; then the group conducts tendering or negotiates a low price.
Online auctions	Companies run auctions of various types on the Internet. Very popular in C2C, but gaining ground in other types of EC.
Product customization	Customers use the Internet to self-configure products or services. Sellers then price them and fulfill them quickly (*build-to-order*).
Electronic marketplaces and exchanges	Transactions are conducted efficiently (more information to buyers and sellers, less transaction cost) in virtual marketplaces (private or public).
Value-chain integrators	Integrators aggregate information and package it for customers, vendors, or others in the supply chain.
Value-chain service providers	Service provider offers specialized services in supply chain operations such as providing logistics or payment services.
Information brokers	Brokers provide services related to EC information such as trust, content, matching buyers and sellers, evaluating vendors and products.
Bartering online	Intermediary administers online exchange of surplus products and/or company receives "points" for its contribution, and the points can be used to purchase other needed items.
Deep discounters	Company (e.g., Half.com) offers deep price discounts. Appeals to customers who consider only price in their purchasing decisions.
Membership	Only members can use the services provided, including access to certain information, conducting trades, etc. (e.g., Egreetings.com).
Supply-chain improvers	Organizations restructure supply chains to hubs or other configurations. Increases collaboration, reduces delays, and smoothes supply chain flows.

MANAGER'S CHECKLIST 5.1

E-Commerce Business Models

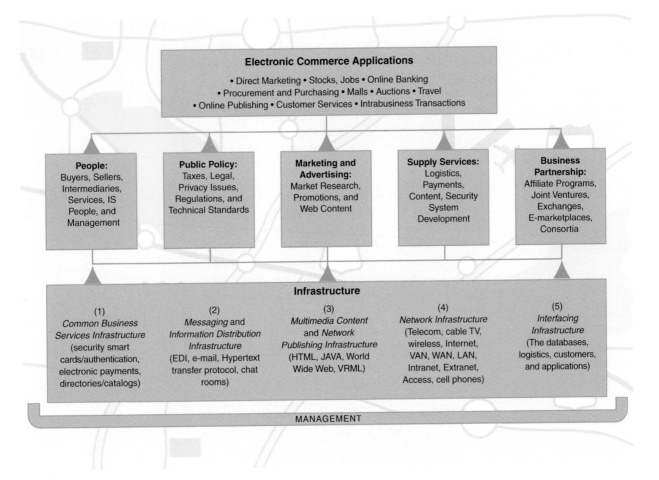

Figure 5.1 **Roadmap:** *A framework for e-commerce.*
Source: Drawn by E. Turban. Based on R. Kalakota and A. B. Whinston, Electronic Commerce: A Manager's Guide
(Reading, MA: Addison-Wesley, 1997), p. 12, and on V. Zwass, "Electronic Commerce: Structures and Issues," International
Journal of Electronic Commerce, *Fall 1996, p. 6.*

3. *Marketing and advertising:* EC usually requires the support of marketing and advertising, like any other business. This is especially important in B2C online transactions where the buyers and sellers usually do not know each other.

4. *Support services:* Many services, ranging from payments to order delivery and content creation, are needed to support EC.

5. *Business partnerships:* Joint ventures, e-marketplaces, and business partnerships
are common in EC. These occur frequently throughout the supply chain (i.e., the
interactions between a company and its suppliers, customers, and other partners).

All of these EC components require good management practices. This means that
companies need to plan, organize, motivate, devise strategy, and restructure processes
as needed.

Benefits and Limitations/Failures of E-Commerce

Few innovations in human history encompass as many benefits to organizations, individuals, and society as does e-commerce. These benefits have just begun to materialize, but they will increase significantly as EC expands. The major benefits to
organizations are the availability of national and international markets and the decreased cost of processing, distributing, and retrieving information. The major benefit
to customers is the access to a vast number of products and services, around the clock.
The major benefit to society is the ability to easily and conveniently deliver information, services, and products to people in cities, in rural areas, and in developing countries. (Additional benefits of e-commerce are listed in Online File W5.1.)

Counterbalancing its many benefits, EC has some limitations, both technological and nontechnological, which have slowed its growth and acceptance. Technological limitations include the lack of universally accepted security standards, insufficient telecommunications bandwidth, and expensive accessibility. Nontechnological limitations include a perception that EC is insecure, unresolved legal issues, and a lack of a critical mass of sellers and buyers. (A more detailed list of limitations and inhibitors is shown in Online File W5.2.) As time passes, the limitations, especially the technological ones, will lessen or be overcome. In addition, appropriate planning can minimize the negative impact of some of them.

Despite its limitations, e-commerce has made very rapid progress. Also, various B2B activities, e-auctions, e-government, e-learning, and some B2C activities are ballooning. As experience accumulates and technology improves, the ratio of EC benefits to cost will increase, resulting in an even greater rate of EC adoption.

> wiley.com/college/turban

Before you go on . . .

1. Define e-commerce and distinguish it from e-business.

2. List the major types of EC (by transaction).

3. Distinguish between business-to-consumer, business-to-business, and intrabusiness EC.

5.2 MAJOR EC MECHANISMS

The major mechanisms for buying and selling on the Internet are electronic catalogs, electronic auctions, and online bartering. (Other mechanisms—e-storefronts, e-mails, and e-marketplaces—are described later.

Electronic Catalogs

Catalogs have been printed on paper for generations. Recently, electronic catalogs on CD-ROM and the Internet have gained popularity. Electronic catalogs consist of a product database, directory and search capabilities, and a presentation function. They are the backbone of most e-commerce sites. For merchants, the objective of electronic catalogs is to advertise and promote products and services. For the customer, the purpose of such catalogs is to provide a source of information on products and services.

Electronic catalogs can be classified according to three dimensions:

1. *The dynamics of the information presentation.* Catalogs can be static or dynamic. *Static catalogs* present information in text and static pictures. *Dynamic* catalogs present information in motion pictures or animation, possibly with supplemental sound.

2. *The degree of customization.* Catalogs can be standard or customized. In *standard catalogs*, merchants offer the same catalog to any customer. *Customized catalogs* tailor content, pricing, and displays to the characteristics of specific customers.

3. *The degree of integration with other business processes or features.* Catalogs can be classified according to the degree of integration with the following business processes or features: order taking and fulfillment; electronic payment systems; intranet workflow software and systems; inventory and accounting systems; and suppliers' or customers' extranet. For example, when you place an order with Amazon.com, your order will be automatically transferred to a computerized inventory check.

For a comparison of paper and online catalogs, see Online File W5.3.

> wiley.com/college/turban

Electronic Auctions (E-Auctions)

An **auction** is a competitive process in which either a seller solicits consecutive bids from buyers or a buyer solicits bids from sellers. The primary characteristic of auctions, whether offline or online, is that prices are determined dynamically by compet-

auction *A competitive process in which either a seller solicits consecutive bids from buyers or a buyer solicits bids from sellers, and prices are determined dynamically by competitive bidding.*

itive bidding. Auctions have been an established method of commerce for generations, and they are well-suited to deal with products and services for which conventional marketing channels are ineffective or inefficient. Electronic auctions generally increase revenues for sellers by broadening the customer base and shortening the cycle time of the auction. Buyers generally benefit from e-auctions by the opportunity to bargain for lower prices and the convenience of not having to travel to an auction site to "attend" the auction. Additional benefits of electronic auctions are shown in Online File W5.4.

wiley.com/college/turban

The Internet provides an efficient infrastructure for executing auctions at lower administrative cost and with many more involved sellers and buyers (see Kambil and van Heck, 2002). Individual consumers and corporations alike can participate in this rapidly growing form of e-commerce. There are several types of electronic auctions, each with its motives and procedures. Auctions are divided here into two major types: *forward* auctions and *reverse* auctions.

forward auction   *An auction that sellers use as a selling channel to many potential buyers; the highest bidder wins the items.*

Forward Auctions.   **Forward auctions** are auctions that *sellers* use as a selling channel to many potential buyers. Usually, items are placed at sites for auction, and buyers will bid continuously for the items. The highest bidder wins the items. Sellers and buyers can be individuals or businesses. The popular auction site eBay.com is a forward auction.

According to Gallaugher (2002) there are two types of forward e-auctions. One is to *liquidate* existing inventory, the other one is to *increase marketing efficiency*. Customers in the first type seek the lowest price on widely available goods or services; customers in the second type seek access to unique products or services. Online File W5.5 graphically demonstrates these two types of forward auctions.

wiley.com/college/turban

reverse auction   *An auction in which one buyer, usually an organization, seeks to buy a product or a service, and suppliers submit bids; the lowest bidder wins.*

Reverse Auctions.   In **reverse auctions**, there is one buyer, usually an organization, that wants to buy a product or a service. Suppliers are invited to submit bids. Online bidding is much faster than conventional bidding, and it usually attracts many more bidders. The reverse auction is the most common auction model for large purchases (in terms of either quantities or price). Everything else being equal, the lowest-price bidder wins the auction. Governments and large corporations frequently mandate this approach, which may provide considerable savings.

(Cartoon by Sidney Harris.)

Auctions are used in B2C, B2B, C2B, e-government, and C2C commerce, and they are becoming popular in many countries. The Internet opens many opportunities for e-auctions. Auctions can be conducted from the seller's site, the buyer's site, or from a third party's site. For example, as described in IT's about Business 5.1, eBay, the best-known third-party site, offers hundreds of thousands of different items in several types of auctions. Over 300 other major companies, including Amazon.com and Dellauction.com, offer online auctions as well.

Bartering

electronic bartering   *The electronically supported exchange of goods or services without a monetary transaction.*

Related to auctions is **electronic bartering**, the electronically supported exchange of goods or services *without a monetary transaction*. Electronic bartering is done through means of individual-to-individual bartering ads that appear in some newsgroups, bulletin boards, and chat rooms. There also are several intermediaries that arrange for corporate e-bartering (e.g., *barterbrokers.com*). These intermediaries try to match online partners to a barter transaction.

Before you go on . . .

1. Describe forward and reverse auctions.
2. How are forward auctions used as a selling channel?
3. Describe the process of using reverse auctions for purchasing.
4. Define electronic bartering.

eBay (*ebay.com*) is the world's largest auction site, and one of the most profitable e-businesses. The successful online auction house has its roots in a 50-year-old novelty item—Pez candy dispensers. Pamela Kerr, an avid collector of Pez dispensers, came up with the idea of trading them over the Internet. When she shared this idea with her boyfriend (now her husband), Pierre Omidyar, he was instantly struck with the soon-to-be-famous e-business auction concept.

In 1995, the Omidyars started the company, later renamed eBay, that has since become the premier online auction house. The business model of eBay was to provide an electronic infrastructure for conducting mostly C2C auctions, although it caters to small businesses as well. Technology replaces the traditional auctioneer as the intermediary between buyers and sellers.

On eBay, people can buy and sell just about anything. It has millions of unique auctions in progress and over 500,000 new items are added each day. The company collects a submission fee upfront, plus a commission as a percentage of the sale amount. The submission fee is based on the amount of exposure you want your item to receive. For example, a higher fee is required if you would like to be among the "featured auctions" in your specific product category, and an even higher fee if you want your item to be listed on the eBay home page under Featured Items.

The seller must specify a minimum opening bid. Sellers might set the opening bid lower than the *reserve price*, a minimum acceptable bid price, in order to generate bidding activity. If a successful bid is made, the seller and the buyer negotiate the payment method, shipping details, warranty, and other particulars. eBay serves as a liaison between the parties; it is the interface through which sellers and buyers can conduct business.

After a few years of successful operations and tens of millions of loyal users, eBay started to do B2C (e-tailing), mostly in fixed prices. By 2003, eBay operated several specialty sites, such as eBay Motors. eBay also operates a *business exchange* in which small- and medium-sized enterprises can buy and sell new and used merchandise, in B2B or B2C modes. In addition, *half.com*, the famous discount e-tailer, is now part of eBay and so is PayPal.com, the person-to-person payment company.

eBay operates *globally*, permitting international trades to take place. Country-specific sites are located in over 25 countries. Buyers from more than 160 other countries also participate. Finally, eBay operates locally: It has over 60 local sites in the United States that enable users to easily find items located near them, to browse through items of local interest, and to meet face-to-face to conclude transactions. As of spring 2004, eBay had over 95 million registered users, and according to company financial statements, eBay expects net revenue of $3 billion in 2004.

Sources: Compiled from press releases at *eBay.com* (2002–2003) and from H. M. Deitel et al., *E-Business and E-Commerce for Managers* (Upper Saddle River, NJ: Prentice Hall, 2001).

QUESTIONS

1. Enter eBay and use the tutorial to learn the auction process eBay uses. Summarize your experience.
2. Does eBay's 2003 change of business model, from pure auctions to adding e-tailing, make sense?
3. Why are wireless auctions promoted?

5.3 BUSINESS-TO-CONSUMER APPLICATIONS

B2C E-commerce began when companies like Amazon.com started selling directly to consumers using the Internet. Here we will look at some of the major categories of B2C applications, which are expected to reach $1 trillion by 2005.

Electronic Retailing Mechanisms: Storefronts and Malls

For generations home shopping from catalogs has flourished, and television shopping channels have been attracting millions of shoppers for more than two decades. Shopping online offers an alternative to catalog and television shopping. **Electronic retailing (e-tailing)** is the direct sale of products and services through electronic storefronts or electronic malls, usually designed around an electronic catalog format and/or auctions.

Like any mail-order shopping experience, e-commerce enables you to buy from home, and to do so 24 hours a day, 7 days a week. However, EC offers a wider variety

electronic retailing (e-tailing) *The direct sale of products and services through electronic storefronts or electronic malls, usually designed around an electronic catalog format and/or auctions.*

of products and services, including the most unique items, often at lower prices. Furthermore, within seconds, shoppers can get very detailed supplementary information on products and can easily search for and compare competitors' products and prices. Finally, using the Internet, buyers can find hundreds of thousands of sellers.

Both goods and services are sold online. Goods that are bought most often online are computers and computer-related items, office supplies, books and magazines, CDs, cassettes, movies and videos, clothing and shoes, and toys. Services that are bought most often online include entertainment, travel services, stocks and bonds trading, electronic banking, insurance, and job matching. (Services will be presented as a separate topic later in this section.) Directories and hyperlinks from other Web sites and intelligent search agents help buyers find the best stores and products to match their needs.

Two popular shopping mechanisms online are electronic storefronts and electronic malls.

Electronic Storefronts.   Hundreds of thousands of solo storefronts can be found on the Internet, each with its own Internet address (URL), at which orders can be placed. Called **electronic storefronts**, they may be an *extension* of physical stores such as Home Depot, The Sharper Image, or Wal-Mart. Or they may be new businesses started by entrepreneurs who saw a niche on the Web, such as Amazon.com, CDNow.com, Uvine.com, Restaurant.com (see the Real-World Case at the end of the chapter), and Alloy.com. Besides being used by retailers (e.g., Officedepot.com), storefronts also are used by manufacturers (e.g., Dell.com). Retailers' and manufacturers' storefronts may sell to individuals (B2C) and/or to organizations (B2B).

There are two types of storefronts, general and specialized. The *specialized* store sells one or a few products (e.g., flowers, wines, or dog toys). The *general* storefronts sell many products (e.g., Amazon.com).

electronic storefront *The Web site of a single company, with its own Internet address, at which orders can be placed.*

Electronic Malls.   An **electronic mall**, also known as a cybermall or e-mall, is a collection of individual shops under one Internet address. The basic idea of an electronic mall is the same as that of a regular shopping mall—to provide a one-stop shopping place that offers many products and services. Each cybermall may include thousands of vendors. For example, *shopping.yahoo.com* and *eshop.msn.com* include tens of thousands of products from thousands of vendors.

Two types of malls exist. First, there are *referral malls* (e.g., *hawaii.com*). You cannot buy in such a mall, but instead you are transferred from the mall to a participating storefront. In the second type of mall (e.g., *shopping.yahoo.com*), you can actually make a purchase. At this type of mall, you might shop from several stores but you make only one purchase transaction at the end; an *electronic shopping cart* enables you to gather items from various vendors and pay for them all together in one transaction. (The mall organizer, such as Yahoo, takes a commission from the sellers for this service.)

As is true for vendors that locate in a physical shopping mall, a vendor that locates in an e-mall gives up a certain amount of independence. Its success depends on the popularity of the mall, as well as on its own marketing efforts. On the other hand, malls generate streams of prospective customers who otherwise might never have stopped by the store.

electronic mall *A collection of individual shops under one Internet address.*

E-Tailing: The Essentials

The concept of retailing implies sales of goods and/or services to individual customers. One of the most interesting properties of e-tailing as a type of retailing is the ability to offer *customized* products to individual customers at a reasonable price and fairly fast (as done by Dell Computer). Many sites (e.g., *nike.com* and *lego.com*) offer product self-configuration from their B2C portals. The most well known B2C site is *Amazon.com*, whose story is presented in IT's about Business 5.2.

Online Service Industries

Selling books, toys, computers, and most other products on the Internet may reduce vendors' selling costs by 20 to 40 percent. Further reduction is difficult to achieve because the products must be delivered physically. Only a few products (such as soft-

IT's ABOUT BUSINESS
5.2: Amazon.com: The King of E-Tailing

Entrepreneur and e-tailing pioneer Jeff Bezos, envisioning the huge potential for retail sales over the Internet, selected books as the most logical product for e-tailing. In July 1995, Bezos started Amazon.com, offering books via an electronic catalog from its Web site. Key features offered by the Amazon.com "superstore" were broad selection, low prices, easy searching and ordering, useful product information and personalization, secure payment systems, and efficient order fulfillment. Early on, recognizing the importance of order fulfillment, Amazon.com invested hundreds of millions of dollars in building physical warehouses designed for shipping small packages to hundreds of thousands of customers.

Over the years since its founding, Amazon.com has continually enhanced its business model by improving the customer's experience. For example, customers can personalize their Amazon accounts and manage orders online with the patented "One-Click" order feature. This personalized service includes an *electronic wallet*, which enables shoppers to place an order in a secure manner without the need to enter their address, credit card number, and so forth, each time they shop. One-Click also allows customers to view their order status and make changes on orders that have not yet entered the shipping process.

In addition, Amazon has been adding services and alliances to attract customers to make more purchases. For example, the company now offers specialty stores, such as its professional and technical store. It also is expanding its offerings beyond books. For example, in June 2002 it became an authorized dealer of Sony Corp. for selling Sony products online. Today you can find almost any product that sells well on the Internet, ranging from beauty aids to sporting goods to cars.

Amazon has more than 500,000 affiliate partners that refer customers to Amazon.com. Amazon pays a 3 to 5 percent commission on any resulting sale. In yet another extension of its services, in September 2001 Amazon signed an agreement with Borders Group Inc., providing Amazon's users with the option of picking up books, CDs, and so on at Borders' physical bookstores. Amazon.com also is becoming a Web-fulfillment contractor for national chains such as Target and Circuit City.

In January 2002, Amazon.com declared its first-ever profit—for the 2001 fourth quarter—and followed that by a profitable first quarter of 2002. Yet its financial success is by no means assured: The company sustained operating losses in the second and third quarters of 2002, though they were smaller than losses in the same quarters in preceding years. In the fourth quarter of 2002, the company again made a profit; 2003 will be the first year with profit in each quarter. Like all businesses, and especially all e-tailing businesses, Amazon.com will continue to walk the fine line of profitability for the foreseeable future.

Sources: Compiled from C. Bayers, "The Last Laugh (of Amazon's CEO)," *Business 2.0*, September 2002, and from M. Daisey, *21 Dog Years: Doing Time @ Amazon.com* (New York: Free Press, 2002).

QUESTIONS

1. What are the critical success factors for Amazon.com?
2. What advantages does it have over other e-tailers (e.g., Wal-Mart Online or *barnesandnoble.com*)?
3. Visit Amazon.com and experience its various customer service offerings. Summarize your encounter.
4. What is the purpose of the alliances Amazon.com has made?

---

ware or music) can be digitized to be delivered online for additional savings. On the other hand, delivery of *services*, such as buying an airline ticket or buying stocks or insurance online, can be done 100 percent electronically, with considerable cost reduction potential. Therefore, online delivery of services is growing very rapidly, with millions of new customers being added annually.

We will take a quick look here at the leading online service industries: banking, trading of securities (stocks, bonds), job matching, travel services, and real estate.

Cyberbanking.   Electronic banking, also known as **cyberbanking**, includes various banking activities conducted from home, a business, or on the road instead of at a physical bank location. Electronic banking has capabilities ranging from paying bills to applying for a loan. It saves time and is convenient for customers. For banks, it offers an inexpensive alternative to branch banking (for example, about 2 cents' cost per

cyberbanking *Various banking activities conducted electronically from home, a business, or on the road instead of at a physical bank location.*

virtual bank   *A banking institution dedicated solely to Internet transactions.*

transaction versus $1.07 at a physical branch) and a chance to enlist remote customers. Many banks now offer online banking, and some use EC as a major competitive strategy. In addition to regular banks with added online services, we are seeing the emergence of **virtual banks**, dedicated solely to Internet transactions, such as *netbank.com*.

International and Multiple-Currency Banking.   International banking and the ability to handle trading in multiple currencies are critical for international trade. Transfers of electronic funds and electronic letters of credit are important services in international banking. An example of support for EC global trade is provided by TradeCard (*tradecard.com*) in conjunction with MasterCard. Banks and companies such as Oanda also provide currency conversion of over 160 currencies. Although some international retail purchasing can be done by giving a credit card number, other transactions may require cross-border banking support. For example, Hong Kong and Shanghai Bank (*hsbc.com.hk*) has developed a special system (called Hexagon) to provide electronic banking in 60 countries. Using this system, the bank has leveraged its reputation and infrastructure in the developing economies of Asia, to rapidly become a major international bank without developing an extensive new branch network.

Online Securities Trading.   Emarketer.com (2003) has estimated that by the year 2004 about 35 million people in the United States will be using computers to trade stocks, bonds, and other financial instruments. In Korea, more than half of stock traders are already using the Internet for that purpose. Why? Because it makes a lot of dollars and "sense": An online trade typically costs the trader between $5 and $15, compared to an average fee of $100 from a full-service broker and $25 from a discount broker. Orders can be placed from anywhere, any time, even from your cell phone, and there is no waiting on busy telephone lines. Furthermore, the chance of making mistakes is small because online trading does away with oral communication of orders. Investors can find on the Web a considerable amount of information regarding specific companies or mutual funds in which to invest (e.g., *money.cnn.com*, *bloomberg.com*).

FIN   **EXAMPLE**   *How Online Trading Works.* Let's say you have an account with Charles Schwab. You access Schwab's Web site (*schwab.com*) from your PC or your Internet-enabled mobile device, enter your account number and password to access your personalized Web page, and then click on "stock trading." Using a menu, you enter the details of your order (buy or sell, margin or cash, price limit, market order, etc.). The computer tells you the current "ask" and "bid" prices, much as a broker would do on the telephone, and you can approve or reject the transaction. Some well-known companies that offer only online trading are E*Trade, Ameritrade, and Suretrade.

wiley.com/college/turban

However, both online banking and securities trading require tight security. Otherwise, your money may be at risk. (See Online File W5.6 for an example.) Most online banks and stock traders use only ID numbers and passwords. Yet even this may not be secure enough. See Section 5.8 on how to improve online security.

The Online Job Market.   The Internet offers a promising new environment for job seekers and for companies searching for hard-to-find employees. Thousands of companies and government agencies advertise available positions of all types of jobs, accept resumes, and take applications via the Internet. The online job market is especially effective for technology-oriented jobs.

   The online job market is used by job seekers to reply online to employment ads, to place resumes on various sites, and to use recruiting firms (e.g., *monster.com*, *jobdirect.com*, *jobcenter.com*). Companies who have jobs to offer advertise openings on their Web sites or search the bulletin boards of recruiting firms. In many countries governments must advertise job openings on the Internet. In addition, hundreds of job-placement brokers and related services are active on the Web.

Travel Services. The Internet is an ideal place to plan, explore, and economically arrange almost any trip. Online travel services allow you to purchase airline tickets, reserve hotel rooms, and rent cars. Most sites also offer a fare-tracker feature that sends you e-mail messages about low-cost flights to your favorite destinations or from your home city. Examples of comprehensive online travel services are Expedia.com, Travelocity.com, and Orbitz.com. Services are also provided online by all major airline vacation services, large conventional travel agencies, car rental agencies, hotels (e.g., *hotels.com*), and tour companies. Priceline.com allows you to set a price you are willing to pay for an airline ticket or hotel accommodations and then attempts to find a vendor that will match your price. A similar service offered by Hotwire.com tries to find the lowest available price for you.

"First of all—you need a Web site."
©2002 *Carole Cable from cartoonbank.com. All rights reserved.*

Real Estate. Real estate transactions are an ideal area for e-commerce. You can view many properties on the screen, and can sort and organize properties according to your preferences and decision criteria. In some locations brokers allow the use of real estate databases only from their offices, but considerable information is now available on the Internet. For example, Realtor.com allows you to search a database of over 1.2 million homes across the United States. The database is composed of local "multiple listings" of all available properties, in hundreds of locations. Those who are looking for an apartment can try Apartments.com.

Customer Service

Whether an organization is selling to organizations or to individuals, in many cases a competitive edge is gained by providing superb customer service. In e-commerce, customer service becomes even more critical, since customers and merchants do not meet face-to-face.

Phases in the Customer Service Life Cycle. Customer service should be approached as a business life cycle process, with the following four phases:

Phase 1: Requirements. Assist the customer to determine needs by providing photographs of a product, video presentations, textual descriptions, articles or reviews, sound bites on a CD, and downloadable demonstration files. Also use intelligent agents to make requirements suggestions.

Phase 2: Acquisition. Help the customer to acquire a product or service (online order entry, negotiations, closing of sale, and delivery).

Phase 3: Ownership. Support the customer on an ongoing basis (interactive online user groups, online technical support, FAQs [frequently asked questions] and answers, resource libraries, newsletters, and online renewal of subscriptions).

Phase 4: Retirement. Help the client to dispose of a service or product (online resale, classified ads).

Many activities can be conducted in each of these phases. For example, when an airline offers information such as flight schedules and fare quotes on its Web site, it is supporting phases 1 and 2. Similarly, when computer vendors provide electronic help desks for their customers, they are supporting phase 3. Dell will help you to auction your obsolete computer, and Amazon.com will help you to sell used books, activities that support phase 4.

EXAMPLE *Fidelity Investments Offers Financial Information and News.* Fidelity Investments provides investors with "the right tools to make their own best investment decisions." The site (*fidelity.com*) has several sections, which include daily updates of financial news, information about Fidelity's mutual funds, material for interactive investment and retirement planning, and brokerage services. This is an example of support given to phase 1 in the online selling of services. The site also helps customers buy Fidelity's products (phase 2), handle their accounts (phase 3), and sell the securities (phase 4).

Facilitating Customer Service. Various tools are available for facilitating online customer service: Companies can use e-mail to send confirmations, product information, and instructions to customers and also to take orders, complaints, and other inquiries. Customers can track the status of their orders, services (such as FedEx shipments, banking or stock-trading activities), or job applications online at the company Web site. They can build individualized pages at the vendor's site, at which customized information can be provided. In company-sponsored chat rooms, customers can interact with each other and with the vendor's personnel, who monitor the chat room. And at Web-based call centers a company can handle customers' inquiries in any form they come (fax, telephone, e-mail, letters) and answer them quickly and automatically, whenever possible. Customers can also interact with the vendor and get quick problem resolution through these communication centers. (See Chapter 4 for details and more tools.) An example of a Web-based call center is included in Online File W5.7 about Canadian Tire's integrated call center.

wiley.com/college/turban

Issues in E-Tailing

Despite e-tailing's ongoing growth, many e-tailers continue to face some major issues related to e-tailing. If not solved, they can slow the growth of an organization's e-tailing efforts. These issues are described below.

1. *Resolving channel conflict.* If a seller is a click-and-mortar company, such as Levi's or GM, it may face a conflict with its regular distributors when it sells directly online. Known as **channel conflict**, this situation can alienate the regular distributors. Channel conflict has forced some companies (e.g., Lego.com) to limit their B2C efforts; others (e.g., some automotive companies) have decided not to sell direct online. An alternative approach is to try to collaborate in some way with the existing distributors whose services may be restructured. For example, an auto company could allow customers to configure a car online, but require that the car be picked up from a dealer, where customers could arrange financing, warranties, and service.

channel conflict *The alienation of existing distributors when a company decides to sell to customers directly online.*

2. *Resolving conflicts within click-and-mortar organizations.* When an established company decides to sell direct online on a large scale, it may create a conflict within its offline operations. Conflicts may arise in areas such as pricing of products and services, allocation of resources (e.g., advertising budget), and logistics services provided by the offline activities to the online activities (e.g., handling of returns of items bought online). As a result of these conflicts, some companies have completely separated the "clicks" (the online portion of the organization) from the "mortar" or "bricks" (the traditional brick-and-mortar part of the organization). Such separation may increase expenses and reduce the synergy between the two organizational parts.

3. *Organizing order fulfillment and logistics.* E-tailers face a difficult problem of how to ship very small quantities to a large number of buyers. This can be a difficult undertaking, especially when returned items need to be handled.

4. *Determining viability and risk of online e-tailers.* Many purely online e-tailers folded in 2000–2002 (see Kaplan, 2002), the result of problems with cash flow, customer acquisition, order fulfillment, and demand forecasting. Online competition, especially in commodity-type products such as CDs, toys, books, or groceries, became very fierce, due to the ease of entry to the marketplace. So a problem most young e-tailers face is to determine how long to operate while you are still losing money and how to finance the losses.

5. *Identifying appropriate revenue models.* One early dot-com model was to generate enough revenue from advertising to keep the business afloat until the customer

base reached critical mass. This model did not work. Too many dot-coms were competing for too few advertising dollars, which went mainly to a small number of well-known sites such as AOL and Yahoo. In addition, there was a "chicken-and-egg" problem: Sites could not get advertisers to come if they did not have enough visitors. To succeed in EC, it is necessary to identify appropriate revenue models. (For further discussion of EC revenue models, see Turban et al., 2004.)

To successfully implement e-tailing and solve the five issues just discussed, it is frequently necessary to conduct market research. Market research is needed for product design, marketing, and advertising decisions and strategy. For a discussion of market research in e-commerce, see Online File W5.8.

wiley.com/college/turban

Before you go on . . .

1. Describe electronic storefronts and malls.

2. What are some general features (critical success factors) that make the delivery of online services (e.g., cyberbanking, securities trading, job hunting, travel services) successful for both sellers and buyers?

3. Describe how customer service is provided online and list its four phases.

4. List the major issues relating to e-tailing.

5.4 ONLINE ADVERTISING

Advertising is an attempt to disseminate information in order to influence a buyer–seller transaction. Traditional advertising on TV or in newspapers is impersonal, one-way mass communication. Direct-response marketing (telemarketing) contacts individuals by direct mail or telephone and requires them to respond in order to make a purchase. The direct-response approach personalizes advertising and marketing, but it can be expensive, slow, and ineffective (and from the consumer's point of view, annoying).

Internet advertising redefines the advertising process, making it media-rich, dynamic, and interactive. It improves on traditional forms of advertising in a number of ways: Internet ads can be updated any time at minimal cost and therefore can be always timely. Internet ads can reach very large numbers of potential buyers all over the world, and they are sometimes cheaper in comparison to print (newspaper and magazine), radio, or television ads. Internet ads can be interactive and targeted to specific interest groups and/or to individuals. Finally, it makes sense to move advertising to the Internet, where the number of viewers is growing.

Nevertheless, the Internet as an advertising medium does have some shortcomings, most of which relate to the difficulty in measuring the effectiveness and cost-justification of the ads. For example, it is difficult to measure the actual results of placing a banner ad or sending a marketing e-mail.

Advertising Methods

The most common online advertising methods are banners, pop-ups, and e-mails. The essentials of these and some other methods are presented next.

Banners. **Banners** are simply electronic billboards. Typically, a banner contains a short text or graphical message to promote a product or a vendor. It may even contain video clips and sound. When customers *click* on a banner, they are *transferred* to the advertiser's home page. Banner advertising is the most commonly used form of advertising on the Internet. Advertisers go to great lengths to design banners that catch consumers' attention.

banners *Electronic billboards, which typically contain a short text or graphical message to promote a product or a vendor.*

keyword banner *Banner advertising that appears when a predetermined word is queried from a search engine.*

random banner *Banner advertising that appears randomly.*

There are two types of banners: **Key word banners** appear when a predetermined word is queried from a search engine. This is effective for companies who want to narrow their target to consumers interested in particular topics. **Random banners** appear randomly; they might be used to introduce new products to the widest possible audience or to promote brand recognition.

A major advantage of banners is that they can be customized to the target audience (a market segment or even an individual user). If the computer system knows who you are or what your profile is, you may be sent a banner that is supposed to match your interests. However, one of the major drawbacks of banners is that limited information is allowed due to their small size. Hence advertisers need to think of creative but short messages to attract viewers. Another drawback is that banners are ignored by many viewers today. A new generation of banner-like ads are the pop-ups.

Pop-Up, Pop-Under, and Similar Ads. Pop-up, pop-under, and similar ads are contained in a new browser window that is automatically launched when one enters or exits a Web site or by other triggers such as a delay during Internet surfing. A **pop-up ad** appears in front of the current browser window. A **pop-under ad** appears underneath the active window; when users close the active window, they see the ad. Pop-ups and pop-unders are sometime difficult to close. These methods are controversial: Many users strongly object to these ads, which they consider intrusive.

pop-up ad *An advertisement that is automatically launched by some trigger and appears in front of the active window.*

pop-under ad *An advertisement that is automatically launched by some trigger and appears underneath the active window.*

E-Mail Advertising. E-mail is emerging as an Internet advertising and marketing channel. It is generally cost-effective to implement and provides a better and quicker response rate than other advertising channels (such as print ads). Marketers develop or purchase a list of e-mail addresses, place them in a customer database, and then send advertisements via e-mail. A list of e-mail addresses can be a very powerful tool because the marketer can target a group of people or even individuals. For example, Restaurants.com (see the Real-World Case at the end of the chapter) uses e-mail to send restaurant coupons to millions of customers. However, as with pop-ups, there is a potential for misuse of e-mail advertising, and some consumers are receiving a flood of unsolicited mail. (We address the topic of unsolicited advertising below.)

Electronic Catalogs and Brochures. As described earlier, the merchant's objective in using online catalogs is to advertise and promote products and services. Sometimes merchants find it useful to provide a *customized electronic catalog* to some individual customers. Each catalog is assembled specifically for the particular buyer, usually a company but sometimes even an individual consumer who buys frequently or in large quantities.

Other Forms of Internet Advertising. Online advertising can be done in several other forms, including posting advertising in chat rooms (newsgroups) and in classified ads (see *infospace.com/info.cls2K/*). Advertising on Internet radio is just beginning, and soon advertising on Internet television will commence. Of special interest is advertising to members of Internet communities. Community sites (such as *geocities.com*) are gathering places for people of similar interests and are therefore a logical place to promote products related to those interests. Another interesting method is wireless ads, which we describe in Chapter 6.

Some Advertising Issues and Approaches

There are many issues related to the implementation of Internet advertising: how to design ads for the Internet, where and when to advertise, and how to integrate online and offline ads. Most such decisions require the input of marketing and advertising experts. Here, we present some illustrative issues in online advertising.

spamming *Indiscriminate distribution of electronic ads without permission of the receiver.*

Unsolicited Advertising. **Spamming** is the indiscriminate distribution of electronic ads without permission of the receiver. E-mail spamming, also known as *unsolicited commercial e-mail (UCE)*, has been part of the Internet for years. Another form of spamming is the pop-up ad. Unfortunately, spamming seems to be getting worse over time. The drivers of spamming and some potential solutions are described in Online File W5.9. Permission marketing is one answer to e-mail spamming.

Permission Marketing.   **Permission marketing** asks consumers to give their permission to voluntarily accept online advertising and e-mail. Typically, consumers are asked to complete an electronic form that asks what they are interested in and requests permission to send related marketing information. Sometimes consumers are offered incentives to receive advertising; at the least, marketers try to send information in an entertaining, educational, or other interesting manner.

Permission marketing is the basis of many Internet marketing strategies. For example, millions of users receive e-mails periodically from airlines such as American and Southwest. Users of this marketing service can ask for notification of low fares from their hometown or to their favorite destinations. Users can easily unsubscribe at any time. Permission marketing is also extremely important for market research (e.g., see Media Metrix at *comscore.com*).

In one particularly interesting form of permission marketing, companies such as Clickdough.com, Getpaid4.com, and CashSurfers.com have built customer lists of millions of people who are happy to receive advertising messages whenever they are on the Web. These customers are paid $0.25 to $0.50 an hour to view messages while they do their normal surfing. They may also be paid $0.10 an hour for the surfing time of any friends they refer to the site.

Viral Marketing.   **Viral marketing** refers to online "word-of-mouth" marketing. The main idea in viral marketing is to have people forward messages to friends, suggesting that they "check this out." A marketer can distribute a small game program, for example, embedded with a sponsor's e-mail, that is easy to forward. By releasing a few thousand copies, vendors hope to reach many more thousands.

Word-of-mouth marketing has been used for generations, but its speed and reach are multiplied manyfold by the Internet. Viral marketing is one of the new models being used to build brand awareness at a minimal cost. It has long been a favorite strategy of online advertisers pushing youth-oriented products.

Unfortunately, though, several e-mail hoaxes have spread via viral marketing. Also, a more serious danger of viral marketing is that a destructive computer virus can be added to an innocent advertisement, game, or message. However, when used properly, viral marketing can be both effective and efficient.

Interactive Advertising and Marketing.   All advertisers, whether online or not, attempt to target their ads to the desired market and, if possible, even to individuals. A good salesperson is trained to interact with sales prospects, asking questions about the features they are looking for and handling possible objections as they come up. Online advertising comes closer to supporting this one-to-one selling process than more traditional advertising media possibly can.

Ideally, in interactive marketing, advertisers present customized, one-on-one ads. The term *interactive* points to the ability to address an individual, to gather and remember that person's responses, and to serve that customer based on his or her previous, unique responses. When the Internet is combined with databases, interactive marketing becomes a very effective and affordable competitive strategy.

Online Promotions: Attracting Visitors to a Site.   A Web site without visitors has little value. The following are three ways to attract visitors to a Web site.

Making the Top of the List of a Search Engine.   Web sites submit their URLs to search engines. The search engine's intelligent program (called a *spider*) crawls through the submitted site, indexing all related content and links. Some lists generated by search engines include hundreds or thousands of items. Users that view the results submitted by a search engine typically start by clicking on the first 10 or so items, and soon get tired. So, for best exposure, advertisers like to be in the top 10 on the list.

wiley.com/college/turban

permission marketing *Method of marketing that asks consumers to give their permission to voluntarily accept online advertising and e-mail.*

viral marketing *Online "word-of-mouth" marketing.*

How does one make the top 10? If a company understands how a search engine's program ranks its findings, it can get to the top of a search engine's list merely by adding, removing, or changing a few sentences on its Web pages. However, this is not easy, as everyone wants to do it, so there are sometimes several thousand entries competing to be in the top 10. It may be easier to pay the search engine to put a banner at the top of the lists (e.g., usually on the right-hand side or the top of the screen at *google.com*'s results).

Online Events, Promotions, and Attractions. People generally like the idea of something funny or something free, or both. Contests, quizzes, coupons, and free samples are therefore an integral part of e-marketing. Running promotions on the Internet is similar to running offline promotions. These mechanisms are designed to attract visitors and to keep their attention. For innovative ideas for promotions and attractions used by companies online, see Strauss et al. (2003).

Online Coupons. Just as in offline advertising, online shoppers can get discounts via coupons. You can gather any discount coupons you want by accessing sites like *hotcoupons.com* or *coupons.com*, selecting the store where you plan to redeem the coupons, and printing them. In the future, transfer of coupons directly to a virtual supermarket (such as Peapod.com or Netgrocer.com) will be available so that you can receive discounts on the items you buy there. Coupons also can be distributed via wireless devices, based on your location. As you approach a restaurant, for example, you may be offered a 15 percent discount electronic coupon to show to the proprietors when you arrive.

Before you go on . . .

1. Describe online advertising, its methods, and benefits.
2. Discuss spamming and permission marketing.
3. What is viral marketing?
4. List popular online promotion methods.

5.5 B2B APPLICATIONS

In *business to business (B2B) applications*, the buyers, sellers, and transactions involve only organizations. Business-to-business comprises about 85 percent of EC volume. It covers a broad spectrum of applications that enable an enterprise to form electronic relationships with its distributors, resellers, suppliers, customers, and other partners. By using B2B, organizations can restructure their supply chains and partner relationships.

There are several business models for B2B applications. The major ones are sell-side marketplaces, buy-side marketplaces, and electronic exchanges.

Sell-Side Marketplaces

sell-side marketplace *B2B model in which organizations sell to other organizations from their own private e-marketplace and/or from a third-party site.*

In the **sell-side marketplace** model, organizations attempt to sell their products or services to other organizations electronically from their own private e-marketplace and/or from a third-party site. This model is similar to the B2C model in which the buyer is expected to come to the seller's site, view catalogs, and place an order. In the B2B sell-side marketplace, however, the buyer is an organization.

The key mechanisms in the sell-side model are: (1) electronic catalogs that can be customized for each large buyer and (2) forward auctions. Sellers such as Dell Computer (*dellauction.com*) use auctions extensively. In addition to auctions from their own Web sites, organizations can use third-party auction sites, such as eBay, to liquidate items. Companies such as Freemarkets.com are helping organizations to auction obsolete and old assets and inventories (see Online File W5.10).

The sell-side model is used by hundreds of thousands of companies and is especially powerful for companies with superb reputations. The seller can be either a manufacturer (e.g., Dell, IBM), a distributor (e.g., *avnet.com*), or a retailer (e.g., *bigboxx.com*). The seller uses EC to increase sales, reduce selling and advertising expenditures, increase delivery speed, and reduce administrative costs. The sell-side model is especially suitable to customization. For example, organizational customers can configure their orders online at *cisco.com*, *dell.com*, and others. Self-customization of orders results in fewer misunderstandings about what customers want and in much faster order fulfillment.

wiley.com/college/turban

Buy-Side Marketplaces

The **buy-side marketplace** is a model in which organizations attempt to buy needed products or services from other organizations electronically. A major method of buying goods and services in the buy-side model is a *reverse auction*. Here, a company that wants to buy items places a *request for quotation (RFQ)* on its Web site or in a third-party bidding marketplace. Once RFQs are posted, sellers (usually preapproved suppliers) submit bids electronically. Such auctions attract large pools of willing sellers, who can be either manufacturers, distributors, or retailers. The bids are routed via the buyer's intranet to the engineering and finance departments for evaluation. Clarifications are made via e-mail, and the winner is notified electronically.

buy-side marketplace *B2B model in which organizations buy needed products or services from other organizations electronically, often through a reverse auction.*

The buy-side model uses EC technology to streamline the purchasing process in order to reduce the cost of items purchased, the administrative cost of procurement, and the purchasing cycle time. Procurements using a third-party buy-side marketplace model are especially popular for medium and small organizations.

E-Procurement. Purchasing by using electronic support is referred to as **e-procurement**. E-procurement uses *reverse auctions* (as discussed above) as well as two other popular mechanisms: group purchasing and desktop purchasing.

e-procurement *Purchasing by using electronic support.*

Group Purchasing. In **group purchasing**, the orders of many buyers are aggregated so that they total to a large volume, in order to merit more seller attention. The aggregated order can then be placed on a reverse auction, and a volume discount can be negotiated. Typically, the orders of small buyers are aggregated by a third-party vendor, such as Shop2gether.com or United Sourcing Alliance (*usa-llc.com*). Group purchasing is especially popular in the health care industry (see *all-health.com*).

group purchasing *The aggregation of purchasing orders from many buyers so that a volume discount can be obtained.*

Desktop Purchasing. A special case of e-procurement known as **desktop purchasing**, suppliers' catalogs are aggregated into an internal master catalog on the buyer's server, so that the company's purchasing agents (or even end users) can shop more conveniently. Desktop purchasing is most suitable for *indirect maintenance, replacement, and operations (MRO) items*, such as office supplies. (The term *indirect* refers to the fact that these items are not inputs to manufacturing.) In the desktop purchasing model, a company has many suppliers, but the quantities purchased from each are relatively small. This model is most appropriate for government entities and for large companies (such as Schlumberger, as described in IT's about Business 5.3, page 146).

desktop purchasing *E-procurement method in which suppliers' catalogs are aggregated into an internal master catalog on the buyer's server for use by the company's purchasing agents.*

Electronic Exchanges

E-marketplaces in which there are many sellers and many buyers are called **public exchanges** (in short, **exchanges**). They are open to all, and frequently are owned and operated by a third party. According to Kaplan and Sawhney (2000), there are four basic types of exchanges:

public exchanges (exchanges) *E-marketplace in which there are many sellers and many buyers, and entry is open to all; frequently owned and operated by a third party.*

1. ***Vertical distributors for direct materials.*** These are B2B marketplaces where *direct materials* (materials that are inputs to manufacturing) are traded, usually in large quantities in an environment of long-term relationship known as *systematic*

IT's ABOUT BUSINESS

POM

5.3: E-Procurement at Schlumberger

Schlumberger is an $8.5 billion company with 60,000 employees in 100 countries. That makes it the world's largest oil-service company. In 2000 the company installed a Web-based automated procurement system in Oilfield Services, its largest division. With this system, employees can buy office supplies and small equipment as well as computers direct from their desktops. The single desktop system streamlined and sped up the purchasing operation, reducing both costs and the number of people involved in the process. The system also enables the company to consolidate purchases for volume discounts from vendors.

The system has two parts: The internal portion uses CommerceOne's BuySite procurement software and runs on the company's intranet. Once the employee selects the item, the system generates the requisition, routes it electronically to the proper people for approval, and turns it into a purchase order. The second part of the system, CommerceOne's MarketSite, transmits the purchase orders to the suppliers. This B2B Internet marketplace connects Schlumberger with hundreds of suppliers with a single, low-cost, many-to-many system.

Negotiation of prices is accomplished with individual vendors. For example, Office Depot's entire catalog is posted on the MarketSite, but the Schlumberger employees see only the subset of previously negotiated products and prices. (In the future, the company plans to negotiate prices in *real time* through auctions and other bidding systems.)

The benefits of the system are evident in both cost and processes. The cost of goods has been reduced, as have the transaction costs. Employees spend much less time in the ordering process, giving them more time for their true work. The system is also much more cost efficient for the suppliers, who can then pass along savings to customers. Procurement effectiveness can be increased because tracing the overall procurement activity is now possible.

Getting the system up and running was implemented in stages and ran at the same time as existing systems. There were no implementation issues for employees (once the system was in place, the old system was disabled), and there were no complaints in regard to the old system being shut down (no one was using the old system anymore).

Sources: Compiled from Ovans (2000) and CommerceOne.com, "Schlumberger Oilfield Services Selects Commerce One Solution to Fully Automate Its Worldwide Procurement Process," February 1, 1999, *commerceone.com/news/releases/schlumberger.html* (accessed July 2003); CommerceOne.com, "Customer Snapshot: Schlumberger," 2003, *commerceone.com/customers/profiles/schlumberger.pdf* (accessed July 2003); and *Schlumberger.com* (2003).

QUESTIONS

1. What are the benefits of the e-procurement system to Schlumberger?
2. How does it empower the buyers?
3. Why would real-time price negotiations be beneficial?

sourcing. Examples are Plasticsnet.com and Papersite.com. Both fixed and negotiated prices are common in this type of exchange.

2. ***Vertical exchanges for indirect materials.*** Here indirect materials in *one industry* are purchased usually on an "as-needed" basis (called *spot sourcing*). Buyers and sellers may not even know each other. ChemConnect.com and Isteelasia.com are examples. In such vertical exchanges, prices are continually changing, based on the matching of supply and demand. Auctions are typically used in this kind of B2B marketplace, sometimes done in private trading rooms, which are available in exchanges like ChemConnect.com (see IT's about Business 5.4).

3. ***Horizontal distributors.*** These are "many-to-many" e-marketplaces for indirect (MRO) materials, such as office supplies, used by *any industry*. Prices are fixed or negotiated in this systematic sourcing-type exchange. Examples are EcEurope.com, Globalsources.com, and Alibaba.com.

4. ***Functional exchanges.*** Here, needed services such as temporary help or extra space are traded on an "as-needed" basis (spot sourcing). For example, Employease.com can find temporary labor using employers in its Employease Network. Prices are dynamic, and they vary depending on supply and demand.

All four types of exchanges offer diversified support services, ranging from payments to logistics. Vertical exchanges are frequently owned and managed by a group

IT'S ABOUT BUSINESS

MKT

5.4: Chemical Companies "Bond" at ChemConnect

Buyers and sellers of chemicals and plastics today can meet electronically in a large vertical exchange called ChemConnect (*chemconnect.com*). Using this exchange, *global* chemical-industry leaders such as British Petroleum, Dow Chemical, BASF, Hyundai, and Sumitomo can reduce trading cycle time and cost and can find new markets and trading partners around the globe.

ChemConnect provides a public trading marketplace and an information portal to more than 9,000 members in 150 countries. In 2003, over 60,000 products were traded in this public, third-party–managed e-marketplace. Chemconnect provides three marketplaces (as of October 11, 2003): a commodity markets platform, a marketplace for sellers, and a marketplace for buyers, as described below.

At the *commodity markets platform*, prequalified producers, customers, and distributors come together in real time to sell and buy chemical-related commodities like natural-gas liquids, oxygenates, olefins, and polymers. They can even simultaneously execute multiple deals. Transactions are done through regional trading hubs.

The *marketplace for sellers* has many tools ranging from electronic catalogs to forward auctions. It enables companies to find buyers all over the world. ChemConnect provides all the necessary tools to expedite selling and achieving the best prices. It also allows for negotiations.

The *marketplace for buyers* is a place where thousands of buyers shop for chemical-related indirect materials (and a few direct materials). The market provides for automated request for proposal (RFP) tools as well as a complete online reverse auction. The sellers' market is connected to the buyers' market, so that sellers can connect to the RFPs posted on the marketplace for buyers. (Note that RFP and RFQ are interchangeables terms; RFP is used more in government bidding.)

In the three marketplaces, ChemConnect provides logistics and payment options. In all of its trading mechanisms, up-to-the-minute market information is available and can be translated to 30 different languages. Members pay transaction fees only for successfully completed transactions. Business partners provide several support services, such as financial services for the market members. The marketplaces work with certain rules and guidelines that ensure an unbiased approach to the trades. There is full disclosure of all legal requirements, payments, trading rules, and so on. (Click on "Legal info and privacy issues" at the ChemConnect Web site.) ChemConnect is growing rapidly, adding members and trading volume.

Source: Compiled from *chemconnect.com* (accessed October 11, 2003).

QUESTIONS

1. What are the advantages of the ChemConnect exchange?
2. Why are there three trading places?
3. Why does the exchange provide information portal services?

---

of big players in an industry (referred to as a *consortium*). For example, Marriott and Hyatt own a procurement consortium for the hotel industry, and ChevronTexaco owns an energy e-marketplace. The vertical e-marketplaces offer services particularly suited to the community they serve.

Since B2B activities involve many companies, specialized network infrastructure is needed. Such infrastructure works either as an Internet/EDI or as extranets (see Chapter 9). A related EC activity, usually done between and among organizations, is collaborative commerce (see Chapters 4 and 8).

Before you go on . . .

1. Briefly differentiate between the sell-side marketplace and the buy-side marketplace.
2. Describe how forward and reverse auctions are used in B2B commerce.
3. Describe the various methods of e-procurement.
4. Describe the role of exchanges in B2B.

5.6 INTRABUSINESS AND BUSINESS-TO-EMPLOYEES EC

intrabusiness *E-commerce done within an organization (between an organization and its employees or among business units).*

E-commerce can be done not only between business partners but also *within* organizations. Such activity is referred to as *intrabusiness* EC or in short, **intrabusiness**. Intrabusiness can be done between a business and its employees (B2E), among units within the business (usually done as collaborative commerce), and among employees in the same business.

Business to Its Employees (B2E) Commerce

Companies are finding many ways to do business electronically with their own employees. They disseminate information to employees over the company intranet, for example. They also allow employees to manage their fringe benefits and take training classes electronically. In addition, employees can buy discounted insurance, travel packages, and tickets to events on the corporate intranet, and they can electronically order supplies and material needed for their work. Also, many companies have electronic corporate stores that sell the company's products to its employees, usually at a discount.

E-Commerce between and among Units within the Business

Large corporations frequently consist of independent units, or *strategic business units (SBUs)*, which "sell" or "buy" materials, products, and services from each other. Transactions of this type can be easily automated and performed over the intranet. An SBU can be considered as either a seller or a buyer. An example would be company-owned dealerships, which buy goods from the main company. This type of EC helps improve the internal supply chain operations.

The major benefits of c-commerce are smoothing the supply chain, reducing inventories along the supply chain, reducing operating costs, increasing customer satisfaction, and increasing a company's competitive edge. The challenges faced by the collaborators are software integration issues, technology selection, trust and security, and resistance to change and collaboration.

E-Commerce between and among Corporate Employees

Many large organizations allow employees to post classified ads on the company intranet, through which employees can buy and sell products and services from each other. This service is especially popular in universities, where it has been conducted since even before the commercialization of the Internet. The Internet is used for other collaborations as well, such as scheduling of employee athletic and social events.

> ### Before you go on . . .
> 1. Describe intrabusiness EC and list its major types.
> 2. Define B2E.

5.7 E-GOVERNMENT AND CONSUMER-TO-CONSUMER EC

e-government *The use of e-commerce to deliver information and public services to citizens, business partners and suppliers of government entities, and those working in the public sector.*

E-Government

As e-commerce matures and its tools and applications improve, greater attention is being given to its use to improve the business of public institutions and governments (country, state, county, city, etc). **E-government** is the use of Internet technology in general and e-commerce in particular to deliver information and public services to citizens, business partners and suppliers of government entities, and those working in the public sector. It is also an efficient way of conducting business transactions with citizens and businesses and within the governments themselves.

E-government offers a number of potential benefits: It improves the efficiency and effectiveness of the functions of government, including the delivery of public services. It enables governments to be more transparent to citizens and businesses by giving access to more of the information generated by government. E-government also offers greater opportunities for citizens to provide feedback to government agencies and to participate in democratic institutions and processes. As a result, e-government may facilitate fundamental changes in the relationships between citizens and governments.

E-government applications can be divided into three major categories: *government-to-citizens (G2C)*, *government-to-business (G2B)*, and *government-to-government (G2G)*. In the first category (G2C), government agencies are increasingly using the Internet to provide various services to citizens. An example is *electronic benefits transfer (EBT)*, in which governments (usually state or national) transfer benefits, such as Social Security and pension payments, directly to recipients' bank accounts or to smart cards. In G2B, governments use the Internet to sell to or buy from businesses. For example, electronic tendering systems using reverse auctions are becoming mandatory, in order to ensure the best price for government procurement of goods and services. G2G includes intragovernment EC (transactions between different governments) as well as services among different governmental agencies. For an example of one e-government initiative in Australia, see IT's about Business 5.5.

IT's ABOUT BUSINESS ── GOV

5.5: E-Government in Western Australia

The focus of the Western Australian (WA) government agency Contract and Management Services (CAMS) is to develop online contract management solutions for the public sector. CAMS Online allows government agencies to search existing contracts to discover how to access the contracts that are in common use by different government agencies (for example, lightbulbs or paper towels bought by various government units). It also enables suppliers wanting to sell to the government to view the current tenders (bids) on the Western Australia Government Contracting Information Bulletin Board and to download tender documents from that site.

CAMS Online also provides government departments and agencies with unbiased expert advice on e-commerce, Internet, and communication services, and how-to's on building a bridge between the technological needs of the public sector and the expertise of the private sector.

WA's e-commerce activities include electronic markets for government buying. The *WA Government Electronic Market* provides online supplier catalogs, electronic purchase orders, and electronic invoicing, EFT, and check and credit card payments (*ecc.online.wa.gov.au/news,19*, September 2002).

Government-to-government e-commerce functions include *DataLink*, which enables the transfer of data using a secure and controlled environment. *DataLink* is an ideal solution for government agencies needing to exchange large volumes of operational information. An intragovernment EC application is a videoconferencing service that offers two-way video and audio links, enabling government employees to meet together electronically from up to eight sites at any one time.

In addition to G2B functions, the G2C Web site also offers online training to citizens. A service called *Westlink* delivers adult training and educational programs to remote areas and schools, including rural and regional communities.

Source: Compiled from business.wa.gov.au (February 2001) and ecc.online.wa.gov.au/news,19 (June/November 2002).

QUESTIONS

1. How is contract management of the Western Australian government agency facilitated by e-commerce tools?

2. Describe the WA online training program.

3. Why would government want to take on a role in promoting e-learning?

Implementing E-Government. Like any other organization, government entities want to move into the digital era, becoming click-and-mortar organizations. However, the transformation from traditional delivery of government services to full implementation of online government services may be a lengthy process.

The business consulting firm Deloitte & Touche conducted a study (Wong, 2000) that identified six stages in the transformation to e-government: *stage 1:* information publishing/dissemination; *stage 2:* "official" two-way transactions, with one department at a time; *stage 3:* multipurpose portals; *stage 4:* portal personalization; *stage 5:* clustering of common services; *stage 6:* full integration and enterprise transformation.

The speed at which a government moves from stage 1 to stage 6 varies, but usually the transformation is very slow. Deloitte & Touche found that in 2000, most governments were still in stage 1 (Wong, 2000).

The implementation issues that are involved in the transformation to e-government depend on which of the six stages of development a government is in, on the plan for moving to higher stages, and on the available funding. In addition, governments are concerned about maintaining the security and privacy of citizens' data, so time and effort must be spent to ensure that security.

In general, implementation of G2B is easier than implementation of G2C. In some countries, such as Hong Kong, G2B implementation is outsourced to a private company that pays all of the startup expenses in exchange for collecting future transaction fees. As G2B services have the potential for rapid cost savings, they can be a good way to begin an e-government EC initiative.

Consumer-to-Consumer E-Commerce

consumer-to-consumer (C2C) *E-commerce in which both the buyer and the seller are individuals (not businesses).*

Consumer-to-consumer (C2C) e-commerce refers to e-commerce in which both the buyer and the seller are individuals (not businesses). C2C is conducted in several ways on the Internet, where the best-known C2C activities are auctions.

C2C Auctions. In dozens of countries, C2C selling and buying on auction sites is exploding. Most auctions are conducted by intermediaries, like ebay.com. Consumers can select general sites such as *800webmall.com* or *auctionanything.com;* they also can use specialized sites such as *buyit.com* or *bid2bid.com.* In addition, many individuals are conducting their own auctions. For example, *greatshop.com* provides software to create online C2C reverse auction communities.

Classified Ads. People sell to other people every day through classified ads in newspapers and magazines. Internet-based classified ads have one big advantage over these more traditional types of classified ads: They offer a national, rather than a local, audience. This wider audience greatly increases the supply of goods and services available and the number of potential buyers. For example, *infospace.com/info.cls2k* contains a list of 3 million job openings and about 500,000 cars, compared with the much smaller numbers you might find locally. Internet-based classifieds often can be edited or changed easily, and in many cases they display photos of the product offered for sale.

The major categories of online classified ads are similar to those found in the newspaper: vehicles, real estate, employment, pets, tickets, and travel. Classified ads are available through most Internet service providers (AOL, MSN, etc.), at some portals (Yahoo, etc.), and from Internet directories, online newspapers, and more. To help narrow the search for a particular item on several sites, shoppers can use search engines. Once users find an ad and get the details, they can e-mail or call the other party for additional information or to make a purchase. Classified sites generate revenue from affiliate sites.

Personal Services. Numerous personal services (lawyers, handy helpers, tax preparers, investment advisors, dating services) are available on the Internet. Some are in the classified ads, but others are listed in specialized Web sites and directories. Some are for free, some for a fee. *Be very careful before you purchase any personal services online.* Fraud or crime could be involved. For example, an online lawyer may not be an expert in the area he or she professes, or may not deliver the service at all.

Support Services to C2C.   When individuals buy products or services from individuals, they usually buy from strangers. The issues of ensuring quality, receiving payments, and preventing fraud are critical to the success of C2C. One service that helps C2C is payments by companies such as PayPal.com (see Section 5.8). Another one is *escrow services*, intermediaries that take the buyer's money and the purchased goods, and only after making sure that the seller delivers what was agreed upon, deliver the goods to the buyer and the money to the seller (for a fee).

Before you go on . . .

1. Define e-government and list its various types.
2. Describe typical G2B activities.
3. Describe the six phases of e-government implementation.
4. Define C2C EC and list some types of C2C activities.

5.8 E-COMMERCE SUPPORT SERVICES

The implementation of EC may require several support services. B2B and B2C applications require payments and order fulfillment; portals require content. Figure 5.2 portrays the collection of the major EC services. They include: e-infrastructure (mostly technology consultants, system developers and integrators, hosting, security,

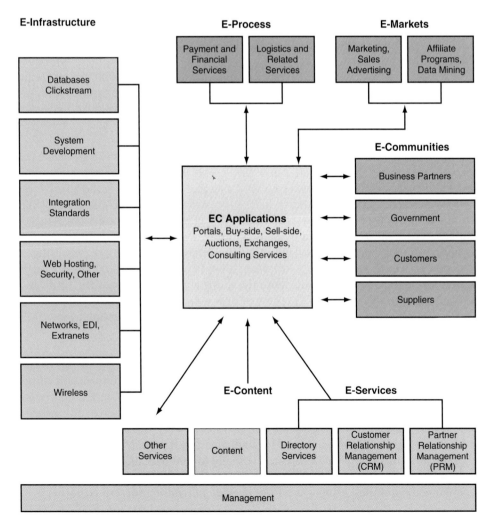

Figure 5.2 *E-commerce support services.*
Source: Drawn by E. Turban. Based on S. Y. Choi et al., The Economics of E-Commerce *(Indianapolis: Macmillan Technical Publications, 1997), p. 18.*

wireless, and networks), e-process (mainly payments and logistics), e-markets (mostly marketing and advertising), e-communities (different audiences and business partners), e-services (CRM, PRM, and directory services), and e-content (supplied by content providers). All of these services support the EC applications in the center of the figure, and all of the services need to be managed.

Here we will focus on two of the above topics—payments and order fulfillment. For details on the other services, see Turban et al. (2004).

Electronic Payments

Payments are an integral part of doing business, whether in the traditional way or online. Unfortunately, in most cases traditional payment systems are not effective for EC, especially for B2B. Cash cannot be used because there is no face-to-face contact. Not everyone accepts credit cards or checks, and some buyers do not have credit cards or checking accounts. Finally, contrary to what many people believe, it may be less secure for the buyer to use the telephone or mail to arrange or send payment, especially from another country, than to complete a secured transaction on a computer. For all of these reasons, a better way is needed to pay for goods and services in cyberspace. This better way is *electronic payment systems*.

Electronic Payment Systems. As in the traditional marketplace, so too in cyberspace, diversity of payment methods allows customers to choose how they wish to pay. Here we will look at some of the most popular electronic payment mechanisms. In Online File W5.11 we consider how to make them secure.

wiley.com/college/turban

Electronic Checks. *Electronic checks (e-checks)* are similar to regular paper checks. They are used mostly in B2B (Reda, 2002). First, the customer establishes a checking account with a bank. When the customer contacts a seller and buys a product or a service, he or she e-mails an encrypted electronic check to the seller. The seller deposits the check in a bank account, and funds are transferred from the buyer's account and into the seller's account.

Like regular checks, e-checks carry a signature (in digital form) that can be verified (see *echeck.net*). Properly signed and endorsed e-checks are exchanged between financial institutions through electronic clearinghouses (see *eccho.org* and *echecksecure.com* for details).

Electronic Credit Cards. *Electronic credit cards* make it possible to charge online payments to one's credit card account. For security, only encrypted credit cards should be used. Credit card details can be encrypted by using the SSL protocol in the buyer's computer (available in standard browsers). (This process is described in Online File W5.11.)

wiley.com/college/turban

Here is how electronic credit cards work: When you buy a book from Amazon, your credit card information and purchase amount are encrypted in your browser. So the information is safe while "traveling" on the Internet. Furthermore, when this information arrives at Amazon, it is not opened but is transferred automatically (in encrypted form) to a clearinghouse, where the information is decrypted for verification and authorization. The complete process of how e-credit cards work is shown in Figure 5.3. Electronic credit cards are used mainly in B2C and in shopping by SMEs (small-to-medium enterprises).

Purchasing Cards. The B2B equivalent of electronic credit cards is *purchasing cards*. In some countries companies pay other companies primarily by means of purchasing cards, rather than by paper checks. Unlike credit cards, where credit is provided for 30 to 60 days (for free) before payment is made to the merchant, payments made with purchasing cards are settled within a week.

Purchasing cards typically are used for unplanned B2B purchases, and corporations generally limit the amount per purchase (usually $1,000 to $2,000). Purchasing cards can be used on the Internet much like regular credit cards. They expedite the process of unplanned purchases, usually as part of *desktop purchasing* (described earlier).

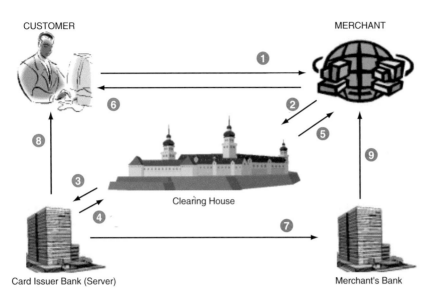

Figure 5.3 *How e-credit cards work. (The number 1–9 indicate the sequence of activities.) Source: Drawn by E. Turban.*

Electronic Cash.   Cash is the most prevalent consumer payment instrument in off-line transactions. Some buyers pay with cash because they do not have checks or credit cards, or because they want to preserve their anonymity. Traditional brick-and-mortar merchants prefer cash since they do not have to pay commissions to credit card companies, and they can put the money to use as soon as it is received. It is logical, therefore, that EC sellers and some buyers may prefer electronic cash. *Electronic cash (e-cash)* appears in three major forms: stored-value money cards, smart cards, and person-to-person payments.

Stored-Value Money Cards.   Although they are in the form of credit cards, **stored-value money cards** actually are a form of e-cash. The cards that you use to pay for photocopies in your library, for transportation, or for telephone calls are stored-value money cards. They allow a fixed amount of prepaid money to be stored. Each time you use the card, the amount is reduced. Millions of travelers, around the world, pay for transportation with such cards. Some of these cards are reloadable, and some are discarded when the money is depleted.

Cards with stored-value money can be also purchased for Internet use. To use such cards, you enter a third-party Web site and provide an ID number and a password, much as you do when you use a prepaid phone card. The money can be used only in participating stores online.

Smart Cards.   Although some people refer to stored-value money cards as smart cards, they are not really the same. True **smart cards** contain a microprocessor (chip) that enables them to store a considerable amount of information (more than 100 times that of a stored-value money card) and to conduct processing. Such cards are frequently *multipurpose*; they can be used as a credit card, debit card, or stored-value money card. In addition, when used in department store chains (as a *loyalty card*), they may contain the purchasing information of shoppers.

Advanced smart cards have the ability to support funds transfer, bill payments, and purchasing from vending machines, or to pay for services such as those offered on television or PCs (Shelter and Procaccino, 2002). Money values can be loaded onto advanced smart cards at ATMs, kiosks, or from your PC. For example, the VISA Cash Card allows you to buy goods or services at participating gas stations, fast-food outlets, pay phones, discount stores, post offices, convenience stores, coffee shops, and even movie theaters. Like stored-value money cards, smart cards are ideal for *micropayments* (small payments of a few dollars or less), but smart cards have additional functions as well. In Hong Kong, the transportation card called Octopus is a stored-value money card that can be used for trains and buses; however, as its capabilities have expanded so that it can be used in stores and vending machines, it is moving to a smart card.

stored-value money card   *A form of e-cash on which a fixed amount of prepaid money is stored; the amount is reduced each time the card is used.*

smart card   *A card that contains a microprocessor (chip) that enables the card to store a considerable amount of information (including stored funds) and to conduct processing.*

A stored-value money card from the Chicago Transit Authority (CTA).

Smart cards can also be used to transfer benefits from companies to their employees (as when retirees get their pension payments) and from governments that pay citizens various entitlements. The money is transferred electronically to a smart card at an ATM, kiosk, or PC.

person-to-person payment *A form of e-cash that enables the transfer of funds between two individuals, or between an individual and a business, without the use of a credit card.*

Person-to-Person Payments. Person-to-person payments are a form of e-cash that enable the transfer of funds between two individuals, or between an individual and a business, without the use of a credit card. They are one of the newest and fastest-growing payment mechanisms. They can be used for a variety of purposes, like repaying money borrowed from a friend, sending money to students at college, paying for an item purchased at an online auction, or sending a gift to a family member.

One of the first companies to offer this service was PayPal. PayPal (now an eBay company) claimed to have had about 20 million customer accounts in 2003, handling more than 35 percent of all transactions of eBay and funneling $8.5 billion in payments through its servers annually (*paypal.com*, accessed September 13, 2003). Other companies offer similar services: AOL QuickCash, One's Bank eMoneyMail, Yahoo PayDirect, and WebCertificate (*webcertificate.com*) are all PayPal competitors.

Virtually all of these person-to-person payment services work in a similar way. First, you select a service and open up an account. Basically, this entails creating a user name, selecting a password, and providing the service with a credit card or bank account number. Next, you add funds from your credit card or bank account to your new account. Now you're ready to send money to someone over the Internet. You access PayPal (for example) with your user name and password, and you specify the e-mail address of the person to receive the money, along with the dollar amount that you want to send. An e-mail is sent to the payee's e-mail address. The e-mail will contain a link back to the service's Web site. When the recipient clicks on the link, he or she will be taken to the service. The recipient will be asked to set up an account to which the money that was sent will be credited. The recipient can then credit the money from this account to either his or her credit card or bank account. The payer pays a small amount (around $1) per transaction.

Electronic Bill Presentment and Payments. An increasing number of people prefer to pay their recurring monthly bills (such as telephone, utilities, credit cards, mortgage, rent, and cable TV) online. The recipients of such payments are even more enthusiastic about such service than the payers, since online payments enable them to reduce processing costs significantly and they receive the funds sooner.

Paying Bills at ATMs. In some countries (e.g., Hong Kong, Singapore) customers can pay bills at regular ATMs. The bills are sent by regular mail or can be viewed online. When you receive the bills, you go to an ATM, slide in your bank card, enter a password, and go to "bill payments" on the menu. All you need to do is insert the account number of the biller and the amount you want to pay; that amount will be charged to your bank card and sent to the biller. You get a printed receipt on the spot. Many merchants give a discount to those who use the service.

Security in Electronic Payments. Two main issues need to be considered under the topic of payment security: what is required in order to make EC payments safe, and the methods that can be used to do so.

Security Requirements. Security requirements for conducting EC are the following:

- ***Authentication.*** The buyer, the seller, and the paying institutions must be assured of the identity of the parties with whom they are dealing.

- ***Integrity.*** It is necessary to ensure that data and information transmitted in EC, such as orders, replies to queries, and payment authorizations, are not accidentally or maliciously altered or destroyed during transmission.

- ***Nonrepudiation.*** Merchants need protection against the customer's unjustified denial of placing an order. On the other hand, customers need protection against merchants' unjustified denial of payments made. (Such denials, of both types, are called *repudiation.*)

- **Privacy.** Many customers want their identity to be secured. They want to make sure others do not know what they buy. Some prefer complete anonymity, as is possible with cash payments.
- **Safety.** Customers want to be sure that it is safe to provide a credit card number on the Internet. They also want protection against fraud by sellers or by criminals posing as sellers.

Security Protection.   Several methods and mechanisms can be used to fulfill the above requirements. One of the primary mechanisms is *encryption* (making messages indecipherable by using a key), which is often part of the most useful security schemes. For more detailed explanation of encryption, see Online File W5.11. Other representative methods are discussed below.

E-Wallets. **E-wallets** (or **digital wallets**) are software mechanisms that provide security measures, combined with convenience, to EC purchasing. The wallet stores the financial information of the buyer, such as credit card number, shipping information, and more. Thus, sensitive information does not need to be re-entered for each purchase. If the wallet is stored at the vendor's site, it does not have to travel on the Net for each purchase, making the information more secure.

The problem is that you need an e-wallet with each merchant. One solution is to have a wallet installed on your computer (e.g., MasterCard Wallet or AOL Wallet). In that case, though, you cannot use the e-wallet to make a purchase from another computer, nor is it a totally secured system. Another solution is a *universal* e-wallet such as Microsoft's Passport (Rosenbaum, 2002) and the Liberty Alliance (Costa, 2002). Universal systems are becoming popular because they provide a *digital identity* as well.

Virtual Credit Cards. A **virtual credit card** allows you to shop with an ID number and a password instead of with a credit card number. Such cards are used primarily by people who do not trust browser encryption sufficiently to use their credit card numbers on the Internet. The virtual credit card gives an extra layer of security. The bank that supports your traditional credit card, for example, can provide you with a transaction number valid for online use for a short period. For example, if you want to make a $200 purchase, you would contact your credit card company to charge that amount to your regular credit card account. You would be given a transaction number that is good for charges up to $200. This transaction number is encrypted for security, but even in the worst possible case (that some unauthorized entity obtained the transaction number), your loss would be limited, in this case to $200.

Payment Using Fingerprints. An increasing number of supermarkets allow their regular customers to pay by merely using their fingerprint for identification. A computer template of your fingerprint is kept in the store's computer system. Each time you shop, your fingerprint is matched with the template at the payment counter. You approve the amount, which is then charged either to your credit card or bank account.

Order Fulfillment

We now turn our attention to another important EC support service—*order fulfillment.* Any time a company sells direct to customers it is involved in various order-fulfillment activities. It must perform the following activities: Quickly find the products to be shipped; pack them; arrange for the packages to be delivered speedily to the customer's door; collect the money from every customer, either in advance, by COD, or by individual bill; and handle the return of unwanted or defective products.

It is very difficult to accomplish these activities both effectively and efficiently in B2C, since a company may need to ship small packages to many customers, and do it quickly. For this reason, both online companies and click-and-mortar companies often have difficulties in their B2C supply chain. Here, we provide a brief overview of order fulfillment. For a more detailed discussion, see Bayles (2001).

wiley.com/college/turban

e-wallets (digital wallets) *A software component in which a user stores secured personal and credit card information for one-click reuse.*

virtual credit card *A payment mechanism that allows a buyer to shop with an ID number and a password instead of with a credit card number, yet the charges are made to the credit card.*

Order fulfillment includes not only providing customers with what they ordered and doing it on time, but also providing all related customer service. For example, the customer must receive assembly and operation instructions to a new appliance. (A nice example is available at *livemanuals.com*.) In addition, if the customer is not happy with a product, an exchange or return must be arranged (see *fedex.com* for how returns are handled via FedEx). Order fulfillment is basically a part of what are called a company's *back-office operations* (activities such as inventory control, shipment, and billing).

In the late 1990s, e-tailers faced continuous problems in order fulfillment, especially during the holiday season. The problems resulted in inability to deliver on time, delivery of wrong items, high delivery costs, and the need to heavily compensate unhappy customers. Several factors can be responsible for delays in deliveries. They range from inability to forecast demand accurately to ineffective supply chains. Some such problems exist also in offline businesses. One factor that is typical of EC, though, is that it is based on the concept of "pull" operations, which begin with an order, frequently a customized one (see Appendix W1.1 on build-to-order). In the pull case it is more difficult to forecast demand, due to unique demands of customized orders and lack of sufficient years of experience.

wiley.com/college/turban

For many e-tailers, taking orders over the Internet could well be the easy part of B2C e-commerce. Fulfillment to customers' doors is the sticky part. Fulfillment can be less complicated in B2B where several effective methods are in use (see Bayles, 2001).

Before you go on . . .

1. List the various electronic payment mechanisms. Which of these are most often used for B2B payments?

2. List the security requirements for EC.

3. Describe the issues in EC order fulfillment.

5.9 ETHICAL AND LEGAL ISSUES IN E-BUSINESS

Ethical standards and their incorporation into law frequently trail technological innovation. E-commerce is taking new forms and enabling new business practices that may bring numerous risks—particularly for individual consumers—along with their advantages. We begin by considering ethical issues relating to e-business.

Ethical Issues

Many of the ethical and global issues related to IT in general apply also to e-business. These are discussed in the Ethics Primer at our Web site and in Chapter 12. In this section we touch on issues particularly related to e-commerce.

wiley.com/college/turban

Privacy.   Most electronic payment systems know who the buyers are; therefore, it may be necessary to protect the buyers' identities. A privacy issue related to employees also involves tracking: Many companies monitor employees' e-mail and have installed software that performs in-house monitoring of Web activities in order to discover employees who extensively use company time for non-business-related activities. Yet many employees don't want to feel like they are under the watchful eye of "Big Brother," even while at work.

Another privacy issue may involve tracking of individuals' activities on the Internet by intelligent agents and "cookies" (a string of characters stored on the user's hard drive to record the history of the user's visits to particular Web sites). Programs such as cookies raise a batch of privacy concerns. The tracking history is stored on your PC's hard drive, and any time you revisit a certain Web site, the computer knows it (see NetTracker at *sane.com*). In response, some users install programs such as Cookie Cutter to have some control over cookies and restore their online privacy.

Loss of Jobs.   The use of EC may result in the elimination of some of a company's employees as well as brokers and agents. The manner in which these unneeded workers, especially employees, are treated may raise ethical issues, such as how to handle the displacement and whether to offer retraining programs.

One of the most interesting EC issues relating to loss of jobs is that of *intermediation*. Intermediaries provide two types of services: (1) matching and providing information and (2) value-added services such as consulting. The first type of services (matching and providing information) can be fully automated, and therefore these services are likely to be assumed by e-marketplaces and portals that provide free services. The second type of services (value-added services) requires expertise, and these can be only partially automated. Intermediaries who provide only (or mainly) the first type of service may be eliminated, a phenomenon called **disintermediation** (elimination of the intermediaries). On the other hand, brokers who provide the second type of service or who manage electronic intermediation, also known as *infomediation*, are not only surviving, but may actually prosper. This phenomenon is called **reintermediation**.

disintermediation *Elimination of intermediaries in EC.*

reintermediation *Occurs where intermediaries such as brokers provide value-added services and expertise that cannot be eliminated when EC is used.*

The Web offers new opportunities for reintermediation by providing services (manual or computerized) required to support or complement EC. First, services are especially valuable when the number of participants is enormous, as with job finding, or when complex information products are exchanged. Second, many brokering services require extensive information processing; electronic versions of these services can offer more sophisticated features at a lower cost than is possible with human labor. Finally, for delicate negotiations, a computer mediator may be more predictable, and hence more trustworthy, than a human. For example, suppose a mediator's role is to inform a buyer and a seller whether a deal can be made, without revealing either side's initial price to the other. An independent auditor can verify that a software-based mediator will reveal only the information it is supposed to; a human mediator's fairness is less easily verified.

Legal Issues Specific to E-Commerce

Many legal issues are related to e-commerce. When buyers and sellers do not know each other and cannot even see each other (they may even be in different countries), there is a chance that dishonest people will commit fraud and other crimes over the Internet. During the first few years of EC, the public witnessed many of these, ranging from the creation of a virtual bank that disappeared along with the investors' deposits, to manipulation of stock prices on the Internet. Unfortunately, fraudulent activities on the Internet are increasing. Representative examples of legal issues specific to e-commerce are discussed below.

Fraud on the Internet.   Internet fraud and its sophistication have grown as much as, and even faster than, the Internet itself. For example, stock promoters falsely spread positive rumors about the prospects of the companies they touted, to boost the stock price. In other cases the information provided might have been true, but the promoters did not disclose that they were paid to talk up the companies. Stock promoters specifically target small investors who are lured by the promise of fast profits.

Stocks are only one of many areas where swindlers are active. Auctions are especially conducive to fraud, by both sellers and buyers. Other areas of potential fraud include selling bogus investments and phantom business opportunities. Financial criminals now have access to many more people, mainly due to the availability of electronic mail and pop-up ads. The U.S. Federal Trade Commission (*ftc.gov*) regularly publishes examples of scams most likely to arrive via e-mail or be found on the Web. Some ways in which consumers and sellers can protect themselves from online fraud are discussed later in this section.

domain name *An Internet address, whose top level identifies the name of the company or organization, follow by .com, .org, etc.*

Domain Names.   Another legal issue involves competition over domain names. Internet addresses are known as **domain names**. Domain names appear in levels. A top-level name is *wiley.com* or *stanford.edu*. A second-level name will be *wiley.com/turban* or *ibm.com.hk* (for IBM in Hong Kong). Top-level domain names are assigned by central nonprofit organizations that check for conflicts and possible infringement of trademarks. Obviously, companies who sell goods and services over the Internet want customers to be able to find them easily, so it is best when the domain name matches the company's name.

Problems arise when several companies that have similar names compete over a domain name. For example, if you want to book reservations at Holiday Inn hotels on a cross-country trip you are planning and you go to *holidayinn.com*, you get the Web site for a hotel at Niagara Falls, New York; to get to the *hotel chain's* Web site, you have to go to *holiday-inn.com*. Several cases of disputed names are already in court. An international arbitration organization is available as an alternative to the courts. The problem of domain names was alleviated somewhat in 2001 after several upper-level names were added to "com" (such as "info" and "coop").

cybersquatting *Registering domain names in the hope of selling them later at a higher price.*

Cybersquatting. Cybersquatting refers to the practice of registering domain names in the hope of selling them later at a higher price. For example, the original owner of *tom.com* received about $8 million for the name. The case of *tom.com* was ethical and legal. But in other cases, cybersquatting can be illegal or at least unethical (see Stead and Gilbert, 2001). Companies such as Christian Dior, Nike, Deutsche Bank, and even Microsoft have had to fight or pay to get the domain name that corresponds to their company's name. The Anticybersquatting Consumer Protection Act (1999) lets trademark owners in the United States sue for statutory damages.

Taxes and Other Fees. In offline sales, most states and localities tax business done within their jurisdiction, through sales taxes and other taxes. Federal, state, and local authorities now are scrambling to figure out how to get a piece of the revenue created by e-business. The problem is particularly complex for interstate and international commerce. For example, some claim that even the state in which a *server* is located deserves to receive some sales tax from an e-commerce transaction. Others say that the state in which the *seller* is located deserves the entire sales tax (or in some countries, value-added tax, VAT).

In addition to sales tax, there is a question about where (and in some cases, whether) electronic sellers should pay business license tax, franchise fees, gross-receipts tax, excise tax, privilege tax, and utility tax. Furthermore, how should tax collection be controlled? Legislative efforts to impose taxes on e-commerce are opposed by an organization named the Internet Freedom Fighters. Their efforts have been successful so far: At the time this edition was written (March 2004), there was a sales tax ban on business done on the Internet in the United States and many other countries, which could remain valid until fall 2006. At that time also, buyers were exempt from tax on Internet access (subject to renewal in 2004).

Copyright. Intellectual property, in its various forms, is protected by copyright laws and cannot be used freely. In EC it is very difficult to protect intellectual property. For example, some people mistakenly believe that if they have bought a piece of software, they have the right to share it with others. What they have bought is the right to use the software, not the right to distribute it—that right remains with the copyright holder. Similarly, it violates copyright laws to copy material from Web sites without permission. For further discussion of issues relating to intellectual property protection, see Chapter 12.

Protection of Buyers and Sellers

There are several ways buyers can be protected against fraud in e-commerce. Representative methods are described next.

Buyer Protection. Some tips for safe electronic shopping are shown in Manager's Checklist 5.2. (The information in this list applies to all Internet shoppers—not just managers!) In short, do not forget that you have shopper's rights. Consult your local or state consumer protection agency for general information on your consumer rights.

- ❏ Look for reliable brand names at sites like *Wal-Mart Online*, *Disney Online*, and *Amazon.com*. Before purchasing, make sure that the site is authentic by entering the site directly and not from an unverified link.
- ❏ Search any unfamiliar selling site for the company's address and phone and fax numbers. Call up and quiz the employees about the seller.
- ❏ Check out the vendor with the local Chamber of Commerce or Better Business Bureau (*bbbonline.org*). Look for seals of authenticity such as TRUSTe.
- ❏ Investigate how secure the seller's site is by examining the security procedures and by reading the posted privacy policy.
- ❏ Examine the money-back guarantees, warranties, and service agreements.
- ❏ Compare prices to those in regular stores. Too-low prices are too good to be true, and some "catch" is probably involved.
- ❏ Ask friends what they know. Find testimonials and endorsements in community sites and well-known bulletin boards.
- ❏ Find out what your rights are in case of a dispute. Consult consumer protections agencies and the National Fraud Information Center (*fraud.org*).
- ❏ Check *consumerworld.org* for a listing of useful resources.

Seller Protection. Online sellers, too, may need protection. They must be protected against consumers who refuse to pay or who pay with bad checks and from buyers' claims that the merchandise did not arrive. They also have the right to protect against the use of their name by others as well as to protect the use of their unique words and phrases, slogans, and Web address (trademark protection). Security features such as authentication, nonrepudiation, and escrow services provide some needed protections. Another seller protection applies particularly to electronic media: Sellers have legal recourse against customers who download without permission copyrighted software and/or knowledge and use it or sell it to others.

Before you go on . . .

1. List some ethical issues in EC.
2. List the major legal issues of EC.
3. Describe buyer protection in EC.
4. Describe seller protection in EC.

5.10 FAILURES AND STRATEGIES FOR SUCCESS

In this concluding section we consider some EC failures and successes. A well known pre-Internet failure involving a U.S. Food and Drug Administration system is presented in Online File W5.12.

wiley.com/college/turban

E-Commerce Failures

Failures of EC initiatives are fairly common. Furthermore, during 2000–2002, large numbers of dot-com companies failed. In this section we will look at some examples of failures and their causes. We will also look into some success factors that can be used to prevent failure.

Internet-Related EC Failures. Pioneering organizations saw the potential for e-commerce, but expertise and EC business models were just developing. Failures of

Lessons From
IT
IT Failures

EC projects started as early as 1996. However, the major wave of Internet-based EC failures started in 2000, as second-round funding (funding subsequent to a firm's original funding but before it goes to the stock market with a stock offering) began to dry up. Here are some examples. (In the list we have highlighted key reasons for the failure.)

- Dr. Koop, a medical portal, was unable to raise the needed advertising money, so the company folded. The diagnosis: death due to *incorrect business model*.
- An Internet mall operated by Open Market was closed in 1996 due to *an insufficient number of buyers*.
- Garden.com closed its doors in December 2000 due to *lack of cash*. Suppliers of venture capital were unwilling to give the company any more money to "burn."
- Several toy companies—Red Rocket, eParties.com, and BabyBucks.com—failed due to *too much competition*. This competition led vendors to lower their prices, which resulted in insufficient profits.
- Living.com, the online furniture store, closed in 2000. The *customer acquisition cost* was too high.
- PaperX.com, an online paper exchange in the UK, folded due to *lack of second-round funding*.
- Webvan, an online grocery and same-day delivery company, made a huge *investment* (over $1 billion) *in infrastructure of warehouses and logistics*. But its income was insufficient to convince investors to fund it further. It collapsed in 2002.
- In late 2000 Chemdex.com, the "granddaddy" of the third-party exchanges, closed down. Ventro.com, its parent company, said that the *revenue growth* was too slow and that a *new business model* was needed. Chemdex was not alone: During 2001–2003 large numbers of exchanges folded or changed their business models.

According to Useem (2000), the major reasons for EC failure are incorrect revenue model, lack of strategy and contingency planning, inability to attract enough customers, lack of funding, channel conflict with distributors, too much online competition in standard (commodity) products (e.g., CDs, toys), poor order-fulfillment infrastructure, and lack of qualified management. To learn more about EC failures, visit *whytheyfailed.com* and *techdirt.com*.

Failed EC Initiatives within Organizations. Whereas failed companies, especially publicly listed ones, are well advertised, failed EC initiatives within companies, especially within private companies, are less known. However, news about some failed EC initiatives has been publicized. For example, Levi Strauss stopped online direct sales of its apparel (jeans and its popular Dockers brand) on its Web site (*levistrauss.com*) after its major distributors and retailers put pressure on the company not to compete with their brick-and-mortar outlets (*channel conflict*). Another EC initiative that failed was a joint venture between Intel and SAP, two world-class companies, which was designed to develop low-cost solutions for SMEs. It collapsed in August 2000 due to low demand and too few customers. Large companies such as Citicorp, Disney, and Merrill Lynch also closed EC initiatives after losing millions of dollars in them.

Success Stories and Lessons Learned

Offsetting the failures are hundreds of EC success stories, primarily in specialty and niche markets (see Athitakis, 2003). Here are some of the reasons for EC success and some suggestions from EC experts on how to succeed:

- Thousands of brick-and-mortar companies are slowly adding online channels with great success. Examples are Uniglobe.com, Staples.com, Homedepot.com, Clearcommerce.com, 1-800-FLOWERS (*800flowers.com*), and Southwest Airlines (*iflyswa.com*).
- As of late 2000, more companies were pursuing mergers and acquisitions (e.g., Ivillage.com with Women.com, though each maintains its separate Web site). Mergers seem to be a growing trend.

- Peter Drucker, the management guru, provides the following advice: "Analyze the opportunities, go out to look, keep it focused, start small (one thing at a time), and aim at market leadership."

- A group of Asian CEOs recommends the following factors that are critical for success: Select robust business models, foster e-innovation, co-brand, carefully evaluate a spinoff strategy, employ ex-dot-com staffers, and focus on the e-generation (young adults) as your market (e.g., *alloy.com* and *bolt.com*).

- Consultant PricewaterhouseCoopers (*pwcglobal.com*) suggests taking extra care to avert technology malfunctions (e.g., inability to handle a surge of orders quickly enough), which erode consumer trust.

- Many experts (e.g., The National Institute for Standards and Technology, NIST) recommend contingency planning and preparing for disasters.

- Huff et al. (1999) suggest the following critical success factors for e-commerce: Add value, focus on a niche and then extend that niche, maintain flexibility, get the technology right, manage critical perceptions, provide excellent customer service, create effective connectedness, and understand Internet culture.

Conclusion

Analyzing successful companies, researchers have suggested that if they do careful planning to reach profitability quickly, many click-and-mortar companies are likely to succeed. Joint ventures and partnerships are very valuable, and planning for satisfactory infrastructure and logistics to meet high demand is needed. In short, do not forget that e-business has a "business" side!

Finally, let's not forget that history repeats itself. When the automobile was invented, there were 240 startup companies between 1904 and 1908. In 1910 there was a shakeout, and today there are only three U.S. automakers. However, the auto industry has grown by hundredfold. The same is happening in EC: Despite the 2000–2003 failures, the total volume of EC activities continued to grow exponentially. For example, *emarketer.com* reported on May 19, 2003, that B2C revenues in 2002 reached $76 billion; a 48 percent increase over 2001. The figure for 2003 was over $96 billion—more than a 30 percent increase over 2002.

Before you go on . . .

1. List five reasons for EC failures.
2. List five suggestions for EC success.

WHAT'S IN IT FOR ME?

ACC

FOR THE ACCOUNTING MAJOR

Accounting personnel will be involved in several EC activities. Designing the ordering system and its relationship with inventory management requires accounting attention. Billing and payments are also accounting-related, as are determining cost and profit allocation. The implications of replacing paper documents by electronic means affect many of the accountant's tasks, especially the auditing of EC activities and systems. Finally, building a cost-benefit and cost-justification system of what products/services to take online and the creation of a chargeback system are critical to the success of EC.

FIN

FOR THE FINANCE MAJOR

The worlds of banking, securities and commodities markets, and other financial services are being reengineered due to EC. Online securities trading and its supporting infrastructure are growing more rapidly than any other EC activity. Many innovations already in place are changing the rules of economic and financial incentives for financial analysts and managers. Online banking, for example, does not recognize state boundaries and may create a new framework for financing global trades. Public financial information is accessible in seconds. All this changes the manner in which finance personnel will operate and excel.

MKT

FOR THE MARKETING MAJOR

A major revolution in marketing and sales is taking place due to EC. In addition to moving from a physical to a virtual marketplace, a radical transformation to one-on-one advertising and sales and to customized and interactive marketing is happening. Marketing channels are being combined, eliminated, or recreated. The EC revolution is creating new products and markets and significantly altering others. Digitization of products and services also has implications for marketing and sales. The direct producer-to-consumer channel is expanding rapidly, and with it the nature of customer service. As the battle for customers intensifies, the marketing and sales personnel are becoming the most critical success factor in many organizations. Online marketing can be a blessing to one company and a curse to another.

POM

FOR THE PRODUCTION/ OPERATIONS MANAGEMENT MAJOR

EC is changing the manufacturing system from product-push mass production to order-pull mass customization. This change requires a robust supply chain, information support, and reengineering of processes that involve suppliers and other business partners. Using extranets, suppliers can monitor and replenish inventories without the need for constant reorders. In addition, the Internet and intranets help reduce cycle times. Many production/operations problems that have persisted for years, such as complex scheduling and coordination as well as excess inventories, are being solved rapidly with the use of Web technologies. Via external and internal networks, companies can now find and manage manufacturing operations in other countries much more easily. Also, the Web is reengineering procurement, by helping companies conduct electronic bids for parts and subassemblies, thus reducing cost. All in all, the job of the progressive production/operations manager is closely tied in with e-commerce.

HRM

FOR THE HUMAN RESOURCES MANAGEMENT MAJOR

HRM majors need to understand the new labor markets and the impacts of EC on old labor markets. Also, the HRM department may use EC tools (e.g., for its own procurement of office supplies). Also, knowing about new government online initiatives and about online training is critical. Finally, understanding legal issues related to EC and employment is important.

SUMMARY

1. **Describe electronic commerce, its scope, benefits, limitations, and types.** E-commerce can be conducted on the Web and on other networks. It is divided into the following major types: business-to-business, collaborative commerce, business-to-consumers, consumers-to-business, consumer-to-consumer, intrabusiness, e-government, and mobile commerce. In each type you can find several business models. E-commerce offers many benefits to organizations, consumers, and society, but it also has limitations (technological and non-technological). The current technological limitations are expected to lessen with time.

2. **Understand the basics of how online auctions and bartering work.** A major mechanism in EC is auctions. The Internet provides an infrastructure for executing auctions at lower cost, and with many more involved sellers and buyers, including both individual consumers and corporations. Two major types of auctions exist: forward auctions and reverse auctions. Forward auctions are used in the traditional process of *selling* to the highest bidder. Reverse auctions are used for *buying*, using a tendering system to buy at the lowest bid. A minor mechanism is online bartering, in which companies or individuals arrange for *exchange* of physical items and/or services.

3. **Describe the major applications of business-to-consumer commerce, including service industries, and the major issues faced by e-tailers.** B2C e-tailing can be pure (such as Amazon.com), or part of a click-and-mortar organization. Direct marketing is done via solo storefronts or in malls. It can be done via electronic catalogs or by using electronic auctions. The leading online B2C service industries are banking, securities trading, job markets, travel, and real estate. The major issues faced by e-tailers are channel conflict, conflict within click-and-mortar organizations, order fulfillment, determining viability and risk, and identifying appropriate revenue models.

4. **Discuss the importance and activities of online advertising.** Like any type of commerce, e-commerce requires advertising support. In EC, though, much of the advertising can be done online by methods such as banner ads, pop-ups, e-mail, electronic catalogs, and customized ads. Permission marketing, interactive and viral marketing, making it to the top of search-engine listings, and online promotions offer additional ways for vendors to reach more customers.

5. **Describe business-to-business applications.** The major B2B applications are selling from catalogs and by forward auctions (the sell-side marketplace), buying in reverse auctions and in group and desktop purchasing (the buy-side marketplace), and trading in electronic exchanges.

6. **Describe intrabusiness and B2E commerce.** EC activities can be conducted inside organizations. Three types are recognized: between a business and its employees, between units of the business, and among employees of the same organizations.

7. **Describe e-government activities and consumer-to-consumer e-commerce.** E-government commerce can take place between government and citizens, between businesses and governments, or among government units. It makes government operations more effective and efficient. EC also can be done between consumers (C2C), but should be undertaken with caution. Auctions are the most popular C2C mechanism. C2C also can be done by use of online classified ads.

8. **Describe the e-commerce support services, specifically payments and logistics.** New electronic payment systems are needed to complete transactions on the Internet. Electronic payments can be made by e-checks, e-credit cards, purchasing cards, e-cash, stored-value money cards, smart cards, person-to-person payments via services like PayPal, electronic bill presentment and payment, and e-wallets. Order fulfillment is especially difficult and expensive in B2C, because of the need to ship relatively small orders to many customers.

9. **Discuss some ethical and legal issues relating to e-commerce.** There is increasing fraud and unethical behavior on the Internet, including invasion of privacy by sellers and misuse of domain names. The value of domain names, taxation of online business, and how to handle legal issues in a multi-country environment are major legal concerns. Protection of customers, sellers, and intellectual property is also important.

10. **Describe EC failures and strategies for success.** Periods of innovation produce both successes and failures. There have been many of both in e-commerce. Major reasons for failure are insufficient cash flow, too much competition, conflicts with existing systems, wrong revenue models, and lack of planning. Despite the failures, overall EC volume is growing exponentially. Five key strategies for EC success are: an appropriate revenue model, sufficient funding for the initial period, selection of the right products to sell online, entry into an area with not too many competitors, and proper planning.

INTERACTIVE / LEARNING

Opening Up E-Wallets on Amazon.com
Go to the Interactivities section on the Student Web Site and access Chapter 5: E-Business and E-Commerce. There you will find an animated simulation of the technologies used for the electronic wallets used by Amazon.com's customers, as well as some hands-on activities that visually explain business concepts in this chapter.

More Resources
More resources and study tools are located on the Student Web Site. You'll find additional chapter materials and links to organizations, people, and technologies for each chapter. In addition, self-quizzes that provide individualized feedback are available for each chapter.

Instructions for accessing the Interactivities on the Student Web Site:

1. Go to
   wiley.com/college/turban
2. Select Turban Rainer Potter's *Introduction to Information Technology, Third Edition*
3. Click on Student Resources Site, in the toolbar on the left

4. Click on Interactivities Web Site
5. Click on Interactivities Web Site and use your password to enter the site (your password card is located in the inside cover of your textbook)

DISCUSSION QUESTIONS

1. Discuss the major limitations of e-commerce. Which of them are likely to disappear? Why?
2. Discuss the reasons for having multiple EC business models.
3. Distinguish between business-to-business forward auctions and buyers' bids for RFQs.
4. Discuss the benefits to sellers and buyers of a B2B exchange.
5. What are the major benefits of e-government?
6. Discuss the various ways to pay online in B2C. Which one(s) would you prefer and why?
7. Why is order fulfillment in B2C considered difficult?
8. Discuss the reasons for EC failures.

PROBLEM-SOLVING ACTIVITIES

1. Assume you're interested in buying a car. You can find information about cars at *autos.msn.com*. Go to *autoweb.com* or *autobytel.com* for information about financing and insurance. Decide what car you want to buy. Configure your car by going to the car manufacturer's Web site. Finally, try to find the car from *autobytel.com*. What information is most supportive of your decision-making process? Write a report about your experience.
2. Consider the opening case about Hi-Life.
   a. How was the corporate decision making improved?
   b. Summarize the benefits to the customers, suppliers, store management, and employees.
   c. The data collected at Activesys can be uploaded to a PC and transmitted to the corporate intranet via the Internet. It is suggested that transmission be done using a wireless system. Comment on the proposal.
3. Compare the various electronic payment methods. Specifically, collect information from the vendors cited in the chapter and find more with *google.com*. Pay attention to security level, speed, cost, and convenience.
4. Prepare a study on how to stop pop-ups. Look at *find.pcworld.com/27401* and *28221, 27424, 27426*. Consider *adsubstract.com, guidescope.com, symantac.com* (Norton). Investigate what AOL and Yahoo offer. What is new in legislation regarding spamming in your country?

INTERNET ACTIVITIES

1. Access *etrade.com* and register for the Internet stock simulation game. You will be bankrolled with $100,000 in a trading account every month. Play the game and relate your experiences to IT.
2. Use the Internet to plan a trip to Paris. Visit *lonelyplanet.com, yahoo.com*, and *expedia.com*.
   a. Find the lowest airfare.
   b. Examine a few hotels by class.
   c. Get suggestions of what to see.
   d. Find out about local currency, and convert $1,000 to that currency with an online currency converter.
   e. Compile travel tips.
   f. Prepare a report.
3. Access *realtor.com*. Prepare a list of services available on this site. Then prepare a list of advantages derived by the users and advantages to realtors. Are there any disadvantages? To whom?
4. Enter *alibaba.com*. Identify the site's capabilities. Look at the site's private trading room. Write a report. How can such a site help a person who is making a purchase?
5. Enter *campusfood.com*. Explore the site. Why is the site so successful? Could you start a competing one? Why or why not?
6. Enter *dell.com*, go to "desktops" and configure a system. Register to "my cart" (no obligation). What calculators are used there? What are the advantages of this process as compared to buying a computer in a physical store? What are the disadvantages?
7. Enter *checkfree.com* and find their services. Prepare a report.

1. Have each team study a major bank with extensive EC strategy. For example, Wells Fargo Bank is well on its way to being a cyberbank. Hundreds of brick-and-mortar branch offices are being closed. In Spring 2003 the bank served more than a 1.2 million cyberaccounts (see *wellsfargo.com*). Other banks to look at are Citicorp, Netbank, and HSBC (Hong Kong). Each team should attempt to convince the class that its e-bank activities are the best.

2. Assign each team to one industry. Each team will find five real-world applications of the major business-to-business models listed in the chapter. (Try success stories of vendors and EC-related magazines.) Examine the problems they solve or the opportunities they exploit.

3. Have teams investigate how B2B payments are made in global trade. Consider instruments such as electronic letters of credit and e-checks. Visit *tradecard.com* and examine their services to SMEs. Also, investigate what Visa and MasterCard are offering. Finally, check Citicorp and some German and Japanese banks.

REAL-WORLD CASE

MARKETING ONLINE DINING CERTIFICATES AT RESTAURANTS.COM

SVC   MKT

THE BUSINESS PROBLEM Restaurants.com was founded in 1999 as an all-purpose dining portal with menus, online video tours, and a reservation feature. Like other dot-coms, the company was losing money. Few restaurants were willing to pay the fees in order to put their Web page on the *restaurants.com* site. The company was ready to pull the plug when its owner learned that CitySpree, which was selling dining certificates (coupons) online, was for sale in a bankruptcy auction. Realizing that Restaurants.com might have a better model for selling dining certificates online than did CitySpree, the owner purchased CitySpree. This enabled him to change the company from "just another dining portal" to a gift-certificate seller.

THE IT SOLUTION Here is how the new business model works: Restaurants are invited to place, for free, dining certificates at *restaurants.com*, together with information about the restaurant, menu, parking availability, and more. The dining certificates traditionally had been found in newspapers or newspaper inserts. Placing them online is free to the restaurants' owners; some use the online coupons to replace the paper coupons, and others supplement the paper coupons with the online version. Restaurants.com *sells* these certificates online, and collects all the fees for itself. The restaurants get broad visibility, since Restaurants.com advertises on Orbitz, Yahoo, and MSN; it even auctions certificates at eBay.

The certificates offer 30–50 percent off the menu price, so they are appealing to buyers. By using a search engine, you can find a restaurant with a cuisine of your choice, and you can look for certificates when you need them. Although you pay $5–$15 to purchase a certificate, you get usually a better discount than is offered in the newspapers. You pay with your credit card, print the certificate, and are ready to dine. Customers are encouraged to register as members, free of charge. Then they can get e-mails with promotions, news, etc. In their personalized account, customers can view past purchases as well. Customers also can purchase gift certificates to be given to others. And bargains can be found: For example, a $50-off-regular-price certificate to New York City's Manhattan Grille was auctioned for only $16.

THE RESULTS The business model worked. By going to eBay, the world largest virtual mall, Restaurants.com found an audience of millions of online shoppers. By e-mailing coupons to customers it saves the single largest cost of most conventional coupon marketers—printing and postage. Finally, the model works best in difficult economic times, when price-conscious consumers are looking for great deals.

The financial results are striking: Revenues doubled during the first five months of operation (late 2001). The company has been profitable since the third quarter of 2002. And by June 2003, the company was selling over 80,000 certificates a month, grossing over $5 million in 2002, and expecting about $10 million in 2003.

Sources: Compiled from M. Athitakis, "How to Make Money on the Net," *Business 2.0* (May 2003), and from *restaurants.com* (June 1, 2003).

QUESTIONS

1. Visit *restaurants.com*. Find an Italian restaurant in your neighborhood and examine the information provided. Assuming you like Italian food, is the gift certificate a good deal?

2. Review the "lessons from failures" described in Section 5.10 and relate them to this case.

3. Speculate on why it was necessary to purchase CitySpree.

4. What motivates restaurants to participate in the new business model when they refused to do so in the old one?

5. Given that anyone can start a competing business, how can Restaurants.com protect its position? What are some of its competitive advantages?

wiley.com/college/turban

E-COMMERCE AND CLUB IT

The people who hang out at Club IT are wired. They regularly use mobile devices such as Blackberry's, PDA's, and camera phones. Online shopping is a regular part of their lives. However, not many clubs have taken advantage of B2C e-commerce activities, and Ruben sees this as an opportunity to gain a competitive advantage in dealing with suppliers as well as guests. Ruben asks you to identify some potential e-commerce technologies and applications to help build Club IT's clientele and community.

ASSIGNMENT

1. Review the technologies and applications for e-payments. Describe a transaction where Club IT would make an e-payment to a supplier. Describe a transaction where Club IT would accept an e-payment from a guest. Do these provide any competitive advantage?

2. Consider the many opportunities for Club IT to advertise its events, its concerts, and other happenings using online advertising. Which of the advertising mechanisms described in the chapter would you recommend to Ruben? Why do you think it would be effective?

3. Currently, Club IT sells advance tickets to its special Friday and Saturday night concerts by phone or in person. Ruben would like to set up a web site to sell tickets, so guests can have 24 X 7 self-service access. Design a prototype web page for Club IT to sell tickets. You can use MS-Word and File | Save As Web page to create a simple web page, or use an online web page wizard to do this. Test your page in your web browser to see how it would appear to online viewers.

**Go to wiley.com/college/turban to access the
CLUB IT Web Site on the Student Web Site**

Mobile, Wireless, and Pervasive Computing

Chapter Preview

The traditional computing environment that requires users to come to a wired computer may be ineffective or inefficient in many situations. The solution is to make computers small enough that they are easy to carry or even to wear. Such mobile devices can communicate with traditional systems and infrastructure via wireline or, even better, wireless networks. The ability to communicate and collaborate any time and from anywhere provides organizations with strategic advantage by increasing productivity, speed, and customer service.

Mobile and wireless computing provide the infrastructure for mobile commerce—conducting e-commerce wirelessly, any time and from any place. They enable location-based e-commerce, which is based on knowing where people are at any given time and on the ability to communicate with them. Mobile and wireless computing are changing how IT is deployed and are creating the foundations of the futuristic computing environment called pervasive computing. All of these topics are explored in this chapter.

Chapter Outline

Learning Objectives

1. Discuss the characteristics, attributes, and drivers of mobile computing and m-commerce.
2. Describe the emergence of Wi-Fi and voice portals.
3. Describe personal service applications of m-commerce.
4. Discuss m-commerce applications in financial services.
5. Describe m-commerce applications in shopping, advertising, and customer service.
6. Describe the use of m-commerce in intrabusiness applications.
7. Discuss the use of mobile computing in enterprise and supply chain applications.
8. Describe location-based commerce (l-commerce).
9. Discuss the key characteristics and current uses of pervasive computing.
10. Describe the major inhibitors and barriers of mobile computing and m-commerce.

NEXTBUS: A SUPERB CUSTOMER SERVICE

Buses in certain parts of San Francisco have difficulty keeping up with the posted schedule, especially in rush hours. The scheduled times become meaningless, and passengers are angry because they waste time waiting for late buses.

San Francisco bus riders carrying an Internet-enabled wireless device, such as a cell phone or PDA, can quickly find out in *real time* when a bus is most likely to arrive at a particular bus stop. Similar systems have been used successfully in several other cities around the United States and in several other countries.

Figure 6.1 shows how the NextBus system works. The core of the system is a GPS satellite that lets the NextBus information center know where a specific bus is at any given time. Based on a bus's location, traffic patterns, and weather conditions, dispatchers can calculate the arrival time at each stop. Users can access that information from their cell phones or PCs. NextBus schedules are also posted in real time on bus shelter signs.

Currently, NextBus is an ad-free customer service, but in the near future advertising may be added. Because the system knows exactly where you are when you request information and how much time you have until your next bus, it could send you to the nearest Starbucks for a cup of coffee, giving you an electronic coupon for a discount on a cup of coffee as you wait.

Passengers in San Francisco are happy with the system; worries about missing the bus are diminished. In rural areas in Finland, where a similar system is used, buses are infrequent and winters are very cold; passengers can stay in a warm coffeehouse not far

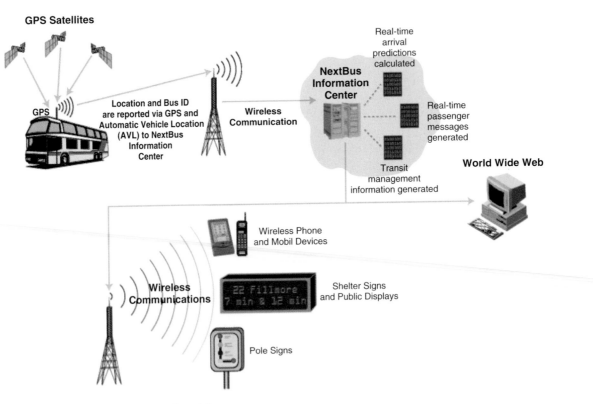

Figure 6.1 *NextBus operational model.*
(Source: NextBus.com/corporate/works/index.htm, *2002. Used with permission of NextBus Information Systems.)*

from the bus stop rather than wait in the cold for a bus that may be an hour late. Also, using such a system, a bus company can do better scheduling, arrange for extra buses when needed, and improve its operations.

Sources: Compiled from P. Murphy, "Running Late? Take the NextBus," *Environmental News Network,* September 7, 1999, *enn.com/enn-features-archive/1999/09/090799/nextbus_4692.asp* (accessed June 2003); *nextbus.com* (accessed September 2003); and ITS America, "NextBus Expands Real-Time Transit Information in the Bay Area With AC Transit," August 9, 2001, *itsa.org/ITSNEWS.NSF/0/ 34c13fd8352c4c3f85256aa400497aad?OpenDocument* (accessed June 2003).

WHAT WE LEARNED FROM THIS CASE

This opening vignette is an example of *location-based e-commerce,* which is an application of *mobile commerce,* in which EC services are provided to customers wherever they are located at the time they need them. This capability, which is not available in regular EC, may change many things in our lives. The vignette also exemplifies *pervasive computing,* in which services are seamlessly blended into the environment without the user being aware of the technology behind them. This application is an implementation of *mobile computing,* a type of computing designed for employees who travel outside the boundaries of their organizations or for travelers of any kind.

Mobile computing and commerce are spreading rapidly, replacing or supplementing wired computing. The wireless infrastructure upon which mobile computing is built may reshape the entire IT field. The technologies, applications, and limitations of mobile computing and mobile commerce are the main focus of this chapter. Later in the chapter, we look briefly at futuristic applications of *pervasive computing.*

6.1 MOBILE COMPUTING AND COMMERCE: OVERVIEW, BENEFITS, AND DRIVERS

The Mobile Computing Landscape

In the traditional computing environment users come to a computer, which is connected to other computers, to networks, and to servers with wires. The need to be linked by wires limits the use of computers and makes it difficult or impossible for people on the move to use them. In particular, salespeople, repair people, service employees, law enforcement agents, and utility workers can be more effective if they can use information technology while at their jobs in the field or in transit. Mobile vacationers also may wish to be connected with home or office. Thus, mobile computing was designed for workers who travel outside the boundaries of their organizations or for any people traveling outside their homes. One can work with a mobile device as long as the battery is working.

> **mobile computing** *A computing model designed for workers who travel outside the boundaries of their organizations or for people traveling outside their homes.*

The first solution to the need for mobile computing was to make computers small enough so that they could be easily carried about. First, the laptop computer was invented; later, smaller and smaller computers, such as PDAs (personal digital assistants) and other handhelds, appeared. Carriable computers, from laptops to PDAs and other portables, are examples of mobile devices. They have become lighter with time and more powerful as far as processing speed and storage. At the end of the workday, mobile workers can download (or upload) information from or to a regular desktop computer in a process known as *synchronization* ("sync"). To speed up the "sync," special connecting cradles (docking stations) were created (see IT's about Business 6.1 later in this chapter).

> **mobile devices** *Portable computers such as PDAs and other handhelds.*

EXAMPLE *Millstone Coffee Goes Mobile.* Millstone Coffee equipped its 300 drivers with handheld devices and mobile applications for use while they are on the road selling roasted coffee beans to 13,000 stores in the United States. Using the devices, the drivers can track inventory, generate invoices, and capture detailed sales and marketing data at each store. The drivers synchronize their   **POM**

handhelds with the company's main system at the end of the day, a process that takes only 2 minutes. This strategy has proven to be cheaper for Millstone than going wireless, at least with the 2002 technology when the decision to implement the new system was made.

The second solution to the need for mobile computing was to replace wires with *wireless communication media.* Wireless systems have been in use in radio, TV, and telephones for a long time. So it was natural to adopt them to the computing environment.

The third solution was a combination of the first two, namely to use mobile devices in a wireless environment. Referred to as wireless mobile computing, this combination enables a real-time connection between a mobile device and other computing environments, such as the Internet or an intranet. This innovation is revolutionizing how people use computers. It is spreading at work and at home. It is also used in education, health care, entertainment, and much more. This new computing model is basically leading to *ubiquity*—meaning that computing is available anywhere, at any time. Note that since many mobile applications now go wireless, the term *mobile computing* today is often used generally to describe wireless mobile computing.

Due to some current technical limitations, we cannot (yet) do with mobile computing all the things that we do with regular computing. On the other hand, we can do things in mobile computing that we cannot do in the regular computing environment. A major boost to mobile computing was provided in 2003 by Intel with its Centrino chip. This chip, which will be a standard feature in most laptops by 2005, includes three important capabilities: (1) a connection device to a wireless local area network, (2) low usage of electricity, enabling users to do more work on a single battery charge, and (3) a high level of security. The Centrino is expected to make mobile computing the common computing environment.

A second driving development of mobile computing is the introduction of the third- and fourth-generation wireless environments known as 3G and 4G. These are described in Online File W6.1.

wireless mobile computing *The combination of mobile devices used in a wireless environment.*

wiley.com/college/turban

Mobile Commerce

While the impact of mobile computing on our lives will be very significant, a similar impact is already occurring in the way we conduct business. This impact is described as mobile commerce (also known as **m-commerce** and **m-business**), which is basically any e-commerce or e-business done in a wireless environment, especially via the Internet. Like regular EC applications, m-commerce can be done via the Internet, private communication lines, smart cards, or other infrastructures.

M-commerce is not merely a variation on existing Internet services; it is a natural extension of e-business. Mobile devices create an opportunity to deliver new services to existing customers and to attract new ones. (A classification of applications by industry is provided at *mobile.commerce.net*. Also see *mobiforum.org*.)

mobile commerce (m-commerce, m-business) *Any e-commerce done in a wireless environment, especially via the Internet.*

Mobile Computing Basic Terminology

Let's build a foundation for further discussion by defining some common mobile computing terms:

- *Global positioning system (GPS).* A satellite-based tracking system that enables the determination of a GPS device's location. (See Section 6.6 for more on GPS.)
- *Personal digital assistant (PDA).* A small handheld computer, such as the family of Palm handhelds and the Pocket PC devices from companies like HP.
- *Short message service (SMS).* A technology that allows for the sending of short text messages (up to 160 characters in 2004) on Internet-connected cell phones. SMS messages can be sent or received concurrently, even during a voice or data call. Used by hundreds of millions of users, SMS is known as the e-mail of m-commerce.

personal digital assistant (PDA) *A small handheld computer.*

short messaging service (SMS) *Technology that allows for sending of short text messages on Internet-connected cell phones.*

- *Bluetooth.* A chip technology wireless standard that enables short-range connection (data and voice) between mobile devices and/or other devices (see *bluetooth.com*). It uses low-power, digital, two-way radio frequency.

- *Wireless Application Protocol (WAP).* A set of communications protocols that enable different kinds of wireless devices to talk to a server installed on a mobile network, so users can access the Internet. WAP offers secured Internet browsing (see Online File W6.2).

- *Smartphones.* Internet-connected cell phones that can support mobile applications. These "phones with a brain" are becoming standard devices. They include WAP microprocessors for Internet access and the capabilities of PDAs as well.

- **WLAN (wireless local area network).** Basically, a wireless version of the Ethernet networking standard. (For discussion of the Ethernet standard, see Technology Guide 4.)

- **Wi-Fi (short for Wireless Fidelity).** Refers to the 802.11b standard on which most of the wireless local area networks (WLANs) run.

With these terms in mind, we can now look more deeply at the attributes and drivers of mobile computing.

Bluetooth *Chip technology that enables short-range connection (data and voice) between wireless devices.*

wiley.com/college/turban

Wireless Application Protocol (WAP) *A set of communications protocols designed to enable different kinds of wireless devices to talk to a server installed on a mobile network, so users can access the Internet.*

smartphone *Internet-connected cell phone that can support mobile applications.*

The Attributes and Drivers of Mobile Computing

Generally speaking, many of the EC applications described in Chapter 5 can be done in m-commerce. However, several *new* applications are possible only in the mobile environment. To understand why this is so, let's examine the major attributes and capabilities of mobile computing and m-commerce.

The Specific Attributes of Mobile Computing and M-Commerce. Mobile computing has two major characteristics that differentiate it from other forms of computing: mobility and broad reach.

Mobility implies portability. Mobile computing is based on the fact that users carry a mobile device with them and can initiate a real-time contact with other systems from wherever they happen to be if they can establish an Internet connection.

Broad reach refers to the fact that in mobile computing people can be reached at any time. Of course, users can block certain hours or certain messages, but when users carry an open mobile device, they can be reached instantly.

These two characteristics, mobility and broad reach, create five value-added attributes that break the barriers of geography and time: ubiquity, convenience, instant connectivity, personalization, and localization of products and services. A mobile terminal can fill the need for real-time information and communication, independent of the user's location (*ubiquity*). With an Internet-enabled mobile device, it is easy and fast to access the Web, intranets, and other mobile devices without booting up a PC or placing a call via a modem (*convenience* and *instant connectivity*). Information can be customized and sent to individual consumers as an SMS (*customization*). And knowing where a user is physically at any particular moment is key to offering relevant advertisement of products and services (*localization*).

Vendors and telecommunication carriers can *differentiate themselves* in the competitive marketplace by offering new, exciting, and useful services based on these attributes. Such services will help vendors attract and keep customers and increase revenues.

Drivers of Mobile Computing and M-Commerce. In addition to the value-added attributes just discussed, the development of mobile computing and m-commerce is driven by the following factors.

Widespread Availability of Mobile Devices. The number of cell phones throughout the world exceeded 1.3 billion in 2003 (*cellular.co.za/stats/stats-main.htm*). It is estimated that within a few years about 70 percent of cell phones in the developed countries will have Internet access. Thus, a potential mass market is developing for mobile computing and m-commerce. Cell phones are also spreading quickly in developing countries. In 2002, for example, the number of cell phones in China exceeded 200 million, virtually equally the number of fixed line phones in that country. This growth enables developing countries to leap-frog to m-commerce.

No Need for a PC.   Because the Internet can be accessed via smartphone or other Internet-connected wireless device, there is no need for a PC to access the Internet. Even though the cost of a PC that is used primarily for Internet access, such as the Simputer (a "simple computer"), can be as low as $300 (or even less), that amount is still a major expense for the vast majority of people in the world. Smartphones and other wireless devices make it unnecessary to have a PC to reach the Internet.

The "Cell Phone Culture."   The widespread use of cell phones is a social phenomenon, especially among the 15-to-25-year-old age group. The use of SMS has been spreading like wildfire in several European and Asian countries. In the Philippines, for example, SMS is a national phenomenon in the youth market. These members of the "cell phone culture" will constitute a major force of online buyers once they begin to make and spend reasonable amounts of money.

Vendor Marketing.   Vendors also are pushing m-commerce. Both manufacturers of mobile devices and mobile communication network operators are advertising the many potential applications of mobile computing and m-commerce, so that they can sell new technologies, products, and services to buyers.

Declining Prices and Increasing Functionalities.   With the passage of time, the price of wireless devices is declining. The per-minute pricing of mobile services is ex-

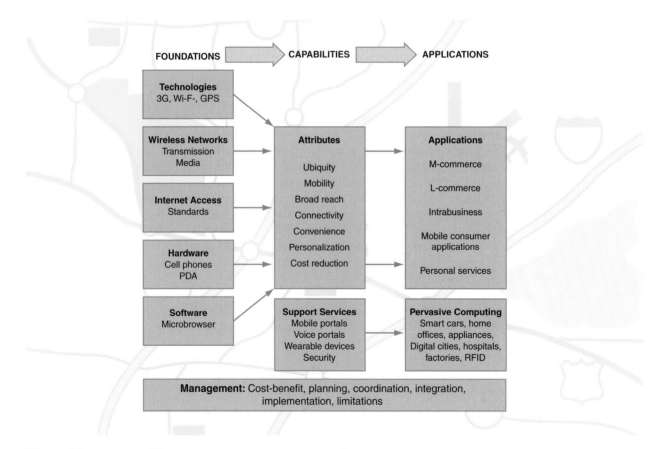

Figure 6.2   *Roadmap: The landscape of mobile computing and commerce.*
(Source: Drawn by E. Turban.)

pected to decline by 50 to 80 percent before 2005. At the same time, functionalities are increasing.

Improvement of Bandwidth.   To properly conduct m-commerce, it is necessary to have sufficient bandwidth for transmitting text; bandwidth is also required for voice, video, and multimedia. The 3G (third-generation) technology provides the necessary bandwidth, at a data rate of up to 2 mbps (millions of bits per second). Wi-Fi moves information even faster, at 11 mbps, and new standards enable even faster speeds (54 mbps).

Mobile computing and m-commerce include many applications. These result from the capabilities of various technologies as shown in Figure 6.2 (page 172), which also describes the major topics discussed in this chapter.

> ## Before you go on . . .
>
> **1.** Define mobile computing and m-commerce.
>
> **2.** Define the following terms: PDA, WAP, SMS, GPS, Wi-Fi, and smartphone.
>
> **3.** List the value-added attributes of mobile computing.
>
> **4.** List at least five major drivers of mobile computing.

6.2 WIRELESS LOCAL AREA NETWORKS, WI-FI, AND VOICE PORTALS

WLANs and Wi-Fi

For the past few years, much of the discussion about mobile computing and m-commerce has revolved around WWANs (wireless wide area networks) with cellular technologies, especially the 3G one. Slowly but surely, another technology—wireless local area networks—has been making its way to the forefront, as the market factors impeding its growth are being addressed. As the name implies, a **wireless LAN (WLAN)** is like a wired LAN but without the cables.

In a typical configuration, a transmitter with an antenna, called a **wireless access point**, connects to a wired LAN from a fixed location or to satellite dishes that provide an Internet connection. A wireless access point provides service to a number of users within a small geographical perimeter (up to a couple hundred feet), known as a "hotspot zone" or **hotspot**. (To support a larger number of users across a larger geographical area, several wireless access points are needed.)

WLANs provide fast and easy Internet or intranet broadband access from public hotspots located at airports, hotels, Internet cafés, and conference centers. WLANs are also being used in universities (recall the Dartmouth University case in Chapter 1), offices, and homes, in place of the traditional wired LANs. In this way, users are free to roam with computing capabilities across the campus, office, or throughout their homes (see *weca.net*).

Users can access a WLAN with their laptops, desktops, or PDAs by adding a wireless network card. As of 2004, most PC and laptop manufacturers incorporate these cards directly in their PCs (as an option). For how to connect your PC or laptop quickly and securely with no wires, see Stafford and Brandt (2002) and also the Virtual Music Company running case.

Most of today's WLANs run on a standard known as **802.11b**. This standard is also known as **Wi-Fi (wireless fidelity)**. WLANs employing this standard have communication speeds of 11 mbps. While most wired networks run at 100 mbps, 11 mbps is actually sufficient for many applications. Two other new standards, 802.11a and 802.11g, support data transmissions at 54 mbps. The 802.11g standard is beginning to show up in commercial products because it is compatible with the 802.11b standard. While PCs

wireless LAN (WLAN) *A local area network (LAN) without the cables; used to transmit and receive data over the airwaves.*

wireless access point *An antenna connecting a mobile device (laptop or PDA) to a wired local area network.*

hotspot *A small geographical perimeter within which a wireless access point provides service to a number of users.*

802.11b *Technical standard, developed by the IEEE, on which most of today's WLANs run; WLANs employing this standard have communication speeds of 11 mbps.*

(Wi-Fi) wireless fidelity *Another name for the 802.11b standard on which most WLANs run.*

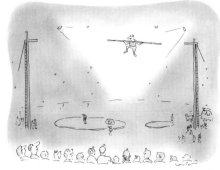

"It appears to be some kind of wireless technology."

can take advantage of 54 mbps, today's (2004) PDAs cannot, because their expansion (network) cards are limited to the 11 mbps speed.

The major benefits of Wi-Fi are its lower cost and its ability to provide simple Internet access. It is the greatest facilitator of the *wireless Internet* (the ability to connect to the Internet wirelessly). The Wi-Fi market got a boost at the end of 2002 when AT&T, Intel, and IBM, along with two global investment firms, joined forces to create Cometa Networks, Inc. (*cometa.com*). Cometa works with major retail chains, hotels, universities, and real estate firms to deploy Wi-Fi hotspots throughout the top 50 U.S. metropolitan areas.

Wireless Personal Area Networks (WPANs). A *wireless personal area network (WPAN)* is a kind of WLAN that people have at their homes or home offices. With such a network, one can connect PCs, PDAs, mobile phones, and digital music players that detect each other and can interact. Also, one can add a digital payment system and personal security technologies. The network maintains constant connectivity among devices (including wearable devices), which is useful in office settings.

Wi-Fi Applications. Each month brings new examples of business that are adding Wi-Fi services. Several examples are presented below.

SVC **MKT** **EXAMPLE** *Wi-Fi in Airports.* Like a number of airports in the United States, the Minneapolis–St. Paul International airport is served by Wi-Fi. The Northstar Crossing concession area, the Northwest Airlines' World Club lounge, the United Airlines' Red Carpet Club, and many of the main terminal concourses provide wireless Internet access to anyone with a laptop or handheld device and a Wi-Fi network card. The Internet service that is hosting Wi-Fi at the airport charges a fee of $7.95 for unlimited daily access.

 MKT **EXAMPLE** *Wi-Fi In-flight.* Lufthansa offers in-flight Wi-Fi service on its long-haul fleet. The hotspots on the aircrafts are connected to the Internet via satellites. A news channel is free; there is a charge of $25 for Wi-Fi use during the flight.

SVC **MKT** **EXAMPLE** *Wi-Fi in Eateries.* In 2002, T-Mobile installed Wi-Fi networks in approximately 2,000 Starbucks stores in the United States. Starbucks has plans to add Wi-Fi to 70 percent of its 6,000 locations worldwide over the next few years. Panera Bread Company has added hotspots in many of its restaurants in St. Louis, Missouri, where Panera is headquartered. McDonald's piloted a program in April 2003 in which it offered Wi-Fi wireless access in 10 restaurants in New York City (*mcdwireless.com*). If you buy a "value meal" you get one hour of free access. Alternatively, you can pay $3 an hour. McDonald's will eventually offer the program in thousands of its restaurants. (If you have an Internet access via AOL or other ISPs, you will get the services free, even without buying the value meal.)

SVC **POM** **EXAMPLE** *Wi-Fi at an Amusement Park.* Using a wireless ticketing system, Universal Studios in Hollywood is shortening the waiting lines for tickets at its front gate. The ticket sellers, armed with Wi-Fi–enabled devices and belt-mounted printers, not only sell tickets but also provide information.

POM **EXAMPLE** *Wi-Fi in Stores.* CVS Corp., the largest retail pharmacy in the United States, uses Wi-Fi–based devices throughout its 4,100 stores. The handheld computers support a variety of in-store applications, including price management, inventory control, and merchandise receiving. Benefits include faster transfer rates, increasing productivity and performance, reduced cost, and improved customer service.

Two factors are standing in the way of even greater commercial Wi-Fi market growth: cost and security. We look at those factors next.

Cost as a Barrier to Commercial Wi-Fi Growth. First, some people question why anyone would pay $30 a month, $7.95 a day, or any other fee for Wi-Fi access when it is readily available in many locations for free. Because it's relatively inexpensive to set up a wireless access point that is connected to the Internet, a number of businesses offer their customers Wi-Fi access without charging them for the service (e.g., Starbucks, Panera Bread, and Border's Books and Music Stores). In fact, there is an organization, Freenetworks.org, aimed at supporting the creation of free community wireless network projects around the globe.

In areas where there is a solid core of high-tech professionals, many "gear heads" have set up their own wireless hotspots that give passersby free Internet connections. This is a part of a new culture known as *war chalking* and *war driving.*

War Chalking and War Driving. Free Wi-Fi Internet hubs are marked in some places by symbols on sidewalks and walls to indicate nearby wireless access. This practice is called *war chalking*. It was inspired by the practice of hobos during the Great Depression who used chalkmarks to indicate which homes were friendly to those seeking handouts of food.

A number of people have also made a hobby or sport out of war driving. *War driving* is the act of locating wireless local area networks while driving around a city or elsewhere (see *wardriving.com*). To war drive, you need a vehicle, a computer or PDA, a wireless card, and some kind of an antenna that can be mounted on top of or positioned inside the car. Because a WLAN may have a range that extends beyond the building in which it is located, an outside user may be able to intrude into the network, obtaining a free Internet connection and possibly gaining access to important data and other resources. The term war driving was coined by computer security consultant Peter Shipley. It derives from the term *war dialing*, a technique in which a hacker programs his or her system to call hundreds of phone numbers in search of poorly protected computer dialups.

Cost as a Barrier to Commercial Wi-Fi Growth. People who engage in war driving highlight the lax security of Wi-Fi hotspots. Security is the second barrier to widespread acceptance of Wi-Fi. Because it uses radio waves, Wi-Fi can be interrupted by walls (resulting in poor quality at times), and it is difficult to protect. Wi-Fi does have a built-in security system, known as *Wireless Encryption Protocol (WEP)*, which encrypts the communications between a client machine (laptop or PDA) and a wireless access point. However, WEP provides weak encryption, meaning that it is secured against casual hacking as long as the person setting up the network remembers to turn on the encryption. Unfortunately, many small business owners and homeowners with wireless LANs fail to do just that. For more on mobile security and WEP, see Online File W6.2.

wiley.com/college/turban

Voice Systems and Portals in Mobile Computing and M-Commerce

The most natural mode of human communication is voice. Voice communication can now be done on the computer using a microphone and a sound card. Voice systems are improving and voice technology applications are growing.

Voice technologies have various advantages, which make them especially useful in mobile computing: The most obvious one is portability; the hands- and eyes-free operations of voice technologies increase the productivity, safety, and effectiveness of mobile computer users, ranging from forklift drivers to military pilots. For users in dirty or moving environments, voice terminals operate better than keyboards because they are more rugged. Voice technologies also enable disabled people to tell a computer to perform various tasks. Another advantage is speed: People can communicate about two-and-a-half times faster talking than typing. In most circumstances, speaking also results in fewer data entry errors than does keyboard data entry.

voice portal *A Web site with audio interface, accessed by making a phone call.*

Voice Portals.   A voice portal is a Web site with an audio interface. Voice portals are not Web sites in the normal sense because they are also accessed through a standard or a cell phone. A certain phone number connects you to a Web site where you can request information verbally. The system finds the information, translates it into a computer-generated voice reply, and tells you what you want to know. Most airlines provide real-time flight status information this way.

An example of this application for mobile computing is the voice-activated 511 travel-information line developed by Tellme.com. It enables callers to request information about weather, local restaurants, current traffic, and other handy information. In addition to retrieving information, some sites provide true interaction. *iPing.com* is a reminder and notification service that allows users to enter information via the Web and receive reminder calls. This service can even call a group of people to notify them of a meeting or conference call.

The real value for mobile computing is that voice portals can help marketers find new customers. When voice portal services are combined with information about users' locations, they make possible location-based m-commerce, a topic we address later in the chapter.

With the development of additional technical standards and the continuing growth of wireless technologies, the number of m-commerce applications is growing rapidly. Applications are derived from providing wireless access to existing B2C, intrabusiness, and CRM applications and from creating new location-based and SMS-based applications. In Sections 6.3 through 6.6 of this chapter, we will study m-commerce applications in a number of diverse categories.

Before you go on . . .

1. Define WLANs.
2. Describe Wi-Fi and cite its applications and advantages.
3. What are war chalking and war driving?
4. Describe wireless voice systems and voice portals.

6.3 MOBILE PERSONAL SERVICE APPLICATIONS

A large number of applications provide personal services to consumers. As an example, consider a person going to an international airport. Tasks such as finding the right check-in desk, checking for delayed flights, finding where to claim lost luggage, and even finding a place to eat or the nearest restroom can be assisted by mobile devices. Online File W6.3 at the book's Web site describes 12 problem areas in an airport that can be solved using mobile devices. Other personal service areas in which wireless devices can be used are described in the following sections. (See also *attws.com*.)

wiley.com/college/turban

Hotel Services Go Wireless

A number of hotels now offer their guests in-room, high-speed, wireline Internet connection. Some of these same hotels are beginning to offer Wi-Fi Internet access in public areas and meeting rooms. One of these is Marriott, which manages 2,500 hotels worldwide. After a seven-month test, Marriott has partnered with STSN (*stsn.com*), an Internet service provider specializing in hotels, to provide Wi-Fi services in the 400 Marriott hotels that already have in-room broadband Internet access. Other hotels in the United States, India (Taj Group hotels), and England (Holiday Inn and Crowne Plaza hotels) are beginning to offer similar services.

While Wi-Fi provides guests with Internet access, to date it has had minimal impact on other sorts of hotel services (e.g., check-in). However, a few hotels are testing use of the Bluetooth technology. Guests are provided with Bluetooth-enabled phones that can communicate with access points located throughout the hotel. This technology can be used for check-in and checkout, for making purchases from hotel vending machines and stores, for tracking loyalty points (see *tesalocks.com*), and for opening room doors in place of keys. In 2001, Classwave signed a deal with Starwood Hotels & Resorts worldwide to enable Bluetooth solutions within Starwood's hotels.

Wireless Telemedicine

Today there are two different kinds of technology used for *telemedicine* applications: (1) storage of data and transferring of digital images from one location to another, and (2) videoconferencing for real-time consultation between a patient in one location and a medical specialist in another. In most of the real-time consultations, the patient is in a rural area and the specialist is in an urban location.

There are a number of impediments to telemedicine. Some states do not allow physicians to provide medical advice across state lines. The threat of malpractice suits is another issue since there is no "hands-on" interaction between the physician and patient. Also, from a technical standpoint, many telemedicine projects are hindered by poor telecommunications support. However, those who are looking ahead are seeing opportunities to meet some of the needs of the aging population by use of emerging technologies. The new mobile technologies, especially the forthcoming generation, not only offer the possibility of overcoming the hurdles imposed by remote locations but also open a number of novel application opportunities.

EXAMPLE *Meds by Wireless.* Typically, physicians write a prescription and you take it to the pharmacy where you wait 15 to 30 minutes for it to be filled. Instead, some new mobile systems allow physicians to enter the patient prescription onto a palm-size device. That information goes by cellular modem (or Wi-Fi) to Med-i-net's (or similar companies') services. There, the information is checked for insurance eligibility and conformity to insurance company regulations. If all checks out, the prescription is transferred electronically to the appropriate pharmacy. For patients who need refills, the system notifies physicians when it is time for the patient to reorder, and the doctor can reissue a prescription with a few clicks.

`POM` `SVC`

EXAMPLE *In-flight Emergencies Aided by Wireless.* In-flight medical emergencies occur more frequently than one might think. Alaska Airlines, for example, deals with about 10 medical emergencies per day. Mobile communications are already being used to attend to medical emergencies occurring on planes. MedLink, a service of MedAire in Phoenix, provides around-the-clock access to board-certified emergency physicians. These mobile services can also remotely control medical equipment, like defibrillators, located on board the plane.

`SVC`

EXAMPLE *Remote Surgery.* The military is engaged in developing mobile telesurgery applications that enable surgeons in one location to remotely control robotic arms for surgery in another location. The technology was proven to be particularly useful in battlefield situations during the 2003 Iraq War.

`SVC`

Mobile Portals

mobile portal *A user interaction channel that aggregates content and services for mobile users.*

A **mobile portal** is a user channel, optimized for mobility, that aggregates and provides content and services for mobile users. The services provided by mobile portals include news, sports, e-mail, entertainment, and travel information; restaurant and event information; leisure-related services (e.g., games, TV and movie listings); community services; and stock trading. A sizeable percentage of the portals also provide downloads and messaging, music-related services, and health, dating, and job information. Mobile portals frequently charge for their services. For example, you may be asked to pay 50 cents to get a weather report over your mobile phone. Alternatively, you may pay a monthly fee for the portal service and get the report free any time you want it.

Increasingly, the field of mobile portals is being dominated by a few big companies. The world's best-known mobile portal, with over 40 million members, mostly in Japan, is i-mode from DoCoMo. The big players in Europe, for instance, are Vodafone, Orange, O2, and T-Mobile. In the United States the big players are Cingular, Nextel, Verizon, and Sprint PCS. Also, mobile-device manufacturers offer their own portals (e.g., Club Nokia portal, my Palm portal). And, finally, the traditional portals (such as Yahoo, AOL, and MSN) have mobile portals as well. Examples of the best "pure" mobile portals (those whose only business is to be a mobile portal) are Room 33 (*room33.com*) in Europe and *zed.com* from Sonera in Finland; compared to the large companies that provide various services, these companies are relatively small.

Other Personal Services Mobile-Computing Applications

Many other personal services mobile computer applications exist for consumers, in a variety of categories. One category of other consumer-related mobile applications is on-

IT's ABOUT BUSINESS   GOV

6.1: The Highway 91 Project

Route 91 is a major eight-lane, east–west highway near Los Angeles. Traffic is especially heavy during rush hours. California Private Transportation Company (CPT) built six express toll lanes along a 10-mile stretch in the median of the existing Highway 91. The express lane system has only one entrance and one exit, and it is totally operated with EC technologies. The system works as follows.

Prepaid subscribers receive an automatic vehicle identification (AVI) device that is placed on the rearview mirror of the car. The device, about the size of a thick credit card, includes a microchip, an antenna, and a battery. A large sign over the tollway tells drivers the current fee for cruising the express lanes. In a recent year it varied from $0.50 in slow traffic hours to $3.25 during rush hours.

Sensors in the pavement let the tollway computer know that a car has entered; the car does not need to slow or stop. The AVI makes radio contact with a transceiver installed above the lane. The transceiver relays the car's identity through fiber-optic lines to the control center, where a computer calculates the fee for that day's trip. The system accesses the driver's account and the fare is automatically deducted from the driver's prepaid account. A monthly statement is sent to the subscriber's home.

Surveillance cameras record the license numbers of cars without AVIs. These cars can be stopped by police at the exit or fined by mail. Video cameras along the tollway also enable managers to keep tabs on traffic, for example, sending a tow truck to help a stranded car. Also, through knowledge of the traffic volume, pricing decisions can be made. Raising the price as traffic increases ensures that the tollway will not be jammed.

The system saves commuters between 40 and 90 minutes each day, so it is in high demand. An interesting extension of the system is the use of the same AVIs for other purposes. For example, they can be used in paid parking lots. Someday you may even be recognized when you enter the drive-through lane of McDonald's and a voice asks you, "Mr. Smart, do you want your usual meal today?"

Source: Compiled from *91expresslanes.com* (2002).

QUESTIONS

1. List the benefits of the Highway 91 project to the company that runs it and to its customers.
2. What other applications of an AVI device can you envision for cars?

line entertainment, as discussed in Online File W6.4. Other examples include online lan-guage translations; information about tourist attractions (hours, prices); and emergency services. For other services for consumers, see the case studies at *mobileinfo.com*.

wiley.com/college/turban

In addition, non-Internet mobile applications, mainly those using smart cards, have existed since the early 1990s. Active use of the cards is reported in transportation, where millions of "contactless" cards (also called *proximity cards*) are used to pay bus and subway fares and road tolls. Amplified remote-sensing cards that have an RF (radio frequency) of up to 30 meters are used in several countries for toll collection. IT's about Business 6.1 (page 178) describes the use of proximity cards in a California highway system.

Before you go on . . .

1. Discuss some of the potential applications of Wi-Fi and Bluetooth technologies in hotels.

2. Describe some potential uses of mobile and wireless technologies in providing medical care.

3. Describe mobile portals and the kind of information they provide for consumers.

6.4 MOBILE APPLICATIONS IN FINANCIAL SERVICES

Other popular mobile applications are in financial services. Mobile financial applica-tions include banking, wireless payments and micropayments, wireless wallets, bill-payment services, brokerage services, and money transfers. In this section we will look at some of the most widely used mobile applications in financial services.

Mobile Banking

Throughout many countries in the world, an increasing percentage of banks offer mo-bile access to financial and account information. Banks in Koreo, Sweden, the United States, Japan, Scotland, and Mexico offer some form of wireless banking services. A study of banks in Germany, Switzerland, and Austria found that over 60 percent of-fered some form of mobile financial services (Hornberger and Kehlenbeck, 2002).

Wireless Electronic Payment Systems

Wireless payment systems transform mobile phones into secure, self-contained purchas-ing tools capable of instantly authorizing payments over the cellular network. In Italy, for example, DPS-Promatic (*dpspro.com*) has designed and installed the first parking meter payable by mobile telephone. In the United States, Cellbucks (*cellbucks.com*) of-fers a mobile payment service to participating sports stadiums. Any fan who is a mem-ber of the Cellbucks Network can dial a toll-free number provided on a menu of choices, enter his or her password and seat location, and then select numbered items from the electronic menu of food, beverages, and merchandise. Once authorized, the purchase is passed on to stadium personnel and is in turn delivered to the fan's seat. An e-mail detailing the transaction is sent to the fan as further confirmation of the order. In Europe and Japan, wireless buying of tickets to movies and other events is popular (Sadeh, 2002).

Micropayments

If you were in Frankfurt, Germany, and took a taxi ride, you could pay the taxi driver using your cell phone. As discussed in Chapter 5, electronic payments for small-purchase amounts (generally less than $10) are called *micropayments*. The demand for wireless micropayments systems is fairly high. An A.T. Kearney study (*cyberatlas.com*) found that more than 40 percent of mobile phone users surveyed would like to use their mobile phone for small cash transactions such as transit fares or vending machines.

MKT

> **EXAMPLE** *Dialing Up Coca-Cola.* Coca-Cola faces fierce competition around the world. By using a radical new strategic information system (SIS) that marries "smart" Coke machines with cellular telephone technology, Coca-Cola has a strong competitive advantage in Singapore. As a result of a joint venture between Singapore Telecommunications, Ltd. and F&N Coca Cola Pte. Ltd. of Singapore, subscribers to the SingTel cellular network can buy drinks from vending machines by using their mobile phones. They punch in an ID number and press the call button or send a short mail message. The machine receives the call or mail, identifies the user, and enables the user to then make the desired selection from the machine. The charge is transferred to the user's telephone bill. The telephone company does not collect a commission from Coke, but does make money on the phone call or electronic message sent. Many of the vending machines in Singapore also accept electronic money cards.

Micropayment technology has wide-ranging applications, such as making payments to parking garages, restaurants, grocery stores, and public transportation. The success of micropayment applications, however, ultimately depends on the costs of the transactions. Transaction costs will be small only if there is a large volume of transactions. Growth in the volume of transactions can be facilitated by wireless e-wallets.

Mobile (Wireless) Wallets

(mobile wallet) m-wallet *A wireless wallet that enables cardholders to make purchases with a single click from their wireless device.*

As discussed in Chapter 5, an *e-wallet* is a piece of software that stores an online shopper's credit card numbers and other personal information so that the shopper does not have to reenter that information for every online purchase. Various companies offer **mobile wallet** (*m-wallet*, also known as *wireless wallet*) technologies that enable

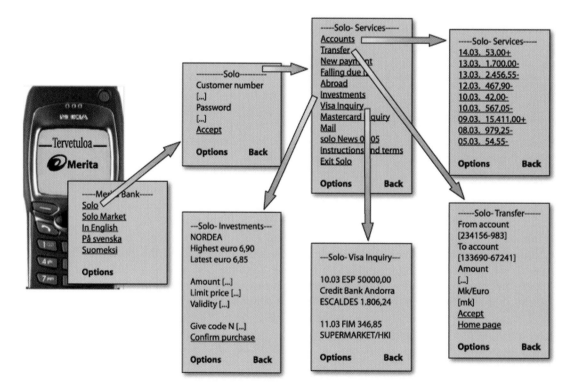

Figure 6.3 *Nordea's WAP Solo banking portal.*
(Source: N. Sadeh, M-Commerce *(New York: Wiley, 2002, Fig. 1.4).)*

cardholders to make purchases with a single click from their mobile devices. One example is the Nokia wallet. This application securely stores information (such as credit card numbers) in the customer's Nokia phone for use in making mobile payments. The information also can be used to authenticate transactions by signing them digitally. Microsoft also offers an e-wallet, Passport, for use in a wireless environment.

Wireless Bill Payments

In addition to paying bills through wireline banking or from ATMs, a number of companies are now providing their customers with the option of paying their bills directly from a cell phone. HDFC Bank of India (*hdfcbank.com*), for example, allows customers to pay their utility bills through SMS. An example of how bill payments can be made using a mobile device is shown in Figure 6.3 (page 180). This service is offered by Nordea, a pioneering provider of wireless banking services in Scandinavia.

Before you go on . . .

1. Describe wireless banking.
2. How can micropayments be made from a mobile device?
3. Describe m-wallets and wireless bill payments.

6.5 MOBILE SHOPPING, ADVERTISING, AND CUSTOMER SERVICE

As in e-commerce, m-commerce B2C applications are concentrated in three major areas—retail shopping, advertising, and providing customer service.

Shopping from Wireless Devices

An increasing number of online vendors allow customers to shop from wireless devices. For example, customers who use Internet-ready cell phones can shop at certain sites such as *mobile.yahoo.com* or *amazon.com*. Shopping from wireless devices enables customers to perform quick searches, compare prices, order, and view the status of their order using their cell phones or wireless PDAs. Wireless shoppers are supported by services similar to those available for wireline shoppers.

> **EXAMPLE**   *Restaurant Ordering from Wireless Devices.* A joint venture between Motorola and Food.com provides an infrastructure for restaurant shopping from wireless devices. Restaurants can use the infrastructure to enable consumers to place an order for pickup or delivery virtually any time, anywhere. Donatos Pizzeria was the first chain to implement the system in 2002.

> **EXAMPLE**   *Wireless Auction Shopping.* Cell phone users can [MKT] [SVC] also participate in online auctions. For example, eBay offers "anywhere wireless" services. Account holders at eBay can access their accounts, browse, search, bid, and rebid on items from any Internet-enabled phone or PDA. The same is true for participants in Amazon.com Auctions.

An example of purchasing movie tickets by wireless device is illustrated in Figure 6.4 (page 182). Notice that the reservation is made directly with the merchant. Then money is transferred from the customer's account to the merchant's account.

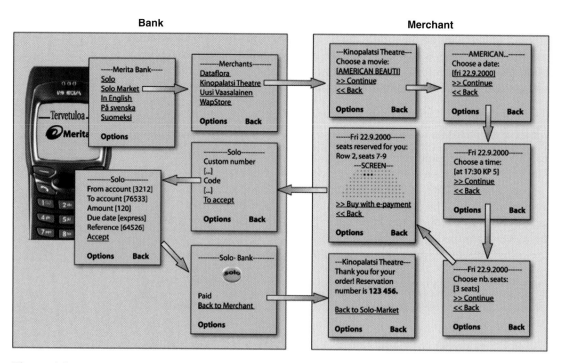

Figure 6.4 *Purchasing movie tickets with WAP Solo.*
(Source: N. Sadeh, M-Commerce *(New York: Wiley, 2002, Fig. 1.5).)*

Location-Based Advertising

Imagine that you are walking near a Starbucks store, but you do not even know that one is there. Suddenly your cell phone beeps with a message: "Come inside and get a 15 percent discount." Your wireless device was detected, and similar to the pop-up ads on your PC, advertising was directed your way.

Knowing the current location of mobile users and their preferences or surfing habits, marketers can send user-specific advertising messages to wireless devices about shops, malls, and restaurants close to where a potential buyer is. SMS messages and short paging messages can be used to deliver this type of advertising to cell phones and pagers. Many companies are capitalizing on targeted wireless advertising, as the examples in Online File W6.5 demonstrate.

Just as in the wireline world, some people are willing to be exposed to mobile advertising—a practice called *permission marketing.* Advertisers sometimes offer incentives to receive mobile advertising. For example, many people in Singapore are willing to listen to a 10-second ad when they dial their cell phone in exchange for 2 minutes of free long-distance time. You also could use permission marketing to shield yourself from location-based advertising. Using the Starbucks example above, for instance, if the permission marketing system knows that you do not drink coffee, you would not be sent a message from Starbucks.

One method of location-based advertising, already in use in a few places, involves putting ads on the top of taxicabs. The ad changes based on the taxi's location. For example, a taxi cruising in the theater district in New York City might show an ad for a play or a restaurant in that area; when the cab goes to another neighborhood, the ad might be for a restaurant or a business in that other area of the city.

Another (future) use of wireless devices for advertising is dynamic billboards. As described by Raskin (2003), ads can be personalized by a system that knows the likes and preferences of passersby. Here's how dynamic billboards, which are still experimental, are expected to work: Your car would be tracked by a GPS, every 20 seconds. A computer would scan the areas in which billboards are visible, and by cross-referencing information about your location and your likes, a personalized ad could be placed on the billboard so you would see it as you pass. For more on location-based commerce, see Section 6.8.

wiley.com/college/turban

IT's ABOUT BUSINESS   SVC   MKT

6.2: How Expedia Is Using Web Services to Provide Customer Service

Expedia.com is a leading online travel service in the United States, with localized versions in the United Kingdom, Canada, and Germany. Expedia operates in a very competitive marketplace with competition from similar services such as Travelocity and Orbitz, ticket discounters such as Priceline and Lastminute.com, traditional travel agencies such as Rosenbluth, and, increasingly, the airlines and hotels themselves. Expedia harnesses the power of Web Services to distinguish itself in this market. As described in Chapter 2, Web Services are universal, prefabricated business process software modules, delivered over the Internet, that users can select and combine through almost any device, enabling disparate systems to share data and services.

Expedia's competitive strategy is driven by nearly every traveler's need to receive up-to-the-second, diverse information at any time and any place. Expedia actively supplies travelers with dynamic and real-time personalized information, such as flight status. This information is *pushed* to travelers (sent to them from Expedia) as well as *pulled* from the company's portal (accessed by the travelers through specific inquiries). Travelers use desktop computers, cell phones, and other Web-enabled devices to receive or access this information. This multichannel provision of timely travel information is the key for attracting new customers and for keeping existing customers.

To make this happen, Expedia needs to connect to many service providers (airlines, hotels, car renting companies), as well as airports, news services, map services, and more. By using Web Services the company solves the integration problem as well as creates device-independent information delivery. This way Expedia can write information only once and then deliver it via whichever method the customer wants—eliminating the need to rewrite the information for each delivery method. Expedia can also tie information into the users' existing "buddy lists" and calendars.

The architecture of the system is flexible enough to work with non-Internet devices. For example, many people with PDAs do not have wireless capabilities. So they can receive information from Expedia by synchronizing the information from a PC to their PDAs and vice versa. By using a system development vendor (Microsoft), Expedia did not have to build services such as authentication, message notification, and calendaring. This enabled the company to be a first-mover in getting these services to market. Using this XML-based service, Expedia adds value to their customers, which provides Expedia with a competitive edge in the travel market.

Sources: Compiled from *expedia.com* and from Microsoft's publicity brochure (2001).

QUESTIONS

1. Identify the customer services provided online.
2. What are the gains to the company?
3. Identify non-Internet mobile computing in this case.

Mobile Support of Consumers

Many companies are using wireless systems to improve customer service for individual consumers. One example is British Airways, which uses wireless customer support to provide a competitive advantage, as described in Online File W6.6. Another example of a company providing wireless customer service is Expedia, which is using the new technology of Web Services as described in IT's about Business 6.2.

wiley.com/college/turban

Before you go on . . .

1. Describe how mobile devices can be used to shop.
2. Explain targeted advertising in the wireless environment.
3. How can a wireless system facilitate B2C customer service?

6.6 MOBILE INTRABUSINESS APPLICATIONS

Although B2C m-commerce gets considerable publicity, most of today's applications actually are used *within* organizations. Preliminary research indicates that employees connected to Wi-Fi increase their productivity by up to 22 percent due to better and faster connectivity (Estrada, 2002). In this section we will look at some intrabusiness applications of mobile technologies—at how companies use mobile computing to support their own employees.

Support of Mobile Workers

Mobile workers are those working outside the corporate premises. Examples of mobile workers are salespeople in the field, traveling executives, telecommuters, people working in warehouses, and repair or installation employees who work at customers' sites or on utility lines. These mobile workers need the same corporate data available to employees working inside the company's offices. Using wireline devices, even portable ones, may be inconvenient or impossible for mobile workers.

The solution is myriad smaller, simple wireless devices—such as the smartphones and handheld companions carried by mobile workers and the in-vehicle information systems installed in cars. Many of these wireless devices are wearable.

wearable devices   *Small computers that can be attached to clothing or the human body.*

Wearable Devices.   Employees who work on buildings, electrical poles, or other difficult-to-climb places may be equipped with small computers that can be attached to a piece of clothing or the human body. These computing devices called **wearable devices**. The following are examples of wearable devices.

- *Screen.* A computer screen is mounted on a safety hat, in front of the wearer's eyes, displaying information to the worker.

- *Camera.* A camera is mounted on a safety hat. Workers can take digital photos and videos and transmit them instantly to a portable computer nearby. Photo transmission to a wearable device or computer is made possible via Bluetooth technology.

  - *Touch-panel display.* In addition to the wrist-mounted keyboard, mobile employees can use a flat-panel screen, attached to the hand, which responds to the tap of a finger or stylus.

  - *Keyboard.* A wrist-mounted keyboard enables typing by the other hand. (Wearable keyboards are an alternative to voice recognition systems, which are also wireless.)

  - *Speech translator.* For those mobile employees who do not have their hands free to use a keyboard, a wearable speech translator is handy.

For an example of wearable devices supporting mobile employees, see IT's about Business 6.3 and *wearable.com.au*.

Wearable computers.
Item 1: *Computer screen mounted in safety helmet.* Item 2: *Camera mounted in safety helmet.* Item 3: *Touch-panel display, attached to hand.* Item 4: *Wrist-mounted keyboard.* Source: Xybernaut.com.

Like e-mail, short messaging services (SMS) on wireless devices can be used to bolster collaboration. Because of its reach, though, SMS has special applications. According to Kontzer (2003), the following are 10 applications of SMS for mobile workers: (1) alerting mobile technicians to system errors, (2) alerting mobile execs to urgent voice messages, (3) confirming with mobile sales personnel that a faxed order was received, (4) informing traveling employees of delays and changes, (5) enabling contract workers to receive and accept project offers, (6) keeping stock traders up to date on urgent stock activity, (7) reminding data services subscribers about daily updates, (8) alerting doctors to urgent patient situations, (9) enabling mobile sales teams to input daily sales figures into corporate database, and (10) sending mobile sales reps reminders of appointments and other schedule details.

Job Dispatch

Mobile devices are becoming an increasingly integral part of workflow applications. For example, nonvoice mobile services can be used to assist in dispatch functions—to assign jobs to mobile employees, along with detailed information about the task. Tar-

IT'S ABOUT BUSINESS
6.3: Wearable Devices for Bell Canada Workers

For years, mobile employees, especially those who had to climb trees, electric poles, or tall buildings, were unable to enjoy or benefit from computing technologies while on the job. With mobile technologies, that has changed.

On a cold, damp November day in Toronto, Chris Holm-Laursen, a field technician with Bell Canada (*bell.ca*), is out and about as usual, but this time with a difference: A small but powerful computer sits in a pocket of his orange mesh vest, a keyboard is attached to the vest's upper-left side, and a flat-panel display screen hangs by his waist. A video camera attached to his safety hat enables him to take pictures without using his hands and send them immediately to the office. A cell phone is attached as well, connected to the computer. A battery pack to keep everything going sits against his back. (See photo, page 184.)

Holm-Laursen and 18 other technicians on this pilot project were equipped like this for 10 weeks during fall 2000. By summer 2003, an increasing number of Bell Canada's employees had been equipped with similar devices. The wearable devices enabled the workers to access work orders and repair manuals wherever they were. The hands-free aspect and the ability to communicate anytime, from any-

where, represent major steps forward for these utility workers. A wide variety of employees in various industries—technicians, medical practitioners, aircraft mechanics, and contractors—are using or testing such devices.

Of course, a practical problem of wearable devices in many countries is the weather: What happens when the temperature is minus 50 degrees or the humidity is 99 percent? Other potential problems also exist: If you are wearing thick gloves, how can you use a keyboard? If it is pouring rain, will the battery short circuit? Various solutions are being developed, such as voice input, tapping on a screen instead of typing, and rainproof electrical systems.

Sources: Compiled from Xybernaut.com, "Xybernaut Mobile Assistant: Productivity Gains in the Telecommunication Field," *xybernaut.com/case_studies/PDFs/Telecommunication_CS.pdf* (accessed January 2004).

QUESTIONS

1. What are some other industrial applications of similar wearable devices?
2. How do you think wearable devices could be used in entertainment?

get areas for mobile delivery and dispatch services include the following: transportation (delivery of food, oil, newspapers, cargo, courier services, tow trucks, and taxis); utilities (gas, electricity, phone, water); field service (computer, office equipment, home repair); health care (visiting nurses, doctors, social services); and security (patrols, alarm installation). Wireless dispatching applications allow improved response with reduced resources, real-time tracking of work orders, increased dispatcher efficiency, and a reduction in administrative work.

EXAMPLE *AirIQ Shows Its "Smarts" through Wireless Dispatching.* AirIQ (*edispatch.com*) offers an interesting dispatching solution. The company's OnLine system combines Internet, wireless, GPS, digital mapping, and intelligent information technologies. The system tracks vital information about a vehicle's direction, speed, and location; those data are provided by a device housed in each of the vehicles being tracked. Managers can view and access information about the fleet on digital maps, monitor on the Internet the location of its vehicles, and maintain top operating condition of their fleet. AirIQ promises savings of about 30 percent in communication costs and increases in workforce efficiency of about 25 percent.

Online File W6.7 provides a detailed description of a job-dispatching system used by U.S. Fleet to benefit both itself and its customers.

wiley.com/college/turban

Other Wireless Intrabusiness Applications. A large number of Internet-based wireless applications have been implemented inside enterprises. Three examples of such intrabusiness applications are described below.

HRM

EXAMPLE *Paying Employees by Cell Phone.* Employees at Telecom Italia Mobile get their monthly pay slips as SMS messages sent to their mobile phone. The money itself is transferred electronically to a designated bank account. The method is much cheaper for the company and results in less paperwork than the old method of mailing monthly pay slips (Republica IT, 2001).

SVC **POM**

EXAMPLE *Photos Sent from the Field.* Kemper Insurance Company has piloted an application that lets property adjusters report from the scene of an accident. Kemper attached a wireless digital imaging system to a camera that lets property adjusters take pictures in the field and transmit them to a processing center (Henning, 2002; Nelson, 2000). The cameras are linked to Motorola's StarTac data-enabled cellular phone service, which sends the information to a database. These applications eliminate delays in obtaining information and in film processing that exist with conventional methods.

SVC **POM**

EXAMPLE *Quality Checkers Report Wirelessly.* Like many national franchises, Taco Bell employs "mystery customers" who visit restaurants to conduct a survey, unknown to the owners. Taco Bell has provided these customers with handheld computers so that they can communicate their reports more quickly to the company's headquarters. The mystery customers answer 35 questions, ranging from the speed of service to food quality. Before the devices, they filled out paper forms that were mailed overnight; the information was then scanned into computers for processing. The information flow using the handhelds is both faster and more accurate.

As these examples indicate, a variety of intrabusiness workflow applications are possible. Manager's Checklist 6.1 shows typical intrabusiness workflow applications before and after the introduction of wireless services. Some of these can be delivered on a wireless intranet; some are offered on the Internet. (For details on intrabusiness applications, see *mdsi-advantex.com* and *symbol.com*. The advantages offered by in-

---

MANAGER'S CHECKLIST 6.1

Intrabusiness Workflow Applications

Before Wireless	With Wireless
Work orders are manually assigned by multiple supervisors and dispatchers.	Work orders are automatically assigned and routed within minutes for maximum efficiency.
Field service technicians commute to dispatch center to pick up paper work orders.	Home-based field service technicians receive first work order via mobile terminal and proceed directly to first assignment.
Manual record keeping of time, work completed, and billing information.	Automated productivity tracking, record keeping, and billing updates.
Field service technicians call for new assignments and often wait because of radio traffic or unavailable dispatcher.	Electronic transmittal of additional work orders with no waiting time.
Completed work orders are dropped off at the dispatch center at the end of the the day for manual entry into the billing tracking system. Uncompleted orders are manually distributed to available technicians. Overtime charges often result.	Technicians close completed work orders from the mobile terminals as they are completed. At the end of the shift, the technicians sign off and go home.

Source: From the publicly distributed brochure, "RALI Mobile," from Smith Advanced Technology, Inc. (2001).

trabusiness wireless solutions can be seen through an examination of workflow applications at *mdsi-advantex.com*.) Also, see Online File W6.8 for examples of the Internet-based intrabusiness wireless applications.

wiley.com/college/turban

Non-Internet Intrabusiness Applications.   Wireless applications in the non-Internet environment have been around since the early 1990s. Examples include such applications as: wireless networking used to pick items out of storage in warehouses via PCs mounted on forklifts; delivery-status updates, entered on PCs inside distribution trucks; and collection of data such as competitors' inventories in stores and customer orders using a handheld (but not networked) device, from which data were transferred to company headquarters each evening. (See the Maybelline case in Chapter 7, Online File W7.7.) Mobile intrabusiness applications are very popular and are typically easier to implement than interbusiness applications.

Other Types of Mobile Work Support.   Wireless devices may support a wide variety of mobile workers. The following example demonstrates one of the varied uses to which mobile computing can be put.

EXAMPLE   *Work on the Farm.* Tractors equipped with sensors, onboard computers, and a global positioning system (GPS) help farmers save time, effort, and money. GPS determines the precise location of the tractor and can direct its automatic steering. Because the rows of planting resulting from GPS guiding are more exact, farmers save both on seed and on fertilizer, due to minimized overlapping and spillage. The sensors also can instantly notify service people of any machine breakdown, enabling faster repair response and less down time (Scanlon, 2003).

The applications of mobile computing will surely grow as the technology matures and as workers think up new ways to apply the functions of wireless devices to their jobs.

Before you go on . . .

1. Describe wearable devices.
2. Describe wireless job dispatch.
3. List some of the major intrabusiness wireless applications.

6.7 MOBILE ENTERPRISE AND SUPPLY CHAIN APPLICATIONS

Mobile computing solutions are also being applied to B2B and supply chain relationships. This section looks at some applications in these areas.

Support of Customers and Business Partners

Successful companies have applied customer service concepts to the support of business partners as well. Increasingly, companies are looking for ways to meld the interests of various organizational units into enterprisewide systems that support both business customers and business partners. Customer relationship management using mobile technologies is one way to do so.

Customer Relationship Management with Mobile Technologies.   Supporting customers is the essence of *customer relationship management (CRM)* systems. Mobile access extends the reach of CRM to both customers and business partners on a 24/7 basis, to wherever recipients are located. According to Eklund

(2002), 12 percent of companies in the United States provided corporate users with mobile access to their CRM systems. Today, it is much more.

In the large CRM software suites (e.g., Siebel's CRM), the two CRM functions that have attracted the most interest are field service and sales force automation. For example, a field service representative on a service call might need to know current availability of various parts in order to fix a piece of machinery. Or a salesperson might be on a sales call and need to know recent billing history for a particular business customer's account. It is these sorts of situations where mobile access to customer and partner data is invaluable.

Sales force automation (SFA) is a technique of using software to automate the business tasks of sales, including order processing, contact management, information sharing, inventory monitoring and control, order tracking, customer management, sales forecast analysis, and employee performance evaluation. Recently, SFA becomes interrelated with CRM, since the salespeople constitute the contact point with customers.

Voice portal technology can also be used to provide enhanced customer service. For example, customers who are away from the office could use a vendor's voice portal to check on the status of deliveries to a job site. Similarly, salespeople could check on inventory status during a meeting to help close a sale. There are a wide variety of CRM applications for voice portal technology. The challenge is in learning how to create the navigation and other aspects of interaction that makes customers feel comfortable with voice-access technology.

Supply Chain Applications

Mobile computing solutions also are used to improve supply chain operations. Such solutions enable organizations to respond faster to supply chain disruptions by proactively adjusting plans or by shifting resources related to critical supply chain events as they occur. With the increased interest in collaborative commerce comes the opportunity to use wireless communication to collaborate along the supply chain. For this to take place, integration is needed.

An integrated messaging system is at the center of B2B communications. By integrating the mobile terminal into the supply chain, it is possible to make mobile reservations of goods, check availability of a particular item in the warehouse, order a particular product from the manufacturing department, or provide security access to obtain confidential financial data from a management information system.

Mobile devices can also facilitate collaboration among members of the supply chain. There is no longer any need to call a partner company and ask someone to find certain employees who work with your company. Instead, you can contact these employees directly, on their mobile devices.

By enabling sales force employees to type orders straight into the ERP while at a client's site, companies can reduce clerical mistakes and improve supply chain operations. By allowing them to check production schedules and inventory levels, and to access product configuration and *available-to-promise/capacity-to-promise (ATP/CTP)* functionality to obtain real-time delivery quotes, they empower their sales force to make more competitive and realistic offers to customers. Today's ERP systems tie into broader supply chain management solutions that extend visibility across multiple tiers in the supply chain. Mobile supply chain management (mSCM) empowers the workforce to leverage these broader systems through inventory management and ATP/CTP functionality, which extend across multiple supply chain partners and take into account logistics considerations. IT's about Business 6.4 illustrates the integration of mobile devices to provide customer data to mobile workers, to help improve customer support, and to improve workflow.

Before you go on . . .

1. Discuss how wireless applications can be used to provide customer support.

2. Describe wireless support along the supply chain.

IT'S ABOUT BUSINESS

MKT POM

6.4: PAVECA of Venezuela Uses Wireless

PAVECA, Venezuela's largest paper goods manufacturer and exporter, manufactures toilet paper, paper towels, tissues, and other paper products. The company enjoys a significant amount of market share. Seeking to maintain its lead, PAVECA chose to use some m-commerce technologies to cut operational costs and improve customer service at the same time.

PAVECA implemented a wireless system that enables sales reps to use their wireless PDAs to connect to the Internet while they are in the field. Via the Internet connection, the salespeople can log directly into the company intranet to get all the information they need in real time. Orders can then be entered into the system in real time. When an order is entered into the PDA, it goes into the ERP system (Chapter 8) and follows a predefined automated workflow. The savings produced by the new system as compared to the manual system were dramatic: Order processing time was reduced by 90 percent, order approval time by 86 percent, shipment time by 50 percent, and the time between orders taken and order posting was reduced from three days to 20 seconds. The faster order processing time not only led to faster order approval but also increased the number of daily shipments out of the warehouse.

While the main goal was to improve workflow, there has been another benefit: better customer service. Because of the direct links and integration, customers get their orders faster, and there is less chance of errors occurring. Customers are happier and more loyal, and are more likely to place additional orders with PAVECA in the future.

Sources: Compiled from Paperloop, Inc., "The Profits of Going Wireless," *Paperloop Magazines,* Paper and Pulp International, Inc. (August 2002).

QUESTIONS

1. What are the benefits of PAVECA's new system?
2. What segments of the supply chain are supported?
3. What are the advantages of using wireless systems?

6.8 LOCATION-BASED COMMERCE

As discussed earlier, **location-based commerce (l-commerce)** refers to the localization of products and services. Location-based services are attractive to both consumers and businesses alike. From a user's point of view, l-commerce offers various benefits: convenience (you can locate what is near you without having to consult a directory, payphone, or map), productivity (you can optimize your travel and time by determining points of interest within close proximity), and safety (you can connect to an emergency service with a mobile device and have the service pinpoint your exact location). From a business supplier's point of view, l-commerce offers an opportunity to provide services that meet customers' needs.

The basic l-commerce services revolve around five key areas: (1) *location*—determining the basic position of a person or a thing (e.g., car or boat); (2) *navigation*—plotting a route from one location to another; (3) *tracking*—monitoring the movement of a person or a thing (e.g., a package or vehicle); (4) *mapping*—creating maps of specific geographical locations; (5) *timing*—determining the precise time at a specific location.

location-based commerce (l-commerce) *M-commerce transactions targeted to individuals in specific locations, at specific times.*

L-Commerce Technologies

Providing location-based services requires the following location-based and network technologies:

- **Position-determining equipment (PDE).** This equipment identifies the location of the mobile device (either through GPS or by locating the nearest base station). The position information is sent to the mobile positioning center (see opening case).

- **Mobile positioning center (MPC).** The MPC is a server that manages the location information sent from the PDE.

- **Location-based technology.** This technology consists of groups of servers that combine the position information with geographic- and location-specific content to provide an l-commerce service. For instance, location-based technology could present a list of addresses of nearby restaurants based on the position of the caller, local street maps, and a directory of businesses.

- *Geographic content.* Geographic content consists of names and images of streets, road maps, addresses, routes, landmarks, land usage, Zip codes, and the like. This information must be delivered in compressed form for fast distribution over wireless networks.

- *Location-specific content.* Location-specific content is used in conjunction with the geographic content to provide the location of particular services. Yellow Page directories showing the location of specific businesses and services exemplify this type of content.

Figure 6.5 shows how these technologies are used in conjunction with one another to deliver location-based services.

Underlying these technologies are global positioning and geographical information systems.

global positioning system (GPS)
A wireless system that uses satellites to enable users to determine their position anywhere on the earth.

Global Positioning System (GPS).   As indicated at the start of the chapter, a **global positioning system (GPS)** is a wireless system that uses three satellites to enable users to determine their position anywhere on the earth. GPS equipment has been used extensively for navigation by commercial airlines and ships and for locating trucks and buses (as in the opening case study).

GPS is supported by 24 U.S. government satellites that are shared worldwide. Each satellite orbits the earth once every 12 hours on a precise path, at an altitude of 10,900 miles. Each satellite broadcasts its position and a time signal from its onboard atomic clock, which is accurate to one-billionth of a second. GPS devices also have accurate clocks that are synchronized with those of the satellites. At any point in time, the exact position of each satellite is known, based on the reception of the broadcast satellite data. Knowing the location of the three satellites enables the calculation of the location of the GPS device that receives the satellite's broadcast.

Cell phones that are equipped with a GPS device can be used as standalone units. The GPS can be plugged into or embedded in other mobile devices. GPS software then computes the latitude and longitude of the receiver (to within 50 feet of its location). For an online tutorial on GPS see *trimble.com/gps.*

Geographical Information System (GIS).   The location provided by GPS is expressed in terms of latitude and longitude. To make that information useful to busi-

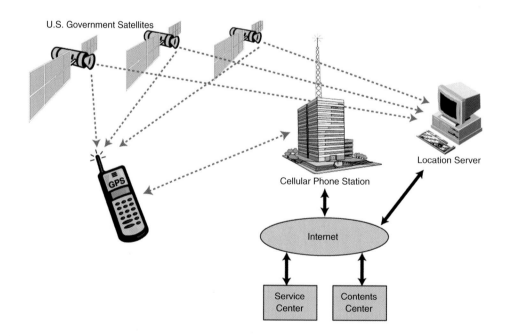

U.S. Government Satellites

GPS

Cellular Phone Station

Location Server

Internet

Service Center

Contents Center

Figure 6.5 *A smartphone with GPS system in l-commerce.*

nesses and consumers it is usually necessary to relate those measures to a certain place or address. This is done by inserting the latitude and longitude onto an electronic map, using software known as a geographical information system (GIS) (see Chapter 3). The GIS data visualization technology integrates GPS data onto digitized map displays. Companies such as *mapinfo.com* provide the GIS core spatial technology, maps, and other data content needed in order to power location-based GPS/GIS services (see Figure 6.6).

An interesting application of GPS/GIS is now available from several car manufacturers (e.g., Toyota, Cadillac) and car rental companies (e.g., Hertz, Avis). Some cars have a navigation system that indicates how far away the driver is from gas stations, restaurants, and other locations of interest. The GPS knows where the car is at any time, so the application can map the route for the driver to a particular destination. Any GPS application can be classified as *telemetry*, a topic discussed further later on.

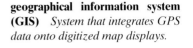

geographical information system (GIS) *System that integrates GPS data onto digitized map displays.*

E-911 Emergency Cell Phone Calls

If someone dials 911 from a regular wired phone, it is easy for the emergency 911 service to pinpoint the location of the phone. But, what happens if someone places a 911 call from a mobile phone? Can the emergency service locate the caller? A few years ago, the U.S. Federal Communications Commission (FCC) issued a directive to wireless carriers, requiring that they establish services to handle wireless 911 (e-911) calls. To give you an idea of the magnitude of this requirement, more than 156,000 wireless 911 calls are made *every day*, representing more than half the 911 calls made daily in the United States. In 2003, 66 million emergency calls were made from cell phones in the United States.

The e-911 directive is to take effect in two phases. Phase I requires carriers, upon appropriate request by a local Public Safety Answering Point (PSAP), to report the telephone number of a wireless 911 caller and the location of the cellular antenna that received the call. Phase II, which is being rolled out over a four-year period from October 2002 to December 2005, requires wireless carriers to provide information that will enable the PSAP to locate a caller within 50 meters, 67 percent of the time and within 150 meters, 95 percent of the time. (The specifics of the phases vary from one wireless carrier—e.g., AT&T, Cingular, Sprint, etc.—to another.) By the end of Phase II, 100 percent of the new cell phones and 95 percent of all cell phones will have these location capabilities. It is expected that many other countries will follow the example of the United States in providing e-911 service.

wireless 911 (e-911) *Calls from cellular phones to providers of emergency services; automatic crash notification (ACN).*

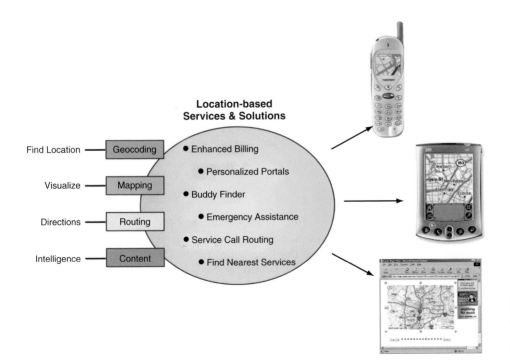

Figure 6.6 *Location-based services involving maps. (Source: Mapinfo.com, accessed October 2001.)*

Telemetry Applications

Telemetry is the science that measures physical remoteness by means of wireless transmission from a remote source (such as a vehicle) to a receiving station. Telemetry has numerous mobile computing applications. Using *mobile telemetry*, technicians can diagnose maintenance problems in equipment. Car manufacturers use the technology for remote vehicle diagnosis and preventive maintenance. Finally, doctors can monitor patients and control medical equipment from a distance.

General Motors Corporation popularized an automotive use of telemetry with its OnStar system (*onstar.com*). Nokia believes that every vehicle will be equipped with at least one Internet Protocol (IP) address by the year 2010. Nokia therefore has set up a business unit called Smart Traffic Products, which is focusing solely on telemetry applications. Smart cars and traffic products are discussed in more detail in Section 6.7.

Barriers to L-Commerce

What is holding back the widespread use of location-based commerce? Several factors come into play:

- **Accuracy.** Some of the location technologies are not as accurate as people expect them to be. However, a good GPS provides a location that is accurate up to 15 meters. Less expensive, but less accurate, technologies can be used instead to find an approximate location (within about 500 meters).

- **The cost-benefit justification.** For many potential users, the benefits of l-commerce do not justify the cost of the hardware or the inconvenience and time required to utilize the service (Hamblen, 2001). After all, they seem to feel, they can just as easily obtain information the "old-fashioned" way.

- **The bandwidth of GSM networks.** GSM bandwidth is currently limited; it will be improved as 3G technology spreads. As bandwidth improves, applications will improve, which will attract more customers.

- **Invasion of privacy.** When "always-on" cell phones are a reality, a number of people will be hesitant to have their whereabouts and movements tracked throughout the day, even if they have nothing to hide. This issue will be heightened when our cars, homes, appliances, and all sorts of other consumer goods are connected to the Internet, as described in the next section.

> **Before you go on . . .**
>
> 1. Describe some of the potential uses of l-commerce.
> 2. Describe GPS and GIS.
> 3. List some of the barriers to l-commerce.

6.9 PERVASIVE COMPUTING

Steven Spielberg's sci-fi thriller *Minority Report* depicts the world of 2054. The film immerses the viewer in the consumer-driven world of pervasive computing 50 years from now. Spielberg put together a think tank, headed by Peter Schwartz, president of Global Business Network (*gbn.com*), to produce a realistic view of the future. The think tank projected out from today's marketing and media technologies to create a society where billboards beckon you by name, newspapers are delivered instantly over broadband wireless networks, holographic hosts greet you at retail stores, and cereal boxes broadcast live commercials. While the technologies in the film were beyond the leading edge, none was beyond the realm of the plausible.

A world in which virtually every object has processing power with wireless or wired connections to a global network is the world of **pervasive computing**. The term pervasive computing also goes by the names *ubiquitous computing, embedded computing,* or *augmented computing.*

The idea of pervasive computing has been around for years. However, the current version was articulated by Mark Weiser in 1988 at the computer science lab of Xerox PARC. From Weiser's perspective, pervasive computing was the opposite of virtual reality. In virtual reality, the user is immersed in a computer-generated environment. In contrast, pervasive computing is invisible "everywhere computing" that is embedded in the objects around us—the floor, the lights, our cars, the washing machine, our cell phones, our clothes, and so on (Weiser, 2002).

pervasive computing *Invisible, everywhere computing that is embedded in the objects around us.*

Invisible Computing Everywhere

By "invisible," Weiser did not mean to imply that pervasive computing devices would not be seen. He meant, rather, that these embedded computers would not intrude on our consciousness. Think of a pair of eyeglasses. The wearer does not have to think about using them. He or she simply puts them on and they augment the wearer's ability to see. This is Weiser's vision for pervasive computing. The user doesn't have to think about how to use the processing power in the object; rather, the processing power automatically helps the user perform a task.

Some new embedded technology is already in use at Prada's "epicenter" stores in New York, San Francisco, and Los Angeles. Prada is a high-end fashion retailer (*prada.com*). At these epicenters, the items for sale have an **RFID (radio frequency identification)** tag attached. The tag contains a processor and an antenna. If a customer wants to know about a particular item, she or he can move with the item toward one of the many displays around the store. The display automatically detects the item and provides sketches, video clips of models wearing the item, and information about the item (color, cut, fabric, materials, and availability). If a customer takes a garment into one of the dressing rooms, the tags are automatically scanned and detected via an antenna embedded in the dressing room. Information about the item will be automatically displayed on an interactive touch screen in the dressing room. The dressing rooms also have a video-based "Magic Mirror." When the customer tries on the garment and turns around in front of the mirror, the images will be captured and played back in slow motion. (See Section 6.8 for a related privacy issue).

RFID (radio frequency identification) *Generic term for technologies that use radio waves to automatically identify the location of individual items equipped with RFID tags.*

A device manufactured and sold by Fitsense Technology (*fitsense.com*), a Massachusetts developer of Internet sports and fitness monitors, also offers "invisible" processing power. With this one-ounce device that is clipped to a shoelace, runners are able to capture their speed and the distance they have run. The device transmits the data via a radio signal to a wrist device that can capture and transmit the data wirelessly to a desktop computer for analysis. Along the same lines, Champion Chip (*championchip.com*), headquartered in the Netherlands, has developed a system that keeps track of the tens of thousands of participants in very popular long-distance (marathon) races.

Active badges can be worn as ID cards by employees who wish to stay in touch at all times while moving around the corporate premises. The clip-on badge contains a microprocessor that transmits its (and its wearer's) location to the building's sensors, which send it to a computer. When someone wants to contact the badge wearer, the phone closest to the person is identified automatically. When badge wearers enter their offices, their badge identifies them and logs them on to their personal computers.

Similarly, *memory buttons* are nickel-sized devices that store a small database relating to whatever it is attached to. These devices are analogous to a barcode, but with far greater informational content and a content that is subject to change. For example, the U.S. Postal Service has placed memory buttons in some residential mailboxes to track and improve delivery schedules.

For a list of the technical foundation of pervasive computing, see Online File W6.9 at the book's Web site.

wiley.com/college/turban

Contextual Computing and Context Awareness

context awareness *Capturing a broad range of contextual attributes to better understand what the consumer needs and what products or services might be of interest.*

contextual computing *Active adaptation of the contextual environment for each user, at each point of computing.*

Location can be a significant differentiator in advertising services such as restaurants. However, knowing that the user is at the corner of the street will not tell you what he or she is looking for. For this, we might need to know the time of day or to access our user's calendar or other relevant *contextual attributes.* **Context awareness** refers to capturing a broad range of contextual attributes to better understand what the consumer needs, and what products or services he or she might possibly be interested in.

Context awareness is part of **contextual computing**, which refers to the enhancement of a user's interactions by understanding the user, the context, and the applications and information being used, typically across a wide set of user goals (Pitkow et al., 2002). Contextual computing is about actively adapting the contextual environment for each user, at each point of computing. Such applications are futuristic at the present time. But as shown in IT's about Business 6.5 they already exist in a research university.

Applications of Pervasive Computing

According to Estrin et al. (2000), 98 percent of all processors on the planet are not in traditional desktop computer systems, nor even in laptops. They are in household appliances, vehicles, and machines. Such existing and future applications of pervasive computing are illustrated in Figure 6.7 (page 196). Notice that all 15 devices can be connected to the Internet. Several of these applications are described in the remainder of this section. We will look at four applications in particular: smart homes, smart appliances, smart cars, and smart things.

Smart Homes

In a *smart home*, your home computer, television, lighting and heating controls, home security system, and many appliances within the home can "talk" to each other via the Internet or a home intranet. These linked systems can be controlled through various devices, including your pager, cellular phone, television, home computer, PDA, or even your automobile. In the United States, tens of thousands of homes are already equipped with home-automation devices, and there are signs that Europe—which has much lower home Internet penetration levels—is also warming to the idea. Some of the tasks and services supported today by home automation systems are described in more detail in Online File W6.10.

wiley.com/college/turban

Smart Appliances

One of the key elements of a smart home is the *smart appliance*, an Internet-ready appliance that can be controlled by a small handheld device or desktop computer via a home intranet (wire or wireless) or the public Internet.

One organization that is focused on smart appliances is the Internet Home Alliance (*internethomealliance.com*). The alliance is made up of a number of appliance manufacturers (e.g., Whirlpool and Sunbeam), computer hardware companies (e.g., IBM and Cisco), retailers (e.g., Best Buy), and vendors specializing in home automation (e.g., Lutron Electronics). The mission of the alliance is to accelerate the process of researching, developing, and testing new home products and services that require a broadband or persistent connection to the Internet.

The appliance manufacturers are interested not only in the sale of appliances but also in servicing them. In most cases, the manufacturer loses touch with a purchased appliance unless the customer registers it for warranty purposes. Potentially, a networked appliance could provide a manufacturer with information that could be used to capture or report on its operation, performance, and usage. In addition, the networked appliance could provide information for diagnostic purposes—for monitoring, troubleshooting, repairing, or maintaining the device.

To date, however, consumers have shown little interest in smart appliances. For now, the appliance manufacturers are focusing on improving people's lives by eliminating

IT'S ABOUT BUSINESS

6.5: Context-Aware Environment at Carnegie Mellon University

Carnegie Mellon University (CMU) is known for its advanced science projects including robotics and artificial intelligence. Students participate in a context-awareness experiment in the following manner: Each participating student is equipped with a PDA from which he or she can access Internet services via the campus Wi-Fi network. The students operate in a context-aware environment whose architecture is shown in the attached figure.

A user's content (left of figure) includes the following: calendar information; current location (position), which is regularly updated using location-tracking technology; weather information, indicating whether it is sunny, raining, or snowing, and the current outside temperature (environment); and social context information, including the student's friends and his or her teachers, classmates, and so forth.

The preferences of each student are solicited and entered into system, as is a personal profile. This is shown as the "preferences and permissions" in the figure. All of the above information helps the system to filter incoming messages, and determine what to show to the students and when. For example, while attending classes the student may block all messages, except from her boyfriend. That is, certain messages will be shown only if the student is in a certain place and/or time; others will not be shown at all.

A user's context information can be accessed by a collection of *personal agents*, each in charge of assisting with different tasks, while locating and invoking relevant Internet services identified through services registries (see the figure). An example of a simple agent is a *restaurant concierge* that gives suggestions to students about places to have lunch, depending on their food preferences, the time they have available before their next class, their location on campus, and the weather. For example, when it is raining, the agent attempts to find a place that does not require going outside of the building where the student is located. The recommendations (usually several choices) appear on the PDA, with an overall rating and a "click for details" possibility.

Source: Compiled from N. Sadeh, *M-Commerce* (New York: Wiley, 2002).

QUESTIONS

1. Does the usefulness of such as service justify the need to disclose private preferences?
2. Can such a system be developed for consumers who are not members of a defined community such as a university?

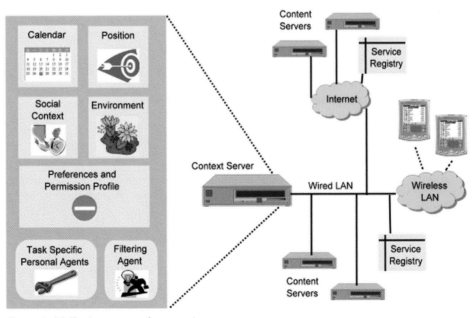

Carnegie Mellon's contextual-computing system.
[Source: N. Sadeh, M-Commerce *(New York: Wiley, 2002).]*

1. Smart building materials:
   • Sense vibrations, temperature, moisture
   • Monitor premises for intruders
   • Cancel street noise
2. Bridge deck erected with smart building materials:
   • Senses, reports traffic, wind loads
   • Monitors structural integrity
3. Autonomous robo-sweeper
4. Wireless communication, including links to GPS satellites, Net access
5. Smart sensor pills:
   • Programmable delivery vehicles for pharmaceuticals
   • Internal sensing applications
6. Embedded automobile devices:
   • Antilock brakes
   • Air bags
   • Evaluate performance
   • Provide net access
7. Fire hydrant measures water flow, senses heat, offers security mechanisms.
8. Autonomous robo-mailbox performing nominally manual labor.
9. Street light senses foot and motor traffic, polices area.
10. Banking/business:
    • ATM machines, cash registers, bar-code readers, credit card devices
    • Security devices offer personal Ids, but also sense vibrations and (body) heat and motion and monitors premises for intruders.
11. Home networks:
    • Most electrical applications, including dishwashers, toasters, cable TV set-top boxes, toys, phones, thermostats, PCs
12. Smart building materials:
    • Smart paint
    • smart concrete
    • Smart gels
13. Smart cement detects earthquake activity.
14. Collar on dog for wireless location via GPS link. Clothes on man (personal cybernetics) offer similar abilities. As well as networking and heat sensors.

Figure 6.7 *Embedded computing devices everywhere.*
[Source: D. Estrin, "Embedding the Internet," Communications of the ACM, May 2000, pp. 38–39.]

repetitive, nonquality tasks. One example is Sunbeam's corded HLT (Home Linking Technology) products that communicate with one another using an embedded technology called PLC (Power Line Communication). For instance, an HTL alarm clock can coordinate an entire morning's routine: The heating system, the coffeemaker, and the lights in the kids' rooms go on, and the electric blanket goes off.

Smart Cars

Every car today has at least one computer on board to operate the engine, regulate fuel consumption, and control exhaust emissions. The average automobile on the road today has 20 or more microprocessors. They are under the hood, behind the dash, in the door panels, and on the undercarriage. Microprocessors control the radio, decide when your transmission should shift gears, remember your seat position, and adjust the temperature in the passenger cabin. They can make the suspension work better, help you see in the dark, and warn when a tire is low. In the shop, the onboard microprocessors are used to diagnose problems. Car computers often operate independently, but some swap data among themselves—a growing trend. The microprocessors in a car require little maintenance, continuing to operate through extreme temperature, vibration, and humidity.

There is also a growing trend to connect car microprocessors to mobile networks and to the Internet. Emergency assistance, driving directions, and e-mail are some of the services these connections can support. To increase safety, drivers can use voice-activated controls, even to access the Web.

The next generation of smart cars is likely to provide even more automated services, especially in emergency situations. Some expect that in the future cars will have a device for *automatic crash notification (ACN)*. This still-experimental device would automatically notify the police of an accident involving an ACN-equipped car and its location. Such systems would determine the speed upon impact, whether the car has rolled over, and whether the driver and passengers were wearing seat belts. Information of this sort might be used by emergency personnel to determine the severity of the accident and what types of services will be needed.

Ideally, smart cars eventually will be able to drive themselves. Known as *autonomous land vehicles (ALVs)*, these cars follow GIS maps and use sensors in a wireless environment to identify obstacles. Such vehicles are already on the roads in California, Pennsylvania, and Germany (on an experimental basis, of course).

General Motors' OnStar system (onstar.com) is the forerunner of smart cars of the future. OnStar already supports many of the services that smart cars will offer.

Smart "Things"

Several other devices and instruments can be made "smart." Some examples are discussed below.

Barcodes. A typical barcode, known as the *Universal Product Code (UPC)*, is made up of 12 digits, in various groups. The first two show the country where it was issued, the next four represent the manufacturer, and the remaining six are the product code assigned by the manufacturer. On a package the code is represented by a series of bars and spaces of varying widths.

Barcodes have worked pretty well over the past 25 years. But they have their limitations. First, they require line-of-sight of the scanning device. This is fine in a store but can pose substantial problems in a manufacturing plant, a warehouse, or on a shipping/receiving dock. Second, they are printed on paper, and so can be ripped, soiled, or lost. Third, the barcode identifies the manufacturer and product, not the item. For example, every carton of milk of a given producer has the same barcode, regardless of when it was produced. This makes a barcode useless in determining things like the expiration date. There is an alternative identification method, called Auto-ID, which overcomes the limitations of barcodes.

Auto Identification (Auto-ID) Center *Joint partnership among global companies and research universities to create an "Internet of things."*

Internet of things *A network that connects computers to objects in order to be able to track individual items as they move from factories to store shelves to recycling facilities, providing near-perfect supply chain visibility.*

wiley.com/college/turban

Auto-ID. This method has been promoted over the past couple of years by the Auto Identification (Auto-ID) Center (*autoidcenter.org*). This center is a joint partnership among more than 87 global companies and three of the world's leading research universities—MIT in the United States, the University of Cambridge in the UK, and the University of Adelaide in Australia. The companies include manufacturers (e.g., Coca-Cola, Gillette, and Canon), retailers (e.g., Wal-Mart, Tesco in the UK), shippers (e.g., UPS and the U.S. Postal Service), standards bodies (e.g., Uniform Code Council), and government agencies (e.g., the U.S. Department of Defense).

The mission of the Auto-ID Center goes well beyond replacing one code with another. Its stated aim is to create an Internet of "things," a network that connects computers to objects—ranging from boxes of laundry detergent to pairs of jeans to airplane engines. This Internet of things will provide the ability to track *individual* items as they move from factories to store shelves to recycling facilities. This will make possible near-perfect supply chain visibility.

The key technical elements of the Auto-ID system and an explanation of how it will work are provided in Online File W6.11. One of the tools of Auto-ID is RFID.

RFID: Capabilities and Cost. As discussed earlier, RFID (radio frequency identification) uses radio waves to automatically identify individual items. Typically, a microchip with product information and an antenna are embedded in an RFID tag. The antenna transmits the identification information by radio waves to an RFID reader; the reader passes the information on to computers that can make use of it.

RFID has been around awhile. In World War II, RFIDs were used to identify friendly aircraft. Today, they are used in wireless tollbooth systems, such as E-Z Pass. In Singapore they are used in a system called Electronic Road Pricing, which charges different prices to drive on different roads at different times, encouraging drivers to stay off busy roads at busy times. Every car has an RFID tag that communicates with card readers on the major roads (similar to Highway 91 in California).

Until now the problem with RFID has been the expense. Tags have cost at least 50 cents, which makes them unusable for low-priced items. A California company called Alien Technology (*alientechnology.com*) has invented a way to mass-produce RFID tags for less than 10 cents apiece for large production runs. In January 2003, Gillette placed an order with Alien Technology for 500 million RFID tags (*RFID Journal*, November 15, 2002). Gillette is using the tags in a number of trial programs. In one of the early trials, Gillette attached the tags to Mach 3 razors shipped to Wal-Mart, whose store shelves are equipped with special RFID readers. The overall success of RFID tags in the marketplace will depend on the outcome of trials such as this.

Large-Scale Pervasive Systems

Smart homes, smart appliances, smart cars, and smart things can certainly make our lives more comfortable and efficient. But pervasive computing has the potential to make an even larger contribution to society when many computing devices are linked together, creating massive intelligent systems. These systems include factories, airports, schools, offices, health-care facilities, and even entire cities.

At the moment, most such systems are experimental and on a relatively small scale. Two examples of large-scale pervasive systems that are already in operation are provided below.

SVC POM

EXAMPLE *Intelligent Elder-Care.* Due to the increased average age of the population in many countries, more elderly people must be cared for and for longer periods of time. Long-term care facilities, where patients require different levels of care, bring the problem of how to provide such care efficiently and effectively. An experimental project called Elite-Care has demonstrated the benefits of using pervasive computing in such settings. At Elite-Care's Estates Cluster Residential Care Facility in Milwaukie, Oregon, pervasive computing is being used to increase the autonomy and care level of all of its residents, regardless of their individual needs.

Elite-Care, a family-owned business (*elite-care.com*), has been built from the ground up to provide "high-tech, high-touch" programs. The entire facility is wired with a 30-mile network (wireline and wireless) of unobtrusive sensors and other devices including: biosensors (e.g., weight sensors) attached to each resident's bed; movement sensors embedded in badges worn by the residents and staff (wearable computers); panic buttons used to call for help; Internet access via touch screens in each room; video conferencing using Webcams; and climate control, lights, and other regulated appliances.

These devices and others allow the staff to monitor patient activity. For example, staff can determine the location of any patient, to tell whether he or she is in an expected area of the facility. Devices that monitor length of absence from bed might alert personnel that the patient has fallen. Medical personnel can watch for weight loss, restlessness at night, and frequency of trips to the bathroom, all of which may indicate certain medical conditions for the elderly. Also, close monitoring of conditions enables staff to give medicine and/or other treatments as needed, rather than at predetermined periods. All of these capabilities enable true one-to-one care, which is both more effective and less expensive.

One of the initial concerns with these monitors was that the privacy of the residents would be unnecessarily invaded. To alleviate these concerns, residents and their families are given the choice of participating or not. Most choose to participate because the families believe that these monitors provide better tracking and care. The monitors also increase the autonomy of all the patients because their use reduces the need for staff to constantly monitor residents in person, especially those with more acute care needs. At the present time such projects are experimental and expensive, but someday they will be affordable to many. (*Source:* Standford, 2000.)

EXAMPLE   *Digital Cities.* The main object of *digital cities* is to
provide computerized services to citizens and visitors any where, any time. Digital cities integrate urban information (both real-time and stored) and create public spaces for people living in or visiting the cities. Digital cities are being developed all over the world. In Europe alone there are over 100 projects (e.g., Amsterdam, Helsinki).

In the city of Kyoto, Japan, for example, the digital city complements and corresponds to the physical city (Ishida, 2002). Three layers are constructed: The first is an *information layer*, where Web archives and real-time sensory data are integrated to provide information anywhere, at any time. The second layer is 2-D and 3-D *interfaces*, which provide views of cars, buses, and pictures that illustrate city services (for attractive and natural presentation). Finally, there is an *interactive layer*. Extensive use of GIS supports the project. One area of emphasis is a digital tour guide for visitors. Also, the system uses *avatars* (animated computer characters) that appear on a handheld device and "walk" with visitors around the city in real time.

Another digital-city experiment is the city of Lancaster (UK), where wireless devices are being used for improved services for both visitors and residents. The experimental Lancaster City Guide is based on a network of Wi-Fi context-sensitive and location-aware applications. One area that was developed first is services for tourists. By knowing where the tourist is (using a GPS) and his or her preferences, the system can recommend tourist sites in the same general area. (This application is similar to the Carnegie Mellon application described in IT's about Business 6.5, page 195.)

Before you go on . . .

1. Define pervasive computing.
2. What is contextual computing?
3. What applications of pervasive computing interest you the most? Explain why.
4. Explain the benefits of auto-ID and RFID.

6.10 INHIBITORS AND BARRIERS OF MOBILE COMPUTING

Several limitations either are slowing the spread of mobile computing or are leaving many m-commerce customers disappointed or dissatisfied (Islam and Fayad, 2003). Here, we consider some representative inhibitors and barriers of mobile computing.

Usability and Other Problems

When mobile Internet users visit mobile Internet sites, the *usability* of the site is critical to attract attention and retain "user stickiness" (the degree to which users stay at a site). There are three dimensions to usability, namely *effectiveness*, *efficiency*, and *satisfaction*. However, users often find current mobile devices to be ineffective, particularly with respect to restricted keyboards and pocket-size screens, limiting their usability. In addition, because of the limited storage capacity and information access speed of most smartphones and PDAs, it is often difficult or impossible to download large files to these devices. The major technical and other limitations that have slowed the spread of m-commerce are summarized in Table 6.1.

Ethical and Legal Issues

Several ethical and legal issues are unique to mobile computing. For example, fashion retailer Benetton Group SpA was considering embedding RFID smart tags into the labels in one of its lines of clothing, to help track shipping, inventory, and sales in the company's 5,000 stores worldwide. (Also, the tags could help prevent shoplifting.) Using the tags, the store would know where each piece of clothing is, at any given time. However, privacy groups expressed concern that the tags could also be used to track buyers; some groups even urged that the company's clothing be boycotted. As a result, Benetton backed away from the plan, at least until an impact study could be done.

According to Hunter (2002), privacy is in great danger in the world of ubiquitous computing. Some people fear that the networking of pervasive computing devices, which could link individuals, businesses, and government, may jeopardize privacy. The Elite-Care project, for example, raised the issue of protecting infor-

Table 6.1   Technical and Other Limitations of Mobile Computing

Limitation	Description
Insufficient bandwidth	Sufficient bandwidth is necessary for widespread use and it must be inexpensive. It will take a few years until 3G is in many places. Wi-Fi solves some of the problem.
Security standards	Universal standards were not available in 2003. It may take 3 or more years to have them.
Power consumption	Batteries with long life are needed for mobile computing. Color screens and Wi-Fi consume more electricity, but new chips are solving some of the power-consumption problems.
Transmission interferences	Weather and terrain problems as well as distance-limited connection exist with some technologies. Reception in tunnels and some buildings is poor.
GPS accuracy	GPS may be inaccurate in a city with tall buildings.
WAP limitations	According to *mofileinfo.com*, in 2002 there were only about 50,000 WAP sites (compared to millions of Web sites). WAP still is a cumbersome process to work with.
Potential health hazards	Potential health damage from cellular radio frequency emission is not known yet. However, more car accidents are related to drivers who were talking (some places bar the use of cell phones while you drive). Also, cell phones may interfere with sensitive medical devices.
Legal issues	Potential legal issues against manufacturers of cell phones and against service providers exist, due to the potential health problems.
Human interface with device	Screens and keyboards are too small, uncomfortable, and tedious for many people to use.
Complexity	Too many optional add-ons are available (e.g., battery chargers, external keyboards, headset, microphone, cradles). Storing and using the optional add-ons can be a problem.

❏ Do not start without appropriate infrastructure.

❏ Do not start a full-scale implementation; use a small pilot for experimentation.

❏ Pick up an appropriate architecture. Some users don't need to be persistently connected, for example.

❏ Talk with a range of users, some experienced and some not, about usability issues.

❏ Users must be involved; use biweekly meetings if possible.

❏ Use wireless experts if you are not one.

❏ Wireless is a different medium from other forms of communication. Remember that people are not used to the wireless way of doing things.

Source: Compiled from M. Hamblen, "Get Payback on Wireless," *Computer World*, January 1, 2001.

mation collected by sensors. Also, privacy is difficult to control in other types of context-aware systems. Security is especially difficult in Wi-Fi systems.

In order for pervasive (ubiquitous) systems to be widely deployed, it is necessary to overcome both the technical and the ethical/legal barriers associated with wireless computing. In addition, vendors will need to find appropriate business models for pervasive computing technologies and to develop experience in deploying ubiquitous systems. Some of this experience is likely to come through trial-and-error.

Failures in Mobile Computing and M-Commerce

As with any other technology, especially a new one, there have been many failures of applications as well as of entire companies in mobile computing and m-commerce. It is important to anticipate and plan for possible failures as well as to learn from them. The case of Northeast Utilities provides some important insights.

EXAMPLE   *Inspectors Go Wireless.* Northeast Utilities, located in Berlin, Connecticut, supplies energy products and services to 1.2 million customers from Maine to Maryland. The company embarked on a wireless project in 1995 in which its field inspectors used wireless devices to track spills of hazardous material and report them to headquarters in real time. After spending a year and a half and $1 million, the project failed (Hamblen, 2001). Some of the lessons learned from the failure of the wireless project are shown in Manager's Checklist 6.2.

Having learned from the failure, Northeast made its next wireless endeavor a success. Today, 15 field inspectors carry rugged wireless laptops that are connected to the enterprise intranet and databases. The laptops are used to conduct various measurements in the field. The laptops transmit the results, in real time, to chemists and people who prepare government reports about hazardous materials spills. All of the information is entered directly into electronic forms without having to be transcribed, saving time and ensuring greater accuracy. The new system is so successful that it has given IT workers the confidence to launch other applications such as sending power-outage reports to executives via smartphones and wireless information to crews repairing street lights (Hamblen, 2001).

Before you go on . . .

1. Discuss the role that usability plays in the adoption of m-commerce.

2. List the technical limitations of m-commerce.

3. List some legal and ethical m-commerce issues.

WHAT'S IN IT FOR ME?

ACC

FOR THE ACCOUNTING MAJOR

Wireless applications help with inventory counting and auditing. They also assist in expediting the flow of information for cost control. Price management, inventory control, and other accounting-related activities can be improved by use of wireless technologies.

FIN

FOR THE FINANCE MAJOR

Banks and other financial institutions can enhance a competitive advantage when providing wireless services. Wireless electronic payments, including micropayments, are made more convenient (any place, any time), and their cost is significantly reduced. Electronic bill payment from mobile devices is becoming more popular, increasing security and accuracy, expediting cycle time, and reducing processing cost.

MKT

FOR THE MARKETING MAJOR

Imagine a whole new world of marketing, advertising, and selling, with the potential to increase sales of products and services by significant amounts. Such is the promise of mobile computing. Of special interest for marketing are location-based advertising and l-commerce as well as the new opportunities resulting from pervasive computing and RFIDs. Finally, wireless also provides new opportunities in sales force automation (SFA), enabling faster and better communications with both customers (CRM) and corporate services.

POM

FOR THE PRODUCTION/ OPERATIONS MANAGEMENT MAJOR

Wireless technologies offer a multitude of opportunities to support mobile employees of all kinds. Wearable computers enable repair personnel working in the field and off-site employees to service customers faster, better, and at less cost. Wireless devices also enable productivity lifts within factories by allowing faster communication and collaboration, and improved managerial planning and control. In addition, mobile computing technologies can decrease risky operations and increase safety by providing quicker warning signs and instant messaging to isolated employees. Finally, using mobile devices, personnel can communicate and collaborate better both internally and externally.

HRM

FOR THE HUMAN RESOURCES MANAGEMENT MAJOR

Mobile computing offers new frontiers in improving HR training and extending it to any place at any time. Payroll notices can be delivered as SMSs. Self-service selection of benefits and updating of personal data can be extended to wireless devices, making these functions even more convenient for employees to handle on their own.

SUMMARY

1. **Discuss the characteristics, attributes, and drivers of mobile computing and m-commerce.** Mobile computing is based on mobility and reach. These characteristics provide ubiquity, convenience, instant connectivity, personalization, and product and service localization. The major drivers of mobile computing are: large numbers of users of mobile devices, especially cell phones; no need for a PC; a developing "cell phone culture"; vendor marketing; declining prices and increasing functionalities; and bandwidth improvement.

2. **Describe the emergence of Wi-Fi and voice portals.** Wi-Fi is a popular emerging standard for wireless local area networks (WLANs). It is fairly fast and inexpensive. It provides Internet access via your own laptop to a number of users within a small transmission area known as a hotspot. Hotspots are available in many public places. Voice portals allow users to access the Internet by voice from a regular or cell telephone.

3. **Describe personal service applications of m-commerce.** M-commerce is being used to provide applications in travel, delivery of medical services, delivery of information (e.g., news, sports, and other information) over wireless devices, and gaming and entertainment. Non-Internet consumer

applications of m-commerce are used mainly in transportation and shopping from vending machines and gas pumps. Such applications typically involve use of various types of smart cards and RFIDs.

4. **Discuss m-commerce applications in financial services.** Many EC applications in the service industries (e.g., banking, travel, and stocks) can be conducted with wireless devices. Applications in financial services are expanding. Mobile banking is popular in many countries. Wireless electronic payment systems and micropayment technology allow purchasing from vending machines any time and place. Wireless m-wallets store the information used to make mobile payments more easily.

5. **Describe m-commerce applications in shopping, advertising, and customer service.** Consumers who shop from wireless devices are supported by services similar to those used by wireline shoppers. In addition, targeted advertising can reach customers in the appropriate place and time. Finally, real-time ubiquitous customer service is provided by m-commerce applications.

6. **Describe the use of m-commerce in intrabusiness applications.** Large numbers of applications of mobile computing are being found in business. Intrabusiness applications such as wearable devices for mobile workers, job dispatching, and more are already evident inside organizations.

7. **Discuss the use of mobile computing in enterprise and supply chain applications.** Enterprise applications in areas such as knowledge management, CRM, sales force automation, and supply chain management are being used to provide competitive market advantage and to facilitate cooperation between business partners.

8. **Describe location-based commerce (l-commerce).** Location-based commerce is emerging in applications such as calculating arrival time of buses (using GPS) and calling for emergency services (wireless 911). In the future, it will be used to target advertising to individuals based on their location. Other innovative applications also are expected.

9. **Discuss the key characteristics and current uses of pervasive computing.** Pervasive computing is the world of "invisible" computing in which virtually every object has an embedded microprocessor that is connected in a wired and/or wireless manner to the Internet. In context-aware computing, a computer captures the contextual variables of the user and the environment and then provides, in real time, various services to users. Current uses of pervasive computing include some early applications in homes, appliances, and cars (e.g., OnStar). Many more applications are still in the experimental stage. Eventually, an Internet of things—homes, appliances, cars, and any manufactured items—will provide a number of life-enhancing, consumer-centric, and B2B applications.

10. **Describe the major inhibitors and barriers of mobile computing and m-commerce.** The major limitations of mobile computing are: small screens on mobile devices, limited bandwidth, high cost, lack of (or small) keyboards, transmission interferences, unproven security, and possible health hazards. Many of these limitations are expected to diminish over time. The primary legal/ethical limitations of m-commerce relate to privacy issues.

INTERACTIVE / LEARNING

Business Unplugged: How to Build a Wi-Fi Network
Go to the Interactivities section on the Student Web Site and access Chapter 6: Mobile, Wireless, and Pervasive Computing. There you will find an animated simulation of a Wi-Fi network, as well as some hands-on activities that visually explain business concepts in this chapter.

More Resources
More resources and study tools are located on the Student Web Site. You'll find additional chapter materials and links to organizations, people, and technologies for each chapter. In addition, self-quizzes that provide individualized feedback are available for each chapter.

Instructions for accessing the Interactivities on the Student Web Site:

1. Go to **wiley.com/college/turban**
2. Select Turban Rainer Potter's *Introduction to Information Technology, Third Edition*
3. Click on Student Resources Site, in the toolbar on the left
4. Click on Interactivities Web Site
5. Click on Interactivities Web Site and use your password to enter the site (your password card is located in the inside cover of your textbook)

DISCUSSION QUESTIONS

1. Discuss how m-commerce can expand the reach of e-business.
2. Discuss why wireless mobile computing may be superior to mobile computing that is *not* wireless.
3. How are GIS and GPS related?
4. List three to four major advantages of wireless commerce to consumers, presented in this chapter, and explain what benefits they provide to consumers.
5. Discuss the ways in which Wi-Fi is being used to support mobile computing and m-commerce. Describe the ways in which Wi-Fi is affecting the use of cellular phones for m-commerce.

6. Describe some m-commerce B2B applications along the supply chain.
7. You can use location-based tools to help you find your car or the closest gas station. However, some people see location-based tools as an invasion of privacy. Discuss the pros and cons of location-based tools.
8. Which of the applications of pervasive computing—smart cars, homes, appliances, consumer products, and other objects—do you think are likely to gain the greatest market acceptance over the next few years? Why?

PROBLEM-SOLVING ACTIVITIES

1. Enter *kyocera-wireless.com*. Take the smart tour and view the demos. What is a smartphone? What are its capabilities? How does it differ from a regular cell phone?
2. Enter *mymobile.aol.com/portal/aolbyphone/index.html*. Run the demo. What types of services are provided? What types of users would be more likely to use a voice portal rather than a smartphone?

3. Using a search engine, try to determine whether there are any commercial Wi-Fi hotspots in your area. Enter *wardriving.com*. Based on information provided at this site, what sorts of equipment and procedures could you use to locate hotspots in your area?

INTERNET ACTIVITIES

1. Explore *nokia.com*. Prepare a summary of the types of mobile services and applications Nokia currently supports and plans to support in the future.
2. Enter *ibm.com*. Search for *wireless e-business*. Research the resulting stories to determine the types of wireless capabilities and applications IBM's software and hardware supports. Describe some of the ways these applications have helped specific businesses and industries.
3. Enter *mapinfo.com* and look for the location-based services demos. Try all the demos. Find all of the wireless services. Summarize your findings.

4. Enter *packetvideo.com* and *microsoft.com/mobile/pocketpc*. Examine their demos and products and list their capabilities.
5. Enter *onstar.com*. What types of *fleet* services does OnStar provide? Are these any different from the services OnStar provides to individual car owners? (Play the movie.)
6. Enter *mdsi-advantex.com* and review the wireless products for the enterprise. Summarize the advantages of the different products.
7. Enter *gii.co.jp/english/cg11183_smart_appliances.html* and look for information about smart appliances.

TEAM ASSIGNMENTS

1. Each team should examine a major vendor of mobile devices (Nokia, Kyocera, Motorola, Palm, Black-Berry, etc.). Each team will research the capabilities and prices of the devices offered by each company and then make a class presentation, the objective of which is to convince the rest of the class why one should buy that company's products.
2. Each team should explore the commercial applications of m-commerce in one of the following areas: financial services, including banking, stocks, and insurance; marketing and advertising; manufacturing;

travel and transportation; human resources management; public services; and health care. Each team will present a report to the class based on their findings. (Start at *mobiforum.org*.)
3. Each team should take one of the following areas—homes, cars, appliances, or other consumer goods like clothing—and investigate how embedded microprocessors are currently being used and will be used in the future to support consumer-centric services. Each team will present a report to the class based on their findings.

The car rental industry is very competitive, and Hertz (*hertz.com*), the world's largest car rental company, competes against hundreds of companies in thousands of locations. The competition focuses on customer acquisition and loyalty.

Hertz has been a "first mover" to information technologies since the 1970s. So it has naturally looked for new technologies to improve its competitive position. Hertz has pioneered the following mobile computing applications:

- *Quick rentals.* Upon arrival at the airport, Hertz's curbside attendant greets you if you have a reservation and transmits your name wirelessly to the renting booth. The renting-booth employee advises the curbside attendant about the location of your car. All you need to do is go to the slot where the car is parked and drive away. This system is now part of a national wireless network that can check credit cards, examine your rental history, determine which airline to credit your loyalty mileage to, and more.

- *Instant returns.* Pioneered by Hertz in 1987, a handheld device connected to a database via a wireless system expedites the car-return transaction. Right in the parking lot, the lot attendant uses a handheld device to calculate the cost of the rental and print a receipt for the renter. You check out in less than a minute, and you do not have to enter the renting booth at all.

- *In-car cellular phones.* Starting in 1988, Hertz began renting cell phones with its cars. Today, of course, this is not the big deal it was in 1988, when it was a major innovation.

- *NeverLost Onboard.* Some cars come equipped with an onboard GPS system, which provides route guidance in the form of turn-by-turn directions to many destinations. The information is displayed on a screen with computer-generated voice prompts. An electronic mapping system is combined with the GPS, enabling you to see on the map where you are and where you are going. Also, consumer information about the locations of the nearest hospitals, gas stations, restaurants, and tourist areas is provided.

- *Additional customer services.* Hertz's customers can download city guides, Hertz's location guide, emergency telephone numbers, city maps, shopping guides, and even reviews of restaurants, hotels, and entertainment into their PDAs and other wireless devices. Of course, driving directions are provided.

- *Car locations.* Hertz is experimenting with a GPS-based car-locating system. This will enable the company to know where a rental car is at any given time, and even how fast it is being driven. Although the company says it wants to collect such information in order to provide discounts based on your usage pattern, this capability is seen by many as an invasion of privacy. On the other hand, some may feel safer knowing that Hertz knows where they are at all times.

Source: hertz.com (2003) and J. A. Martin, "Mobile Computing: Hertz In-Car GPS," *PC World*, March 13, 2003, *pcworld.com/howto/article/0,aid,109560,00.asp* (accessed June 2003).

QUESTIONS

1. Which of these wireless applications are intra-business in nature? Which are customer-centered applications?
2. Identify any finance- and marketing-oriented applications.
3. What are the benefits to Hertz of knowing exactly where each of its cars is? As a renter, how do you feel about this capability?

CLUB IT — wiley.com/college/turban

PERVASIVE COMPUTING AT CLUB IT

Club IT's wait staff are known for the fun times they help create for the guests. You notice though, that they spend a lot of time walking orders to the kitchen and the bar. You think of the extra time they could spend with guests if they could transmit orders and be notified when ready with wireless communications. You remember seeing an ad for a product called Wireless Waitress when you were browsing through some industry publications in Lisa's office, and so you decide to so some more investigation of this product.

ASSIGNMENT

1. Visit the Wireless Waitress Web Site (http://www.thewirelesswaitress.com), view the demonstration

and read about its capabilities for nightclubs. Describe some of the features you learned about that would be useful to Club IT.

2. If Lisa and Ruben decided to purchase and install Wireless Waitress, would it change the dynamics in the club? What are some advantages to using a product such as Wireless Waitress? What are some disadvantages?

3. What are some mobile consumer or personal service applications that could be implemented at Club IT to bring in more guests more often? Consider technologies such as hot-spots, location-based services, uses for SMS and MMS, and other m-commerce possibilities. As an example, view the cell phone emulator here: http://www.wapsilon.com, and enter Club IT's URL onto the phone to see a prototype Club IT web page.

Go to wiley.com/college/turban to access the CLUB IT Web Site on the Student Web Site

Transaction Processing, Functional Applications, and Integration

Chapter Preview

In previous chapters we introduced many information technologies to show the benefits they provide to the modern organization. In this chapter we show how separate technologies are woven into *systems* common in today's organizations.

First we introduce the most common and basic type of system, known as the *transaction processing system (TPS)*. Such systems deal with the repetitive core business processes of organizations, such as order fulfillment and payroll. The objectives of TPSs are to increase the efficiency and effectiveness of the core business processes, to reduce corporate cost, and to improve customer service. We also discuss a common type of system that draws from the TPS, the management information system (MIS). We detail how MISs are used in all functional areas. These applications can increase productivity, reduce costs, enhance customer relations, and in general increase the efficiency and knowledge of managers in all parts of the organization. Finally we look at how the various functional applications can be integrated in two or more departments, or even throughout the entire organization (also addressed in Chapter 8).

Chapter Outline

Learning Objectives

1. Describe the drivers and characteristics of functional information systems.
2. Describe MISs.
3. Describe the transaction processing system and how it is supported by IT.
4. Describe the support provided by IT and the Web to accounting and finance.
5. Describe the support provided by IT and the Web to marketing and sales.
6. Describe the support provided by IT and the Web to production/operations management, including logistics.
7. Describe the support provided by IT and the Web to human resources management.
8. Describe the benefits and issues of integrating functional information systems.

WIRELESS INVENTORY MANAGEMENT SYSTEM AT DARTMOUTH-HITCHCOCK MEDICAL CENTER

Dartmouth-Hitchcock Medical Center (DHMC) is a large medical complex in New Hampshire with hospitals, a medical school, and over 600 practicing physicians in its many clinics. DHMC is growing rapidly and is encountering a major problem in the distribution of medical supplies. These supplies used to be ordered by nurses. But there is a shortage of nurses. So having them spending valuable time ordering supplies left nurses less time for their core competency—nursing. Furthermore, having nurses handling supply orders led to inventory management problems: Busy nurses tended to over-order in an effort to spend less time managing inventory. On the other hand, they frequently waited until the last minute to order supplies, which led to costly rush orders.

One solution would have been to transfer the task of inventory ordering and management to other staff. But doing so would have required hiring additional personnel, and DHMC was short on budget. Also, the coordination with the nurses to find what is needed and when, as well as maintaining the stock, would have been cumbersome. The size of the medical center and the fact that there are over 27,000 different inventory items made any solution difficult.

THE IT SOLUTION

Realizing that their problem related to the supply chain, DHMC looked to IT for solutions. The idea that DHMC chose was to connect wireless handheld devices with a purchasing and inventory management information system. Here is how the new system (as of the summer of 2002) works: The medical center has a wireless LAN (Wi-Fi) into which handhelds are connected. Information about supplies can be uploaded and downloaded from the handheld devices to the network from anywhere within the range of the Wi-Fi. In remote clinics without Wi-Fi, the handhelds are docked into wireline network PCs.

DHMC established a "par level" (the level at which supplies must be reordered) for each item in stock. The par levels were based on actual usage reports and in collaboration between the nurses and the materials management staff. Nurses simply scan each item when it is consumed, and the software automatically adjusts the recorded inventory level. When a par level is reached for any inventory item, an order to the supplier is generated automatically. When the inventory level of an item at each nursing station dips below the *station's* par level, a shipment is arranged from the central supply room to that nursing station. The system also allows for nurses to make restocking requests, which can be triggered by scanning an item or scanning the supply cart where items are stocked at each nursing station. The system works for the supplies of all non-nursing departments as well (e.g., human resources or accounting).

The system is integrated with other applications from the same software vendor (PeopleSoft Inc.). One such application is Express PO, which enables purchasing managers to review standing purchase orders, e-procurement, and contract management.

THE RESULTS

Inventory levels were reduced by 50 percent, paying for the system in just a few months. Materials purchasing and management now are consistent across the enterprise, the time spent by nurses on tracking materials has been drastically reduced, and access to current information has been improved. All of these results contributed to reduced costs and improved patient care.

Sources: Compiled from S. Grimes, "Declaration Support: The B.P.M. Drumbeat," *Intelligent Enterprise*, April 23, 2003, and *peoplesoft.com* (site visited October 2003).

The DHMC case provides some interesting observations about implementing IT: First, IT can support the routine processes of inventory management, enabling greater efficiency and more focus on core competencies. The new system at DHMC also helped to modernize and redesign some of the center's business processes (e.g., distribution, procurement).

Although the system's major application is in inventory management, it is able to support several business processes (e.g., reordering, inventory counts, and billing patients), not just one. The software vendor provided ready-made modules that could be *integrated* with each other (e.g., inventory management with purchasing and contract management). The integration also included connection to suppliers, using the Internet. This IT solution has proved useful for an organization whose business processes cross the traditional functional departmental lines. In this case, nursing is considered an operations/production function; inventory control, purchasing, and contract management are finance/accounting functions.

WHAT WE LEARNED FROM THIS CASE

7.1 FUNCTIONAL INFORMATION SYSTEMS

To offer service in the digital economy, companies must continuously upgrade their functional information systems by using state-of-the-art technology. Furthermore, the functional processes must be improved as needed. Finally, as we will show in Chapter 8, supply chain software is needed in some segments of the supply chain. These segments may include functional information systems.

Functional information systems for accounting, sales and marketing, POM, and so on get much of their data from *transaction processing systems (TPSs)*—the systems that process an organization's routine transactions. Also, many applications in business intelligence, e-commerce, CRM, and other areas use data and information from two or more functional information systems. Therefore, there is a need to integrate the functional systems applications among themselves, with the TPS, and with other applications. These relationships are shown in Figure 7.1, which also provides a pictorial roadmap of the topics discussed in this chapter. (Not showing in the figure are applications discussed in other chapters, such as e-commerce and knowledge management.)

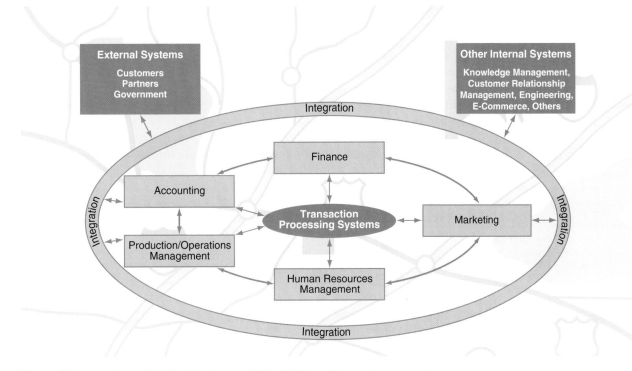

Figure 7.1   *Roadmap: The functional areas, TPS, CRM, and integration connection.*

Functional Systems for Managers: Management Information Systems

Functional information systems support various types of employees, ranging from professionals to managers. Functional information systems can be divided into two general categories: function-specific and function-general. Here we will discuss the most common type of function-general system, management information systems (MISs).

management information system (MIS) *A system that provides information to managers (usually mid-level) in the functional areas, in order to support managerial tasks of planning, organizing, and controlling operations.*

The Role of the MIS. As described in Chapter 2, management information systems (MISs) provide information to managers (usually mid-level ones, such as department heads) in the functional areas, in order to support managerial tasks of planning, organizing, and controlling operations. The information is provided in routine reports such as daily sales, monthly expenditures, or weekly payroll. (The term *MIS* is occasionally used as a blanket concept for all information systems combined—the same as IT by our definition. Historically, there were MIS departments in business organizations and in colleges. Today, the broad concept is referred to as IS or IT, and MIS is reserved for the specific use described above.)

As shown in Figure 7.1, information about each business transaction (everything from purchase of raw materials, to hiring of employees, to paying of bills, to sale of merchandise, and more) comes into the MIS, mainly from the various function-specific transaction processing system databases (described below). Other internal and external databases may supply additional data needed to create management reports.

MIS Reports. Each MIS generates reports in its functional area. These reports are used for applications in the specific area and in other functional areas. The MIS also sends information to the corporate data warehouse and can be used for decision support (Chapter 3). An MIS produces mainly routine reports, ad-hoc (on-demand) reports, and exception reports, as described below.

Routine Scheduled Reports. Routine periodic reports are produced at scheduled intervals, ranging from hourly quality control reports to reports on monthly absenteeism rates.

ad-hoc (on-demand) reports *Nonroutine reports.*

drill-down reports *Reports that show a greater level of detail than is included in routine reports.*

key-indicator reports *Reports that summarize the performance of critical activities.*

comparative reports *Reports that compare performances of different business units or time periods.*

exception reports *Reports that include only information that exceeds certain threshold standards.*

Ad-hoc (On-Demand) Reports. Managers frequently need special information that is not included in the routine reports, or they need the same information that is included in the routine reports but at different times ("I need the report today, for the last three days, not for one week"). Such out-of-the routine reports are called ad-hoc (on-demand) reports. They also may include requests for drill-down reports, which show a greater level of detail; for key-indicator reports, which summarize the performance of critical activities; or for comparative reports, which compare, for example, performances of different business units or time periods.

Exception Reports. Some high-level managers prefer exception reports. Exception reports include only information that exceeds certain threshold standards—for example, reports on expense items that are larger than 5 percent of the budget, or sales that fall 3 percent or more short of the quota.

To implement *management by exception*, management first sets standards (such as the level of expenditure). Then systems are set up to monitor performance (via the incoming data about business transactions such as expenditures), compare actual performance to the standards, and identify predefined exceptions. Managers are alerted to the exceptions via exception reports. (Expenditures that fall within the accepted range of standards would not be reported.) Reporting exceptions saves high-level managers time (since they need not read the long, complete reports) and helps them concentrate on the essentials. The exceptions themselves then need to be managed (e.g., make adjustments to fix negative deviations in performance). Operations-level managers, of course, need to read routine reports.

The major functional areas in many companies are the *production-operations, marketing, human resources, accounting,* and *finance* departments.

Information Systems for Specific Functional Areas

As noted earlier in this section, information systems can also be function-specific. Traditionally, information systems were designed within each functional area, to support the area by increasing its internal effectiveness and efficiency. As shown in Figure 7.1, typical function-specific systems are accounting, finance, marketing, operations (POM), and human resources management. We will explore these traditional functional information systems in Sections 7.3 through 7.6.

However, the traditional functional structure may not be the best structure for some organizations, because certain business processes involve activities that are performed in several functional areas. Product orders, for example, may involve business activities in the marketing department, in finance, in the production/operations and logistics area, and in accounting. If the flow of work and information among departments does not work well, delivery of the product may be slow or customer service may suffer. An integrated enterprise information system can help communication, coordination, and control. The integrated approach is discussed in Section 7.7 and in Chapter 8.

Major Characteristics of Functional Information Systems

Before we demonstrate how IT facilitates the work of the specific functional areas, it will be helpful to examine four characteristics that functional information systems of various types share. These characteristics are:

1. *Frequently composed of smaller systems.* A functional information system frequently consists of several smaller information systems that support specific activities performed in the functional area.

2. *Integrated or independent.* The specific IS applications in any functional area can be integrated to form a coherent departmental functional system, or they can be completely independent. Or, some of the applications within each area can be integrated across departmental lines to match the structure of a business process.

3. *Interfacing.* Functional information systems may interface with each other to form the organizationwide information system. Some functional information systems interface with the environment outside the organization. For example, a human resources information system can collect data about the labor market.

4. *Supportive of different organizational levels.* Information systems applications support the three levels of an organization's activities: operational, managerial, and strategic (see Chapter 2).

Since functional applications receive much of the data that they process from the corporate *transaction processing system,* we present this system first.

Before you go on . . .

1. What is a functional information system? List its major characteristics.

2. Define a management information system (MIS) and describe its role in an organization.

3. How does the MIS system support management by exception? How does it support on-demand reports?

4. Why is it advisable to integrate functional systems?

7.2 TRANSACTION PROCESSING INFORMATION SYSTEMS

The core operations of organizations are enabled by transaction processing systems. These core operations may involve two or more functional areas.

Computerization of Routine Transaction Processes

In every organization certain business transactions provide its mission-critical activities. Such transactions occur when a company produces a product or provides a service. For example, to produce toys, a manufacturer needs to buy materials and parts, pay for labor and electricity, build the toys, receive orders from customers, ship them to customers, bill customers, and collect money. Every transaction may generate additional transactions. For example, purchasing materials will change the inventory level, and paying an employee reduces the corporate cash on hand.

Because the computations involved in most transactions are simple and the transaction volume is large and repetitive, such transactions are fairly easy to computerize. As defined in Chapter 2, the information system that supports routine core transactions is referred to as a **transaction processing system (TPS)**. The transaction processing system monitors, collects, stores, processes, and disseminates information for all routine core business transactions. These data are inputs to functional information systems applications. They also may be inputs to decision support systems, customer relationship management, knowledge management, and e-commerce (e.g., data on customers and their online purchasing history, and suppliers' information in B2B).

Transaction processing occurs in all functional areas. Some TPSs occur only within one area (such as POM production plans or HRM recruiting plans), others (such as payroll) cross several areas. Online File W7.1 provides a list of TPS activities mapped on the major functional areas. The information systems that automate transaction processing can be part of the departmental systems and/or part of the enterprisewide information system.

transaction processing system (TPS) *Information system that supports routine, core business transactions.*

wiley.com/college/turban

Objectives of a TPS

The primary goal of a TPS is to provide all the information needed by law, by management, and/or by organizational policies to keep the business running properly and efficiently. More specifically, a TPS has to efficiently handle high volume, avoid errors due to concurrent operations, be able to handle large variations in volume (e.g., during peak times), avoid downtime, never lose results, and maintain privacy and security (Bernstein and Newcomer, 1997). A TPS must also closely interface with many EC applications, including e-payment, e-procurement, and e-marketing. To meet these goals, a TPS is usually automated and is constructed with the major characteristics listed in Manager's Checklist 7.1.

It should be emphasized that TPSs usually yield the most tangible benefits of IT investments. They were the first to be computerized so they have had more improvement opportunities. Also, their information volume is high, so even a small improvement may result in a high payoff.

Activities and Methods of TPSs

Regardless of the specific data processed by a TPS, a fairly standard process occurs, whether in a manufacturing firm, in a service firm, or in a government organization. First, data are collected by people or sensors and entered into the computer via any input device. Generally speaking, organizations try to automate the TPS data entry as much as possible because of the large volume involved.

Next, the system processes data in one of two basic ways: *batch* or *online processing*. In **batch processing**, the firm collects data from transactions as they occur, placing them in groups or batches. The system then prepares and processes the batches periodically (say, every night). Batch processing is particularly useful for operations that require processing for an extended period of time. Once a batch job begins, it continues until it is completed or until an error occurs.

In **online processing**, data are processed, without batching, after a transaction occurs, frequently but not necessarily in real time. *Master files* containing key information are placed on hard drives, where they are directly accessible. *Transaction files* containing information about activities of these business entities (such as orders placed by customers) are held in online files until they are no longer needed for everyday transaction processing activity. This ensures that the transaction data are avail-

batch processing *TPS that processes data in batches at fixed periodic intervals.*

online processing *TPS that processes data after transactions occur, frequently in real time.*

MANAGER'S
CHECKLIST 7.1

**The Major
Characteristics of a TPS**

❑ Typically, *large amounts of data* are processed.

❑ The *sources of data are mostly internal*, and the output is intended mainly for an *internal audience*. This characteristic is changing somewhat, since trading partners may contribute data and may be permitted to use TPS output directly.

❑ The TPS processes information on a *regular basis:* daily, weekly, biweekly, and so on.

❑ *Large storage (database) capacity* is required.

❑ *High processing speed* is needed due to the high volume.

❑ The TPS *monitors and collects past data.*

❑ Input and output *data are structured*. Since the processed data are fairly stable, they are formatted in a standard fashion.

❑ A *high level of detail* (raw data, not summarized) is usually observable, especially in input data but often in output as well.

❑ *Low computation complexity* (simple mathematical and statistical operations) is usually evident in a TPS.

❑ A high level of *accuracy, data integrity*, and *security* is needed. Sensitive issues such as privacy of personal data are strongly related to TPSs.

❑ *High reliability* is required. The TPS can be viewed as the lifeblood of the organization. Interruptions in the flow of TPS data can be fatal to the organization.

❑ *Inquiry processing* is a must. The TPS enables users to query files and databases (even online and in real time).

able to all applications, and that all data are kept up-to-the-minute. These data can also be processed and stored in a data warehouse (Chapter 3). The entire process is managed by a *transaction manager* (see Subrahmanyam, 2002 for details).

The flow of information in a typical TPS is shown in Figure 7.2. An event, such as a customer purchase, is recorded by the TPS program. The processed information can be either a report or an activity in the database. In addition to a scheduled report, users can query the TPS for nonscheduled information (such as, "What was the impact of our price cut on sales during the first five days, by day?"). The system will provide the appropriate answer by accessing a database containing transaction data.

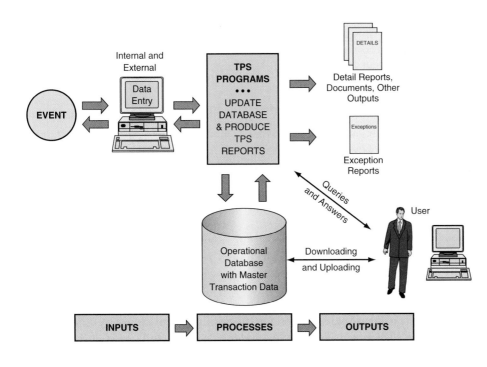

Figure 7.2 *The flow of information in transaction processing.*

Web-Based and Online Transaction Processing Systems

Transaction processing systems may be fairly complex, involving customers, vendors, telecommunications, and different types of hardware and software. Traditional TPSs are centralized and run on a mainframe. However, innovations such as online transaction processing require a client/server architecture and may be Web-based.

In *online transaction processing (OLTP),* business transactions are processed online as soon as they occur. For example, when you pay for an item at a POS at a store, the system records the effects of the sale by reducing the inventory on hand by a unit, increasing the store's cash position by the amount you paid, and increasing sales figures for the item by one unit—by means of online technologies and all in real time.

With OLTP and Web technologies such as an extranet, suppliers can look at the firm's inventory level or production schedule in real time and, in partnership with their customers, can assume responsibility for inventory management. Customers too can enter data into the TPS to track orders, arrange for payments, and even query the TPS directly, as described in the following examples:

`SVC` `POM`   **EXAMPLE**   *Monitoring Copies at Kinko's.* When you make a copy at Kinko's, the copying transaction generates the need for a payment transaction. In the past you received a card that you inserted into a monitor device attached to each copy machine. This card recorded the number of copies that you made, and you then stood in line to pay. The cashier placed the device in a reader to see how many copies were made, and your bill was computed. Kinko's cost was high in this system, especially when only a few copies were made, and some customers were not happy to stand in line to pay for only a few copies. Today, using Kinko's new system, you insert your credit card (or a stored-value card purchased from a machine) into a control device attached to each machine, make the copies, print a receipt, and go home. You no longer need to see a Kinko's employee to complete your purchase.

`SVC` `POM`   **EXAMPLE**   *TPS at UPS Stores.* Seconds after you enter an address and a Zip code into a terminal at a UPS Store, software generates a shipping label and a receipt. Your shipping record stays in the database, so if you later send another package to the same person, you do not need to repeat the address.

`SVC` `POM`   **EXAMPLE**   *Expediting Order Processing at Sprint.* Sprint Inc. has improved its order processing for new telephones. In the past it took a few days for a customer to get a new telephone line; with its new system, Sprint can process an order in only a few hours, or even minutes. The order application now can be executed on electronic forms on a salesperson's desktop or laptop computer; the process takes less than 10 minutes and experiences fewer errors.

Typical Tasks in Transaction Processing

Transaction processing exists in all functional areas. In later sections (7.3 through 7.6) we will describe the key TPS activities in major functional areas. Here we describe in some detail one application that crosses several functional areas—order processing.

Order Processing.   Orders for goods and/or services flow from customers to a company by phone, on paper, or electronically. Fast and effective order processing is recognized as a key to customer satisfaction. Orders can also be internal—from one department to another. Once orders arrive, an order processing system needs to receive, document, route, summarize, and store the orders. A computerized system can also track sales by product, by zone, or by salesperson, providing sales or marketing information that may be useful to the organization. As described in Chapter 6, more and more companies are providing systems for their salespeople that enable them to enter orders from a customer's site using wireless devices. Orders also can be processed by using innovative IT technologies such as global positioning systems, as shown in IT's about Business 7.1.

IT's ABOUT BUSINESS [SVC] [POM]

7.1: Automatic Vehicle Location and Dispatch System in Singapore

Taxis in Singapore are tracked by a global positioning system. The GPS allows dispatchers to get an instant fix on the geographical position of each taxi at any given time (see attached figure).

Here's how the system works: Customer orders are usually received via a cell phone, regular telephone, fax, or e-mail. Customers can also dispatch taxis from special kiosks (called CabLinks) located in shopping centers and hotels. Other booking options include portable taxi-order terminals placed in exhibition halls. Frequent users enter orders from their offices or homes by keying in a PIN number over the telephone. That number automatically identifies the user, together with his or her pickup point. Infrequent customers use an operator-assisted system.

The computerized ordering system is connected to the GPS. Once an order has been received, the GPS finds a vacant cab nearest to the caller; a display panel in the taxi alerts the driver to the pickup address. The driver has 10 seconds to push a button to accept the order. If he does not, the system automatically searches out the next-nearest taxi for the job.

The system completely reengineered taxi order processing. First, the transaction time for processing an order for a frequent user is much shorter, even during peak demand, since users are immediately identified. Second, taxi drivers are not able to pick and choose which trips they want to take, since

the system will not provide the commuter's destination. This reduces the customer's average waiting time significantly, while minimizing the travel distance of empty taxis. Finally, customers who use terminals do not have to wait a long time just to get a telephone operator (a situation that exists during rush hours, rain, or any other time of high demand for taxis).

The system has produced benefits for taxi companies as well. It has increased the capacity for taking incoming calls by 1,000 percent, providing a competitive edge to those cab companies that use the system. It also reduces misunderstandings between drivers and dispatchers, and driver productivity has increased since they are able to utilize their time more efficiently. Three major taxi companies with about 50,000 taxis are connected to the system.

Source: Compiled from Z. Liao, "Real Time Taxi Dispatching Using GPS," *Communications of the ACM*, May 2003, and from the author's experience.

QUESTIONS

1. What tasks do computers execute in this order-processing system?
2. What kinds of priorities can be offered to frequent taxi customers?

Location tracking of taxicabs in Singapore.

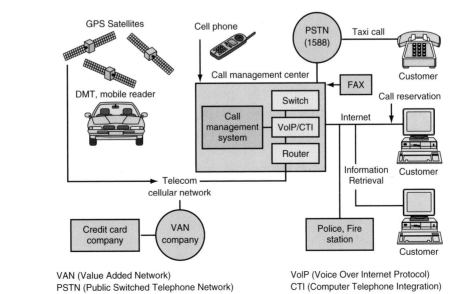

VAN (Value Added Network)
PSTN (Public Switched Telephone Network)

VoIP (Voice Over Internet Protocol)
CTI (Computer Telephone Integration)

Table 7.1 Typical TPS Activities

Activities	Description
The ledger	The entire group of an organization's financial accounts. Contains all of the assets, liabilities, and owner's (stockholders') equity accounts.
Accounts payable and receivable	Records of all accounts to be paid and those owed by customers. Automated system can send reminder notes about overdue accounts.
Receiving and shipping records	Transaction records of all items sent or received, including returns.
Inventory-on-hand records	Records of inventory levels as required for inventory control and taxation. Use of barcodes improves ability to count inventory periodically.
Fixed-assets management	Records of the value of an organization's fixed assets (e.g., buildings, cars, machines), including depreciation rate and major improvements made in assets, for taxation purposes.
Payroll	All raw and summary payroll records.
Personnel files and skills inventory	Files of employees' history, evaluations, and record of training and performance.
Reports to government	Reports on compliance with government regulations, taxes, etc.
Other periodic reports and statements	Financial, tax, production, sales, and other routine reports.

Other TPS Activities. Other typical TPS activities are summarized in Table 7.1. Most of these routine tasks are computerized.

Transaction Processing Software

There are dozens of commercial TPS software products on the market. Many are designed to support Internet transactions. The discussion of software selection in Chapter 11 applies to selection of TPS products as well. But the selection of a TPS software product has some unique features. Therefore, one organization, the Transaction Processing Performance Council (*tpc.org*), has been trying to assist in this task. This organization is conducting *benchmarking* for TPS by establishing objective measures of TPS performance. It checks hardware vendors, database vendors, middleware vendors, and so forth for performance standards (such as speed of execution or cost of certain services). Recently it also started to evaluate e-commerce transaction software (at *tpc.org/tpcw* see "transactional Web e-commerce benchmark").

Before you go on . . .

1. Define TPS.
2. List the key objectives of a TPS.
3. Describe order taking as a TPS activity.
4. Describe how TPS operates on the Web.

7.3 MANAGING THE ACCOUNTING AND FINANCE SYSTEMS

In many companies the accounting and finance departments are one entity; generally in larger companies they may be two separate functions. A primary mission of the accounting/finance functional area is to manage money flows into, within, and out of organizations. This is a very broad mission since money is involved in all functions of an organization. The accounting and finance functions also oversee all auditing-related activities.

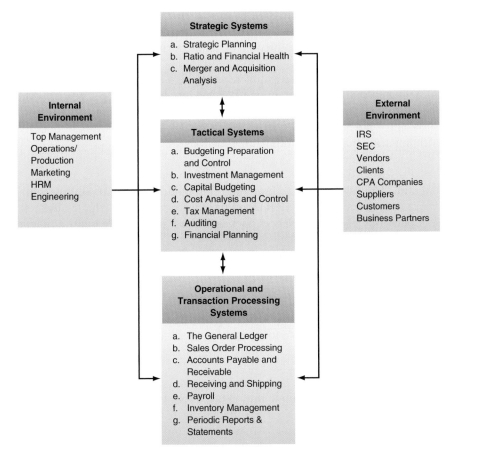

Figure 7.3 *Major activities of the accounting/finance system.*

The general structure of an accounting/finance system is presented in Figure 7.3. It is divided into three levels: strategic, tactical, and operational. Information technology can support almost all the activities listed, as well as the communication and collaboration of accounting/finance with internal and external environments. We describe some selected activities in the remainder of this section.

Financial Planning and Budgeting

Appropriate management of financial assets is a major task in financial planning and budgeting. Managers must plan for both the acquisition of resources and their maintenance and use. Financial planning, like any other functional planning, is tied to the overall organizational planning. Here we discuss representative planning and budgeting areas.

Financial and Economic Forecasting. Knowledge about the availability and cost of money is a key ingredient for successful financial planning. Especially important is the projection of cash flow, which tells organizations what funds they need and when, and how they will acquire them.

Funds for running organizations come from several sources, including stockholders' investments, sale of bonds, loans from banks, sales of products and services, and income from investments. Decisions about sources of funds for financing ongoing operations and for capital investment can be supported by decision support and expert systems.

Financial and economic analysis is also facilitated by intelligent systems such as neural computing (Chapter 10). Many software packages are available with which an organization can conduct economic and financial forecasting. Economic and financial forecasts are also available for a fee, frequently over the Internet.

Budgeting. The best-known part of financial planning is the annual budget, which allocates the financial resources of an organization among participants and activities.

The budget is the financial expression of the organization's plans. It allows management to allocate resources in the way that best supports the organization's mission and goals. IT enables the introduction of financial intelligence into the budgeting process.

Several software packages are available to support budget preparation and control and to facilitate communication among participants in the budget process. Many of these products now are Web-based. One of the latest trends is industry-specific packages such as for hospitals, banks, or retailing. Budgeting software is frequently bundled with financial analysis and reporting functions.

Capital Budgeting. *Capital budgeting* is the financing of asset acquisitions. Capital budgeting analysis uses standard financial models, such as net present value (NPV), internal rate of return (IRR), and payback period, to evaluate alternative investment decisions. Most spreadsheet packages like Excel include built-in functions of these models.

Managing Financial Transactions

An accounting/finance information system is also responsible for gathering the raw data necessary for the accounting TPS, transforming the data into information, and making the information available to users. Many packages exist to execute routine accounting transaction processing activities. Several are available free on the Internet (try *tucows.com*).

Many software packages are integrated. In these integrated systems, the accounting/finance activities are combined with other TPSs such as those of marketing and production/operations management. The data collected and managed for the accounting/finance transaction processing system are also inputs for the other functional information systems. One such integrated system is MAS 90 from *bestsoftwareinc.com/mass90/index*. It is a collection of standard accounting modules. Another integrated accounting software package is *peachtree.com* (from Best Software), which offers a sales ledger, purchase ledger, cash book, sales order processing, invoicing, stock control, job casting, fixed-assets register, and more. Other accounting packages can be found at *2020software.com* and *findaccountingsoftware.com*.

The accounting/finance TPS also provides a complete, reliable audit trail of all transactions transmitted through the network. This feature is vital to accountants and auditors. (For more, see the "Control and Auditing" section below.)

E-Commerce Applications of Financial Transactions. Companies doing e-commerce need to access financial data of customers (e.g., credit line), inventory levels, and manufacturing databases (to see available capacity, to place orders, etc.). Great Plains (*bestsoftware.com*) offers 50 modules to choose from, to meet the most common financial, project, distribution, manufacturing, and e-business needs.

Diversified financial transactions also lend themselves to e-commerce applications, especially Web-based ones. In Chapter 5, we described e-banking, electronic transactions of stock markets, e-financial services, and more. Many of these can also be done in a wireless environment. Here we provide a few other examples.

Global Stock Exchanges. Financial markets are moving toward global, 24-hour, distributed electronic stock exchanges that will use the Internet for both the transactions and multicasting of real-time stock prices.

Handling Multiple Currencies. Global trade involves financial transactions in different currencies. Conversion ratios of some currencies change daily. A Web-based system (e.g., from SAP AG) takes financial data from different countries and in seconds converts the currencies to U.S. dollars. Reports based on these data, which used to take weeks to generate, now take minutes. The system handles a multiplicity of languages as well.

E-Bonds.   The World Bank is now using *e-bonds*, a system for marketing, distributing, and trading bonds over the Internet. The system expanded in 2003 to include electronic applications to currency and derivatives trading.

Online Factoring.   *Factoring* involves activities conducted by special financial companies that buy accounts receivable, usually at a discount. Factoring of receivables gives the selling company an immediate cash inflow. The factoring company takes on the risks and expenses of collecting the debts. Factoring on the Web is becoming very popular.

Electronic Bill Presentment and Payments.   One of the most successful areas of e-commerce is that of electronic presentment and payments. In its simplest form it is an electronic payment of bills. However, third-party companies provide a service in which they calculate, print, and electronically present bills to customers, who pay these bills electronically.

Electronic Re-presentment of Checks.   Companies face a problem of dealing with some bad checks (due to insufficient funds) that they receive from customers. Paper checks that do not clear are usually re-presented (manually or electronically). Electronic re-presentment can be organized as part of cash management information systems. Such systems consolidate checks from different banks and conduct a return analysis (analysis of why checks are not honored, who is likely to pass bad checks, etc.) (Giesen, 2003).

Virtual Close.   Companies close their books (accounting records) quarterly, mainly to meet regulatory requirements. Some companies want to be able to close their books at any time, on short notice. Called a **virtual close**, the ability to close the books quickly may give almost real-time information on the financial health of a company. An advanced IT program developed by Cisco will soon enable organizations, even large multinational corporations, to close their books in a matter of hours. For details see Online File W7.2.

virtual close   *The ability of a company to close its accounting records quickly and on short notice.*

wiley.com/college/turban

Expense Management Automation.   **Expense management automation (EMA)** refers to systems that automate the data entry and processing of travel and entertainment expenses. These expenses can account for 20 percent of the operating expenses of large corporations (Degnan, 2003). EMA systems are Web-based applications that replace the paper forms and rudimentary spreadsheet. These systems let companies quickly and consistently collect expense information, enforce company policies and contracts, and reduce unplanned purchases of airline and hotel services. The software forces travelers to be organized before a trip starts. In addition to benefits to the companies, employees benefit from quick reimbursement (since expense approvals are not held up by sloppy or incomplete documentation).

expense management automation (EMA)   *Systems that automate data entry and processing of travel and entertainment expenses.*

Investment Management

Organizations invest large amounts of money in stocks, bonds, real estate, and other assets. Investment management is a difficult task. For one thing, there are thousands of investment alternatives. On the New York Stock Exchange alone, there are more than 2,000 stocks, and millions of possible combinations for creating portfolios. The investment environment also includes opportunities in other countries. Another factor that contributes to the complexity of investment management is that investments made by many organizations are subject to complex regulations and tax laws. Investment decisions are based on economic and financial forecasts and on various multiple and conflicting objectives (such as high yield, safety, and liquidity).

Investment decisions need to be made quickly and frequently as opportunities arise. Decision makers can be in different locations, and they need to collaborate. Therefore, computerization is especially popular in financial institutions that are involved in investments, as illustrated in IT's about Business 7.2 (page 220).

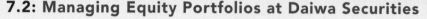

IT'S ABOUT BUSINESS

7.2: Managing Equity Portfolios at Daiwa Securities

FIN

Daiwa Securities of Japan (*daiwa.co.jp*) is one of the world's largest and most profitable multinational securities firms. Many of the company's traders are engineers and mathematicians who use computers to constantly decide about buying and selling securities for the company's own portfolio.

Daiwa believes that identifying mispricings in the stock markets holds great profit potential. Toward this end the company uses leading-edge computerized decision support systems to look for securities that are underpriced by the market. The software compares stock price performance of individual companies to that of other companies in the same market sector. In an attempt to minimize risk, the model then suggests a buy, sell, or sell-short solution for each investigated security.

The company is using what is called an *arbitrage* approach, which looks for the opportunity to make profits with very little risk. It may keep undervalued stocks, but it sells short overvalued stocks and futures. The buy–sell recommendations are derived by a system that is based on modern portfolio theory. The system uses two models: one for the short term (3 to 10 days) and one for the longer term (3 to 6 weeks). It follows over 1,200 stocks and includes many variables, some of which are very volatile.

Changes in the model can be made quickly on the Excel spreadsheet it uses. Complex statistical tools are used to perform the computations.

The system attempts to minimize the risk of the portfolio yet maximize its profit. Since these two goals usually contradict each other, trade-offs must be considered. The system is based on neural networks and fuzzy logic. The advantage of neural networks is that they can closely approximate the underlying processes that may be moving the financial markets in a particular direction.

To motivate its traders to use the system, Daiwa pays generous bonuses for successful trades. As a matter of fact, some young MBA and Ph.D. traders have commanded bonuses of hundreds of thousands of dollars each year.

Sources: Compiled from A. Pittaras, "Automated Modeling," *PC AI* (January–February 1996), and from *daiwa.co.jp* (press releases 2000).

QUESTIONS

1. What is the logic of the arbitrage strategy?
2. Why would bonuses be used to motivate employees to use the system?

In addition, data-mining tools and neural networks (Chapter 10) are used by many institutional investment managers to analyze historical databases, so they can make better predictions.

The following are the major areas of support that IT can provide to investment management.

Access to Financial and Economic Reports. Investment decisions require managers to evaluate financial and economic reports provided by federal and state agencies, universities, research institutions, financial services, and corporations. There are hundreds of such Web sources, many of which are free. Most of these services are useful both for professional investment managers and for individual investors.

To cope with the large amount of online financial data, investors use three supporting tools: (1) Internet search engines for finding financial data, (2) Internet directories and yellow pages, and (3) software for monitoring, interpreting, and analyzing financial data and for alerting management.

Financial Analysis. Financial analysis can be executed with a spreadsheet program or with commercially available ready-made decision support software. Or, it can be more sophisticated, involving intelligent systems. Other information technologies can be used as well. For example, Morgan Stanley and Company uses virtual reality on its intranet to display the results of risk analysis in three dimensions. Seeing data in three-dimensional makes it easier for investment managers to make comparisons and intuitive connections than would seeing a two-dimensional chart.

One area of analysis that is becoming popular is referred to as **financial value chain management (FVCM)**. In this approach, financial analysis is combined with opera-

financial value chain management (FVCM) *The combination of financial analysis with operations analysis, which analyzes all financial functions in order to provide better financial control.*

tions analysis. All financial functions and transactions are analyzed (including international trades). Combining financial and operations analysis provides better financial control. For example, if the organization runs its operations at a lower-than-planned level, it is likely to need less money. If it exceeds the operational plan, it may well be all right to exceed the budgeted amounts for that plan. (For details see Aberdeen.com, 2002.)

Control and Auditing

The major reason new or small organizations go out of business is their inability to forecast and/or secure sufficient *cash flow*. Underestimated expenses, overspending, fraud, and financial statement mismanagement can lead to disaster. Good planning is necessary, but not sufficient; it must be supplemented by skillful control. Control activities in organizations take many forms, including control and auditing of the information systems themselves. Information systems play an extremely important role in supporting organizational control, as we show throughout the text.

Specific forms of financial control are presented next.

Budgetary Control.   Once the annual budget has been decided upon, it is divided into monthly allocations. Managers at various levels monitor departmental expenditures and compare them against the budget and operational progress of the corporate plans. Numerous software programs can be used to support budgetary control; most of them are combined with budget preparation packages.

Simple reporting systems summarize ongoing expenditures and provide exception reports, flagging any expenditure that exceeds the budget by a certain percent or that falls significantly below the budgeted amount. More sophisticated software attempts to tie expenditures to program accomplishment.

Auditing.   The major purpose of auditing is to ensure the accuracy and condition of the financial health of an organization. Internal auditing is done by the organization's accounting/finance personnel. They also prepare for periodic external auditing by CPA companies. There are several types of auditing, including financial (verifies accuracy of financial records), operational (validates effectiveness of auditing procedures), and concurrent (runs a continuous operational audit).

IT can facilitate auditing. For example, intelligent systems can uncover fraud by finding financial transactions that significantly deviate from previous payment profiles. Also, IT provides real-time financial data whenever needed in order to expedite auditing (e.g., by using scanners to count inventory items) (see *peoplesoft.com/go/pt_financials*).

Financial Ratio Analysis.   A major accounting/finance function is to watch the financial health of the company by monitoring and assessing a set of financial ratios. These ratios are mostly the same as those used by external parties when they are deciding whether to invest in an organization, loan money to it, or buy it. But internal parties have access to much more detailed data for use in calculating financial ratios.

The collection of data for ratio analysis is done by the transaction processing system. Computation of the ratios can be done by computerized financial analysis models. The *interpretation* of the ratios, and especially the prediction of their future behavior, requires expertise and is sometimes supported by expert systems.

Product Pricing.   The pricing of products is an important corporate decision since it determines competitiveness and profitability. The marketing department may wish to reduce prices in order to increase market share, but the accounting/finance system must check the relevant cost in order to provide guidelines for such price reductions. Decision support models can facilitate product pricing. See the example of intelligent price setting in retailing at Online File W7.3.

wiley.com/college/turban

Contract Management.   Service and supply contracts used by IT departments are valued in the millions of dollars. Errors in the contract details can be costly, which is one of the main reasons companies invest in contract management software. *Contract* *management software* helps companies identify unauthorized spending (e.g., purchases from suppliers that are not under contract), suppliers that overcharge, and unutilized services that have automatically renewing terms. Contract management software can also take some of the labor out of creating new contracts.

According to a 2003 report by Boston-based AMR Research, adopters of contract management software have realized an annual return on investment of 150 to 200 percent. For a CIO, says AMR analyst Pierre Mitchell, contract management can be particularly helpful as hardware and software ages to the point of obsolescence. "Companies should definitely look at all of the software maintenance contracts in their portfolio," Mitchell says. "Is it worth paying $100,000 a year to continue to support an AS400 (an IBM mainframe computer) that generates five reports a year?" (Surmacz, 2003).

Profitability Analysis and Cost Control.   Many companies are concerned with the profitability of individual products or services. No company can remain in business long if it does not manage its operations to produce sufficient profit to cover its expenses. Profitability analysis decision support software (see Chapter 10) allows accurate computation of profitability. It also allows allocation of overhead (costs indirectly associated with the production of goods or services). One way to control cost is by properly estimating it. This is done by special software.

For more applications of transaction processing systems in the financial/accounting area, see Online File W7.4.

wiley.com/college/turban

> ## Before you go on . . .
>
> **1.** Describe financial planning and budgeting and tell how it is supported by IT.
>
> **2.** How does IT facilitate financial transactions?
>
> **3.** Describe how IT can support investment management.
>
> **4.** What kind of support can IT provide to financial audit and control?

7.4 MANAGING MARKETING AND SALES SYSTEMS

In Chapters 1 through 6 we emphasized the increasing importance of a customer-focused approach and the trend toward customization and consumer-based organizations. How can IT help manage the marketing and sales systems that are needed to support the customer-focused approach?

First we need to understand how products reach customers, which takes place through a series of marketing entities known as *channels*. **Channel systems** are all the systems involved in the process of getting a product or service to customers and dealing with all customers' needs. The complexity of channel systems can be observed in Figure 7.4, which shows seven major interrelated marketing channel systems.

channel systems   *The systems involved in the process of getting a product or service to customers and dealing with all customers' needs.*

We describe only a few of the many channel-system activities and related systems here, organizing them into three groups: customer relations, distribution channels and in-store innovations, and marketing management. A fourth topic, telemarketing, is presented in Online File W7.5 on the Web site.

wiley.com/college/turban

Customer Relations: "The Customer Is King/Queen"

It is essential for companies today to know who their customers are and to treat them like royalty. Information systems that help companies focus on new and innovative products and services, successful promotions, customization, and superb customer service are becoming a necessity for many organizations. In this section we will describe some applications related to *customer-centric* organizations. More are described in Chapter 8, where customer relationship management (CRM) is presented.

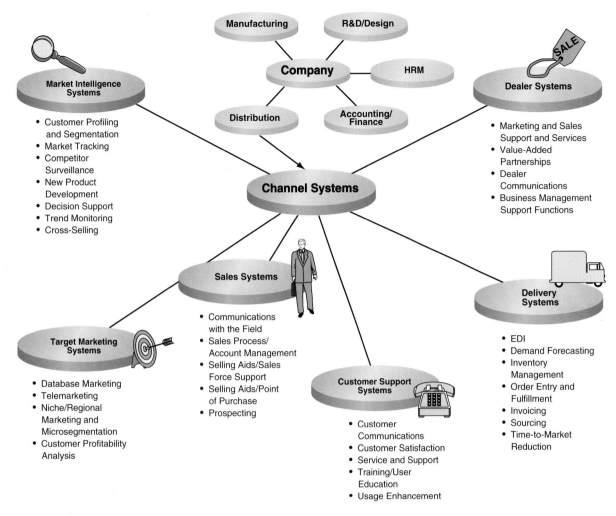

Figure 7.4 *Marketing channel systems and the IT support to each (bulleted items).*

Customer Profiles and Preference Analysis.   Information about existing and potential customers is critical for success. Sophisticated information systems are being developed to collect data on customers, their demographics (age, gender, income level), and preferences.

Customer online behavior can be tracked by cookies (small data files placed on a user's hard drive by a Web server). Then (as explained in Chapter 5), the customer's online behavior can be analyzed and used for marketing purposes. By checking the demographics of its millions of customers and their locations, America Online (AOL), for example, can match appropriate ads of advertisers with specific customers. The effectiveness of such ads is very high. Even more powerful is the combination of offline and online data (e.g., see *doubleclick.com*).

Prospective Customer Lists and Marketing Databases.   All firms need to know who their customers are, and IT can help create customer databases of both existing and potential customers. It is possible today to purchase computerized lists from several sources and then merge them electronically. These prospective-customer lists then can be analyzed and sorted by any desired classification for direct mailing, e-mailing, or telemarketing. Customer data can be stored in a corporate database or in special marketing databases for future analysis and use.

Mass Customization.   Increasingly, today's customers want customized products. Some manufacturers offer different product configurations, and in some products dozens of options are available. The result is *mass customization*, as practiced successfully by Dell Computer and many other companies (see Online Appendix W1.1). Customization is possible both in manufactured goods and in services.

wiley.com/college/turban

Table 7.2 The Changing Face of Marketing

	Old Model Mass and Segmented Marketing	New Model Customization
Relationships with customers	Customer is a passive participant in the exchange	Customer is an active co-producer
Customer needs	Articulated	Articulated and unarticulated
Segmentation	Mass market and target segments	Segments looking for customized solutions and "segments one" (a segment of only one person)
Product and service offerings	Line extensions and modification	Customized products, services, and marketing
New-Product development	Marketing and R&D drive new-product development	R&D focuses on developing the platforms that allow consumers to customize
Pricing	Fixed prices and discounting	Customer-determined pricing (e.g., Priceline.com; auctions) Value-based pricing models
Communication	Advertising and public relations	Integrated, interactive, and customized marketing communication, education, and entertainment
Distribution	Traditional retailing and direct marketing	Direct (online) distributions and rise of third-party logistics services
Branding	Traditional branding and co-branding	Use of the customer's name as the brand (e.g., My brand or Brand 4 ME)
Basis of competitive advantage	Marketing power	Marketing finesse and "capturing" the customer as "partner" while integrating marketing, operations, R&D, and information

Source: Y. Wind, "The Challenge of Customization in Financial Services," *Communications of the ACM* (July 2001), p. 41.

Wind (2001) analyzed the impact of customization on marketing and the resultant changes (see Table 7.2). As shown throughout this book, these changes are being supported by IT. For example, the Web can be used to expedite the ordering and fulfillment of customized products, as demonstrated in IT's about Business 7.3, about building a Jaguar.

Personalization. Using digital cameras, retailers can find what people are doing while they visit physical stores. Similarly, tracking software can find what people are doing in a virtual store. These technologies provide information that is used for real-time marketing and also for m-commerce (see Chapter 6 and also Sadeh, 2002). Personalized product offers then are made based on where the customer spent the most online time and on what he or she purchased. Also *cross-selling* (or *up-selling*) efforts can be automatically made, in which advertising of related products is provided. For example, if you are buying a car, car insurance is automatically offered (Strauss et al., 2003). Or, if you buy a mystery book at Amazon.com, the company's software will automatically recommend similar books bought by other readers.

Advertising and Promotions. The Internet opens the door to new advertising methods and approaches. As was shown in Chapter 5, online advertising mainly via e-mail, pop-ups, and banners, is growing rapidly, and innovative methods such as viral marketing that are possible only on the Internet are being implemented. Wireless and pervasive computing applications also are changing the face of advertising. For example, in order to measure attention to advertising, a mobile-computing device called Arbitron is carried by customers (Gentile, 2002). Whoever is wearing the device automatically logs advertising seen or heard any time, anywhere in their daily travels. This device provides accurate feedback on ads (in almost real time) and information that can be used to target certain types of advertising methods to certain types of people.

IT's ABOUT BUSINESS

7.3: Build Your Jaguar Online

Prospective Jaguar car buyers can design, see an image of, and price the car of their dreams online. As of October 2000, you can configure the car at *jaguar.com* in real time. Cars have been configured online since 1997, but Jaguar was first in the industry to offer comprehensive services, delivered in many languages.

Using a virtual car, users can view more than 1,250 possible exterior combinations, rotating the car through 360 degrees by moving directional arrows. As you select the model, color, trim, wheels, and accessories, both image and price information automatically update. The design choices are limited to current models. Up to 10 personalized car selections per customer can be stored in a "virtual garage." Customers can "test" virtual cars and conduct comparisons of different models. Once the buyer makes a decision, the order is forwarded to a dealer of his or her choice.

Like most other car manufacturers, Jaguar will not let you consummate the purchase online. To negotiate final price, customers can go to a Jaguar dealer or use Auto By Tel (*autobytel.com*), which connects nearby dealers to the customer. However, Jaguar's system helps get customers to the point of purchase. It helps them *research* the purchase and explore, price, and visualize options. Customers thus familiarize themselves with the Jaguar before even visiting a showroom. The ability to see a 3-D photo of the self-designed car is an extremely important customer service. Finally, the production order for the customer-configured car can be transmitted electronically to the production floor, reducing the time-to-delivery cycle.

The IT support for this innovation includes a powerful configuration database integrated with Jaguar's production system (developed by Ford Motor Company and Trilogy Corp.) and the "virtual car" (developed by Global Beach Corp.).

As of mid-2000, most car manufacturers had introduced Web-based make-to-order systems. In order to avoid channel conflicts, these systems typically involve the dealers in the actual purchase. All major car manufacturers are attempting to move car ordering to the Web.

Sources: Compiled from *jaguar.com* press releases (October–November 2000 and February 2003); *ford.com* (2003) (go to Services); and *autobytel.com* (2002).

QUESTIONS

1. Why would car manufacturers be interested in the Web if the actual purchase is done at the dealers' site?

2. What are the benefits to customers?

Distribution Channels and In-Store Innovations

Organizations distribute their products and services through several available distribution channels: A company may use its own outlets or distributors; products can be delivered directly to customers by trucks; digitizable products can be distributed online or can be delivered on CD ROMs. The Web is revolutionizing distribution channels. Here we look at some representative IT applications relating to distribution channels.

New IT-Supported Distribution Channels.   In addition to the Internet, IT enables other new or improved channels through which to distribute goods or services. For example, by connecting mapping technology with databases of local employers, retailers and fast-food marketers are providing goods and services to employees during their lunch breaks. Using the Internet, retailers can offer special incentives (e.g., coupons) to lunchtime shoppers in their area (see *sbs.com*).

EXAMPLE   *Japanese Kiosks Start Selling Digital Music.*   Japan Telecom Co., Ltd. and East Japan Railway Co. have launched a music distribution service, called "Digi-Break," at three major train stations in Tokyo. Using the service, rail passengers can purchase and download songs from kiosks in the train stations onto their personal minidisk players. Japan Telecom runs a data center that distributes the music to the kiosks via high-speed optical fiber networks. Each tune costs from 200 yen (US$1.61) to 500 yen, and the terminal also prints out jacket pictures and song lyrics. It takes approximately 20 to 40 seconds to record each song and about 30 seconds to print out the picture and lyrics. The venture now offers approximately 500 songs, and plans to add around 40 titles per month. The railway company plans eventually to expand the music distribution service to include other digital content, such as games and books, using the same terminals. (*Source:* cnn.com, 2001.)

Improving Shopping and Checkout at Retail Stores. The modern shopper is often pressed for time, and most are unhappy about waiting in long lines. Using information technology, it is possible to reengineer the shopping and the checkout process.

SVC **MKT**   **EXAMPLE**   *In-store Information Kiosks Are Replacing Catalogs.* In-store information kiosks enable customers to view catalogs in stores, conduct product searches, and even compare prices with those of competitors. Kiosks at some stores (e.g., 7-Eleven stores in some countries) can be used to place orders on the Internet. (For details about use of in-store kiosks, see Sweeney, 2001.)

SVC **POM**   **EXAMPLE**   *Providing Product Information to Buyers.* Several companies use handheld wireless devices (or in-store kiosks) where shoppers can scan the barcode UPC of the product they want to buy, giving them all the product information, including options such as maintenance agreements. The desired purchase order is sent to the cashier with the buyer's credit card information. By the time shoppers arrive at the cashier, the bill and the merchandise are ready.

SVC **ACC**   **EXAMPLE**   *Expediting Check Writing.* Some stores that have many customers who pay by check (e.g., large grocery stores, Wal-Mart stores, Costco) have installed checkwriters. Shoppers hand a blank check to the cashier, who runs it through a machine attached to the cash register. The machine prints the name of the store as the payee and the amount, the shopper signs the check, and in seconds the check is validated and the shopper is out of the store with the merchandise.

U-Scan Kiosk

wiley.com/college/turban

   EXAMPLE   *Self-Checkout from Retail Stores.* Many retailers are installing self-checkout machines. Home Depot and K-Mart are examples. Not only does the retailer save the cost of checkout employees' salaries, but customers are happier for saving time. (And some enjoy "playing cashier" briefly.) A major device is U-Scan, which is being used in many supermarkets (see photo).

Marketing Management

Many marketing management decision applications are supported by computerized information systems. Here are some representative applications of marketing management. (Online File W7.6 shows the marketing management decision framework.)

Pricing of Products or Services. Sales volumes are largely determined by the prices of products or services. Price is also a major determinant of profit. Pricing is a difficult decision, and prices may need to be changed frequently. For example, in response to price changes made by competitors, a company may need to adjust its prices or take other actions.

Pricing decisions are supported by a number of computerized systems. Many companies are using online analytical processing (OLAP; see Chapter 10) to support pricing and other marketing decisions. An example is a price-optimization model used to support prices at Longs Drug Stores (as described in Online File W7.3). Web-based comparison engines enable vendors to see how their prices compare with others, and they enable customers to select a vendor at the price they want. For an overview on pricing and the Internet, including quick price testing, see Baker et al. (2001).

wiley.com/college/turban

Salesperson Productivity.   Salespeople differ from each other: Some excel in selling certain products, while others excel in selling to a certain type of customer or in a certain geographical zone. This information, which is usually collected in the sales and marketing TPS, can be analyzed, using a comparative performance system, in which sales data by salesperson, product, region, and even the time of day are evaluated. Actual current sales can be compared to historical data and to standards. Multidimensional spreadsheet software facilitates this type of analysis. Assignment of salespeople to regions and/or products and the calculation of bonuses can also be supported by this system.

In addition, sales productivity can be boosted by Web-based systems. For example, in a Web-based call center, when a customer calls a sales rep, the rep can look at the customer's history of purchases, demographics, services available where the customer lives, and more. This information enables reps to work faster, while providing better customer service.

Sales Force Automation.   As discussed briefly in Chapter 6, the productivity of salespeople in the field also can be greatly increased by what is known as *salesforce automation*—using software to automate the business tasks of sales. Business processes that often are automated in SFA include order processing, contract management, information sharing, inventory monitoring and control, order tracking, customer care and management, sales forecast analysis, and employee performance evaluation. Of special interest in the context of B2E e-commerce is the support provided to employees when they are in the field. For example, SFA empowers the field sales force to close deals at the customer's office and to configure marketing strategies at home. Many companies, ranging from Maybelline to Kodak, have equipped their salesforces with mobile SFA devices. For an example of SFA used by Maybelline, see Online File W7.7.

wiley.com/college/turban

Sales force automation can be boosted in many ways by using Web-based tools. For example, Netgain (from *netgainservices.com*) lets a multimedia company's design their services and their sales teams collaborate over the Web, passing off sales leads, bringing in new sales reps to clinch different parts of a deal, and tracking reports on sales progress.

Sales Productivity Software.   Sales automation software helps automate the routine parts of a salesperson's job. Such Web-based software can manage the flow of messages and assist in writing contracts, scheduling, and making appointments. Of course it provides word processing and e-mail; and it helps with mailings and follow-up letters. Electronic stamps (e.g., *stamp.com*) can assist with mass mailings. Sales productivity software is especially helpful to small businesses, enabling them to rapidly increase sales and growth.

sales automation software *Software that helps automate the routine parts of a salesperson's job.*

Profitability Analysis.   As discussed earlier, finance and accounting personnel constantly analyze profitability of products and services. Advertising and marketing managers also often need to know the profit contribution of certain products and services in order to plan cost-effective marketing efforts. For example, profit performance analysis software available from Oracle (*oracle.com*) is designed to help managers assess and improve the profit performance of their line of business, products, distribution channels, sales regions, and other dimensions critical to managing the enterprise. Northwest Airlines, for example, uses expert systems and DSS to set prices based on profitability. They also use a similar system to audit commissions to travel agents.

In addition, identification of profitable customers and the frequency with which they interact with the organization can be derived from special promotional programs, such as hotels' frequent-stayer programs. Since this is derived from large amounts of data, computer help (including DSSs and/or intelligent systems) is needed. This information can also be used for loyalty and other programs.

Sales Analysis and Trends. The marketing TPS collects sales figures that can be segregated along several dimensions for early detection of problems and opportunities, by searching for trends and relationships. For example, if sales of a certain product show a continuous decline in certain regions but not in other regions, management can investigate the declining region. Similarly, an increasing sales volume of a new product calls attention to an opportunity if it is found to be statistically significant. This application demonstrates the reliance of decision making on the TPS. Also, data mining can be used to find relationships and patterns in large databases.

New Products, Services, and Market Planning. The introduction of new or improved products and services can be expensive and risky. An important question to ask about a new product or service is, "Will it sell?" An appropriate answer calls for careful analysis, planning, and forecasting. These can best be executed with the aid of IT because of the large number of determining factors and the uncertainties that may be involved. Market research also can be conducted on the Internet, as described in Chapter 5.

A related issue is the speed with which products are brought to market. An example of how Procter & Gamble expedites the time-to-market by using the Internet is provided in Online File W7.8.

wiley.com/college/turban

Web-Based Systems in Marketing. The use of Web-based systems in support of marketing and sales has grown rapidly, as demonstrated by the Procter & Gamble case earlier. A summary of some Web-based impacts is provided in Online File W7.9.

wiley.com/college/turban

Before you go on . . .

1. Describe the support IT provides to customer-related research.
2. How does IT support customization and personalization?
3. Describe how IT facilitates product distribution.
4. What marketing management activities can be enhanced with IT? How?

7.5 MANAGING PRODUCTION/OPERATIONS AND LOGISTICS

The production and operations management (POM) function in an organization is responsible for the processes that transform inputs into useful outputs and for the operation of the business. In comparison to the other functional areas, the POM area is very diversified and so are its supporting information systems. It also differs considerably among organizations. (See Online File W7.10 for a model of the IS applications in the production/operations area. Note that the internal interfaces are on the left and the external ones on the right.)

wiley.com/college/turban

Because of the breadth and variety of POM functions, here we present only four IT-supported POM topics: in-house logistics and materials management, planning production and operations, computer-integrated manufacturing (CIM), and product life cycle management (PLM).

In-house Logistics and Materials Management

Logistics management deals with ordering, purchasing, inbound logistics (receiving), and outbound logistics (shipping) activities. In-house logistics activities are a good example of processes that cross several primary and support activities in the value chain. Both conventional purchasing and e-procurement are used. All of the related activities can be supported by information systems. For example, many companies today are moving to some type of e-procurement (Chapter 5).

Inventory Management. *Inventory management* determines how much inventory to keep. Overstocking can be expensive (due to storage costs and the costs of spoilage and obsolescence). However, keeping insufficient inventory is also expensive (due to last-minute orders and lost sales).

Two basic decisions are made by operations personnel: when to order, and how much to order. Inventory models, such as the economic order quantity (EOQ) model, support these decisions. A large number of commercial inventory software packages that automate the application of these inventory models are available at low cost.

Many large companies (e.g., Wal-Mart) allow their suppliers to monitor their inventory levels and ship products when needed, eliminating the need for sending purchasing orders. Such a strategy, in which the supplier monitors inventory levels and replenishes when needed, is called **vendor-managed inventory (VMI)**. The monitoring can be done by using mobile agents over the Internet. It can be also done by using Web services (as Dell Computer is doing).

vendor-managed inventory (VMI) *Strategy in which the supplier monitors a vendor's inventory levels and replenishes products when needed.*

In Chapter 8 we demonstrate how IT and EC help in reducing inventories.

Quality Control. Quality-control systems used by manufacturing units provide information about the quality of incoming material and parts, as well as the quality of in-process semifinished and finished products. Such systems record the results of all inspections. They also compare actual results to metrics.

Quality-control data may be collected by Web-based sensors and interpreted in real time, or they can be stored in a database for future analysis. Periodic reports are generated (such as percentage of defects, percentage of rework needed), and management can compare performance among departments on a regular basis or as needed.

Planning Production and Operations

The POM planning in many firms is supported by IT. Some major areas of planning and their computerized support are described here.

Material Requirements Planning. Inventory systems that use an EOQ approach are designed for those individual items for which demand is completely independent (for example, the number of identical PCs a computer manufacturer will sell). However, in manufacturing operations, the demand for some items can be interdependent. For example, a company may make three types of chairs that all use the same legs, screws, and bolts. Thus, the demand for legs, screws, and bolts depends on the total demand for all three types of chairs and their shipment schedules.

The planning process that integrates production, purchasing, and inventory management of interdependent items is called **material requirements planning (MRP)**. Usually computerized, MRP software facilitates the plan for acquiring (or producing) interdependent parts, subassemblies, or materials. MRP is computerized because of the complex interrelationship among many products and their components, and the need to change the plan each time that a delivery date or the order quantity is changed. Several MRP packages are commercially available.

material requirements planning (MRP) *A planning process that integrates production, purchasing, and inventory management of interdependent items.*

MRP deals only with production scheduling and inventories. More complex planning also involves allocation of related resources (e.g., money, labor). In such a case, more complex, integrated software is available—MRP II.

Manufacturing Resource Planning. A POM system called **manufacturing resource planning (MRP II)** adds functionalities to a regular MRP. It integrates an enterprise's production, inventory management, purchasing, financing, and labor activities. For example, in addition to output similar to that of MRP, MRP II determines the costs of parts and the cash flow needed to pay for parts. It also estimates costs of labor, tools, equipment repair, and energy. Finally, it provides a detailed,

manufacturing resource planning (MRP II) *A planning process that integrates an enterprise's production, inventory management, purchasing, financing, and labor activities.*

computerized budget for the parts involved and a schedule for the workers. MRP II evolved to ERP, which is described in Chapter 8.

Just-in-Time Systems. In mass customization and build-to-order production, the just-in-time concept is frequently used. **Just-in-time (JIT)** is a principle fo production and inventory control in which materials and parts arrive when and where needed for production or use. This approach attempts to minimize waste of all kinds (of space, labor, materials, energy, and so on). For example, if materials and parts arrive at a workstation *exactly when needed,* there is no need for inventory, there are no delays in production, and there are no idle production facilities or underutilized workers. JIT also makes continuous improvement possible. Many JIT systems are supported by software.

Other Areas. Many other areas of planning production and operations are improved by IT. These include: production planning optimization, factory layout planning and design, project management, troubleshooting, and work management.

just-in-time *A principle of production and inventory control in which materials and parts arrive when and where needed for production or use.*

Computer-Integrated Manufacturing

computer-integrated manufacturing (CIM) *Manufacturing approach that integrates several computerized systems, such as CAD, CAM, MRP, and JIT, into a whole, in a factory.*

Computer-integrated manufacturing (CIM) is an approach that integrates various computerized factory systems. CIM has three basic goals: (1) *simplification* of all manufacturing technologies and techniques, (2) *automation* of as many of the manufacturing processes as possible, and (3) *integration and coordination* of all aspects of design, manufacturing, and related functions via computer hardware and software. Typical technologies to be integrated are MRP, JIT, computer-aided design (CAD), computer-aided engineering (CAE), group technology (GT), and flexible-manufacturing systems (FMS).

The CIM Model. CIM starts with a plan. This plan comes from the CIM model, which describes the CIM vision, standards, and architecture. The basic CIM model is shown in Figure 7.5.

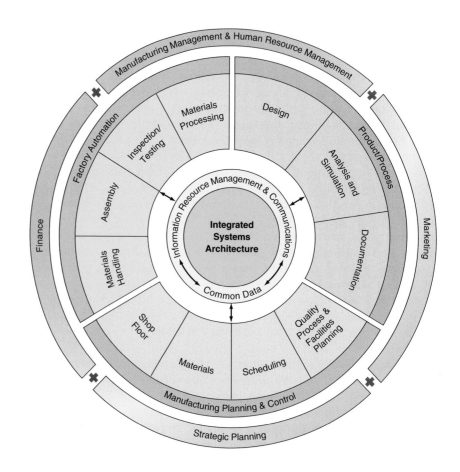

Figure 7.5 *The CIM model: integration of all manufacturing activities under unified management.* [Source: *Reprinted from the CASA/SME Manufacturing Enterprise Wheel, with permission from the Society of Manufacturing Engineers, Dearborn, Michigan (1999), 3rd ed.*]

The CIM model is derived from the *CIM enterprise wheel* developed by the Technical Council of the Society of Manufacturing Engineers. Its outer circle represents general business management. The inner circles represent four major "families" of processes that make up CIM: (1) product and process definition, (2) manufacturing planning and control, (3) factory automation, and (4) information resource management. Each of these five dimensions is a composite of more specific manufacturing processes, and each dimension is interrelated with the others. Thus, when planning a CIM system, no dimension can be ignored.

The hub of the wheel (the solid gold circle and the lighter gold circle around it) represents the IT resources and technologies necessary for the integration of CIM. Without an integrated plan, trying to implement CIM would be next to impossible. There must be communication, data sharing, and cooperation among the different levels of management and functional personnel.

For examples and resources, see *tech.purdue.edu/cimt*.

Product Life Cycle Management (PLM)

Even within a single organization, product design and development can prove tedious and time-consuming. When multiple organizations are involved, the process can become very complex. **Product life cycle management (PLM)** is a business strategy that enables manufacturers to share product-related data as part of product design and development efforts and in support of supply chain operations. In PLM, Web-based and other new technologies are applied to *product development* to automate its *collaborative aspects*. By overlapping formerly disparate functions, such as a manufacturing process and the logistics that support it, a dynamic collaboration takes place among the functions, essentially forming a single large product team from the product's inception.

An example of a Web-based PLM product (from PTC Corp.) for designing popular ATV bikes is provided in Figure 7.6. The collaboration is achieved via "ProjectLink" (at the center of the figure). Using this PLM, bikemaker Cannondale Corp. was able to design its 2003 model significantly faster.

PLM is a big step for an organization, requiring it to integrate a number of different processes and systems. Ultimately, its overall goal is to move information through

product life cycle management (PLM) *A business strategy that enables manufacturers to collaborate on product design and development efforts, using Web-based strategies.*

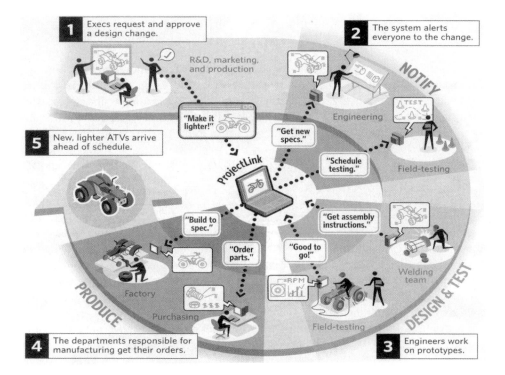

Figure 7.6 *How product life cycle management works.* [Source: *A. Raskin, "A Faster Ride to Market," Business 2.0 (October 2002), p. 50.]*

an organization as quickly as possible in order to reduce the time it takes to get a product to market and to increase profitability.

Before you go on . . .

1. Describe logistics and inventory activities supported by IT.
2. Describe some IT-enabled production planning.
3. How is CIM related to IT?
4. What is PLM? What are its benefits? How is it supported by IT?

7.6 MANAGING HUMAN RESOURCES SYSTEMS

Initial human resources information system (HRIS) applications were mainly related to transaction processing systems (e.g., record-keeping of vacation days and benefits management). In recent years, as organizational systems generally have moved to intranets and the Web, so have HRIS applications, and their popularity has grown.

Many HRIS applications today are delivered via an HR portal. For example, numerous organizations use their Web portals to advertise job openings and conduct online hiring and training. Ensher et al. (2002) describe the impact of the Internet on acquiring, rewarding, developing, protecting, and retaining human resources. Their findings are summarized in Table 7.3.

In this section, we look at how IT is being used in some key HRM functions: recruitment, HR maintenance and development, and HR planning and management.

Recruitment

Recruitment is finding employees, testing them, and deciding which ones to hire. Some companies are flooded with viable applicants, while others have difficulty finding the right people. Information systems can be helpful in both cases. In addition, IT can help in related activities such as testing and screening job applicants. Here are some examples.

Using the Web for Recruitment. With millions of resumes available online, it is not surprising that companies are trying to find appropriate candidates on the Web, usually with the help of specialized search engines. Also, hundreds of thousands of jobs are advertised on the Web. Many matching services exist (see Internet Activity #2). Online recruiting is able to "cast a wide net" to reach more candidates, which may bring in better applicants. In addition, the costs of online recruitment are usually lower. Other benefits of online recruitment for employers, plus some disadvantages, are shown in Online File W7.11.

wiley.com/college/turban

Online recruitment may be facilitated by intelligent systems, as described below.

HRM   **EXAMPLE**   *Resumix Helps HR Recruiters.* From the time a position becomes available or a resume is received, Resumix (*resumix.yahoo.com;* take the hiring gateway tour) helps recruiters match candidates and jobs while dispersing the mechanics of processing job applications. The core of this powerful system is Resumix's Knowledge Base. A computerized intelligent system, it goes beyond simply matching words; instead, it *interprets* a candidate's resume, determining skills based on context and matching those skills to the position criteria.

For example, you might be looking for a product manager. Being a member of the AMA (American Marketing Association) might be one of the desirable properties for the job. However, with a basic key word search, you might get candidates who have

Table 7.3   Comparison of Traditional Human Resources to E-Human Resources

Key HR Process	Traditional HR	E-HR
Acquiring Human Resources		
Recruitment and selection	Paper resumes and paper postings Positions filled in months Limited by geographical barriers	Electronic resumes and Internet postings Positions filled in weeks or days Unlimited access to global barriers
Selection	Costs directed at attracting candidates Manual review of resumes Face-to-face (FTF) process	Costs directed at selecting candidates Electronic review of resumes (scanning) Some distance interviewing (mostly still FTF)
Rewarding Human Resources		
Performance evaluation	Supervisor evaluation Face-to-face evaluation	360-degree evaluation Appraisal software (online and hardcopy)
Compensation and benefits	Time spent on paperwork (benefits changes) Emphasis on salary and bonuses Naïve employees Emphasis on internal equity Changes made by HR	Time spent on assessing market salaries Emphasis on ownership and quality of worklife Knowledgeable employees Emphasis on external equity Online changes made by employees
Developing Human Resources		
Training and development	Standardized classroom training Development process is HR-driven	Flexible online training Development process is employee-driven
Career management	HR lays out career paths for employees Reactive decisions Personal networking (local area only)	Employees manage their careers in concert with HR Proactive planning with technology Electronic and personal networking
Protecting Human Resources		
Health and safety	Building and equipment safety Physical fatigue Mostly reactive programs Limited to job-related stressors Focus on employee–management relations	Ergonomic considerations Mental fatigue and wellness Proactive programs to reduce stress Personal and job-related stressors Focus on employee–employee relations
Employee relations/legal	Stronger union presence Sexual harassment/discrimination Task performance monitoring	Weaker union presence Equal employment opportunity Use of technology monitoring/big brother Intellectual property/data security Inappropriate uses of technology
Retaining Human Resources		
Retention strategies	Not a major focal point	Currently the critical HR activity Online employee opinion surveys Cultivating an effective company culture Mundane tasks done by technology, freeing time for more interesting work
Work–family balance	Not a major focal point	Development and monitoring of programs Providing childcare and eldercare Erosion of work–home boundaries

Source: E. A. Ensher et al., "Tales From the Hiring Line," *Organizational Dynamics* (October–December 2002), p. 240, Table 1.

listed with AMA, but are really members of the American Medical Association or American Meatpackers Association. Those are not relevant to your search. Resumix Knowledge Base would select only the candidates with relevant skills. (*Source: resumix.com,* accessed March 13, 2004.)

HRM Portals and Salary Surveys.   One advantage of the Web is the large amount of information related to job matching that is available there. There are, for example, many private and public HR-related portals. These portals provide services such as a job search engine that can be used to search an index of jobs that are posted on corporate-member sites. For example, several large companies (e.g., IBM, Xerox,

GE) jointly created a career portal called DirectEmployers.com. Commercial, public online recruiters, such as Monster.com, help corporate recruiters find candidates for difficult-to-fill positions.

Another application for HR portals is salary surveys. Salary surveys help companies determine how much to pay their employees. Companies used to pay HR consultants up to $10,000 for a one-time survey. Now they can conduct such surveys themselves by utilizing data (some are free) from vendors such as Salary.com.

Human Resources Maintenance and Development

Once recruited, employees become part of the corporate human resources pool, which needs to be maintained and developed. Some HR maintenance and development activities supported by IT are the following.

Performance Evaluation. Most employees are periodically evaluated by their immediate supervisors. Peers or subordinates may also evaluate others. Evaluations are usually recorded on paper or electronic forms. Using such information manually is a tedious and error-prone job. But once digitized, evaluations can be used to support many decisions, ranging from rewards to transfers to layoffs. Corporate managers can analyze employees' performances with the help of expert systems, which provide an unbiased and systematic interpretation of performance over time. Performance evaluation is related to wage review.

HRM

EXAMPLE *Paperless Wage Review System at HP.* Hewlett-Packard's Atlanta-based U.S. Field Services Operations Group (USFO) has developed a paperless wage review (PWR) system. The Web-based system uses intelligent agents to deal with quarterly reviews of HP's 15,000 employees. The agent software lets USFO managers and personnel access employee data from both the personnel and functional databases. The PWR system tracks employee review dates and automatically initiates the wage review process. It sends wage review forms to first-level managers by e-mail every quarter.

Similarly, many universities evaluate professors online. The evaluation form appears on the screen, and the students fill it in. Results can be tabulated in seconds.

Training and HR Development. IT also plays an important role in training and retraining (see the discussion on e-learning, Chapter 4). Some of the most innovative developments are in the areas of *intelligent computer-aided instruction (ICAI)* and application of multimedia support for instructional activities. For example, training salespeople is an expensive and lengthy proposition. To save money on training costs, companies are providing sales-skills training over the Internet or intranet. Online File W7.12 provides examples of the variety of employee training programs available on the Internet and intranets.

wiley.com/college/turban

Human Resources Planning and Management

Managing human resources in large organizations requires extensive planning and detailed strategy. For example, in some industries, labor negotiation is a particularly important aspect of human resources planning. For most companies, administering employee benefits is also a significant part of the human resources function. Here are some examples of how IT can help.

Payroll and Employees' Records. The HR department is responsible for payroll preparation, which can be executed in-house or may be outsourced. It is done usually with the help of computers that also print the payroll checks or transfer the money electronically to the employees' bank accounts. The HR department is also responsible for all personnel record keeping and its privacy and security. In most companies this is done electronically.

Benefits Administration.   Employees' work contributions to their organizations are rewarded by salary/wage, bonuses, and other benefits. Benefits include those for health and dental care as well as contributions for pensions.

Managing the benefits system can be a complex task, due to its many items offered and the tendency of organizations to allow employees to choose and trade off benefits. In large companies, using computers for benefits selection and management can save a tremendous amount of labor and time for HR staff. Also, data entered by employees themselves have usually fewer errors.

Employees can self-register for specific benefits using the corporate portal or voice technology. Employees self-select desired benefits from a menu. The system specifies the value of each benefit and the available benefits balance of each employee. Some companies use intelligent agents to assist employees in choosing benefits and to monitor their actions. Expert systems can answer employees' questions and offer online advice. Simpler systems allow for self-updating of personal information such as changes in address, family status, and so forth.

For a comprehensive resource of HRM on the Web, see *shrm.org/hrlinks*.

Employee Relationship Management.   In their effort to better manage employees, companies are developing **employee relationship management (ERM)** (also called *human capital management, HCM*) applications. ERM applications are an employee version of CRM services. For example, a typical ERM application would be a call center for employees' problems. Self-services such as tracking personal information and online training are very popular in ERM. Facilitated by the Web, ERM applications streamline the HR process. For example, investment in ERM applications is seen as cost-effective because improved relationships with employees results in better retention and higher productivity.

> **employee relationship management (ERM)** *An employee-focused version of CRM services.*

> ### Before you go on . . .
>
> 1. Describe how IT supports the various activities of recruiting.
> 2. Explain how IT can facilitate human resources maintenance and development.
> 3. Describe some HRM planning and management activities that can be enhanced with IT.

7.7 INTEGRATING FUNCTIONAL INFORMATION SYSTEMS

For many years most IT applications were developed in the functional areas, independent of each other. Many companies developed their own customized systems that dealt with standard procedures to execute transaction processing/operational activities. These procedures are fairly similar, regardless of what company is performing them. Therefore, the trend today is to buy commercial, off-the-shelf functional applications or to lease them from application service providers (ASPs). The smaller the organization, the more attractive such options are. Indeed, several hundred commercial products are available to support each of the major functional areas or in an industry.

Development tools are also available to build custom-made applications in a specific functional area. For example, there are software packages for building financial applications, a hospital pharmacy management system, or a university student registration system. Some software vendors specialize in one or a few areas or in an industry. For example, Lawson Software concentrates on retailing.

However, execution of many tasks in organizations requires interactions and exchange of information between and among different departments. This may be difficult to do if there is no compatibility of hardware and software. Therefore, software integration is critical.

Approaches to Integration

To build information systems along business processes, which cross functional lines, requires a different approach. Matching business processes with a collection of several functional off-the-shelf packages may be a solution in some areas. For example, it may be possible to easily integrate manufacturing, sales, and accounting software if they all come from the same software vendor. However, combining existing packages from several vendors may not be practical or effective.

To build applications that will easily cross functional lines and reach separate databases often requires new approaches such as Web Services and integrated software suites, such as Oracle 9i. (See Online File W7.13 for an illustration of the Oracle 9i integration platform.)

Information systems integration tears down barriers between various business units and corporate headquarters as well as barriers among departments. Integration also reduces duplication of effort. One of the key factors for integration, especially with business partners, is agreement on appropriate standards (see *openapplications.org*). Reaching consensus on standards is sometimes no easy task but is generally worth the effort.

wiley.com/college/turban

IT's ABOUT BUSINESS POM

7.4: Web-Based Integrated Employees and Customer Portals at Europcar

Europcar International (*europcar.com*), the largest European-based car rental agency, changed the structure of its entire organization. In doing so, it also changed its everyday work processes and methods. To support these changes, the company combined 55 different mainframe and minicomputer systems into a single client/server center known as Greenway. Located at corporate headquarters near Paris, the $400 million system initially combined data from nine different countries within Europe. Today it has expanded to a global system (118 countries in 2004).

The 55 original independent systems used various data types, many of which were incompatible. Europcar was interested in integrating the business processes, customer preferences, and related data into a single system. To complicate matters, the company had to simultaneously develop a uniform set of business practices (e.g., corporate standards) to support the new single business entity. Furthermore, Europcar had to consider the variety of languages spoken in the nine countries involved, as well as different cultures and currencies.

Key business processes—including reservations, billing, fleet management, cost control, and corporate finance—were all integrated into Greenway. The system serves employees via an employee portal and customers via a customer portal. Reservations for corporate clients can be made on the corporate portal, and a smart card is available to enable customers to check in and out rapidly. As Europcar has expanded to 100 countries worldwide (as of 2003), its information system has expanded considerably as well.

Europcar originally grew through the acquisition of geographically and culturally disparate entities. Through reengineering, IT helps support these entities to present more of a multicountry team-based organization. By 2004, several thousand Europcar employees at about 1,000 offices worldwide were using Greenway.

Sources: Based on *europcar.com/English* (press releases 2000–2004; last access March 13, 2004).

QUESTIONS

1. What are some of the difficulties of integrating 55 systems from nine countries speaking different languages?
2. What functional areas can you identify in the integrated system?
3. What is the role of the different portals?

Integrated information systems can be easily built in a small company. In large organizations, and especially in multinational corporations, integration may require more effort, as shown in IT's about Business 7.4.

Another approach to integration of information systems is to use enterprise resources planning (ERP) software. However, ERP requires a company to fit its business processes to the software. As an alternative to ERP, companies can choose the best-of-breed systems on the market. Or they can use their own home-grown systems and integrate them. The latter approach may not be simple, but it may be more effective, especially if it is done using components (see Technology Guide 6).

By whatever method it is accomplished, integrating information systems helps to reduce cost, increase employees' productivity, and facilitate information sharing and collaboration, which are necessary for improving customer service.

Integrating Front-Office and Back-Office Operations

In Chapters 2 and 5 we discussed the need to integrate front-office with back-office operations. This is a difficult task. It is easier to integrate the front-office operations among themselves and the back-office operations among themselves (which is basically what systems such as MAS 90 are doing).

Software suites from various vendors offer some front-office and back-office integration solutions. Oracle Corp., for example, is continuously expanding its front-office software, which offers a capability of connecting back-office operations with it. To do so, the software uses new integration approaches, such as process-centric integration. **Process-centric integration** refers to integration solutions designed, developed, and managed from a business-process perspective, instead of from a technical or middleware perspective. Oracle's 9i product, for example, offers not only internal integration of the back office and front office, but also integration with business partners. Among its capabilities are:

process-centric integration *System integration solutions designed, developed, and managed from a business-process perspective.*

- *Field sales online.* A Web-based customer management application.
- *Service contracts.* Contract management and service options (with ERP).
- *Mobile sales and marketing.* Wireless groupware for connecting different management groups.
- *Call center and telephony suite.* A Web-based call center.
- *Internet commerce.* An order-taking and payment unit interconnected with ERP back-office applications. It is also tightly connected to the call center for order taking.
- *Business intelligence.* Identification of most-valuable customers, analysis of why customers leave, and evaluation of sales forecast accuracy.

Many other vendors offer complete enterprise packages. IBM's WebSphere architecture is another integration software product that includes front-office (WebSphere Portal), back-office, and supportive infrastructure. SAP-AG, in its ERP R/3 product, offers more than 70 integrated modules, as will be shown in our next chapter.

Before you go on . . .

1. List the major reasons for integration of functional software.
2. What is the advantage of a comprehensive package like that of 9i?
3. Why is it important to integrate an organization's back-office and front-office operations?

WHAT'S IN IT FOR ME?

FOR THE ACCOUNTING MAJOR

Executing TPSs effectively is a major concern of any accountant. It is also necessary to understand the various activities of all functional areas and how they are interconnected. The large CPA firms employ thousands of people in implementing ERP integrated solutions. By studying this chapter, you can learn some innovations that can be used to improve the operations of the accounting area.

FIN

FOR THE FINANCE MAJOR

The use of IT helps financial analysts and managers perform their tasks better. One of the major areas is analyzing cash flows and securing the financing required for smooth operations. Financial applications can support risk analysis, investment management, and global transactions involving different currencies and fiscal regulations.

MKT

FOR THE MARKETING MAJOR

Marketing and sales expenses are usually a target in a cost-reduction program. This chapter provides examples of how to reduce these costs through IT yet keep strong marketing and sales capabilities. Sales force automation not only improves salespeople's productivity (and thus reduces costs) but also makes possible improved customer service.

POM

FOR THE PRODUCTION/ OPERATIONS MANAGEMENT MAJOR

Execution of the production tasks, materials handling, and inventories in short time intervals, at a low cost, and with high quality is critical for competitiveness and can be achieved only if properly supported by IT. Also, interaction with other functional areas, especially sales, can be greatly improved by IT. Use of methods such as CIM and PLM offers efficiencies throughout the entire design and manufacturing processes.

HRM

FOR THE HUMAN RESOURCES MANAGEMENT MAJOR

Human resources managers can benefit from understanding how to improve efficiency and effectiveness by using IT for some of the routine HR functions. The HRM department needs to understand the flow of information to and from the HRM department to the other functional areas. Finally, the integration concept and its implementation have a major impact on skills requirements, scarcity of employees, and the need to deal with resistance to change, all of which are related to the tasks performed by the HRM department.

SUMMARY

1. **Describe the drivers and characteristics of functional information systems.** The major business functional areas are production/operations management, marketing, accounting/finance, and human resources management. Each is supported by many specific information systems, which aim to improve functional productivity.

2. **Describe MISs.** A management information system (MIS) is a system designed to support mid-level managers in functional areas. MISs generate reports (routine, ad-hoc, drill-down, key-indicator, and comparative) and provide information to managers regardless of their functional areas. Some high-level managers see only exception reports.

3. **Describe the transaction processing system and how it is supported by IT.** The backbone of most information systems applications is the transaction processing system (TPS), which keeps track of the routine mission-central operations of an or-

ganization. IT automates many of the TPS tasks. For example, orders can be submitted online, sales are recorded at point of sale, and results are recorded instantly. IT makes TPS paperless and in real time.

4. **Describe the support provided by IT and the Web to accounting and finance.** Financial information systems deal with topics such as financial planning and budgeting, investment management, financing operations, raising capital, factoring, and financial control. Customer relations are improved by better communication and flow of information; distribution is made faster and cheaper; and marketers can reach more people, even in other countries, and sell online at reduced costs. Accounting information systems cover applications in areas such as bookkeeping functions, electronic bill payment and re-presentment of checks, financial ratio analysis, cost control auditing, product pricing, and

profitability analysis. The "virtual close" is another accounting information system application.

5. **Describe the support provided by IT and the Web to marketing and sales.** Channel systems deal with all activities related to customer orders, sales, advertising and promotion, market research, customer service, and product and service pricing. Using IT can increase sales, customer satisfaction, and profitability.

6. **Describe the support provided by IT and the Web to production/operations management, including logistics.** The major areas of IT support to production/operations management are in logistics and materials management, planning of production and operations, computer-integrated manufacturing (CIM), and product life cycle management (PLM). Logistics and materials management involves inventory management and quality control. Production and operations planning includes use of MRP, MRP II, and JIT. CIM integrates various computerized factory systems. PLM enables manufacturers to collaborate in product design and development stages.

7. **Describe the support provided by IT and the Web to human resources management.** All tasks related to human resources development can be supported by human resources information systems. These tasks include employee recruitment and selection, hiring, performance evaluation, salary and benefits administration, training and development, labor negotiations, keeping of payroll and benefits records, and work scheduling. Web-based HR systems are extremely useful for recruiting and training.

8. **Describe the benefits and issues of integrating functional information systems.** Integrated functional information systems are necessary to ensure effective and efficient execution of activities that cross functional lines or that require functional cooperation. Integrating applications is difficult. It can be done in different ways, such as buying off-the-shelf applications, leasing applications from ASPs, or building custom systems. A promising new approach is that of Web Services.

INTERACTIVE / LEARNING

Inventory Management: Taking a Look at the Supply Chain
Go to the Interactivities section on the Student Web Site and access Chapter 7: Transactional Processing, Functional Applications, and Integration. There you will find an animated simulation of supply chain management, as well as some hands-on activities that visually explain business concepts in this chapter.

More Resources
More resources and study tools are located on the Student Web Site. You'll find additional chapter materials and links to organizations, people, and technologies for each chapter. In addition, self-quizzes that provide individualized feedback are available for each chapter.

Instructions for accessing the Interactivities on the Student Web Site:

1. Go to wiley.com/college/turban
2. Select Turban Rainer Potter's *Introduction to Information Technology, Third Edition*
3. Click on Student Resources Site, in the toolbar on the left
4. Click on Interactivities Web Site
5. Click on Interactivities Web Site and use your password to enter the site (your password card is located in the inside cover of your textbook)

DISCUSSION QUESTIONS

1. Why is it logical to organize IT applications by functional areas?
2. Describe the role of a TPS in a service organization.
3. Discuss how IT facilitates the budgeting process.
4. Why are information systems critical to sales-order processing?
5. What is the role of software in PLM? Can PLM be done manually?

6. Discuss the benefits of online self-service by employees and customers. How can these activities be facilitated by IT?

7. Discuss the need for integration of applications from different functional areas and the difficulty of doing it.

PROBLEM-SOLVING ACTIVITIES

1. Argot International (a fictitious name) is a medium-sized company in Peoria, Illinois, with about 2,000 employees. The company manufactures special machines for farms and food-processing plants, buying materials and components from about 150 vendors in six different countries. It also buys special machines and tools from Japan. Products are sold either to wholesalers (about 70) or directly to clients (from a mailing list of about 2,000). The business is very competitive.

   The company has the following information systems in place: financial/accounting, marketing (primarily information about sales), engineering, research and development, and inventory management. These systems are independent of each other although they are all connected to the corporate intranet.

   Argot is having profitability problems. Cash is in high demand and short supply, due to strong business competition from Germany and Japan. The company wants to investigate the possibility of using information technology to improve the situation. However, the vice president of finance objects to the idea, claiming that most of the tangible benefits of information technology are already being realized.

   You are hired as a consultant to the president. Respond to the following:
   a. Prepare a list of 10 potential applications of information technologies that you think could help the company.
   b. From the description of the case, would you recommend any portals? Be very specific. Remember, the company is in financial trouble.
   c. Can Web Services help Argot? If yes, how?

2. Enter *resumix.yahoo.com*. Take the demo. Prepare a list of all the product's capabilities. As a job candidate, can you prepare your resume to be better processed by Resumix? How?

3. The chart shown in Online File W7.9 shows the flow of routine activities in marketing. Explain in what areas IT can be most valuable.

INTERNET ACTIVITIES

1. Surf the Net and find free accounting software (try *shareware.cnet.com*, *rkom.com/free.htm*, *tucows.com*, *passtheshareware.com*, and *freeware-guide.com*). Download the software and try it. Write a report on your findings.

2. Enter the Web sites *tps.com* and *nonstop.compaq.com*, and find information about software products available from those sites. Identify the software that allows Internet transaction processing. Prepare a report about the benefits of the products identified.

3. Examine the capabilities of the following (and similar) financial software packages: Financial Analyzer (from Oracle) and CFO Vision (from SAS Institute).

Prepare a report comparing the capabilities of the software packages.

4. Surf the Internet and find information from three vendors on sales-force automation (try *sybase.com* and *salesforce.com*). Prepare a report on the state of the art.

5. Enter *microsoft.com/businessSolutions/Solomon/default.mspx*. View three of the demos in different functional areas of your choice. Prepare a report on the capabilities.

6. Enter *sage.com/solutions/solutions.htm*. Identify functional software, CRM software, and e-business software products. Are these standalone or integrated?

TEAM ASSIGNMENTS

1. Each group should visit or investigate a large company in a different industry and identify its marketing channel systems. Prepare a diagram that shows the seven components in Figure 7.4. Then find how IT supports those components. Finally, suggest improvements in the existing channel system that can be supported by IT technologies and that are not in use by the company today. Each group presents its findings.

2. The class is divided into groups of four. Each group member represents a major functional area: accounting/finance, sales/marketing, production/operations management, and human resources. Find and describe several examples of processes that require the integration of functional information systems in a company of your choice. Each group will also show the interfaces to the other functional areas.

3. Each group is to investigate an HRM software vendor (Oracle, Peoplesoft, SAP, Lawson Software). The group should prepare a list of all HRM functionalities supported by the software. Then the groups make a presentation to convince the class that its vendor is the best.

REAL-WORLD CASE   DOLLAR GENERAL USES INTEGRATED SOFTWARE

ACC
HRM
SVC

THE BUSINESS PROBLEM Dollar General (*dollargeneral.com*) operates more than 6,000 general stores in the United States, fiercely competing with Wal-Mart, Target, and hundreds of small stores in the sale of food, apparel, home-cleaning products, health and beauty aids, and more. The chain doubled in size between 1996 and 2002. Due to its rapid expansion, it has had some problems in addition to the stiff competition. For example, moving into new states means different sales taxes, and these need to be closely monitored for changes. Personnel management also became more difficult with the organization's growth. An increased number of purchasing orders aggravated problems in the accounts payable department, which was using manual matching of purchasing orders, invoices, and what was actually received in the receiving department before bills were paid.

The IT department was flooded with requests to generate reports on topics ranging from asset management to general ledgers. It became clear that a better information system was needed. Dollar General started by evaluating information requirements that would be able to solve the various problems that cut into the company's profit. A major factor in deciding which software to buy was the integration requirement among the existing functional information systems, especially the financial applications. This led to the selection of the Financials suite from Lawson Software.

THE IT SOLUTION The company started to implement applications one at a time. Before 1998, the company installed the suite's asset management, payroll, and some HR applications (which allow the tens of thousands of employees to monitor and self-update their benefits). After 1998, the accounts payable and general ledger modules of Lawson Software were activated. The accounting modules allow employees to route, extract, and analyze data in the accounting/finance area with little reliance on IT personnel. During 2001–2003, Dollar General added the marketing and operation activities to the integrated system.

Here are a few examples of how various parts of the new system work: All sales data from the point-of-sale scanners of some 6,000 stores are pulled each night, together with financial data, into the business intelligence application for financial and marketing analysis. This provides synergy with the sales audit system (from STS Software). All sales data are processed nightly by the STS system, broken to hourly journal entries, processed and summarized, and then entered into the Lawson's general ledger module.

The original infrastructure was mainframe based (IBM AS 400). In 2001 the system was migrated from the old legacy system to the Unix operating system, and then to a Web-based infrastructure, mainly in order to add Web-based functionalities and tools.

A development tool embedded in Lawson's Financials allowed users to customize applications without touching the computer programming code. For example, an employee-bonus application was not available in Lawson's software but was added to Financial's payroll module to accommodate Dollar General's bonus system. A customized application that allowed additions and changes in dozens of geographical areas also solved the organization's state sales-tax collection and reporting problem.

THE RESULTS The system is very scalable, so there is no problem in adding stores, vendors, applications, or functionalities. In 2003, the system was completely converted to Web-based, enabling authorized vendors, for example, to log on the Internet and view the status of their invoices by themselves. The Internet/EDI (see Chapter 9) enables small vendors to use the system. (An EDI is too expensive for small vendors, but the EDI/Internet is affordable.) Also, the employees can update personal data from any Web-enabled desktop in the store or at home. Future plans call for adding an e-purchasing (procurement) module using a desktop purchasing model.

Sources: Compiled from D. M. Amato-McCoy, "Dollar General Rings Up Back-Office Efficiencies with Financial Suite," *Stores* (October 2002) and from *lawson.com* (site accessed May 17, 2003).

QUESTIONS

1. Explain why the old, nonintegrated functional system created problems for the company. Be specific.
2. The new system cost several million dollars. Why, in your opinion, was it necessary to install it?
3. Lawson Software Smart Notification Software (*lawson. com*) is being considered by Dollar General. Find information about the software and write an opinion for adoption or rejection.
4. Another new product of Lawson is Services Automation. Would you recommend it to Dollar General? Why or why not?

CLUB IT   wiley.com/college/turban

FUNCTIONAL SYSTEMS AT CLUB IT

Lisa and Ruben look forward to the time when they can get useful and timely numbers on Club IT operations. Dollar and volume numbers for food and beverage operations, payroll, concert events, and marketing campaigns are difficult to compile with their current information systems. They realize that they must first implement functional systems before they can expect to get reliable information for planning, organizing, and controlling activities in the club. Given your creative work on information analysis so far, Lisa asks you to research and prepare a presentation on functional systems at Club IT.

ASSIGNMENT

1. Describe the transaction of ordering a drink from an information perspective. What functional information systems are touched by this transaction? What information is involved? What support can the Web provide?

2. There are a number of TPS tailored to the food and beverage service industry. Take a look online at some of these systems and describe how it would benefit Lisa and Ruben in running Club IT. Here are several to start with:
   - RestaurantPlus (http://www.restaurantplus.com/)
   - Micros (http://www.micros.com/)
   - NextPOS (http://www.nextpos.com)

3. Prepare *pro forma* reports for Lisa and Ruben to show them the benefits of getting reports from integrated functional systems:
   - a routine, scheduled report
   - an ad-hoc report
   - an exception report

Go to wiley.com/college/turban to access the CLUB IT Web Site on the Student Web Site

Enterprise Systems: From Supply Chains to ERP to CRM

Chapter Preview

Enterprise systems support more than one department and frequently the entire organization. Most notable are systems that support the supply chain. The success of many organizations—private, public, and military—depends on their ability to manage the flow of materials, information, and money into, within, and out of the organization. Such a flow is referred to as a supply chain.

In this chapter we describe the nature and types of enterprise systems, and particularly those that support supply chains. First we examine why problems occur there, then we outline some IT-based solutions, most of which are provided by integrated software. Next we show how e-commerce can cure problems along the supply chain. Finally, we discuss customer relationship management (CRM) as an enterprise system.*

* This chapter was revised with the assistance of Christy Cheung, City University of Hong Kong.

Chapter Outline

8.1 Essentials of Enterprise Systems and Supply Chains

8.2 Supply Chain Problems and Solutions

8.3 Computerized Enterprise Systems: MRP, MRP II, SCM, and Software Integration

8.4 Enterprise Resource Planning and Supply Chain Management

8.5 CRM and Its Support by IT

Learning Objectives

1. Understand the essentials of enterprise systems and computerized supply chain management.
2. Describe the various types of supply chains.
3. Describe some major problems of managing supply chains and some innovative solutions.
4. Describe some major types of software that support activities along the supply chain.
5. Describe the need for integrated software and how ERP does it.
6. Describe CRM and its support by IT.

CHEVRONTEXACO MODERNIZED ITS SUPPLY CHAIN WITH IT

ChevronTexaco, the largest U.S. oil company, is multinational in nature. Its main business is drilling, refining, transporting, and selling gasoline (oil). In this competitive business, a saving of even a quarter of a penny per gallon totals up to millions of dollars. Two problems have plagued the oil industry: running out of gasoline at individual pumps, and a delivery that is aborted because a tank at the gas station is too full (called "retain"). Run-outs and retains, known as the industry's "twin evils," have been a target for improvements for years, with little success.

The causes of the twin evils have to do with the supply chain: Gasoline flows in the supply chain start with oil hunting, drilling, and extraction. After the oil is taken from the ground, it is delivered to and then processed in refineries, and finally it goes to storage and eventually to the customer. The difficulty is to match the three parts of the supply chain: oil acquisition, processing, and distribution.

ChevronTexaco owns oil fields and refineries, but it also buys both crude and refined oil to meet peak demand. Purchases are of two types: those that are made through long-term contracts and those that are purchased "as needed," in what is called the *spot market*, at prevailing prices (usually higher than contract purchases).

In the past, ChevronTexaco acted like a mass-production manufacturing company, just trying to make oil products and then sell them (a supply-driven strategy). The problem with this strategy is that each time you make too much or too little, you are introducing extra costs into the supply chain.

The company decided to change its business model from supply driven to demand driven. Namely, instead of focusing on how much oil it would process and "push" to customers, the company started thinking about how much oil its customers wanted and then about how to get it. This change necessitated a major transformation in the business and extensive support by information technologies.

To implement the IT support, the company installed in each tank in each gas station an electronic monitor. The monitor transmits real-time information about the oil level, through a cable, to the station's IT-based management system. That system then transmits the information via a satellite to the main inventory system at the company's main office. There, an advanced DSS-based planning system processes the data to help refining, marketing, and logistics decisions. This DSS also includes information collected at trucking and airline companies, which are major customers. Using an enterprise resource planning (ERP) and business planning system, ChevronTexaco determines how much to refine, how much to buy in spot markets, and when and how much to ship to each retail station.

To combine all of these data, it is necessary to integrate the supply and demand information systems, and this is where the ERP software is useful. These data are used by planners at various points across the supply chain (e.g., refinery, terminal management, station management, transportation, and production) who process and share data constantly. This data processing and data sharing are provided by the various information systems.

Recent IT projects support the supply chain and extend it to a global reach. These projects include the NetReady initiative that enables the operations of 150 e-business projects, the Global Information Link (GIL2) that enables connectivity throughout the company, the e-Guest project that enables sharing of information with business partners, and a global human resources information system.

The integrated system that allows data to be shared across the company has improved decision making at every point in the customer-facing and processing parts of the supply chain. It resulted in an increase in the company's profit by more than $300 million in 1999 and by more than an additional $100 million each year after.

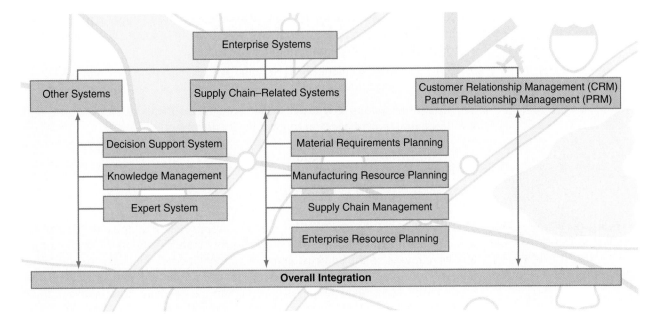

Figure 8.1 *Roadmap: Overview of enterprise systems.*

According to Worthen (2002), studies indicate that companies in the top 20 percent of the oil industry operate their supply chains twice as efficiently as average companies. These successful companies also carry half as much inventory, can respond to a significant rise in demand (20 percent or higher) twice as fast, and know how to minimize the number of deliveries to the gas stations. ChevronTexaco is in this category.

Sources: Compiled from J. Worthen, "Drilling for Every Drop of Value," *CIO Management* (June 1, 2002), p. 39; and from *chevrontexaco.com*, see "Information Technology" (site accessed January 2004).

The ChevronTexaco case illustrates the need to drastically improve the management of the supply chain. All decision makers along the supply chain need to share information and collaborate. Doing so is not a simple task, as will be seen in this chapter, but IT solutions enable even a large multinational company to manage its supply chain.

WHAT WE LEARNED FROM THIS CASE

ChevronTexaco successfully implemented the concepts of *supply chain management*, and *enterprise resource planning*. Figure 8.1 shows how these two topics are interrelated. Such a system is an enterprise system. In addition, the figure shows other enterprise systems. Some are described in other chapters (Chapters 3–7, and 10). Enterprise systems such as supply chains, ERP, and CRM are the subjects of this chapter.

8.1 ESSENTIALS OF ENTERPRISE SYSTEMS AND SUPPLY CHAINS

Enterprise systems (also called **enterprisewide systems**) are systems or processes that involve the entire enterprise or major portions of it. This is in contrast to functional systems, which are confined to one department (functional area) each.

enterprise systems (enterprisewide systems) *Systems or processes that involve the entire enterprise or major portions of it.*

Several enterprise systems can be found in organizations. Typical examples are:

* Enterprise resource planning (ERP), which supports the internal supply chain.
* Extended ERP, which supports business partners as well. Most ERP systems today are extended.
* Customer relationship management (CRM), which provides customer care.
* Partner relationship management (PRM), which is designed to provide care to business partners.

- Decision support systems (DSSs), whose purpose is to support decision making throughout the enterprise, frequently with the help of a data warehouse. This category includes executive information systems.
- Knowledge management (KM) systems, whose objective is to support knowledge creation, storage, maintenance, and distribution throughout the enterprise.

The first three systems are described in this chapter; PRM is described in Chapter 9, KM in Chapter 3, and decision support in Chapter 10.

Relevant Definitions

The following definitions are helpful as you read this chapter:

supply chain *The flow of materials, information, money, and services from raw material suppliers, through factories and warehouses, to the end customers; includes the organizations and processes involved.*

Supply Chain. As discussed in Chapter 2, **supply chain** refers to the flow of materials, information, money, and services from raw material suppliers, through factories and warehouses, to the end customers. A supply chain also includes the *organizations* and *processes* that create and deliver products, information, and services to end customers. It includes many tasks, such as purchasing, payment flow, materials handling, production planning and control, logistics and warehousing, inventory control, and distribution and delivery.

supply chain management (SCM) *The planning, organizing, and optimization of one or more of the supply chain's activities.*

Supply Chain Management. The function of **supply chain management (SCM)** is to plan, organize, and optimize one or more of the supply chain's activities. Today the concept of SCM is usually supported by IT (see Vakharia, 2002).

SCM Software. SCM software refers to software intended to support specific segments of the supply chain, such as in manufacturing, inventory control, scheduling and transportation. This software concentrates on improving decision making, optimization, and analysis.

e-supply chain *A supply chain that is managed electronically, usually with Web-based software.*

E-Supply Chain. When a supply chain is managed electronically, usually with Web-based software, it is referred to as an **e-supply chain.** As will be shown in this chapter, improvements in supply chains frequently involve attempts to convert a traditional supply chain to an e-supply chain, namely to automate the information flow in the chain (see Poirier and Bauer, 2000).

The Flows in the Supply Chain

There are typically three flows in the supply chain: materials, information, and financial.

1. *Materials flows.* These are all physical products, raw materials, supplies, and so forth, that flow along the chain. The concept of material flows also includes *reverse* flows—returned products, recycled products, and disposal of materials or products. A supply chain thus involves a *product life cycle* approach, from "dirt to dust."
2. *Information flows.* All data related to demand, shipments, orders, returns, and schedules, and changes in the data just cited, are information flows.
3. *Financial flows.* The financial flows are all transfers of money, payments, credit card information and authorization, payment schedules, e-payments, and credit-related data.

In some supply chains there are fewer flows. For example, in service industries there may be no physical flow of materials, but frequently there is flow of documents (hard and/or soft copies). In fact, the digitization of software, music, and other digital content may result in a supply chain without any physical flow. Notice, however, that in such a case, there are two types of information flows: one that replaces materials flow (e.g., digitized software) and one that is the supporting information (orders, billing, etc.).

In managing the supply chain it is necessary to coordinate all the above flows among all the parties involved in the supply chain.

The Structure and Components of Supply Chains

The term *supply chain* comes from a picture of how the partnering organizations are linked together. A typical supply chain, which links a company with its suppliers and its distributors and customers, is shown in Figure 8.2. Note that the supply chain involves three segments:

1. *Upstream*, where sourcing or procurement from external suppliers occur
2. *Internal*, where packaging, assembly, or manufacturing take place
3. *Downstream*, where distribution or dispersal take place, frequently by external distributors

As noted earlier, a supply chain is more than just the movement of tangible inputs; it also includes the movement of information and money and the procedures that support the movement of a product or a service. Finally, the organizations and individuals involved are part of the chain as well.

Supply chains come in all shapes and sizes. They may be fairly complex, as shown in Figure 8.3 (page 248). As can be seen in the figure, the supply chain for a car

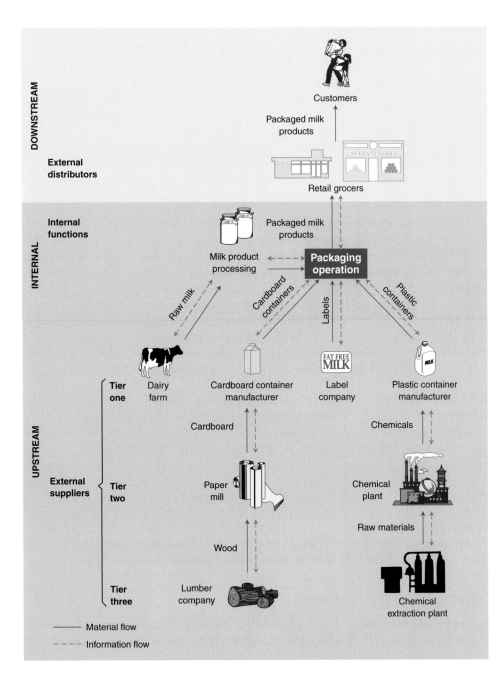

Figure 8.2 *The supply chain of a dairy.*
[Source: D. Reid and N. R. Sanders, Operations Management *(New York: Wiley, 2002), p. 80.]*

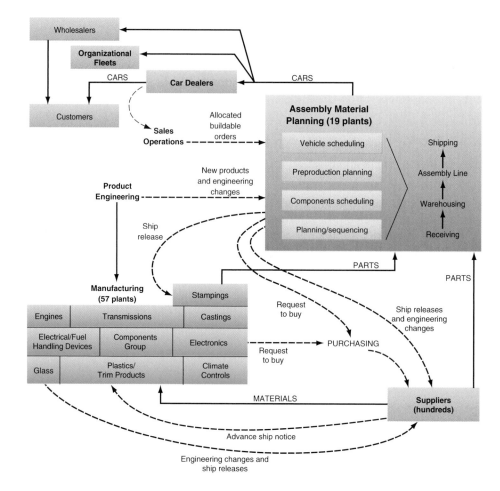

Figure 8.3 *An automotive supply chain.*
[Source: Modified from Introduction to Supply Chain Management *by Handfield and Nichols, 1999. Reprinted by permission of Pearson Education, Inc., Upper Saddle River, NJ.]*

manufacturer includes many suppliers, manufacturing plants (for parts) and assembly plants (for cars), dealers, direct business customers (fleets), wholesalers (some of which are virtual), customers, and support functions such as product engineering and purchasing. For the sake of simplicity we do not show here the flow of information and payments.

Notice that in Figure 8.3 the chain is not strictly linear, as it is in Figure 8.2. Here, we see some loops in the process. In addition, sometimes the flow of information and even goods can be bidirectional. For example, not shown in this figure is the *return* of damaged or unwanted products (known as *reverse logistics*). For the automaker, that would be cars returned to the dealers in cases of defects or recalls by the manufacturer.

Tiers of Suppliers.   An examination of Figure 8.2 shows that there are several potential tiers of suppliers. In some processes (e.g., in providing raw milk), there is only one tier of suppliers. However, in many other processes there are several tiers of suppliers. The idea of tiers of suppliers means that a supplier may have one or more subsuppliers, and the subsupplier may have its own subsupplier(s), and so on. For example, making cardboard containers involves three tiers: The cardboard container manufacturer (tier one) gets its material from the paper mill (tier two), which gets its material from the lumber company (tier three). Some supply chains can have up to a dozen tiers.

Coordinating subsuppliers can be a complex task. Use of B2B exchanges (Chapter 5), extranets, and PRM (Chapter 9) can help provide needed coordination.

Types of Supply Chains

The supply chains shown in Figures 8.2 and 8.3 are those of manufacturing companies. Such companies may have warehouses in different locations, making the chain even more complex. Types of supply chain can be classified into four categories: integrated make-to-stock, continuous replenishment, build-to-order, and channel assembly. Details are provided in Online File W8.1.

wiley.com/college/turban

Benefits of Proper Supply Chain Management

The flow of goods, services, information, and financial resources is usually designed not only to effectively transform raw items to finished products and services, but also to do so in an *efficient manner*. IT makes a major contribution to both efficiency and effectiveness of information flows (see Section 8.3).

The goals of modern SCM are to reduce uncertainty and risks along the supply chain, thereby decreasing inventory levels and cycle time, and improving business processes and customer service. All of these benefits contribute to increased profitability and competitiveness, as demonstrated in the opening case. The benefits of supply chain management have long been recognized both in business and in the military. To enjoy the above benefits it is necessary to overcome the limitations and problems described in the next section of the chapter.

Before you go on . . .

1. Define and list enterprise systems

2. Define a supply chain and supply chain management (SCM).

3. List the major components of supply chains.

4. List the benefits of effective SCM.

8.2 SUPPLY CHAIN PROBLEMS AND SOLUTIONS

Supply chain problems have been recognized in business, services, government, and the military for generations. Some even caused companies to go out of business. The problems are most evident in complex or long supply chains and in cases where many business partners are involved.

A well-known military case is the difficulties the German army encountered in World War II in the long supply chain to its troops in remote Russian territories, especially during the winter months. These difficulties resulted in a major turning point in the war and the beginning of the Germans' defeat. Note that during the 1991 war in Kuwait and the 2003 war in Iraq, the allied armies had superb supply chains that were managed by the latest computerized technologies (including DSS and intelligent systems). These chains were a major contributor to the swift victories.

In the business world there are numerous examples of supply chain problems, such as companies that were unable to meet demand, had too large and expensive inventories, and so on. Some of these companies paid substantial penalties, and others even went out of business. On the other hand, some world-class companies such as Wal-Mart, Federal Express, and Dell have excellent supply chains with innovative IT-enhanced applications.

Problems along the Supply Chain

Problems along the supply chain can occur between business units within a single enterprise; they also can occur between (and among) enterprises. A major symptom of ineffective supply chains is poor customer service, which hinders people or businesses from getting products or services when and where needed or gives them poor-quality products. Other symptoms are high inventory costs, loss of revenues, extra cost of expediting shipments, and more. Let's look at an example.

POM

EXAMPLE   *Problems with "Santa's Supply Chain."* An example of a supply chain problem was the difficulty of fulfilling toy orders received electronically during the 1999 holiday season. During the last months of that year, on-line toy retailers, including eToys (now KBkids.com), Amazon.com, and ToysRUs, conducted a massive advertising campaign for Internet ordering. This included $20 to $30 discount vouchers for shopping online.

Customer response was overwhelming, and the retailers that underestimated it were unable to get the necessary toys from the manufacturing plants and warehouses and deliver them to the customers' doors by Christmas Eve. ToysRUs, for example, offered each of its unhappy customers a $100 store coupon as compensation. Despite its generous gift, over 40 percent of the unhappy ToysRUs customers said they would not shop online at ToysRUs again (*Interactiveweek.com*, February 3, 2000).

Reasons for Supply Chain Problems.   The problems along the supply chain stem mainly from two sources: (1) from uncertainties and (2) from the need to coordinate several activities, internal units, and business partners. Here we will address several of the uncertainties that contribute to supply chain problems. Throughout the chapter we will consider how IT can help enterprises improve supply chain coordination and reduce uncertainties.

A major source of supply chain uncertainties is the *demand forecast*, as demonstrated by the 1999 toy season example. The actual demand may be influenced by several factors such as competition, prices, weather conditions, technological developments, customers' general confidence, and more. These are external, usually uncontrollable factors. ChevronTexaco, as seen earlier, overcame this uncertainty by measuring demand in real time and using a demand-driven production strategy.

Other supply chain uncertainties are delivery times, which depend on many factors, ranging from production machine failures to road conditions and traffic jams that may interfere with shipments. Quality problems in materials and parts may also create production delays, which lead to supply chain problems.

One of the major difficulties to properly setting inventory levels in various parts of the supply chain is known as the bullwhip effect.

bullwhip effect *Erratic shifts in orders up and down the supply chain.*

The Bullwhip Effect.   The bullwhip effect refers to erratic shifts in orders up and down the supply chain. This effect was initially observed by Procter & Gamble (P&G) with its disposable diapers product (Pampers). While actual sales in retail stores were fairly stable and predictable, orders from distributors to the manufacturer, P&G, had wild swings, creating production and inventory problems. An investigation revealed that distributors' orders were fluctuating because of poor demand forecast, price fluctuation, order batching, and rationing within the supply chain. These dysfunctions resulted in unnecessary and costly inventories in various locations along the supply chain, fluctuations in P&G orders to their suppliers, and flow of inaccurate information. Distorted information can lead to tremendous inefficiencies, excessive inventories, poor customer service, lost revenues, ineffective shipments, and missed production schedules (Donovan, 2002/2003).

The bullwhip effect is not unique to P&G, however. Firms ranging from Hewlett-Packard in the computer industry to Bristol-Myers Squibb in pharmaceuticals have experienced a similar phenomenon. Basically, demand variables can become magnified when viewed through the eyes of managers at each link in the supply chain. If each distinct entity makes ordering and inventory decisions with an eye to its own interest above those of the chain, stockpiling may be simultaneously occurring at as many as seven or eight locations along the supply chain. Study has shown that such hoarding has led in some cases to as many as 100 days of inventory that is waiting, "just in case" (versus 10–20 days in the normal case).

A 1998 industry study projected that $30 billion in savings could materialize in grocery industry supply chains alone, by sharing information and collaborating. Thus, companies are trying to avoid the "sting of the bullwhip" as well as to solve other SCM problems.

Solutions to Supply Chain Problems

Supply chain problems can be very costly for companies, and therefore organizations are motivated to find innovative solutions. During the oil crises in the 1970s, for example, Ryder Systems, a large trucking company, purchased a refinery to control the upstream part of the supply chain and ensure timely availability of gasoline for its trucks. Such a strategy is known as **vertical integration**. It is effective in some cases but ineffective in others. (Ryder sold the refinery later, because of its inability to manage a business it did not know and the fact that oil became more plentiful.) In the remaining portion of this section we will look at some of the possible solutions to supply chain problems, many of which are supported by IT.

vertical integration *Strategy of integrating the upstream part of the supply chain with the internal part, typically by purchasing upstream suppliers, in order to ensure timely availability of supplies.*

Using Inventories to Solve Supply Chain Problems. Undoubtedly, the most common solution used by companies to solve supply chain problems is *building inventories*, as "insurance" against supply chain uncertainties. The main problem with this approach is that it is very difficult to correctly determine inventory levels for each product and part. If inventory levels are set too high, the cost of keeping the inventory will be very large. (And, as we have seen, high inventories at multiple points in the supply chain can result in the bullwhip effect.) If the inventory is too low, there is no insurance against high demand or slow delivery times, and revenues (and customers) may be lost. In either event, the total cost—including cost of keeping inventories, cost of lost sales opportunities, and bad reputation—can be very high. Thus, companies make major attempts to optimize and control inventories, as discussed in the story about Littlewoods Stores, one of Britain's largest retailers of high-quality clothing, available in Online File W8.2.

wiley.com/college/turban

Information Sharing. Another common way to solve supply chain problems, and especially to improve demand forecasts, is *sharing information* along the supply chain. Such sharing can be facilitated by EDI, extranets, and groupware technologies, as part of interorganizational information systems (IOSs, Chapter 9) or *c-commerce* (Chapter 5). Such information sharing is frequently referred to as the *collaborative supply chain* (see Simatupang and Sridharan, 2002).

One of the most notable examples of information sharing is between large manufacturers and retailers. For example, Wal-Mart provides Procter & Gamble access to daily sales information from every store for every item P&G makes for Wal-Mart. Then P&G is able to manage the *inventory replenishment* for Wal-Mart's stores. By monitoring inventory levels, P&G knows when inventories fall below the threshold for each product at any Wal-Mart store. These data trigger an immediate shipment.

Such information sharing between Wal-Mart and P&G is done automatically. It is part of a **vendor-managed inventory (VMI)** strategy. P&G has similar agreements with other major retailers. The benefit for P&G is accurate and timely demand information. Thus, P&G can plan production more accurately, minimizing the 'bullwhip effect." To do so, in 2000 P&G deployed a Web-based "Ultimate-Supply System," which replaced 4,000 different EDI links to suppliers and retailers in a more cost-effective way. The VMI is an example of supply chain collaboration.

vendor-managed inventory (VMI) *Strategy used by retailers of allowing suppliers to monitor the inventory levels of their products in the retailers' stores and to replenish inventory when needed.*

Changing a Linear Supply Chain to a Hub. In linear supply chains, information is processed in a sequence, which slows down its flow. One solution is to change the linear chain into a hub, as the Chapter 1 example about Orbis Corp. (page 7) demonstrated. Recall that ProductBank.com is a digitized hub of photos, to which manufacturers, ad agencies, retailers, and printers have access. Each partner in the supply chain can directly access the images in the data bank. With the electronic hub, the transaction cost per picture (usually paid by the manufacturer) is 30 to 40 percent lower, and the cycle time is 50 to 70 percent shorter than in the traditional linear supply chain model (*productbank.com.au*). Orbis's information system is concentrated around its own supply chain; other companies provide similar services to entire industries (see *Webcor.com* and the Asite case in Chapter 9).

Supply Chain Collaboration. Proper supply chain and inventory management requires coordination of all the different activities and links of the supply chain. Successful coordination enables goods to move smoothly and on time from suppliers to manufacturers to customers, which enables a firm to keep inventories low and costs down. Collaboration of supply chain partners is needed since companies depend on each other but do not always work together toward the same goal. Both suppliers and buyers must participate together in the design or redesign of the supply chain to achieve their shared goals. As part of the collaboration effort, business partners must learn to *trust* each other.

To properly control the uncertainties associated with supply chain problems, it is necessary to identify and understand their causes, determine how uncertainties in some activities will affect other activities up and down the supply chain, and then formulate specific ways to reduce or eliminate the uncertainties. Combined with this is the need for an effective and efficient communication environment among all business partners (see Chapter 9). A rapid flow of information along a supply chain tends to improve efficiency. For example, computerized point-of-sale (POS) information can be transmitted in real time to distribution centers, suppliers, and shippers. Having real-time information enables firms to achieve optimal inventory levels.

An example of a well-known supply chain collaboration, the CPFR, is provided in Online File W8.3.

wiley.com/college/turban

Other IT-Assisted Solutions to SCM Problems. Some other generic IT-assisted solutions to solve supply chain management problems are provided in Table 8.1.

Large companies employ several methods to achieve supply chain superiority. Wal-Mart, for example, is well-known for its ability to collaborate with companies across its supply chain. It is able to combine information from its suppliers with demand and inventory data from its stores, in order to minimize operating cost and reduce prices. Nestlé USA even created a vice-president-level position exclusively to manage business with Wal-Mart (Worthen, 2002). For an example of how another large company, Dell, manages its supply chain, see Online File W8.4.

wiley.com/college/turban

Several other mechanisms, such as supply chain teams and virtual factories, are potent in helping to solve supply chain problems; all are IT-enabled. For support of global supply chains see Chapter 9.

Table 8.1 IT-Supported Solutions to Supply Chain Problems

Problem Area	Solution
Slow communication	Use wireless devices to find vehicle locations, to expedite salespeople's contact with headquarters. Use hub supply chain to enable online access to information.
Difficult product configuration	Use DSS and intelligent systems for rapid and accurate analysis.
Select and coordinate suppliers	Use DSS to determine which suppliers to use; determine how to create strategic partnerships.
Supplies arrive when needed	Use just-in-time approach and collaboration with suppliers.
Handle peak demands	Use IT-enabled outsourcing. Use DSS to determine what to outsource and when to buy and not make (see ChevronTexaco opening case).
Expedite lead time for buying and selling	Use e-commerce tools and business intelligence models.
Too many or too few suppliers	Use optimization model to decide and employ e-procurement.
Supplier relationships	Improve supplier relationships by using portals, Web-based call center, and other CRM and PRM tools.
Control inventory levels	Manufacture only after order received (online). Use VMI and Web-services.
Forecast fluctuating demand	Use collaboration (like CPFR) or intelligent systems (see ChevronTexaco opening case).
Expedite flows in the chain	Automate material, information, and money flows.

Supply Chain Teams.   The change of the linear supply chain to a hub (Chapters 1, 5, and 9) points to the need to create **supply chain teams**. A supply chain team is a group of tightly integrated businesses that work together to serve the customer. Each task is done by the member of the team who is best positioned, trained, and capable of doing that specific task, regardless of which company the member works for.

supply chain team   *A group of tightly integrated businesses that work together to serve the customer; each task is done by the member of the team who is best capable of doing the task.*

For example, in a supply chain team, the team member that deals with the delivery will handle a delivery problem, even if he or she works for the delivery company rather than for the retailer whose product is being delivered. This way, redundancies will be minimized. The delivery company will deal with the customer about a delivery problem, rather than passing the problem along to the retailer, who would end up having to contact the delivery company. Thus, the retailer will not have to spend valuable resources following up on the delivery. The task assignment to team members can be facilitated by IT tools such as workflow software and groupware.

Virtual Factories.   A **virtual factory** is a collaborative enterprise application that provides a computerized model of a factory. In the virtual factory, proposed designs can be tested, relationships with suppliers can be simulated, and manufacturing processes and how they are connected can be modeled. If potential problems in these areas are spotted in the digital model of the factory, solutions can be worked out in the virtual model before they are implemented in the real-world factory. Usually, the virtual factory application would connect suppliers to the B2B system and clearly present the needed demand to suppliers. That "demand visibility" can help the company to focus on two important key performance indicators, lead times and transaction cost. Uniting the entire supply chain and creating visibility between suppliers and buyers can help the companies forecast and plan demand more effectively. Virtual factories also enable all companies involved to work together collaboratively using common tools, and they provide greater flexibility and responsiveness by getting information and goods flowing much more quickly.

virtual factory   *Collaborative enterprise application that provides a computerized model of a factory.*

EXAMPLE   ***Work in a Virtual Factory.*** Adaptec Inc. and Taiwan Semiconductor Manufacturing Co. (TSMC) are using Extricity Alliance (from Extricity Software) to connect their internal systems through the Internet and to create a smoothly choreographed virtual factory. By means of this system-to-system communication over the Internet, the two companies accomplish several supply chain management activities, including sharing forecasts, managing orders, issuing work-in-progress reports, and transmitting shipping notices and engineering-design changes. This process results in shorter product lead times, more direct control over processes, and more accurate capacity planning.

Wireless Solutions.   In the last few years we have seen an increased number of wireless solutions to supply chain problems, as illustrated in IT's about Business 8.1 (page 254).

Ethical Issues Relating to Supply Chain Solutions.   Conducting a supply chain management project may result in the need to lay off, retrain, or transfer employees. Should management notify the employees in advance regarding such possibilities? And what about those older employees who are difficult to retrain? Other ethical issues may involve sharing of personal information, which may be required for a collaborative organizational culture. But, how can it be forced on resisting employees? Finally, individuals may have to share computer programs that they designed for their personal use on the job. Such programs may be considered the intellectual property of the individuals. (Should the employees be compensated for the programs' use by others?)

To provide the solutions discussed in this section, IT utilizes a number of software packages. These are described in the next two sections.

All of us are familiar with the service at restaurants, and many of us have encountered inconvenient scenarios such as long waits, cold food, or even receiving a wrong order. These inconveniences are the result of a conventional process that works like this: A server takes your drink order and then walks to the bar to place the order. He or she knows that it will take about five minutes for your drink to be prepared; in the meantime, the server takes an order from someone else and then heads back to the bar. The server might make a couple of such trips, with stops at your table to apologize for delays, until your drink is ready.

Eventually the server comes to your table and takes your food order. That order is written on a piece of paper, which the server carries to the kitchen and places on a revolving wheel. The chef rotates each new order into view when he or she is ready to begin preparing the next order. By the time your order is rotated into view, which may be 10 or 15 minutes after it is placed, the server may be told that the kitchen is out of this selection. He or she comes to your table and asks you to reorder. Sometimes the server makes a mistake writing your order or the chef reads the handwritten order incorrectly. In such a case, after a long wait, you are very frustrated at getting the wrong food. In the end, no one is happy.

At Royal Mile Pub in Silver Springs, Maryland, the situation is different, thanks to pervasive computing. Royal Mile is a medium-size restaurant (about 20 tables) with a bar that carries a wide selection of beverages. What is different about Royal Mile is that the servers' little green order pads have been replaced with iPaq PDAs (see photo) connected to the kitchen using wireless networking.

The new system works as follows: Most menu items are visible on the PDA, which also has handwriting capabilities for writing in special instructions (e.g., "dressing on the side"). To take drink or food orders for standard orders requires only one or two keystrokes.

The server glances at the screen to verify that the correct item has appeared. Experienced servers can be trained in about 15 minutes on how to use the devices.

The Wi-Fi system (Chapter 6) within the restaurant transmits the orders, which appear immediately on screens in the bar and the kitchen. After transmitting an order, the server can move to the next table rather than hurrying off to hand the orders to the cooks or bartenders.

The PDA interface immediately tells servers which menu items are unavailable, thus eliminating another source of customer and server dissatisfaction. Because the kitchen becomes aware of orders immediately, the food arrives more quickly. The system also totals each bill, eliminating arithmetic errors. Because they make half as many trips out of the serving area, servers can spend more time with each customer and handle more tables, enabling more pleasant customer relationships and higher tip income.

In addition, the owner is enthusiastic about the system's effects on his business. The order system costs about $30,000 to install. Its benefits include fewer errors, better inventory control, and smaller payrolls. The system has reduced the error rate from several wrong meals per night to about one every two nights. Improvements have occurred not only in reducing the number of wasted (and replacement) meals, but also in customer satisfaction.

In addition, as orders transmit, they are processed against the inventory database. This integration allows kitchen managers to track raw material purchases against the food orders and identify waste or other delivery and processing problems. Integration with the inventory control systems is fundamental to realizing cost reductions, improved workflow, and inventory and personnel management.

Finally, only three food servers are needed with the new system, meaning lasting salary cost reductions and lower overhead. Also, three data-entry stations on the servicing floor for processing credit card charges were reduced to one, freeing up space on the serving floor.

Sources: Compiled from V. Stanford, "Pervasive Computing Puts Food on the Table," *Pervasive Computing* (January 2003), and *royalmilepub.com* (accessed January 2004).

PPT 8800 from Symbol Technologies, another type of personal digital assistant, used for the same purpose as an iPaq PDA.

QUESTIONS

1. Why would customers appreciate this pervasive computing system?
2. If such a system is beneficial to all, why haven't all restaurants adopted it?
3. Draw the supply chain within the restaurant's order system.

8.3 COMPUTERIZED ENTERPRISE SYSTEMS: MRP, MRP II, SCM, AND SOFTWARE INTEGRATION

The concept of the supply chain is interrelated with the computerization of its activities, which has evolved over 50 years.

The Evolution of Computerized Aids

Historically, many of the supply chain management activities were done manually using paper, telephones, and faxes, but this can be very inefficient. Therefore, since the time when computers first began to be used for business, people have wanted to automate the processes along the supply chain.

The first software programs, which appeared in the 1950s and early 1960s, supported short segments along the supply chain. Typical examples are inventory management systems, scheduling, and billing. The supporting software was called *supply chain management (SCM) software* (see Section 8.4). The major objectives were to expedite processing, reduce errors, and reduce costs. As was shown in Chapter 7, such applications were developed in the functional areas, independently of each other, and they became more and more sophisticated with the passage of time. Of special interest were inventory management systems and financial decision-making formulas (e.g., for capital budgeting).

In a short time it became clear that interdependencies exist among some of the supply chain activities. One early realization was that production scheduling is related to inventory management and purchasing plans. As early as the 1960s, the material requirements planning (MRP) model was devised. This planning model essentially integrates production, purchasing, and inventory management of interrelated products (see Chapter 7). It became clear that computer support could greatly enhance the use of this model, which may require daily updating. This resulted in commercial MRP software packages coming on the market.

material requirements planning (MRP) *A planning model that integrates production, purchasing, and inventory management of interrelated products.*

MRP packages were (and still are) useful in many cases, helping to drive inventory levels down and streamlining portions of the supply chain. However, they also failed in many cases. One of the major reasons for the failures was the realization that schedule-inventory-purchasing operations are closely related to both financial and labor resources. This realization resulted in an enhanced MRP methodology (and software) called manufacturing resource planning (MRP II), which adds labor requirements and financial planning to MRP (see Sheikh, 2002).

manufacturing resource planning (MRP II) *An enhanced planning model that adds labor requirements and financial planning to MRP.*

During this evolution there was more and more integration of functional information systems. This evolution continued, leading to the *enterprise resource planning (ERP)* concept, which integrates the transaction processing and other routine activities of all functional areas in the entire enterprise. ERP initially covered all routine transactions within a company, including internal suppliers and customers. Later it was expanded, in what is known as *extended ERP software*, to incorporate external suppliers and customers. We'll look at ERP in more detail in Section 8.4.

The next step in this evolution, which started in the late 1990s, is the inclusion of business intelligence and other software. At the beginning of the twenty-first century, the integration expanded to include markets and communities.

Notice that throughout this evolution there has been increasing integration along several dimensions (e.g., more functional areas, combination of transaction processing and decision support, and inclusion of business partners). Therefore, before we describe the essentials of ERP and SCM software it may be beneficial to analyze the reasons for activities and software integration.

Why Systems Integration?

Twentieth-century computer technology was *functionally* oriented. Managing the twenty-first-century enterprise cannot be done effectively with such technology. Functional systems may not let different departments communicate with each other in the same language. Worse yet, crucial sales, inventory, and production data often have to be painstakingly entered manually into separate computer systems every time a person who is not a member of a specific department needs ad-hoc information related to the specific department. In many cases employees using functionally oriented technology simply do not get the information they need, or they get it too late.

Sandoe et al. (2001) list the following major benefits of systems integration (in order of importance):

- *Tangible benefits.* Inventory reduction, personnel reduction, productivity improvement, order management improvement, financial-close cycle improvements, IT cost reduction, procurement cost reduction, cash management improvements, revenue/profit increases, transportation logistics cost reduction, maintenance reduction, and on-time delivery improvement
- *Intangible benefits.* Information visibility, new/improved processes, customer responsiveness, standardization, flexibility, globalization, and business performance

Internal versus External Integration.   There are two basic types of systems integration—internal and external. *Internal integration* refers to integration within a company between (or among) applications, and/or between applications and databases. For example, an organization may integrate inventory control with an ordering system, or a CRM suite with the database of customers. Large companies that have hundreds of applications may find it extremely difficult to integrate the newer Web-based applications with the older legacy systems.

External integration refers to integration of applications and/or databases among business partners—for example, the suppliers' catalogs with the buyers' e-procurement system. Another example of external supply chain integration is product-development systems that allow suppliers to dial into a client's intranet, pull product specifications, and view illustrations and videos of a manufacturing process. (For further discussion, see Chapter 9 and Hagel, 2002.) External integration is especially needed for B2B and for partner relationship management (PRM) systems, as will be discussed in Chapter 9.

Before you go on . . .

1. Describe MRP and MRP II.
2. Describe the need for, and types of, integration.

8.4 ENTERPRISE RESOURCE PLANNING AND SUPPLY CHAIN MANAGEMENT

One of the most successful tools for managing supply chains, especially internal ones, is enterprise resource planning (ERP).

What Is ERP?

With the advance of enterprisewide client/server computing comes a new challenge: how to control all major business processes in real time with a single software architecture. The most common *integrated software* solution of this kind is known as **enterprise resource planning (ERP)** or just **enterprise systems**. This software integrates the planning, management, and use of all resources in the entire enterprise. It is comprised of sets of applications that automate routine back-end operations (such as financial, inventory management, and scheduling) to help enterprises handle jobs such as order fulfillment. For example, there is a module for cost control, for accounts payable and receivable, and for fixed assets and treasury management. ERP promises benefits ranging from increased efficiency to improved quality, productivity, and profitability. (See Ragowsky and Somers, 2002, for details.)

ERP's major objective is to *integrate all departments and functional information flows across a company* onto a single computer system that can serve all of the enterprise's needs. For example, improved order entry allows immediate access to inventory, product data, customer credit history, and prior order information. Such availability of information raises productivity and increases customer satisfaction. ERP systems are in use in thousands of large and medium companies worldwide, and some ERP systems are producing dramatic results (see *erpassist.com*).

enterprise resource planning (ERP) (enterprise systems) *Software that integrates the planning, management, and use of all resources in the entire enterprise.*

> **EXAMPLE** *Multiple Benefits at Master Product Co.* ERP helped Master Product Company increase customers' satisfaction and, consequently, sales by 20 percent and decrease inventory by 30 percent, thus increasing productivity (Caldwell, 1997).

> **EXAMPLE** *Consolidation Applications via ERP.* ExxonMobil consolidated 300 different information systems by implementing SAP R/3 in its U.S. petrochemical operations alone.

For businesses that want to use ERP, one option is to self-develop an integrated system, either by linking together existing functional packages or by programming a new, custom-built system. Another option, which is often quicker and/or less expensive, is to use commercially available integrated ERP software. The leading ERP software is **SAP R/3** (from SAP AG Corp.). This highly integrated software package contains more than 70 business activities modules. Oracle, Computer Associates, and PeopleSoft also make similar products. All of these products include Web modules.

Yet another way for a business to implement ERP is to lease ERP systems from *application service providers (ASPs)*. A major advantage of the leasing approach is that even a small company can enjoy ERP: A small company can lease only relevant modules, rather than buy an entire ERP package. Some companies, such as Starbucks, have chosen a *best-of-breed* approach—building their own customized ERP with ready-made components leased or purchased from several vendors.

SAP R/3 *The leading ERP software (from SAP AG Corp.); a highly integrated package containing more than 70 business activities modules.*

The Software Content of ERP. As indicated above, an ERP system is composed of modules for managing all the routine activities performed by a business. For example, an ERP suite for a manufacturing company would include modules that cover activities such as production scheduling, inventory management, entering sales orders, coordinating shipping, and providing after-sales customer service. The modules in an ERP suite are accessed through a single interface.

Vendors offer dozens of different ERP modules. It is a collection of integrated functional applications, plus some enterprisewide applications. A list of representative ERP modules is provided in Online File W8.5.

First-Generation ERP

The first generation of ERP concentrated on activities within the enterprise that were routine and repetitive in nature. Large companies have been successful in integrating several hundred applications using first-generation ERP software. ERP forces discipline and organization around business processes, making the alignment of IT and business goals more likely. Such change is related to business process redesign (Chapter 11). Also, by implementing ERP a company can discover and clean up the "dusty corners" of its business.

However, ERP is not a "wonder drug" for business ills. It has some drawbacks: It can be extremely complex to implement. Also, companies often need to change existing business processes to fit ERP's format. Finally, some companies require only a few of the ERP 's software modules yet must purchase the entire package (unless they decide to lease individual modules from ASPs). For these reasons, ERP software may not be attractive to everyone.

As of the late 1990s, ERP systems began to be extended along the supply chain to suppliers and customers. These extended systems can incorporate functionality for customer interactions and for managing relationships with suppliers and vendors, making the system less inward-looking. (For a comprehensive treatment of ERP, see Lucas and Bishop, 2002.)

But ERP originally was never meant to fully support supply chains, even when suppliers and customers were added. ERP solutions are centered around *business transactions*. As such, they do not provide the computerized models needed to respond rapidly to real-time changes in supply, demand, labor, or capacity, nor to effectively integrate with e-commerce and other applications. This deficiency has been overcome by the second generation of ERP.

Second-Generation ERP

The objective of second-generation ERP is to leverage existing information systems in order to increase efficiency in handling transactions, improve decision making, and transform ways of doing business into e-business. Let's explain.

The reports generated by first-generation ERP systems gave planners statistics about business transactions, costs, and financial performance. However, the planning systems in ERP were rudimentary. Reports from first-generation ERP systems provided a snapshot of the business at a point in time. But they did not support *continuous* planning, which is central to supply chain planning. Continuous planning is more like a video than a snapshot: It continues to refine and enhance the plan as changes and events occur, up to the very last minute before the plan is executed. Attempting to come up with an optimal plan using first-generation ERP-based systems has been compared to steering a car by looking in the rear-view mirror.

SCM software *Applications programs specifically designed to improve decision making in segments of the supply chain.*

This weakness of first-generation ERP created the need for planning systems oriented toward decision making. **SCM software** is specifically designed to improve decision making in segments of the supply chain. Its focus on decision making is in contrast to the focus in ERP on streamlining the flow of routine information. (For further description of the differences between SCM and ERP software, see Online File W8.6.)

wiley.com/college/turban

Combining ERP with SCM Software. Use of ERP and SCM software is not necessarily an either-or decision. Rather, the two can be combined and used together. To illustrate how ERP and SCM may work together, consider the task of order processing. There is a fundamental difference between SCM and ERP in order processing: The ERP approach is, "How can I best take or fulfill your order?" In contrast, the question that SCM software asks is, "Should I take your order?" The answer might be "no" if taking the order would lose money for the company or interfere with production. Thus, SCM software focuses on planning, optimization, and decision making in segments of the supply chain.

Thus, the *analytical* SCM information systems have emerged as a *complement* to ERP systems, to provide intelligent decision support or business intelligence (Chapter

10) capabilities. An SCM system is designed to overlay existing systems and to pull data from every step of the supply chain. It is therefore able to provide a clear, organizational-level picture of where the enterprise is heading.

EXAMPLE   *How IBM Is Using SCM.* An example of a successful SCM effort is IBM's restructuring of its *global supply chain*. The goal of the restructuring was to achieve quick responsiveness to customers and to do it with minimal inventory. To support this effort, IBM developed a supply chain analysis tool, called the Asset Management Tool (AMT), for use by a number of IBM business units and their channel partners. IBM is using AMT to analyze and improve such issues as inventory budgets and turnover, customer-service targets, and new-product introductions. AMT integrates graphical process modeling, analytical performance optimization, simulation, activity-based costing, and enterprise database connectivity into a system that allows quantitative analysis of interenterprise supply chains. AMT benefits include savings of over $750 million in material costs and price-protection expenses each year (Yao et al., 2000). The system was also a prerequisite to a major e-procurement initiative at IBM.

Creating a plan from an SCM system allows companies to quickly assess the impact of their actions on the entire supply chain, including customer demand. But this can be done only if ERP software is added. Therefore, it makes sense to integrate ERP and SCM.

Alternative Ways to Integrate ERP and SCM.   How is integration of ERP and SCM done? One approach is to work with different software products from different vendors. For example, a business might use SAP as an ERP and add to it Manugistics' manufacturing-oriented SCM software, as shown in the Warner-Lambert case in Online File W8.3. Such an approach requires fitting together different software, which may be a complex task unless special connectors provided by middleware vendors exist.

wiley.com/college/turban

The second approach is for ERP vendors to add decision support and analysis capabilities, known as *business intelligence*, to their major product. Business intelligence (as defined in Chapters 3 and 10) refers to analysis performed by DSS, ESS, data mining, and intelligent systems. Using a combined product from a single vendor solves the integration problem. However, most ERP vendors offer a combined product for another reason: It is cheaper for the customers. The added business intelligence functionalities, which create the *second-generation ERP*, include not only decision support, but also CRM, e-commerce, and data warehousing and mining. Some systems include a *knowledge management* component as well. In 2003, vendors started to add PLM (see Chapter 7) in an attempt to optimize the supply chain. An example of an ERP application that includes an SCM module is provided in IT's about Business 8.2 (page 260).

Integrating ERP with Other Enterprise Systems

In addition to integrating ERP with SCM systems, ERP can be integrated with other enterprise systems, most notably with e-commerce. IT's about Business 8.3 (page 261) describes the integration of ERP and EC at Cybex International.

ERP is a most common enterprisewide information system in medium and large organizations. Another enterprise system, which is adopted even by some small companies, is customer relationship management (CRM).

ERP Failures and Their Prevention

Despite improvements over the years, ERP projects, especially large ones, may fail. The following are some examples of ERP failures. See the Real-World Case at the end of Chapter 11 (page 358 for another example of an ERP failure.

Lessons From

IT Failures

IT'S ABOUT BUSINESS
POM

8.2: Colgate-Palmolive Uses ERP to Smooth Its Supply Chain

Colgate-Palmolive is the world leader in oral-care products (toothpaste, toothbrushes, and mouthwashes) and a major supplier of personal-care products (baby care, deodorants, shampoos, and soaps). In addition, the company's Hill's Health Science Diet is a leading pet-food brand worldwide. Foreign sales account for about 70 percent of Colgate's total revenues.

To stay competitive, Colgate continuously seeks to streamline its supply chain, through which thousands of suppliers and customers interact with the company. At the same time, Colgate faces the challenges of accelerating new-product development, which has been a factor in driving faster sales growth and improved market share. Also, Colgate is devising ways to offer consumers a greater choice of better products at a lower cost to the company. To better manage the complexities of its manufacturing and the supply chains, Colgate embarked on an ERP imple-

mentation. The new system allows the company to access more timely and accurate data and to reduce costs. The structure of the ERP is pictured below.

An important factor for Colgate was whether it could use the ERP software across the entire spectrum of the business. Colgate needed the ability to coordinate globally and act locally. Colgate's U.S. division installed SAP R/3 for this purpose.

Source: Compiled from R. Kalakota and M. Robinson, *E-Business: Roadmap for Success* (Boston, MA: Addison Wesley, 2001).

QUESTIONS

1. What is the role of the ERP for Colgate-Palmolive?
2. Who are the major beneficiaries of the new system?
3. Comment on the structure of the ERP.

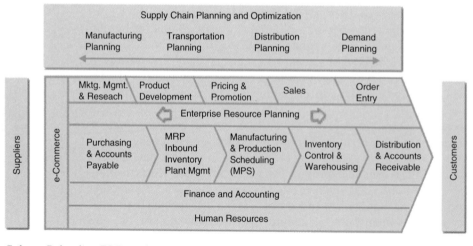

Colgate-Palmolive ERP implementation.
[*Source: R. Kalakota and M. Robinson,* E-Business 2.2 *(Boston, MA: Addison Wesley, 2001).]*

POM | EXAMPLE | ***ERP Integration Problems at Hershey.*** In late 1999, Hershey Foods Corporation reported a 19 percent drop in third-quarter net earnings, due to computer problems. The major problem, according to the company, was its new order-and-distribution system, which used software from both SAP (the ERP) and Siebel Systems (the CRM). Since the integrated system went live in July 1999, Hershey had been unable to fill all orders and get products onto shelves on time. The problems continued for several months, causing Hershey to lose market share and several hundred million dollars.

POM | EXAMPLE | ***Rushing Resulted in Damage.*** In November 1999, Whirlpool Corp. reported major delays in shipment of appliances due to "bugs" in its new ERP. Orders for quantities smaller than one truckload met with snags in the

8.3: Integrating EC and ERP at Cybex

Cybex International (*cybex.com*), a global maker of fitness machines, was unable to meet the demand for its popular fitness machines, which increased dramatically in the late 1990s. To maintain its market share, the company had to work with rush orders from its nearly 1,000 suppliers. The cost of responding to rush orders was extremely high. This problem was a result of a poor demand forecast for the machine's components. The demand forecast was produced using three different legacy systems that Cybex had inherited from merger partners.

After examining existing vendors' supply chain software, Cybex decided to install an ERP system (from PeopleSoft Inc.) for its supply chain planning and manufacturing applications. In conjunction with the software installation, the company analyzed and redesigned some of its business processes. It also reduced the number of suppliers from 1,000 to 550.

In the new system, customers' orders are accepted at the corporate Web site. Each order is electronically forwarded to one of the company's two specialized manufacturing plants. The ERP uses its *planning module* to calculate which parts are needed for each model. Then, the ERP's *product configurator* constructs, in just a few seconds, a component list and a bill-of-materials needed for each order.

The ERP system helps with other processes as well. For example, Cybex can e-mail to a vendor a detailed purchase order with engineering changes clearly outlined. These changes are visible to everyone; if one engineer is not at work, his or her knowledge remains in the system and is easy to find. Furthermore, dealers now know that they will get deliveries in less than two weeks. They can also track the status of each order (see www.*peopletalkonline.com*, July–September 2003), which allows Cybex to provide superb customer care.

The system also helps Cybex to better manage its 550 suppliers. For example, the planning engine looks at price variations across product lines, detecting opportunities to negotiate price reductions by showing suppliers that their competitors offer the same products at lower prices. Also, by giving suppliers projected long- and short-term production schedules, Cybex helps ensure that all parts and materials are available when needed. This also reduces the inventory level at Cybex. Furthermore, suppliers that cannot meet the required dates are replaced after quarterly reviews.

Despite recent intense industry price-cutting, Cybex has remained very profitable, mainly due to its improved supply chain. Some of the most impressive results were the following: Cybex cut its bill-of-material count from thousands to hundreds; reduced the number of vendors from 1,000 to 550; cut paperwork by two-thirds; and reduced build-to-order time from four to two weeks.

Implementing the system cost money, of course. In addition to the cost of the software, the technology staff increased from three to 12. Yet the company feels that the investment was worthwhile, especially because it provided for much greater harmony between Cybex and its customers and suppliers.

Sources: Compiled from M. Sullivan et al., "Case Studies: Digital Do-Overs," *Forbes.com* (October 7, 2002), and from press releases at *cybex.com*.

QUESTIONS

1. What are the relationships between the EC applications and ERP?
2. What is the role of the planning module?
3. What are the critical success factors for implementation?

---

areas of order processing, tracking, and invoicing. According to *cnet.com* (site accessed February 16, 2001), SAP gave Whirlpool a red light twice prior to the date on which the project would go live, saying the supply chain software was not ready, but Whirlpool ignored the signals.

EXAMPLE   *Did ERP Bankrupt FoxMeyer?* FoxMeyer, a **SVC** major distributor of prescription drugs to hospitals and pharmacies, filed for bankruptcy in 1996. In August 2001 FoxMeyer sued both SAP and Accenture Consulting for $500 million each, claiming that the ERP system they constructed led to its demise. Many customers sued FoxMeyer as well. (See the complete case in Online File W8.7.)

wiley.com/college/turban

ACC | **EXAMPLE** | *Gore's ERP Cost Too Much.* W. L. Gore and Associates filed a lawsuit against PeopleSoft and Deloitte & Touche because the ERP project that the two companies developed for W.L Gore cost twice the original estimate. The cost runup was due to difficulties in integration and special requirements for the ERP.

According to *thespot4sap.com*, in order to avoid failures and ensure success, it is necessary for the partners involved in ERP implementation (the software vendor, the management consultant, the implementing company, and the support-service vendors) to hold open and honest dialogue at the start of each project. Included in this initial dialogue should be consideration of the following factors: the company's expectations; the ERP product capabilities and limitations; the level of change the company has to go through to make the system fit; the level of commitment within the organization to see the project through to completion; the risks presented by politics within the organization, and (if applicable) the capabilities, responsibilities, and role of the implementing IT consultants. In addition, the organization and the IT consultants should nail down the critical success factors (CSFs) of the implementation. Failures can also be minimized if appropriate cost-benefit and cost justification is done in advance. Yet another way to avoid failures, or at least to minimize their cost, is to use application service providers (ASPs). Online File W8.8 describes the use of ASPs as a way to outsource ERPs. ERP implementation may be affected by cultural and global factors, which are described in the next chapter.

wiley.com/college/turban →

In whatever form it is implemented, ERP has played a critical role in getting organizations to focus on business processes, thus facilitating business process changes across the enterprise. For manufacturers, in particular, by tying together multiple plants and distribution facilities, ERP solutions have facilitated a change in thinking. This change in thinking has its ultimate expression in an enterprise that is better able to expand operations and manage its supply chain.

Before you go on . . .

1. Define ERP and describe its functionalities.
2. List the additions provided by second-generation ERP.
3. Describe the logic of integrating ERP and SCM software.
4. List some reasons for ERP failures.

8.5 CRM AND ITS SUPPORT BY IT

customer relationship management (CRM) *An enterprisewide effort to acquire and retain customers, often supported by IT.*

As explained in Chapter 1, **customer relationship management (CRM)** is an enterprisewide effort to acquire and retain customers. CRM recognizes that customers are the core of a business and that a company's success depends on effectively managing relationships with them (see Greenberg, 2002). CRM focuses on building long-term and sustainable customer relationships that add value both for the customer and the company. (See Romano and Fjermestad, 2001/2002, *crm-forum.com*, and *crmassist.com*.)

What Is CRM?

Greenberg (2002) and others provide more than 10 definitions of CRM. Why are there so many definitions? The reason is that CRM is new and still evolving. Also, it is an interdisciplinary field, so each discipline (e.g., marketing, management) defines CRM differently.

Evaluation of CRM.   In general, CRM is an approach that recognizes that customers are the core of the business and that the company's success depends on effectively managing relationships with them. In other words: "CRM is a business strategy to select and manage customers to optimize long-term value. CRM requires a customer-centric business philosophy and culture to support effective marketing, sales and services processes" (Thompson, 2003). It overlaps somewhat with the concept of *relationship marketing*, but not everything that could be called relationship marketing is in fact CRM. CRM is much broader in that it includes a *one-to-one* relationship between a customer and a seller. To be a genuine one-to-one marketer, a company must be willing and able to change its behavior toward a specific customer, based on what it knows about that customer. So, CRM is basically a simple idea: *Treat different customers differently*. It is based on the fact that no two customers are exactly the same.

CRM involves much more than just sales and marketing, because a firm must be able to change how its products are configured or its service is delivered, based on the needs of individual customers. (For example, see the Real-World Case at the end of this chapter.) Smart companies have always encouraged the active participation of customers in the development of products, services, and solutions. For the most part, however, being customer oriented has traditionally meant being oriented to the needs of the *typical* customer in the market—the average customer. In order to build enduring one-to-one relationships in a CRM initiative, a company must continuously interact with customers *individually*. One reason so many firms are beginning to focus on CRM is that this kind of marketing can create high customer loyalty and, additionally, help the firm's profitability. Involvement of almost all other departments and especially engineering (design), accounting, and operations is critical in CRM.

Types of CRM

We distinguish among three major types of CRM *activities* involved: operational, analytical, and collaborative. *Operational CRM* is related to typical business functions involving customer services, order management, invoice/billing, and sales/marketing automation and management. *Analytical CRM* involves activities that capture, store, extract, process, interpret, and report customer data to a corporate user, who then analyzes them as needed. *Collaborative CRM* deals with all the necessary communication, coordination, and collaboration between vendors and customers. Typical CRM activities and their IT support are listed in Online File W8.9.

wiley.com/college/turban

Classifications of CRM Applications.   Another way of looking at CRM is to focus on the tools used by the CRM applications. The Patricia Seybold Group (2002) distinguishes among customer-facing, customer-touching, and customer-centric intelligence CRM applications. These three categories of applications are described below and are shown in Figure 8.4 (page 264). The exhibit also shows how customers interact with these applications.

1. *Customer-facing applications.*   These include all the areas where customers interact with the company: call centers, including help desks; sales force automation; and field service automation. Such CRM applications basically automate the information flow or they support employees in these areas.

2. *Customer-touching applications.*   In this category, customers interact directly with the applications. Notable are self-service, campaign management, and general purpose e-commerce applications.

3. *Customer-centric intelligence applications.*   These are applications that are intended to analyze the results of operational processing and use the results of the analysis to improve CRM applications. Data reporting and warehousing and data mining are the prime topics here.

To this classification of CRM applications we add the following fourth category:

4. *Online networking applications.*   Online networking refers to methods that provide the opportunity to build personal relationships with a wide range of people in business. These include chat rooms and discussion lists.

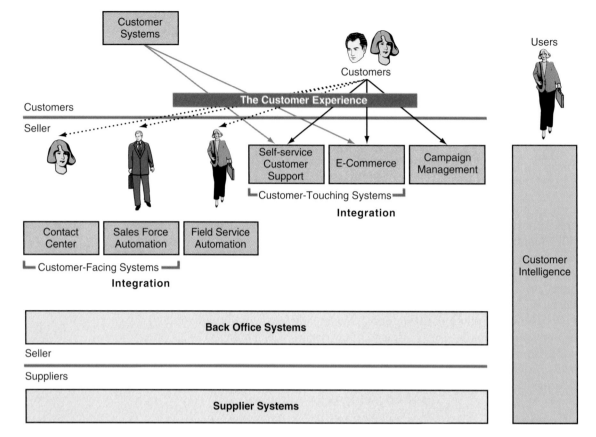

Figure 8.4 *CRM applications.*
[Source: Patricia Seybold Group, An Executive Guide to CRM *(March 21, 2002).]*

(Further details on the first three categories can be found at *psgroup.com*, in the free download of *An Executive's Guide to CRM.*)

E-CRM

e-CRM (electronic CRM) *The use of Web browsers, the Internet, and other electronic touchpoints to manage customer relationships.*

CRM has been practiced manually by corporations for generations. However, since the mid-1990s various types of information technologies have enhanced CRM. CRM technology is an evolutionary response to changes in the business environment, making use of new IT devices and tools. The term **e-CRM** (electronic CRM) was coined in the mid-1990s, when businesses started using Web browsers, the Internet, and other electronic touchpoints (e-mail, POS terminals, call centers, and direct sales) to manage customer relationships. E-CRM covers a broad range of topics, tools, and methods, ranging from the proper design of digital products and services to pricing and loyalty programs (e.g., see *e-sj.org, Journal of Service Research,* and *ecrmguide.com*). The use of e-CRM technologies has made customer service, as well as service to partners, much more effective and efficient.

Through Internet technologies, data generated about customers can be easily fed into marketing, sales, and customer service applications and analysis. E-CRM also includes online applications that lead to segmentation and personalization. The success or failure of these efforts can now be measured and modified in real time, further elevating customer expectations. In the world connected by the Internet, e-CRM has become a requirement for survival, not just a competitive advantage.

The Scope of E-CRM. We can differentiate three levels of e-CRM:

1. *Foundational service.* This includes the *minimum necessary* services such as Web site responsiveness (e.g., how quickly and accurately the service is provided), site effectiveness, and order fulfillment.

2. *Customer-centered services.* These services include order tracking, configuration and customization, and security/trust. These are the services that *matter the most* to customers.

3. *Value-added services.* These are *extra services* such as online auctions and online training and education.

Customer Service on the Web. A primary activity of e-CRM is customer service on the Web, which can take many forms. We describe some of these different kinds of Web-based customer services below. (For fuller details, see Greenberg, 2002.)

Search and Comparison Capabilities. With the hundreds of thousands of online stores, it is difficult for customers to find what they want, even inside a single electronic mall. Search and comparison capabilities are provided internally in large malls (e.g., *smartmall.biz*) or by independent comparison sites (*mysimon.com*). Some of these shopping aids were described in Chapter 4; for others, see Turban et al. (2004).

Free Products and Services. One approach companies use to differentiate themselves is to give away some product or service. For example, Compubank.com once offered free bill payments and ATM services. Companies can offer free samples over the Internet, as well as free entertainment, customer education, and more.

Technical and Other Information and Services. Interactive experiences can be personalized to induce the consumer to commit to a purchase or to remain a loyal customer. For example, General Electric's Web site provides detailed technical and maintenance information and sells replacement parts for discontinued models for those who need to fix outdated home appliances. Such information and parts are quite difficult to find offline. Another example is Goodyear, which provides information about tires and their use at *goodyear.com*. The ability to download manuals and problem solutions at any time is another innovation of electronic customer service.

Customized Products and Services. Dell Computer revolutionized the purchasing of computers by letting customers configure their own systems. This mass customization process is now used extensively by online vendors. Consumers are shown prepackaged "specials" and are given the option to "custom-build" products using software configurators.

Other companies have found ways that are unique to their industries to offer customized products and services online. Web sites such as *gap.com* allow you to "mix and match" your entire wardrobe. Web sites such as *hitsquad.com*, *musicalgreetings.com*, or *surprise.com* allow consumers to handpick individual titles from a library and customize a CD, a feature that is not offered in traditional music stores. Instant delivery of any digitized entertainment is a major advantage of EC.

Account or Order Status Tracking. Customers can view their account balances or check merchandise shipping status at any time from their computers or cell phones. If you ordered books from Amazon, for example, you can find the anticipated arrival date. Many companies follow this model and provide similar services.

All of these examples of customer service on the Web demonstrate an important aspect of CRM: a focus on the individual customer.

Other Tools for Customer Service. There are many innovative Web-related tools to enhance customer service and CRM. Here are the major ones.

Personalized Web Pages. Many companies allow customers to create their own individual Web pages. These pages can be used to record purchases and preferences, as well as problems and requests. For example, using intelligent agent techniques, American Airlines generates personalized Web pages for each of about 800,000 registered travel-planning customers.

Also, customized information (such as product and warranty information) can be efficiently delivered when the customer logs on to the vendor's Web site. Not only can the customer pull information as needed, but the vendor also can push information to the customer. Transaction information stored in the vendor's database, can be used to support marketing of more products, for example.

FAQs.   Frequently asked questions (FAQs) are the simplest and least expensive tool for dealing with repetitive customer questions. Customers use this tool by themselves, which makes the delivery cost minimal. However, any nonstandard question requires an e-mail.

E-Mail and Automated Response.   The most popular tool of customer service is e-mail. Inexpensive and fast, e-mail is used mostly to answer inquiries from customers but also to disseminate information (e.g., confirmations), to send product information, and to conduct correspondence regarding any topic.

Chat Rooms.   Another tool that provides customer service, attracts new customers, and increases customers' loyalty is a chat room. For example, retailer QVC offers a chat room where customers can discuss their QVC shopping experiences (see the Real-World Case at the end of this chapter).

Call Centers.   One of the most important tools of customer service is the *call center*. Call centers are typically the "face" of the organization to its customers. For example, investment company Charles Schwab's call center effectively handles over 1 million calls from investment customers every day.

New technologies are extending the functionality of the conventional call center to e-mail and to Web interaction. For example, *epicor.com* combines Web channels, such as automated e-mail reply, Web knowledge bases, and portal-like self-service, with call center agents or field service personnel. Such centers are sometimes called *telewebs*.

Troubleshooting Tools.   Large amounts of time can be saved by customers if they can solve problems by themselves. Many vendors provide Web-based troubleshooting software to assist customers in this task. The vendors dramatically reduce their expenses for customer support when customers are able to solve problems without further intervention of customer service specialists.

Wireless CRM.   Many CRM tools and applications are going wireless. As shown in Chapter 6, mobile sales force automation is becoming popular. In addition, use of wireless devices by mobile service employees is enabling these employees to provide better service while they are at the customer's site. Also, using SMS and e-mail from handheld devices is becoming popular as a means of improving CRM. Overall, we will see many of CRM services going wireless fairly soon. For example, the Expedia case (in Chapter 6, page 183) illustrates a wireless CRM application.

Lessons From
IT Failures

CRM Failures

As with many IT innovations, there have been a large number of CRM failures, which have been reported in the media. For example, according to *Zdnetindia.com/news* (2000), the founder and CEO of Customer.com estimated that 42 percent of the top 125 CRM sites experienced failures. Numerous failures have also been reported by *thinkanalytics.com, cio.com, CRM-forum.com*, and many more. However, according to *itgreycells.com*, CRM failures are declining, from a failure rate of up to 80 percent in 1998 to about 40 percent in 2003.

Some of the major issues relating to CRM failures are the following:

- Difficulty in measuring and valuing intangible benefits. There are only a few tangible benefits to CRM.
- Failure to identify and focus on specific business problems.

❑ Conduct a survey to determine how the organization responds to customers.

❑ Carefully consider the four components of CRM: sales, service, marketing, and channel/partner management.

❑ Survey how CRM accomplishments are measured; use defined metrics. Make sure quality, not just quantity, is addressed.

❑ Consider how CRM software can help vis-á-vis the organization's objectives.

❑ Decide on a strategy: refining existing CRM processes, or reengineering the CRM.

❑ Evaluate all levels in the organization but particularly frontline agents, field service, and salespeople.

❑ Prioritize the organization's requirements as one of the following: *must*, *desired*, and *not important*.

❑ Select appropriate CRM software. There are more than 60 vendors. Some (like Siebel) provide comprehensive packages; others provide only certain functions. Decide whether to use the best-of-breed approach or to go with one vendor. ERP vendors (e.g., PeopleSoft and SAP) also offer CRM products.

Source: Compiled from D. DeFazio, "The Right CRM for the Job," *Technologydecisions.com* (November 2000).

- Lack of active senior management (non-IT) sponsorship.

- Poor user acceptance. This issue can occur for a variety of reasons such as unclear benefits (i.e., CRM is a tool for management, but it may not help a rep sell more effectively) and usability problems.

- Trying to automate a poorly defined process.

Strategies to deal with these and other problems are offered by many. (For example, see *cio.com* for CRM implementation. Also see *conspectus.com* for "10 steps for CRM success.")

CRM failures can create substantial problems. Some companies are falling behind in their ability to handle the volume of site visitors and the volume of buyers. Managerial guidelines for implementing CRM and avoiding CRM failure are provided in Manager's Checklist 8.1.

WHAT'S IN IT FOR ME?

Accounting information systems (part of the back-end systems) are a central component in any ERP package. As a matter of fact, all large CPA firms actively consult with clients on ERP and other enterprise systems implementation, using thousands of specially trained accounting majors. Also, many supply chain issues, ranging from inventory management and valuation to risk analysis, are in the realm of accountants. Finally, many SCM software packages are available to support the accountant's job.

ACC

FOR THE ACCOUNTING MAJOR

Finance activities and modeling are integral portions of MRP II and ERP. Flows of funds (payments), at the core of most supply chains, must be done efficiently and effectively. Financial arrangements are especially important along global supply chains where currency conventions and financial regulations must be considered.

FIN

FOR THE FINANCE MAJOR

MKT

FOR THE MARKETING MAJOR

The downstream part of supply chains is where marketing, distribution channels, and customer service are conducted. An understanding of how this portion of the supply chain is related to the other portions is critical. Supply chain problems hurt customer satisfaction and marketing efforts, so you need to understand the nature of such problems and their solutions. Also, learning about CRM, its options, and implementation is important for designing customer services and advertising.

POM

FOR THE PRODUCTION/ OPERATIONS MANAGEMENT MAJOR

Supply chain management is usually the responsibility of the POM department since it involves material handling, inventory control, logistics, and other activities done by that department. The POM department started the trend of software integration with MRP. Many of the SCM innovations are in the realm of the POM department. As a matter of fact, almost all POM majors will deal with supply chain issues and its software support.

HRM

FOR THE HUMAN RESOURCES MANAGEMENT MAJOR

Interactions among employees along the supply chain, especially between business partners from different countries, are important for supply chain effectiveness. It is necessary, therefore, for the HRM expert to understand the flows of information and the collaboration issues in SCM. In addition, the HRM manager is usually actively involved in setting up the CRM program, which may serve employees as well.

SUMMARY

1. **Understand the essentials of enterprise systems and computerized supply chain management.** Enterprise systems are information systems that support several departments and/or the entire enterprise. The most notable is ERP, which supports supply chains. Supply chains connect suppliers to a manufacturing company, departments inside a company, and a company to its customers. The supply chain must be completely managed, from the raw material to the end customers. Typical supply chains involve three segments: upstream, internal, and downstream. Most supply chains are supported by a variety of IT application programs.

2. **Describe the various types of supply chains.** The major types of supply chains are integrated make-to-stock (manufacture to inventory), continuous replenishment, build-to-order, and channel assembly. Each type can be global or local.

3. **Describe some major problems in managing supply chains and some innovative solutions.** It is difficult to manage the supply chain due to the uncertainties in demand and supply and the need to coordinate several business partners' activities. One of the major problems is known as the bullwhip effect, in which lack of coordination results in large, unnecessary inventories. A number of solutions are supported by IT, such as appropriate inventory management, vertical integration, information sharing, VMI, supply chain hubs, supply chain collaboration, supply chain teams, virtual factories, and wireless lsolutions.

4. **Describe some major types of software that support activities along the supply chain.** During the last 50 years, software support for supply chain management has increased both in coverage and scope. MRP pulled together production, purchasing, and inventory management of intrerelated products. MRP II software added labor requirement and financial planning to the MRP model. The next step was to integrate routine transactions, including internal suppliers/customers and external suppliers/customers, in ERP and extended ERP software. The latest step in the evolution of integrated supply chain software is the addition of business intelligence and CRM applications.

5. **Describe the need for integrated software and how ERP does it.** ERP software, which is designed to improve standard business transactions, is enhanced with decision-support capabilities as well as Web interfaces, and it provides an integrated framework of all functional activities in the enterprise. ERP enables different functional applications to work seamlessly so that data can flow automatically (from production to marketing, for example). ERP also provides easy interfaces to legacy systems as well as to partners' systems.

6. **Describe CRM and Its support by IT.** CRM is an enterprisewide activity through which an organization takes care of its customers and their needs. It is based on the idea of one-to-one relationships with customers. CRM is done by providing many services, most of which are IT-supported and many of which are delivered on the Web.

INTERACTIVE / LEARNING

Increasing Sales, Decreasing Inventory, Improving Productivity

Go to the Interactivities section on the Student Web Site and access Chapter 8: Enterprise-wide Systems. There you will find an animated simulation of an ERP system, as well some hands-on activities that visually explain business concepts in this chapter.

More Resources

More resources and study tools are located on the Student Web Site. You'll find additional chapter materials and links to organizations, people and technologies for each chapter. In addition, self-quizzes that provide individualized feedback are available for each chapter.

Instructions for accessing the Interactivities on the Student Web Site:

1. Go to wiley.com/college/turban
2. Select Turban Rainer Potter's *Introduction to Information Technology, Third Edition*
3. Click on Student Resources Site, in the toolbar on the left
4. Click on Interactivities Web Site
5. Click on Interactivities Web Site and use your password to enter the site (your password card is located in the inside cover of your textbook)

DISCUSSION QUESTIONS

1. Distinguish between ERP and SCM software. In what ways do they complement each other? Relate them to system integration.
2. Discuss how cooperation between a company that you are familiar with and its suppliers can reduce inventory cost.
3. Find examples of how organizations improve their supply chains in two of the following: manufacturing, hospitals, retailing, education, construction, agribusiness, and shipping. Discuss the benefits to the organizations.
4. It is said that supply chains are essentially "a series of linked suppliers and customers; every customer is in turn a supplier to the next downstream organization, until the ultimate end-user." Explain. Use of a diagram is recommended.
5. Explain the bullwhip effect. In which type of business it is likely to occur most? How can the effect be controlled?
6. Discuss why Web-based call centers are critical for a successful CRM.

PROBLEM-SOLVING ACTIVITIES

1. Identify the supply chain(s) and the flow of information described in the opening case. Draw it. Also, answer the following.
   a. "The company's business is not to make the product, but to sell the product." Explain this statement.
   b. Why was it necessary to use IT to support the change?
   c. Identify all the segments of the supply chain.
   d. Identify all supporting information systems in this case.
2. Enter *aberdeen.com* and observe its "online supply chain community" (go to *supply chain access*). Most of the information there is free. Prepare an outline of the major resources available in the site.
3. Go to a bank and find out the process and steps of obtaining a mortgage for a house. Draw the supply chain. Now assume that some of the needed information, such as the value of the house and the financial status of the applicant, is found in a publicly available database (such a database exists in Hong Kong, for example). Draw the supply chain in this case. Explain how such a database can shorten the loan approval time.

INTERNET ACTIVITIES

1. Enter *ups.com*. Examine some of the IT-supported customer services and tools provided by the company. Write a report on how UPS contributes to supply chain improvements.
2. Enter *supply-chain.org*, *cio.com*, *findarticles.com*, and *google.com* and search for recent information on supply chain management integration.
3. Enter one or more of the following Web sites: *logictool.com*, *isourceonline.com*, *supplychaintoday.com*, and *tilion.com*. Find information on the bullwhip effect and on the strategies and tools used to lessen the effect.
4. Enter *mySap.com*. Identify its major components. Also review the Advanced Planning and Optimization tool. How can each benefit the management of a supply chain?
5. Enter *i2.com* and review its SCM products that go beyond ERP. Examine the OCN Network and Rhythm. Write a report.
6. Enter *siebel.com*. View the demo on e-business. Identify all e-business–related initiatives. Why is the company considered as the leader of CRM software?
7. Enter *anntaylor.com* and identify the customer service activities offered there.

TEAM ASSIGNMENTS

1. Each group in the class will be assigned to a major ERP/SCM vendor such as SAP, PeopleSoft, Oracle, etc. Members of the groups will investigate topics such as: (a) Web connections, (b) use of business intelligence tools, (c) relationship to CRM and to EC, (d) major capabilities, and (e) availability of ASP services by the specific vendor.

   Each group will prepare a presentation for the class, trying to convince the class why the group's software is best for a local company known to the students (e.g., a supermarket chain).
2. Assign each team to one type of supply chain, such as build-to-order or continuous replenishment. The team should find two examples of the assigned type, draw the supply chains, and explain the IT and EC solutions used.
3. Create groups to investigate the major CRM software vendors, their products, and the capabilities of those products in the following categories. (Each group represents a topical area or several companies.)
   - Sales force automation (Oracle, Onyx, Siebel, Saleslogix, Pivotal)
   - Call centers (Clarify, LivePerson, NetEffect, Inference, Peoplesoft)
   - Marketing automation (Annuncio, Exchange Applications, MarketFirst, Nestor)
   - Customer service (Brightware, Broadvision, Primus, Silknet)
   - Sales configuration (Exactium, Newtonian)

   Start with *searchcrm.com* and *crmguru.com* (to ask questions about CRM solutions). Each group must present arguments to the class to convince class members to use the product(s) the group investigated.

REAL-WORLD CASE   QVC PROVIDES SUPERB CRM

MKT

QVC (*qvc.com*) is known for its TV shopping channels. The leading TV-based mail-order service, QVC is selling on the Web too. It is a very competitive business, since retail selling is done in several marketing channels. In 2000, QVC served more than 6 million customers, answered 125 million phone calls, shipped about 80 million packages, and handled more than a billion page views on its Web site. QVC's business strategy is to provide top-notch customer service in order to keep its customers loyal. QVC also appointed a senior vice president for customer service. The problem was how to provide top-notch customer care and do it economically.

To manage its huge business (about $4.4 billion a year), QVC must use the latest IT support. For example, QVC operates four state-of-the-art call centers, one for overseas operations. However, before using technology to boost loyalty and sales, QVC had to develop a strategy to put its customers at the core of corporate decision making. "Exceeding the expectations of every customer" is a sign you can see all over QVC's premises. As a mat-

ter of fact, the acronym QVC stands for Quality, Value, and Convenience—all from the customers' perspective.

In pursuit of this goal, QVC created a truly excellent service organization. Among other things, QVC provides education (demonstrating product features and functions), entertainment, and companionship. Viewers build a *social* relationship with show hosts, upon which the *commercial* relationship is built. Now QVC is also attempting to build a social relationship with its customers on the Web (see *qvc.com*).

QVC knows that building trust on the TV screen is necessary, but not sufficient to draw customers. So everyone in the company contributes to the customer service goals. QVC's president checks customers' letters. All problems are fixed quickly. Everything is geared toward the long run. In addition, to make CRM work, QVC aligns senior executives, IT executives, and functional managers so that they work toward the same goals, collaborate, have plans that do not interfere with others' plans, and so forth. Also the company adopts the latest

IT applications and offers training to its customer service reps in the new applications and in CRM continuously.

QVC is using metrics to measure customer service. These include: friendliness of the call center reps; how knowledgeable the reps are about the products; clarity of the instructions about how to order and how to use the products purchased; the number of people a customer has to speak with to get a satisfactory answer; and how often a customer has to call a second time to get a problem resolved.

Data on customer service are collected in several ways, including tracking of telephone calls and Web-site movements. Cross-functional teams staff the call center, so complete knowledge is available in one place. Corrective actions are taken quickly, to prevent repeat problems in the future.

To get the most out of the call center's employees, QVC strives to keep them very satisfied. They must enjoy the work in order to provide excellent customer service. The employees are called "customer advocates," and they are handsomely rewarded for innovative ideas.

In addition to call centers, QVC uses computer-telephony integration technology (CTI), which identifies the caller's phone number and matches it to customer information in the database. This information pops up on the rep's screen when a customer calls. The rep can greet the customer by saying, "Nice to have you at QVC again, David. I see that you have been with us twice this year, and we want you to know that you are important to us. Have you enjoyed the jacket you purchased last June?"

To know all about the customer history, QVC maintains a large data warehouse. Customers' buying history is correlated by Zip code with psychodemographic data from Experian, a company that analyzes consumer information. This way, QVC can know instantly, for example, whether a new product is a hit with wealthy retirees or with young adults. The information is used for e-procurement, advertising strategy, and more. QVC also uses viral marketing (word-of-mouth of its loyal customers). In order not to bother its customers, QVC does not send any mail advertisements.

Sources: Compiled from "Nice Guys Finish First—Customer Relationship Management," *Darwin Magazine* (October 2000), and from *qvc.com* (accessed March 18, 2004).

QUESTIONS

1. Enter *qvc.com* and identify actions that the company takes to increase trust in its e-business. Also, look at all customer-service activities. List as many as you can find.

2. List the advantages of buying online versus buying over the phone after watching QVC. What are the disadvantages?

3. Enter the chat room of *qvc.com* and the bulletin board. What is the general mood of the participants? Are they happy with QVC? Why or why not? What is the advantage of having customers chat live online?

4. QVC is using a data warehouse to provide customer service (e.g., find what customers purchased in the past). Explain how this is done. The data warehouse now operates in real time. Why?

SCM, CRM, AND CLUB IT

Club IT's management has a good relationship with their suppliers, though occasionally running out of club soda or napkins or the expensive bulbs for their lighting systems reduces profits. Ruben remembers reading about SCM and ERP systems in his information technology class in college, but he's not really sure if Club IT is big enough to be concerned about managing its supply chain or planning enterprise-wide resource utilization. You are tasked with identifying opportunities to better manage inventory—from beverages to bulbs to blenders. First, though, you need to better understand a nightclub's supply chain.

ASSIGNMENT

1. Who is in Club IT's upstream supply chain? Identify products Club IT consumes in providing services to guests. Then, use a tool like Visio, Word or PowerPoint to draw a diagram that shows the flow of these goods through the supply chain to Club IT.

2. What are some potential problems in the supply chain? Remember, an oversupply of fruit juice is just as problematic as an undersupply. What kinds of information can be used by Club IT management to prevent these problems?

3. Club IT has a members' only card that gives perks to frequent guests to reward their loyalty. Currently, it is an entirely paper-based system. Investigate the possibilities of using CRM to provide even more recognition and service to frequent guests. For example, view a demonstration or attend an online "webinar" about CRM software and identify its benefits to Club IT. Find a demo or webinar by searching for *CRM* and *webinar* or *online demo*.

Go to wiley.com/college/turban to access the CLUB IT Web Site on the Student Web Site

Interorganizational and Global Information Systems

Chapter Preview

For many years information systems were used mostly *within* organizations. Interorganizational systems (IOSs)—information systems that connect two or more organizations—were few and confined mostly to travel, banking, and large corporations. This situation changed as the Internet and e-commerce grew in popularity. Information systems that involve two or more organizations can be very complex, especially global ones and those that involve many organizations. Yet the benefits can be significant, especially when the Internet and new technologies such as XML and Web Services are used. In this chapter we describe the various types of IOSs, the required infrastructure, and the major issues involved in IOS implementation.

Chapter Outline

9.1 Interorganizational Systems

9.2 Global Information Systems

9.3 B2B Exchanges and Hubs

9.4 Virtual Corporations and IT Support

9.5 Electronic Data Interchange (EDI)

9.6 Extranets, XML, and Web Services

9.7 IOS Implementation Issues

Learning Objectives

1. Define and classify IOSs.
2. Define and classify global information systems.
3. Present the major issues surrounding global information systems.
4. Describe B2B exchanges and hubs.
5. Describe virtual corporations and their IT support.
6. Describe EDI and EDI/Internet and their benefits and limitations.
7. Describe extranets, XML, and Web Services.
8. Present major IOS implementation issues.

HOW DELL IS USING WEB SERVICES TO IMPROVE ITS SUPPLY CHAIN

Dell Inc. (dell.com) has many assembly plants. In these plants, located in various countries and locations, Dell makes PCs, servers, printers, and other computer hardware. The assembly plants rely on third-party logistics companies (3PLs), called "vendor-managed hubs," whose mission is to collect and maintain inventory of components from all of Dell's component manufacturers (suppliers). The supply chain is shown in Figure 9.1.

In the past Dell submitted a weekly demand schedule to the 3PLs, who prepared shipments of specific components to the plants based on expected demand. Components management is critical to Dell's success for various reasons: Components become obsolete quickly, and their prices are constantly declining (by an average of 0.6 percent a week). So the fewer components a company keeps in inventory, the lower its costs. In addition, the costs of components make up about 70 percent of a computer's cost, so managing components' cost can have a major impact on the bottom line. Because it is expensive to carry, maintain, and handle inventories, it is tempting to reduce inventory levels as low as possible. However, some inventories are necessary, both at the assembly plants and at the 3PLs' premises. Without such inventories Dell cannot meet its "five-day ship to target" goal (computer must be on a shipper's truck no later than five days after an order is received).

To minimize inventories, it is necessary to have considerable collaboration and coordination among all parties of the supply chain. For Dell, the supply chain includes hundreds of suppliers that are in many remote countries, speak different languages, and use different hardware and software platforms. Many have incompatible information systems that do not "talk" to each other.

In the past Dell suppliers operated with 45 days of lead time. (That is, they had 45 days to ship an order after it was received.) To keep production lines running, Dell had to carry 26 to 30 hours of buffer inventory at the assembly plants, and the 3PLs

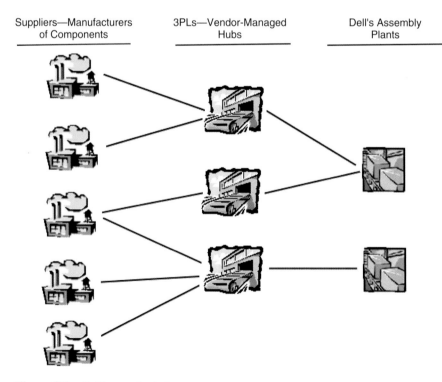

Suppliers—Manufacturers of Components   3PLs—Vendor-Managed Hubs   Dell's Assembly Plants

Figure 9.1 *Dell's supply chain.*
[Source: Drawn by E. Turban.]

had to carry 6 to 10 days of inventory. To meet its delivery target, Dell created a 52-week demand forecast that was updated every week as a guide to its suppliers.

All of these inventory items amount to large costs (due to the millions of computers produced annually).

THE IT SOLUTION

Dell started to issue updated manufacturing schedules for each assembly plant, every 2 hours. These schedules reflected the actual orders received during the previous two hours. The schedules list all the required components, and they specify exactly when components need to be delivered, to which plant, and to what the location of the plant (building number and exact door dock). These manufacturing schedules are published as Web Services and can be accessed by suppliers via Dell's extranet. Then, the 3PLs have 90 minutes to pick, pack, and ship the required parts to the assembly plants.

Dell introduced another Web Services system that facilitates checking the reliability of the suppliers' delivery schedules early enough in the process that corrective actions can take place. Dell can, if necessary, temporarily change production plans to accommodate delivery difficulties of components.

THE RESULTS

As a result of the new systems, inventory levels at Dell's assembly plants have been reduced from 30 hours to between 3 and 5 hours. This improvement represents a reduction of about 90 percent in the cost of keeping inventory. The ability to lower inventories also resulted in freeing up floor space that previously was used for storage. This space is now used for additional production lines, increasing factory utilization (capacity) by a third.

The inventory levels at the 3PLs have also been reduced, by 10 to 40 percent, increasing profitability for all. The more effective coordination of supply-chain processes across enterprises has also resulted in cost reduction, more satisfied Dell customers (who get computers as promised), and less obsolescence of components (due to lower inventories). As a result, Dell and its partners have achieved a more accelerated rate of innovations, which provides competitive advantage. Dell's partners are also happy that the use of Web Services has required only minimal investment in new information systems.

Sources: Compiled from J. Hagel, III, *Out of the Box* (Boston: Harvard Business School Press, 2002), and from *dell.com*, press releases (2000–2003).

WHAT WE LEARNED FROM THIS CASE

Dell's success depends in large part on the information systems that connect its manufacturing plants with its suppliers and logistics providers. The construction and operation of interorganizational information systems (IOSs) that serve two or more organizations is the subject of this chapter. In today's economy, such IOSs often are global. A new interorganizational information technology, Web Services, has been successfully applied to improve the information systems that connect Dell and its vendors and the vendors and their parts' and components' manufacturers. To achieve efficient and effective communication of information, companies may select technologies such as EDI and extranets, both of which are described in this chapter. Also described are some relevant IOS implementation issues.

9.1 INTERORGANIZATIONAL SYSTEMS

An **interorganizational information system (IOS)** involves information flow among two or more organizations. Its major objective is efficient processing of transactions, such as transmitting orders, bills, and payments. As we will show in this chapter, an IOS can be local or global, dedicated to only one activity (e.g., transfer of funds) or intended to support several activities (e.g., to facilitate trade, communication, and collaboration).

interorganizational information system (IOS) *An information system that supports information flow among two or more organizations.*

Interorganizational systems have developed in direct response to two business pressures (drivers): the desire to reduce costs and to improve the effectiveness and timeliness of business processes. More specifically, by connecting the information systems of business partners, IOSs enable both partners to: reduce the costs of routine business transactions; improve the quality of the information flow by reducing or eliminating errors; compress cycle time in the fulfillment of business transactions; eliminate paper processing and its associated inefficiencies and costs; and make the transfer and processing of information easy for users.

A major characteristic of an IOS is that the customer–supplier relationship frequently is determined in advance (as in the case of Dell), with the expectation that it will be ongoing. Advance arrangements result in agreements between organizations on the nature and format of the business documents and payments that will be exchanged. Both parties also know which communication networks will be integral to the system. Interorganizational systems may be built around privately or publicly accessible networks.

When IOSs use telecommunications companies for communication, they typically employ *value-added networks (VANs)*. These are *private*, third-party networks that can be tailored to specific business needs. However, use of *publicly accessible* networks is growing with the increased use of the Internet.

Types of Interorganizational Systems

Interorganizational information systems include a variety of business activities, from data interchange to messaging services to funds transfers. The most prominent types of interorganizational systems are the following.

- *B2B trading systems.* These systems are designed to facilitate trading between (among) business partners. The partners can be in the same or in different countries. B2B trading systems were covered in Chapter 5, where we described both company-centric (private) e-marketplaces and many-to-many public exchanges.
- *Global systems.* Global information systems connect two or more companies in two or more countries. The airline reservations system, SABRE, is an example of a huge global system.
- *Electronic funds transfer (EFT).* In EFT, telecommunications networks transfer money among financial institutions.
- *Groupware.* Groupware technologies (Chapter 4) facilitate communication and collaboration between and among organizations.
- *Integrated messaging.* A single transmission system can be used to deliver electronic mail and fax documents between organizations (see Chapter 4).
- *Shared databases.* Trading partners sometimes share databases in order to reduce time in communicating information between parties and to arrange cooperative activities (see Chapters 4, 5, and 9).
- *Systems that support virtual corporations.* These IOSs provide support to virtual corporations—two or more business partners, in different locations, sharing costs and resources to provide a product or service.

IOS Support Technologies

IOSs are also classified by the technology used. Four major IOS technologies are described in this chapter. They are:

- *Electronic data interchange (EDI).* The electronic movement of business documents between business partners. EDI can be Internet-based, in which case it is known as EDI/Internet.
- *Extranets.* Extended intranets that link business partners.

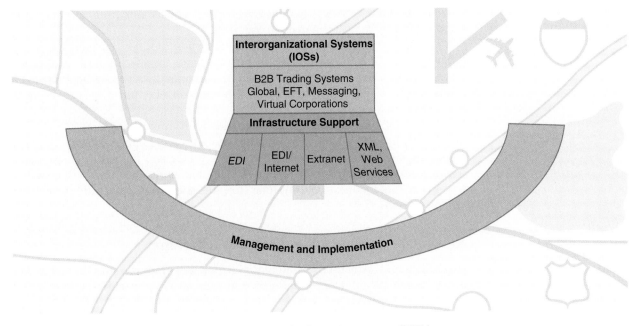

Figure 9.2   *Roadmap: Overview of interorganizational information systems (IOSs).*

- *XML.* An emerging B2B standard, promoted as a companion or even a replacement for EDI systems.
- *Web Services:* the emerging technology for integrating B2B and intrabusiness applications.

The IOS systems and their supporting technologies are the subject of this chapter. Figure 9.2 provides an overview of these topics and their relationships.

Before you go on . . .

1. Define an interorganizational information system (IOS).
2. List the major types of IOSs.
3. List the IT technologies that can support IOSs.

9.2 GLOBAL INFORMATION SYSTEMS

Interorganizational systems that connect companies located in two or more countries are referred to as **global information systems**. Multinational companies, international companies, and virtual global companies typically need global information for their B2B operations. Companies that have global B2C operations usually use the Internet.

Multinational companies are those that operate in several countries. Examples are Coca-Cola, McDonald's, IBM, and SAP/AG (a German company). Multinational organizations may have sales offices and/or production facilities in several countries. They may conduct operations in locations where factory workers are plentiful and inexpensive, or where highly skilled employees are available at low salaries, or where there is a need to be close to the market. SAP/AP, for example, has a large research and development division in Silicon Valley, California, and distribution and sales offices in dozens of countries.

International companies are those that do business with other companies in different countries. For example, Toyota Motor Company (Japan) works with many sup-

global information systems *Interorganizational systems that connect companies located in two or more countries.*

pliers in the United States. Boeing Corporation solicits bids from and does contract work with manufacturers in over 40 countries.

Virtual global companies are joint ventures whose business partners are located in different countries. The partners form a company for the specific purpose of producing a product or service. Such companies can be temporary, with a one-time mission (such as building an oil pipeline), or they can be permanent. (For more on virtual companies, see Section 9.4.)

All of the above companies use some global information systems. Global systems involve multiple organizations in multiple countries. Examples include airline reservation systems such as SABRE (*sabre.com*), police and immigration systems, electronic funds transfer (EFT) systems (including networks of ATMs), and many commercial and educational systems for international organizations such as the United Nations.

Benefits of Global Information Systems

Regardless of its structure, a company with global operations relies heavily on IT. The major benefits of global information systems for such organizations, made possible by IT, are:

1. *Effective communication at a reasonable cost.* The partners are far from each other, yet they are able to work together, make decisions, monitor transactions, and provide controls. Business partners communicate through e-mail, EDI, and extranets. Communication is even more critical if the partners speak different languages. Intelligent IT systems can provide automatic translation.

2. *Effective collaboration to overcome differences in distance, time, language, and culture.* Collaboration can be enhanced with groupware software (Chapter 6), group decision support systems (see Chapter 11), extranets, and teleconferencing devices (Chapter 6).

3. *Access to databases of business partners and ability to work on the same projects while their members are in different locations.* Information technologies such as video teleconferencing and screen sharing (Chapter 6) are useful for this purpose.

Issues in Global IS Design

The task of designing any effective interorganizational information system is complicated. It is even more complex when the IOS is a global system, because of differences in cultures, economies, and politics among parties in different countries.

Although the potential for a global economy certainly exists, some countries are erecting artificial borders through local language preference, local regulation, and access limitations. In addition, barriers of various sorts must be dealt with before global information systems can achieve their potential. Some issues to consider in designing global IOSs are cultural differences, localization, economic and political differences, and legal issues.

Cultural Differences.   *Culture* consists of the objects, values, and other characteristics of a particular society. It includes many different aspects ranging from tradition, to legal and ethical issues, to what information is considered offensive. When companies plan to do business in countries other than their own, they must consider the cultural environment. A well-known example is GM's car Nova. *No va* means "no go" in Spanish. GM did not pay attention to this issue, and the model's sales in Spanish-speaking countries suffered as a result.

Localization.   Many companies use different names, colors, sizes, and packaging for their overseas products and services. This practice is referred to as *localization*. In order to maximize the benefits of global information systems, the localization approach should also be used in the design and operation of such systems. For example, many Web sites offer different language and/or currency options, as well as special content. Europcar, for example, has more than 40 Web portals, each in its own language (see page 236).

Economic and Political Differences. Countries also differ considerably in their economic and political environments. One result of such variations is that the information infrastructures may differ from country to country. For example, many countries own the telephone services; others control communications very tightly. France, for example, insisted for years that French should be the sole language on French Web sites. Additional languages are now allowed, but French must also appear in every site. China controls the content of the Internet, blocking some Web sites from being viewed in China.

Legal Issues. Legal systems differ considerably among countries. Examples are copyrights, patents, computer crimes, file sharing, privacy, and data transfer. All of these issues have the potential to affect what is transmitted via global information systems, and so they must be considered. The impact of legal, economic, and political differences on the design and use of global information systems can be clearly seen in the issue of cross-border data transfer.

Transfer of Data across International Borders. Several countries, such as Canada and Brazil, impose strict laws to control **cross-border data transfer**, the flow of corporate data across nations' borders. These countries usually justify their laws as protecting the privacy of their citizens, since corporate data frequently contain personal data. Other justifications are intellectual property protection and keeping jobs within the country by requiring that data processing be done there.

cross-border data transfer *The flow of corporate data across nations' borders.*

The transfer of information in and out of a nation raises an interesting legal issue: Whose laws have jurisdiction when records are in a different country for reprocessing or retransmission purposes? For example, if data are transmitted by a Polish company through a U.S. satellite to a British corporation, whose laws control what data, and when? In order to solve some of these issues, governments are developing laws and standards to cope with the rapid increase of information technology, and international efforts to standardize these laws and standards are underway (e.g., see *www.oecd.org*). Some issues of cross-border data transfer are shown in Online File W9.1.

wiley.com/college/turban

Characteristics and Problems along Global Supply Chains

A special issue for global companies and their global information systems is how to optimize their supply chains. Supply chains that involve suppliers and/or customers in other countries are referred to as *global supply chains* (e.g., see Harrison, 2001, and Handfield and Nichols, 1999). E-commerce has made it much easier to find suppliers in other countries (e.g., by using electronic bidding) as well as to find customers in other countries (see Handfield et al., 2002, and Turban et al., 2004).

Global supply chains are usually longer than domestic ones, and they may be complex. Therefore, interruptions and uncertainties are likely. Some of the issues that may create difficulties in global supply chains are legal issues, customs fees and taxes, language and cultural differences, fast changes in currency exchange rates, and political instabilities. An example of difficulties in a global supply chain can be seen in IT's about Business 9.1 (page 280).

Information technologies have proven to be extremely useful in supporting global supply chains, but one needs to carefully design global information systems (Harrison, 2001). For example, TradeNet in Singapore connects sellers, buyers, and government agencies via electronic data interchange (EDI). (TradeNet's case is described in detail in Online File W9.2.) A similar network, TradeLink, is operating in Hong Kong, using both EDI and EDI/Internet and attempting to connect about 70,000 potential trading partners.

wiley.com/college/turban

IT's ABOUT BUSINESS

[MKT]

9.1: LEGO Struggles with Global Issues

Lego Company of Denmark *lego.com* is a major producer of toys, including electronic ones. It is the world's best-known toy manufacturer (voted as "the toy of the century") and has thousands of Web sites created by fans all over the world.

In 1999 the company decided to market its Lego Mindstorms on the Internet. This product is a unique innovation. Its users can build a *Lego robot* using more than 700 traditional Lego elements, program it on a PC, and transfer the program to the robot. Lego sells its products in many countries using several regional distribution centers.

When the decision to do global electronic commerce was made, the company had the following concerns. (Note that although this is a B2C example, many of the problems are common to B2B as well.)

- It did not make sense to go to all countries, since sales are very low in some countries and some countries offer no logistical support services. In which countries should Lego sell the product?
- A supportive distribution and service system would be needed for e-commerce sales, including returns and software support.
- There was an issue of merging the offline and online operations versus creating a new centralized unit, which seemed to be a complex undertaking.
- Existing warehouses were optimized to handle distribution to commercial buyers, not to individual customers. E-commerce sales to individual customers would need to be accommodated.
- It would be necessary to handle returns around the globe.
- Lego products were selling in different countries in different currencies and at different prices. Should the product be sold on the Net at a single price? In which currency? How would this price be related to the offline prices?
- How should the company handle the direct mail and track individual shipments?

- Invoicing must comply with the regulations of many countries.
- Should Lego create a separate Web site for Mindstorms? What languages should be used there?
- Some countries have strict regulations regarding advertising and sales to children. Also laws on consumer protection vary among countries. Lego needed to understand and deal with these differences.
- How should the company handle restrictions on electronic transfer of individuals' personal data?
- How should the company handle the tax and import duty payments in different countries?

In the rush to get its innovative product to market, Lego did not solve all of these issues before it introduced the direct Internet marketing. The resulting problems forced Lego to close the Web site for business in 1998. It took about a year to solve all global trade-related issues and eventually reopen the site. By 2001 Lego was selling online many of its products, priced in U.S. dollars, but the online service was available in only 15 countries.

As of 2003 Lego.com has been operating as an independent unit, allowing online design of many products (e.g., see "Train Configurator"). The site offers many Web-only deals, and it is visited by over 4 million unique visitors each day.

Sources: Compiled from *lego.com*, from L. Damsgaard and J. Horluck, "Designing www.LEGO.com/ shop: Business Issues and Concerns," case 500–0061, *European Case Clearing House* (2000), and from R. Stoll, "How We Built LEGO.com," *Practical Internet* (March 2003).

QUESTIONS

1. Visit Lego's Web site and see the latest online marketing activities.
2. Is the Web the proper way to go global?
3. Why does it make sense to sell the Lego products on the Internet? (See Chapter 5 for insights.)

IT provides not only EDI and other communication infrastructure options, but also online expertise in sometimes difficult and fast-changing regulations. IT also can be instrumental in helping businesses find trading partners (via electronic directories and search engines, as in the case of *alibaba.com* and *chemconnect.com*). In addition, IT can help solve language problems through use of automatic Web page translation (see Online File W9.3).

wiley.com/college/turban

In order to overcome logistics problems along the supply chain, especially a global one, companies are outsourcing these services to logistics vendors. Global information systems help enable tight communication and collaboration among supply chain members, as shown in IT's about Business 9.2.

IT'S ABOUT BUSINESS

POM

9.2: How BikeWorld Uses Global Information Systems to Fulfill Orders

BikeWorld (San Antonio, Texas) is a small company (16 employees) known for its high-quality bicycles and components, expert advice, and personalized service. The company opened its Web site (*BikeWorld.com*) in February 1996, using it as a way to expand its reach to customers outside of Texas, including other countries.

BikeWorld encountered two of Internet retailing's biggest problems: fulfillment and after-sale customer service. Sales of its high-value bike accessories over the Internet steadily increased, including global markets. But the time BikeWorld spent processing orders manually, shipping packages, and responding to customers' order status inquiries was overwhelming for the company.

In order to focus on its core competency (making bicycles and their components), BikeWorld decided to outsource its order fulfillment. FedEx offered reasonably priced, quality express delivery, exceeding customer expectations while automating the fulfillment process. Whit Snell, BikeWorld's founder, knew that his company needed the help that FedEx's global systems could provide: "To go from a complete unknown to a reputable worldwide retailer was going to require more than a fair price. We set out to absolutely amaze our customers with unprecedented customer service. FedEx gave us the blinding speed we needed," Snell said.

The nearby figure shows the five steps in the fulfillment process. (Explanations are provided in the figure.) Notice that the logistics vendor (FedEx), with its sophisticated information system, provides services to the customers (such as order tracking).

Four years after BikeWorld ventured online, its sales volume more than quadrupled. The company had sales of over $8 million in 2003 and is consistently profitable. Thanks to its outsourcing of order fulfillment, and to FedEx's world-class information systems, BikeWorld has a fully automated and scalable fulfillment system; has access to real-time order status data, which enhances customer service and leads to greater customer retention; and has the capacity to service global customers.

Source: Compiled from FedEx (2000).

QUESTIONS

1. Identify the necessary IOSs between FedEx and the customers.
2. Identify the necessary IOSs between BikeWorld and FedEx.
3. Visit *fedex.com* and find out how FedEx can help any company in global trade.
4. Describe the delivery process used by FedEx.

BikeWorld's order fulfillment process.
[Source: FedEx (2000).]

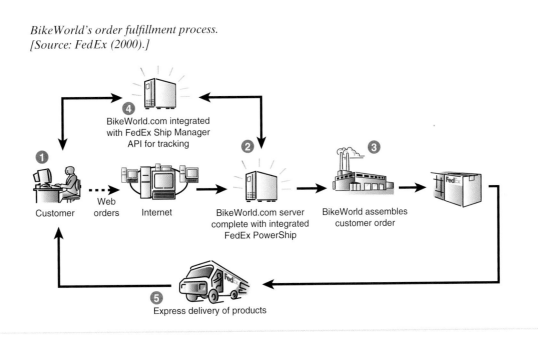

1 — Customer / Web orders / Internet

4 — BikeWorld.com integrated with FedEx Ship Manager API for tracking

2 — BikeWorld.com server complete with integrated FedEx PowerShip

3 — BikeWorld assembles customer order

5 — Express delivery of products

As IT technologies advance and global trade expands, more organizations will find the need to implement global information systems. We next look at two other types of IOSs (which sometimes are global)—B2B exchanges and hubs.

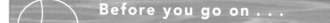

Before you go on . . .

1. Define a global information system.
2. List some of the difficulties in managing global supply chains.
3. How can global information systems facilitate global trade?

9.3 B2B EXCHANGES AND HUBS

IOSs are viewed by many as wireline or wireless connections between organizations. Actually they are much more than that: These systems provide for *all interactions* among organizations including communication, collaboration, and even trading. Two IT innovations that help organizations communicate, collaborate, and trade are B2B exchanges and hubs.

B2B Exchanges

Considerable support to B2B supply chains can be provided by electronic exchanges. *B2B exchanges*, as discussed in Chapter 5, can be either *private* (one buyer and many sellers, or one seller and many buyers) or *public* (many sellers and buyers). In either case, the communications and transactions are done on IOSs. The IOS in a private exchange is usually controlled by the sole seller or buyer; it is usually an extranet or EDI. In a public exchange, the IOS can be the Internet, usually with a virtual private network (VPN).

A system of public exchanges is shown in Figure 9.3. Notice that in this example there are three interconnected exchanges (designated by the ovals in the center of the figure). In other cases there may be only one exchange for an entire industry.

B2B public exchanges provide an alternative to private exchanges. As described in Chapter 5, the public exchange manager provides all the necessary information systems to

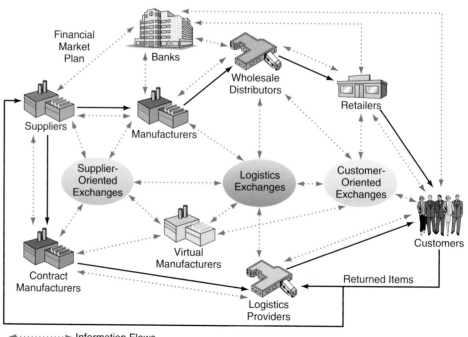

Figure 9.3 *Web-based supply chain involving trading exchanges.*

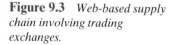

the participants. Thus, buyers and sellers merely have to "plug in" in order to trade. The technology used by the B2B exchange depends on its size and the nature of transactions.

B2B public exchanges are sometimes the initial point for contacts between business partners. Once such contact is made, the partners may move to a private exchange or to the private trading rooms provided by many public exchanges to do their subsequent trading activities.

Electronic Hubs

B2B exchanges are used mainly to facilitate trading among companies. In contrast, a *hub* is used to facilitate communication and coordination among business partners, frequently *along the supply chain*. Hubs are structured in such a way that each partner can access a Web site, usually a portal, which is used for an exchange of information. Furthermore, each partner can deposit new information, make changes, or get and leave messages. In some hubs it is possible to conduct trade as well. A structure of an electronic hub is shown in Figure 9.4. An example of a company that provides an electronic hub as well as some public exchange capabilities is Asite, as described in IT's about Business 9.3 (page 284).

Before you go on . . .

1. What is a B2B exchange?

2. Why is a B2B exchange considered an IOS?

3. Define a B2B hub and contrast it with an exchange.

4. List the major benefits of a hub to the participating companies. (Hint: See IT's about Business 9.3, page 284.)

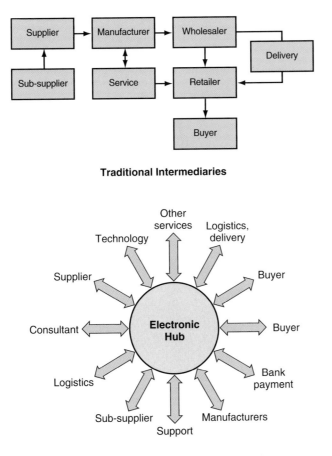

Traditional Intermediaries

Electronic Hub

Figure 9.4 *Electronic hub compared to traditional intermediaries.*
[Source: Drawn by E. Turban and J. Lee.]

IT'S ABOUT BUSINESS

9.3: Asite's B2B Exchange and E-Hub for the Construction Industry

Asite (*www.asite.com*) is a B2B exchange for the construction industry in the United Kingdom. The construction industry is typified by a high degree of physical separation and fragmentation, and communication among the members of the supply chain (e.g., contractors, subcontractors, architects, supply stores, and building inspectors) has long been a primary problem. Founded in February 2000 by leading players in the construction industry, Asite understands two of the major advantages of the Internet: the ability it provides to communicate more effectively, and the increase in processing power that Internet technologies make possible. Taking advantage of the functions of an online portal as information broker, Asite developed a comprehensive portal for the construction industry. The company's goal is to be the leading information and transaction hub in the European construction industry.

Asite drew on partner organizations with profound industry knowledge and expertise. It made the decision not to build its own technology, but to establish partnerships with technology vendors that have highly specialized products. It formed core partnerships with Commerce One, which provides the busi-

ness solution for the portal; Microsoft, which provides the technology platform and core applications; and Attenda, which designed and manages Asite's Internet infrastructure.

Asite set up seven interconnected marketplaces within its portal. These marketplaces serve the needs of the participants in the construction industry—building owners, developers, trade contractors, general contractors, engineers, architects, and materials suppliers—from design through procurement to materials delivery (see the nearby figure). Participating firms need nothing more sophisticated than a browser to connect to Asite's portal. This ease of access makes it particularly well suited to an industry such as construction, which is distinguished by a high proportion of small, and even single-person, firms.

Asite's partnerships allow it to seamlessly interact with other e-marketplaces. The open standards espoused by vendors in these e-marketplaces enable Asite's technology to be easily incorporated with participating firms' back-end technologies. Such linkages allow full visibility of the supply and demand chains.

The participants in Asite's E-Marketplace.
[Source: Aberdeen Group, Inc.]

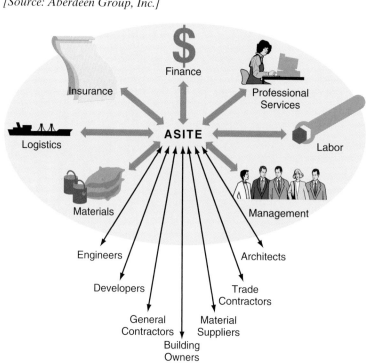

The combination of strong backing from industry participants, experienced management from the construction industry, and the commitment to working with best-of-breed technology infrastructure providers is helping construction firms streamline their supply chains.

Sources: Compiled from Aberdeen Group (2001) and *asite.com* (2004).

QUESTIONS

1. What type of IOS is this (per Section 9.1)?
2. What are the advantages to the participating companies?
3. Enter *asite.com* and read about any new developments (within the last 6 months).
4. What is the exchange's revenue model?

9.4 VIRTUAL CORPORATIONS AND IT SUPPORT

Another variation of an interorganizational information system is one that supports virtual corporations.

A **virtual corporation (VC)** is an organization composed of two or more business partners, in different locations, sharing costs and resources for the purpose of producing a product or service. The VC can be temporary, with a one-time mission such as launching a satellite, or it can be permanent. Permanent virtual corporations are designed to create or assemble a broad range of productive resources rapidly, frequently, and concurrently. Each partner in a VC creates a portion of a product or service, in an area in which they have special advantage (such as expertise or low cost). The major characteristics of VCs are listed in Online File W9.4.

The concept of VCs is not new, but recent developments in IT allow new implementations. The modern VC can be viewed as a *network* of creative people, resources, and ideas connected via online services and/or the Internet, who band together to produce products or services. In a VC the resources of the business partners remain in their original locations but are integrated for the VC's use. Because the partners are in different locations, they need IOSs to support communication and collaboration.

virtual corporation (VC) *An organization composed of two or more business partners, in different locations, sharing costs and resources for the purpose of producing a product or service; can be temporary or permanent.*

wiley.com/college/turban

How IT Supports Virtual Corporations

IT can support virtual corporations in several ways. The most obvious are those that allow communication and collaboration among the dispersed business partners. For example, e-mail, desktop videoconferencing, screen sharing, and several other groupware technologies (such as Lotus Notes) support interorganizational collaboration. Standard transactions are supported by EDI, EFT, and extranets. The Internet is the infrastructure for these and other technologies. Modern database technologies and networking permit business partners to access each other's databases. In general, most VCs cannot exist without information technology.

EXAMPLE   *Five Companies Join IBM's Ambra.* IBM's Ambra was formed to produce and market a PC clone. At Ambra's headquarters in Raleigh, North Carolina, 80 employees use global telecommunications networks to coordinate the activities of five companies that are partners in the virtual company.

Wearnes Technology of Singapore is doing engineering design and subsystem development services and manufacture for Ambra PC components. SCI Systems assembles the Ambra microcomputers in its assembly plants on a build-to-order basis from order data received by its computers from AI Incorporated. AI, a subsidiary of Insight Direct, a national telemarketing company based in Tempe, Arizona, receives orders for Ambra computers from customers over its 800-number telephone lines or its Web site. Merisel Enterprises provides the product and delivery database used by AI and handles Ambra order fulfillment and customer delivery. Finally, another IBM subsidiary provides field service and customer support.

POM

POM

| EXAMPLE | *No Need to Buy Office Furniture for Turnstone.*

Steelcase Inc. is a major U.S. maker of office furniture. It formed a virtual corporation subsidiary called Turnstone that sells its products through catalogs designed and printed by a third-party company (and now also available on the Web). Turnstone's customers e-mail or phone in credit card orders to a telemarketing company based in Denver, Colorado, which transmits the order data to computers at warehouses operated by Excel Logistics, Inc. in Westerville, Ohio. From there, subcontracted carriers ship the products to manufacturing plants. Excel's computer systems handle all order processing, shipment tracking, and inventory control applications. Marketing, financial management, and coordinating the virtual company's business partners are the only major functions left to Turnstone's managers.

Before you go on . . .

1. Define virtual corporations (VCs).

2. Describe the support IT provides to VCs.

9.5 ELECTRONIC DATA INTERCHANGE (EDI)

One of the early contributions of IT to facilitate B2B e-commerce and other IOSs is electronic data interchange (EDI).

Traditional EDI

EDI *A communication standard that enables the electronic transfer of routine documents between business partners.*

EDI is a communication standard that enables the electronic transfer of routine documents, such as purchasing orders, between business partners. It formats these documents according to agreed-upon standards. EDI has been around for about 30 years in the non-Internet environment.

EDI often serves as a catalyst and a stimulus to improve the standard of information that flows between organizations. It reduces costs, delays, and errors inherent in a manual document-delivery system.

Major Components of EDI.   The following are the major components of EDI:

- *EDI translators.* An EDI translator converts data into a standard format before it is transmitted.

- *Business transactions messages.* EDI primarily transfers messages about repetitive business transactions. These include purchase orders, invoices, credit approvals, shipping notices, confirmations, and so on.

- *Data formatting standards.* Because EDI messages are repetitive, it makes sense to use formatting (coding) standards. In the United States and Canada, EDI data are formatted according to the ANSI X.12 standard. An international standard developed by the United Nations is called EDIFACT.

The Process and Benefits of EDI.   The process of EDI (as compared with a non-EDI process) is shown in Figure 9.5. The figure shows that in EDI, computers talk to computers. Messages are coded using the standards before they are transmitted using a converter. Then, the message travels over a VAN or the Internet (secured). When received, the message is automatically translated into a business language.

The benefits of this process are that data entry errors are minimized (only one entry, and an automatic check by the computer), the length of the message can be shorter, the messages are secured, and EDI fosters collaborative relationships and

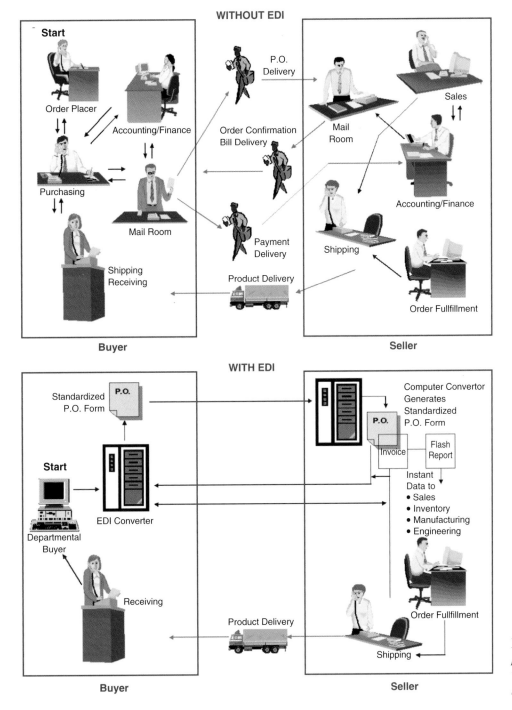

Figure 9.5 *Comparing purchasing order (PO) fulfillment with and without EDI. [Source: Drawn by E. Turban.]*

strategic partnerships. Other benefits are: reduced cycle time, better inventory management, increased productivity, enhanced customer service, minimized paper usage and storage, and increased cash flow (per *1edisource.com*).

Applications of Traditional EDI

Traditional EDI has changed the business landscape of many industries and large corporations. It is used extensively by large corporations, sometimes in a global network such as the one operated by General Electric Information System (which has over 100,000 corporate users). Well-known retailers such as Home Depot, Toys R Us, and Wal-Mart would operate very differently without EDI, because it is an integral and essential element of their business strategies. Thousands of global manufacturers, including Procter & Gamble, Levi Strauss, Toyota, and Unilever, have been using EDI to redefine relationships with their customers through such practices as quick-response retailing and just-in-time (JIT) manufacturing. These highly visible, high-impact applications of EDI by large companies have been extremely successful.

Limitations of Traditional EDI

However, despite the tremendous impact of traditional EDI among industry leaders, the set of adopters represented only a small fraction of potential EDI users. In the United States, where several million businesses participate in commerce every day, only about 100,000 companies have adopted traditional EDI. Furthermore, most of these companies have had only a small number of their business partners on EDI, mainly due to its high cost. Therefore, in reality, few businesses have benefited from traditional EDI.

Various factors held back more universal implementation of traditional EDI. For example: Significant initial investment is needed, and ongoing operating costs are high (due to use of expensive, private VANs). Another cost is the purchase of a converter, which is required to translate business transactions to EDI code. Other major issues for some companies relate to the fact that the traditional EDI system is inflexible. For example, it is difficult to make quick changes, such as adding business partners, and a long startup period is needed. Further, business processes must sometimes be restructured to fit EDI requirements. Finally, multiple EDI standards exist, so one company may have to use several standards in order to communicate with different business partners.

These factors suggest that traditional EDI—relying on formal transaction sets, translation software, and VANs—is not suitable as a long-term solution for most corporations. Therefore, a better infrastructure was needed; *Internet-based EDI* is such an infrastructure.

Internet-Based EDI

Internet-based (or Web-based) EDI is becoming very popular. Let's see why this is the case.

Why Internet-Based EDI?   When considered as a channel for EDI, the Internet appears to be a most feasible alternative for putting online B2B trading within reach of virtually any organization, large or small. There are a number of reasons for firms to create EDI ability over the Internet.

- *Accessibility.* The Internet is a publicly accessible network with few geographical constraints. Its largest attribute, large-scale connectivity (without the need for any special company networking architecture), is a seedbed for growth of a vast range of business applications.

- *Reach.* The Internet's global network connections offer the potential to reach the widest possible number of trading partners of any viable alternative currently available.

- *Cost.* The Internet's communication cost can be 40 to 70 percent lower than that of VANs. Transmission of sensitive data can be made secure with VPN (see Technology Guide 4).

- *Use of Web technology.* Using the Internet to exchange EDI transactions is consistent with the growing interest of business in delivering an ever-increasing variety of products and services via the Web. Internet-based EDI can complement or replace many current EDI applications.

- *Ease of use.* Internet tools such as browsers and search engines are very user-friendly, and most employees today know how to use them.

- *Added functionality.* Internet-based EDI has several functionalities not provided by traditional EDI, which include collaboration, workflow, and search engine capabilities (see Boucher-Ferguson, 2002). A comparison between EDI and EDI/Internet is provided in Figure 9.6.

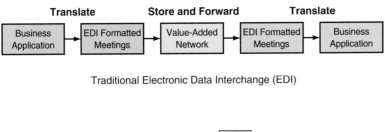

Traditional Electronic Data Interchange (EDI)

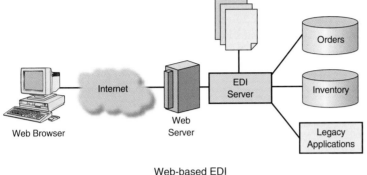

Web-based EDI

Figure 9.6 *Traditional and Web-based EDI.*
[Source: Drawn by E. Turban.]

Types of Internet-Based EDI. The Internet can support EDI in a variety of ways. For example, Internet e-mail can be used to transport EDI messages in place of a VAN. To this end, standards for encapsulating the messages within Secure Internet Mail Extension (S/MIME) exist and need to be used. Another way to use the Internet for EDI is to create an extranet that enables a company's trading partners to enter information into a Web form, the fields of which correspond to the fields in an EDI message or document.

Alternatively, companies can use a Web-based EDI hosting service, in much the same way that companies rely on third parties to host their EC sites. Harbinger Express (*harbinger.net*) is an example of those companies that provide third-party hosting services.

The Prospects of Internet-Based EDI

Companies that used traditional EDI in the past have had a positive response to Internet-based EDI. With traditional EDI, companies have to pay for network transport, translation, and routing of EDI messages into their legacy processing systems. The Internet serves as a cheaper alternative transport mechanism. The combination of the Web, XML, and Java makes EDI affordable even for small, infrequent transactions. Whereas EDI is not interactive, the Web and Java were designed specifically for interactivity as well as ease of use.

The following examples demonstrate the application range and benefits of Internet-based EDI.

EXAMPLE *Rapid Growth at CompuCom.* CompuCom Systems, a leading IT services provider, was averaging 5,000 transactions per month with traditional EDI. In just a short time after the transition to Web-based EDI, the company was able to average 35,000 transactions. The system helped the company to grow rapidly.

POM

EXAMPLE *Recruitment at Tradelink.* Tradelink of Hong Kong had a traditional EDI that communicated with government agencies regarding export/import transactions, but was successful in recruiting only several hundred of the potential 70,000 companies to the traditional system. After switching to an Internet-based system, Tradelink registered thousands of new companies to the system; hundreds were being added monthly, reaching about 15,000 by 2003.

POM

EXAMPLE *Better Collaboration at Atkins Carlyle.* Atkins Carlyle Corp. a wholesaler of industrial, electrical, and automotive parts, buys from 6,000 suppliers and has 12,000 customers in Australia. The large suppliers were using three different traditional-EDI platforms. By moving to an Internet-based EDI, the company was able to collaborate with many more business partners, reducing the transaction cost by about $2 per message.

Note that many companies no longer refer to their IOSs as EDI. However, the *properties* of EDI are embedded in new e-commerce initiatives such as collaborative commerce, extranets, PRM, and electronic exchanges. The new generation of EDI/ Internet is built around XML (see next section).

Before you go on . . .

1. Define EDI.

2. List the major benefits of EDI.

3. List the limitations of traditional EDI.

4. Explain the benefits of Internet-based EDI.

9.6 EXTRANETS, XML, AND WEB SERVICES

Companies involved in an IOS need to be connected in a secure and effective manner and their applications must be integrated with each other. This can be done by using extranets, XML, and Web services.

The Extranet

extranet *A network that links business partners to one another over the Internet by providing access to certain areas of each other's corporate intranets.*

In building IOSs, it is necessary to connect the internal systems of different business partners, which are usually connected to the partners' corporate intranets. A common solution is to use an extranet. Although extranets continue to evolve, they are generally understood to be networks that link business partners to one another over the Internet by providing access to certain areas of each other's corporate intranets. This arrangement is shown in Figure 9.7. (An exception to this definition is an extranet that

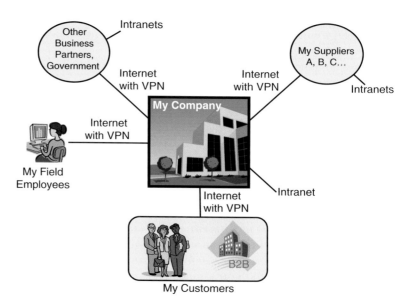

Figure 9.7 *The structure of an extranet.*

offers individual customers or suppliers one-way access to the intranet of a company.) The term *extranet* comes from "extended intranet."

The main goal of extranets is to foster collaboration between business partners. An extranet is open to selected B2B suppliers, customers, and other business partners, who access it through the Internet. Extranets enable people who are located outside a company to work together with the company's internally located employees. An extranet enables external business partners and telecommuting employees to enter the corporate intranet, via the Internet, to access data, place orders, check status, communicate, and collaborate.

The Components, Structure, and Benefits of Extranets. An extranet uses the same basic infrastructure components as the Internet, including servers, TCP/IP protocols, e-mail, and Web browsers. In addition, extranets use virtual private network (VPN) technology to make communication over the Internet more secure. The Internet-based extranet is far less costly than proprietary networks. It is a nonproprietary technical tool that can support the rapid evolution of electronic communication and commerce.

Why would a company allow a business partner access to its intranet? To answer this question, let's look at Dr. Pepper in the following example.

EXAMPLE *Dr. Pepper Notifies Bottlers of Price Changes.* [POM]
Dr. Pepper/Seven Up, the $1.7 billion division of Cadbury Schweppes, uses an extranet to improve efficiency for its diverse community of 1,400 independent and franchise bottlers. The Bottler Hub/Extranet is made available to Dr. Pepper's entire group of registered bottlers and retailers. The extranet has helped automate the process of communicating price changes to retailers, in real time.

Such automation was necessary for Dr. Pepper because the company depends on contract bottlers, who set the pricing of Dr. Pepper products in stores. Customer retailers such as Wal-Mart had complained about the bottlers' practice of faxing weekly price changes. Because many bottlers were mom-and-pop organizations and did not have the resources to modernize the process, Dr. Pepper decided to put in an extranet-based centralized system that would make the pricing information available online to retail outlets.

Dr. Pepper also uses its extranet for other purposes. The company also collects sales data online, enabling merchants to report how many cases of soda they sell. The data are used to measure sales growth and to analyze brands and packages that are sold by a bottler within a territory to the major retail chains. The information is also used to help the national accounts department find opportunities to sell more Dr. Pepper/Seven Up brands within a particular account.

As seen in the example, the extranet enables effective and efficient real-time collaboration. It also enables partners to perform self-service activities such as checking the status of orders or inventory levels.

Types of Extranets. Depending on the business partners involved and the purpose, there are three major types of extranets, described below.

A Company and Its Dealers, Customers, or Suppliers. Such an extranet is centered around one company. An example would be the FedEx extranet that allows customers to track the status of a package. To do so, customers use the Internet to access a database on the FedEx intranet. By enabling a customer to check the location of a package, FedEx saves the cost of having a human operator do that task over the phone. Similarly, Toshiba uses an extranet with its dealers, as shown in IT's about Business 9.4 (page 292).

IT's ABOUT BUSINESS POM MKT

9.4: Extranet Enables E-Commerce at Toshiba America

Toshiba America, a maker of fax machines and copiers, works with 300 dealers that sell its consumer-electronics products. Dealers who needed product parts used to place a daily telephone or fax order before 2:00 P.M. for next-day delivery; they were charged $25 per overnight shipment. To handle other needs, Toshiba's Electronic Imaging Division (EID) had to spend $1.3 million annually on communications. A cumbersome order-entry system was created in 1993, but no significant improvement was achieved.

In August 1997, Toshiba created a Web-based order-entry system for product parts using an extranet that connects to Toshiba's intranet. Dealers can now place orders for parts until 5:00 P.M. for next-day delivery. The company placed a physical warehouse in Memphis, Tennessee, near FedEx headquarters, to ensure quick delivery. On the company intranet, dealers can also check accounts receivable balances and pricing arrangements and can read service bulletins, press releases, and so on.

Once an order is submitted, a computer checks for the part's availability. If the part is available, the order is sent electronically to Toshiba's warehouse in Memphis. Once at the warehouse site, the order pops up on a handheld wireless radio frequency (RF) monitor for quick fulfillment. Within a few hours, the part is packed, verified, and packaged for FedEx, as shown in the nearby figure.

The extranet also allows sales reps to interact more effectively with dealers. The dealers can be kept up-to-date about orders and inventory and can manage their volume discount quotes online.

Using the IOS, Toshiba has cut the cost per express order to about $10. EID's networking costs

Toshiba's Automated Customer Service Process

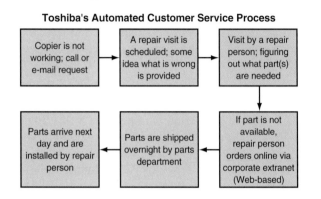

[*Source: Drawn by E. Turban.*]

have been reduced by more than 50 percent (to $600,000 a year). The low shipping cost results in overnight delivery of 98 percent of its orders, which increases customer satisfaction. As of 2003, the extranet was processing close to 90 percent of all dealers' orders.

Sources: Compiled from L. McCreary, "Toshiba America Information Systems Inc.," *CIO Web Business Magazine* (July 1999); and from *toshiba.com/US* (2003).

QUESTIONS

1. What are the benefits of Toshiba's intranet to the dealers?
2. What are the wireless devices used for?
3. What role does FedEx play in the order-fulfillment process?

An Industry's Extranet. The major players in an industry may team up to create an extranet that will benefit all. The world's largest industry-based, collaborative extranet is used by General Motors, Ford, and DaimlerChrysler. That extranet, called the Automotive Network Exchange (ANX), links the carmakers with more than 10,000 suppliers. The suppliers can then use a B2B marketplace, Covisint (*covisint.com*, now a division of Freemarkets.com) located on ANX, to sell directly and efficiently to the carmakers, cutting communications costs by as much as 70 percent.

Joint Ventures and Other Business Partnerships. In this type of extranet, the partners in a joint venture use the extranet as a vehicle for communications and collaboration. An example is Bank of America's extranet for commercial loans. The partners involved in making such loans are a lender, loan broker, escrow company, title company, and others. The extranet connects lenders, loan applicants, and the loan organizer, Bank of America. A similar case is Lending Tree (*lendingtree.com*), a company that provides mortgage quotes for your home and also sells mortgages online, which uses an extranet for its business partners (e.g., the lenders).

Benefits of Extranets.   As extended versions of intranets, extranets offer benefits similar to those of intranets, as well as other benefits. The major benefits of extranets include faster processes and information flow, improved order entry and customer service, lower costs (e.g., for communications, travel, and administrative overhead), and overall improvement in business effectiveness. Details of how these benefits are achieved are summarized in Online File W9.4.

Extranets are fairly permanent in nature, where all partners are known in advance. For on-demand relationships and one-time trades, companies can instead use B2B exchanges and hubs.

wiley.com/college/turban

XML

An emerging technology that supports IOSs and is being used to integrate systems of business partners is a language known as XML and its variants (see Raisinghani, 2002; Linthicum, 2000). **XML (eXtensible Markup Language)** is a simplified version of a general data description language known as SGML (Standard Generalized Markup Language). XML is used to improve compatibility between the disparate systems of business partners by defining the meaning of data in business documents. XML is considered "extensible" because the markup symbols are unlimited and self-defining. This new standard is promoted as a new platform for B2B and as a companion or even a replacement for EDI systems. It has been formally recommended by the World Wide Web Consortium (www.*W3C.org*).

XML (eXtensible Markup Language) *A simplified version of the general data description language, SGML; used to improve compatibility between the disparate systems of business partners by defining the meaning of data in business documents.*

XML Differs from HTML.   People sometimes wonder if XML and HTML are the same. The answer is, they are not. The purpose of HTML is to help build Web pages and display data on Web pages. The purpose of XML is to describe data and information. It does not say *how* the data will be displayed (which HTML does). XML can be used to send complex messages that include different files (and HTML cannot). See Technology Guide 2 for details.

Benefits of XML.   XML was created in an attempt to overcome limitations of EDI implementation discussed earlier. XML can overcome EDI barriers for three reasons:

1. *Flexibility.* XML is a flexible language. Its flexibility allows new requirements and changes to be incorporated into messages, thus expanding the rigid ranges of EDI.
2. *Understandability.* XML message content can be easily read and understood by people using standard browsers. Thus, message recipients do not need EDI translators. This feature enables SMEs to receive, understand, and act on XML-based messages.
3. *Less specialized.* In order to implement EDI, it is necessary to have highly specialized knowledge of EDI methodology. Implementation of XML-based technologies requires less-specialized skills.

The benefits of XML are demonstrated in IT's about Business 9.5 (page 294).

XML supports IOSs and makes B2B e-commerce a reality for many companies that were unable to use the traditional EDI. For more information see *xml.com.*

Another technology that supports IOSs and uses XML in its core is Web services.

Web Services

As described in Chapter 2, **Web Services** are universal, prefabricated business process software modules, delivered over the Internet, that users can select and combine through almost any device, enabling disparate systems to share data and services. Web Services can support IOSs by providing easy integration for different internal and external systems. (Also see Chapter 11 and Technology Guide 2.) Such

Web Services *Universal, prefabricated business process software modules, delivered over the Internet, that users can select and combine through almost any device, enabling disparate systems to share data and services.*

IT'S ABOUT BUSINESS [FIN] [ACC]

9.5: Fidelity Uses XML to Standardize Corporate Data

Fidelity Investments has made all its corporate data XML-compatible. The effort helped the world's largest mutual fund company and online brokerage eliminate up to 75 percent of the hardware and software devoted to middle-tier processing and speeded the delivery of new applications.

The decision to go to XML began when Fidelity developed its Powerstreet Web trading service. At the time, Fidelity determined it would need to offer its most active traders much faster response times than its existing brokerage systems allowed. The move to XML brought other benefits as well. For example, the company was able to link customers who have 401k plans, brokerage accounts, and IRAs under a common log-in. In the past, they required separate passwords.

Today, two-thirds of the hundreds of thousands of hourly online transactions at *fidelity.com* use XML to link the Web to back-end systems. Before XML, comparable transactions took seconds longer because they had to go through a different proprietary data translation scheme for each back-end system from which they retrieved data.

Fidelity's XML strategy is critical to bringing new applications and services to customers faster than rivals. By using XML as a common language into which all corporate data—from Web, database, transactional, and legacy systems—are translated, Fidelity is saving millions of dollars on infrastructure and development costs. Fidelity no longer has to develop translation methods for communications between the company's many systems. XML also has made it possible for Fidelity's different databases—including Oracle for its customer account information and IBM's DB2 for trading records—to respond to a single XML query.

Source: Compiled from "Fidelity Retrofits All Data for XML," *InternetWeek* (August 6, 2001); and from *fidelity.com.*

QUESTIONS

1. Why did Fidelity decide to use XML?
2. Why is it possible to develop applications faster with XML?
3. XML is used in this case for both B2B and B2C. Explain why.

integration enables companies to develop new applications, as the following example demonstrates.

[FIN] [POM] **EXAMPLE** *Web Services Facilitate Communication at Allstate.* The Allstate Financial Group, with 41,000 employees and $29 billion in annual sales, used Microsoft.NET to create AccessAllstate.com (*accessallstate.com*), a Web portal that allows its 350,000 sales representatives to access information about Allstate investment, retirement, and insurance products.

Before the portal was developed, independent agents had to call Allstate customer service representatives for information, and transactions were done via mail, fax, or phone. The necessary information resided on five policy-management information systems running on mainframe computers—substantial technology investments that Allstate was not willing to lose. But because Web Services enables easy communications between applications and systems, Allstate did not have to lose its mainframe investment. The agents use the Web portal to access the policy-management systems residing on the mainframe. Web Services make this connection seamless and transparent to the agents.

AccessAllstate.com has about 13,000 registered users and receives 500,000 hits per day. By unlocking the information on Allstate's proprietary mainframes, the company increases revenues and reduces costs. The Web portal eliminates the need to call the service center to perform common account service tasks. Allstate estimates that the portal will pay for itself through lower call center and mailing costs. The company is also making all printed correspondence available online via the portal. [*Source:* Compiled from B. Grimes, "Microsoft.NET Case Study: Allstate Financial Group," *PC Magazine* (March 25, 2003), and *allstate.com* (site accessed December 2, 2003).]

9.7 IOS IMPLEMENTATION ISSUES

Due to their complexity and the involvement of two or more organizations, IOSs and global systems face issues relating to partner relationship management, collaborative commerce, and facilitating global trade.

Partner Relationship Management

Every company that has business partners has to manage the relationships with them. Partners need to be identified, recruited, and maintained. Communication needs to flow between the organizations. Information needs to be updated and shared. Actually, all of the efforts that are made to apply CRM to relationships with business partners can be categorized as **partner relationship management (PRM)**.

Before the spread of Internet technology, there were few automated processes to electronically support business partnerships. Organizations were limited to manual methods of phone, fax, and mail. EDI was used by large corporations, but usually only with their largest partners. Also, there was no systematic way of conducting PRM. Internet technology changed the situation by offering a way to connect different organizations easily, quickly, and affordably.

What PRM Does.   PRM solutions connect companies with their business partners (suppliers, customers, services) using Web technology to securely distribute and manage information. At its core, a PRM application facilitates partner relationships. Specific functions include: partner profiles, partner communications, management of customer leads, targeted information distribution, connecting the extended enterprise, partner planning, centralized forecasting, group planning, e-mail and Web-based alerts, messaging, price lists, and community bulletin boards. As described in Chapter 3, many large companies offer suppliers or partners portals for improved communication and collaboration. (For more on PRM, see *channelwave.com*, *www.it-telecomsolutions.com*, and Coupey, 2001.)

partner relationship management (PRM) *All of the efforts made to apply customer relationship management (CRM) to relationships with business partners.*

EXAMPLE   *Supporting PRM at SkyMall. SkyMall.com* (now a subsidiary of Gem-Star TV Guide International) is a retailer that sells from catalogs on board airplanes, over the Internet, and by mail order. It relies on its catalog partners to fill the orders. For small vendors that do not handle their own shipments and for international shipments, SkyMall contracts with distribution centers owned by fulfillment outsourcer Sykes Enterprise.

To coordinate the logistics of sending orders to thousands of customers, SkyMall uses integrated EC order-management software called Order Trust. SkyMall leases this software and pays transaction fees for its use. As orders come in, SkyMall conveys the data to Order Trust, which disseminates the information to the appropriate partners (either a vendor or a Sykes distribution center). A report about the shipment is then sent to SkyMall, and SkyMall pays Order Trust the transaction fees. This arrangement has allowed SkyMall to increase its online business by more than 3 percent annually without worrying about order fulfillment. The partners (the makers of the products) also benefit by receiving the electronically transmitted orders quickly.

IT's ABOUT BUSINESS

MKT POM

9.6: CRM/PRM Initiatives at New Piper Aircraft

Today, New Piper Aircraft is the only general-aviation manufacturer offering a complete line of business and pleasure aircraft (from trainers and high-performance aircraft for personal and business use to turbine-powered business aircraft). But in 1992, the company (then Piper Aircraft) was making fewer than 50 planes per year and had $15 million in bank debt and only $1,000 in cash. By 2001, the company delivered 441 planes and took in $243 million in revenue.

The fundamental reason for the company's success was its new ownership and management that realized that its ability to provide assistance to customers and partners needed to be completely overhauled. The company purchased Siebel Systems' MidMarket, a CRM software tool, and customized it for PRM. The results were the PULSE Center. PULSE stands for Piper Unlimited Liaison via Standards of Excellence. The system tracks all contacts and communications between New Piper and its dealers and customers. It also helps meet the growing needs of its partner- and customer-care programs.

In less than one year after implementation, the Web-based call center's productivity increased 50 percent, the number of lost sales leads was reduced 25 percent, and sales representatives handled 45 percent more sales. Before the system was instituted, an 11-person call center used spiral notebooks crammed into numerous cabinets to store the data and contacts; it took 30 minutes to locate a contact. Today, the call center tracks 70,000 customers among 17 dealers, and contact information is available in less than a minute.

Development of the PULSE Center took place in stages. The first three phases had been completed by October 2002: Phase 1—loading current aircraft owners, dealers, fleet customers aircraft, and new customer service employees into the system to develop the organization infrastructure; Phase 2—enabling the Customer Service Center to process activities; and Phase 3—enabling dealers to access sales opportunities pertinent to their territory.

The company is now (January 2004) in Phase 4 and beginning Phase 5. Phase 4 is the opening of the Dealer Web Portal, which will allow partners (aircraft dealers) access to particular areas of PULSE and provide the technology to make online service requests. Phase 5 will streamline entry of warranty claims. Phase 6, the Partner Web Portal, will allow key suppliers access to areas of the PULSE system and assist in communication with those suppliers. Phase 7 will provide for ordering parts online, and Phase 8 will be the Customer Web Portal giving customers access to open service requests, online logbooks, and product and survey information.

Piper's Vice President for Customers, Dan Snell, says, "New Piper's goal is to lead the industry with respect to quality, excellence, and customer care. It is a challenging mission, but certainly not daunting, and will be achieved through initiatives such as PULSE."

Sources: Compiled from D. Galante, "Case Studies: Digital Do-Overs," *Forbes* (October 7, 2002), pp. 2–3; and "New Piper, Piper Rolls Out Further Customer Relations Initiatives," *New Piper* news releases (2002, 2004).

QUESTIONS

1. Describe the major features of the CRM/PRM program.
2. Why does the company need such an elaborate program? How would you justify it?
3. How can one system serve both individual customers and business customers, including dealers?

A Gartner Group survey about CRM, conducted in December 2002, showed that of all sales-related applications, PRM programs had the highest return on investment (*Business Wire*, 2003). For this reason, companies are interested in finding ways to use it extensively, as shown in IT's about Business 9.6.

supplier relationship management (SRM) *All of the efforts made to apply CRM to relationships with suppliers.*

Supplier Relationship Management. One of the major categories of PRM is **supplier relationship management (SRM)**, the efforts made to apply CRM to relationships with suppliers. For many companies (e.g., retailers and manufacturers), the ability to work properly with suppliers is a major critical success factor. PeopleSoft, Inc. (*peoplesoft.com*) developed a model for managing relationships with suppliers in real time.

PeopleSoft's SRM model. PeopleSoft's SRM model is generic and could be considered by any large company. It includes 12 steps, illustrated in Figure 9.8. The de-

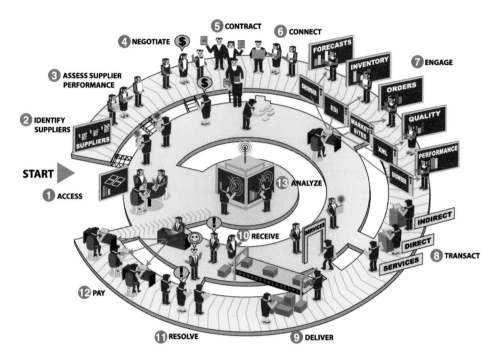

Figure 9.8   *Supplier relationship management (SRM). [Source: B. Schecterle, "Managing and Extending Supplier Relationships,"* People Talk *(April–June 2003).]*

tails of the steps are shown in Online File W9.5. The core idea of this model is that an e-supply chain is based on integration and collaboration. The supply chain processes are connected, decisions are made collectively, performance metrics are based on common understanding, information flows in real time (whenever possible), and the only thing a new partner needs in order to join the SRM system is just a Web browser.

wiley.com/college/turban

Collaborative Commerce

As described in Chapter 4, *collaborative commerce (c-commerce)* refers to non–selling/buying electronic transactions between and among organizations. An example would be a company collaborating electronically with a vendor that is designing a product or part for this company. C-commerce implies communication, information sharing, and collaboration done electronically by means of tools such as groupware and specially designed collaboration tools. That means that IOSs and c-commerce coexist. Use of c-commerce requires some IOS technology, such as an extranet, EDI, or groupware. Let's look at some areas of collaboration using IOSs.

Retailer-Suppliers.   As discussed in Chapter 8, large retailers like Wal-Mart collaborate with their major suppliers to conduct production and inventory planning and forecasting of demand. Such forms of collaboration enable the suppliers to improve their production planning as well.

Product Design.   All the parties that are involved in a specific product design use software tools that enable them to share data and collaborate in product design. One such tool is screen sharing (see Chapter 4), in which several people can work on the same document on a computer screen while in different locations. Changes made in one place are visible to others instantly. Documents that can be processed through a collaborative product design IOS include blueprints, bills of material, accounting and billing documents, and joint reports and statements.

Collaborative Manufacturing.   Manufacturers can create dynamic collaborative production networks by means of IOSs. For example, original equipment manufacturers (OEMs) outsource components and subassemblies to suppliers. (For example, if you buy a Kenmore product from Sears, Sears does not make the product; it just buys and resells it. Some other manufacturer, such as Maytag, is the OEM.) In the past, these relationships often created problems in coordination, workflows, and communication. Web-based collaborative IOSs have improved the outsourcing process and are especially useful in tracking changes that may be initiated by any partner along the supply chain.

Facilitating Global Trade

As countries' borders begin to disappear in global trading, language translation is becoming very important. This topic is very important in e-commerce, where appropriate translation of Web pages is a critical success factor. The use of intelligent systems in automatic language translation has been progressing rapidly since the mid-1990s. For details see Online File W9.4.

wiley.com/college/turban

Many other systems and applications are used to facilitate international trade. An example is the use of intelligent systems to fight money laundering across international borders, or the use of a hybrid intelligent system for developing global marketing strategy. As international trade is expanding, mainly due to the Internet and trading blocks like the European Union and NAFTA, expertise will be needed in many areas, ranging from legal issues to export and import licenses. Such expertise can be provided to a global audience online. Also, expert systems can provide to users in developing countries the advice of top experts in the fields of medicine, safety, agriculture, and crime fighting. These various systems and applications work with different types of IOSs and technologies.

WHAT'S IN IT FOR ME?

ACC

FOR THE ACCOUNTING MAJOR

Accounting rules and regulations and cross-border transfer of data are critical for global trade. IOSs can facilitate such trade. No less important are the issues of taxation, government reports, and more. Creating information systems such as EDI-based may require the attention of accountants. Finally, fraud detection in global settings (e.g., transfers of funds) can be facilitated by appropriate controls and auditing.

FIN

FOR THE FINANCE MAJOR

Many finance-related issues exist in implementing IOSs. For one thing, establishing EDI and extranet relationships means structuring payment agreements. Global supply chains may involve complex financial arrangements, which may require legal considerations. Understanding how information systems work among different companies and what support they provide is essential to any trade, including global ones. Finally, EFT systems are an essential part of modern business.

MKT

FOR THE MARKETING MAJOR

As competition intensifies globally, finding new markets including global ones becomes critical. Use of IOSs, B2B exchanges, and so forth provides an opportunity to improve marketing and sales. Understanding the capabilities of these technologies and their implementation issues will enable the marketing department to excel. Marketing is also involved in the design and implementation of PRM and in creating the sales side of virtual corporations.

POM

FOR THE PRODUCTION/ OPERATIONS MANAGEMENT MAJOR

Being in charge of procurement, production/operations managers must understand how supporting information systems interface with business partners' systems. In addition, collaboration in design, manufacturing, and logistics requires knowledge of how modern information systems can be connected. Finally, supply chain collaboration frequently requires joining EDI agreements or B2B exchanges and hubs.

Preparing and training employees to work with business partners (frequently in foreign countries) requires knowledge about how IOSs operate. Sensitivity to cultural differences and extensive communication and collaboration can be facilitated with IT.

SUMMARY

1. **Define and classify IOSs.** Information systems that involve two or more organizations are referred to as interorganizational information systems (IOSs). They can be local or global, dedicated to only one activity (e.g., transfer funds), or intended to support several activities (e.g., to facilitate trade, communication, or collaboration). IOSs are classified into the following types: B2B trading, global systems, EFT, integrated messaging, shared databases, and systems that support virtual corporations. Technologies that support IOSs are EDI, extranets, groupware, XML, and Web Services.

2. **Define and classify global information systems.** Global information systems exist when at least two parties of an information system are in different countries. Three types of companies that use global information systems exist: multinational (one company operates in two or more countries), international (at least one business partner is in a different country), and virtual global (partners in at least two countries form one company jointly).

3. **Present the major issues surrounding global information systems.** Some of the major issues that affect global information systems are cultural issues, political and economic issues (including currency conversion), legal issues such as cross-border data transfer, different languages, and logistics. Global supply chains are usually longer, requiring complex supporting information systems.

4. **Describe B2B exchanges and hubs.** Communication and collaboration among companies can be done via IOSs that are organized as either public or private B2B exchanges (usually designed for trading) or hubs (designed to improve the supply chain).

5. **Describe virtual corporations and their IT support.** Virtual corporations are joint ventures involving several companies that create one entity for a special purpose. Since working groups of the VC are in different locations, IT is needed to facilitate coordination and collaboration.

6. **Describe EDI and EDI/Internet and their benefits and limitations.** EDI provides a systematic framework for information exchange between business partners. It both translates routine business documents to national or international standard formats and provides a secure transmission over VANs. The major benefits include minimization of errors and cycle time, increased understanding and collaboration among business partners, reduced cost of processing information, better customer service, and improved employee productivity. The major limitations are high cost and complexity, long training periods required, high investment and operating costs, and inflexibility. EDI/Internet overcomes most of the above limitations by using the Internet and its tools to reduce cost and to increase flexibility and ease of use.

7. **Describe extranets, XML, and Web services.** Extranets connect the intranets of business partners by using the Internet (over secure VPNs). This connection enables partners to conveniently enter portions of their partners' intranets. XML is a standard, used mainly for B2B transactions, that enables communication among business partners, regardless of the software they use. Web Services support IOSs and facilitate integration of B2B applications by enabling disparate systems to share data and services.

8. **Present major IOS implementation issues.** Some representative issues are developing appropriate partner relationship management, c-commerce, and the use of automatic language translation and other methods to facilitate global trade.

INTERACTIVE / LEARNING

How Much Does that Bottle of Dr. Pepper Cost?
Go to the Interactivities section on the Student Web Site and access Chapter 9: Interorganizational and Global Information Systems. There you will find an animated simulation of an extranet that allows Dr. Pepper to notify bottlers of price changes, as well some hands-on activities that visually explain business concepts in this chapter.

Instructions for accessing the Interactivities on the Student Web Site:

1. Go to
wiley.com/college/turban

2. Select Turban Rainer Potter's *Introduction to Information Technology, Third Edition*
3. Click on Student Resources Site, in the toolbar on the left
4. Click on Interactivities Web Site
5. Click on Interactivities Web Site and use your password to enter the site (your password card is located in the inside cover of your textbook)

More Resources

More resources and study tools are located on the Student Web Site. You'll find additional chapter materials and links to organizations, people and technologies for each chapter. In addition, self-quizzes that provide individualized feedback are available for each chapter.

DISCUSSION QUESTIONS

1. Discuss some reasons for the complexity of global trade and the potential assistance of IT.
2. In what way is a B2B exchange related to a global supply chain? To a global information system?
3. Discuss the major differences between a B2B exchange and a B2B hub.
4. Compare an EDI to an extranet and discuss the major differences.

5. When a company opens a private marketplace (for selling and/or buying), it may use EDI, an extranet, EDI-Internet, or just the Internet with regular encryption. Discuss the *criteria* a company needs to consider when making this decision.
6. Discuss the manner in which cross-border data transfer can be a limitation to a company that has manufacturing plants in other countries.

PROBLEM-SOLVING ACTIVITIES

1. Enter *peoplesoft.com* and find material on the different IOSs discussed in this chapter. Prepare a report.
2. General Electric Information Systems is the largest provider of EDI services. Investigate what services GEIS and other EDI vendors provide. If you were to evaluate their services for your company, how would you plan to approach the evaluation? Prepare a report.

3. Examine the Lego case and *lego.com*. Design the conceptual architecture of the relevant IOSs you think Lego needs. Concentrate on the marketing portion of the supply chain, but point out some of the suppliers of plastic, paper, electronics, and wood that Lego uses.

INTERNET ACTIVITIES

1. Enter *i2.com* and review the products presented there. Explain how some of the products facilitate collaboration.
2. Enter *collaborate.com* and read about recent issues related to collaboration. Prepare a report.
3. Enter *smarterwork.com*. Find out how collaboration is done. Summarize the benefits of this site to the participants. Then enter *vignette.com*; look at the prod-

ucts listed under Collaboration. Compare the two sites.
4. Enter *1edisource.com* and see the demo of Web-Source. What are the benefits of this product?
5. Visit *edi-information.com* and prepare a list of educational and source material offered there.
6. Visit *xml.com* and *google.com* and find recent applications of XML. Prepare a report.

TEAM ASSIGNMENTS

1. Have each team locate several organizations that use IOSs, including one with a global reach. Students should contact the companies to find what IOS tech-

nology support they use (e.g., an EDI, extranet, etc.). Then find out what issues they faced in implementation. Prepare a report.

2. Team members will work on the EDI-XML connection. Start with *XML-EDI.org* and *xmlglobal.com* (see the tutorials at those sites) and find more resources.

Prepare a report to convince management of a hypothetical company to use XML/EDI.

HOW VOLKSWAGON RUNS ITS SUPPLY CHAIN IN BRAZIL

THE BUSINESS PROBLEM Like many other companies, Volkswagen (VW) works with several vendors in its assembly plants. However, there were problems in coordination and communication with some vendors. Vendors' materials were shipped to VW factories, where VW employees assembled trucks. But the supply chain was long, and problems with materials often developed. Each time there was a problem, VW had to wait for a partner to come to the plant to solve the problem. Also, materials arrived late, and so VW held large inventories to have extra materials on hand in the event of a delayed shipment. Finally, quality was frequently compromised.

THE IT SOLUTION In its Brazilian plant truck 100 miles northwest of Rio de Janeiro, Volkswagen (VW) radically altered its supply chain in 2002. The Rio plant is relatively small: Its 1,000 workers are scheduled to produce 100 trucks per day. Only 200 of the 1,000 workers are Volkswagen employees; they are responsible for overall quality, marketing, research, and design. The other 800 workers, who are employees of suppliers such as Rockwell International and Cummins Engines, do the specific assembly work. The objective of the lean supply chain was to reduce the number of defective parts, cut labor costs, and improve efficiency.

Volkswagen's major suppliers are assigned space in the VW plant, but they supply their own components, supplies, and workers. Workers from various suppliers build the truck as it moves down the assembly line. The system is illustrated in the nearby figure. At the first stop in the assembly process, workers from Iochepe-Maxion mount the gas tank, transmission lines, and steering blocks. As the chassis moves down the line, employees from Rockwell mount axles and brakes. Then workers from Remon put on wheels and adjust tire pressure. The MWM/Cummins team installs the engine and transmission. Truck cabs, produced by the Brazilian firm Delga Automotivea, are painted by Eisenmann, and then finished and upholstered by VDO, both of Germany. Volkswagen employees do an evaluation of the final truck.

THE RESULTS Volkswagen's innovative supply chain has already improved quality and driven down costs, as a result of each supplier having accepted responsibility for

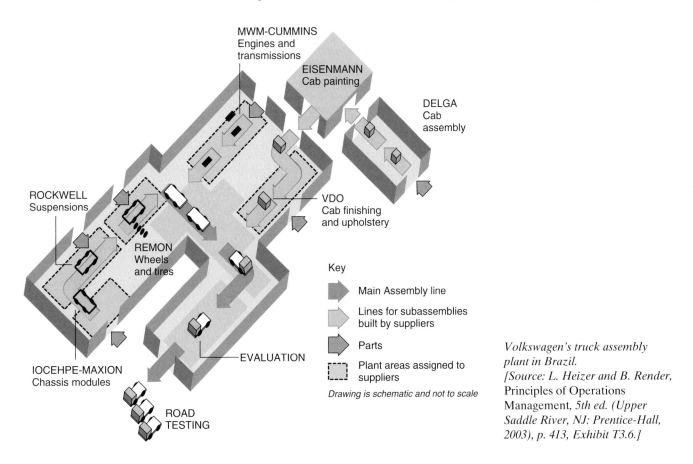

Volkswagen's truck assembly plant in Brazil.
[Source: L. Heizer and B. Render, Principles of Operations Management, *5th ed. (Upper Saddle River, NJ: Prentice-Hall, 2003), p. 413, Exhibit T3.6.]*

its units and workers' compensation. Encouraged by these results, VW is trying a similar approach in plants in Buenos Aires, Argentina, and with Skoda, in the Czech Republic. Volkswagen's new level of integration in supply chain management may be the wave of the future.

Source: Compiled from L. Heizer and B. Render, *Principles of Operations Management*, 5th ed. (Upper Saddle River, NJ: Prentice-Hall, 2003), pp. 412–414; and from *vw.com*.

QUESTIONS

1. Draw the supply chain of VW's manufacturing plant.
2. What IOSs might be necessary to support such an arrangement? Distinguish between upstream, internal, and downstream supply chain activities. (See Chapter 8 for review of these terms.)

CLUB IT   wiley.com/college/turban

COMMUNICATING WITH CLUB IT'S BUSINESS PARTNERS

One morning, Ruben walks into the office talking excitedly about the potential for XML to help Club IT solve its data integration problems. Fortunately, you have already studied XML and are aware of its utility even for small, infrequent transactions. Club IT is upgrading its office software to a new version that supports XML-based documents and data tagging, so it is time to investigate how you can exploit these new features for interorganizational communication.

ASSIGNMENT

1. Visit Microsoft's Web Site and search for articles describing XML features in their latest version of Office. Read about using XML in Word documents to tag data that can then directly update an Access database. Using data items from a patron transaction (for example, buying a drink), prepare an XML DTD (document type definition, an XML-style data description) to describe this transaction.

2. Sysco is one of the major purveyors in the food and beverage industry. They have a new service, eSysco (esysco.com) to provide online web ordering and tracking. Visit the Sysco Web Site and determine whether the eSysco service is a major consideration in choosing a purveyor.

3. While Club IT does not have global business partners, it does need to maintain records and initiate transactions with a number of governing bodies. Issues such as HVAC (heating, ventilation and air conditioning) and fire safety, DJ's music and royalty fees, city ordinances and noise laws, and alcohol liability and underage drinking require club management to stay current and provide timely reports. Choose a city and identify an ordinance and its reporting requirements Club IT would be subject to if they were located there. Describe how intranets, extranets or IOS could help Club IT stay in compliance.

Go to wiley.com/college/turban to access the CLUB IT Web Site on the Student Web Site

Managerial Support Systems

Chapter Preview

A manager's primary function is making decisions. Decision support systems, one type of managerial support system, assist managers in making decisions by allowing extensive, user-driven data analysis via a variety of modeling techniques. Intelligent systems, another type of managerial support system, range from expert systems to artificial neural networks. These systems can be used by themselves or in conjunction with other systems to increase productivity, quality, and customer service and to reduce cycle time. Intelligent systems can also facilitate communication and collaboration within and among organizations. These systems help us to communicate better with people who speak other languages as well as to communicate with computers. In addition, intelligent systems help us quickly find, compare, and analyze data.

Learning Objectives

1. Describe the concepts of management, decision making, and computerized support for decision making.
2. Describe decision support systems (DSSs) and their benefits, and describe the structure of DSSs.
3. Describe computerized support for group decision making.
4. Describe organizational decision support and executive support systems.
5. Describe artificial intelligence (AI).
6. Define an expert system and its components.
7. Describe natural language processing and natural language generation.
8. Describe artificial neural networks (ANNs) and their major applications.

NEW BALANCE MAKES SURE THAT SHOES FIT

New Balance (*newbalance.com*) is a $1.3 billion privately held athletic shoe company. As recently as 2001, New Balance executives did not have the tools to deliver accurate forecasts for the number of shoes it would sell through its various outlets.

The company's forecasting process worked like this: The person in charge of the forecasting department was supposed to collect forecasts from about half of the company's 160 sales representatives, compile them, and create overall predictions of what shoes the company's factories should turn out and when. However, she was lucky to get 20 forecasts back each month.

The problem for the sales representatives was that filling out the sheets consumed a lot of time—as much as a day for the forecasts for larger accounts. Reps had to pore through reams of printouts to plug answers into the company's spreadsheet. For salespeople paid on commission, the process took money out of their wallets.

The problems multiplied for the forecasters. The format of the company's spreadsheet was not protected. That meant, first of all, that reps would delete columns, type in the wrong style names, and move information around as they saw fit. It took at least a day for New Balance forecasters to validate the data from each sales rep's forecast, put the data into the correct form, and collate and analyze it.

In reality, New Balance forecasters produced their forecasts without the input of sales reps. This seat-of-the-pants approach caused sudden spikes in orders to factories for some products and backlogs of others. There would be deep valleys of production, when inventory that had piled up was sold off. The worst problem was that New Balance could not get orders to customers on time.

Also, the company used these forecasts to push sales quotas down from headquarters. The quota typically was the prior year's number plus some estimate of growth for the coming year. Because the quotas had little basis in reality, the sales force paid little attention to them.

New Balance turned to a decision support system (DSS) to give it the ability to manage its production planning by account, region, sales person, and other criteria. The DSS helped New Balance forecasters take into account such predictors of demand as general economic indicators, current orders, and historic sales data. The company produced forecast numbers for each shoe style. These forecasts could be given to the company's manufacturing managers to guide how they planned for production capacity.

With the new DSS, information about customers can now be gathered for each sales rep from corporate databases. The reps download that information from a secure Web site as each month ends. Using the data and consulting with customers, each sales rep updates the forecast of each customer's orders, not just for the rest of the current year, but for the following year as well.

Then, instead of using a malleable spreadsheet, sales reps enter their revisions in a locked-down template created by corporate forecasters. This template makes it easier for sales reps to fill out required information, and it is easy for forecasters to "roll up" all the sales reps' forecasts. In four hours, corporate forecasters can send out consolidated reports and breakouts by account and product.

The DSS has produced several beneficial results for New Balance. For the first time, the company can tell which representatives can best predict orders and which representatives can best manage problems with key accounts. Basically, the DSS has added accountability to everyone's role.

Second, New Balance now has a much more accurate picture each month of what its production should be. Because New Balance has a six-month lead time for delivery from its factories and overseas suppliers, rapid information and more accurate forecasts enable the company to react more quickly to retailers' needs. Since the implementation of the DSS, the number of shoes left in inventory when the company discontinues a style has dropped on average by 8 percent.

Third, using the DSS, the company discovered that its best-selling shoe sales had shifted from the $120-to-$160 basketball shoes to less-expensive, multipurpose shoes that cost between $60 and $90 per pair. So, the company produced styles in this price range in all widths.

Fourth, company executives now routinely call individual sales reps whose top accounts have fallen behind on purchases. The source of the executives' information is the "Top Accounts" report, an update distributed at noon every Monday that gives company executives a detailed look at sales figures for the past, present, and forecasted future. Executives have a wealth of information: a report for each style of shoe in New Balance's lineup; the to-date sales for the year and the month for each major retailer that New Balance serves; the sales of that shoe (or its predecessor) for the same period last year at that retailer; the orders for that retailer that have not been filled by New Balance's factory or warehouse; and what the sales rep had forecast for the current month. The sales force has access to the same report, meaning that everyone is on the same page and there are far fewer surprises.

The bottom line? Worldwide sales have more than doubled from $560 million in 1997 to $1.3 billion in 2002. New Balance now stands second only to Nike in the sale of running shoes. For all types of athletic shoes, New Balance ranks third, behind Nike and Reebok.

Source: Compiled from L. Barrett and S. Gallagher, "New Balance: Shoe Fits," *Baseline Magazine* (November 1, 2003).

WHAT WE LEARNED FROM THIS CASE

The opening case illustrates that a solution to complex production and other problems can be enhanced with the use of a decision support system (DSS). In fact, the DSS software supported several important decisions. We also learned that decisions are supported both in operational and HRM areas. Furthermore, much of the case illustrates the concepts of optimization and quantitative analysis. Finally, the Web is playing an increasing role in facilitating the use of such systems.

This chapter is dedicated to describing computer and Web support to *managerial decision makers*. We begin by reviewing the manager's job and the nature of today's decisions, which help explain why computerized support is needed. Then we present the concepts and methodology of the computerized decision support system for supporting individuals, groups, and whole organizations. Next, we introduce several types of intelligent systems and their role in decision support. Finally, we describe the topic of decision support in the Web environment. A discussion of intelligent agents and their role in decision support appears in an online appendix to the chapter.

10.1 MANAGERS AND DECISION MAKING

Management is a process by which organizational goals are achieved through the use of resources (people, money, energy, materials, space, time). These resources are considered to be *inputs*; the attainment of the goals is viewed as the *output* of the process. Managers oversee this process in an attempt to optimize it. A manager's success is often measured by the ratio between inputs and outputs for which he or she is responsible. This ratio is an indication of the organization's *productivity*.

The Manager's Job

To understand how information systems support managers, it is necessary first to briefly describe the manager's job. Managers do many things, depending on their position in the organization, the type and size of the organization, organizational policies and culture, and the personalities of the managers themselves. Despite this variety, managers have three basic roles (Mintzberg, 1973):

- **Interpersonal roles.** Figurehead, leader, liaison
- **Informational roles.** Monitor, disseminator, spokesperson
- **Decisional roles.** Entrepreneur, disturbance handler, resource allocator, negotiator

Early information systems mainly supported the informational roles. In recent years, information systems have been developed that support all three roles. In this chapter, we are mainly interested in the support that IT can provide for decisional roles.

Decision Making

A *decision* refers to a choice made between two or more alternatives. Decisions are diverse and are made continuously by both individuals and groups. When making a decision, either organizational or personal, the decision maker goes through a systematic process. Simon (1977) described the process as composed of three major phases: *intelligence*, *design*, and *choice*. A fourth phase, *implementation*, was added later. A conceptual presentation of the four-stage decision-making process is shown in Figure 10.1, which illustrates what tasks are included in each phase. Note that there is a continuous flow of information from intelligence to design to choice (bold lines), but at any phase there may be a return to a previous phase (broken lines).

The decision-making process starts with the *intelligence phase*, in which managers examine a situation and identify and define the problem. In the *design phase*,

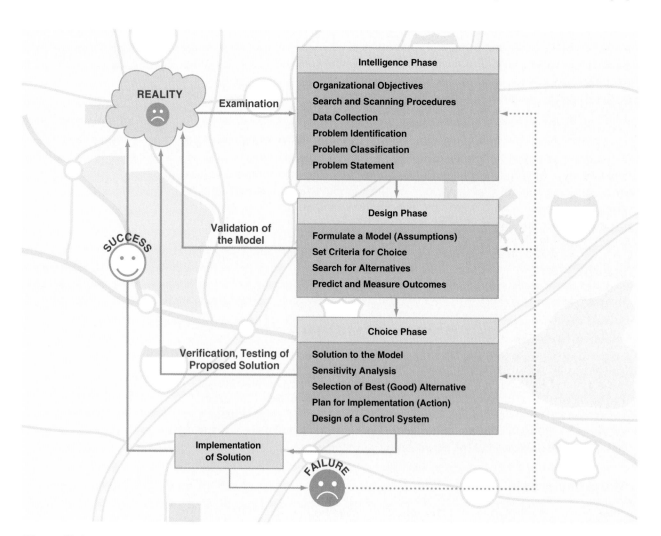

Figure 10.1 *Roadmap: The process and phases in decision making.*

decision makers construct a model that simplifies the problem. This is done by making assumptions that simplify reality and by expressing the relationships among all variables. The model is then validated, and decision makers set criteria for the evaluation of alternative potential solutions that are identified. The *choice phase* involves selecting a solution, which is tested "on paper." Once this proposed solution seems to be feasible, we are ready for the last phase—*implementation*. Successful implementation results in resolving the original problem or opportunity. Failure leads to a return to the previous phases. Computer-based decision support attempts to automate several tasks in the decision-making process, in which modeling is the core.

Modeling and Models. A model (in decision making) is a *simplified representation*, or abstraction of reality. It is simplified because reality is too complex to copy exactly, and because much of its complexity is actually irrelevant to a specific problem. With modeling, one can perform virtual experiments and an analysis on a model of reality, rather than on reality itself.

model (in decision making) *A simplified representation, or abstraction of reality.*

The benefits of modeling in decision making are:

* The cost of virtual experimentation is much lower than the cost of experimentation conducted with a real system.

* Models allow for the simulated compression of time. Years of operation can be simulated in seconds of computer time.

* Manipulating the model (by changing variables) is much easier than manipulating the real system. Experimentation is therefore easier to conduct, and it does not interfere with the daily operation of the organization.

* Today's environment holds considerable uncertainty. Modeling allows a manager to better deal with the uncertainty by introducing many "what-ifs" and calculating the risks involved in specific actions.

Why Managers Need IT Support

It is difficult to make good decisions without valid and relevant information. Information is needed for each phase and activity in the decision-making process. Despite the widespread availability of information, making decisions is growing increasingly difficult due to the following trends:

* The *number of alternatives* to be considered in ever *increasing*, due to innovations in technology, improved communications, the development of global markets, and the use of the Internet and e-business. A key to good decision making is to explore and compare many relevant alternatives. The more alternatives that exist, the more computer-assisted search and comparisons are needed.

* Typically, decisions must be made *under time pressure*. Frequently it is not possible to manually process the needed information fast enough to be effective.

* Due to increased uncertainty in the decision environment, decisions are becoming more complex. It is usually necessary to *conduct a sophisticated analysis* in order to make a good decision. Such analysis requires the use of modeling.

* It is often necessary to rapidly access remote information, consult with experts, or have a group decision-making session, all without large expense. Decision makers can be in different locations and so is the information. Bringing them all together quickly and inexpensively may be a difficult task.

These trends cause difficulties in making decisions, but a computerized analysis can be of enormous help. For example, a decision support system (discussed in Section 10.2) can examine numerous alternatives very quickly, can provide a systematic risk analysis, can be integrated with communications systems and databases, and can be used to support group work. All this can be done with relatively low cost.

What Information Technologies Are Available to Support Managers?

In addition to discovery, communication, and collaboration tools (Chapter 4) that provide indirect support to decision making, several other information technologies have been successfully used to support managers. The Web can facilitate them all. Collectively, they are referred to as **management support systems (MSSs)**.

The first of these MSS technologies are *decision support systems*, which have been in use since the mid-1970s. They provide support primarily to analytical, quantitative types of decisions. Second, *executive support systems* represent a technology developed initially in the mid-1980s, mainly to support the informational roles of executives. A third technology, *group decision support systems*, supports managers and staff working in groups. A fourth technology is *intelligent systems*. These four technologies and their variants can be used independently, or they can be combined, each providing a different capability. They are frequently related to data warehousing. A simplified presentation of such support is shown in Figure 10.2.

As Figure 10.2 shows, managers need to find, filter, and interpret information to determine potential problems or opportunities and then decide what to do about them. The figure shows the support of the various MSS tools (circled) as well as the role of a data warehouse, which was described in Chapter 3.

We will discuss decision support systems in Section 10.2, but before we get too far along in the chapter, let's take a look at some representative examples of how companies use IT to support decision making.

management support systems (MSSs) *Major IT technologies designed to support managers: decision support systems, executive support systems, groupware technologies, and intelligent systems.*

FIN   **EXAMPLE**   *Wells Fargo Targets Customers.* Wells Fargo (*wellsfargo.com*) has become so good at predicting consumer behavior that it practically knows what customers want before they realize it themselves. The bank developed a decision support system (DSS) in-house. The DSS collects data on every transaction—whether it is over the phone, at an ATM, in a bank branch, or online—and combines that data with personal data that the customer provides. Wells Fargo then analyzes the data and models the customer's behavior to come up with prospective offerings, like a low-cost second mortgage, just at the right time for the customer. The result: Compared with the industry average of 2.2 products per customer, Wells Fargo sells four (Hovanesian, 2003).

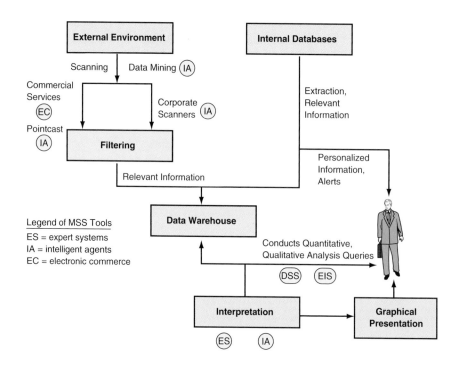

Figure 10.2 *Computerized support for decision making.*

EXAMPLE *Schwab Targets the Rich.* In 2000, Charles Schwab `FIN` (*schwab.com*) changed its strategy to target high-net-worth investors. This meant turning itself from a discount brokerage into a full-service investment firm. To avoid the $20-million-per-year cost of hiring analysts, it made a onetime, $20 million investment in a decision support system. Schwab Equity Ratings, an online intelligent DSS, offers recommendations for buying and selling more than 3,000 stocks. It automatically sends e-mail alerts to Schwab customers and to Schwab analysts. Schwab says the system picks stocks as efficiently as its human counterparts. In addition, the system does away with conflicts of interest. In the wake of Wall Street scandals, the DSS makes investors feel safer (Edwards, 2003).

EXAMPLE *Lowering Costs in Health Care.* For Owens & `ACC` Minor (*owens-minor.com*), one of the largest suppliers for the health care industry, success means driving down the price of thousands of hospital supplies. The company `SVC` uses its decision support system to help customers hunt for bargains. The DSS lets hospitals track purchases they make with hundreds of competing medical suppliers. The DSS pinpoints lower pricing on similar items, helping customers take advantage of discounts already negotiated. Hospitals keep better tabs on their bills and cut costs an average of 2 to 3 percent. For Owens & Minor, the DSS attracts new customers, and when existing customers find lower prices, they order more (Ante, 2003).

These examples exhibit the diversity of decisions that decision support systems can support. We now address additional aspects of decision making to put our discussion of DSSs in context.

A Framework for Computerized Decision Analysis

To better understand management support systems, it helps if we classify decisions along two major dimensions: problem structure and the nature of the decision (Gorry and Scott-Morton, 1971). Figure 10.3 gives an overview of decision making along these two dimensions.

Nature of Decision

Type of Decision	Operational Control	Management Control	Strategic Planning	Support Needed
Structured	Accounts receivable, order entry **1**	Budget analysis, short-term forecasting, personnel reports, make-or-buy analysis **2**	Financial management (investment), warehouse location, distribution systems **3**	MIS, management science models, financial and statistical models
Semistructured	Production scheduling, inventory control **4**	Credit evaluation, budget preparation, plant layout, project scheduling, reward systems design **5**	Building new plant, mergers and acquisitions, new product planning, compensation planning, quality assurance planning **6**	DSS
Unstructured	Selecting a cover for a magazine, buying software, approving loans **7**	Negotiating, recruiting an executive, buying hardware, lobbying **8**	R & D planning, new technology development, social responsibility planning **9**	DSS ES neural networks
Support Needed	MIS, management science	Management science, DSS, EIS, ES	EIS, ES, neural networks	

Figure 10.3 *Decision support framework. Technology is used to support the decisions shown in the column at the far right and in the bottom row.*

Problem Structure. The first dimension is *problem structure*, where decision-making processes fall along a continuum ranging from highly structured to highly unstructured decisions. (See the left column in Figure 10.3.) *Structured decisions* refer to routine and repetitive problems for which standard solutions exist. In a structured problem, the first three of the decision process phases (intelligence, design, and choice) are laid out in a particular sequence, and the procedures for obtaining the best (or at least a good enough) solution are known. Common solution criteria are cost minimization or profit maximization.

At the other extreme of problem complexity are *unstructured decisions*. These are "fuzzy," complex problems for which there are no cut-and-dried solutions. An unstructured problem is one in which intelligence, design, and choice are not organized in a particular sequence. In such a problem, human intuition often plays an important role in making the decision. Typical unstructured problems include planning new service offerings, hiring an executive, or choosing a set of research and development projects for the next year.

In between structured and unstructured problems are *semistructured* problems, in which only some of the decision process phases are structured. These problems require a combination of standard solution procedures and individual judgment. Examples of semistructured problems are annual evaluation of employees, setting marketing budgets for consumer products, performing capital acquisition analysis, and trading bonds.

The Nature of Decisions. The second dimension of decision support deals with the *nature of decisions*. We can define three broad categories that encompass all managerial decisions: (1) *operational control*—the efficient and effective execution of specific tasks; (2) *management control*—the acquisition and efficient use of resources in accomplishing organizational goals; and (3) *strategic planning*—the long-range goals and policies for growth and resource allocation. These are shown along the top row of Figure 10.3.

The Decision Matrix. The three primary classes of problem structure and the three broad categories of the nature of decisions can be combined in a nine-cell decision-support matrix, as shown in Figure 10.3. Lower-level managers usually perform the structured and operational control-oriented tasks (cells 1, 2, and 4). Tasks in cells 6, 8, and 9 are mainly the responsibility of senior executives. The tasks in cells 3, 5, and 7 are usually the responsibility of middle managers and professional staff.

Computer Support for Structured Decisions. Computer support for the nine cells in the matrix is shown in the right-hand column and the bottom row of Figure 10.3. Structured and some semistructured decisions, especially of the operational and management control type, have been supported by computers since the 1950s. Decisions of this type are made in all functional areas, but particularly in finance and operations management.

Problems that lower-level managers encounter on a regular basis typically have a high level of structure. Examples include capital budgeting (e.g., replacement of equipment), allocation of resources, distribution of merchandise, and inventory control. For each type of structured decision, prescribed solutions have been developed through the use of mathematical formulas. This approach is called *management science* or *operations research*, and it is also executed with the aid of computers.

optimization *A management science approach that attempts to find the best possible solution.*

wiley.com/college/turban

wiley.com/college/turban

Management Science. The *management science* approach takes the view that managers can follow a fairly systematic process for solving problems. Therefore, it is possible to use a scientific approach to managerial decision making. This approach, which also centers on modeling, is presented in Online File W10.1. For a list of management science problems and tools, see Online File W10.2. Management science frequently attempts to find the best possible solution, an approach known as **optimization**.

Before you go on . . .

1. Describe the decision-making process proposed by Simon.
2. Why do managers need IT support?
3. Describe the decision matrix.

10.2 DECISION SUPPORT SYSTEMS

Broadly defined, a **decision support system (DSS)** is a computer-based information system that combines models and data in an attempt to solve semistructured and some unstructured problems with extensive user involvement. As the examples in Section 10.1 demonstrate, companies are using DSSs to improve decision making for many reasons.

Characteristics and Capabilities of DSSs

Most DSSs at least have some of the attributes shown in Manager's Checklist 10.1. DSSs also employ mathematical models and have a related, special capability known as sensitivity analysis.

Sensitivity Analysis. **Sensitivity analysis** is the study of the impact that changes in one (or more) parts of a model have on other parts. Usually we check the impact that changes in input variables have on result variables.

Sensitivity analysis is extremely valuable in DSSs because it makes the system flexible and adaptable to changing conditions and to the varying requirements of different decision-making situations. It provides a better understanding of the model and the problem it purports to describe. It may increase the users' confidence in the model, especially when the model is not so sensitive to changes. A *sensitive model* means that small changes in conditions dictate a different solution. In a *nonsensitive model*, changes in conditions do not significantly change the recommended solution. This means that the chances for a solution to succeed are very high.

What-If Analysis. A model builder must make predictions and assumptions regarding the input data, many of which are based on the assessment of uncertain futures.

decision support system (DSS) *A computer-based information system that combines models and data in an attempt to solve semistructured and some unstructured problems with extensive user involvement.*

sensitivity analysis *The study of the impact that changes in one (or more) parts of a model have on other parts.*

MANAGER'S CHECKLIST 10.1

The Capabilities of a DSS

- ❏ A DSS provides support for decision makers at all management levels, whether individuals or groups, mainly in semistructured and unstructured situations, by bringing together human judgment and objective information.
- ❏ A DSS supports several interdependent and/or sequential decisions.
- ❏ A DSS supports all phases of the decision-making process—intelligence, design, choice, and implementation—as well as a variety of decision-making processes and styles.
- ❏ A DSS is adaptable by the user over time to deal with changing conditions.
- ❏ A DSS is easy to construct and use in many cases.
- ❏ A DSS promotes learning, which leads to new demands and refinement of the current application, which leads to additional learning, and so forth.
- ❏ A DSS usually utilizes quantitative models (standard and/or custom made).
- ❏ Advanced DSSs are equipped with a knowledge management component that allows the efficient and effective solution of very complex problems.
- ❏ A DSS can be disseminated for use via the Web.
- ❏ A DSS allows the easy execution of *sensitivity analyses*.

what-if analysis *The study of the impact of a change in the assumptions (input data) on the proposed solution.*

The results depend on these assumptions, which are frequently subjective, made by one or a few people. **What-if analysis** attempts to check the impact of a change in the assumptions (input data) on the proposed solution. For example, what will happen to the total inventory cost *if* the originally assumed cost of carrying inventories is not 10 percent but 12 percent? In a well-designed DSS, managers themselves can interactively ask the computer these types of questions as many times as needed.

goal-seeking analysis *Study that attempts to find the value of the inputs necessary to achieve a desired level of output.*

Goal-Seeking Analysis. **Goal-seeking analysis** represents a "backward" solution approach. It attempts to find the value of the inputs necessary to achieve a desired level of output. For example, let us say that a DSS initial solution yielded a profit of $2 million. Management may want to know what sales volume and additional advertising would be necessary to generate a profit of $3 million, and so could do a goal-seeking analysis to find out.

These types of decision support analyses are important, as IT's about Business 10.1 shows.

Structure and Components of DSS

Every DSS consists of at least data management and model management subsystems, a user interface, and end users. A few advanced DSSs also contain a knowledge

IT'S ABOUT BUSINESS [MKT] [HRM]
10.1: DSS Helps Lowe's Strategy

Lowe's (*lowes.com*), the number-two home-improvement retailer in the United States, has its sights set on number-one Home Depot. Lowe's has located 72 percent of its stores within 10 miles of a Home Depot. Lowe's has 875 stores to Home Depot's 1,568. Lowe's annual revenue is $26.5 billion compared to Home Depot's $58.2 billion. But what really has the attention of executives at Lowe's is that Lowe's averages $294 of sales per square foot whereas Home Depot averages $370. Lowe's is using a decision support system and a data warehouse to narrow the gap. The overall goal is to sell big home-improvement projects and all the goods that go with them.

Unlike many other retailers, including Home Depot, Lowe's does not use techniques such as "pallet drops" and "dump bins" where merchandise is put at the end or middle of aisles to move it quickly. Instead, Lowe's uses its DSS to plan out its stores. "Planograms"—DSS-driven shelf plans—influence where and at what level it puts every product it sells. With the help of the DSS and the data warehouse, the company checks past sales histories of the products it sells: which generate the most profit, where they get the best attention, what season gets the most action, and so forth.

Lowe's carefully considers what goes where. In its fashion-lighting section, for example, products at the end of the aisles at Lowe's might be chandeliers with Italian crystal beads, with prices topping $200. In the aisle itself, lighting fixtures hang against realistic backdrops depicting a living room. Pricier items are typically at eye level. Lowe's lighting aisle uses "atmospherics" to increase the willingness of customers to buy and to target women buyers. The key is to allow a customer to visualize a home-improvement project, easily find items specific to that project, and then purchase them.

The company also allows key national suppliers access to its store layouts for aisles such as lighting and fashion plumbing. Through Lowe's DSS, Lowe's national suppliers can then create planograms for aisles they control. Lowe's also analyzes data to track sales and target customers. For instance, if a customer buys a chain saw, he will receive direct mail on other items he is likely to purchase, such as replacement chains or garden supplies.

In 2002, Lowe's added $74 million to its bottom line, store sales grew almost 20 percent, and the company earned 5.6 cents on every dollar, up from 4.6 cents in the previous year.

Source: L. Dignan, "Lowe's Big Plan," *Baseline Magazine* (June 16, 2003).

QUESTIONS

1. What are the advantages of the DSS and data warehouse to Lowe's?
2. Do you think the DSS and data warehouse will provide a sustainable competitive advantage for Lowe's, or will Home Depot develop the same technologies?

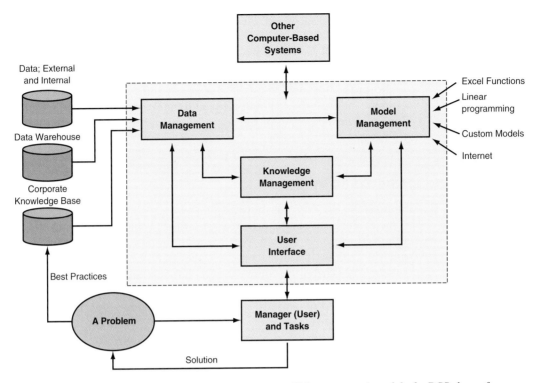

Figure 10.4 *The DSS and its computing environment. This conceptual model of a DSS shows four main software components and their relationships with other systems.*

management component. (see Figure 10.4). Each subsystem (component) consists of the following:

- **Data management subsystem.** A DSS data management subsystem is similar to any other data management system. It contains all the data that flow from several sources. The data usually are extracted prior to their entry into a DSS database or a data warehouse. In some DSSs, there is no separate database, and data are entered into the DSS model as needed.

- **Model management subsystem.** A model management subsystem contains completed models and the building blocks necessary to develop DSS applications. This includes standard software with financial, statistical, management science, or other quantitative models. A model management subsystem also contains all the custom models written for the specific DSS. These models provide the system's analytical capabilities.

  Also included is a *model-based management system (MBMS)* whose role is analogous to that of a DBMS. (See Technology Guide 3.) The major functions (capabilities) of an MBMS are shown in Online File W10.3.

wiley.com/college/turban

- **User interface.** The term *user interface* covers all aspects of the communications between a user and the DSS. The user interface provides much of the power, flexibility, and ease of use of the DSS. Most interfaces today are Web-based, and some are supplemented by voice.

- **Users.** The person faced with the problem or decision that the DSS is designed to support is referred to as the *user*, the *manager*, or the *decision maker*. A DSS has two broad classes of users: managers and staff specialists (such as financial analysts, production planners, and market researchers).

- **Knowledge-based subsystems.** Many unstructured and semistructured problems are so complex that they require expertise for their solutions. Such expertise can be provided by a knowledge-based system, such as an expert system. Therefore, the more advanced DSSs are equipped with a component called a *knowledge-based* (or *intelligent*) *subsystem*. Such a component can provide the required expertise for solving some aspects of the problem or can provide knowledge that can enhance the operation of the other DSS components.

The knowledge component consists of one or more expert (or other intelligent) systems, or it draws expertise from the organizational knowledge base. A DSS that includes such a component is referred to as an *intelligent DSS*, a *DSS/ES*, or a *knowledge-based DSS (KBDSS)*.

Except for the users, the DSS components are all software. They are housed in a computer and can be facilitated by additional software (such as multimedia). Tools like Excel include some of the components and therefore can be used for DSS construction by end users.

How DSSs Work

Figure 10.4 also illustrates how the DSS works. When user has a business problem, he or she evaluates it via the processes described in Figures 10.1 and 10.2. A DSS system is then constructed. As you recall from Chapters 3 and 4, DSS users get their data from the data warehouse, databases, and other data sources. These data are entered into the DSS (from the sources on the left side and the models on the right side, as shown in Figure 10.4). Knowledge can also be gathered from the corporate knowledge base. As more problems are solved, more knowledge is accumulated in the organizational knowledge base.

The Web is a perfect medium for deploying decision support capabilities on a global basis. IT's about Business 10.2 illustrates that these Web-based DSSs can benefit both users and developers.

IT's ABOUT BUSINESS   FIN

10.2: Web-Based DSS at a Luxembourg Bank

SEB Private Bank is the Luxembourg subsidiary of Swedish Bank SEB, an elite international bank that is quickly moving to take advantage of big growth opportunities in Europe with Internet banking. SEB is finding that customers on the Internet conduct more transactions than others, a trend that could deliver high profitability. The bank sees its greatest and most attractive opportunity in Europe. There SEB already participates in a growing investment market and distinguishes itself with high-performance financial tools that empower managers to offer superior customer service. The bank has set an ambitious goal of having 5 million Internet customers by the end of 2004 with the help of a pan-European Internet partner.

To move into real-time 24/7 operations, SEB Private Bank decided to investigate a DSS software product called Web-FOCUS (from Information Builders.) The software allows users to quickly build self-service production reporting and business analysis systems, features that sounded promising for SEB Private Bank's needs. Everything from standard to customized reports can be developed quickly and delivered immediately, internally or externally, by intranets, extranets, and over the Internet. As a result, the entire *decision-making process* is shifted onto a real-time transaction platform. The bank developed over 600 reports, of which more than 150 are used by the bank's managers on a daily basis.

The DSS generates messages to leading stock exchanges, which in turn deliver a return message to the application, giving current financial updates. This streamlines the bank's reaction times with the outside world, giving up-to-the-minute information.

But having this intelligent information source is one thing; making full use of it is another. SEB Private Bank sees the increasing use of its intranet, with its Web-based architecture, as a move toward fewer paper reports. For example, through this system, the bank's managers can easily check the inventory value of a client's assets; when the DSS is asked to evaluate a portfolio, it can quickly produce a result.

With reliable security and high value-added services, SEB Private Bank feels well positioned to expand its markets with new expatriate investor business.

Source: informationbuilders.com/applications/seb.html (accessed November 11, 2003).

QUESTIONS

1. What other applications can be developed with such a DSS?

2. How does the DSS contribute to superior customer service?

Emerging Types of DSS

Although organizations have been using decision support systems since the 1980s, new types are being developed. We discuss two of these types, frontline DSSs and real-time decision support, in this section.

Frontline Decision Support Systems. **Frontline decision making** is the process by which companies automate decision processes and push them down into the organization and sometimes out to partners. It *empowers employees* by letting them devise strategies, evaluate metrics, analyze impacts, and make operational changes.

Frontline decision making automates simple decisions (like freezing the account of a customer who has failed to make payments) by predefining business rules and events that trigger them. At more complex decision points (such as inventory allocation), frontline decision making gives managers the necessary context-available alternatives, business impacts, and success measurements to make the right decision.

Frontline decision making provides users with the right questions to ask, the location of needed data, and metrics that translate data into corporate objectives, and it suggests actions that can improve performance. Analytical application products are now emerging to support these actions. As the next example shows, UPS is providing a frontline DSS application to its customers.

> **frontline decision making** *The process by which companies automate decision processes and push them down into the organization and sometimes out to partners.*

EXAMPLE *UPS Provides Frontline DSS to Customers.* [POM]
United Parcel Service (UPS) is providing a frontline DSS application, called CampusShip, to its customers. Workers can now operate virtual post offices on their desktops. Whether in the office or on the road, an employee using CampusShip can build an online address list, print labels, track a package, and e-mail shipping notifications. To provide controls on the service, CampusShip lets managers set rules on who can ship what. The free service, which is bundled in with other UPS services that customers buy, now has a total of 300,000 users at 6,000 companies (Haddad, 2003).

Real-Time Decision Support. Business decisions today must be made at the right time, and frequently under time pressure. To do so, managers need to know what is going on in the business at any moment and be able to quickly select the best decision alternatives. In recent years, special decision support software has been developed for this real-time purpose (Bates, 2003). These tools appear under different names such as *business activity monitoring (BAM)* and *extreme analytical frameworks (EAF)*.

DSSs were designed initially to support individual decision makers. However, many organizational decisions are made by groups, such as an executive committee. Next we see how IT can support such situations.

Group Decision Support Systems

Decision making is frequently a shared process. When a decision-making group is supported electronically, the support is referred to as *group decision support*. Two types of groups may be supported: a "one-room" group whose members are in one place (e.g., a meeting room) and a **virtual group**, whose members are in different locations.

A **group decision support system (GDSS)** is an interactive computer-based system that facilitates a group's efforts to find solutions to semistructured and unstructured problems. The objective of a GDSS is to support the *process* of arriving at a decision. Important characteristics of a GDSS, according to DeSanctis and Gallupe (1987), are shown in Online File W10.4.

The first generation of GDSSs was designed to support face-to-face meetings in what is called a **decision room**—a face-to-face setting for a group DSS, in which terminals are available to the participants. Such a GDSS is described in Online File W10.5.) A virtual GDSS application is described in IT's about Business 10.3 (page 316).

> **virtual group** *A group whose members are in different locations.*
>
> **group decision support system (GDSS)** *An interactive computer-based system that supports the process of finding solutions by a group of decision makers.*
>
> **decision room** *A face-to-face setting for a group DSS, in which terminals are available to the participants.*

wiley.com/college/turban

wiley.com/college/turban

IT's ABOUT BUSINESS

POM

10.3: Virtual Meetings at the World Economic Forum

The World Economic Forum (WEF, at *www.weforum.org*) is a consortium of top business, government, academic, and media leaders from virtually every country in the world. WEF's mission is to foster international understanding. Until 1998, the members conferred privately or debated global issues only at the forum's annual meeting in Davos, Switzerland, and at regional summits. Follow-up was difficult because of the members' geographic dispersion and conflicting schedules.

A WEF online strategy and operations task force developed a collaborative computing system to allow secure communication among members, making the nonprofit group more effective in its mission. Now WEF is making faster progress toward solutions for the global problems it studies. The GDSS and its complementary videoconferencing system, called the World Electronic Community (WELCOM), give members a secure channel through which to send e-mail, read reports available in a WEF library, and communicate in point-to-point or multipoint videoconferences. Forum members now hold real-time discussions and briefings on pressing issues and milestones, such as, for example, the 2003 Iraqi war.

The WELCOM system was designed with a graphical user interface (GUI) to make it easily accessible to inexperienced computer users. (Many WEF members might not be computer-literate or proficient typists.) The forum also set up "concierge services," based in Boston, Singapore, and Geneva, for technical support and to arrange videoconferences and virtual meetings. To handle any time/any place meetings, members can access recorded forum events and discussions that they may have missed. One of the most heavily used features of the system is an extensive library. The site also operates a knowledge base ("knowledge navigator") and a media center.

As of 2001, the system was moved completely onto the Web. With Webcasting, all sessions of the annual meetings can be viewed in real time. The virtual meetings are done in a secured environment, and private chat rooms are also available.

Source: weforum.org (accessed November 10, 2003).

QUESTIONS

1. How does the GDSS contribute to the mission of the World Economic Forum?
2. How important do you think security is to this GDSS? Why?

Before you go on . . .

1. Distinguish between sensitivity analysis and goal-seeking analysis.
2. What are the components of a DSS?
3. Describe group decision support systems.

10.3 ENTERPRISE AND EXECUTIVE DECISION SUPPORT SYSTEMS

Two types of enterprise decision support systems are described here: systems that support whole organizational tasks and systems that support decisions made by top-level managers and executives.

Organizational Decision Support System

organizational decision support system (ODSS) *A DSS that focuses on an organizational task or activity involving a sequence of operations and decision makers.*

Hackathorn and Keen (1981) first defined an **organizational decision support system (ODSS)** as one that focuses on an *organizational* task or activity involving a *sequence* of operations and decision makers, such as developing a divisional marketing plan or doing capital budgeting. Each individual's activities must mesh closely with other people's work. The computer support was primarily seen as a vehicle for improving communication and coordination, in addition to problem solving.

There are three major characteristics of an ODSS: (1) It affects several organizational units or corporate problems. (2) It cuts across organizational functions or hierarchical layers. (3) It involves computer-based technologies and usually involves communication technologies. Also, an ODSS often interacts or integrates with enterprisewide information systems such as executive support systems.

Executive Information (Support) Systems

The majority of personal DSSs support the work of professionals and middle-level managers. Organizational DSSs (ODSSs) provide support primarily to planners, analysts, researchers, and to some managers. Notice that top executives are not included on either of these lists. For a DSS to be used by top managers it must meet executives' needs. An **executive information system (EIS)**, also known as an *executive support system (ESS)*, is a computer-based technology designed in response to the specific needs of executives.

An EIS serves the information needs of top executives by providing rapid access to timely information and direct access to management reports. An EIS is very user friendly, is supported by graphics, and provides the capabilities of *exception reporting* (reporting of only the results that deviate from a set standard) and *drill down* (investigating information in increasing detail). It is also easily connected with online information services and electronic mail. EISs may include analysis support, communications, office automation, and intelligence support.

> **executive information system (EIS)** *A computer-based technology designed in response to the specific needs of executives; also known as an* executive support system (ESS).

Capabilities and Characteristics of ESSs

Executive support systems vary in their capabilities and benefits. Capabilities common to many ESSs are summarized in Table 10.1. One of these capabilities, the monitoring of critical success factors (CSFs), is measured by key performance indicators (KPIs) as shown in Online File W10.6. ESSs can be enhanced with multi-dimensional analysis and presentation, friendly data access, user-friendly graphical interface, imaging capabilities, intranet access, e-mail, Internet access, and modeling.

wiley.com/college/turban

Some of the capabilities discussed in this section are now part of a business intelligence product (discussed in Chapter 3), as shown in Figure 10.5 (page 318).

Enterprise Decision Simulator

An interesting example of enterprise decision support is the so-called "corporate war room." This concept has been used by the military for a long time to plan campaigns.

Table 10.1   The Capabilities of an ESS

Capability	Description
Drill-down	Ability to go to details, at several levels; can be done by a series of menus or by direct queries (using intelligent agents and natural language processing).
Critical success factors (CSF)	The factors most critical for the success of business. These can be organizational, industry, departmental, etc.
Key performance indicators	The specific measures of CSFs. Examples are provided (KPIs) in Online File W10.6.
Status access	The latest data available on KPI or some other metric, ideally in real time.
Trend analysis	Short-, medium-, and long-term trend of KPIs or metrics, which are projected using forecasting methods.
Ad-hoc analysis	Analyses made any time, upon demand and with any desired factors and relationships.
Exception reporting	Reports that highlight deviations larger than certain thresholds. Reports may include only deviations. Based on the concept of management by exception.

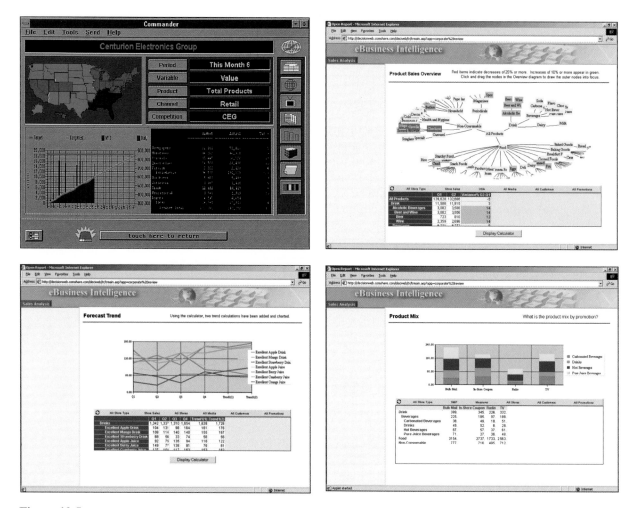

Figure 10.5   *Sample screens from Comshare Decision (now part of Geac Computer Corp.)—a modular system for generating business intelligence reports.*

It has now been transformed by SAP for use in industry, as described in the following example.

EXAMPLE

The Management Cockpit. The Management Cockpit is a strategic management room that enables top-level decision makers to pilot their businesses better. The aim is to create an environment that encourages more efficient management meetings and boosts team performance via effective communication. To help achieve this goal, key performance indicators and information relating to critical success factors are displayed graphically on the walls of a meeting room (see nearby photo). The cockpit-like arrangement of instrument panels and displays helps managers grasp how all the different factors in the business interrelate.

Executives can call up this information on their laptops, of course, but a key element of the concept is the Management Cockpit Room. There, on the four walls—Black, Red, Blue, and White—graphics depict performance as reflected in mission-critical factors. The Black Wall shows the principal success factors and financial indicators; the Red Wall, market performance; the Blue Wall, the performance of internal processes and employees; and the White Wall, the status of strategic projects. The Flight Deck, a six-screen high-end PC, enables executives to drill down to detailed information. The Cockpit environment is integrated with SAP's ERP products and reporting systems. External information can be easily imported to the room to allow competitive analysis.

Board members and other executives can hold meetings in this room. Managers will also meet there with the comptroller to discuss current business issues. For this purpose, the Management Cockpit can implement various what-if scenarios. The Management Cockpit provides a common basis for information and communication. It also supports efforts to translate a corporate strategy into concrete activities by identifying performance indicators. (*Sources:* Compiled from *sap.com*, and from *metis.no/info/cases/ it_man_cockpit.html*.)

Before you go on . . .

1. What are some of the capabilities of executive support systems?
2. What is an enterprise decision simulator?

10.4 INTELLIGENT SUPPORT SYSTEMS: THE BASICS

Intelligent support systems is a term that describes the various commercial applications of artificial intelligence (AI).

Artificial Intelligence and Intelligent Behavior

Artificial intelligence (AI) is a subfield of computer science. It is concerned with two basic ideas: first, studying the thought processes of humans, and second, representing those processes via machines (computers, robots, and so on). Since the events of 9/11, AI has been getting lots of attention, due to its potential to assist in fighting terrorism (Kahn, 2002). AI also is gaining attention as the number of intelligent devices in the marketplace grows.

One well-publicized definition of AI is "behavior by a machine that, if performed by a human being, would be considered *intelligent*." So, what is *intelligent behavior*? The following capabilities are considered to be signs of intelligence: learning or understanding from experience, making sense of ambiguous or contradictory messages, and responding quickly and successfully to a new situation.

AI's ultimate goal is to build machines that will mimic human intelligence. An interesting test to determine whether a computer exhibits intelligent behavior was designed by Alan Turing, a British AI pioneer. According to the Turing test, a computer could be considered "smart" only when a human interviewer, conversing with both an unseen human being and an unseen computer, cannot determine which is which. At this time, the intelligent systems exemplified in commercial AI products are far from exhibiting any significant intelligence.

The potential value of AI can be better understood by contrasting it with natural (human) intelligence. AI has several important commercial advantages over natural intelligence, but also some limitations, as shown in Table 10.2 (page 320).

The Commercial AI Technologies

The development of machines that exhibit intelligent characteristics draws upon several sciences and technologies, ranging from linguistics to mathematics. Artificial intelligence

artificial intelligence (AI) *A subfield of computer science concerned with studying the thought processes of humans and representing those processes via machines.*

Turing test *A test for artificial intelligence, in which a human interviewer, conversing with both an unseen human being and an unseen computer, cannot determine which is which; named for English mathematician Alan Turing.*

Table 10.2 Comparison of the Capabilities of Natural vs. Artificial Intelligence

Capabilities	Natural Intelligence	Artificial Intelligence
Preservation of knowledge	Perishable from an organizational point of view.	Permanent.
Duplication and dissemination of knowledge	Difficult, expensive, takes time.	Easy, fast, and inexpensive once knowledge is in a computer.
Total cost of knowledge	Can be erratic and inconsistent. Incomplete at times.	Consistent and thorough.
Documentability of process and knowledge.	Difficult, expensive.	Fairly easy, inexpensive.
Creativity	Can be very high.	Low; uninspired.
Use of sensory experiences	Direct and rich in possibilities.	Must be interpreted first; limited.
Recognizing patterns and relationships	Fast, easy to explain.	Machine learning still not as good as people in most cases, but in some cases can do better than people.
Reasoning	Making use of wide context of experiences.	Good only in narrow, focused, and stable domains.

itself is not a commercial field; it is a collection of concepts and ideas that are appropriate for research.

The major intelligent systems are: expert systems, natural language processing, speech understanding, robotics and sensory systems, fuzzy logic, neural computing, computer vision and scene recognition, and intelligent computer-aided instruction. In addition, two or more of the above can be combined into a *hybrid* intelligent system. The major intelligent systems are listed in Table 10.3.

Software and Intelligent Agents. As described in Chapters 4 and 5, software and intelligent agents play a major role in supporting such work on computers as search, alerts, monitoring Web activities, and suggestions to users. Intelligent agents also support computer work in general, such as configuring complex product and diagnosing malfunctions in networks. Coverage of the topic of intelligent agents is provided in Online Appendix W10.1.

wiley.com/college/turban

Table 10.3 The Intelligent Systems

Name	Short Description
Expert system (ES)	Computerized advisory systems usually based on rules.
Natural language processing (NLP)	Enables computers to recognize and even understand human languages.
Speech understanding	Enables computers to recognize words and understand short voice sentences.
Robotic and sensory systems	Programmable combination of mechanical and computer program. Recognize their environments via sensors.
Computer vision and scene recognition	Enable computers to interpret the content of pictures captured by cameras.
Machine learning	Enables computers to interpret the content of pictures captured by sensors (see next three items).
Handwriting recognition	Enables computers to recognize characters (letters, digits), written by hand.
Neural computing (networks)	Using massive parallel processing, able to recognize patterns in large amount of data.
Fuzzy logic	Enables computers to reason with partial information.
Intelligent agents	Software programs that perform tasks for a human or machine master.
Semantic Web	An intelligent software program that "understands" content of Web pages.

Before you go on . . .

1. Describe what is meant by intelligent behavior.
2. Compare artificial and natural intelligence.

10.5 EXPERT SYSTEMS

When an organization has a complex decision to make or a problem to solve, it often turns to experts for advice. These experts have specific knowledge and experience in the problem area. They are aware of alternative solutions, chances of success, and costs that the organization may incur if the problem is not solved. Companies engage experts for advice on such matters as equipment purchase, mergers and acquisitions, and advertising strategy. The more unstructured the situation, the more specialized and expensive is the advice.

Expert systems (ESs) are an attempt to mimic human experts by applying reasoning methodologies or knowledge in a specific domain. Expert systems can either *support* decision makers or completely *replace* them. Expert systems are the most widely applied and commercially successful AI technology.

Typically, an ES is decision-making software that can reach a level of performance comparable to a human expert in some specialized and usually narrow problem area. The basic idea behind an ES is simple: *Expertise* is transferred from an expert (or other source of expertise) to the computer. This knowledge is then stored in the computer, and users can call on the computer for specific advice as needed. The computer can make inferences and arrive at a conclusion. Then, like a human expert, it offers advice or recommendations and explains, if necessary, the logic behind the advice. ESs can sometimes perform better than any single expert can.

> **expert system (ES)** *A computer system that attempts to mimic human experts by applying reasoning methodologies or knowledge in a specific domain.*

Expertise and Knowledge

Expertise is the extensive, task-specific knowledge acquired from training, reading, and experience. It enables experts to make better and faster decisions than nonexperts in solving complex problems. Expertise takes a long time (possibly years) to acquire, and it is distributed in organizations in an uneven manner.

The transfer of expertise from an expert to a computer and then to the user involves four activities:

1. *Knowledge acquisition.* Knowledge is acquired from experts or from documented sources.

2. *Knowledge representation.* Acquired knowledge is organized as rules or frames (object-oriented) and stored electronically in a knowledge base.

3. *Knowledge inferencing.* Given the necessary expertise stored in the knowledge base, the computer is programmed so that it can make inferences. The reasoning function is performed in a component called the **inference engine**, which is the brain of the ES.

4. *Knowledge transfer.* The inferenced expertise is transferred to the user in the form of a recommendation.

> **inference engine** *Component of an expert system that performs a reasoning function.*

A unique feature of an ES is its ability to *explain* its recommendations. The explanation and justification is done in a subsystem called the *justifier* or the *explanation subsystem*. For example, it presents the sequence of rules used by the inference engine to generate a recommendation.

The Benefits and Limitations of Expert Systems

During the past few years, the technology of expert systems has been successfully applied in thousands of organizations worldwide to problems ranging from AIDS research

Table 10.4   Benefits of Expert Systems

Benefit	Description
Increased output and productivity	ESs can configure components for each custom order, increasing production capabilities.
Increased quality	ESs can provide consistent advice and reduce error rates.
Capture and dissemination of scarce expertise	Expertise from anywhere in the world can be obtained and used.
Operation in hazardous environments	Sensors can collect information that an ES interprets, enabling human workers to avoid hot, humid, or toxic environments.
Accessibility to knowledge and help desks	ESs can increase the productivity of help-desk employees, or even automate this function.
Reliability	ESs do not become tired or bored, call in sick, or go on strike. They consistently pay attention to details.
Ability to work with incomplete or uncertain information	Even with an answer of "don't know," an ES can produce an answer, though it may not be a definite one.
Provision of training	The explanation facility of an ES can serve as a teaching device and knowledge base for novices.
Enhancement of decision-making and problem-solving capabilities.	ESs allow the integration of expert judgment into analysis (e.g., diagnosis of machine malfunction and even medical diagnosis).
Decreased decision-making time	ESs usually can make faster decisions than humans working alone.
Reduced downtime	ESs can quickly diagnose machine malfunctions and prescribe repairs.

to the analysis of dust in mines. Why have ESs become so popular? It is because of the large number of capabilities and benefits they provide. The major benefits are listed in Table 10.4.

Despite their many benefits, available ES methodologies are not always straightforward and effective. Expert systems may not be able to arrive at any conclusions. For example, even some fully developed complex expert systems are unable to fulfill about 2 percent of the orders presented to them. Finally, expert systems, like human experts, sometimes produce incorrect recommendations.

The Components of Expert Systems

The following components exist in an expert system: knowledge base, inference engine, blackboard (workplace), user interface, and explanation subsystem (justifier). In the future, systems will include a knowledge-refining component. The relationships among components are shown in Figure 10.6. The major components of expert systems are described below.

- *Knowledge base.* The *knowledge base* contains knowledge necessary for understanding, formulating, and solving problems. It includes two basic elements: (1) *facts*, such as the problem situation and theory of the problem area, and (2) *rules* that direct the use of knowledge to solve specific problems in a particular domain.

- *Inference engine.* The *inference engine* is the brain of the ES. This component is essentially a computer program that provides a methodology for reasoning and formulating conclusions.

- *User interface.* The *user interface* allows for user–computer dialogue. That dialogue can be best carried out in a natural language, usually in a question-and-answer format and sometimes supplemented by graphics. The dialogue triggers the inference engine to match the problem symptoms with the knowledge in the knowledge base and then generate advice.

- *Blackboard.* The *blackboard* is an area of working memory set aside for the description of a current problem, as specified by the input data. It is also used for recording intermediate results. It is a kind of database.

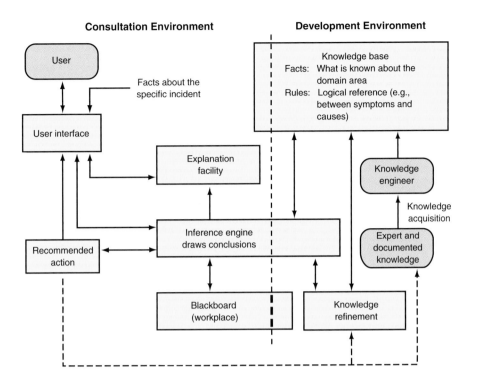

Consultation Environment   **Development Environment**

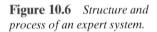

Figure 10.6 *Structure and process of an expert system.*

- **Explanation subsystem.** The *explanation subsystem* can trace responsibility for arriving at a conclusion and explain the ES's behavior. It interactively answers questions such as the following: *Why* was a certain question asked by the expert system? *How* was a certain conclusion reached? *What* is the plan to reach the solution?

Human experts have a *knowledge-refining* system; that is, they can analyze their own performance, learn from it, and improve it for future consultations. Similarly, such evaluation is necessary in computerized learning so that the program will be able to improve by analyzing the reasons for its success or failure. Such a component is not available in commercial expert systems at the moment, but it is being developed in experimental systems.

Applications of Expert Systems

Expert systems are in use today in all types of organizations. Expert systems are especially useful in 10 generic categories, displayed in Table 10.5.

Table 10.5   Ten Generic Categories of Expert Systems

Category	Problem Addressed
Interpretation	Inferring situation descriptions from observations.
Prediction	Inferring likely consequences of given situations.
Diagnosis	Inferring system malfunctions from observations.
Design	Configuring objects under constraints.
Planning	Developing plans to achieve goal(s).
Monitoring	Comparing observations to plans, flagging exceptions.
Debugging	Prescribing remedies for malfunctions.
Repair	Executing a plan to administer a prescribed remedy.
Instruction	Diagnosing, debugging, and correcting student performance.
Control	Interpreting, predicting, repairing, and monitoring systems behavior.

IT's ABOUT BUSINESS

10.4: Con-Way Central Automates Truck Dispatching

Line-haul, the movement of freight over long distances between service centers for redistribution, used to force freight dispatchers at Con-Way (*con-way.com*) into a perpetual tug-of-war between the promise of on-time overnight delivery (a nonnegotiable customer expectation) and efficiency. For efficiency, routes must have the fewest miles, maximize trailer loads, and ensure that drivers, who are nonunion, can get home when their daily shift ends. Dispatchers had to gather and sort through a stack of mainframe printouts showing what freight needed to move between 200 locations across 25 states and Canada during the next 12 hours.

Dispatchers reviewed tonnage, available drivers and trucks, and trailer capacity at each of the 40 locations assigned to each dispatcher. Seven dispatchers typically had to plot the nightly routes that would transport 50,000 shipments of heavy freight on 2,100 trucks from their origin points to midway freight-assembly centers. In addition, the stressful dispatcher position was difficult to fill and had a learning curve as long as 18 months. The procedures and business rules that the dispatchers followed were undocumented, making the company uncomfortably dependent on the knowledge in the dispatchers' heads.

Con-Way decided to develop an expert system for its dispatching process. The system ultimately took five years and $3 million to develop, test, and deploy. But it was certainly worth the effort and expense.

Today, Con-Way's expert system digests on average 80,000 customer pickup orders and change requests every day. Its optimization model plots delivery across all the service centers and determines which shipments should be loaded on which truck—all this in seven minutes! The expert system now has a Web interface that allows dispatchers to view the line-haul plot onscreen rather than in stacks of printouts.

The incremental efficiencies generated repaid in the first two years the investment in the system. Even without that hard-dollar return on investment, Con-Way would have funded the project simply because it could not sustain the status quo. The expert system routinely extracts efficiency improvements of 1 to 3 percent over results achieved with manual route planning. These incremental gains add up to $4 to $5 million in savings annually. These savings come from paying fewer drivers, moving trucks fewer miles, packing more freight per trailer, and reducing damage from rehandling freight. Con-Way also has been able to reduce its dispatchers by three people (through attrition) and can keep the group small as the company adds business.

Customers benefit by improvement in on-time delivery. While Con-Way is reluctant to attribute its 99 percent on-time performance directly to the expert system, the company realizes that freeing dispatchers from the tedium of routing has given them more time to prevent delays. Another customer benefit is the later cutoff time for submitting orders. Con-Way does not market the extended time to its customers, as it wants to avoid being overwhelmed by last-minute calls. Still, when an urgent situation arises, a customer has until the end of the day to call Con-Way and schedule a pickup, a unique and valuable competitive advantage.

Source: R. Pastore, "Cruise Control," *CIO Magazine* (February 1, 2003).

QUESTIONS

1. List the advantages of Con-Way's expert system and the functional areas of the company that are enjoying the advantages.
2. Why was having all dispatching knowledge "in the heads of the dispatchers" a problem for Con-Way?
3. How would you feel if you were a dispatcher and the company decided to develop this expert system?

IT's about Business 10.4 shows how a trucking company uses its expert system. For additional examples of ES applications, see Online File W10.7. For other examples, by industry, see *exsys.com* (in the case studies).

wiley.com/college/turban

Before you go on . . .

1. Describe the transfer of expertise from human expert(s) to a computer and then to a user.
2. What are the benefits and limitations of expert systems?

10.6 OTHER INTELLIGENT SYSTEMS

An expert system's major objective is to provide expert advice. Other intelligent systems can be used to solve problems or provide capabilities in areas in which they excel. Several such technologies are described next: natural language processing, artificial neural networks, and fuzzy logic.

Natural Language Processing and Voice Technologies

Natural language processing (NLP) refers to communicating with a computer in English or whatever language you speak. To understand a natural language inquiry, a computer must have the knowledge to analyze and then interpret the input. This may include linguistic knowledge about words, domain knowledge (knowledge of a narrowly defined, specific area, such as student registration or air travel), commonsense knowledge, and even knowledge about the users and their goals. Once the computer understands the input, it can take the desired action.

In this section we briefly discuss two types of NLP: natural language understanding (also called speech or voice recognition) and natural language generation (also called voice synthesis). NL understanding is the input side and NL generation is the output side of the natural-language-processing coin.

natural language processing (NLP) *Communicating with a computer in English or whatever language you may speak.*

Natural Language Understanding. **Natural language understanding** or **speech (voice) recognition** allows a computer to comprehend instructions given in ordinary English (or other language), via the keyboard or by voice, so that computers are able to understand people. The goal of natural language understanding is to have a system that not only recognizes voice input but also understands it. Speech recognition is deployed today in wireless PDAs as well as in many applications in stores and warehouses (Kumagai, 2002, and Amato-McCoy, 2003).

natural language understanding/speech (voice) recognition *The ability of a computer to comprehend instructions given in ordinary language, via the keyboard or by voice.*

Advantages and Limitations of Natural Language Understanding. Natural language understanding offers several advantages:

- ***Ease of access.*** Many more people can speak than can type. As long as communication with a computer depends on typing skills, many people may not be able to use computers effectively.

- ***Speed.*** Even the most competent typists can speak more quickly than they can type. It is estimated that the average person can speak twice as quickly as a proficient typist can type.

- ***Manual freedom.*** Obviously, communicating with a computer through typing occupies your hands. There are many situations in which computers might be useful to people whose hands are otherwise engaged, such as product assemblers, pilots of aircraft, and busy executives. Speech recognition also enables people with hand-related physical disabilities to use computers.

However, there are limitations of natural language understanding, which limit its use. The major limitation is the inability of such a system to recognize long sentences, or the long time needed to accomplish it. The better the system is at speech recognition, the higher is its cost. Also, in voice recognition systems, you cannot manipulate icons and windows, so speech may need to be combined with a keyboard entry, which slows communication.

Natural Language Generation. **Natural language generation** or **voice synthesis** is a technology that enables computers to produce ordinary English language, by "voice" or on the screen, so that people can understand computers more easily. As the term *synthesis* implies, sounds that make up words and phrases are electronically constructed from basic sound components and can be made to form any desired voice pattern.

The current quality of synthesized voice is very good, but the technology remains somewhat expensive. Anticipated lower cost and improved performance of synthetic

natural language generation/voice synthesis *Technology that enables computers to produce ordinary language, by "voice" or on the screen, so that people can understand computers more easily.*

voice should encourage more widespread commercial interactive voice response (IVR) applications, especially those on the Web. Opportunities for its use will encompass almost all applications that can provide an automated response to a user, such as inquiries by employees pertaining to payroll and benefits. A number of banks already offer voice service to their customers, informing them about their balance, which checks were cashed, and so on. Many credit card companies provide similar services, telling customers about current account balances, recent charges, and payments received. For a list of other voice synthesis and voice recognition applications, see Table 10.6.

Artificial Neural Networks

artificial neural networks (ANNs)
Computer technology, modeled after concepts from biological neural systems, that attempts to simulate massively parallel processing of interconnected elements in a network architecture.

neural computing *The application of artificial neural network technology.*

Artificial neural networks (ANNs) use a limited set of concepts from biological neural systems. The goal is to simulate massively parallel processing of interconnected elements in a network architecture. The artificial neuron receives inputs analogous to the electrochemical impulses biological neurons receive from other neurons. The output of the artificial neuron corresponds to signals sent out from a biological neuron. These artificial signals can be changed, like the signals from the human brain. Neurons in an ANN receive information from other neurons or from external sources, transform or process the information, and pass it on to other neurons or as external outputs. The application of artificial neural network technology is referred to as **neural computing**.

Table 10.6 Examples of Voice Technology Applications

Applications	Companies	Types of Devices Used
Answering inquiries about reservations, schedules, lost baggage, etc.	Scandinavian Airlines, other airlines	Output
Informing credit card holders about balances and credits, providing bank account balances and other information to customers	Citibank, many other banks	Output
Verifying coverage information	Delta Dental Plan (CA)	Output
Requesting pickups, ordering supplies	Federal Express	Input
Giving information about services, receiving orders	Illinois Bell, other telephone companies	Output and input
Enabling stores to order supplies, providing price information	Domino's Pizza	Output and input
Allowing inspectors to report results of quality assurance tests	General Electric, Rockwell International, Austin Rover, Westpoint Pepperell, Eastman Kodak	Input
Allowing receivers of shipments to report weights and inventory levels of various meats and cheeses	Cara Donna Provisions	Input
Conducting market research and telemarketing	Weidner Insurance, AT&T	Input
Notifying people of emergencies detected by sensors	U.S. Department of Energy, Idaho National Engineering Lab, Honeywell	Output
Notifying parents about cancellation of classes and of when students are absent	New Jersey Department of Education	Output
Calling patients to remind them of appointments, summarizing and reporting results of tests	Kaiser-Permanente HMO	Output
Activating radios, heaters, etc. by voice	Car manufacturers	Input
Logging in and out to payroll department by voice	Taxoma Medical Center	Input
Prompting doctors in the emergency room to conduct all necessary tests, reporting of results by doctors	St. Elizabeth's Hospital	Output and input
Sending and receiving patient data by voice, searching for doctors, preparing schedules and medical records	Hospital Corporation of America	Output and input

Benefits and Applications of Neural Networks. The value of neural network technology includes its usefulness for pattern recognition, learning, and the interpretation of incomplete inputs.

With **pattern recognition**, neural networks analyze large quantities of data in order to establish patterns and characteristics in situations where the logic or rules are not known. An example would be loan applications. By reviewing many historical cases of applicants' questionnaires and the "yes or no" decisions made, the ANN can create "patterns" or "profiles" of applications that should be approved or denied. The computer can then match a new application against the pattern. If the application comes close enough to existing profiles, the computer classifies it as a "yes" or "no"; otherwise it goes to a human for a decision. Neural networks are especially useful for financial applications such as determining when to buy or sell stock, predicting bankruptcy, and predicting exchange rates.

Beyond its role as an alternative computing mechanism and in data mining, neural computing can be combined with other computer-based information systems to produce powerful hybrid systems, as illustrated in IT's about Business 10.5.

pattern recognition *The ability of a neural network to establish patterns and characteristics in situations where the logic or rules are not known, by analyzing large quantities of data.*

Fuzzy Logic

Fuzzy logic is computer reasoning that deals with uncertainties by simulating the process of human reasoning. It allows the computer to behave less precisely and logically than

fuzzy logic *Computer reasoning that deals with uncertainties by simulating the process of human reasoning.*

IT's ABOUT BUSINESS [FIN]

10.5: Banks Are Cracking Down on Credit Card Fraud

Only 0.2 percent of Visa International's turnover in 1995 was lost to fraud, but at $655 million it is a loss well worth addressing. Visa (*visa.com*) is now concentrating its efforts on reversing the number of fraudulent transactions by using neural computing.

Most people stick to a well-established pattern of credit card use and only rarely splurge on expensive nonessentials. Neural networks are designed to notice when a card that is usually used to buy gasoline once a week is suddenly used to buy a number of tickets to the hottest show on Broadway. Unusual charges may be denied, or the card may be inactivated. In some cases, the merchant may be told to confiscate the card and alert the authorities.

In 1995, Visa's cardholder risk identification system (CRIS) conducted over 16 billion transactions. By 2003, VisaNet (Visa's data warehouse and e-mail operations) and CRIS were handling more than 8,000 transactions per second or about 320 billion transactions a year. By fall 2003, CRIS was able to notify banks of fraud within a few seconds of a transaction. Rapid notification allows banks to cancel credit cards before additional items are charged, saving banks and merchants money. The only downside to CRIS is that occasionally the system prompts a call to a cardholder's spouse when an out-of-the-ordinary item is charged, such as a surprise vacation trip or a diamond ring. After all, no one wants to spoil surprises for loved ones.

Visa's participating member banks believe the neural network technology has been successful in combating fraud. Bank of America uses the cardholder risk identification system (CRIS) and has cut fraudulent card use by up to two-thirds. Toronto Dominion Bank found that losses were reduced, and overall customer service improved, with the introduction of neural computing. Another bank recorded savings of $5.5 million in six months. Visa spent $2 million to implement CRIS and says that the system paid for itself in one year by preventing fraudulent credit card use.

Sumitomo Credit Service Co., a credit card issuer in Japan, is using a similar neural network-based system, Falcon, from HNC Corp (now owned by Fair Isaac, *fairisaac.com*). The product works well reading Japanese characters, protecting 18 million cardholders in Japan.

Sources: Customer success stories at *hnc.com* (November 10, 2003) and *visa.com* (press releases, accessed November 15, 2003).

QUESTIONS

1. What is the advantage of CRIS over an automatic check against the balance in the account?
2. What is the advantage of CRIS against a set of rules such as "Call a human authorizer when the purchase price is more than 200 percent of the average previous bill"?

conventional computers do. The rationale behind this approach is that decision making is not always a matter of black and white, true or false. It often involves gray areas where the term *maybe* is more appropriate. In fact, creative decision-making processes are often unstructured, playful, contentious, and rambling. At the present time, there are only a few examples of pure fuzzy logic applications in business, mainly in predicting system behavior.

Before you go on . . .

1. What are the advantages and disadvantages of natural language understanding?

2. What are the advantages and disadvantages of artificial neural networks?

3. What is fuzzy logic?

WHAT'S IN  FOR ME?

ACC

FOR THE ACCOUNTING MAJOR

Intelligent systems are used extensively in auditing to uncover irregularities. They are also used to uncover and prevent fraud. Today's CPAs use intelligent systems for many of their duties, ranging from risk analysis to cost control. Intelligent agents are also used for several mundane tasks such as managing accounts or monitoring employees' Internet usage.

FIN

FOR THE FINANCE MAJOR

People have been using computers for decades to solve financial problems. Innovative decision support applications exist in stock market decisions, bond refinancing, debt risk assessment, analysis of financial conditions, business failure prediction, financial forecasting, investment in global markets, and more. Intelligent systems were found to be superior to other computerized methods in many instances. Intelligent agents can facilitate the use of spreadsheets and other computerized systems used in finance. Finally, intelligent systems can help in reducing fraud in credit cards, stocks, and other financial services.

MKT

FOR THE MARKETING MAJOR

Marketing personnel utilize DSS models in many applications, for example from allocating advertising budgets to evaluating alternative routings of salespeople. New marketing approaches such as targeted marketing and marketing transaction databases are heavily dependent on IT in general and on intelligent systems in particular. Intelligent systems are particularly useful in mining customer databases and predicting customer behavior. Successful applications are noted in almost any area of marketing and sales, from analyzing the success of one-to-one advertising to supporting customer help desks. With the increased importance of customer service, the use of intelligent agents is becoming critical for providing fast response.

POM

FOR THE PRODUCTION/ OPERATIONS MANAGEMENT MAJOR

Decision support systems support complex operations and production decisions, from inventory to production planning. Many of the early expert systems were developed in the production/operations management field for tasks ranging from diagnosis of machine failures and prescription of repairs to complex production scheduling and inventory control. Some companies, such as DuPont and Kodak, have deployed hundreds of expert systems in the planning, organizing, and control of their operational systems.

Human resource personnel use intelligent systems for many applications. For example, intelligent agents can find resumes of applicants posted on the Web and sort them to match needed skills. Expert systems are used in evaluating candidates (tests, interviews). Intelligent systems are used to facilitate training and to support self-management of fringe benefits. Neural computing is used to predict employee performance on the job as well as to predict labor needs. Voice recognition systems provide benefits information to employees.

HRM

FOR THE HUMAN RESOURCES MANAGEMENT MAJOR

SUMMARY

1. **Describe the concepts of management, decision making, and computerized support for decision making.** Management is a process by which organizational goals are achieved through the use of resources (people, money, energy, materials, space, time). Managers have three basic roles: interpersonal, informational, and decisional. When making a decision, either organizational or personal, the decision maker goes through a four-step process: intelligence, design, choice, and implementation.

   Several information technologies have been successfully used to directly support managers. Collectively, they are referred to as management support systems (MSSs). These technologies include decision support systems, executive support systems, group decision support systems, and intelligent systems.

2. **Describe decision support systems (DSSs) and their benefits, and describe the structure of DSSs.** A decision support system is a computer-based information system that combines models and data in an attempt to solve semistructured and some unstructured problems with extensive user involvement. DSS benefits include (among others): support for decision makers at all levels of management; support of all phases of the decision-making process; promotion of learning; and extensive, user-driven data analysis, usually through modeling. DSSs consist of data management and model management components, a user interface, end users, and sometimes knowledge management components.

3. **Describe computerized support for group decision making.** A group decision support system (GDSS) is an interactive computer-based system that facilitates the solving of semistructured and unstructured problems by a group of decision makers. The objective of a GDSS is to support the *process* of arriving at a decision.

4. **Describe organizational decision support and executive support systems.** An organizational decision support system (ODSS) focuses on an organizational task or activity involving a sequence of operations and decision makers. It aims to solve problems as well as to improve communication and coordination or organizational activities.

   An executive information system (EIS) serves the information needs of top executives. It provides rapid access to timely information and direct access to management reports. An EIS is very user friendly, is supported by graphics, and provides the capabilities of exception reporting and drill-down.

5. **Describe artificial intelligence (AI).** Artificial intelligence involves studying the thought processes of humans and attempting to represent those processes in machines (computers, robots, and so on). AI's ultimate goal is to build machines that will mimic human intelligence.

6. **Define an expert system and its components.** Expert systems (ESs) are an attempt to mimic the reasoning abilities of human experts. An ES is decision-making software that can reach a level of performance comparable to a human expert in some specialized and usually narrow problem area.

   The components of expert systems include: the knowledge base; the inference engine; the user interface; the blackboard (an area of working memory); and the explanation subsystem. It is expected that in the future ESs will also have a knowledge-refining system that can analyze performance and improve on it.

7. **Describe natural language processing and natural language generation.** Natural language understanding or speech recognition allows a computer to comprehend instructions given in ordinary language, via the keyboard or by voice, so that computers are able to understand people. Natural language generation or voice synthesis strives to allow computers to produce ordinary language, on the screen or by voice, so people can understand computers more easily.

8. **Describe artificial neural networks (ANNs) and their major applications.** Artificial neural networks simulate massively parallel processing of interconnected elements in a network architecture. The value of neural network technology includes its usefulness for pattern recognition, learning, and the interpretation of incomplete inputs.

INTERACTIVE / LEARNING

How Much Popcorn Should the Local Blockbuster Video Store Keep In Stock?

Go to the Interactivities section on the Student Web Site and access Chapter 10: Managerial Support Systems. There you will find some hands-on activities that explain the decision support systems used by industries ranging from retail to healthcare.

More Resources

More resources and study tools are located on the Student Web Site. You'll find additional chapter materials and links to organizations, people and technologies for each chapter. In addition, self-quizzes that provide individualized feedback are available for each chapter.

DISCUSSION QUESTIONS

1. Your company is considering opening a branch in China. List several typical activities in each phase of the decision (intelligence, design, choice, and implementation).

2. American Can Company announced that it was interested in acquiring a company in the health maintenance organization (HMO) field. Two decisions were involved in this act: (1) the decision to acquire an HMO, and (2) the decision of which one to acquire. How can a DSS, ES, and ESS be used in such situation?

3. A major difference between a conventional decision support system and an ES is that the former can explain a *how* question whereas the latter can also explain a *why* question. Discuss.

4. Compare and contrast neural computing and conventional computing.

5. Fuzzy logic is frequently combined with expert systems and/or neural computing. Explain the logic of such integration.

PROBLEM-SOLVING ACTIVITIES

1. Sofmic (fictitious name) is a large software vendor. About twice a year, Sofmic acquires a small, specialized software company. Recently, a decision was made to look for a software company in the area of data mining. Currently, there are about 15 companies that would gladly cooperate as candidates for such acquisitions.

   Bill Gomez, the corporate CEO, asked that a recommendation for a candidate for acquisition be submitted to him within one week. "Make sure to use some computerized support for justification, preferably from the area of AI," he said. As a manager responsible for submitting the recommendation to Gomez, you need to select a computerized tool for conducting the analysis. Respond to the following points:

   a. Prepare a list of all the tools that you would consider.

   b. Prepare a list of the major advantages and disadvantages of each tool, as it relates to this specific case.

   c. Select a computerized tool.

   d. Mr. Gomez does not assign grades to your work. Instead, if you make a poor recommendation, you may be out of a job. Therefore, carefully justify your recommendation.

2. Table 10.5 provides a list of 10 categories of ES. Compile a list of 10 examples from the various functional

areas in an organization (accounting, finance, production, marketing, human resources, and so on) that will show functional applications as they are related to the 10 categories.

3. *Debate:* Prepare a table showing all the arguments you can think of that justify the position that computers cannot think. Then, prepare arguments that show the opposite.

1. Enter the sites of *microstrategy.com, hyperion.com,* and *businessobjects.com* and identify each company's major DSS products. Find success stories of customers using these products.
2. Enter *asymetrix.com*. Learn about their decision support and performance management tool suite (Toolbook Assistant). Explain how the software can increase competitive advantage.
3. Prepare a report on the use of expert systems in help desks. Collect information from *ginesys.com, exsys.com, ilog.com,* and *pcai.com.*

4. At MIT (*media.mit.edu*) there is a considerable amount of interest in intelligent agents. Find the latest activities regarding IA. (Look at research and projects.)
5. Visit *sas.com/technologies/analytics/datamining/miner/ neuralnet.html*. Identify links to real-world applications in finance, manufacturing, health care, and automotive (hint: see the list of industries on the left side of the page). Prepare a report on current applications.

1. Prepare a report regarding DSSs and the Web. As a start go to *dssresources.com*. (Take the DSS tour.) Each group represents one vendor such as *microstrategy. com, sas.com,* and *ca.com*. Each group should prepare a report that aims to convince a company why its DSS Web tools are the best.
2. Find recent application(s) of intelligent systems in an organization. Assign each group member to a major functional area. Then, using a literature search, material from vendors, or industry contacts, each member should find two or three recent applications (within the last six months) of intelligent systems in this area.

Try the journals *Expert Systems* and *IEEE Intelligent Systems*.)
   a. The group will make a presentation in which it will try to convince the class via examples that intelligent systems are most useful in its assigned functional area.
   b. The entire class will conduct an analysis of the similarities and differences among the applications across the functional areas.
   c. The class will vote on which functional area is benefitting the most from intelligent systems.

REAL-WORLD CASE
SINGAPORE AND MALAYSIA AIRLINES EXPERT SYSTEMS

THE BUSINESS PROBLEM Airlines fly around the globe, mostly with their native crew. Singapore Airlines (*singaporeair.com*) and Malaysia Airlines (*malaysiaairlines. com*) are relatively small airlines, but they serve dozens of different countries. If a crewmember is ill on route, there is a problem of quickly finding a replacement. This is just one example why crew scheduling may be complex. Regulatory constraints, contract agreements, and crew preferences complicate the scheduling task. Disturbances such as weather conditions, or maintenance problems also make crew management difficult.

THE IT SOLUTION Singapore Airlines uses Web-based intelligent systems such as expert systems and neural computing to manage the company's flight crew scheduling and handle disruptions to the crew rosters. The Integrated Crew Management System (ICMS) proj-

ect, implemented in Singapore in 1997, consists of three modules: one roster assignment module for cockpit crew, one for the cabin crew, and a crew-tracking module. The first two modules automate the tracking and scheduling of the flight crew's timetable. The second module tracks the positions of the crew; it includes an intelligent system that handles crew pattern disruptions.

For example, crews are rearranged if one member falls ill while in a foreign port; the system will find a backup in order to prevent understaffing on the scheduled flight. The intelligent system then determines the best way to reschedule the different crew members' rosters. When a potentially disruptive situation occurs, the intelligent system automatically draws upon the knowledge stored in the database and advises the best course of action. This might mean repositioning the crew or calling in backup staff. The crew tracking system includes a crew disruption-handling module which provides decision support capabilities in real time.

A similar Web-based system is used by Malaysia Airlines as of summer 2003 to optimize flight crew utilization. Also called ICMS, it leverages optimization software from *ilog.com*. Its Crew Pairing Optimization (CPO) module utilizes optimization components to ensure compliance with airline regulations, trade union agreements, and company policies and to minimize the costs associated with crew accommodations and transportation. The CPO also efficiently plans and optimizes manpower utilization and activities associated with long-term planning and daily operations. The Crew Duty Assignment (CDA) module provides automatic assignment of duties to all flight crews. The system considers work rules, regulatory requirements, and crew requests to produce an optimal monthly crew roster.

THE RESULTS Despite the difficult economic times, both airlines are competing successfully in the region, and their balance sheets are better than most other airlines.

Source: ilog.com (accessed November 18, 2003).

QUESTIONS

1. Why do airlines need optimization systems for crew scheduling?
2. What role can experts' knowledge play in this case?
3. What are the similarities between the systems in Singapore and Malaysia?

CLUB IT — wiley.com/college/turban

FUTURE PLANNING AT CLUB IT

Club IT's interior remodel has been completed for a few months now, and it seems to be paying off in a higher door figure and more repeat patrons. Lisa and Ruben face many decisions for the future operations of their club. Should they expand? Should they raise drink prices? Are they staffed at the right levels? How effective are their live DJ's? Once they organize their information systems and data collection becomes systematic, they will have useful inputs for making better management decisions. You want to make sure they have the right decision making tools as well as the ability to use them productively, so you set about building some examples.

ASSIGNMENT

1. To help Lisa and Ruben decide whether or not to add more tables and chairs to the club, describe several typical activities in each phase of this decision (intelligence, design, choice, and implementation).

2. Create a spreadsheet to help Ruben do sensitivity analysis on drinks prices. Assume an initial net profit margin of 50% at a price of $5. Club IT averages 220 patrons per night and sells about three drinks per patron. In your formula, create several scenarios raising the price by x% and reducing the average number of drinks by y%. Make a recommendation regarding drink prices.

3. Review the *planograms* Lowes uses to place their merchandise in the store. How could Club IT use this to optimize the club's layout?

Go to wiley.com/college/turban to access the CLUB IT Web Site on the Student Web Site

Acquiring IT Applications and Infrastructure

Chapter Preview

Competitive organizations move as quickly as they can to acquire new information technologies (or modify existing ones) that can lead to improved efficiencies and strategic advantage. But acquisition now goes beyond building new systems in-house, and information technology resources go beyond software and hardware. The old model of firms building their own systems is being replaced with a broader perspective of IT resources acquisition that provides companies with a number of options regarding who will build systems, who will maintain them, and how critical applications will be acquired and on what financial terms. Decisions must be made about which IT tasks will remain in-house, and even whether the entire IT resource should be provided and managed by other companies. This chapter describes the process of IT resource acquisition from a managerial perspective. Special attention is given to the available options and how to evaluate them. Also, relationships with vendors and partners are discussed. We will also take a close look at planning and justifying the need for information systems.

The related technological issues, starting with an examination of the traditional systems development life cycle—the "how" of constructing information systems—are described in Technology Guide 6.

Chapter Outline

11.1 The Landscape and Framework of IT Application Acquisition

11.2 Planning for and Justifying Information System Applications

11.3 Strategies for Acquiring IT Applications: Available Options

11.4 Outsourcing and Application Service Providers

11.5 Criteria for Selecting an Acquisition Approach

11.6 Vendor and Software Selection and Other Implementation Issues

11.7 Connecting to Databases and Business Partners

Learning Objectives

1. Describe the process of IT acquisition or development.
2. Describe the IT planning process.
3. Describe the IT justification process and methods.
4. List the major IT acquisition options and the criteria for option selection.
5. Describe the use of criteria for selecting an acquisition approach.
6. Describe the role of ASPs.
7. Describe the process of vendor and software selection.
8. Understand some major implementation issues.
9. Understand the issue of connecting IT applications to databases, other applications, networks, and business partners.

WEB SERVICES GET SWEDISH BANKING APPLICATIONS TALKING TO EACH OTHER

THE BUSINESS PROBLEM

Centrala Studie Stodsnamnden (CSN) is the Swedish government's banking authority responsible for providing student loans and grants to Swedes who are pursuing higher education. Each year, CSN loans out SEK$2.5 billion to a half-million people and delivers a host of financial services to thousands more. In January 2002, at the start of the new school semester, when online traffic to the organization is typically four to five times greater than in other months, CSN's Web site went down. Students were forced to phone CSN representatives directly to receive help with new loan and grant applications and payback information. The voice-response system, that was designed to meet a much lower demand, had proved inadequate.

A group of technicians led by the production team worked hard to stabilize the Web site and ease the burden caused by overuse of the voice-response system. "We found the load problem and tried to tame it by adding servers, but the solution was like patchwork—and in the following weeks we could see the same pattern with instability occur," says Orjan Carlsson, Chief Architect of CSN's information technology department. Consistently poor Web site performance coupled with long waits on the telephone was enough to cause a public outcry.

THE IT SOLUTION

Given CSN's heterogeneous enterprise environment—which comprised everything from IBM mainframes to UNIX-based applications, to systems running Microsoft Windows NT—a solution that could support cross-platform communication was a necessity. Only a flexible, scalable, open-standards–based integration architecture could supply the level of interoperability the organization desired, especially for the high volume during the start of a semester.

A locally based IBM team worked closely with CSN to investigate solution possibilities. Together, the technical teams decided that the best way for the organization to realize cross-platform, program-to-program communication was through Web Services built on IBM WebSphere. This architecture allows CSN's disparate applications to exchange information with each other without human intervention. The team implemented a system that also eliminated the organization's reliance on an outsourced application service provider for its voice-response system. The system leverages Web Services to enable the Windows NT–based voice-response system to execute transactions that are easily recognized by CSN's back-end (back-office) operations.

THE RESULTS

The new Web Services–enabled system allows CSN to deliver student account status and transaction information to phones (voice response) and to CSN's portal at a significantly reduced cost. "Web Services are essential for us today and in the future," says Carlsson. According to Carlsson, Web Services enable a loosely coupled architecture, resulting in a highly integrated solution.

Reuse of code also gives CSN an advantage. One interface can serve several business systems using different channels, making it easy to modify existing channels or add new ones, a feature that significantly reduces total cost of ownership. CSN dramatically saves on developer costs as well as gets new functionality to market faster and with more frequency. The result is a flexible and scalable Web services–enabled architecture that is essentially transparent to end users, giving CSN the cross-platform communication system it needs to operate efficiently, serve its customers, and lower costs.

Source: Compiled from *http://www-3.ibm.com/software/success/cssdb.nsf/CS/LEOD-5KKTRX?OpenDocument&Site=admain* (site accessed November 25, 2003).

WHAT WE LEARNED FROM THIS CASE

The case demonstrates how a need for a new IT application arises: An organization needed to solve a business problem. The question then becomes which IT applications to build and how to do it. The trend today is to use some technology partners (IBM in this case) from which to buy or lease software, to outsource the job to, or to work together with. We also saw that software suites (in this case, WebSphere) can be used to expedite construction. We also learned that a new technology, Web Services, eased the job of system integration. In this chapter we will describe the major steps and tasks of system acquisition or development. The technical aspects of these topics are described in Technology Guide 6.

11.1 THE LANDSCAPE AND FRAMEWORK OF IT APPLICATION ACQUISITION

Our attention in this chapter is focused on information systems *acquisition*. We include in "acquisition" all approaches to obtaining systems: *buying, leasing,* or *building.* The acquisition issue is complex for various reasons: There is a large variety of IT applications, they keep changing over time, and they may involve several business partners. In addition, there is no single way to acquire IT applications: They can be developed in-house, outsourced (obtained from an external organization), or a combination of the two. Another strategy that is becoming very popular is to build applications from components. When components are used, the appropriate ones must be found, and even a single application may have many components from several different vendors.

The diversity of IT applications requires a variety of development methodologies and approaches. For example, small EC storefronts can be developed with HTML, Java, or other programming languages. Or they can be quickly implemented with commercial packages or leased from application service providers (ASP) for a small monthly fee. Larger applications can be outsourced, or developed in-house. Building medium-to-large applications requires extensive integration with existing information systems such as corporate databases, intranets, enterprise resource planning (ERP), and other application programs.

The Acquisition Process

The acquisition process of a typical IT application has five major steps, which are shown in the five arrows and corresponding boxes of Figure 11.1 (page 336). In general terms, the acquisition process begins with strategic planning and justification activities (Step 1, described in Section 11.2). One of the major outputs of this first step is the set of recommended applications (the *application portfolio*). The objective of IT application development is to create these applications and implement them. The steps in the acquisition process are outlined and discussed below.

Step 1: Planning for and Justifying Information Systems. Information systems are built as enablers of some business process(es). Therefore, their planning must be aligned with that of the organization's overall business plan. Furthermore, each application must be carefully analyzed to ensure that it will have the needed functionality and that its benefits justify its cost. Both of these activities may be complex, but they are necessary especially for systems that require high investment to acquire, operate, and maintain. As noted above, the application portfolio is an output of this step of the planning process. This step is usually done in-house (with consultants if needed). All other steps can be done in-house or outsourced.

Step 2: IT Architecture Creation—A Systems Analysis Approach. The major objective of this step is to create the IT architecture. *IT architecture*, as described in Chapter 2, is the conceptualization of how the organization's information needs are met by the capabilities of the specific applications. A detailed description of this step is provided in Technology Guide 6 (see Section TG6.1).

The results obtained from Step 2 are routed to the strategic planning level (e.g., to a steering committee). As a result, the application portfolio may be changed. For

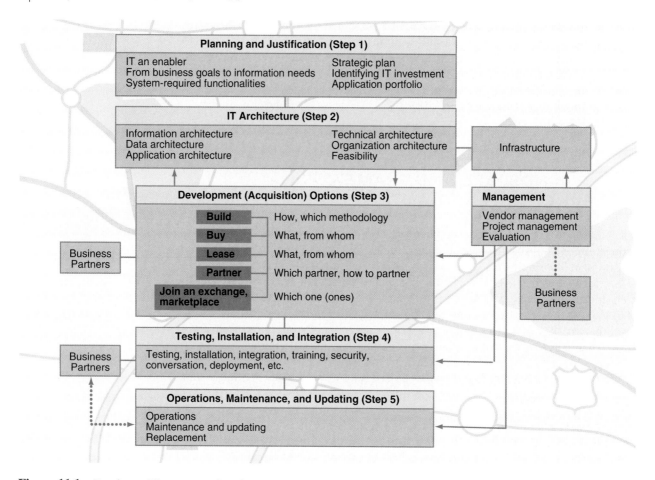

Figure 11.1 *Roadmap: The process of application acquisition.*

example, the steering committee may defer or scale down risky applications. Once the architecture is compiled and the application portfolio is finalized, a decision about *how* to develop these applications has to be made.

Step 3: Select a Development Option and Acquire the Application.   IT applications can be developed through several approaches which will be described in this chapter and in Technology Guide 6. The major options are:

- Build the system in-house. (This can be done in several ways.)
- Buy an application and install it (with or without modifications).
- Lease software from an application service provider (ASP) or lease via *utility computing*.
- Enter into a partnership or alliance that will enable the company to use someone else's application.
- Join a third-party e-marketplace, such as an auction site, a bidding (reverse auction) site, or an exchange, that provides needed capabilities to participants.
- Use a combination of these listed approaches.

The consideration criteria for the various methodologies are presented in Section 11.5. Once an option is decided on, the system is acquired. At the end of this step, an application is ready to be installed and deployed.

Step 4: Installing, Connecting, and More.   IT applications need to be connected to the corporate intranet and/or extranets, to databases, and to other applications. Connection to business partners or public exchanges may also be required. Details of the connection process are provided in Section 11.6.

During this step the applications are also tested, and user reactions are examined. Once the applications pass all of the tests, they can be deployed. In the deployment process one may deal with issues such as conversion strategies, training, and resistance to change (see Whitten et al., 2003).

Step 5: Operation and Maintenance.   Operation and maintenance can be done in-house and/or outsourced (Kendall and Kendall, 2002). Maintenance can be a big problem due to rapid changes in the IT technology field.

Managing the Development Process.   The development process can be fairly complex, and it must be managed properly. For medium-to-large applications a project team is usually created to manage the process and the vendors. Collaboration with business partners is also critical. As shown in various chapters, some IT failures are the result of delays and lack of cooperation by business partners. For example, you can install a superb e-procurement system, but if your vendors will not use it properly, the system will collapse.

Appropriate management also includes periodic evaluations of system performance. Standard project management techniques and tools are useful for this task.

Before you go on . . .

1. List and briefly discuss the five steps of the information systems acquisition process.

2. Describe the role of project management.

11.2 PLANNING FOR AND JUSTIFYING INFORMATION SYSTEM APPLICATIONS

Information system applications may be expensive. Therefore, an organization must analyze the need for applications and justify it in terms of cost and benefits. Because most organizations operate with tight budgets, this analysis must be carefully done. The investigation is usually divided into two parts. First, it is necessary to explore the need for each system. Second, it is necessary to justify it from a cost-benefit point of view. The need for information systems is usually related to organizational planning and to the analysis of its performance vis-à-vis its competitors. The cost-benefit justification must look at the wisdom of the specific IT investment vis-à-vis investing in alternative projects.

Both of these topics are complex, involving many issues. For example, organizational and IT planning may involve business processes redesign (e.g., see El Sawy, 2001). Both issues are also related to marketing and corporate strategy. For example, Ward and Peppard (2002) developed a framework for deciding on what IT applications to choose, based on their strategic versus high potential values. Such investigation is the subject of special IS courses and will not be dealt with here. However, what is important to stress is that such an investigation ends with a prioritized list of IT applications, called the **application portfolio**, which is a mix of existing and potential applications. These applications need to be acquired (or possibly modified if they already exist). Each of these applications may go through the process described in this chapter.

application portfolio *The set of recommended applications resulting from the planning and justification process in application development.*

IT Planning

Planning the acquisition of IT resources, including applications and infrastructure, does not start with bits and bytes or with a Web site. Rather, it starts with gaining a holistic perspective on what the firm aims to achieve and how it will do so.

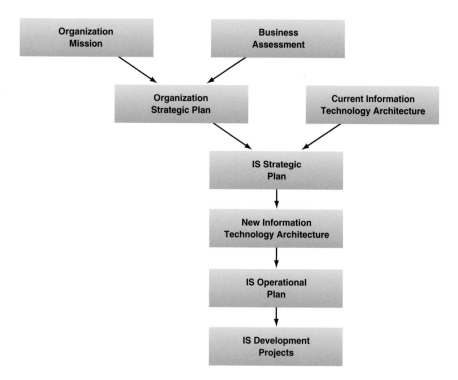

Figure 11.2 *The information systems planning process.*

This process begins with analysis of the *organizational strategic plan*, as shown in Figure 11.2. (Figure 11.2 shows the first two steps from Figure 11.1.) The organization's strategic plan states the firm's overall mission, the goals that follow from that mission, and the broad steps necessary to reach these goals. The strategic planning process matches the organization's objectives and resources to meet its changing markets and opportunities.

The organizational strategic plan and the existing IT architecture provide the inputs in developing the *IT strategic plan*. The *IT architecture* delineates the way an organization's information resources should be used to accomplish its mission. It encompasses both technical and managerial aspects of information resources. The technical aspects include hardware and operating systems, networking, data and data management systems, and applications software. The managerial aspects specify how managing the IS department will be accomplished, how functional area managers will be involved, and how IS decisions will be made. (See Technology Guide 6, Section TG6.1, for more technical details on IT architecture.)

The organization's strategic plan is supported by and must be aligned with the IT strategic plan.

IT strategic plan *A set of long-range goals that describe the IT infrastructure and major IS initiatives needed to achieve the goals of the organization.*

The IT Strategic Plan. The **IT strategic plan** is a set of long-range goals that describe the IT infrastructure and major IS initiatives needed to achieve the goals of the organization. The IT strategic plan must meet three objectives:

1. It must be aligned with the organization's strategic plan.
2. It must provide for an IT architecture that enables users, applications, and databases to be seamlessly networked and integrated.
3. It must efficiently allocate IS development resources among competing projects, so the projects can be completed on time, within budget, and have the required functionality.

The IT strategic plan also states the *mission* of the IS department, which defines the department's underlying purpose. The mission helps to answer questions related to the following three major issues:

1. *Efficiency.* Do the IS department and IT resources help the organization reach its goals with minimum resources?
2. *Effectiveness.* Do the IS department and IT resources help the functional area managers (and executives) do the right things?

3. *Competitiveness.* Do the IS department and IT resources engage in projects that will enhance the organization's competitive position?

The mission of the IS department requires a great deal of input from *all* of the organization's functional area managers, and often from higher organizational officers as well. This input will help to define the appropriate role of the IS department in accomplishing the organization's goals. This requires tight alignment.

IT Alignment with Organizational Plans and IT Strategy. A survey of 420 organizations, conducted by National Computing Centre (NCC) in 2003 (*ncc.co.uk*, 2003), found that keeping IT strategy aligned with business strategy was their number-one strategic concern.

The IT strategic plan must be aligned with overall organizational planning, whenever relevant, so that the IT unit and other organizational personnel are working toward the same goals, using their respective competencies (Ward and Peppard, 2002). The primary task of IT planning is therefore to identify information systems applications that fit the objectives and priorities established by the organization. Figure 11.3 graphically illustrates the alignment of business strategy, IT strategy, and IS operation plan (discussed below).

Challenges for IT Alignment. Despite the theoretical importance of IT alignment, organizations continue to demonstrate limited actual alignment. People3 (as reported by *Database*, 2003) reported that about 65 percent of companies have either a negative or neutral view of the ability of IT and business managers to work together in supporting corporate goals and objectives. Alignment is a complex management activity, and its complexity increases in accordance with the increasing complexity of organizations. To overcome such difficulties, companies can use software, as described in Online File W11.1.

wiley.com/college/turban

The IS Operational Plan. Note the bidirectional relationships among the three plans. For example, the IT strategic plan may require a new IT architecture, or modified IT architecture may be sufficient. The *IS operational plan* is a clear set of projects that will be executed by the IS department and by functional area managers in support of the IT strategic plan. A typical IS operational plan contains the following:

- ***Mission.*** The mission of the IS function (derived from the IT strategy).

- ***IS environment.*** A summary of the information needs of the functional areas and of the organization as a whole.

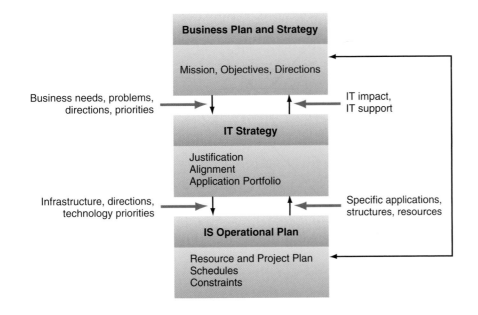

Figure 11.3 *The alignment among business and IT strategies and IS operational plan.*

- *Objectives of the IS function.* The IS function's current best estimate of its goals.
- *Constraints on the IS function.* Technological, financial, personnel, and other resource limitations on the IS function.
- *The application portfolio.* A prioritized inventory of present applications and a detailed plan of projects to be developed or continued during the current year.
- *Resource allocation and project management.* Listing of who is going to do what, how, and when.

Evaluating and Justifying IT Investment: Benefits, Costs, and Issues

Essentially, justifying IT investment includes three aspects: *assessment of costs, assessment of benefits (values),* and *comparison of the two.* This comparison is frequently referred to as *cost-benefit analysis.* Cost-benefit analysis is not a simple task, as Figure 11.4 shows. Before we elaborate on the figure, it will be useful to look at IT investment categories.

IT Investment Categories. One basic way to segregate IT investment is to distinguish between investment in infrastructure and investment in specific applications.

The IT *infrastructure,* as defined in Chapter 2, includes the physical facilities, components, services, and management that support the information systems of an entire organization. The infrastructure provides the foundation for all of the IT applications in the enterprise. Examples are a data center, networks, data warehouse, and a corporate knowledge base. Infrastructure investments are made for a long time, and the infrastructure is shared by many applications throughout the enterprise. (For more on the nature and types of IT infrastructure, see Broadbent and Weill, 1997.)

The IT *applications,* as defined in Chapter 2, are computer programs designed to support a specific task, a business process, or another application program—for example, providing a payroll or taking a customer's order. The number of potential IT applications is very large. Applications can be in one functional department (as shown in Chapter 7), or several departments can share an application. Shared applications are

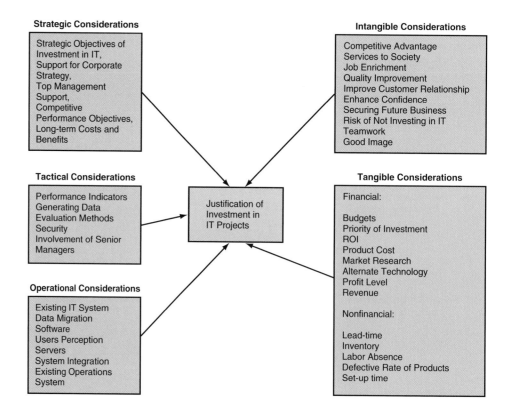

Figure 11.4 *A model for investment justification. [Source: A. Gunasekaran, et al., "A Model for Investment Justification in Information Technology Products,"* International Journal of Information Management *(March 2001), p. 354.]*

harder to evaluate in terms of their costs and benefits. (For details, see Devaraj and Kohli, 2002.)

Costing IT Investment. Placing a dollar value on the cost of IT investments may not be as simple as it sounds. One of the major issues is to allocate fixed costs among different IT projects. *Fixed costs* are those costs that remain the same regardless of change in the activity level. For IT, fixed costs include *infrastructure* cost, cost of IT services, and IT management cost. For example, the salary of the IT director is fixed, and adding one more application will not change it.

Another issue is the fact that the cost of a system does not end when the system is installed. Costs for keeping it running, dealing with bugs, and improving and changing the system may continue for some time. Such costs can accumulate over many years, and sometimes they are not even anticipated when the investment is made. An example is the cost of the Y2K reprogramming projects that amounted to billions of dollars to organizations worldwide.

In costing an organization's IT investment one should consider the total cost of ownership.

Total Cost of Ownership (TCO). Total cost of ownership (TCO) is a formula for calculating the cost of acquiring, operating, and controlling an IT system, even one as simple as a PC. The cost includes *acquisition cost* (hardware and software), *operations cost* (maintenance, training, operations, evaluation, technical support, installation, downtime, auditing, virus damage, and power consumption), and *control cost* (standardization, security, central services). The TCO can be 100 percent higher that just the cost of the hardware, especially for PCs.

total cost of ownership (TCO) *Formula for calculating the cost of acquiring, operating, and controlling an IT system.*

Evaluating the Benefits. Multiple kinds of values can be used to measure benefits. For example, the return of a capital investment measured in numeric (e.g., dollar or percentage) terms is one common measure. Other measures could be improved efficiency, improved customer or partner relations, and improved decision making.

However, evaluating the benefits of IT projects is typically more complex than calculating their costs. Benefits may be harder to quantify, especially since many of them are intangible. In addition, the fact that organizations use IT for several different purposes further complicates the analysis of benefits. In addition, the probability of obtaining a return from an IT investment also depends on the probability of implementation success. These probabilities reflect the fact that many systems are not implemented on time, within budget, or with all the features originally envisioned for them. Thus, the value of the benefits in most cases will be less than that originally anticipated. As in the case of costs, with benefits too we need to look at the *total benefits of ownership*, including the intangible ones.

The Problem of Intangible Benefits. In many cases IT projects generate intangible benefits—benefits that may be very desirable but difficult to place an accurate monetary value on. Intangible benefits include increased quality, faster product development, greater design flexibility, better customer service, or improved working conditions for employees. For example, many people would agree that e-mail improves communications, but it is not at all clear how to measure the value of this improvement. Managers are very conscious of the bottom line, but no manager can prove that e-mail is responsible for so many cents per share of the organization's total profits.

intangible benefits *Benefits from IT that may be very desirable but difficult to place an accurate monetary value on.*

A cost-benefit analysis could ignore intangible benefits, but doing so implies that their value is zero. Ignoring intangible benefits may lead the organization to reject IT investments that could substantially increase revenues and profitability. Therefore, financial analyses need to consider not just tangible benefits but also intangible benefits in such a way that the decision reflects their potential impact.

The most straightforward solution to the problem of evaluating intangible benefits in cost-benefit analysis is to make *rough estimates* of monetary values for all intangible benefits, and then conduct a NVP or similar financial analysis. The simplicity of this approach is attractive, but in many cases the assumptions used in these estimates are debatable. If the technology is acquired because decision makers assigned too high a value to intangible benefits, the organization could find that it has wasted some valuable resources. On the other hand, if the valuation of intangible benefits is too low, the organization might reject the investment and then find that it is losing market share to competitors who did implement the technology. For approaches that deal with intangible benefits see Online File W11.2.

wiley.com/college/turban

Conducting Cost-Benefit Analysis

Conducting a cost-benefit analysis and justification can be done in several ways. Here are some approaches, starting with generic ones:

Using NPV in Cost-Benefit Analysis. Organizations often use *net present value (NPV)* calculations for cost-benefit analyses. Using the NPV method, analysts convert future values of benefits to their present-value equivalent by "discounting" them at the organization's cost of funds. They then can compare the present value of the future benefits to the cost required to achieve those benefits, to determine whether the benefits exceed the costs. NPV analysis works well in situations where the costs and benefits are well defined or "tangible" enough to convert them into monetary values.

Return on Investment. Another traditional tool for evaluating capital investment is *return on investment (ROI)*. It measures the effectiveness of management in generating profits with its available assets. The ROI measure is a percentage, and the higher the percentage return, the better. It is calculated essentially by dividing net income attributable to a project by the average assets invested in the project. (An example of detailed studies of the ROI of a portal, commissioned by Plumtree Software and executed by META group, can be found at *plumtree.com* and at *metagroup.com*.)

However, traditional capital investment methods such as NPV and ROI have some limitations when we deal with IT investments, and especially with e-business ones. Therefore, other methods, such as conducting a business case, may be useful.

The Business Case Approach. One method used to justify investments in projects, and even in entire new companies, is referred to as the *business case approach*. The concept of a business case received lots of attention in the mid-1990s when it was used to justify funding for investment in dot-coms. By 2003, it had become clear that one of the reasons for the collapse of the dot-com bubble was improper business cases submitted to investors. Nevertheless, if done correctly, business cases can be a useful tool.

A *business case* is a written document that is used by managers to garner funding for one or more specific applications or projects. Its major emphasis is the justification for a specific required investment, but it also provides the bridge between the initial plan and its execution. Its purpose is not only to get approval and funding, but also to provide the foundation for tactical decision making and technology risk management. A business case is usually conducted in existing organizations that want to embark on new IT projects (for example, an e-procurement project). The business case helps to clarify how the organization can best use its resources to accomplish the IT strategy. It helps the organization concentrate on justifying the investment, on risk management, and on fit of an IT project with the organization's mission.

A business case for IT investment can be very complex. However, sometimes an IT project is necessary in order for the organization to stay in business, and in those instances, the business case is very simple: "We must do it, we have no choice." For example, the U.S. Internal Revenue Service is requiring businesses to switch to electronic systems for filing their tax returns. Similarly, sometimes an organization must invest because its competitors have done so and if it does not follow, it will lose customers. Examples are e-banking and some CRM services.

Other Cost-Evaluation Methods. Several other cost-benefit methods exist. They are summarized in Table 11.1.

Table 11.1 Cost-Benefit Analysis Methods

Method	Description
Benchmarks	Focuses on objective measures of performance (often available from industry trade associations or consulting firms). *Metric benchmarks* provide numeric measures of performance; *best-practice benchmarks* focus on how IS activities are actually performed by successful organizations.
Management by maxim	Brings together corporate executives, business-unit managers, and IT executives to identify IT infrastructure investments that correspond to organizational strategies and objectives (Broadbent and Weill, 1997).
Real-option valuation	Stems from the field of finance. Looks for projects that create additional opportunities in the future ("have a real-option value"), even if current costs exceed current benefits (Benaroch, 2002).
Balanced scorecard method	Evaluates the overall health of organizations and projects, by looking at the organization's short- and long-term financial metrics, customers, internal business processes, and learning and growth (Kaplan and Norton, 1996).
Activity-based costing approach	Applies principles of activity-based costing (ABC) (which allocates costs based on each product's use of company activities in making the product) to IT investment analysis (Gerlach et al., 2002).
EIAC model	Methodology for implementing IT payoff initiatives, composed of nine phases, divided into four categories: exploration (E), involvement (I), analysis (A), and communication (C) (Devaraj and Kohli, 2002).

Before you go on . . .

1. What are some problems associated with IT costing?
2. What difficulties accompany the intangible benefits from IT?
3. Define NPV and ROI methods.
4. Describe a business case approach.

11.3 STRATEGIES FOR ACQUIRING IT APPLICATIONS: AVAILABLE OPTIONS

There are several options for acquiring IT applications. The major options are: buy, lease, and develop in-house. Each of these is described in this section, with some other minor methods.

Buy the Applications (Off-the-Shelf Approach)

Standard features required by IT applications can be found in many commercial packages. Buying an existing package can be a cost-effective and time-saving strategy compared with in-house application development. The "buy" option should be carefully considered and planned for to ensure that all critical features for current and future needs are included in the selected package. Otherwise such packages may quickly become obsolete.

However, organizational needs are rarely fully satisfied by one software package. It is therefore sometimes necessary to acquire multiple packages to fulfill different needs. These packages may then need to be integrated with each other as well as with existing software (See Section 11.6).

The buy option is especially attractive if the software vendor allows for modifications. However, the option may not be attractive in cases of high obsolescence rates or high software cost. The advantages and limitations of the buy option are summarized in Manager's Checklist 11.1 (page 344). When the buy option is not appropriate, one should consider leasing.

MANAGER'S CHECKLIST 11.1

Advantages and Limitations of the "Buy" Option

Advantages of the "Buy" Option
❏ Many different types of off-the-shelf software are available.
❏ Much time can be saved by buying rather than building.
❏ The company can know what it is getting before it invests in the product.
❏ The company is not the first and only user.
❏ Purchased software may avoid the need to hire personnel specifically dedicated to a project.
Limitations of the "Buy" Option
❏ Software may not exactly meet the company's needs.
❏ Software may be difficult or impossible to modify, or it may require huge business process changes to implement.
❏ The company will not have control over software improvements and new versions.
❏ Purchased software can be difficult to integrate with existing systems.
❏ Vendors may drop a product or go out of business.

Lease the Applications

Compared with the buy option and the option to develop applications in-house (to be discussed soon), the "lease" option can result in substantial cost and time savings. Leased packages may not always exactly fit the application requirements (the same is true with the buy option). But many common features that are needed by most organizations are usually included in leased packages.

In those cases where extensive maintenance is required or where the cost of buying is very high, leasing is more advantageous than buying. Leasing can be especially attractive to SMEs that cannot afford major investments in IT software. Large companies may also prefer to lease packages in order to test potential IT solutions before committing to heavy investments. Also, because there is a shortage of IT personnel with appropriate skills for developing novel IT applications (such as EC or wireless), many companies choose to lease instead of develop software in-house. Even those companies that have in-house expertise may not be able to afford the long wait for strategic applications to be developed in-house. Therefore, they lease (or buy) applications from external resources to establish a quicker presence in the market.

Types of Leasing Vendors. Leasing can be done in one of two ways. The first way is to lease the application from an outsourcer and install it on the company's premises. The vendor can help with the installation and frequently will offer to also contract for the operation and maintenance of the system. Many conventional applications are leased this way. The second way, using an application system provider (ASP), is becoming more popular. ASPs are explored in Section 11.4.

Utility Computing. Tapping into computing resources with a simplicity equal to plugging an electrical lamp into an outlet has been a goal of many companies for years. The approach is known as **utility computing** (or *on-demand computing*). The idea is to provide unlimited computing power and storage capacity that can be used and reallocated for any application—and billed on a pay-per-use basis.

utility computing *Unlimited computing power and storage capacity that can be obtained on demand and billed on a pay-per-use basis.*

Utility computing consists of a pool of "self-managing" IT resources that can be continually reallocated to meet the organization's changing business and service needs. These resources can be located anywhere and managed by an organization's IT staff or a third-party service provider. Equally important, usage of these resources can be tracked and billed down to the level of an individual user or group.

As shown in Figure 11.5, utility computing consists of three layers of tools and two types of value-added services. Each tool must be seamlessly integrated to create a

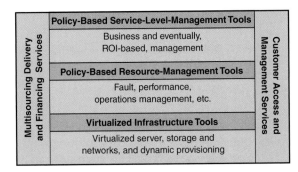

Figure 11.5 *Utility computing.*

comprehensive solution, but will usually be implemented separately. These three tools are:

1. *Policy-based service-level-management tools.* These coordinate, monitor, and report on the ways in which multiple infrastructure components come together to deliver a business service.

2. *Policy-based resource-management tools.* These automate and standardize all types of IT management best practices, from initial configuration to ongoing fault management and asset tracking.

3. *Virtualization tools.* These allow server, storage, and network resources to be deployed and managed as giant pools, and seamlessly changed as needs change.

Utility computing still faces daunting obstacles. One obstacle is the immaturity of the tools. Another is the fact that each vendor prefers to tout its own unique variation on the utility-computing vision, with different (often confusing) names and terminology. However, utility computing will inevitably prompt considerable vendor consolidation. It will also accelerate acceptance of ASPs, which may distribute it.

Develop the Applications In-House (Insourcing)

A third development strategy is to develop ("build") applications in-house. Although this approach is usually more time-consuming and may be more costly than buying or leasing, it often leads to a better fit with the specific organizational requirements. Companies that have the resources and time to develop their own IT applications in-house may follow this approach as a strategy to differentiate themselves from the competition, which may be using standard applications that are bought or leased. In-house development, however, is a challenging task, as many applications are novel, have users from outside the organization, and involve multiple organizations.

In-House Development Approaches. There are two major approaches to in-house development: building from scratch or building from components.

1. *Build from scratch.* This option should be considered only for specialized applications for which components are not available. It is an expensive and slow process, but it will provide the best fit.

2. *Build from components.* Companies with experienced IT staff can use standard components (e.g., a secure Web server), some software languages (e.g., Java, Visual Basic, or Perl), and third-party subroutines to create and maintain applications on their own. (Or, companies can outsource the entire development process to an integrator that assembles the components.) From a software standpoint, using components offers the greatest flexibility and can be the least expensive option in the long run. However, it can also result in a number of false starts and wasted experimentations. For this reason, even those companies with experienced staff are frequently better off modifying and customizing one of the packaged solutions as part of the "buy" option. For details about using components see Technology Guide 6.

In building in-house one can use various methodologies, described below.

Systems Development Life Cycle (SDLC).   Large IT projects, especially ones that involve infrastructure, are developed according to a systematic set of procedures known as the *systems development life cycle* (SDLC). Details about this approach are provided in Technology Guide 6.2.

Prototyping Methodology.   With a *prototyping* methodology, an initial list of basic system requirements is defined and used to build a prototype, which is then improved in several iterations based on users' feedback. This approach can be very rapid.

Many companies have used this approach to develop their IT and especially their EC applications mainly for two reasons: (1) Time is important, and they want to be the first to market. (2) It is usually beneficial to involve the users (employees, suppliers, and customers) in the design of the applications. By quickly building a prototype instead of a full-fledged application, a company can, for example, establish an online presence more quickly than its competitors. The initial prototype is then improved and developed further based on the users' feedback.

The prototyping approach, however, is not without drawbacks. There is a risk of getting into an endless loop of prototype revisions, as users may never be fully satisfied. Such a risk should be planned for because of the rapid changes in IT technology and business models. Another drawback is the risk of idiosyncratic design; the prototype may be revised based on the feedback of only a small group of users who are not necessarily representative of the entire user population. Such a risk can be alleviated by embedding a systematic feedback mechanism in the application itself, such as click trails and online feedback forms to elicit input from as many users as possible.

In-house development can be done by IS department personnel or by end users.

End-User Development

In the early days of computing, an organization housed its computer in a climate-controlled room, with locked doors and restricted access. The only people who interacted with the computer (most organizations had only one computer) were specialists: programmers, computer operators, and data entry personnel. Over the years, computers became cheaper, smaller, and more widely dispersed throughout the organization. Now almost everybody who works at a desk or in the field has a computer.

Along with this proliferation of hardware, many computer-related activities shifted out into the work area. Users now handle most of their own data entry. They create many of their own reports and print them locally, instead of waiting for them to arrive in the interoffice mail after a computer operator has run them at a remote data center. They provide unofficial training and support to other workers in their area. Users also design and develop an increasing proportion of their own applications, sometimes even relatively large and complex systems.

Beneficial as this trend is to both workers and the organization as a whole, end-user computing has some limitations. End users may not be skilled enough in computers, so quality and cost may be jeopardized unless proper controls are installed. Also, many end users do not take time to document their work and may neglect proper security measures.

End-User Computing and Web-Based Systems Development.   The development of client/server applications in the 1980s and 1990s was characterized by user-driven systems development. Either directly or indirectly, end users made decisions for systems designers and developers on how the programs should operate. Web-based systems development in the twenty-first century, however, is application driven rather than user driven. The end user can still determine what the *requirements* will be and has some input into the design of the applications. But because of the nature of the technologies used in Web-based application design, the function, not the user, determines what the application will look like and how it will perform.

Ansett Australia, one of Australia's leading airlines, had chosen IBM Global Services Australia to manage its end-user computing support functions. Ansett (*ansett.com.au*), based in Melbourne, operates an extensive range of domestic airline services and also flies to Japan, Hong Kong, Taiwan, Bali, and Fiji.

Ansett Australia's General Manager for IT Infrastructure and Operations, Hal Pringle, said that IBM Global Services Australia's appointment significantly improved desktop services to the airline's end users while at the same time delivering substantial cost savings. Such service was previously delivered by a mixture of external contractors and in-house staff.

Mr. Pringle said the decision to hire an external provider of end-user computing (EUC) support arose from a benchmarking study conducted earlier by Ansett. The study showed that a move to a single external provider of the caliber of IBM Global Services Australia would do the following: achieve a more consistent end-to-end delivery of applications; assist the implementation of best-practice EUC support at the best cost; deliver substantial cost savings; allow Ansett to better manage EUC supply and demand;

and deliver a more consistent and better quality support service to end users.

"The study highlighted the fact that Ansett had in effect 'outgrown' the level of end-user service provided at that time, and that a quantum leap in service was required to ensure a full return on our end-user computing investment," Pringle said.

"Improving delivery of services to end users and enhancing end-user productivity are becoming key focus areas for many Australian corporations. I am very pleased that we have been chosen to deliver these additional services to Ansett," said Mr. Bligh, General Manager of IBM Global Services Australia, Travel and Transportation Services.

Sources: Compiled from Sachdeva (2000) and *ansett. com.au* (site visited December 2003).

QUESTIONS

1. What strategic advantages can Ansett Australia gain by ensuring consistent and reliable support to its end-user computing?
2. Why does a large company like Ansett use a vendor to manage EUC?

An innovative way of managing end-user computing is described in IT's about Business 11.1. In this case, an outside provider helped to *manage* the end-user computing.

Other Acquisition Options

A number of other acquisition options are available to IT developers, and in particular for e-commerce applications.

Join an E-Marketplace or an E-Exchange. With this option, the company "plugs" itself into an e-marketplace. For example, a company can place its catalogs in Yahoo's marketplace. Visitors to Yahoo's store will find the company's products and will be able to buy them. The company pays Yahoo a monthly fee for the catalog space (Yahoo is "hosting" the company's selling portal.)

Join a Third-Party Auction or Reverse Auction. Similar to the previous option, a company can plug into a third-party auction or reverse auction site fairly quickly. Many companies use this option for certain e-procurement activities. Or, a company can join a B2B exchange that offers auctions, as described in Chapter 5.

Engage in Joint Ventures. There are several different partnership or joint venture arrangements that may facilitate EC application development. For example, four banks in Hong Kong have developed a joint e-banking system. In some cases, companies can team up with a company that already has the needed application in place.

Join a Public Exchange or a Consortium. Alternatively, a company can join a public exchange (Chapter 5), for selling and/or buying, by simply plugging into the public exchange. Another option is for a company to join a consortium (a vertical exchange owned by a group of big players in an industry), which may have applications developed to fit the needs of companies in the industry.

Hybrid Approach. A hybrid approach combines the best of what the company does internally with an outsourced strategy. Hybrid models work best when the outsourced partner offers higher security levels, faster time-to-market, and service level agreements.

Criteria for selecting a development strategy are provided in Section 11.5. However, before proceeding to that topic, let's look further at the recent trend of outsourcing and ASPs.

Before you go on . . .

1. List the major acquisition and development strategies.

2. Compare the buy option against the lease option.

3. List the in-house development approaches.

4. Describe end-user development and cite its advantages and limitations.

5. List other acquisition options.

11.4 OUTSOURCING AND APPLICATION SERVICE PROVIDERS

Outsourcing

Small or medium-sized companies with few IT staff and smaller budgets are best served by outside contractors. Outside contractors have also proven to be a good selection for large companies in certain circumstances. Use of outside contractors or external organizations to acquire IT services is called **outsourcing**. Large companies may choose outsourcing when they want to experiment with new IT technologies without a great deal of up-front investment, to protect their own internal networks, or to rely on experts. Outsourcers can perform any or all tasks in IT development. For example, they can plan, program, build applications, integrate, operate, and maintain.

outsourcing *Use of outside contractors or external organizations to acquire IT services.*

Several types of vendors offer services for creating and operating IT system including e-commerce applications:

- *Software houses.* Many software companies, from IBM to Oracle, among others, offer a range of outsourcing services for developing, operating, and maintaining IT applications.

- *Outsourcers and others.* IT outsourcers, such as EDS, offer a variety of services. Also, the large CPA companies and management consultants (e.g., Accenture) offer some outsourcing services.

- *Telecommunications companies.* Increasingly, the large telecommunications companies are expanding their hosting services to include the full range of IT and EC solutions. MCI, for example, offers Web Commerce services for a monthly fee.

While the trend to outsource is rising, so is the trend to do it offshore, mainly in India and China. Offshore outsourcing is certainly less expensive, but it includes risks as well (see *cio.com*, "The 10 most important issues in 2003," and Overby, 2003).

One of the most common types of IT outsourcing is the use of application service providers.

Application Service Providers

An **application service provider (ASP)** is an agent or vendor who assembles the software needed by enterprises and packages them with outsourced development, operations, maintenance, and other services (see Kern and Kreijger, 2001). The essential difference between an ASP and an outsourcer is that an ASP will manage application servers in a centrally controlled location, rather than on a customer's site. Applications are then accessed via the Internet or VANs through a standard Web browser interface. Such an arrangement provides a full range of services for the company using the ASP: Applications can be scaled, upgrades and maintenance can be centralized, physical security over the applications and servers can be guaranteed, and the necessary critical mass of human resources can be efficiently utilized.

Monthly fees are paid by the end-user businesses to the ASP. In general, the fees include payment for the application software, hardware, service and support, maintenance, and upgrades. The fee can be fixed or be based on utilization. According to Scott McNealy, Sun Microsystems' CEO, by 2005, "if you're a CIO with a head for business, you won't buy software or computers anymore. You'll rent all your resources from a service provider" (staff interview, *CIO Magazine*, November 2000).

ASPs are especially active in enterprise computing and EC applications, which may be too complex to build and too cumbersome to modify and maintain. Therefore, the major providers of ERP software, such as SAP and Oracle, are offering ASP options. IBM, Microsoft, and Computer Associates also offer ASP services.

Benefits of Leasing from ASPs.   Leasing from an ASP is a particularly desirable option for SME businesses, for which in-house development and operation of IT applications can be time-consuming and expensive. Leasing from ASPs saves various expenses (such as labor costs) in the initial development stage. It also helps reduce the software maintenance and upgrading and user training costs in the long run. A company can select another software product from the ASP to meet its changing needs and does not have to invest further in upgrading the existing one. Thus, overall business competitiveness can be strengthened through reducing the time-to-market and enhancing the ability to adapt to changing market conditions. ASPs are particularly effective for IT applications for which timing and flexibility are crucial.

Leasing from ASPs does have its disadvantages. Many companies are concerned with the adequacy of protection offered by the ASP against hackers, theft of confidential information, and virus attacks. Also, leased software often does not provide the perfect fit for the desired application. It is also important to ensure that the speed of the Internet connection is compatible with that of the application, to avoid distortions in its performance. For example, it is not advisable to run heavy-duty applications on a modem link below a T1 line or a high-speed DSL.

From the ASP vendor's point of view, the benefits presented by the ASP model are many. For one, in the long-distance carrier and Internet service providers (ISP) markets, revenues are squeezed due to heavy competition. These companies are looking to generate revenues from sources other than connectivity and transport, and ASP services offer a new outlet. An interesting institution is the *ASP Industry Consortium*, whose founding members include AT&T, Cisco, Citrix Systems, Compaq, Ernst & Young, Verizon, IBM, Marimba, Sharp Electronic, Sun Microsystems, UUNET, and Verio.

application service provider (ASP)
An agent or vendor who assembles the software needed by enterprises and packages them with outsourced development, operations, maintenance, and other services.

Before you go on . . .

1. What type of companies provide outsourcing service?

2. Define ASPs and list their advantages to companies using them.

3. List some disadvantages of ASPs.

MANAGER'S CHECKLIST 11.2

Criteria for Determining Which Application Development Approach to Use

❏ The functionalities of packages	❏ How to measure benefits
❏ Information requirements	❏ Personnel needed
❏ User friendliness	❏ Forecasting and planning for technological evolution
❏ Hardware and software resources	❏ Scaling
❏ Installation	❏ Sizing
❏ Maintenance services	❏ Performance
❏ Vendor quality and track record	❏ Reliability
❏ Estimated costs	❏ Security

11.5 CRITERIA FOR SELECTING AN ACQUISITION APPROACH

A major issue faced by any company is which method(s) of acquisition to select. To do so the company must consider many criteria, such as those provided in Manager's Checklist 11.2. Some criteria may conflict with others, so the company must decide which criteria are most important to its needs. For discussion of the criteria in the checklist, see Online File W11.3.

wiley.com/college/turban

Additional Criteria for Selecting an ASP Vendor. In addition to the general criteria cited in Manager's Checklist 11.2, one should look at the following additional criteria when selecting an ASP vendor.

- *Database format and portability.* The physical structure of ASP application databases should be compatible with the client company's existing applications.

- *Application and data storage.* The client company should inquire how the application and its data are stored. Using dedicated servers may be more costly than sharing them with others, but dedicated servers reduce the security risk.

- *Scope of service.* Terms of fundamental services such as routine maintenance, availability of redundant servers, and default file backups should be clearly defined and agreed upon.

- *Support services.* User training is a very important support service. Other support services include phone, Web, and e-mail help hotlines. However, not all support services are free of charge. It is also important to ascertain whether the services are provided by the ASP itself or subcontracted to other companies.

- *Integration.* Integration is particularly important for applications such as enterprise resource planning (ERP), accounting, and customer relationship management (CRM). The effort required for integration and the assistance provided by the ASP for achieving the integration are critical selection factors.

Using all the previous criteria, one can select one or more methods for acquiring systems. (The topic of selecting specific vendors and software is described in the next section.) Comparison of the various methods is given in Table 11.2. (For description of additional systems development methods, see Technology Guide 6.)

> ### Before you go on . . .
>
> 1. List five criteria for assessing a buy option. (Hint: Consult Manager's Checklist 11.1.)
> 2. List five criteria for selecting a development option. (Hint: Consult Manager's Checklist 11.2.)
> 3. List criteria for selection of an ASP.

Table 11.2   Advantages and Disadvantages of Various Systems Acquisition Methods

Advantages	Disadvantages
Traditional Systems Development (SDLC)	
• Forces staff to systematically go through every step in a structured process.	• May produce excessive documentation.
• Enforces quality by maintaining standards.	• Users may be unwilling or unable to study the specifications they approve.
• Has lower probability of missing important issues in collecting user requirements.	• Takes too long to go from the original ideas to a working system.
	• Users have trouble describing requirements for a proposed system.
Prototyping	
• Helps clarify user requirements.	• May encourage inadequate problem analysis.
• Helps verify the feasibility of the design.	• Not practical with large number of users.
• Promotes genuine user participation.	• User may not give up the prototype when the system is completed.
• Promotes close working relationship between systems developers and users.	• May generate confusion about whether the system is complete and maintainable.
• Works well for ill-defined problems.	• System may be built quickly, which may result in lower quality.
• May produce part of the final system.	
End-User Development	
• Bypasses the IS department and avoids delays.	• May eventually require maintenance assistance from IT department.
• User controls the application and can change it as needed.	• Documentation may be inadequate.
• Directly meets user requirements.	• Poor quality control.
• Increased user acceptance of new system.	• System may not have adequate interfaces to existing systems.
• Frees up IT resources.	
• May create lower-quality systems.	
External Acquisition (Buy or Lease)	
• Software can be tried out.	• Controlled by another company with its own priorities and business considerations.
• Software has been used for similar problems in other organizations.	• Package's limitations may prevent desired business processes.
• Reduces time spent for analysis, design, and programming.	• May be difficult to get needed enhancements.
• Has good documentation that will be maintained.	• Lack of intimate knowledge in the purchasing company about how the software works and why it works that way.

11.6 VENDOR AND SOFTWARE SELECTION AND OTHER IMPLEMENTATION ISSUES

Vendor and Software Selection

Few organizations, especially SMEs, have the time, financial resources, or technical expertise required to develop today's complex IT or e-business systems. This means that many applications are built with hardware, software, hosting services, and development expertise provided by outside vendors. Thus, a major aspect of developing an IT application revolves around the selection and management of these vendors and their software offerings. Martin et al. (2000) identified six steps in selecting a software vendor and an application package.

Step 1: Identify Potential Vendors.   Potential software application vendors can be identified from software catalogs, lists provided by hardware vendors, technical and trade journals, consultants experienced in the application area, peers in other companies, and Web searches.

These sources often yield so many vendors and packages that one must use some preliminary evaluation criteria to eliminate all but a few of the most promising ones from further consideration. For example, one can eliminate vendors that are too small or that have no track record or have a questionable reputation. Also, packages may be eliminated if they do not have the required features or will not work with available hardware, operating system, communications network, or database management software.

Step 2: Determine the Evaluation Criteria.

The most difficult and crucial task in evaluating a vendor and a software package is to determine a set of detailed criteria for choosing the best vendor and package. Some areas in which detailed criteria should be developed are characteristics of the vendor, functional requirements of the system, technical requirements the software must satisfy, amount and quality of documentation provided, and vendor support of the package.

request for proposal (RFP) *Document that is sent to potential vendors inviting them to submit a proposal describing their software package and how it would meet the company's needs.*

These criteria should be set out in a **request for proposal (RFP)**, a document that is sent to potential vendors inviting them to submit a proposal describing their software package and how it would meet the company's needs. The RFP provides the vendors with information about the objectives and requirements of the system: It describes the environment in which the system will be used, the general criteria that will be used to evaluate the proposals, and the conditions for submitting proposals. The RFP may also request a list of current users of the package who may be contacted, describe in detail the form of response that is desired, and require that the package be demonstrated at the company's facilities using specified inputs and data files.

Step 3: Evaluate Vendors and Packages.

The multivendor responses to an RFP generate massive volumes of information that must be evaluated. The goal of this evaluation is to determine the gaps between the company's needs (as specified by the requirements) and the capabilities of the vendors and their application packages. Often, the vendors and packages are given an overall score by assigning an importance weight to each of the criteria, ranking the vendors on each of the weighted criteria (say 1 to 10), and then multiplying the ranks by the associated weights. A short list of potential suppliers can be chosen from those vendors and packages with the highest overall scores.

Step 4: Choose the Vendor and Package.

Once a short list has been prepared, negotiations can begin with vendors to determine how their packages might be modified to remove any discrepancies with the company's IT needs. Thus, one of the most important factors in the decision is the additional development effort that may be required to tailor the system to the company's needs or to integrate it into the company's computing environment. Additionally, the opinions of the users who will work with the system and the IT personnel who will have to support the system have to be considered.

Selecting software depends on the nature of the software. Thus, several selection methods exist. For a list of general criteria, see Manager's Checklist 11.3. For an example of selecting enterprise systems, see Sarkis and Sundarraj (2003).

Step 5: Negotiate a Contract.

The contract with the software vendor is very important. It specifies both the price of the software and the type and amount of support to be provided by the vendor. The contract will be the only recourse if the system or the vendor does not perform as expected. Furthermore, if the vendor is modifying the software to tailor it to the company's needs, the contract must include detailed specifications (essentially the requirements) of the modifications. Also, the contract should describe in detail the acceptance tests the software package must pass.

Contracts are legal documents, and they can be quite tricky. Experienced contract negotiators and legal assistance may be needed. Many organizations have software-purchasing specialists who assist in negotiations and write or approve the contract. They should be involved in the selection process from the start. If an RFP is used, these purchasing specialists may be very helpful in determining its form and in providing boilerplate sections of the RFP.

- ❏ Cost and financial terms
- ❏ Upgrade policy and cost
- ❏ Vendor's reputation and availability for help
- ❏ Vendor's success stories (visit their Web site, contact clients)
- ❏ System flexibility
- ❏ Ease of Internet interface
- ❏ Availability and quality of documentation
- ❏ Necessary hardware and networking resources
- ❏ Required training (check if provided by vendor)
- ❏ Security
- ❏ Learning (speed of) for developers and users
- ❏ Graphical presentation
- ❏ Data handling
- ❏ System-required hardware

Step 6: Establish a Service Level Agreement. Service level agreements (SLAs) are formal agreements regarding the division of work between a company and its vendors. Such divisions are based on a set of agreed-upon milestones, quality checks, and "what-if" situations; they describe how checks will be made and what is to be done in case of disputes. If the vendor is to meet its objectives of installing IT applications, it must develop and deliver support services to meet these objectives. An effective approach to managing vendors must achieve both facilitation and coordination. SLAs do this by (1) defining the partners' responsibilities, (2) providing a framework for designing support services, and (3) allowing the company to retain as much control as possible over their own systems.

service level agreements (SLAs)
Formal agreements regarding the division of work between a company and its vendors.

Management should be willing to incur the time and expense to select the appropriate components and/or applications. Do not compromise quality and be ready to spend time. IT applications can be ruined quickly if the wrong application is developed. All it may take is one bad component to cause a major disaster.

Other Implementation Issues

The following implementation issues are related to IT resource acquisition.

- *In-house or outsource Web site?* Many large enterprises are capable of running their own publicly accessible Web sites for advertising purposes. However, Web sites for online selling may involve complex integration, security, and performance issues. For those companies venturing into such Web-based selling, a key issue is whether the site should be built in-house, thus providing more direct control, or outsourced to a more experienced provider. Outsourcing services, which allow companies to start small and evolve to full-featured functions, are available through many ISPs, telecommunication companies, Internet malls, and software vendors.

- *Consider an ASP.* The use of ASPs is a must for SMEs and should be considered by many large companies as well. However, care must be used in selecting a vendor due to the newness of the concept.

- *Do a detailed IT architecture study.* Some companies rush this process, and this can be a big mistake. If the high-level conceptual planning is wrong, the entire project is at great risk.

- *Security and ethics.* During the application development process, pay close attention to security. It is likely that vendors and business partners will be involved. Protecting customers' privacy is a must, and the issue of what and how to use clickstream and other data is essential.

- *Evaluate the alternatives to in-house systems development.* In-house systems development requires highly skilled employees to undertake a complex process. Organizations may sometimes find it preferable to acquire IT resources rather than build in-house. Methods for acquiring IT resources outside the information systems department include purchase, lease, outsourcing, use of ASPs, and end-user development.

Before you go on . . .

1. List the major steps of selection of a vendor and a software package.
2. Describe a request for proposal (RFP).
3. Describe SLAs.
4. List three major implementation issues.

11.7 CONNECTING TO DATABASES AND BUSINESS PARTNERS

EC applications must be connected to internal information systems, infrastructure (including databases), ERP, and so on. They also must be connected to such items as the partners' systems or to public exchanges. Such connections are referred to as *integration* and are the subject of this section. (See also Chapters 7 and 8 for additional discussion.)

Connecting to Databases

Many IT applications need to be connected to a database. For example, when you receive a customer's order, you want to immediately find out if the item is in stock. To do so, you need to connect your ordering system to your inventory system. Several possibilities exist regarding such a connection. The connection technology enables customers with a Web browser to access catalogs in the seller's database, request specific data, and receive an instant response. Here the application server manages the client's requests. The application server also acts as the front-end to complex databases.

Connecting to Business Partners

Connecting to business partners is critical to the success of IT, especially for B2B e-commerce. As described in Chapter 9, such connection is done via EDI, EDI/Internet, and extranets.

Connection to business partners is done usually along the supply chain. It typically involves connecting a company's front- and back-office e-commerce applications, as shown in Figure 11.6.

In addition to the networking problem, one must deal with issues of connectivity, compatibility, security, scalability, and more. Connecting to business partners can be particularly important, as shown in IT's about Business 11.2.

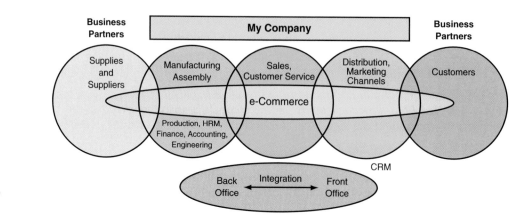

Figure 11.6 *Connecting to databases.*

IT'S ABOUT BUSINESS

11.2: Boeing Designs a New Aircraft

Boeing (*boeing.com*) is at a critical time in its history. European aerospace rival Airbus (*airbus.com*) has overtaken Boeing in commercial-airplane deliveries, and the two companies have different strategies for next-generation airplanes. Airbus is betting on a 550-seat aircraft called the A380. In contrast, Boeing is planning for a 200- to 300-passenger jet designed to consume 20 percent less fuel than bigger jets and fly longer routes previously limited to larger planes. Boeing has named its new jet the 7E7 Dreamliner. The company plans to start production of the 7E7 in 2006, with aircraft to be in service by 2008.

The 7E7 represents a dramatic shift in how Boeing builds planes. The company, which used to design and build the bulk of its aircraft, will outsource 70 percent of the airplane to suppliers. This outsourcing will require cross-company, global collaboration.

Boeing is designing the Dreamliner for half the cost of its last flagship airplane (the Boeing 777). To accomplish that, Boeing will use—and will insist that key suppliers use—software that lets designers around the world collaborate electronically in designing every manufacturing process and every component, from wings to seat-back trays. As a result of this collaboration, the company anticipates improved effi-

ciency in the plane's development process. Designers will use a single set of data, so the data will not have to be reproduced for multiple purposes as in the past. In addition, planners will be able to simulate digitally the plane's life cycle from design through production. The ability to quickly model iterations of a design will reduce errors and redundant work in achieving the best design. Boeing is using a "relational design," which means that the digital models it builds will be made up of virtual components—digital versions of the chairs, metal, and screws used to build a plane. For example, if designers move the location of the windows, the associated parts will move with it, speeding the process. Also, models can also be used to test component combinations to see, for example, if the design can handle certain loads.

Source: Compiled from B. Bacheldor, "Boeing's Flight Plan," Informationweek, February 16, 2004.

QUESTIONS

1. In your opinion, which strategy, Boeing's or Airbus's, will be the more successful? Can both strategies be successful at the same time? Support your answer.
2. How is Boeing using IT to support its strategy?

Before you go on . . .

1. List some internal systems that usually need to be connected to new applications.
2. Why is it especially important to connect to databases?
3. What is mainly connected between business partners?

WHAT'S IN IT FOR ME?

Accounting personnel help perform the cost-benefit analyses on proposed projects to assess their economic feasibility. They may also monitor ongoing project costs to keep the budget on track. Accounting personnel undoubtedly will find themselves involved with systems development at various points throughout their careers.

ACC

FOR THE ACCOUNTING MAJOR

Finance personnel are frequently involved with the financial issues that accompany any large-scale systems development project (e.g., budgeting). Also, they will be involved in cost-benefit and risk analyses. They need to stay abreast of the emerging techniques used to determine project costs and return on investment. Due to the intensity of data

FIN

FOR THE FINANCE MAJOR

and information in their various functions, finance departments themselves are also common recipients of new systems.

MKT

FOR THE MARKETING MAJOR

Marketing, in most organizations, is data- and information-intensive, so the marketing function is also a hotbed of systems development. Marketing personnel, like their co-horts in other functional areas, will find themselves participating on systems development teams. Such involvement increasingly means aiding in the development of systems, especially Web-based systems, that reach out directly from the organization to the customer.

POM

FOR THE PRODUCTION/ OPERATIONS MANAGEMENT MAJOR

Participation on development teams is also a common role for production/operations people. Manufacturing is becoming increasingly computer controlled and integrated with other allied systems, from design to logistics to inventory control to customer support. Production systems interface frequently with marketing, finance, and HRM systems; they may be part of a larger, enterprisewide system. Also, many end users in POM develop their own systems or collaborate with IT personnel on specific applications.

HRM

FOR THE HUMAN RESOURCES MANAGEMENT MAJOR

The human resources department is closely involved with several aspects of the systems acquisitions process. New systems may require hiring new employees, changing job descriptions, or terminating employees, tasks handled by HR. If the organization hires consultants for the development project or outsources it, the human resources department may handle contracts with consultants or outsourcing vendors.

SUMMARY

1. **Describe the process of IT acquisition or development.** Information systems acquisition includes all approaches to obtaining systems: buying, leasing, or building. The objective of IT application acquisition is to create (or buy) applications and implement them. The process of acquiring IT applications can be divided into five steps: planning and justification; IT architecture creation; selecting development options; testing, installing, and integrating new applications; and conducting operations and maintenance. This process needs to be managed.

2. **Describe the IT planning process.** Information systems planning begins with reviewing the strategic plan of the organization. That plan states the firm's overall mission, the goals that follow from the mission, and the broad steps necessary to reach these goals. The organizational strategic plan and the existing IT architecture provide the inputs in developing the *IT strategic plan*, which describes the IT architecture and major IS initiatives needed to achieve the goals of the organization. The IT strategic plan also states the mission of the IS department, which defines its underlying purpose. The IT strategic plan may also require a new IT architecture, or the existing IT architecture may be sufficient. In either case, the IT strategic plan leads to the *IS operational plan*, which is a clear set of projects that will be executed by the IS/IT department and by functional area managers in support of the IT strategic plan.

3. **Describe the IT justification process and methods.** The justification process is basically a comparison of the expected costs versus the benefits of each application. While measuring cost may not be complex, measuring benefits is, due to the many intangible benefits involved. Several methodologies exist for evaluating costs and benefits, including total costs of ownership (TCO), total benefits of ownership (TBO), net present value (NPV), return on investment (ROI), and the business case approach.

4. **List the major IT acquisition options and the criteria for option selection.** The major options are buy, lease, and build (develop in-house). Other options are joint ventures and use of e-marketplaces or exchanges (private or public). Building in-house can be done by using the SDLC, by using prototyping or other methodologies, and it can be done by outsourcers, the IS department employees, or end users (individually or together).

5. **Describe the use of criteria for selecting an acquisition approach.** In deciding how to acquire applications, companies must consider several, sometimes many, criteria. These criteria may conflict among themselves (e.g., quality and price).

Companies need to make sure that all criteria are considered and to evaluate the importance of each criterion for the company.

6. **Describe the role of ASPs.** ASPs lease software applications, usually via the Internet. Fees for the leased applications can be the same each month or can be based on actual usage (like electricity). (This is the basic idea of utility computing which will be provided by ASPs or by software vendors.)

7. **Describe the process of vendor and software selection.** The process of vendor and software selection is composed of six steps: identify potential vendors, determine evaluation criteria, evaluate vendors and packages, choose the vendor and package, negotiate a contract, and establish service level agreements.

8. **Understand some major implementation issues.** Most of the implementation issues are related to decisions regarding selection of development options and vendor and software selection. Also, security and ethics need to be considered.

9. **Understand the issue of connecting IT applications to databases, other applications, networks, and business partners.** New applications need to be connected to existing applications, databases, and so on inside the organization. They may also be connected to partners' information systems. Issues of connectivity, compatibility, and security make connections difficult. Several tools and methods exist to alleviate the problem.

INTERACTIVE / LEARNING

Interactive Learning

To Outsource or Not to Outsource?
Go to the Interactivities section on the Student Web Site and access Chapter 11: Acquiring or Building IT Application and Infrastructure. There you will find some hands-on activities that help explore the implementation issues associated with outsourcing.

More Resources
More resources and study tools are located on the Student Web Site. You'll find additional chapter materials and links to organizations, people, and technologies for each chapter. In addition, self-quizzes that provide individualized feedback are available for each chapter.

Instructions for accessing the Interactivities on the Student Web Site:

1. Go to **wiley.com/college/turban**
2. Select Turban Rainer Potter's *Introduction to Information Technology, Third Edition*
3. Click on Student Resources Site, in the toolbar on the left
4. Click on Interactivities Web Site
5. Click on Interactivities Web Site and use your password to enter the site (your password card is located in the inside cover of your textbook)

DISCUSSION QUESTIONS

1. Discuss the advantages of a lease option over a buy option.
2. Why is it important for all business managers to understand the issues of IT resource acquisition?
3. List some of the new options for acquiring IT resources. (See Table 11.1.)
4. Why should techniques like prototyping be considered sometimes as useful additions to, rather than replacements for, the SDLC?
5. Discuss the issue of assessing intangible benefits and the proposed solutions.
6. Discuss the role of ASPs. Why is their attractiveness increasing? (Hint: Consider utility computing.)

1. Enter *ecommerce.internet.com*. Find the product review area. Read reviews of three software payment solutions. Assess them as possible components.
2. Enter *ibm.com* and find information about how IBM measures the ROI on WebSphere. Then examine ROI from CIOView Corporation (*CIOview.com*).

Identify the variables included in the analysis (at both *ibm.com* and *CIOview.com*). Prepare a report about the fairness of such a tool.
3. Enter *sap.com* and use the Casebuilder Calculator for a hypothetical (or real) IT project. Write a report on your experience.

1. Enter *ibm.com/software*. Find their WebSphere product. Read recent customers' success stories. What makes this software so popular?
2. Enter the Web sites of the GartnerGroup (*gartnergroup.com*), The Yankee Group (*yankeegroup.com*), and CIO (*cio.com*). Search for recent material about ASPs and outsourcing, and prepare a report on your findings.
3. Enter the Web site of IDC (*idc.com*) and find how the company evaluates ROI on intranets, supply chain, and other IT projects.

4. Visit the Web site of Resource Management Systems (*rms.net*) and take the IT investment Management Approach Assessment Self-Test (*rms.net/self_test.htm*) to compare your organization's IT decision-making process with those of best-practices organizations.
5. Enter *cio.com* and *cosn.org/tco*. Find information about the total cost of ownership model. Write a report on the state of the art.
6. Enter *plumtree.com* and see how they conduct ROI on portals. List major elements of the analysis.

1. Assessment of the functionality of an application is a part of the planning process (Step 1). Select three to five Web sites catering to the same type of buyer (for instance, several Web sites that offer CDs or computer hardware), and divide the sites among the teams. Each team will assess the functionality of their assigned Web sites by preparing an analysis of the different sorts of functions provided by the sites. In addition, the team should compare the strong and weak points of each site from the buyer's perspective.

2. Divide into groups, with each group visiting a local company (include your university). At each firm, study the systems acquisition process. Find out the methodology or methodologies used by each organization and the type of application each methodology applies. Prepare a report and present it to the class.
3. As a group, design an information system for a startup business of your choice. Describe your chosen IT resource acquisition strategy, and justify your choices of hardware, software, telecommunications support, and other aspects of a proposed system.

HOW NIKE'S $400 MILLION SUPPLY CHAIN MANAGEMENT SOFTWARE SYSTEM FAILED

THE BUSINESS PROBLEM In certain retail stores, fans of Nike's Air Terra Humara 2 running shoe hit the jackpot. Once selling for over US $100, they were selling for less than $50 in fall 2001. The lower price was the aftermath of the breakdown in Nike's supply chain, a breakdown attributed to a software problem.

Nike's demand-forecast application was supposed to forecast demand and plan supplies of raw material and finished products. But the application apparently overestimated the demand for certain shoes in some locations and underestimated demand in others. As a result, some raw

materials were overpurchased and inventory levels of other materials were insufficient. Certain models of shoes (like Air Terras) were overmanufactured, while the most-demanded ones were undermanufactured. To speed the latter to market, Nike had to spend around $5 a pair in air freight cost, compared to the usual cost of 75 cents a pair by ocean. In all, Nike attributed some $100 million in lost sales in the third quarter of 2001 alone to this problem.

THE IT SOLUTION Nike had decided to buy the application software from i2, a major supply chain software producer. But Nike insisted on modifying the i2 standard software and customizing it to its needs. Specifically, Nike wanted a forecast by style level (several hundred kinds), by color, and by size. This resulted in a need to make thousands of forecasts, very rapidly, to quickly respond to changing market conditions and consumer preferences.

THE RESULTS What went wrong? To meet Nike's need it was necessary to make significant modifications to the standard software. Nike wanted the software fast. The reprogramming was apparently done too fast. The software had "bugs" in it when it was deployed. Almost any new software contains bugs that need to be fixed; appropriate testing is critical, and it is a time-consuming task. Nike and i2 apparently failed to recognize what was achievable.

Customizing standard software requires a systematic process, should be done only when absolutely necessary, and must be planned for properly. None of these requirements was met. Furthermore, Nike could have dis-covered the problem early enough if it had used appropriate deployment procedures.

To avoid disasters such as Nike's, companies must fully understand what they are trying to achieve and why. They must use performance-level indicators to properly measure the system during testing. Incidentally, Nike fixed the problem after an undisclosed amount of time and money in 2002.

Sources: Compiled from J. Sterlicchi and E. Wales, "Custom Chaos: How Nike Just Did It Wrong," *Business Online* (June 2001; *BolWeb.com*), and *nike.com* (press releases, 2002).

QUESTIONS

1. How can a company determine if it really needs to customize software?
2. Whose responsibility is it to properly test and deploy the software—the software vendor's or the user's?
3. Based on what you learned in this chapter, how can such incidents be minimized?

ACQUIRING INFORMATION SYSTEMS FOR CLUB IT

Ruben and Lisa have asked you to meet with them next week and give them your assessment of their current information systems and a recommendation on how to proceed in upgrading and adding information management capabilities. Over the last few months, you have learned much about the nightclub business and opportunities for Club IT to improve its information technology capabilities. You have some definite ideas on how IT could be improved at Club IT, and you also realize it takes thorough analysis and planning to be successful.

ASSIGNMENT

1. Describe the overall IT strategy you recommend to Lisa and Ruben for leveraging IT for better cus-tomer service and informed decision making at Club IT.

2. Choose a functional information system consistent with this strategy that would have a high impact on the information management and success of Club IT, such as a wireless ordering system, web-based supply chain management, or a customer relationship management system. Tell Ruben and Lisa why this system is the best place to start implementing their IT strategy.

3. Describe the advantages and disadvantages to Club IT of the three system acquisition options available, and make a recommendation on which option best fits Club IT's needs.

Go to wiley.com/college/turban **to access the**

CLUB IT Web Site on the Student Web Site

IT Ethics, Impacts, and Security

Chapter Preview

Now that you are acquainted with the major capabilities of IT and the substantial benefits it can provide to organizations, we will explore some of the major issues that are involved in putting these systems to work for you, no matter what function you perform in your company. Specifically, the issues can be of ethical, behavioral, organizational, societal, or technical nature. Of the many implementation issues, we will look here at those that are most frequently encountered and will view them from several perspectives: What are these issues? Why do they appear? Why are they important? What can we do about them? Answers to these and other questions can be found in this chapter. Finally, *information systems security* must be practiced by all people at home, at school, and at work. Therefore, we conclude the chapter and the book with a look at that topic.

Learning Objectives

1. Describe the major ethical issues related to information technology and identify situations in which they occur.
2. Identify the major impacts of information technology on organizational structure, power, jobs, supervision, and decision making.
3. Understand the potential dehumanization of people by computers and other potential negative impacts of information technology.
4. Identify some of the major societal effects of information technology.
5. Describe the many threats to information security.
6. Understand the various defense mechanisms used to protect information systems.
7. Explain IT auditing and planning for disaster recovery.

ONLINE MUSIC AND INTELLECTUAL PROPERTY RIGHTS

Before the advent of the Web, people made audiotape copies of music and videos. Few individuals had either the interest or the means to create and distribute copies to larger populations. For the most part, these activities were ignored by the music producers, distributors, and artists who had the legal rights to the content.

Then came the Web and a variety of enterprising music-distribution sites such as MP3.com and Napster.com. MP3.com enabled users to listen to music from any computer with an Internet connection, without paying royalties. Using peer-to-peer (P2P) technology, Napster supported the distribution of music and other digitized content among millions of users. When asked whether they were doing anything illegal, MP3.com and Napster claimed that they were simply supporting what had been done for years and were not charging for their services. Other companies extended the concept to other digitizable media such as videos and movies.

The popularity of MP3.com, Napster, and P2P services became too great for the content creators and owners to ignore. Music sales declined (and as of 2004 are still declining). To the creators and owners, the Web was becoming a vast copying machine for pirated software, CDs, movies, and the like. If left undeterred, MP3.com's and Napster's services could result in the loss of many thousands of jobs and millions of dollars in revenue.

A SERIES OF "SOLUTIONS" FROM THE MUSIC INDUSTRY

Solution 1 In December 2000, EMusic (*emusic.com*) filed a copyright infringement lawsuit against MP3.com. They claimed ownership of the digital rights to some of the music made available at MP3.com. Other companies—Warner Bros. Music Group, EMI Group PLC, BMG Entertainment, and Sony Music Entertainment—followed suit. A year later, Napster faced similar legal claims.

Result 1 MP3.com suspended operations in April 2000 and settled its lawsuit, paying the litigants $20 million each. Napster suspended service and settled its lawsuits for $26 million.

After Napster's demise, a host of other companies (e.g., Morpheus, Grokster, Gnutella, and Kazaa) began offering decentralized peer-to-peer file sharing. Some P2P companies moved to other countries, trying to escape U.S. copyright laws, but legal problems followed them. However, sales of music continued to decline as an estimated 60 million Americans were swapping songs over P2P services.

Solution 2 On Monday, September 8, 2003, the Recording Industry Association of American (RIAA) sued 261 American computer users, accusing them of using P2P file-sharing services to illegally distribute and download large amounts of copyrighted music over the Internet. One of the suits involved a 12-year-old girl, Brianna LaHara, who had just started the seventh grade at St. Gregory the Great Catholic School in Manhattan.

Result 2 On September, 24, 2003, Sharman Networks, Ltd., the company behind the Kazaa file-sharing software, sued the major record labels, accusing them of using unauthorized versions of its software in their efforts to find users of Kazaa software. Sharman is incorporated in the South Pacific island nation of Vanuatu, with main offices in Sydney, Australia.

In October 2003, Verizon (a large Internet service provider) and Charter Communications (a large cable company) sued to prevent the RIAA from obtaining the identities of their customers who have allegedly traded songs illegally online. In addition, the American Civil Liberties Union (ACLU) filed court documents accusing the RIAA of illegally using thousands of subpoenas to unmask alleged copyright infringers. The ACLU said that the RIAA violated due process and constitutional rights shielding Internet users' anonymity.

As for the RIAA lawsuits, about 98 percent of those sued settled out of court, for approximately $2,000 to $3,000 each. When Brianna LaHara settled her suit on September 10, 2003, she paid the RIAA $2,000 and agreed not to share files online. MusicRebellion.com immediately signed her up for its pay service and gave her $2,000 in free songs.

Following the RIAA's lawsuits, universities moved to block music sharing. MIT, Northeastern, and UCLA are among the universities that complied with subpoenas from the RIAA to provide identifying information on those thought to be pirating music. Other universities used different methods. When the U.S. Naval Academy cracked down on illegally downloaded music, 100 midshipmen were stripped of their computers. Penn State limits students in residence halls to 1.5 gigabytes of inbound or outbound network traffic a week. The University of Florida developed its own software, called Icarus, to monitor bandwidth use.

Solution 3 On September 23, 2003, BMG Music, one of the RIAA's member companies, released a music CD with copy protection, the first time it had done so in the United States. Copyproof CDs are the "killer application" in the music industry's war against digital piracy. The essential idea is to manufacture discs that can be played on stereo audio machines but cannot be copied onto computer hard drives. (Converting CD audio to MP3 files is called "ripping.")

Result 3 Ingenious hackers around the world attack each type of copy protection. For example, CDfreaks.com has posted detailed instructions for cracking Macrovision's SafeAudio, a CD protection product. Also, hackers in Germany disabled Sony's Key2audio protection scheme by covering the data track of a CD, which resides near the outer edge of the disc, with ink from a felt-tip marker.

THE CURRENT PICTURE

There are currently a number of online services—including a legitimate reincarnation of Napster—that offer music at lower prices. Unlike most music stores, these services allow customers to sample any song or album for free. Usually, customers can buy any song for less than a dollar each or an album of songs for about $10. You can create your own albums, mixing the tracks you want and burning your play lists onto CDs or copying them to a portable audio player. Four of the biggest services are iTunes (from Apple; see *apple.com/itunes*), BuyMusic (*buymusic.com*), MusicMatch (*musicmatch.com*), and Napster (now a division of Roxio, *roxio.com*; see *napster.com*).

And the P2P file-sharing services? Use of these services has declined, but all are still in business. Interestingly, two of the original programmers of Kazaa are readying the release of Skype (*skype.com*), an application that uses P2P technology to allow users to make phone calls over the Internet for free. By April 2004, Skype had been downloaded 9.5 million times.

Sources: Compiled from D. Kushner, "Digital Entertainment Post-Napster," *MIT Technology Review* (November 2002); J. Schwartz, "Music's Struggle with Technology," *New York Times* (September 22, 2003); C. Metz, "The Changing Face of Online Music," *PC Magazine* (September 24, 2003); Associated Press, "Makers of Kazaa Are Suing Record Labels," *eWeek* (September 24, 2003); S. Lubell, "Campuses Move to Block Music Sharing," *New York Times* (October 2, 2003); S. Olsen, "Charter Files Suit Against RIAA," *msnbc.com* (October 6, 2003); Associated Press, "Reborn Napster Unveils Test Version," *msnbc.com* (October 9, 2003); P. Burrows, "Napster Lives Again—Sort Of," *Business Week* (October 20, 2003); J. Greene, "Music Magic," *Business Week* (November 10, 2003); E. Hellweg, "The Skype Is Calling," *MIT Technology Review* (November 19, 2003).

WHAT WE LEARNED FROM THIS CASE

All commerce involves a number of legal, ethical, and regulatory issues. Copyright, trademark, and patent infringement, freedom of thought and speech, theft of property, and fraud are not new issues in the world of commerce. However, as this opening case illustrates, electronic commerce adds to the scope and scale of these issues. It also raises a number of questions about what constitutes illegal behavior versus unethical, intrusive, or undesirable behavior.

E-commerce is one of the many IT phenomena that have affected individuals, organizations, and society. This chapter examines the impacts that IT has made on these groups. First, though, we present some of the legal and ethical issues related to the emerging electronic technologies and discuss various legal and technical remedies and safeguards. The chapter also looks at the issue of IS vulnerability and at ways of protecting information resources. Figure 12.1 provides a roadmap of these topics in this chapter.

12.1 ETHICAL ISSUES

ethics *A branch of philosophy that deals with what is considered to be right and wrong.*

Ethics is a branch of philosophy that deals with what is considered to be right and wrong. Over the years, philosophers have proposed many ethical guidelines. It is important to realize that what is unethical is not necessarily illegal. Thus, in most instances, an individual or organization faced with an ethical decision is not considering whether to break the law.

In today's complex environment, interpretations of "right" and "wrong" are not always clear. Many companies and professional organizations develop their own codes of ethics. A **code of ethics** is a collection of principles intended as a guide for the members of a company or an organization. The diversity of IT applications and the increased use of information technologies have created a variety of ethical issues, as illustrated throughout this text. Ethical issues can be categorized into four types: privacy, accuracy, property, and accessibility.

code of ethics *A collection of principles intended as a guide for the members of a company or an organization.*

1. *Privacy issues:* collection, storage, and dissemination of information about individuals
2. *Accuracy issues:* authenticity, fidelity, and accuracy of information collected and processed
3. *Property issues:* ownership and value of information (intellectual property)
4. *Accessibility issues:* right to access information and payment of fees to access it

Representative questions and issues in each category are listed in Manager's Checklist 12.1. Fourteen ethics scenarios are presented in Online Appendix W12.1. Of these, we focus here on the issues of privacy and intellectual property.

wiley.com/college/turban

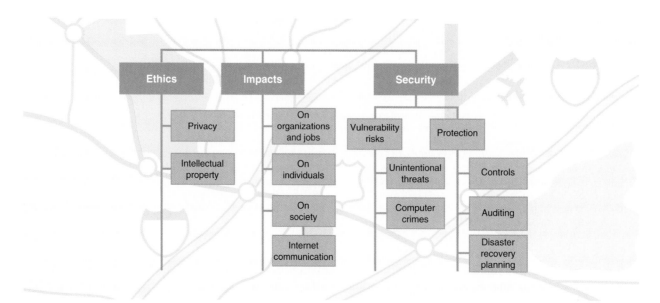

Figure 12.1   *Roadmap: An overview of ethics, impact, and security topics.*

Privacy Issues

- ❏ What information about oneself should an individual be required to reveal to others?
- ❏ What kind of surveillance can an employer use on its employees?
- ❏ What things can people keep to themselves and not be forced to reveal to others?
- ❏ What information about individuals should be kept in databases, and how secure is the information there?

Accuracy Issues

- ❏ Who is responsible for the authenticity, fidelity, and accuracy of information collected?
- ❏ How can we ensure that information will be processed properly and presented accurately to users?
- ❏ How can we ensure that errors in databases, data transmissions, and data processing are accidental and not intentional?
- ❏ Who is to be held accountable for errors in information, and how should the injured party by compensated?

Property Issues

- ❏ Who owns the information?
- ❏ What are the just and fair prices for its exchange?
- ❏ How should one handle software piracy (copying copyrighted software)?
- ❏ Under what circumstances can one use proprietary databases?
- ❏ Can corporate computers be used for private purposes?
- ❏ How should experts who contribute their knowledge to create expert systems be compensated?
- ❏ How should access to information channels be allocated?

Accessibility Issues

- ❏ Who is allowed to access information?
- ❏ How much should be charged for permitting accessibility to information?
- ❏ How can accessibility to computers be provided for employees with disabilities?
- ❏ Who will be provided with equipment needed for accessing information?
- ❏ What information does a person or an organization have a right or a privilege to obtain, and under what conditions and with what safeguards?

Protecting Privacy

In general, **privacy** is the right to be left alone and the right to be free of unreasonable personal intrusions. *Information privacy* is the right to determine when, and to what extent, information about oneself can be communicated to others. This right applies to individuals, groups, and institutions.

privacy *The right to be left alone and to be free of unreasonable personal intrusions.*

The definition of privacy can be interpreted quite broadly. However, the following two rules have been followed fairly closely in past court decisions in many countries:

1. The right of privacy is not absolute. Privacy must be balanced against the needs of society.

2. The public's right to know is superior to the individual's right of privacy.

These two rules show why it is difficult in some cases to determine and enforce privacy regulations. The right to privacy is recognized today in all U.S. states and by the federal government, either by statute or common law. Some representative issues of privacy are discussed next.

electronic surveillance *The tracking of people's activities, online or offline, with the aid of computers.*

Electronic Surveillance. According to the American Civil Liberties Union (ACLU), the tracking of people's activities, online or offline, with the aid of computers—that is, **electronic surveillance**—is a major problem. The ACLU estimates that tens of millions of computer users are being monitored, most without their knowledge. Employees have very limited protection against employers' surveillance. Although several legal challenges are now underway, the law appears to support employers' rights to read electronic mail and other electronic documents.

Surveillance is also a concern for private individuals (via personal e-mail, for example), whether done by corporations, government bodies, or criminal elements. Many Americans are pondering the right balance between personal privacy and electronic surveillance in terms of threats to national security. The terrorist attacks of 9/11 and the anthrax attack that year made many Americans change their positions, moving toward allowing more government surveillance. The next two examples show the two sides of the controversy about surveillance.

SVC

EXAMPLE *Tracking Junior with a Microchip.* Solusat (*solusat.com.mx*), the Mexican distributor of the VeriChip, has launched a service to implant microchips in children as an anti-kidnapping device. The VeriChip is a rice-size microchip that is injected beneath the skin and transmits a 125-kilohertz radio frequency signal. The chip is being marketed as an emergency ID. Mexico's Foundation of Investigations of Robbed and Missing Children has estimated that 133,000 Mexican children have been abducted over the past five years. Solusat envisions placing walk-through scanners—similar to metal-detector portals used in airports—in malls, bus stations, and other areas where a missing child may appear. The chip could also be used to identify children who are found unconscious, drugged, dead, or too young to identify themselves (Scheeres, 2003).

GOV

EXAMPLE *Are You Ready for Constant Electronic Surveillance?* Increasingly, ours is a world of ID checks, surveillance cameras, body scans, fingerprint databases, e-mail sifters, cell phone interceptors, nanny-cams, wireless heart monitors, and swipe-in school and workplace IDs. Three-quarters of U.S. firms now acknowledge that they monitor employees' e-mail, Web browsing, phone calls, and computer files.

Consider an 18-year-old French boy, who was swimming one day in a public pool near his home. At some point, he blacked out and the lifeguards failed to notice. However, 12 large machine eyes deep underwater were watching him sink to the bottom. The swim center had installed an electronic surveillance system called Poseidon, a network of cameras that feeds a computer programmed to use a set of complex algorithms to distinguish between normal and distressed swimming. Poseidon covers a pool's entire swimming area and can distinguish among blurry reflections, shadows, and actual swimmers. When the computer detects a possible problem, it instantly activates a beeper to alert lifeguards and displays the exact incident location on a monitor. Sixteen seconds after Poseidon noticed the boy, the lifeguards had him out of the pool and had initiated CPR. He recovered fully.

In Great Britain, municipalities have installed closed-circuit television cameras (CCTVs) almost everywhere. The country currently has more than four million CCTVs, one for every 15 people. The average visitor to London is now captured on video 300 times in a single day. British authorities have concluded that all Britons should assume that all their behavior outside the home is monitored. The actual effectiveness of the cameras is not clear, but the British public seems to approve of the cameras (Shenk, 2003). For more information, see *urbaneye.net*.

Personal Information in Databases. Information about individuals is being kept in many databases. Perhaps the most visible locations of such records are credit-reporting agencies. Other places where personal information might be stored are banks and financial institutions; cable TV, telephone, and utilities companies; employers; apartment companies; mortgage companies; equipment rental companies; hospitals; schools and universities; supermarkets, retail establishments, and mail-order houses; government agencies (Internal Revenue Service, Census Bureau, your state, your municipality); libraries; and insurance companies. Also, data from questionnaires you fill out on the Internet (e.g., when you try to win a prize) are usually stored in a database.

There are several concerns about the information you provide to these record-keepers. Do you know where the records are? Are the records accurate? Can you change inaccurate data? How long will it take to make a change? Under what circumstances will personal data be released? How are the data used? To whom are they given or sold? How secure are the data against access by unauthorized people?

Information stored in databases can be a problem, as the following example illustrates.

EXAMPLE   *States Shy Away from Crime-Fighting Database.* Seisint (*seisint.com*) is building a giant database, called the Matrix. The database grew out of concerns, after the September 11, 2001, terrorist attacks, that law enforcement agencies across the nation were doing a poor job of sharing information. Matrix cross-references confidential government records from participating states with both public and private databases, creating exhaustive dossiers on individuals for use by law enforcement. As Georgia officials wrestle with sending confidential driver's license records to the Matrix database, Alabama and Louisiana have withdrawn from the multistate effort, citing concerns about privacy. Officials are worried about the potential for inaccurate data. Georgia has already sent prison, sex offender, and other public criminal information to Matrix, but transmitting confidential driver's license data has caused much more controversy. Only eight states remain of the original 14 in the federally funded Matrix project (Stanford and Ledford, 2003).

GOV

Information on Internet Bulletin Boards and Newsgroups.   Every day there are more and more *electronic bulletin boards*, *newsgroups*, and *electronic discussions* such as chat rooms, both on the Internet and within corporate intranets. How does society keep owners of bulletin boards from disseminating information that may be offensive to readers or simply untrue? The difficulty we have addressing this problem highlights the conflict among freedom of speech, privacy, and ethics, a continuing dynamic in American society.

Privacy Codes and Policies.   One way to protect privacy is to develop privacy policies or codes. These are an organization's guidelines with respect to protecting the privacy of customers, clients, and employees. In many corporations, senior management has begun to understand that, with the ability to collect vast amounts of personal information on customers, clients, and employees, comes an obligation to ensure that the collected information—and therefore, the individual—is protected. A sampling of privacy policy guidelines is given in Manager's Checklist 12.2 (page 368).

Having a privacy policy in place can help organizations avoid legal problems. However, privacy codes and policies can be violated, as the following example shows.

privacy policies/codes *An organization's guidelines with respect to protecting the privacy of customers, clients, and employees.*

EXAMPLE   *JetBlue Apologizes to Its Customers.* JetBlue Airways (*jetblue.com*) apologized for giving information on 1.5 million passengers to a Defense Department contractor to test a security system. The information included itineraries, names, addresses, and phone numbers. The contractor then used another service, Acxiom Corporation (*acxiom.com*), to add Social Security numbers, economic status, occupation, and other information.

JetBlue said the test had nothing to do with the government's controversial Computer Assisted Passenger Pre-Screening System II (CAPPS II). CAPPS II uses a

MANAGER'S CHECKLIST 12.2

Privacy Policy Guidelines: A Sampler

Data Collection

☐ Data should be collected on individuals only for the purpose of accomplishing a legitimate business objective.

☐ Data should be adequate, relevant, and not excessive in relation to the business objective.

☐ Individuals must give their consent before data pertaining to them can be gathered. Such consent may be implied from the individual's actions (e.g., applications for credit, insurance, or employment).

Data Accuracy

☐ Sensitive data gathered on individuals should be verified before it is entered into the database.

☐ Data should be accurate and, where and when necessary, kept current.

☐ The file should be made available so the individual can ensure that the data are correct.

☐ If there is disagreement about the accuracy of the data, the individual's version should be noted and included with any disclosure of the file.

Data Confidentiality

☐ Computer security procedures should be implemented to provide reasonable assurance against unauthorized disclosure of data. They should include physical, technical, and administrative security measures.

☐ Third parties should not be given access to data without the individual's knowledge or permission, except as required by law.

☐ Disclosures of data, other than the most routine, should be noted and maintained for as long as the data are maintained.

☐ Data should not be disclosed for reasons incompatible with the business objective for which they are collected.

massive secret database of information to assess individuals' security-threat levels. However, the flap over JetBlue's action illustrated the nervousness of passengers and federal officials concerning the launch of the CAPPS II system. The government has already agreed not to include financial data and similar personal data in the CAPPS II profile. But privacy advocates say they are not convinced that the new system will not infringe on personal privacy.

JetBlue's CEO acknowledged that the airline violated its own privacy policy by releasing passenger information (Phillips, 2003).

International Aspects of Privacy. There are major differences among countries with respect to privacy regulations. For example, the existing inconsistency of standards could obstruct the flow of information among countries in the European Union. To overcome this problem, the European Community Commission (ECC) has issued guidelines to all its member countries regarding the rights of individuals to access information about themselves and to correct errors. The ECC data protection laws that took effect in 1998 are stricter than U.S. laws and therefore may create problems for multinational corporations, which may face lawsuits for privacy violation.

The transfer of data in and out of a nation without knowledge of the authorities or individuals involved raises a number of privacy issues. Whose laws have jurisdiction when records are in a different country for reprocessing or retransmission purposes? For example, if data are transmitted by a Polish company through a U.S. satellite to a British corporation, which country's privacy laws control what data and when? Questions like these will become increasingly more complicated and more common as time goes on. Governments must make an effort to develop laws and standards to cope with rapidly changing information technologies in order to solve some of these privacy issues.

Protecting Intellectual Property

The issue of protecting intellectual property is an important one for those who make their livelihoods in knowledge fields. **Intellectual property** is the intangible property created by individuals or corporations, which is protected under *trade secret, patent*, and *copyright*, laws.

A **trade secret** is intellectual work, such as a business plan, that is a company secret and is not based on public information. An example is a corporate strategic plan. Laws about trade secrets are legislated at the state level in the United States. A **patent** is a document that grants the holder exclusive rights on an invention or process for 20 years. **Copyright** is a statutory grant that provides the creators of intellectual property with ownership of it for the life of the creator plus 70 years. Owners are entitled to collect fees from anyone who wants to copy the property. The U.S. Federal Computer Software Copyright Act (1980) provides protection for *source* and *object code* of computer software, but one problem is that it is not clear what is eligible for protection. For example, copyright law does not protect similar concepts, functions, and general features (such as pull-down menus, colors, or icons).

The most common intellectual property related to IT deals with software. The copying of software without making payment to the owner (such as giving a disc to a friend to install on his or her computer) is a copyright violation, and a major problem for software vendors.

intellectual property   *The intangible property created by individuals or corporations, which is protected under* trade secret, patent, *and* copyright, *laws.*

trade secret   *Intellectual work, such as a business plan, that is a company secret and is not based on public information.*

patent   *A document that grants the holder exclusive rights on an invention or process for 20 years.*

copyright   *A grant that provides the creator of intellectual property with ownership of it for the life of the creator plus 70 years.*

Before you go on . . .

1. Define ethics and list its four categories as they apply to IT.
2. Describe the issue of privacy as it is affected by IT.
3. What does a code of ethics contain?
4. Describe the issue of intellectual property protection.

12.2 IMPACTS OF IT ON ORGANIZATIONS AND JOBS

The use of information technologies, most recently the Web, has brought many organizational changes in areas such as structure, authority, power, job content, employee career ladders, supervision, and the manager's job. In this section, we look at how IT is changing organizational structure and jobs.

How Will Organizations Change?

IT may cause a nearly complete change in organizations, including their structure, supervision, and power distribution.

Flatter Organizational Hierarchies.   IT allows for the increased productivity of managers, an increased span of control (more employees per supervisor), and a decreased number of managers and experts. It is reasonable to assume, then, that fewer managerial levels will exist in many organizations, and there will be fewer staff and line managers. This trend is already evidenced by the continuing phenomenon of the "shrinking of middle management."

Flatter organizational hierarchies will also result from reduction in the total number of employees, reengineering of business processes, increased productivity of employees, and the ability of lower-level employees to perform higher-level jobs with the support of information systems. Starting in the late 1980s and accelerating since then, many organizations are getting smaller and leaner.

Changes in Supervision.   The fact that an employee's work is performed online and stored electronically introduces the possibility for greater electronic supervision.

For professional employees whose work is often measured by their completion of projects, "remote supervision" implies greater emphasis on completed work and less on personal contacts and office politics. This emphasis is especially true if employees work in geographically dispersed locations, including homes, away from their supervisors.

Power and Status. Knowledge is power—this fact has been recognized for generations. The latest developments in computerized systems are changing the power structure within organizations. The struggle over who will control corporate information resources has become one of the most visible conflicts in many organizations, both private and public. Expert systems, for example, may reduce the power of certain professional groups because the employee's knowledge will be in the public domain. On the other hand, individuals who control e-commerce applications may gain considerable prestige, knowledge, power, and status. As a result, a power redistribution is underway in many organizations.

How Will Jobs Change?

One issue of concern to all employees is the impact of IT on their jobs. The content of jobs, career ladders, functional areas, and managerial duties will undoubtedly be affected. Changes will occur particularly in jobs of intermediaries, such as insurance, real estate, and travel agents. Many jobs will be eliminated. Many other changes will take place that we can only speculate about at this point.

Job Content. Job content is important not only because it is related to organizational structure, but also because it is related to employee satisfaction, compensation, status, and productivity. Changes in job content occur when work is redesigned—for example when business process restructuring is attempted, or when e-commerce changes the marketing distribution system. Certainly many jobs are being redesigned to take advantage of the Web and emerging information technologies. These will, in turn, require higher levels of computing literacy from workers and need for retraining.

Many additional job-related questions could surface as a result of using IT. For example: What will be the impact of IT on job qualifications and on training requirements? How can jobs that use IT be designed so that they present an acceptable level of challenge to users? How might IT be used to personalize or enrich jobs? What principles should be used to allocate functions to people and machines, especially those functions that can be performed equally well by either one? Should cost or efficiency be the sole or major criterion for such allocation?

Employee Career Ladders. Increased use of IT in organizations could have a significant and somewhat unexpected impact on career ladders. Today, many highly skilled professionals have developed their abilities through years of experience, holding a series of positions that expose them to progressively more difficult and complex situations. The use of e-learning and intelligent tutoring systems may shortcut a portion of this learning curve by capturing and more efficiently managing the use of knowledge.

However, several questions relating to employee career paths are subject to thought and debate: How will high-level human expertise be acquired with minimal experience in lower-level tasks? What will be the effect on compensation at all levels of employment? How will human resources development programs be structured? What career paths will be offered to employees in a rapidly changing technological environment?

The Manager's Job. One of the most important tasks of managers is making decisions. As seen in Chapter 10, IT can change the manner in which many decisions are made, and consequently change managers' jobs.

Many managers have reported that information technology has finally given them time to get out of the office and into the field. They also have found that they can spend more time planning activities instead of "putting out fires." Information gathering for decision making can now be done much more quickly with search engines and intranets. Web-based intelligent agents can monitor the environment, and scan and interpret information.

Managers used to work on a large number of problems simultaneously, moving from one to another as they waited for more information on their current problem or until some external event interrupted them. IT tends to reduce the time necessary to complete any step in the decision-making process. Therefore, managers today can work on fewer tasks during each day and complete more of them.

Another possible impact on the manager's job could be a change in leadership requirements. What are generally considered to be good qualities of leadership may be significantly altered with the use of IT. For example, when face-to-face communication is replaced by electronic mail and computerized conferencing, leadership qualities attributed to physical presence may be lessened. As a result, effective leadership may be perceived to be more closely linked to effective computer-based communication.

Before you go on . . .

1. List the major organizational impacts of IT.
2. How might jobs change?
3. How is the manager's job likely to change?

12.3 IMPACTS ON INDIVIDUALS AT WORK

IT may have a variety of impacts on individuals at work. This section discusses some of the ways that IT may affect individuals, their perceptions, and their behaviors.

Will My Job Be Eliminated?

One of the major concerns of every employee, part-time or full-time, is job security. This issue is not new; it has frequently been brought to the attention of the public since the beginning of the Industrial Revolution and the introduction of automation.

For years, unemployment has been a major concern of countries that use little automation (developing countries). However, since the 1990s, this concern has spread to industrialized countries as well. Due to difficult economic times, increased global competition, demands for customization, and increased consumer sophistication, many companies have increased their investments in IT. In fact, as computers gain in intelligence and capabilities as time passes, the competitive advantage of replacing people with machines is increasing rapidly. For this reason, some people believe that society is heading toward massive unemployment; others disagree.

The answers to the employment debate will be provided in part by future developments in IT. They are also influenced by national and cultural differences. Some countries (or communities within countries) have unemployment rates of 50 percent or more (e.g., East Timor, Kosovo). While the unemployment rates in other countries may seem low, these rates must be measured against the need of people in society for work, as well as the ability or intention of the government to provide a social safety net. For example, Hong Kong lacks such a comprehensive safety net, and many who would be eligible claimants believe it beneath their dignity to claim benefits anyway. When unemployment reaches 3 or 4 percent in Hong Kong, as during the recent Asian financial crisis, this is considered a very high rate. In other countries, for example, in North America and Western Europe, 3 to 4 percent may be considered unimaginably low.

Dehumanization and Psychological Impacts

dehumanization *Loss of identity.*

A frequent criticism of traditional data processing systems was their impersonal nature and their potential to *dehumanize* and depersonalize the activities that have been computerized. Many people felt, and still feel, a loss of identity, a **dehumanization**, because of computerization: They feel like "just another number" because computers reduce or eliminate the human element that was present in non-computerized systems.

On the other hand, while the major objective of newer technologies, such as e-commerce, is to increase productivity, they can also create personalized, flexible systems that allow individuals to include their opinions and knowledge in the system. These technologies attempt to be people oriented and user friendly.

The Internet threatens to have an even more isolating influence than has been created by television. If people are encouraged to work and shop from their living rooms, then some unfortunate psychological effects, such as depression and loneliness, could develop. Some people have become so addicted to the Web that they have dropped out of their regular social activities, at school, work, or home, creating new societal and organizational problems.

Another possible psychological impact relates to distance learning. In some countries, it is legal to educate children at home through IT. Some argue, however, that the lack of social contacts could be damaging to the social, moral, and cognitive development of school-age children who spend long periods of time working alone on the computer.

(Cartoon by Sidney Harris.)

information anxiety *Disquiet caused by an overload of information.*

Another one of the negative impacts of the information age is **information anxiety**. This disquiet caused by an overload of information can take several forms, such as frustration with our *inability to keep up with the amount of data* present in our lives. Information anxiety can take other forms as well. One is frustration with the quality of the information available on the Web, which frequently is not up-to-date or is incomplete. Another is frustration or guilt associated with not being better informed or being informed too late ("How did others manage to know this before I did?").

Impacts on Health and Safety

Computers and information systems are a part of the environment that may adversely affect individuals' health and safety. To illustrate, we will discuss the effects of three issues: job stress, video display terminals, and long-term use of the keyboard.

An increase in workload and/or responsibilities can trigger *job stress*. Although computerization has benefited organizations by increasing productivity, it has also created an ever-increasing workload for some employees. Some workers feel overwhelmed and start feeling anxious about their jobs and their performance. These feelings of stress and anxiety can adversely affect workers' productivity. Management's responsibility is to help alleviate these feelings by providing training, redistributing the workload among workers, or hiring more individuals.

Exposure to *video display terminals (VDTs)* raises the issue of the risk of radiation exposure, which has been linked to cancer and other health-related problems. Exposure to VDTs for long periods of time is thought to affect an individual's eyesight, for example. Also, lengthy exposure to VDTs has been blamed for miscarriages in pregnant women. However, results of the research done to investigate these charges have been inconclusive.

Other potential health and safety hazards are *repetitive strain injuries* such as backaches and muscle tension in the wrists and fingers. *Carpal tunnel syndrome* is a painful form of repetitive strain injury that affects the wrists and hands. It has been associated with the long-term use of keyboards.

Lessening the Negative Impacts on Health and Safety. Designers are aware of the potential problems associated with prolonged use of computers. Consequently, they have attempted to design a better computing environment. Research in

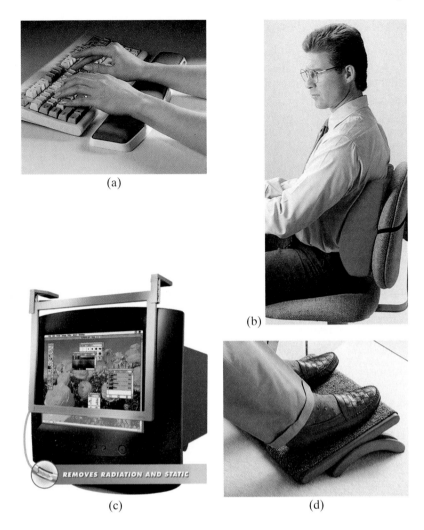

(a)

(b)

(c)

(d)

Figure 12.2 *Ergonomic products protect computer users. (a) Wrist support. (b) Back support. (c) Eye-protection filter (optically coated glass). (d) Adjustable foot rest.*

the area of **ergonomics**, the science of adapting machines and work environments to people, provides guidance for these designers. For instance, ergonomic techniques focus on creating an environment for the worker that is safe, well lit, and comfortable. Devices such as antiglare screens have helped alleviate problems of fatigued or damaged eyesight, and chairs that contour the human body have helped decrease backaches. Some sample ergonomic products are shown in Figure 12.2.

ergonomics *The science of adapting machines and work environments to people.*

Before you go on . . .

1. List the major potential impacts of IT on the individual's job.

2. List potential impacts on an individual's health and safety.

12.4 SOCIETAL IMPACTS AND INTERNET COMMUNITIES

Several positive and some negative social implications of IT could be far-reaching. IT has already had many direct beneficial effects on society. Some such benefits include the use of IT for complicated human and social problems such as medical diagnosis, computer-assisted instruction, government-program planning, environmental quality control, and law enforcement. For an overview see Lubbe and Van Heerden (2003). This section discusses a number of societal impacts of information technology.

Opportunities for People with Disabilities

The integration of artificial intelligence technologies, such as speech and vision recognition, into a computer and especially into Web-based information systems can create new employment opportunities for people with disabilities. For example, those who cannot type are able to use a voice-operated keyboard, and those who cannot travel can work at home.

Adaptive equipment for computers permits people with disabilities to perform tasks they would not normally be able to do. Figure 12.3 shows a PC for a user with hearing impairment, a PC for a visually challenged user, and a PC for a motor-disabled user. In Thailand, students at a vocational school developed a special telephone for sight-impaired people because they wanted to help them to live on more equal terms with the rest of society and not need to depend on help from others (Boonnoon, 2000).

Other devices help improve the quality of life for disabled people in more mundane, but useful, ways: a two-way writing telephone, a robotic page-turner, a hair-brusher, and a hospital-bedside video trip to the zoo or the museum. Several organizations deal with IT and people with disabilities. An example is *halftheplanet.org*.

Quality-of-Life Improvements

On a broader scale, IT has significant implications for the *quality of life*. An increase in organizational efficiency may result in more leisure time for workers. The workplace can be expanded from the traditional nine-to-five job at a central location to 24 hours a day at any location. This expansion provides a flexibility that can significantly improve the quality of leisure time, even if the total amount of leisure time is not increased. Here we discuss some major areas of improvement in quality of life.

Robot Revolution on the Way. Robots are becoming more common. "Cyber-pooches," nursebots, and more may be our companions before we know it. Around the world, quasi-autonomous devices have become increasingly common on factory floors, in hospital corridors, and in farm fields. Military applications are also being developed. The Pentagon is researching self-driving vehicles and bee-like swarms of small surveillance robots, each of which would contribute a different view or angle of a combat zone.

(a)   (b)   (c)

Figure 12.3 *Enabling people with disabilities to work with computers. (a)* A PC for a blind sight-impaired user, *equipped with an Oscar optical scanner and a Braille printer, both by TeleSensory. The optical scanner converts text into ASCII code or into proprietary word processing format. Files saved on disc can then be translated into Braille and sent to the printer. Visually impaired users can also enlarge the text on the screen by loading a TSR software magnification program.*
(b) The deaf hearing-impaired challenged user's PC *is connected to a telephone via an Ultratec Intele-Modem Baudot/ASCH modem. The user is sending and receiving messages to and from someone at a remote site who is using a telecommunications device for deaf people (right).*
(c) This motor-disabled person *is communicating with a PC using a Pointer Systems optical head pointer to access all keyboard functions on a virtual keyboard shown on the PC's display. The user can "strike" a key in one of two ways. He can focus on the desired key for a user-definable time period (which causes the key to be highlighted), or he can click an adapted switch when he chooses the desired key. (Source: J. J. Lazzaro, "Computers for the Disabled,"* Byte, *June 1993.)*

However, it probably will be a long time before we see robots making decisions by themselves, handling unfamiliar situations, and interacting with people. Nevertheless, robots abound that can do practical tasks. Carnegie Mellon University, for example, has developed self-directing tractors that harvest hundreds of acres of crops around the clock in California, using global positioning systems combined with video image processing that identifies rows of uncut crops. Robots are especially helpful in various environments, as illustrated in IT's about Business 12.1.

Improvements in Health Care.   IT has brought about major improvements in health-care delivery, ranging from better and faster diagnoses, to expedited research and development of new drugs, to more accurate monitoring of critically ill patients. One technology that has made a special contribution is artificial intelligence. For example, expert systems support diagnosis of diseases, and machine vision is enhancing the work of radiologists. Recently, surgeons started to use virtual reality to plan complex surgeries and have used a surgical robot to perform long-distance surgery. Cardiologists also can interpret patients' hearts' vital signs from a distance (see *micromed.com*). Now, doctors can discuss complex medical cases not only on the telephone, but also with the support of pictures and sound.

The medical industry has long been using advanced technologies to diagnose and treat health problems. For example, there is an "ingestible camera" pill that, when swallowed, takes color images from inside the intestines and transmits the images wirelessly to a device worn on a patient's belt for later examination (go to *givenimaging.com* and see the M2A capsule). In addition, new computer simulations recreate the sense of touch, allowing doctors-in-training to perform virtual procedures without risking harm to an actual patient (see *technologyreview.com/articles/amato0401.asp*).

IT's ABOUT BUSINESS   POM   GOV
12.1: The Working Lives of Robots

LAYING FIBER-OPTIC CABLES Cities around the world are moving into the digital era by installing fiber-optic cables. To attract high-tech businesses, cities must provide fiber-optic access to all commercial buildings. Installing fiber-optic cable is difficult: Workers cut up the street, creating noise, dust, and traffic problems. The disruption to people may take weeks, or even months, just to complete one city block. Now, robots are changing the cable-installation process.

City Net Telecommunications (*citynettelecom.com*) uses the existing sewer system to lay the cables. This way no trenches need to be dug in the streets. Pioneering work was done in Albuquerque, New Mexico, Omaha, Nebraska, and Indianapolis, Indiana (in spring 2001). How did the robots help? Robots are waterproof and do not have noses, and so they are not bothered by working in the sewer. They do not complain, nor do they get sick. As a matter of fact, they work faster than humans when it comes to laying the fiber-optic cables inside the sewer system.

What does it cost? The company claims that laying the fiber-optic cable with robots costs about the same as the old method. The major advantage is that it can be done 60 percent faster and without disruption to people's lives.

SEARCHING FOR DEEP-WATER SHIPWRECKS. The Republic, a 150-year-old steamship, sailed from New York in 1865, just after the Civil War, carrying 59 passengers and crew and a mixed cargo meant to help New Orleans recover from the war. About 100 miles off Georgia, battling a hurricane, it sank in waters almost 2,000 feet deep. Its cargo of lost coins, experts say, may now be worth up to $150 million.

After a long search by a small robot that used sonar to find the wreck and took thousands of pictures, Odyssey Marine Exploration of Tampa, Florida, was ready for its larger robot. To salvage the treasure, Odyssey is using a tethered, seven-ton robot. This robot first vacuumed away the sand from the wreckage, and then using its mechanical arms, has begun hauling up a fortune in gold and silver coins.

Sources: Compiled from J. Schwartz, "A Robot That Works in the City Sewer," *New York Times* (March 8, 2001); and W. Broad, "Salvagers Say a Shipwreck Trove Is Worth Millions," *New York Times* (November 30, 2003).

QUESTIONS

1. If robots are so effective, what will be the impact on unemployment when more tasks are robotized?
2. What will people do if robots take over?

Of the thousands of other applications related to health care, it is interesting to point out the administrative systems, which range from insurance fraud detection, to nursing scheduling, and financial and marketing management. We see in IT's about Business 12.2, that IT can dramatically affect health care in a variety of ways.

The Internet is a gold mine of medical information. For example, a site about cancer (*cancer.med.upenn.edu*) features a huge array of documents, reviews, descriptions of personal experiences, suggested diets, and links to global resources for people who suffer from cancer or who are interested in oncology. It offers information on the latest research studies and cancer pain management. It also helps families cope with emotional and financial burdens.

IT's ABOUT BUSINESS [SVC]

12.2: Transforming Health Care

Health care costs 14 percent of the U.S. gross national product ($1.4 *trillion* annually). As the population ages, this percentage is expected to increase. If this trend continues, by 2050 (when you are about 70 years old and in need of health care yourself), health-care costs may consume one-third of the U.S. GNP, and the costs of your individual health care could be prohibitive. Consider these facts:

- Hospitals spend only 2.5 percent of their budgets on IT, where other industries spend three to four times that percentage.
- Only 28 percent of physicians use a computer to access patient information.
- Over 40 percent of a doctor's day is spent searching for information.
- Almost one-half of critical patient information is missing when doctors need it.

Health-care institutions face intense pressure to reduce costs and improve health care. IT systems can help with these problems, but there is enormous resistance to them, partly as a result of large up-front costs and partly as a result of physician resistance.

Two IT systems that help solve these problems include electronic medical records systems (EMR) and computerized physician order-entry systems (CPOE). The goal of EMR systems is to eliminate paper. By doing so, EMR will help prevent errors, enforce standards, make health-care workers more efficient, simplify record keeping, and improve patient care. These systems digitize all paper records, including images such as X-rays, CT scans, and MRI scans. Once an EMR system is in place, the next step is a CPOE system. CPOE systems allow a doctor to request medications, lab tests, and radiology procedures. The doctor gets an automatic notification about test results.

Health-care information has to be available any time, anywhere. Therefore, wireless systems are being installed to go along with EMR and CPOE systems. Hospital wireless systems typically involve setting up wireless access points (see Technology Guide 4) in patient wards, treatment facilities, and in corridors in which patients and doctors travel. Wirelessly enabled laptops on top of carts are rolled from bed to bed as needed so that doctors and nurses can access medical records and order tests and medications wherever they are. These shared laptops complement existing networked desktops at nurses' stations and other locations. Wireless tablets and PDAs supplement the laptops.

One hospital is using information technology with impressive results. In 2003, the Maimonides Medical Center (*maimonidesmed.org*) in Brooklyn, NY, finished a $44 million implementation of sophisticated EMR and CPOE systems with wireless connectivity. Today, every one of Maimonides' doctors logs on to order medications and tests, checks lab results, and tracks treatment. One in every five prescriptions is flagged by the system for a possible problem—an allergy or an adverse drug interaction. The average turnaround time for administering medicine to inpatients now has been cut from 5 hours to 90 minutes. Physicians receive all reports from the radiology department online within 24 hours (formerly, it was 5 days), and they no longer have to reorder tests for the estimated 15 percent of film records that previously were lost. Last year, revenue increased $50 million, and hospital officials attribute most of that increase in revenue to the new IT systems. In addition, the annual cost of the hospital's malpractice insurance has dropped one million dollars, a savings also credited to the new IT systems.

Source: Compiled from S. D. Scalet, "Saving Money, Saving Lives," *CIO Magazine* (August 1, 2003).

QUESTIONS

1. What are the advantages of EMR, CPOE, and wireless systems in hospitals?
2. What are the problems with implementing such systems?

There are numerous Web sites devoted to all kinds of specific health topics. The best-known health supersite is WebMD (*webmd.com*). Specific sites include the following: iEmily (*iEmily.com*) provides information on the physical and mental health of teenage girls. TeenGrowth (*teengrowth.com*), KidsHealth (*kidshealth.org*), and ZapHealth (*zaphealth.com*) provide articles on general, sexual, and emotional health, as well as fitness, sports, family, and safety issues. Organized like interactive magazines, these sites also offer discussion forums, chat rooms, and hyperlinks to other related resources.

Finally, the outbreak of Severe Acute Respiratory Syndrome (SARS) demonstrated the use of IT in supporting the social and psychological needs of patients. Technologies such as Web cameras, audio/video phones, and Web-conferencing software enabled patients to stay in touch with their relatives and friends while under quarantine.

Crime Fighting and Other Benefits.   Other quality-of-life improvements brought about by IT relate to crime fighting and other government-services benefits. Here are some examples of how computer applications can benefit society:

- Since 1997, information about sex offenders has been available on the Internet, so that people can be aware of whether previously convicted offenders are living in their localities.

- Los Angeles County has a sophisticated computer program for reporting and tracking over 150,000 gang members in the county. The program significantly helps reduce gang crime.

- Electronic imaging and electronic fax enhance searches for missing children. In addition to its Web site (*missingkids.com*), which attracts more than a million hits each day, the Center for Missing and Exploited Children can send high-quality photos plus text to many fax machines and to portable machines in police cars. Computers have improved the quality of fax transmission and increased the number of people who receive the announcements.

- A geographical information system helps the San Bernardino Sheriff's Department to better visualize crime patterns and allocate resources.

- Electronic Sensors and computers reduce traffic congestion in many major cities, from Los Angeles to Tokyo.

- Police can now track emergency (911) calls made from cell phones equipped with GPS systems.

Technology and Privacy

Throughout the book we have provided examples of invasion of privacy by IT applications. Here we discuss some additional examples related to societal impacts.

Scanning Crowds for Criminals.   One major debate involves situations in which police are using technology to reduce crime. In January 2001, for example, during the Super Bowl game in Tampa, Florida, video cameras took a picture of each of 100,000 fans when they entered the stadium. No one knew about it, so permissions were not obtained. Within seconds, thousands of photos were compared with digital portraits of known criminals and suspected terrorists; several matches were found. The technology is not new, but its magnitude and speed is. Never before had such a large number of people been photographed and the photos analyzed in such a short time. Is this technology Big Brother watching over you, or just a friendly uncle? The ACLU says it is Big Brother. The police say it is the uncle, trying to protect the public. With whom do you agree?

Cookies and Individual Privacy.   A Microsoft product called *Passport* has raised some of the same concerns as cookies. Passport is an Internet strategy that lets consumers permanently enter a profile of information along with a password and use this information and password repeatedly to access services at multiple sites. Critics say that Passport affords the same opportunities as cookies to invade an individual's privacy by permitting unauthorized people (e.g., Microsoft employees or vendors) to look at your personal data. Critics also feel that the product gives Microsoft an unfair competitive edge in EC.

Digital Millennium Copyright Act and Privacy Concerns. As described in the chapter-opening case, the Recording Industry Association of America (RIAA) blames online music piracy for falling sales of CDs. The RIAA has tried to use the Digital Millennium Copyright Act (DMCA) to get ISPs to reveal the identity of customers who illegally swap pirated files. This act has raised some public concern about giving too much power to copyright holders at the expense of Internet users.

The Digital Divide

digital divide *The gap in computer technology in general, and now in Web technology, between those who have such technology and those who do not.*

The term digital divide refers to the gap in computer technology in general, and now in Web technology in particular, between those who have such technology and those who do not. A digital divide exists both within and among countries. According to reports by the United Nations, more than 90 percent of all Internet hosts are in developed countries, where only 15 percent of the world's population resides. Nearly 60 percent of the U.S. population has Internet access, with a distribution highly correlated with household income.

The U.S. federal and state governments are attempting to close this gap within the country, by encouraging training and by supporting education and infrastructure improvements (see *ecommerce. gov*). Many other government and international organizations are also trying to close the digital divide around the world. As technologies develop and become less expensive, the speed at which the gap can be closed will accelerate. For example, it is still expensive to have a DSL-based broadband line to access the Internet as of 2004, but some predict that it could cost as little as $10/month in 2005. Yet even this amount would be expensive in some countries where wages are only few dollars a day. Cell phones will also increase inexpensive access to the Internet as will Web TV.

"I was sad because I had no onboard fax until I saw a man who had no mobile phone."
© *The New Yorker Collection 1993 Warren Miller from cartoonbank.com. All rights reserved.*

cybercafés *Public places in which Internet terminals are available, usually for a small fee.*

Cybercafés and Public Web Terminals. One of the developments that can help close the digital divide is Internet kiosks in public places and cybercafés. In the United States, computers with Internet access usually are also available at public libraries.

Cybercafés are public places such as a coffee house in which Internet terminals are available, usually for a small fee. Cybercafés come in all shapes and sizes, ranging from a chain of cafés (*easyeverything.com* and *easy.com*) that include hundreds of terminals in one location (e.g., 760 in one New York setting), to a single computer in a corner of many restaurants. According to *cybercaptive.com*, in 2003 there were more than 6,000 cybercafés, public Internet access points, and kiosks in 169 countries.

Computers have popped up in many other public locations: discos, laundromats, karaoke bars, bookstores, CD stores, hotel lobbies, and convenience stores. Some facilities give free access to patrons; others charge a small fee. The number of publicly accessed Wi-Fi hotspots is increasing rapidly, and some do not charge fees (see Chapter 6).

Free Speech versus Censorship

Several surveys indicate that the issue of censorship is one of the most important to Web surfers. Censorship is an important concern in Europe and the United States (e.g., see the GVU User Surveys at *gvu.gatech.edu/user_surveys/*). On the Internet, *censorship* refers to government's attempt to control, in one way or another, material that is broadcast.

Take, for example, the question, "How much access should children have to Web sites, newsgroups, and chat rooms containing 'inappropriate' or 'offensive' materials, and who should control this access?" This is one of the most hotly debated issues between the advocates of censorship and the proponents of free speech. The proponents of free speech contend that there should be no government restrictions on Internet content. They say that parents should be responsible for monitoring and controlling their children's travels on the Web. The advocates of censorship feel that government legislation is required to protect children from offensive material. According to Lee (2001), about 20 countries are filtering Internet pornography.

In addition to concern for children, there is also a concern about hate sites, about defamation of character, and about other offensive material. On December 10, 2002, in a landmark case, Australia's highest court gave a businessman the right to sue in Australia for defamation over an article published in the United States and posted on the Internet. This reasoning basically equates the Net to any other published material. The publisher, Dow Jones & Co., said that it will defend those sued in a jurisdiction (Australia) that is far removed from the country in which the article was prepared (the United States).

The advocates of censorship also believe that it is the responsibility of ISPs to control the content of the data and information that flow across their networks and computers. The difficulty is that ISPs have no easy way of monitoring the content or determining the age of the person viewing the content. The only way to control "offensive" content is to block it from children and adults alike. This is the approach that America Online (AOL) has taken, for instance, in blocking sites pandering to hate crime and serial killer enthusiasts.

Controlling Spam

Spamming refers to the practice of indiscriminately broadcasting messages over the Internet (e.g., junk mail and pop-up screens). At some of the largest ISPs, spam now comprises 25 to 50 percent of all e-mail (Black, 2002). This volume significantly impairs bandwidth, slowing down the Internet in general and in some cases shutting down ISPs completely. ISPs are required to offer spam-blocking software. Recipients of spam have the right to request termination of future spam from the same sender and to bring civil action if necessary. On December 16, 2003, President Bush signed a law to restrict junk commercial e-mail, or spam. The law, which took effect on January 1, 2004, bans sending spam using false identities and misleading subject lines. It requires all commercial e-mail messages to include a valid postal address and gives recipients the opportunity to opt out of receiving more messages.

spamming *The practice of indiscriminately broadcasting messages over the Internet.*

Virtual Communities

A *community* is a group of people with some interest in common who interact with one another. A virtual (Internet) community is one in which the interaction among group members takes place by using the Internet. Virtual communities parallel typical physical communities such as neighborhoods, clubs, or associations, except that people do not meet face-to-face. Instead, they meet online. Virtual communities offer several ways for members to interact and collaborate, including communication, information sharing, and e-commerce. Similar to the click-and-mortar e-commerce model, many *physical communities* also have a Web site for Internet-related activities.

virtual (Internet) community *Groups of people with similar interests who interact and communicate via the Internet.*

Characteristics of Communities. Pure-play Internet communities (those that exist solely online) may have thousands or even millions of members. This is one major difference from purely physical communities, which are usually smaller. Another difference is that offline communities are frequently confined to one geographical location, whereas only a few online communities are geographically constrained.

Virtual communities can be classified in several ways. The most common classification includes four types of Internet communities: communities of *transactions*, communities of *interest*, communities of *practice* (or relations), and communities of *fantasy*. Examples of these types of communities are provided in Table 12.1. A number of examples of online communities are presented in Online File W12.1.

IT's about Business 12.3 (page 380) demonstrates how an online game company successfully generates profit through building an online community.

wiley.com/college/turban

Table 12.1 Types of Virtual Communities

Community Type	Description
Transactions	Facilitates buying and selling (e.g., *ausfish.com.au*). Combines information portal with infrastructure for trading. Members are buyers, sellers, intermediaries, etc. Focused on a specific commercial area (e.g., fishing).
Purpose or interest	No trading, just exchange of information on a topic of mutual interest. Examples: Investors consult The Motley Fool (*fool.com*) for investment advice; music lovers go to *mp3.com*; *Geocities.yahoo.com* is a collection of several areas of interest in one place.
Relations or practice	Members are organized around certain life experiences. For example, *ivillage.com* caters to women. Professional communities also belong to this category. For examples, see *isworld.org* for information systems faculty, students, and professionals.
Fantasy	Members share imaginary environments. Examples: sport fantasy teams at *espn.com*.; Geocities members can pretend to be medieval barons at *geocities.com/timessquare/4076*.

Sources: Compiled from A. G. Armstrong and J. Hagel, "The Real Value of Online Communities," *Harvard Business Review* (May–June 1996); and from J. Hagel and A. G. Armstrong, *Net Gain: Expanding Markets through Virtual Communities* (Boston: Harvard Business School Press, 1997).

IT's ABOUT BUSINESS

12.3: Net Fun: Online Game Player Community

Net Fun (*netfun.com*) is an entertainment Web site founded in 1994. In 1996, the firm launched its flag-ship product, CyberCity. Installing CyberCity on the user's PC enables the user to access the variety of online games available from the Web site. CyberCity also provides other functions such as chat rooms, scoreboards, and searching for online game-playing partners. The site provides a three-dimensional (3-D) virtual reality interface between the user and the games and other facilities available on the Web site.

Membership shot up quickly, reaching 180,000 within two years. At that time, the total Internet user population was only around one million. However, the firm was incurring substantial losses. By 1997 losses had mounted up to over $2.56 million, and the firm changed ownership. In 1998, the new owner of the firm, Peggy Chan, changed its revenue model from advertising-based to subscription-based. Membership dropped rapidly by almost 95 percent to a low of 10,000 but then gradually picked up again to 25,000 in 1999, 34,000 in May 2001, and about 45,000 in July 2003. As of April 2002, Net Fun became a prof-itable firm with a digital product delivered online.

Net Fun operates in the Chinese multiplayers online games (MPOG) industry. Although there are numerous players operating in the MPOG industry and many of them offer free online games, surprisingly almost none focus exclusively on classical Chinese games (e.g., Mahjong). The global Chinese online game player community is the target of Net Fun, as the user market was huge, and the competition was not keen.

Net Fun is also a virtual community in which game players can interact with each other through game com-petitions, chat rooms, private messaging, and even on-line voice messaging. The high level of customer "stickiness" to the online games Web site helped the firm successfully switch a failing advertising-based rev-enue model to a successful subscription-based model.

Sources: Compiled from Lee (2002) and *netfun.com* (2003).

QUESTIONS

1. Why are advertising revenue models generally in-effective (see Chapter 5)?
2. Are the community aspects helpful? Why or why not? How could such a site be even more profitable?

Before you go on . . .

1. Discuss the ways that IT can improve your quality of life.
2. How can IT improve health care and crime fighting?
3. What is the digital divide?
4. What is a virtual community?

12.5 IS VULNERABILITY AND COMPUTER CRIMES

Information resources are scattered throughout the organization. Furthermore, employees travel with and take home corporate computers and data. Information is transmitted to and from the organization and among the organization's components. IS physical resources, data, software, procedures, and any other information resources may therefore be vulnerable, in many places at any time.

Before we describe the specific problems with information security and some proposed solutions, it is necessary to know the key terminology in the field. Table 12.2 provides an overview of that terminology.

Information Systems Breakdowns

Most people are aware of some of the dangers faced by businesses that are dependent on computers. Information systems, however, can be damaged for many other reasons. The following incidents illustrate representative cases of breakdowns in information systems.

Incident 1. On September 12, 2002, Spitfire Novelties fell victim to what is called a "brute force" credit card attack. On a normal day, the Los Angeles–based company generates between 5 and 30 transactions. That Thursday, Spitfire's credit card transaction processor, Online Data Corporation, processed 140,000 fake credit card charges, worth $5.07 each. Of these, 62,000 were approved. The total value of the approved charges was around $300,000. Spitfire found out about the transactions only when they were called by one of the credit card owners who had been checking his statement online and had noticed the $5.07 charge.

Brute force credit card attacks require minimal skill. Hackers simply run thousands of small charges through merchant accounts, picking numbers at random. (For details on larger credit card scams, see *money.cnn.com/2003/02/18/technology/creditcards/index.htm.*)

Incident 2. In January 2003 a hacker stole from the database of Moscow's MTS (mobile phone company) the personal details (passport number, age, home address, tax ID number, and more) of 6 million customers, including Russia's president V. V. Putin. The hacker then sold this database of information on CD ROMs for about $15 each. The database can be searched by name, phone number, or address. The information can be used for crimes such as **identify theft**, where someone uses the personal information of others to create a false identify and then uses it for some fraud (e.g., to get a fake credit card). However, in Russia neither the theft of such information nor its sale was illegal (see Walsh, 2003).

identify theft *Crime in which someone uses the personal information of others to create a false identify and then uses it for some fraud.*

Table 12.2   IT Security Terms

Term	Definition
Backup	An extra copy of the data and/or programs, kept in a secured location(s).
Decryption	Transformation of scrambled code into readable data after transmission.
Encryption	Transformation of data into scrambled code prior to its transmission.
Exposure	The harm, loss, or damage that can result if something has gone wrong in an information system.
Fault tolerance	The ability of an information system to continue to operate (usually for a limited time and/or at a reduced level) when a failure occurs.
Information system controls	The procedures, devices, or software that attempt to ensure that the system performs as planned.
Integrity (of data)	A guarantee of the accuracy, completeness, and reliability of data. System integrity is provided by the integrity of its components and their integration.
Risk	The likelihood that a threat will materialize.
Threats (or hazards)	The various dangers to which a system may be exposed.
Vulnerability	Given that a threat exists, the susceptibility of the system to harm caused by the threat.

Incident 3. On March 15, 2003, a student hacked into the University of Houston's computer system and stole Social Security numbers of 55,000 students, faculty, and staff. The student was charged with unauthorized access to protected computers using someone else's ID, with intent to commit a federal crime. The case is still in the courts, and prison time is a possibility.

Incident 4. The eBay ad read "BlackBerry sold AS IS!" So, Mr. Smith bought the wireless device for just $15.50. After putting a battery in the device, he found more than 200 internal company e-mails from financial services firm Morgan Stanley and a database of more than a thousand names, job titles (from vice-presidents to managing directors), e-mail addresses, and phone numbers (some of them home numbers) for Morgan Stanley executives worldwide. The seller, who remains anonymous, was a former vice president of mergers and acquisitions for Morgan Stanley who had left the company months earlier (Zetter, 2003).

These incidents illustrate the vulnerability of information systems, the diversity of causes of computer security problems, and the substantial damage that can be done to organizations anywhere in the world as a result. The fact is that computing is far from secure (e.g., see the 2003 FBI report in Richardson, 2003).

System Vulnerability

Information systems are made up of many components that may be housed in several locations. Thus, each information system is vulnerable to many potential *hazards* or *threats*. Figure 12.4 presents a summary of the major threats to the security of an information system.

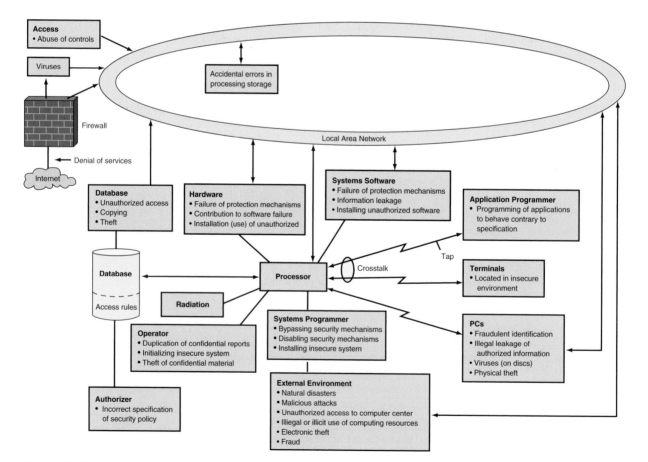

Figure 12.4 *Security threats.*

The vulnerability of information systems is increasing as we move to a world of networked and especially wireless computing. Theoretically, there are hundreds of points in a corporate information system that can be subject to some threat. And actually, there are thousands of different ways that information systems can be attacked or damaged. These threats can be classified as *unintentional* or *intentional*.

Unintentional Threats.   Unintentional threats can be divided into three major categories: human errors, environmental hazards, and computer system failures.

Many computer problems result from *human errors*. Errors can occur in the design of the hardware and/or information system. They can also occur in the programming, testing, data collection, data entry, authorization, and instructions. Human errors contribute to over half of the control- and security-related problems in many organizations.

Environmental hazards include earthquakes, severe storms, floods, power failures or strong fluctuations, fires (the most common hazard), defective air conditioning, explosions, radioactive fallout, and water-cooling-system failures. Such hazards may disrupt normal computer operations and result in long waiting periods and exorbitant costs while computer programs and data files are recreated.

Computer systems failures can occur as the result of poor manufacturing or defective materials. Unintentional malfunctions can also happen for other reasons, ranging from lack of experience to inappropriate testing.

Intentional Threats.   Computer systems may be damaged as a result of intentional actions as well. Examples of intentional threats include: theft of data; inappropriate use of data (e.g., manipulating inputs); theft of mainframe computer time; theft of equipment and/or programs; deliberate manipulation in handling, entering, processing, transferring, or programming data; labor strikes, riots, or sabotage; malicious damage to computer resources; destruction from viruses and similar attacks; and miscellaneous computer abuses and Internet fraud. Intentional threats can even be against whole countries. Many fear the possibility of *cyberattacks* by some countries against others.

Computer Crimes

The number, magnitude, and diversity of computer crimes are increasing. According to the Computer Security Institute (*gocsi.com*), 64 percent of all corporations experienced computer crimes in 1997. The figures in the years 1998 through 2003 were even higher—about 96 percent in 2003 (per Richardson, 2003). Lately, increased fraud related to the Internet and e-commerce is in evidence. For FBI computer crime statistics for 2002/2003, see Richardson (2003).

Types of Computer Crimes and Criminals.   Crimes can be performed by *outsiders* who penetrate a computer system (frequently via communication lines) or by *insiders* who are authorized to use the computer system but are misusing their authorization. Hacker is the term used to describe an outside person who has penetrated a computer system, usually with no criminal intent. A cracker is a *malicious hacker*, who may represent a serious problem for a corporation.

hacker *An outside person who has penetrated a computer system, usually with no criminal intent.*

Crackers may involve unsuspecting insiders in their crimes. In a strategy called social engineering, computer criminals or corporate spies get around security systems by building an inappropriate trust relationship with insiders for the purpose of gaining sensitive information or unauthorized access privileges.

cracker *A malicious hacker.*

social engineering *Getting around security systems by tricking computer users into revealing sensitive information or gaining unauthorized access privileges.*

A large proportion of computer crimes are performed by insiders. According to Richardson (2003) the likely sources of attacks on U.S. companies are: independent hackers (82%), disgruntled employees (78%), U.S. competitors (40%), foreign governments (28%), and foreign corporations (25%).

In addition to computer crimes against organizations there is an alarming increase of fraud committed against individuals, on the Internet. These are a part of cybercrimes.

Cybercrimes.   The Internet environment provides an extremely easy landscape for conducting illegal activities. These are known as cybercrimes, meaning they are exe-

cybercrimes *Illegal activities executed on the Internet.*

cuted on the Internet. Hundreds of different methods and "tricks" are used by innovative criminals to get money from innocent people, to buy without paying, to sell without delivering, to abuse people or hurt them, and much more.

According to Sullivan (2003), between January 1 and April 30, 2003, agencies of the U.S. government uncovered 89,000 victims from whom Internet criminals bilked over $176 million. As a result, on May 16, 2003, the U.S. Attorney General announced that 135 people were arrested nationwide and charged with cybercrime. The most common crimes were investment swindles and identity theft. The Internet with its global reach has also resulted in a growing amount of cross-border fraud, as we see in IT's about Business 12.4.

Identity theft. A growing cybercrime is *identity theft,* in which a criminal (the *identity thief*) poses as someone else. The thief steals Social Security numbers and credit card numbers, usually obtained from the Internet, to commit fraud (e.g., to buy products or

IT's ABOUT BUSINESS

12.4: Cross-Border Cybercrimes

As use of the Internet grows, so do cross-border scams. Most complaints involved advance-fee loans, foreign cash offers, and sweepstakes. Scammers based in one country elude authorities by victimizing residents of others, using the Internet.

For example, David Lee, a 41-year-old Hong Kong resident, replied to an advertisement in a respected business magazine that offered him free investment advice. He was directed to the Web site of Equity Mutual Trust (Equity) where he was able to track the impressive daily performance of a fund that listed offices in London, Switzerland, and Belize. From that Web site he was linked to sister funds and business partners. Lee also was linked to what he believed was the well-known investment-fund evaluator company Morningstar (*morningstar.com*). Actually, the site was an *imitation* that replicated the original site. The imitation site provided a very high, but false, rating on the Equity Mutual Trust funds. Finally, Lee was directed to read about Equity and its funds in the respected *International Herald Tribune*'s Internet edition; the article appeared to be news but was actually an advertisement.

Convinced that he would receive very high short-term gains, he mailed $16,000, instructing Equity to invest in the Grand Financial Fund. Soon he grew suspicious when letters from Equity came from different countries, telephone calls and e-mails were not answered on time, and the daily Internet listings dried up.

When Lee wanted to sell, he was advised to increase his investment and shift to a Canadian company, Mit-Tec, allegedly a Y2K-bug troubleshooter. The Web site he was directed to looked fantastic. But this time Lee was careful. He contacted the financial authorities in the Turks and Caicos Islands—where

Equity was based at that time—and was referred to the British police.

Soon he learned that chances were slim that he would ever see his money again. Furthermore, he learned that several thousand victims had paid a total of about $4 billion to Equity. Most of the victims live in Hong Kong, Singapore, and other Asian countries. Several said that the most convincing information came from the Web sites, including the "independent" Web site that rated Equity and its funds as safe, five-star funds.

What can be done? In June 2003, 29 nations belonging to the Organization for Economic Cooperation and Development (OECD) announced an agreement on unified guidelines for far greater cooperation in persecuting online scammers and in enforcement of existing laws. There will be information sharing and collaboration among investigators from different countries (e.g., relaxing privacy rules that in most nations, including the United States, now strictly limit the information that can be shared). Participating countries will try to pass laws adopting the guidelines. For example, in the United States, which has the most victims of cross-border fraud, Congress is considering a bill that would give the FTC new authority to prosecute this crime.

Sources: Compiled from P. Davidson, "29 Nations Team Up versus Cross-Border Scams," *USA Today* (International Edition), June 17, 2003; and from *ftc.org*.

QUESTIONS

1. Is there anything that Mr. Lee could do?
2. Do you think that the agreement among the OECD nations will be an effective deterrent to cross-border crime? Why or why not?

consume services) that the victim is required to pay for later. The biggest problem for the person whose identity was stolen is to restore the damaged credit rating. For details and commercial solutions, see *idthief.com*.

Cyberwar. There is an increasing interest in the threat of cyberwar, in which a country's information systems could be paralyzed by a massive attack of destructive software. The target systems can range from the information systems of business, industry, government services, and the media to military command systems.

One aspect of cyberwar is *cyberterrorism*, which refers to Internet terrorist attacks. These attacks, like cyberwar, cause risk to the national information infrastructure. In the United States, the Critical Infrastructure Protection Board (CIPB) is preparing protection plans, policies, and strategies to deal with cyberterrorism. For more details and debates, see *cdt.org/security/critinfra* and *ciao.gov*.

cyberwar *War in which a country's information systems could be paralyzed from a massive attack by destructive software.*

Methods of Attack on Computing Facilities

There are many methods of attack on computing facilities, and new ones appear regularly. Table 12.3 lists and describes these methods. Of the many methods of attack on computing facilities, the CSI/FBI reports (per Richardson, 2003) that viruses and denial of service (DoS) attacks are among the most frequent.

Viruses. The most publicized and most common attack method is the computer virus. It receives its name from the program's ability to attach itself to ("infect") other computer programs, without the owner of the program being aware of the infection (see Figure 12.5, page 386). When the software is used, the virus spreads, causing damage to that program and possibly to others.

According to Bruno (2002), 93 percent of all companies experienced virus attacks in 2001, with an average loss of $243,845 per company. A virus can spread throughout

virus *Software that can attach itself to ("infect") other computer programs without the owner of the program being aware of the infection.*

Table 12.3 Methods of Attack on Computer Systems

Method	Definition
Virus	Secret instructions inserted into programs (or data) that are innocently run during ordinary tasks. The secret instructions may destroy or alter data, as well as spread within or between computer systems.
Worm	A program that replicates itself and penetrates a valid computer system. It may spread within a network, penetrating all connected computers.
Trojan horse	An illegal program, contained within another program, that "sleeps" until some specific event occurs, then triggers the illegal program to be activated and cause damage.
Salami slicing	A program designed to siphon off small amounts of money from a number of larger transactions, so the quantity taken is not readily apparent.
Superzapping	A method of using a utility "zap" program that can bypass controls to modify programs or data.
Trap door	A technique that allows for breaking into a program code, making it possible to insert additional instructions.
Logic bomb	An instruction that triggers a delayed malicious act.
Denial of services	Too many requests for service, which crashes the site.
Sniffer	A program that searches for passwords or content in a packet of data as they pass through the Internet.
Spoofing	Faking an e-mail address or Web page to trick users to provide information or send money.
Password cracker	A password that tries to guess passwords (can be very successful).
War dialing	Programs that automatically dial thousands of telephone numbers in an attempt to identify one authorized to make a connection with a modem; then one can use that connection to break into databases and systems.
Back doors	Invaders to a system create several entry points; even if you discover and close one, they can still get in through others.
Malicious applets	Small Java programs that misuse your computer resources, modify your file, send fake e-mail, etc.

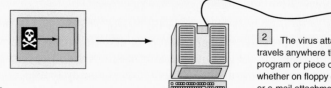

Just as a biological virus disrupts living cells to cause disease, a computer virus—introduced maliciously—invades the inner workings of computers and disrupts normal operations of the machines.

2 The virus attaches itself and travels anywhere that the host program or piece of data travels, whether on floppy disk, networks, or e-mail attachments.

1 A virus starts when a programmer writes a program that embeds itself in a host program.

3 The virus is set off by either a time limit or some set of circumstances, possibly a simple sequence of computer operations by the user. Then it does whatever the virus programmer intended, whether it is to print "Have a nice day" or erase data.

Figure 12.5 *How a computer virus can spread.*

a computer system very quickly. Due to the availability of public-domain software, widely used telecommunications networks, and the Internet, viruses can also spread to many organizations around the world, as shown in the incidents listed earlier. Some of the most notorious viruses are international, such as Michelangelo, Pakistani Brain, Chernobyl, and Jerusalem. (For the history of viruses and how to fight them, see Zetter and Miastkowski, 2000.)

When a virus is attached to a legitimate software program, the legitimate software acts as a **Trojan horse**, a program that contains a hidden function that presents a security risk. The name is derived from the Trojan horse in Greek legend. Trojan horse programs that present the greatest danger are those that make it possible for someone else to access and control a person's computer over the Internet.

The following example discusses several recent types of malicious software.

Trojan horse *A software program containing a hidden function that presents a security risk.*

EXAMPLE   ***Recent Malicious Software.*** Destructive software programs (viruses, worms, and their variants) are flooding the Internet. Here are some examples of the 2003 vintage: *SQL Slammer* is a worm that carries a self-regenerating mechanism that enables it to multiply quickly across the Internet. It is so good at replicating that it quickly generates a massive amount of data. Slammer slowed Internet traffic mainly in South Korea, Japan, Hong Kong, and some European countries in January 2003. It is a variation of *Code Red*, a virus that slowed traffic on the Internet in July 2001. On May 18, 2003, a new virus that masqueraded as an e-mail from Microsoft technical support attacked computers in 89 countries. In June 2003, a high-risk virus *w32/Bugbear* started to steal VISA account information (see "Bugbear worm steals . . . ," 2003).

---

denial-of-service (DoS) *A cyberattack in which an attacker sends a flood of data packets to the target computer, with the aim of overloading its resources.*

Denial of Service. In a **denial-of-service (DoS)** attack, an attacker uses specialized software to send a flood of data packets to the target computer, with the aim of overloading its resources. Many attackers rely on software that has been created by other hackers and made available free over the Internet.

A recent example of a DoS attack is the one on RIAA (Recording Industry Association of America) whose site (*riaa.org*) was rendered largely unavailable for a week starting January 24, 2003. The attack was done mainly by those who did not like the RIAA's attempts to fight pirated music done by file sharing. Due to the widespread availability of free intrusion tools and scripts and the overall interconnectivity on the Internet, the intruder population now consists of virtually anyone with minimal computer experience.

1. Define and give an example of cybercrime.
2. Distinguish between viruses and Trojan horses.
3. What is a denial-of-service attack?

12.6 PROTECTING INFORMATION RESOURCES

Organizations and individuals can protect their systems in many ways. Let's look first at what organizations can do to protect information resources.

A "crime" means breaching the law. In addition to breaking regular laws related to physically stealing computers or conducting fraud, computer criminals may break the specially legislated computer crime laws. According to the FBI, an average robbery involves about $3,000; an average white-collar crime involves $23,000; but an average computer crime involves about $600,000.

Legislation can be helpful but not sufficient. Therefore, the FBI has formed the *National Infrastructure Protection Center (NIPC)*. This joint partnership between government and private industry is designed to protect the nation's infrastructure—its telecommunications, energy, transportation, banking and finance, emergency, and governmental operations. The FBI has also established *Regional Computer Intrusion Squads*, which focus on intrusions to public switched networks, major computer network intrusions, privacy violations, industrial espionage, pirated computer software, and other cybercrimes. Another national organization is the *Computer Emergency Response Team (CERT)* at Carnegie Mellon University (*cert.org*).

Information security problems are increasing rapidly, causing damage to many organizations. Protection is expensive and complex. Therefore, companies must not only use controls to prevent or detect security problems, they must do so in an organized way, assigning responsibilities and authority throughout the organization.

Controls

Knowing about major potential threats to information systems is necessary, but understanding ways to defend against these threats is equally critical (see *cert.org*). The major difficulties of protecting information are listed in Manager's Checklist 12.3 (page 388). Because of its importance to the entire enterprise, organizing an appropriate defense system is one of the major activities of any prudent CIO and of the functional managers who control information resources. As a matter of fact, IT security is the business of *everyone* in an organization.

Protection of information resources is accomplished mostly by inserting *controls* (defense mechanisms). These are intended to prevent accidental hazards, deter intentional acts, detect problems as early as possible, enhance damage recovery, and correct problems. The important point is that defense should stress *prevention*; defense does no good *after the crime*.

Since there are many security threats, there are also many defense mechanisms. *Security controls* are designed to protect all the components of an information system, specifically data, software, hardware, and networks. Any defense strategy may involve the use of several controls. In our discussion the defense controls are divided into two major categories: *general controls* and *application controls*. Both categories have several subcategories.

General controls are established to protect the system regardless of the specific application. For example, protecting hardware and controlling access to the data center are independent of the specific application. The major categories of general controls are physical controls, access controls, data security controls, communications (networks) controls, and administrative controls. Table 12.4 (page 388) shows the various types of general controls.

general controls *Security controls established to protect a computer system regardless of the specific application.*

MANAGER'S CHECKLIST 12.3

The Difficulties in Protecting Information Resources

- ❑ Hundreds of potential threats exist.
- ❑ Computing resources may be situated in many locations.
- ❑ Many individuals control information assets.
- ❑ Computer networks can be outside the organization and difficult to protect.
- ❑ Rapid technological changes make some controls obsolete as soon as they are installed.
- ❑ Many computer crimes are undetected for a long period of time, so it is difficult to learn from experience.
- ❑ People tend to violate security procedures because the procedures are inconvenient.
- ❑ Many computer criminals who are caught go unpunished, so there is no deterrent effect.
- ❑ The amount of computer knowledge necessary to commit computer crimes is usually minimal. As a matter of fact, one can learn hacking, for free, on the Internet.
- ❑ The cost of preventing hazards can be very high. Therefore, most organizations simply cannot afford to protect against all possible hazards.
- ❑ It is difficult to conduct a cost-benefit justification for controls before an attack occurs since it is difficult to assess the value of a hypothetical attack.

Table 12.4   General and Application Controls for Protecting Information Systems

Type of Control	Description of Purpose
General Controls	
Physical controls	Physical protection of computer facilities and resources.
Access controls	Restriction of unauthorized user access to computer resources; concerned with user identification. Can use any of the following identifiers: something the user *knows* (e.g., password), something user *has* (e.g., smart card, token), something the user *is* (*biometrics*—photo of face, fingerprints, iris scan, retinal scan, voice scan).
Data security controls	Protecting data from accidental or intentional disclosure to unauthorized persons, or from unauthorized modification or destruction.
Administrative controls	Issuing and monitoring security guidelines.
Communications (network) controls	
Border security	Major objective is access control.
Firewalls	System that enforces access-control policy between two networks.
Virus controls	Antivirus software (see *antivirus.com, cert.org, pgp.com, symantec.com, ncsa.com, rsa.com, mcafee.com, iss.net, tis.com*).
Intrusion detection	Major object is to detect unauthorized access to network.
Virtual private networking	Uses the Internet to carry information within a company and among business partners but with increased security by uses of encryption, authentication, and access control.
Authentication	Major objective is proof of identity.
Authorization	Permission issued to individuals and groups to do certain activities with information resources, based on verified identity.
Application Controls	
Input controls	Prevent data alteration or loss.
Processing controls	Ensure that data are complete, valid, and accurate when being processed and that programs have properly executed.
Output controls	Ensure that the results of computer processing are accurate, valid, complete, and consistent.

Application controls are safeguards that are intended to protect specific applications. General controls do not protect the *content* of each specific application. Therefore, controls are frequently built into the applications (that is, they are part of the software) and are usually written as validation rules. Application controls include three major categories: input controls, processing controls, and output controls. Table 12.4 shows the various types of application controls.

application controls *Security controls intended to protect specific applications.*

Securing Your PC

Your PC at home is connected to the Internet and needs to be protected. Therefore, solutions such as antivirus software (e.g., Norton Antivirus) and a personal firewall are essential. (You can get a free Internet connection firewall with Microsoft Windows or pay $30–$50 for products such as McAfee Firewall.)

Concluding Thoughts About Computer Security

It is clear from our discussion how important security is for organizations. What security technologies do organizations use the most? According to a CSI/FBI report (Richardson, 2003), 99 percent of all companies use antivirus software, 92 percent use access control, 98 percent use firewalls, 91 percent use physical security, 73 percent use intrusion detection, 69 percent use encrypted files, 58 percent use encrypted login, 47 percent use reusable passwords, and only 11 percent use biometrics. While some measures are commonly used, others, especially new ones such as biometrics, are not yet in regular use.

Auditing Information Systems

Security controls are established to ensure that information systems work properly. Controls can be installed in the original system, or they can be added once a system is in operation. Installing controls is necessary but not sufficient. In addition, it is necessary to answer questions such as the following: Are controls installed as intended? Are they effective? Has any breach of security occurred? If so, what actions are required to prevent recurrence?

These questions must be answered by independent and unbiased observers. Such observers perform the task of information systems *auditing*. In an information systems environment, an **audit** is an examination of information systems, their inputs, outputs, and processing.

audit (in IS) *An examination of information systems, their inputs, outputs, and processing.*

Types of Auditors and Audits. There are two types of auditors and audits: internal and external. Information systems auditing is usually a part of accounting *internal auditing* and is frequently done by corporate internal auditors. An *external auditor* reviews the findings of the internal audit and the inputs, processing, and outputs of information systems. The external audit of information systems is frequently a part of the overall external auditing performed by a certified public accounting (CPA) firm.

Information systems auditing is a broad topic, so we present only its essentials here. Auditing looks at all potential hazards and controls in information systems. It focuses attention on topics such as new systems development, operations, maintenance, data integrity, software applications, security and privacy, disaster planning and recovery, purchasing, budgets and expenditures, chargebacks, vendor management, documentation, insurance and bonding, training, cost control, and productivity. Guidelines are available to assist auditors in their jobs, such as those from the Institute of Internal Auditors (*theiia.org*).

How Is Auditing Executed? IS auditing procedures can be classified into three categories: auditing *around* the computer, auditing *through* the computer, and auditing *with* the computer.

Auditing around the computer means verifying processing by checking for known outputs using specific inputs. This approach is best used in systems with limited outputs.

IT's ABOUT BUSINESS   SVC

12.5: 9/11 Disaster Recovery at Empire Blue Cross/Blue Shield

Empire Blue Cross and Blue Shield (*empireblue.com*) provides health insurance coverage for 4.7 million people in the northeastern United States. It is a regional arm of the Blue Cross/Blue Shield Association (*bcbs.com*). On September 11, 2001, the company occupied an entire floor of the World Trade Center (WTC). Information assets there included the e-business development center as well as the enterprise network of 250 servers and a major Web-enabled call center. Tragically, nine employees and two consultants lost their lives in the terrorist attack. But the company's operations were not interrupted. Let's see why.

The company had built redundancy into all its applications and had moved much of its business to Internet technology for connecting workforce, clients, and partners. Forty applications are available on its corporate intranet. Web-enabled call centers handle 50,000 calls each day, and Web-based applications connect the huge system of hospitals and health-care providers.

Immediately after the terrorist attack, a senior server specialist in Albany, NY, made a quick decision to switch the employee profiles to the Albany location. This action saved the company days of downtime and the need to rebuild the profiles by hand. As employees moved to temporary offices, they were able to log on as if they were sitting at their desks in the WTC.

The disaster recovery protocol, shown in the nearby figure, worked without a glitch. Calls to the customer support center in the WTC were rerouted to centers in Albany and Long Island; customers' access to the Web site experienced no interruptions; and 150 servers, 500 laptops, and 500 workstations were ordered within an hour of the attack, to replace the equipment lost in the attack. In off-facility sites, the main data center was not affected; the backup tapes allowed full restoration of data. The network restructured automatically when the private enterprise network was destroyed, and all necessary information needed at the main off-site data center was rerouted, bypassing the WTC.

Besides building redundancy in the system, the company had also tested different disaster scenarios frequently, making sure everything worked. As a result, the company and the technology were prepared to deal with the disaster. Everything was backed up, so once the servers were rebuilt, all information was available and all applications were functioning within days, thanks to a 300-member IT team working around the clock. Three days after the attack, a new virtual private network was running, enabling employees to work from home.

Source: Compiled from C. Levin, "The Insurance Plan That Came to the Rescue," *PC Magazine* (January 29, 2002).

QUESTIONS

1. Explore the usefulness of Internet technology for disaster planning. What is its advantage over older technologies?

2. Why are people the most important asset when a disaster strikes?

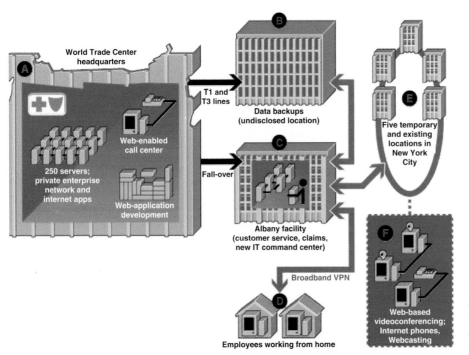

The disaster recovery protocol of Blue Cross.
(Source: C. Levin, "The Insurance Plan That Came to the Rescue," PC Magazine, *January 29, 2002.)*

In *auditing through the computer*, inputs, outputs, and processing are checked. Auditors review program logic, test data, and controlling processing and reprocessing. *Auditing with the computer* means using a combination of client data, auditor software, and client and auditor hardware. It allows the auditor to perform tasks such as simulating payroll program logic using live data.

Disaster Recovery Planning

The best defense is to be prepared for various eventualities. An important element in any security system is a *disaster recovery plan*. Destruction of most or all of an organization's computing facilities can cause significant damage. Therefore, it is difficult for many organizations to obtain insurance for their businesses without showing a satisfactory disaster prevention and recovery plan for the information systems.

Disaster recovery is the chain of events linking planning to protection to recovery. The purpose of a recovery plan is to keep the business running after a disaster occurs (*business continuity*). Planning should focus first on recovery from a total loss of all computing capabilities. All critical applications must be identified in the plan and their recovery procedures addressed. The plan should be written so that it will be effective in case of disaster, not just to satisfy the auditors. The plan should be kept in a safe place; copies should be given to all key managers; and the plan should be audited periodically.

> **disaster recovery** *The chain of events linking planning to protection to recovery.*

Disaster avoidance is an approach oriented toward prevention. The idea is to minimize the chance of avoidable disasters (such as arson or other human threats). For example, many companies use a device called *uninterrupted power supply (UPS)*, which provides power in case of a power outage.

> **disaster avoidance** *A security approach oriented toward prevention.*

Backup Arrangements. In the event of a major disaster, it is often necessary to move a centralized computing facility to a **backup location**, where an extra copy of data and/or programs are kept. At external **hot sites**, vendors provide access to a fully configured backup data center. The World Trade Center tragedy on September 11 illustrated the importance of backup arrangements, especially hot sites, as we see in IT's about Business 12.5 (page 390).

> **backup location** *Location where, in the event of a major disaster, an extra copy of data and/or key programs are kept.*
>
> **hot site** *Location at which vendors provide access to a fully configured backup data center.*

Before you go on . . .

1. Describe the two major types of controls for information systems.
2. Distinguish between authentication and authorization.
3. What is information system auditing?
4. What is the purpose of a disaster recovery plan?

WHAT'S IN  FOR ME?

Auditing information systems is a growing area of special interest, as is Web-based auditing. Also, security of data is of major concern to the accountant. Accountants are also involved in fraud prevention and detection programs. Disaster recovery planning is usually done with the assistance of accountants.

ACC

FOR THE ACCOUNTING MAJOR

The finance and banking industry depends heavily on computers and their networks. Security is one of the major requirements for the development of new technologies such as electronic (home) banking and smart cards. Also, payment systems are critical for e-commerce, and their security and auditing is of the utmost importance. Finally, banking and financial institutions are prime targets for computer criminals, as is fraud

FIN

FOR THE FINANCE MAJOR

involving stocks and bonds sold over the Internet. Finance personnel must be aware of both the hazards and the available controls.

MKT
FOR THE MARKETING MAJOR

Marketers clearly do not want to be sued because of invasion of privacy in data collected for the marketing database, nor do they want their innovative marketing strategies to fall into the hands of competitors. Also, since customers' privacy can be easily invaded while their data are kept in the marketing database or collected at the point-of-sale, marketers need to learn how to prevent such incidents.

POM
FOR THE PRODUCTION/ OPERATIONS MANAGEMENT MAJOR

Can telecommuting increase productivity? To what extent do security efforts reduce productivity? How can efficiency be increased with new organizational structures? The answers to these and other questions require the attention of production/operations management personnel to the topics discussed in this chapter.

HRM
FOR THE HUMAN RESOURCES MANAGEMENT MAJOR

The impacts of IT on individuals, as discussed in this chapter, are especially important to HR professionals. Motivation, supervision, career development, recruiting, and more are all affected by IT. Without an understanding of these issues, it is difficult to manage human resources. Also, HR personnel should be interested in finding how to identify potential computer criminals in the recruiting process.

SUMMARY

1. **Describe the major ethical issues related to information technology, and identify situations in which they occur.** The major ethical issues related to IT are privacy, accuracy, property (including intellectual property), and accessibility to information. Privacy may be violated when data are held in databases or are transmitted over networks. Privacy policies that address issues of data collection, data accuracy, and data confidentiality can help organizations avoid legal problems. Intellectual property is the intangible property created by individuals or corporations, which is protected under trade secret, patent, and copyright laws. The most common intellectual property related to IT deals with software. The copying of software without making payment to the owner (such as giving a disc to a friend to install on his or her computer) is a copyright violation, and a major problem for software vendors.

2. **Identify the major impacts of information technology on organizational structure, power, jobs, supervision, and decision making.** Information technology can make organizations flatter and change authority, job content, and status of employees. As a result, the manager's job and methods of supervision and decision making may drastically change.

3. **Understand the potential dehumanization of people by computers and other potential negative impacts of information technology.** The major negative impacts of IT are in the areas of job

loss, invasion of privacy, and dehumanization. In terms of their impact on health and safety, computers can increase stress and certain health risks. Ergonomically designed computing facilities can greatly reduce the risks associated with computer use. Properly planned information systems can decrease the dehumanization, and shifts in workloads can reduce stress.

4. **Identify some of the major societal effects of information technology.** The major positive impacts of IT are its contribution to employment of the disabled, improvements in health care, delivery of education, crime fighting, and increased productivity. However, the effect on employment levels in general is debatable. Individual privacy is a concern because IT systems can perform surveillance in so many ways. For example, cookies enable merchants to match products to individuals, but this technology can invade your privacy. The digital divide is the gap between those who have computer technology and those who do not. Many governments are working to close this gap. The Internet has always permitted free speech. However, concerns are growing about Internet content such as pornography and the increasing amount of spam. A virtual community is one in which interaction between group members takes place by using the Internet.

5. **Describe the many threats to information security.** Data, software, hardware, and networks can be threatened by many internal and external hazards.

The damage to an information system can be caused either accidentally or intentionally. Most computer criminals are insiders, but outsiders (such as hackers and crackers) can cause major damage as well. Cybercrimes, including identity theft, have proliferated as Internet usage has grown. The two most common methods of attack on computing facilities are viruses and denial-of-service attacks.

6. **Understand the various defense mechanisms used to protect information systems.** Information systems are protected with controls such as security procedures, physical guards, or detection software. These can be classified as controls used for prevention, deterrence, detection, damage control, recovery, and correction of information systems. Biometric controls are used to control access by checking physical characteristics (e.g., fingerprints and retinas) to identify authorized users. Other controls include antivirus software and firewalls.

7. **Explain IT auditing and planning for disaster recovery.** Information systems auditing is done in a similar manner to accounting/finance auditing, around, through, and with the computer. A detailed internal and external IT audit may involve hundreds of issues and can be supported by both software and checklists. Related to IT auditing is the preparation for disaster recovery, which specifically addresses how to avoid, plan for, and quickly recover from a disaster.

INTERACTIVE / LEARNING

Big Brother or Necessary Security Measures?
Go to the Interactivities section on the Student Web Site and access Chapter 12: Ethics, Impacts, and Security. There you will find some animated, hands-on activities that help you make some decisions about ethical issues like privacy and electronic tracking at a hospital, manufacturing plant, and office.

More Resources
More resources and study tools are located on the Student Web Site. You'll find additional chapter materials and links to organizations, people, and technologies for each chapter. In addition, self-quizzes that provide individualized feedback are available for each chapter.

Instructions for accessing the Interactivities on the Student Web Site:

1. Go to wiley.com/college/turban
2. Select Turban Rainer Potter's *Introduction to Information Technology, Third Edition*
3. Click on Student Resources Site, in the toolbar on the left
4. Click on Interactivities Web Site
5. Click on Interactivities Web Site and use your password to enter the site (your password card is located in the inside cover of your textbook)

DISCUSSION QUESTIONS

1. The Internal Revenue Service (IRS) buys demographic market research data from private companies. These data contain income statistics that could be compared to tax returns. Many U.S. citizens feel that their rights are being violated by the agency's use of such information. Is this unethical behavior on the part of the IRS? Discuss.

2. Northeast Utilities (Hartford, Connecticut) (*nu.com*) has its meter readers gather information about services needed on its customers' homes, such as a driveway or fence requiring repairs. The company sells the data to other companies that would stand to gain from the information. Customers are then solicited via direct mail, telemarketing, and so on for the services that the meter readers record as being needed. While some customers welcome this approach, others consider it an annoyance because they are not interested in the particular repairs. Assess the value of the company's IT initiative against the potential negative effects of adverse public reaction.

3. Many hospitals, health maintenance organizations (HMOs), and federal agencies are converting all patients' medical records from paper to electronic storage (using imaging technology). Once the conversion

is made, Web technology and electronic storage can enable quick access to most records. However, the availability of these records in a database and on networks may also enable unauthorized people to view one's private data. To protect privacy fully may cost too much money or result in much slower accessibility to the records. What policies could health-care administrators use in such situations? Discuss.

4. Robots take jobs away from people. Describe the considerations that management will be faced with when it needs to decide whether to use robots in an organization.

5. Discuss the benefits of a virtual community to its members, society, and e-commerce.

6. Some insurance companies will not insure a business unless the firm has a computer disaster recovery plan. Explain why.

PROBLEM-SOLVING ACTIVITIES

1. An information security manager routinely monitored the contents of electronic correspondence among employees. She discovered that many employees were using the system for personal purposes. Some messages were love letters to fellow employees, and others related to a football betting pool. The security manager prepared a list of the employees, with samples of their messages, and gave them to management. Some managers punished their employees for having used the corporate e-mail for personal purposes. Some employees, in turn, objected to the monitoring, claiming that they should have the same right to privacy as they have using the company's interoffice mail system.
   a. Is monitoring of e-mail by managers ethical? (It is legal.) Support your answer.
   b. Is the use of e-mail by employees for personal communication ethical? Support your answer.
   c. Is the security manager's submission of the list of abusers to management ethical? Why or why not?
   d. Is punishing the abusers ethical? Why or why not?
   e. What should the company do in order to rectify the situation?
2. The theft of laptop computers at conventions, hotels, and airports is a major problem. These categories of protection exist: physical devices (e.g., *targus.com*), encryption (e.g., *networkassociates.com*), and security policies (e.g., at *ebay.com*). Find more information on

this problem and on the solutions. Summarize the advantages and limitations of each method.

3. Mr. Jones worked as a customer support representative for a small software company but was fired in late 2002. In early 2003, the company discovered that someone was logging onto its computers at night via a modem and had altered and copied files. During the investigation, the police traced the calls to Mr. Jones's home and found copies there of proprietary information valued at several million dollars. Mr. Jones's access code was canceled the day he was terminated. However, the company suspects that he obtained the access code of another employee.
   a. How might the crime have been committed? Why were the controls ineffective? (State any relevant assumptions.)
   b. What can the company, or any company, do in order to prevent similar incidents in the future?
4. If you do not have Windows XP, which has a firewall, you can install a firewall for free. Your mission is to do just that. Use ZoneAlarm (*zonelabs.com*) or Tiny Personal Firewall (*fwnetwork.com*). For Apple users, use Open Door (*opendoor.com*).
5. In spring 2000 the U.S. government developed an internal intrusion detection network (see *cdt.org/security/fidnet*) to protect itself from hackers and crackers. The Center for Democracy and Technology (*cdt.org*) objected, claiming invasion of privacy. Research the status of the project (FIDNet) and discuss the claims of the center.

INTERNET ACTIVITIES

1. Visit the following virtual communities: *geocities.yahoo.com*, *well.com*, and *electricminds.org*. Join one of the communities. Become a member of the community and report on your experiences.
2. Enter *scambusters.org*. Find out what the organization does. Learn about e-mail scams and Web site scams. Report your findings.
3. Enter *epic.org/privacy/tools.html*, and examine the following groups of tools: Web encryption, disk encryption, and PC firewalls. Explain how these tools can be used to facilitate the security of your PC.

4. Enter *sensar.com* and learn about iris scanning. Also, check what Microsoft is doing with biometric controls.
5. Research the status of how IT is helping people with disabilities. As a start, visit the following sites: *usdoj.gov/crt/ada/adahom1.htm*, *halftheplanet.org*, and *ican.com*. Write a status report on the latest innovations in this area.
6. Download freeware from *junkbusters.com* and learn how to prohibit unsolicited e-mail (spam). Describe how your privacy is protected.

TEAM ASSIGNMENTS

1. Research the Melissa virus attack in 1999. Explain how the virus worked and what damage it caused. Examine Microsoft's attempts to prevent similar future attacks. Investigate similarities between the 2003 viruses (Slammer, Bugbear, etc.) and earlier ones (e.g., "I Love You" and Melissa). What preventive methods are offered by security vendors? (Check *symantec.com*, *mcafee.com*, and *antivirus.com*, for example.) Teams should take one virus each and one security vendor each. Discuss your virus and the merits of your security vendor.

2. The State of California maintains a database of people who allegedly abuse children. (The database also includes names of the alleged victims.) The list is made available to dozens of public agencies, and it is considered in cases of child adoption and employment decisions. Because so many people have access to the list, its content is easily disclosed to unauthorized persons. In 1996, an alleged abuser and her child, whose case had been dropped but whose names had remained on the list, sued the State of California for invasion of privacy. With the class divided into groups, answer the following four questions in terms of a database of sex offenders.

   a. Is there a need to include names of people on the list in cases that were dismissed or declared unfounded?

   b. Who should make the decision about what names should be included and what the criteria should be for inclusion?

   c. What is the potential damage (if any) to the abusers?

   d. Should the State of California abolish the list? Why or why not?

3. China has strengthened its control of the Internet with an extension of its criminal laws to cover the revealing of state secrets and spreading of computer viruses. The new laws were drafted in order "to promote the healthy development of the Internet and protect national security." China also makes it an offense "to use the Internet to promote religious cults, hurt national unity, or undermine the government" (W. Kazer, writing for the *South China Morning Post*, December 30, 2000).

   These laws raise as many concerns as they solve existing problems. Clearly, governments have a strong need to protect their vital interests, but the new laws seem quite sweeping. The vagueness of expressions like "hurting national unity" may be particularly awkward—the intention is to prevent secession, but what constitutes a "nation" is itself arguable. Create groups to debate the following issues.

   a. What impacts do you think these new laws will have for citizens of China?

   b. Are the laws really enforceable? (For example, check out anonymous Web surfing at *anonymizer.com*.)

   c. Does China need laws to promote the healthy development of the Internet? Would the laws in this problem help or hurt the healthy development of the Internet?

   d. In general, what aspects of Internet development do you find unhealthy?

   e. Would you want to regulate the Internet's development? Certain aspects of the Internet's development? If so, which ones? How would you regulate the development of the Internet or parts of the Internet?

REAL-WORLD CASE · THE AUSTRALIAN FISHING COMMUNITY

Recreational fishing in Australia is popular both for residents and for international visitors. Over 700,000 Australians regularly fish. The Australian Fishing Shop (AFS) (*ausfish.com.au*) is a small e-tailer, founded in 1994, initially as a hobby site carrying information about recreational fishing. Recently, the site has evolved into a fishing portal, and it has created a devoted community behind it.

A visit to the site will immediately show that the site is not a regular storefront but that it actually provides considerable information to the recreational fishing community. In addition to sale of products (rods, reels, clothing, boats, and fishing-related books, software, and CD ROMs) and services (fishing charters and holiday packages), the site provides the following information:

- Hints and tips for fishing
- What's new
- A photo gallery of people's catches
- Chat boards—general and specialized
- Directions of boat builders, tackle manufacturing, etc.
- Recipes for cooking fish
- Information about newsgroups and a mailing list
- Free giveaways, competitions

- Links to fishing-related government bodies, other fishing organizations (around the globe and in Australia), and daily weather maps and tides reports
- General information site and FAQs
- List of fishing sites around the globe
- Contact details by phone, post, and e-mail
- Free e-mail Web page hosting

In addition there is an auction mechanism for fishing equipment, and answers are provided to inquiries.

The company is fairly small (gross income of about AU$500,000 a year). How can such a small company survive? The answer can be found in its strategy of providing value-added services to the recreational fishing community. These services attract over 1.6 million visitors each month, from all over the world, of which about 1 percent make a purchase. Also, several advertisers sponsor the site. This is sufficient to survive. Another interesting strategy is to aim at the *global market*. Most of

the profit is derived from customers in the United States and Canada who buy holiday and fishing packages.

In terms of products, the company acts basically as a referral service to vendors, so it does not have to carry an inventory. When AFS receives an order, it orders the products from its suppliers. It then manually aggregates the orders from the suppliers and packs and sends them via a delivery service to customers. Some orders are shipped directly from vendors to the customers.

Source: Based on information found at *ausfish.com.au* (site accessed November 2003).

QUESTIONS

1. Why is this considered an Internet community?
2. How does the community aspect facilitate revenue?
3. Compare the services offered at the AFS Web site with services offered by companies in other countries, such as *daytickets.co.uk*, *fishing-boating.com*, and *pvisuals.com*.

INFORMATION AND ETHICS AT CLUB IT

After reading about the impacts of IT on society, you realize that all of these new technologies and data acquisition and analysis systems you have read about and considered for Club IT also have social and ethical impacts. Dehumanization, privacy and security, accuracy of information . . . these and more are directly related to everything you have considered.

ASSIGNMENT

1. Because the DJ's are contractors, not employees of Club IT, they have an individual obligation to pay the recording companies royalties for the music they play in the club. Lisa wants to make sure this is happening. You wonder too, how does a DJ keep track of everything played to make sure royalties are being paid? Who are they paid to? Do some research on the Web to answer these questions. BMI (*bmi.com*), an organization that

collects and pays music licensing fees, is a good place to start.

2. Consider the data that is collected at Club IT on transactions with patrons, employees, and suppliers. Prepare a draft privacy of information policy for Club IT.

3. Many new technologies would be useful to Club IT. For example, location-based technologies could notify patrons and VIP members who are near the club of new happenings at Club IT. Bracelets with RFID tags could monitor who stays and how long. A CRM could yield a wealth of data on patrons' preferences. The list keeps growing as new applications emerge. What are the privacy risks involved in these technologies? Are the benefits greater than the risks?

Go to wiley.com/college/turban to access the CLUB IT Web Site on the Student Web Site

Computer Hardware

Learning Objectives

1. Identify the major hardware components of a computer system.
2. Describe the design and functioning of the central processing unit.
3. Discuss the relationships between microprocessor component designs and performance.
4. Describe the main types of primary and secondary storage.
5. Distinguish between primary and secondary storage along the dimensions of speed, cost, and capacity.
6. Define enterprise storage and describe the various types of enterprise storage.
7. Describe the evolution of computer hardware.
8. Describe the hierarchy of computers according to power and their respective roles.
9. Differentiate the various types of input and output technologies and their uses.
10. Describe what multimedia systems are and what technologies they use.
11. Discuss the general trends in hardware technology.
12. Discuss strategic issues that link hardware design to business strategy.

TG1.1 INTRODUCTION

Decisions about hardware focus on three interrelated factors: capability (power and appropriateness for the task), speed, and cost. The incredible rate of innovation in the computer industry further complicates hardware decisions. Computer technologies can become obsolete much more quickly than other organizational technologies.

This technology guide will help you better understand the computer hardware decisions in your organization, and your personal computing decisions as well. Many of the design principles presented here apply to any size computer, as do the dynamics of innovation and cost that affect corporate as well as personal hardware decisions.

As we noted in Chapter 2, *computer-based information systems (CBISs)* are composed of hardware, software, databases, telecommunications, procedures, and people. The components are organized to input, process, and output data and information. *Hardware* refers to the physical equipment used for the input, processing, output, and storage activities of a computer system. It consists of the following:

- *Central processing unit (CPU).* Manipulates the data and controls the tasks performed by the other components.
- *Primary storage.* Internal to the CPU; temporarily stores data and program instructions during processing.
- *Secondary storage.* External to the CPU; stores data and programs for future use.
- *Input technologies.* Accept data and instructions and convert them to a form that the computer can understand.
- *Output technologies.* Present data and information in a form people can understand.
- *Communication technologies.* Provide for the flow of data from external computer networks (e.g., the Internet and intranets) to the CPU, and from the CPU to computer networks.

The first four of these components are discussed in the following sections. Communication technologies are the subject of Technology Guide 3 and of Chapters 4 and 6.

central processing unit (CPU) *Hardware that performs the actual computation or "number crunching" inside any computer.*

microprocessor *The CPU, made up of millions of transistors embedded in a circuit on a silicon wafer or* chip.

Before you go on . . .

1. Decisions about information technology focus on what three factors?
2. Define hardware and list the components of hardware.

TG1.2 THE CENTRAL PROCESSING UNIT

control unit *Portion of the CPU that controls the flow of information.*

arithmetic-logic unit (ALU) *Portion of the CPU that performs the mathematic calculations and makes logical comparisons.*

registers *High-speed storage areas in the CPU that store very small amounts of data and instructions for short periods of time.*

The **central processing unit (CPU)** performs the actual computation or "number crunching" inside any computer. The CPU is a **microprocessor** (for example, a Pentium 4 by Intel) made up of millions of microscopic transistors embedded in a circuit on a silicon wafer or *chip*. (Hence, microprocessors are commonly referred to as chips.)

As shown in Figure TG1.1, the microprocessor has different parts, which perform different functions. The **control unit** sequentially accesses program instructions, decodes them, and controls the flow of data to and from the ALU, the registers, the caches, primary storage, secondary storage, and various output devices. The **arithmetic-logic unit (ALU)** performs the mathematic calculations and makes logical comparisons. The **registers** are high-speed storage areas that store very small amounts of data and instructions for short periods of time.

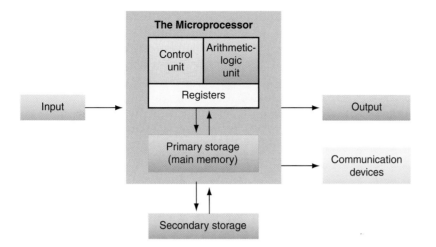

Figure TG1.1 *Parts of a microprocessor.*

How the CPU Works

In the CPU, inputs come in and are stored until needed. When needed, they are retrieved and processed, and the output is stored and then delivered somewhere. Figure TG1.2 illustrates this process, which works as follows.

- The inputs are data and brief instructions about what to do with the data. These instructions come from software in other parts of the computer. Data might be entered by the user through the keyboard, for example, or read from a data file in another part of the computer. The inputs are stored in registers until they are sent to the next step in the processing.

- Data and instructions travel in the chip via electrical pathways called *buses*. The size of the bus—analogous to the width of a highway—determines how much information can flow at any time.

- The control unit directs the flow of data and instructions within the chip.

- The arithmetic-logic unit (ALU) receives the data and instructions from the registers and makes the desired computation. These data and instructions have been translated into **binary form**, that is, only 0s and 1s. The CPU can process only binary data.

- The data in their original form and the instructions are sent to storage registers and then are sent back to a storage place outside the chip, such as the computer's hard drive (discussed below). Meanwhile, the transformed data go to another register and then on to other parts of the computer (to the monitor for display or to storage, for example).

binary form   *The form in which data and instructions can be read by the CPU—only 0s and 1s.*

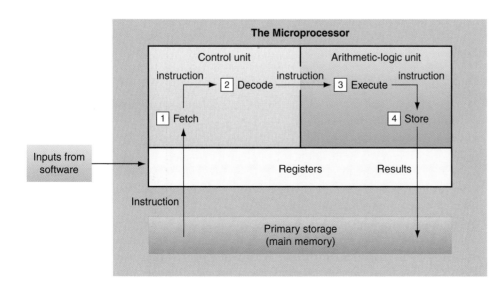

Figure TG1.2 *How the CPU works.*

machine instruction cycle *The cycle of computer processing, whose speed is measured in terms of the number of instructions a chip processes per second.*

clock speed *The preset speed of the computer clock that times all chip activities, measured in megahertz and gigahertz.*

word length *The number of bits (0s and 1s) that can be processed by the CPU at any one time.*

bus width *The size of the physical paths down which the data and instructions travel as electrical impulses on a computer chip.*

line width *The distance between transistors; the smaller the line width, the faster the chip.*

wiley.com/college/turban

Moore's Law *Prediction by Gordon Moore, an Intel co-founder, that microprocessor complexity would double approximately every two years.*

Intel offers excellent demonstrations of how CPUs work (see *intel.com/education/mpworks/INDEX.HTM* and *www97.intel.com/scripts-tji/index.asp*).

This cycle of processing, known as a **machine instruction cycle**, occurs millions of times per second or more. It is faster or slower, depending on the following four factors of chip design:

- *Clock speed.* The **clock speed** is the preset speed of the clock that times all chip activities, measured in *megahertz* (MHz, millions of cycles per second) and *gigahertz* (GHz, billions of cycles per second). The faster the clock speed, the faster the chip. (For example, all other factors being equal, a 1.0 GHz chip is twice as fast as a 500 MHz chip.)

- *Word length.* The **word length** is the number of bits (0s and 1s) that can be processed by the CPU at any one time. The majority of current chips handle 32-bit word lengths; the Pentium 4 is designed to handle 64-bit word lengths. Therefore, the Pentium 4 chip will process 64 bits of data in one machine cycle. The larger the word length, the faster the chip.

- *Bus width.* The **bus width** is the size of the physical paths down which the data and instructions travel as electrical impulses. The wider the *bus*, the more data can be moved and the faster the processing. The bus width in Intel's Itanium II chip has increased from 133 MHz in 1998 to 533 MHz today.

- *Number of transistors on the chip.* We want to pack as many transistors into the chip as possible. If the chip is very compact and efficiently laid out, then data and instructions do not have far to travel while being stored or processed. The distance between transistors is known as **line width**. Line width is expressed in nanometers (billionths of a meter). Currently, most CPUs are designed with 180-nanometer technology (0.18 microns), but chip manufacturers are moving to 130-nanometer technology (0.13 microns). The smaller the line width, the more transistors can be packed onto a chip, and the faster the chip.

Although these four factors are quantifiable, differences in the factors between one chip and another make it difficult to compare the speeds of different processors. As a result, Intel and other chip manufacturers have developed a number of benchmarks to compare processor speeds. (For information about these benchmarks, see the discussion of processor benchmarks in Online File W-TG1.1.)

Advances in Microprocessor Design

Innovations in chip designs are coming at a faster and faster rate, as described by **Moore's Law**. Gordon Moore, an Intel Corporation co-founder, predicted in 1965 that microprocessor complexity would double approximately every two years. His prediction has been amazingly accurate, as shown in Figure TG1.3.

The advances predicted from Moore's Law come mainly from the following changes:

- Increasing miniaturization of transistors.

- Making the physical layout of the chip's components as compact and efficient as possible (decreasing line width).

- Using materials for the chip that improve the *conductivity* (flow) of electricity. The traditional silicon is a semiconductor of electricity—electrons can flow through it at a certain rate. New materials such as *gallium arsenide* and *silicon germanium* allow even faster electron travel and some additional benefits, although they are more expensive to manufacture than silicon chips.

- Targeting the amount of basic instructions programmed into the chip. There are four broad categories of microprocessor architecture: *complex instruction set computing (CISC)*, *reduced instruction set computing (RISC)*, *very long instruction word (VLIW)*, and the newest category, *explicitly parallel instruction computing*

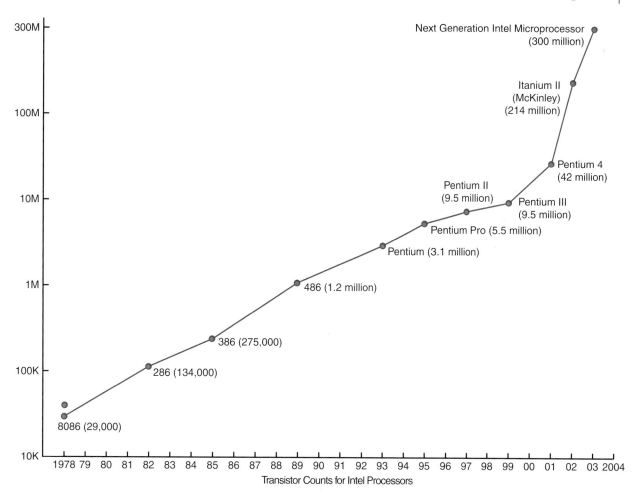

Figure TG1.3 *Moore's Law as it relates to transistor count in Intel microprocessors.*

(EPIC). Most chips are designated as CISC and have very comprehensive instructions, directing every aspect of chip functioning. RISC chips eliminate rarely used instructions. Computers that use RISC chips rely on their software to contain the special instructions. VLIW architectures reduce the number of instructions on a chip by lengthening each instruction. With EPIC architectures, the processor can execute certain program instructions in parallel. Intel's Pentium 4 is the first implementation of EPIC architecture. (For a more technical discussion of these architectures, see Online File W-TG1.2.)

wiley.com/college/turban

In addition to increased speeds and performance, Moore's Law has had an impact on costs. For example, in 1998 a personal computer with a 16 MHz Intel 80386 chip, one megabyte of RAM (discussed later in this chapter), a 40-megabyte hard disk (discussed later in this chapter), and a DOS 3.31 operating system (discussed in Chapter 3), cost $5,200. In mid 2004, a personal computer with a 3.4 GHz Intel Pentium 4 chip, one gigabyte of RAM, a 120-gigabyte hard disk, the Windows XP operating system, and a 17-inch flat-screen monitor cost about $2,000.

Although organizations certainly benefit from microprocessors that are faster, they also benefit from chips that are less powerful but can be made very small and inexpensive. **Microcontrollers** are chips that are embedded in countless products and technologies, from cellular telephones to toys to automobile sensors. Microprocessors and microcontrollers are similar except that microcontrollers usually cost less and work in less-demanding applications. Thus, the scientific advances in CPU design affect many organizations on the product and service side, not just on the internal CBIS side. New types of chips continue to be produced. (For a discussion of advanced chip technologies, see Online File W-TG1.3.)

microcontrollers *Computer chips, embedded in products and technologies, that usually cost less and work in less-demanding applications than microprocessors.*

wiley.com/college/turban

1. Briefly describe how a microprocessor functions.
2. What factors determine the speed of the microprocessor?
3. How are microprocessor designs advancing?

TG1.3 COMPUTER MEMORY

The amount and type of memory that a computer possesses has a great deal to do with its general utility, often affecting the type of program it can run and the work it can do, its speed, and both the cost of the machine and the cost of processing data. There are two basic categories of computer memory. The first is *primary storage*, so named because small amounts of data and information that will be immediately used by the CPU are stored there. The second is *secondary storage*, where much larger amounts of data and information (an entire software program, for example) are stored for extended periods of time.

Memory Capacity

bit *Short for binary digit (0s and 1s), the only data that a CPU can process.*

byte *An 8-bit string of data, needed to represent any one alphanumeric character or simple mathematical operation.*

As already noted, CPUs process only 0s and 1s. All data are translated through computer languages (covered in Technology Guide 2) into series of these binary digits, or bits. A particular combination of bits represents a certain alphanumeric character or simple mathematical operation. Eight bits are needed to represent any one of these characters. This 8-bit string is known as a byte. The storage capacity of a computer is measured in bytes. (Bits are used as units of measure typically only for telecommunications capacity, as in how many million bits per second can be sent through a particular medium.)

The hierarchy of memory capacity is as follows:

* **Kilobyte.** *Kilo* means one thousand, so a kilobyte (KB) is approximately one thousand bytes. Actually, a kilobyte is 1,024 bytes (2^{10} bytes).
* **Megabyte.** *Mega* means one million, so a megabyte (MB) is approximately one million bytes (1,048,576 bytes, or $1,024 \times 1,024$, to be exact). Most personal computers have hundreds of megabytes of RAM memory (a type of primary storage, discussed in a later section).
* **Gigabyte.** *Giga* means one billion; a gigabyte (GB) is actually 1,073,741,824 bytes ($1,024 \times 1,024 \times 1,024$ bytes). The storage capacity of a hard drive (a type of secondary storage, discussed shortly) in modern personal computers is often many gigabytes.
* **Terabyte.** One trillion bytes (actually, 1,078,036,791,296 bytes) comprise a terabyte.
* **Petabyte.** Approximately 10^{15} bytes.
* **Exabyte.** Approximately 10^{18} bytes.

To get a feel for these amounts, consider the following examples. If your computer has 512 MB of RAM (a type of primary storage), it can store 536,870,912 bytes of data. A written word might, on average, contain 6 bytes, so this translates to approximately 90 million words. If your computer has 120 GB of storage capacity on its hard drive (a type of secondary storage) and the average page of text has about 2,000 bytes, your hard drive could store some 60 million pages of text.

Primary Storage

Primary storage, or *main memory*, as it is sometimes called, stores for very brief periods of time three types of information: data to be processed by the CPU, instructions for the CPU as to how to process the data, and operating system programs that manage various aspects of the computer's operation. Primary storage takes place in chips mounted on the computer's main circuit board (the *motherboard*), located as close as physically possible to the CPU chip. (See Figure TG1.4.) As with the CPU, all the data and instructions in primary storage have been translated into binary code.

There are four main types of primary storage: (1) register, (2) random access memory (RAM), (3) cache memory, and (4) read-only memory (ROM). The logic of primary storage is that those components that will be used immediately are stored in very small amounts as close to the CPU as possible. Remember, as with CPU chip design, the shorter the distance the electrical impulses (data) have to travel, the faster they can be transported and processed. The four types of primary storage, which follow this logic, are described next.

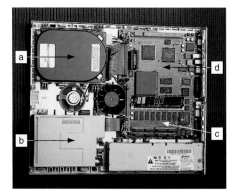

Figure TG1.4 *Internal workings of a common personal computer: (a) hard disk drive; (b) floppy disk drive; (c) RAM; (d) CPU board with fan.*

Registers. As indicated earlier, registers are part of the CPU. They have the least capacity, storing extremely limited amounts of instructions and data only immediately before and after processing.

Random Access Memory. Random access memory (RAM) is the part of primary storage that holds a software program and small amounts of data for processing. When you start most software programs on your computer, the entire program is brought from secondary storage into RAM. As you use the program, small parts of the program's instructions and data are sent into the registers and then to the CPU. RAM stores more information than the registers and is farther away from the CPU, but it stores less than secondary storage and is much closer to the CPU. Again, getting the data and instructions as close to the CPU as possible is key to the computer's speed, as is the fact that the RAM is a type of microprocessor chip. As we shall discuss later, the chip is much faster (and more costly) than are secondary storage devices.

RAM is temporary and *volatile*; that is, RAM chips lose their contents if the current is lost or turned off (as in a power surge, brownout, or electrical noise generated by lightning or nearby machines). RAM chips are located directly on the computer's main circuit board or in other chips located on peripheral cards that plug into the main circuit board.

The two main types of RAM are *dynamic RAM (DRAM)* and *static RAM (SRAM)*. DRAM memory chips offer the greatest capacities and the lowest cost per bit, but are relatively slow. SRAM costs more than DRAM but has a higher level of performance, making SRAM the preferred choice for performance-sensitive applications, including the external L2 and L3 caches (discussed below) that speed up microprocessor performance.

An emerging technology is *magnetic RAM (MRAM)*. MRAM is nonvolatile and uses magnetism, rather than electricity, to store data. DRAM wastes a lot of electricity because it needs to be supplied with a constant current to store data, whereas MRAM requires only a tiny amount of electricity to store data. MRAM combines the high speed of SRAM, the storage capacity of DRAM, and the nonvolatility of flash memory. MRAM will begin to replace DRAM late in 2003.

random access memory (RAM) *The part of primary storage that holds a software program and small amounts of data when they are brought from secondary storage.*

Cache Memory. Cache memory is a type of high-speed memory where the computer can temporarily store blocks of data used more often and that a processor can access more rapidly than main memory (RAM). It augments RAM in the following way: Many modern computer applications (Microsoft XP, for example) are very complex and have huge numbers of instructions. It takes considerable RAM capacity (usually a minimum of 128 megabytes) to store the entire instruction set. Or you may be using an application that exceeds your RAM. In either case, your processor must go to secondary storage to retrieve the necessary instructions. To alleviate this problem, software is often written in smaller blocks of instructions. As needed, these blocks can be brought from secondary storage into RAM. This process is still slow, however.

cache memory *A type of primary storage where the computer can temporarily store blocks of data used more often and which a processor can access more rapidly than main memory (RAM).*

Cache memory is a place closer to the CPU where the computer can temporarily store those blocks of instructions used most often. Blocks used less often remain in RAM until they are transferred to cache; blocks used infrequently stay stored in secondary storage. Cache memory is faster than RAM because the instructions travel a shorter distance to the CPU.

There are three types of cache memory in the majority of computer systems—Level 1 (L1) cache and Level 2 (L2) cache are located in the processor, and Level 3 (L3) cache is located on the motherboard but not actually in the processor. L1 cache is smaller and faster than L2 cache, which is in turn smaller and faster than L3 cache.

Read-only Memory. There is a need for greater security when storing certain types of critical data or instructions. Most people who use computers have lost data at one time or another due to a computer "crash" or a power failure. What is usually lost is whatever is in RAM, cache, or the registers at the time, because these types of memory are volatile. Cautious computer users frequently save data to nonvolatile memory (secondary storage). In addition, most modern software applications have autosave functions. Programs stored in secondary storage, even though they are temporarily copied into RAM when used, remain intact because only the copy is lost and not the original.

read-only memory (ROM) *Type of primary storage where certain critical instructions are safeguarded; the storage is nonvolatile and retains the instructions when the power to the computer is turned off.*

Read-only memory (ROM) is the place (a type of chip) where certain critical instructions are safeguarded. ROM is nonvolatile and retains these instructions when the power to the computer is turned off. The read-only designation means that these instructions can be read only by the computer and cannot be changed by the user. An example of ROM instructions are those needed to start or "boot" the computer once it has been shut off. There are variants of ROM chips that can be programmed (PROM), and some that can be erased and rewritten (EPROM). These are relatively rare in mainstream organizational computing, but are often incorporated into other specialized technologies such as video games (PROM) or robotic manufacturing (EPROM).

flash memory *A form of rewritable read-only memory that is compact, portable, and requires little energy.*

Another form of rewritable ROM storage is called **flash memory**. This technology can be built into a system or installed on a personal computer card (known as a *flash card*). These cards, though they have limited capacity, are compact, portable, and require little energy to read and write. Flash memory via flash cards is very popular for small portable technologies such as cellular telephones, digital cameras, handheld computers, and other consumer products.

Secondary Storage

secondary storage *Memory capacity that can store very large amounts of data for extended periods of time.*

Secondary storage is designed to store very large amounts of data for extended periods of time. Secondary storage can have memory capacity of several terabytes or more and only small portions of that data are placed in primary storage at any one time. Secondary storage has the following characteristics:

- It is nonvolatile.
- It takes much more time to retrieve data from secondary storage than it does from RAM because of the electromechanical nature of secondary storage devices.
- It is cheaper than primary storage (see Figure TG1.5).
- It can take place on a variety of media, each with its own technology, as discussed next.

The overall trends in secondary storage are toward more direct-access methods, higher capacity with lower costs, and increased portability.

magnetic tape *A secondary storage medium on a large open reel or in a smaller cartridge or cassette.*

sequential access *Data access in which the computer system must run through data in sequence in order to locate a particular piece.*

Magnetic Media. **Magnetic tape** is kept on a large open reel or in a smaller cartridge or cassette. Although this is an old technology, it remains popular because it is the cheapest storage medium and can handle enormous amounts of data. The downside is that it is the slowest for retrieval of data, because all the data are placed on the tape sequentially. **Sequential access** means that the system might have to run through the majority of the tape, for example, before it comes to the desired piece of data.

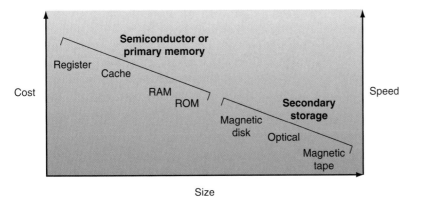

Figure TG1.5 *Primary memory compared to secondary storage.*

Magnetic tape storage often is used for information that an organization must maintain, but uses rarely or does not need immediate access to. Industries with huge numbers of files (e.g., insurance companies) use magnetic tape systems. Modern versions of magnetic tape systems use cartridges and often a robotic system that selects and loads the appropriate cartridge automatically. There are also some tape systems, like digital audio tapes (DAT), for smaller applications such as storing copies of all the contents of a personal computer's secondary storage ("backing up" the storage).

Magnetic disks are a form of secondary storage on a magnetized disk divided into tracks and sectors that provide addresses for various pieces of data. They come in a variety of styles and are popular because they allow much more rapid access to the data than does magnetic tape. Magnetic disks, called *hard disks* or fixed disk drives, are the most commonly used mass storage devices because of their low cost, high speed, and large storage capacity. Fixed disk drives read from, and write to, stacks of rotating (at up to 15,000 RPM) magnetic disk platters mounted in rigid enclosures and sealed against environmental or atmospheric contamination. These disks are permanently mounted in a unit that may be internal or external to the computer.

All disk drives (including removable disk modules, floppy disk drives, and optical drives) are called **hard drives** and store data on platters divided into concentric tracks. Each track is divided further into segments called *sectors*. To access a given sector, a read/write head pivots across the rotating disks to locate the right track, calculated from an index table, and the head then waits as the disk rotates until the right sector is underneath it.

Every piece of data has an address attached to it, corresponding to a particular track and sector. Any piece of desired data can be retrieved in a nonsequential manner, by **direct access** (which is why hard disk drives are sometimes called *direct access storage devices*). The read/write heads use the data's address to quickly find and read the data. (See Figure TG1.6.) Unlike magnetic tape, the system does not have to read through all the data to find what it wants.

The read/write heads are attached to arms that hover over the disks, moving in and out (see Figure TG1.6). They read the data when positioned over the correct track and when the correct sector spins by. Because the head floats just above the surface of the disk (less than 25 microns), any bit of dust or contamination can disrupt the device.

magnetic disks *A form of secondary storage on a magnetized disk divided into tracks and sectors that provide addresses for various pieces of data; also called hard disks.*

hard drives *A form of secondary storage that stores data on platters divided into concentric tracks and sectors, which can be read by a read/write head that pivots across the rotating disks.*

direct access *Data access in which any piece of data be retrieved in a nonsequential manner by locating it using the data's address.*

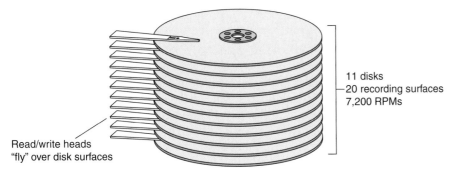

11 disks
20 recording surfaces
7,200 RPMs

Read/write heads "fly" over disk surfaces

Figure TG1.6 *Read/write heads.*

When this happens, it is called a *disk crash* and usually results in catastrophic loss of data. For this reason, hard drives are hermetically sealed when manufactured.

A modern personal computer typically has many gigabytes of storage capacity in its internal hard drive. Data access is very fast, measured in milliseconds. For these reasons, hard disk drives are popular and common. Because they are somewhat susceptible to mechanical failure, and because users may need to take all their hard drive's contents to another location, many users like to back up their hard drive's contents with a portable hard disk drive system, such as Iomega's Jaz.

Disk Drive Interfaces. To take advantage of the new, faster technologies, disk drive interfaces must also be faster. Most PCs and workstations use one of two high-performance disk interface standards: *Enhanced Integrated Drive Electronics (EIDE)* or *Small Computer Systems Interface (SCSI)*. EIDE offers good performance, is inexpensive, and supports up to four disks, tapes, or CD-ROM drives. SCSI drives are more expensive than EIDE drives, but they offer a faster interface and support more devices. SCSI interfaces are therefore used for graphics workstations, server-based storage, and large databases. (For discussions of other interfaces, including fibre channel, firewire, Infiniband, and the universal serial bus, see Online File W-TG1.4.)

Magnetic Diskettes. **Magnetic diskettes**, or *floppy disks* as they are commonly called, function similarly to hard drives, but are much slower. They have much less capacity, ranging from 1.44 megabytes for a standard high-density disk to several gigabytes for a disk formatted for a Zip drive (on which the data are compressed). Further, although they are individually inexpensive, floppy disks are less cost-efficient than hard drive storage. However, the big advantage of floppy disks has been that they are portable.

Optical Storage Devices. Unlike magnetic media, **optical storage devices** do not store data via magnetism. Rather, a laser reads the surface of a reflective plastic platter. Optical disk drives are slower than magnetic hard drives, but are less susceptible to damage from contamination and are also less fragile.

In addition, optical disks can store much more information, both on a routine basis and also when combined into storage systems. Optical disk storage systems can be used for large-capacity data storage. These technologies, known as optical jukeboxes, store many disks and operate much like the automated phonograph record changers for which they are named.

Types of optical disks include compact disk read-only memory (CD-ROM), digital video disk (DVD), and fluorescent multilayer disk (FMD-ROM).

Compact Disk, Read-Only Memory. **Compact disk, read-only memory (CD-ROM)** storage devices feature high capacity, low cost, and high durability. However, because it is a read-only medium, the CD-ROM can be only read and not written on. *Compact disk, rewritable (CD-RW)* adds rewritability to the recordable compact disk market, which previously had offered only write-once CD-ROM technology.

Digital Video Disk. The **digital video disk (DVD)** is a five-inch disk with the capacity to store about 135 minutes of digital video. DVD provides sharp detail, true color, no flicker, and no snow. DVDs have advantages over videocassettes, including better quality, smaller size (meaning they occupy less shelf space), and lower duplicating costs. DVDs can also perform as computer storage disks, providing storage capabilities of 17 gigabytes. DVD players can read current CD-ROMs, but current CD-ROM players cannot read DVDs. The access speed of a DVD drive is faster than a typical CD-ROM drive.

A company called Flexplay (*flexplay.com*) is producing *disposable DVDs*. These DVDs have a preset viewing window of time that begins when the disk is removed from its packaging. After this time (usually 48 hours), the disk will no longer be readable by a DVD player and can be thrown away. The company feels that disposable DVDs will eliminate late rental fees, the hassle of returning the DVD to the store, and scratched disks.

wiley.com/college/turban

magnetic diskettes *A form of easily portable secondary storage on flexible Mylar disks; also called* floppy disks.

optical storage devices *A form of secondary storage in which a laser reads the surface of a reflective plastic platter.*

compact disk, read-only memory (CD-ROM) *A form of secondary storage that can be only read and not written on.*

digital video disk (DVD) *An optical storage device used to store digital video or computer data.*

Fluorescent Multilayer Disk. A new optical storage technology called **fluorescent multilayer disk (FMD-ROM)** greatly increases storage capacity. The idea of using multiple layers on an optical disk is not new, as DVDs currently support two layers. However, by using a new fluorescent-based optical system, FMDs can support 20 layers or more. FMDs are clear disks; in the layers are fluorescent materials that give off light. The presence or absence of these materials tells the drive whether there is information there or not. All layers of an FMD can be read in parallel, thereby increasing the data transfer rate.

fluorescent multilayer disk (FMD-ROM) *An optical storage device with much greater storage capacity than DVDs.*

Memory Cards. PC **memory cards** are credit-card-size devices that can be installed in an adapter or slot in many personal computers. The PC memory card functions as if it were a fixed hard disk drive. The cost per megabyte of storage is greater than for traditional hard disk storage, but the cards do have advantages. They are less failure-prone than hard disks, are portable, and are relatively easy to use. Software manufacturers often store the instructions for their programs on a memory card for use with laptop computers. The Personal Computer Memory Card International Association (PCMCIA) is a group of computer manufacturers who are creating standards for these memory cards. Even smaller cards, called *memory sticks* or *keychain memory*, also fit into PC ports and can store up to one gigabyte.

memory cards *Credit-card-size storage devices that can be installed in an adapter or slot in many personal computers.*

Memory stick storage device.

Expandable Storage. **Expandable storage devices** are removable disk cartridges, with capacity ranging from 100 megabytes to several gigabytes per cartridge, and access speed similar to that of an internal hard drive. Although more expensive than internal hard drives, expandable storage devices combine hard disk storage capacity and diskette portability. Expandable storage devices are ideal for backup of the internal hard drive, as they can hold more than 80 times as much data and operate five times faster than existing floppy diskette drives.

expandable storage devices *Removable disk cartridges, used as backup storage for internal hard drives of PCs.*

Enterprise Storage Systems

The amount of digital information is doubling every two years. As a result, many companies are employing enterprise storage systems. An **enterprise storage system** is an independent, external system with intelligence that includes two or more storage devices. Enterprise storage systems provide large amounts of storage, high-performance data transfer, a high degree of availability, protection against data loss, and sophisticated management tools.

enterprise storage system *An independent, external system with intelligence that includes two or more storage devices.*

The price/performance ratio for enterprise storage systems' hardware has improved even faster than for chips. In 1956, the first disk storage unit weighed more than 1000 pounds, was the size of two refrigerators, leased for $3,200 per month, and stored five megabytes. In 2003, the one-inch-square, half ounce IBM Microdrive cost about $500 and stored approximately two gigabytes.

There are three major types of enterprise storage systems: redundant arrays of independent disks, storage area networks, and network-attached storage .

Redundant Arrays of Independent Disks. Hard drives in all computer systems are susceptible to failures caused by temperature variations, head crashes, motor failure, controller failure, and changing voltage conditions. To improve reliability and protect the data in their enterprise storage systems, many computer systems use **redundant arrays of independent disks (RAID)** storage products. RAID links groups of standard hard drives to a specialized microcontroller. The microcontroller coordinates the drives so they appear as a single logical drive, but they take advantage of the multiple physical drives by storing data redundantly, thus protecting against data loss due to the failure of any single drive.

redundant arrays of independent disks (RAID) *An enterprise storage system that links groups of standard hard drives to a specialized microcontroller that coordinates the drives so they appear as a single logical drive.*

storage area network (SAN) *An enterprise storage system architecture for building special, dedicated networks that allow rapid and reliable access to storage devices by multiple servers.*

Storage Area Network. A **storage area network (SAN)** is an architecture for building special, dedicated networks that allow rapid and reliable access to storage devices by multiple servers. **Storage over IP**, sometimes called *IP over SCSI* or *iSCSI*, is

storage over IP *Technology that uses the Internet Protocol to transport stored data between devices within a SAN; sometimes called IP over SCSI or iSCSI.*

Table TG1.1 Secondary Storage

Type	Advantages	Disadvantages	Application
Magnetic Storage Devices			
Magnetic tape	Lowest cost per unit stored.	Sequential access means slow retrieval speeds.	Corporate data archiving.
Hard drive	Relatively high capacity and fast retrieval speed.	Fragile; high cost per unit stored.	Personal computers through mainframes.
RAID	High capacity; designed for fault tolerance and reduced risk of data loss; low cost per unit stored.	Expensive, semipermanent installation.	Corporate data storage that requires frequent, rapid access.
SAN	High capacity; designed for large amounts of enterprise data.	Expensive.	Corporate data storage that requires frequent, rapid access.
NAS	High capacity; designed for large amounts of enterprise data.	Expensive.	Corporate data storage that requires frequent, rapid access.
Magnetic diskettes	Low cost per diskette, portability.	Low capacity; very high cost per unit stored; fragile.	Personal computers.
Memory cards	Portable; easy to use; less failure-prone than hard drives.	Expensive.	Personal and laptop computers.
Memory sticks	Extremely portable and easy to use.	Relatively expensive.	Consumer electronic devices; moving files from portable devices to desktop computers.
Expandable storage	Portable; high capacity.	More expensive than hard drives.	Backup of internal hard drive.
Optical Storage Devices			
CD-ROM	High capacity; moderate cost per unit stored; high durability.	Slower retrieval speeds than hard drives; only certain types can be rewritten.	Personal computers through corporate data storage.
DVD	High capacity; moderate cost per unit stored.	Slower retrieval speeds than hard drives.	Personal computers through corporate data storage.
FMD-ROM	Very high capacity; moderate cost per unit stored.	Faster retrieval speeds than DVD or CD-ROM; slower retrieval speeds than hard drives.	Personal computers through corporate data storage.

storage visualization software
Software used with SANs to graphically plot an entire network and allow storage administrators to monitor all devices from a single console.

network-attached storage (NAS)
An enterprise storage system in which a special-purpose server provides file storage to users who access the device over a network.

a technology that uses the Internet Protocol to transport stored data between devices within a SAN. **Storage visualization software** is used with SANs to graphically plot an entire network and allow storage administrators to view the properties of, and monitor, all devices from a single console.

Network-Attached Storage. A **network-attached storage (NAS)** device is a special-purpose server that provides file storage to users who access the device over a network. The NAS server is simple to install (i.e., plug-and-play), and works exactly like a general-purpose file server, so no user retraining or special software is needed.

Table TG1.1 compares the advantages and disadvantages of the various secondary storage media.

Before you go on . . .

1. Describe the four main types of primary storage.

2. Describe different types of secondary storage.

3. How does primary storage differ from secondary storage in terms of speed, cost, and capacity?

4. Describe the three types of enterprise storage systems.

TG1.4 EVOLUTION OF COMPUTER HARDWARE

Computer hardware has evolved through four stages, or generations, of technology. Each generation has provided increased processing power and storage capacity, while simultaneously exhibiting decreases in costs. The generations are distinguished by different technologies that perform the processing functions.

The *first generation* of computers, from 1946 to about 1956, used *vacuum tubes* to store and process information. Vacuum tubes consumed large amounts of power, generated much heat, and were short-lived. Therefore, first-generation computers had limited memory and processing capability.

The *second generation* of computers, from 1957 to 1963, used *transistors* for storing and processing information. Transistors consumed less power than vacuum tubes, produced less heat, and were cheaper, more stable, and more reliable. Second-generation computers, with increased processing and storage capabilities, began to be more widely used for scientific and business purposes.

Third-generation computers, from 1964 to 1979, used integrated circuits for storing and processing information. Integrated circuits are made by printing numerous small transistors directly on silicon chips. These devices are called *semiconductors*. Third-generation computers introduced software that could be used by nontechnical people, thus enlarging the computer's role in business.

Early to middle *fourth-generation* computers, from 1980 to 1995, used *very-large-scale integrated (VLSI) circuits* to store and process information. The VLSI technique allowed the installation of hundreds of thousands of circuits (transistors and other components) on a small chip. With *ultra-large-scale integration (ULSI)*, 10 million transistors could be placed on a chip. These computers are relatively inexpensive and are still widely used in business and everyday life.

Late *fourth-generation* computers, from 1996 to the present, use *grand-scale integrated (GSI)* circuits to store and process information. With GSI, one billion transistors can be placed on a chip.

The first four generations of computer hardware were based on the Von Neumann architecture, which processed information sequentially, one instruction at a time. The *fifth generation* of computers, developed about the same time as late fourth-generation computers, uses *massively parallel processing* to process multiple instructions simultaneously. A major application of massively parallel computers is in data mining of large databases (discussed in Chapter 3). Massively parallel computers use flexibly connected networks linking thousands of inexpensive, commonly used chips to address large computing problems, attaining supercomputer speeds. With enough chips networked together, massively parallel machines can perform more than one trillion floating point operations per second—a teraflop. A *floating point operation (flop)* is a basic computer arithmetic operation, such as addition or subtraction, on numbers that include a decimal point.

Modern computers are late fourth-generation machines and they are of all sizes. We now discuss the various types of modern computers, from largest to smallest—the computer hierarchy.

Before you go on . . .

1. What are the four generations through which computer hardware has evolved?
2. What technology did each generation use to store and process information?

TG1.5 COMPUTER HIERARCHY

The traditional way of comparing classes of computers is by their processing power. Analysts typically divide computers (called the *platform* in the computer industry) into six categories: supercomputers, mainframes, midrange computers (minicomputers and servers), workstations, notebooks and desktop computers, and appliances. Recently, the lines between these categories have blurred. This section presents each class of computer, beginning with the most powerful and ending with the least powerful. We describe the computers and their respective roles in modern organizations.

Supercomputers

The term **supercomputer** does not refer to a specific technology, but to the fastest computing engines available at any given time. Supercomputers generally address computationally demanding tasks on very large data sets. Rather than transaction processing and business applications—the forte of mainframes and other multiprocessing platforms—supercomputers typically run military and scientific applications, although their use for commercial applications, such as data mining, has been increasing. Supercomputers generally operate at four to ten times faster than the next most powerful computer class, the mainframe. (For a more technical overview of supercomputers, see Online File W-TG1.5.)

A supercomputer.

wiley.com/college/turban

supercomputers *Computers with the most processing power available; used primarily in scientific and military work for computationally demanding tasks on very large data sets.*

mainframes *Relatively large computers used in large enterprises for extensive computing applications that are accessed by thousands of users.*

Mainframe Computers

Although mainframe computers are increasingly viewed as just another type of server, albeit at the high end of the performance and reliability scales, they remain a distinct class of systems differentiated by hardware and software features. **Mainframes** remain popular in large enterprises for extensive computing applications that are accessed by thousands of users. Examples of mainframe applications include airline reservation systems, corporate payroll, and student grade calculation and reporting. Analysts predict that Internet-based computing will lead to continued growth in the mainframe market.

Mainframes are less powerful and generally less expensive than supercomputers. The cost of mainframe capacity (measured in dollars per MIP) has fallen from $9,410 in 1997, to $2,260 in 2000, to $490 in 2004.

A mainframe system may have up to several gigabytes of primary storage. Online and offline secondary storage (see the earlier discussion of Enterprise Storage Systems) may use high-capacity magnetic and optical storage media with capacities in the terabyte range. Typically, several hundreds or thousands of online computers can be linked to a mainframe. Today's most advanced mainframes perform at more than 5,000 MIPs and can handle more than one billion transactions per day.

Some large organizations that began moving away from mainframes toward distributed systems now are moving back toward mainframes because of their centralized administration, high reliability, and increasing flexibility. This process is called *recentralization*. The reasons for the shift include supporting the high transaction levels associated with e-commerce, reducing the total cost of ownership of distributed systems, simplifying administration, reducing support-personnel requirements, and improving system performance. In addition, mainframe computing provides a secure, robust computing environment in which to run strategic, mission-critical applications. (For a more technical discussion of mainframes, see Online File W-TG1.6.)

A mainframe computer.

wiley.com/college/turban

Midrange Computers

minicomputers *Relatively small, inexpensive, and compact midrange computers that perform the same functions as mainframe computers, but to a more limited extent.*

servers *Smaller midrange computers that support networks, enabling users to share files, software, and other network devices.*

Larger midrange computers, called **minicomputers**, are relatively small, inexpensive, and compact computers that perform the same functions as mainframe computers, but to a more limited extent. In fact, the lines have blurred between minicomputers and mainframes in price and performance. Minicomputers typically support computer networks, enabling users to share files, software, peripheral devices, and other network resources. Minicomputers can provide flexibility to organizations that do not want to spend IT dollars on mainframes, which are less scalable.

Smaller midrange computers are called **servers**. They typically are used to support networks, enabling users to share files, software, and other network devices. Organizations with heavy e-commerce requirements and very large Web sites often run their Web and e-commerce applications on multiple servers in *server farms*. As companies pack greater numbers of servers in their server farms, they are using pizza-box-size servers called *rack servers* that can be stacked in racks. These computers run cooler, and therefore can be packed more closely, requiring less space. To further increase density, companies are using a server design called a blade. A *blade* is a card about the size of a paperback book on which memory, processor, and hard drives are mounted.

Workstations

Computer vendors originally developed desktop engineering workstations, or *workstations* for short, to provide the high levels of performance demanded by engineers. That is, **workstations** run computationally intensive scientific, engineering, and financial applications. Workstations are typically based on *RISC* (reduced instruction set computing) *architecture* and provide both very high-speed calculations and high-resolution graphic displays. These computers have found widespread acceptance within the scientific community and, more recently, within the business community. Workstation applications include electronic and mechanical design, medical imaging, scientific visualization, 3-D animation, and video editing. By the second half of the 1990s, many workstation features were commonplace in PCs, blurring the distinction between workstations and personal computers.

workstations *Powerful desktop-sized computers that run computationally intensive scientific, engineering, and financial applications.*

Microcomputers

Microcomputers (also called *micros, personal computers*, or *PCs*) are the smallest and least expensive category of general-purpose computers. They can be subdivided into four classifications based on their size: desktops, thin clients, notebooks and laptops, and mobile devices.

microcomputers *The smallest and least expensive category of general-purpose computers; also called* micros, personal computers, *or* PCs.

Desktop PCs. The *desktop personal computer* has become the dominant method of accessing workgroup and enterprisewide applications. It is the typical, familiar microcomputer system that has become a standard tool for business and, increasingly, the home. It is usually modular in design, with separate but connected monitor, keyboard, and CPU. In general, modern microcomputers have between 256 megabytes and 1 gigabyte of primary storage, one 3.5-inch floppy drive, a CD-ROM (or DVD) drive, and up to 100 gigabytes or more of secondary storage.

Most desktop systems currently use Intel 32-bit technology (but are moving to 64-bit technology), running some version of Windows. An exception is the Apple Macintosh, which runs Mac OS (operating system) on a PowerPC processor.

Thin-Client Systems. **Thin-client systems** are desktop computer systems that do not offer the full functionality of a PC (called a **fat client**, as opposed to a thin client). Compared to a PC, or fat client, thin clients are less complex, particularly because they lack locally installed software, and thus are easier and less expensive to operate and support than PCs. The benefits of thin clients include fast application deployment, centralized management, lower cost of ownership, and easier installation, management, maintenance, and support. Disadvantages include user resistance and the need to upgrade servers and buy additional server applications and licenses.

thin-client systems *Desktop computer systems that do not offer the full functionality of a PC.*

fat-client systems *Desktop computer systems that offer full functionality.*

Another type of thin client is a **network computer**, which is a system that provides access to Internet-based applications via a Web browser and can download software, usually in the form of Java applets. With PC vendors lowering their systems costs and simplifying maintenance, NCs remain niche products. However, vendors continue to manufacture thin-client systems for use at retail stations, kiosks, and other sites that require access to corporate repositories but little desktop functionality.

network computer *A type of thin client system; has less functionality than a desktop PC but provides access to Internet-based applications via a Web browser and can download software.*

Table TG1.2 compares the classes of computers discussed so far.

Laptop and Notebook Computers. As computers become much smaller and vastly more powerful, they become portable, and new ways of using them open up.

Table TG1.2   Comparing Computers—Desktop and Larger

Type	Processor Speed	Amount of RAM	Physical Size	Common Role/Use
Supercomputer	Up to 40 trillion FLOPS	Many gigabytes	Like a small car	Scientific calculation, complex system modeling, and simulation
Mainframe	2,500–10,000 MIPS	Up to several gigabytes	Like a refrigerator	Enterprisewide systems, corporate database management
Midrange Computers:				
Minicomputer	Up to 2,500 MIPS	Up to several gigabytes	Like a file cabinet	Department-level or small company; dedicated to a particular system (e.g., e-mail)
Server	100–1,000 MIPS	Up to several gigabytes	Fits on desktop	Supports computer networks; e-commerce
Workstation	50–250 MIPS	512 megabytes to 2 gigabytes	Fits on desktop	Engineering/CAD software development
Microcomputer	10–100 MIPS	Up to 1 gigabyte	Fits on desktop	Personal/workgroup productivity, communication

A notebook computer

laptop and notebook computers
Small, easily transportable, light-weight microcomputers that fit easily into a briefcase.

mobile devices *Portable, light-weight platforms for computing and communications, including personal digital assistants (PDAs), handheld personal computers, and mobile phone handsets with wireless and Internet access.*

An Internet-connected cell phone.

Laptop and notebook computers are small, easily transportable, lightweight micro-computers that fit easily into a briefcase. In general, vendors refer to notebook computers as computers that are smaller than laptop computers. They are designed for maximum convenience and transportability, allowing access to processing power and data outside an office environment. They cost more than desktops for similar functionality.

Mobile Devices.   Emerging platforms for computing and communications include such **mobile devices** as handheld computers, often called personal digital assistants (PDAs) or *handheld personal computers*, and mobile phone handsets with new wireless and Internet access capabilities formerly associated with PDAs. Other emerging platforms (game consoles and cable set-top boxes) are consumer electronics devices that are expanding into computing and telecommunications. Mobile devices are becoming more popular and more capable of augmenting, or even substituting for, desktop and notebook computers.

Table TG1.3 describes the various types of mobile devices. In general, mobile devices have the following characteristics:

- They cost much less than PCs.
- Their operating systems are simpler than those on a desktop PC.
- They provide good performance at specific tasks but do not replace the full functions of a PC.
- They provide both computer and/or communications features.
- They offer a Web portal that is viewable on a screen.

Computing Devices

As technology has improved, ever-smaller computing/communication devices have become possible. Technology such as wearable computing/communication devices (à la *Star Trek*)—which for generations seemed like science fiction—has now become reality. This section briefly looks at some of these new computing devices. (For more discussion, see Chapter 6.)

Wearable Computers.   As discussed in Chapter 6, *wearable computers* (wearable devices) are designed to be worn and used on the body. Industrial applications of wearable computing include systems for factory automation, warehouse management, and performance support, such as viewing technical manuals and diagrams while

Table TG1.3   Mobile Devices and Their Uses

Device	Description and Use
Handheld companions	Devices with a core functionality of accessing and managing data; designed as supplements to notebooks or PCs.
PC companions	Devices primarily used for personal information management (PIM), e-mail, and light data-creation capabilities.
Personal companions	Devices primarily used for PIM activities and data-viewing activities.
Classic PDAs	Handheld units designed for PIM and vertical data collection.
Smartphones	Mobile phones with added PDA, PIM, data, e-mail, or messaging creation/service capabilities.
Vertical application devices	Devices with a core functionality of data access, management, creation, and collection; designed for use in vertical markets.*
Pen tablets	Business devices with pen input and tablet form for gathering data in the field or in a mobile situation.
Pen notepads	Pen-based for vertical data collection applications.
Keypad handhelds	Business devices with an alphanumeric keypad used in specialized data-collection applications.

*Vertical markets refer to specific industries, such as manufacturing, finance, health care, etc.

building or repairing something. The technology is already widely used in diverse industries such as freight delivery (e.g., the computer that your Federal Express person carries), aerospace, securities trading, and law enforcement. Governments have been examining such devices for military uses.

Embedded computers are placed inside other products to add features and capabilities. For example, the average mid-sized automobile has more than 3,000 embedded computers (called controllers) that monitor every function from braking to engine performance to seat controls with memory.

Other small-sized computing devices include active badges and memory buttons. As described in Chapter 6, *active badges* can be worn as ID cards by employees who wish to stay in touch at all times while moving around the corporate premises. *Memory buttons* are nickel-sized devices that store a small database relating to whatever it is attached to. These devices are similar to a bar code, but with far greater informational content and a content that is subject to change.

An even smaller form of computer is the *smart card*. As discussed in Chapter 5, smart cards are similar in size to ordinary plastic credit cards. However, smart cards contain a small processor and memory that allow them to be used in everyday activities such as personal identification and banking. Uses for smart cards are appearing rapidly: People can "deposit money" into the card's memory for "withdrawal" at retail stores. Many states and private health maintenance organizations are issuing smart health cards that contain the owner's complete health history, emergency data, and health insurance policy data. Smart cards are being used to transport data between computers, replacing floppy disks. Adding a small transmitter to a smart card can allow businesses to locate any employee and automatically route phone calls to the telephone nearest to him or her.

Another type of computing device is the *radio frequency identification tag (RFID)*. As described in Chapter 6, an RFID tag contains an antenna that, when activated by a reader, can send or receive information. RFID can be read without a line of sight to an item, making it easier to obtain automated reads and to do so in large quantities instead of one by one as with barcodes. RFID also automatically collects far more data than is possible today—not just product information, but even temperature, humidity, and shocks. However, there are disadvantages: The tags are still costly. Also, RFID readers do not come in a wide enough variety for different types of products; wireless networks in the stores interfere with readers; and readers are not fast enough. As prices decline and functionalities improve, use of RFID tags is expected to grow.

Before you go on . . .

1. Describe the computer hierarchy from the largest to the smallest computers.

2. What type of desktop PC has the least amount of processing power?

3. Give examples of the uses of supercomputers and handheld computers.

TG1.6 INPUT AND OUTPUT TECHNOLOGIES

Input technologies allow people and other technologies to put data into a computer. The two main types of input devices are human data-entry devices and source-data automation devices. *Human data-entry* devices include keyboards, mouse, trackball, joystick, touchscreen, stylus, and voice-recognition. *Source-data automation* devices input data with minimal human intervention. Source-data automation technologies speed up data collection, reduce errors, and gather data at the source of a transaction or other event. Table TG1.4 describes the various input devices.

Table TG1.4 Input Devices

Input Device	Description
Human Data-Entry Devices	
Keyboards	Most common input device (for text and numerical data).
Mouse	Handheld device used to point cursor at point on screen, such as an icon; user clicks button on mouse instructing computer to take some action.
Optical mouse	Mouse is not connected to computer by a cable; mouse uses camera chip to take images of surface it passes over, comparing successive images to determine its position.
Trackball	User rotates a ball built into top of device to move cursor (rather than moving entire device such as a mouse).
Touchpad	User moves cursor by sliding finger across a sensitized pad and then can tap pad when cursor is in desired position to instruct computer to take action (also called *glide-and-tap pad*).
Joystick	Joystick moves cursor to desired place on screen; commonly used in workstations that display dynamic graphics and in video games.
Touchscreen	Users instruct computer to take some action by touching a particular part of the screen; commonly used in information kiosks such as ATM machines.
Stylus	Pen-style device that allows user either to touch parts of a predetermined menu of options or to handwrite information into the computer (as with some PDAs); works with touch-sensitive screens.
Voice-recognition	Converts voice wave sounds into digital input for computer; critical technology for physically challenged people who cannot use other input devices.
Source-Data Automation Input Devices	
Automated teller machines	Interactive devices that enable people to make bank transactions from remote locations.
Point-of-sale terminals	Computerized cash registers that also may incorporate touch screen technology and barcode scanners (see below) to input data such as item sold, price, etc.
Barcode scanners	Devices scan black-and-white barcode lines printed on merchandise labels.
Optical mark reader	Scanner for detecting presence of dark marks on predetermined grid, such as multiple-choice test answer sheets.
Magnetic ink character reader	Read magnetic ink printed on checks which identify the bank, checking account, and check number.
Optical character recognition	Software that converts text into digital form for input into computer.
Sensors	Collect data directly from the environment and input data directly into computer; examples include your car's airbag activation sensor and radio-frequency-identification tags.
Cameras	Digital cameras capture images and convert them into digital files.
Retinal scanning displays	Projects an image, pixel by pixel, directly onto a viewer's retina; used with mobile devices; see Microvision's (*mvis.com*) Nomad and Xybernaut's (*xybernaut.com*) Poma.

Table TG1.5   Output Devices

Output Device	Description
Monitors	
Cathode ray tubes	Video screens on which an electron beam illuminates pixels on display screen.
Liquid crystal display (LCDs)	Flat displays that have liquid crystals between two polarizers to form characters and images on a backlit screen.
Organic light-emitting	Displays that are brighter, thinner, lighter, cheaper, faster diodes (OLEDs), and take less power to run than LCDs.
Retinal scanning displays	Project image directly onto a viewer's retina; used in medicine, air traffic control, and controlling industrial machines.
Printers	
Impact	Slow, noisy, subject to mechanical failure, but inexpensive.
Nonimpact	
Laser	Use laser beams to write information on photosensitive drums; produce high-resolution text and graphics.
Inkjet	Shoot fine streams of colored ink onto paper; less expensive than laser printers, but offer less resolution quality.
Plotters	Use computer-directed pens for creating high-quality images, blueprints, schematics, drawing of new products, etc.
Voice Output	Converts digital data to intelligible speech.

The output generated by a computer can be transmitted to the user via several output devices and media. These devices include monitors, printers, plotters, and voice. Table TG1.5 describes the various output devices.

Multimedia

Multimedia technology is the computer-based integration of text, sound, still images, animation, and digitized motion video. It merges the capabilities of computers with televisions, VCRs, CD players, DVD players, video and audio recording equipment, and music and gaming technologies. Multimedia usually represents a collection of various input and output technologies, a system unto itself, as shown in Figure TG1.7.

High-quality multimedia processing requires the most powerful and sophisticated microprocessors available. Firms like Intel produce generations of chips especially designed for multimedia processing. Because of the variety of devices that can make up a multimedia system, standards such as the Multimedia Personal Computer (MPC) Council certification are important in ensuring that the devices are compliant and compatible.

Extensive memory capacity—both primary and secondary storage—is essential for multimedia processing, particularly with video. Video typically requires using compression techniques to reduce the amount of storage needed. Even with compression techniques, those who work extensively with video processing often must augment their secondary storage with devices like writeable CD drives or external hard drives. Later in the book we discuss the business uses of multimedia technology.

multimedia technology
Computer-based integration of text, sound, still images, animation, and digitized motion video.

Before you go on . . .

1. Distinguish between human data-input devices and source-data automation.

2. What are the differences between various types of monitors?

3. What are the main types of printers? How do they work?

4. Describe the concept of multimedia, and give an example of a multimedia system.

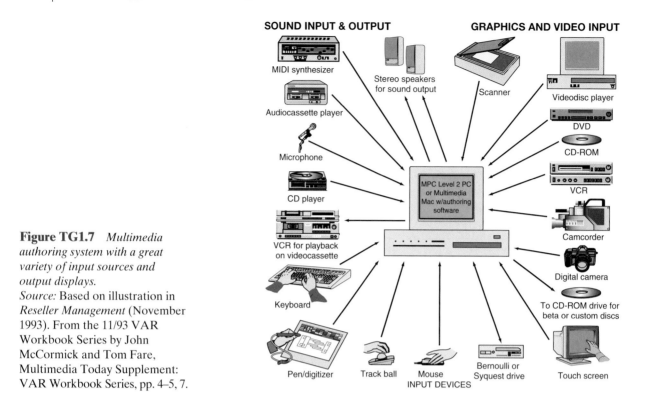

Figure TG1.7 *Multimedia authoring system with a great variety of input sources and output displays.*
Source: Based on illustration in *Reseller Management* (November 1993). From the 11/93 VAR Workbook Series by John McCormick and Tom Fare, Multimedia Today Supplement: VAR Workbook Series, pp. 4–5, 7.

TG1.7 GENERAL TECHNOLOGICAL TRENDS

To fully understand hardware, we should have an idea of how fast hardware is changing. In this section we discuss the general trends in hardware technology.

Cost-Performance Ratio of Chips: Improvement by a Factor of at Least 100

In about 10 years, a computer will cost the same as it costs today, but will be over 50 times more powerful (in terms of processing speed, memory, storage, etc.). At the same time, labor costs could double, so the cost-performance ratio of computers versus manual work will improve by a factor of 100. This means that computers will have increasingly greater comparative advantage over people in performing certain types of work.

Storage

Whereas Moore's Law addresses improvements in processing speed, improvements in storage contribute similarly to the cost-performance ratio. Devices are becoming much smaller and storing increasing amounts of information. For example, memory sticks in 2003 are capable of storing 150 gigabytes in a device the size of a credit card.

Self-Healing Computers

IBM is developing computers, called *self-healing computers*, that have the ability to repair themselves and keep running without human intervention. One such computer (named BlueSky), a supercomputer at the National Center for Atmospheric Research, performs at over six teraflops (trillions of floating point operations per second). (See *scd.ucar.edu/computers/gallery/ibm/bluesky/bluesky.html*.)

Sensor Webs

A **sensor web** consists of a group of pods (small metal boxes) set up to collect various kinds of information, communicate with nearby pods, and in some cases, communicate wirelessly with outside devices. Each pod contains a microprocessor, cellular communications technology, and various sensing components (e.g., to sense temperature, moisture, motion, pressure, etc.). A complete description of how a sensor web works can be found at *sensorwebs.jpl.nasa.gov*. Sensor webs collect information and interact with the environment based on what they detect. Agribusiness companies are using sensor webs in precision agriculture, to control irrigation for example.

> **sensor web** *A group of pods (small metal boxes) set up to collect various kinds of information, communicate with nearby pods, and in some cases, communicate wirelessly with outside devices.*

Nanotechnology

Nanotechnology refers to the creation of materials, devices, and systems at a scale of 1 to 100 nanometers (billionths of a meter). In the near future, still-experimental computers will be constructed on a nanotechnology scale and could be used literally anywhere. They will require very little power, yet they will have huge storage capacities and be immune to computer viruses, crashes, and other problems. In an interesting application, one company, Nano Tex, is incorporating nanotechnology into its fabrics so they will be wrinkle and stain resistant. For a demonstration, see *nano-tex.com/products/flash/Nano-Care.swf*.

> **nanotechnology** *The creation of materials, devices, and systems at a scale of 1 to 100 nanometers (billionths of a meter).*

Quantum Computing

Researchers are looking into using the basic quantum states of matter as a fundamental unit of computing. If successful, quantum computers will be hundreds of times faster than today's supercomputers.

Before you go on . . .

1. Describe how the cost/performance ratio of chips will improve by a factor of 100.
2. What are self-healing computers?
3. What are sensor webs? How are they used?
4. What is nanotechnology?

TG1.8 STRATEGIC HARDWARE ISSUES

This technology guide has explained how hardware is designed and how it works. But it is what the hardware enables, how it is advancing, and how rapidly it is advancing that are the more complex and important issues for most businesspeople. In many industries, exploiting computer hardware is a key to competitive advantage. Successful hardware exploitation comes from thoughtful consideration of the following questions:

- How do organizations keep up with the rapid price/performance advancements in hardware? For example, how often should an organization upgrade its computers and storage systems? Will upgrades increase personal and organizational productivity? How can organizations measure such increases?

- Portable computers and advanced communications technologies (discussed in Technology Guide 3) have enabled employees to work from home or from anywhere. Will these new work styles benefit employees and the organization? How do organizations manage such new workstyles?

Before you go on . . .

1. How do you think the various types of computer hardware affect personal productivity? Organizational productivity?
2. What do you think might be disadvantages of advances in microprocessor design?

WHAT'S IN IT FOR ME?

FOR ALL BUSINESS AND NONBUSINESS MAJORS

There are practically no professional jobs in business today that do not require computer literacy and skills for personal productivity. And there are no industries that do not use computer technology for one form of competitive advantage or another.

Clearly, the design of computer hardware has profound impacts for businesspeople. It is also clear that personal and organizational success can depend on an understanding of hardware design and a commitment to knowing where it is going and what opportunities and challenges innovations will bring. Because these innovations can occur so rapidly, hardware decisions at the individual level and at the organizational level are difficult.

At the *individual level*, most people who have a home or office computer system and want to upgrade it, or people contemplating their first computer purchase, are faced with the decision of *when* to buy as much as *what* to buy and at what cost.

At the *organizational level*, these same issues plague IS professionals, but they are more complex and more costly. Most organizations have many different computer systems in place at the same time. Innovations may come to different classes of computers at different times or rates, and managers must decide when old hardware *legacy systems* still have a productive role in the IS architecture, or when they should be replaced.

IS management at the corporate level is one of the most challenging careers today, due in no small part to the constant innovation in computer hardware. That may not be your career objective, but an appreciation of that area is beneficial. After all, the people who keep you equipped with the right computing hardware, as you can now see, are very important allies in your success.

SUMMARY

1. **Identify the major hardware components of a computer system.** Today's computer systems have six major components: the central processing unit (CPU), primary storage, secondary storage, input technologies, output technologies, and communications technologies.

2. **Describe the design and functioning of the central processing unit.** The CPU is made up of the arithmetic-logic unit that performs the calculations, the registers that store minute amounts of data and instructions immediately before and after processing, and the control unit that controls the flow of information on the microprocessor chip. After processing, the data in their original form and the instructions are sent back to a storage place outside the chip.

3. **Discuss the relationships between microprocessor component designs and performance.** Microprocessor designs aim to increase processing speed by minimizing the physical distance that the data (as electrical impulses) must travel, and by increasing the bus width, clock speed, word length, and number of transistors on the chip.

4. **Describe the main types of primary and secondary storage.** There are four types of primary storage: registers, random access memory (RAM), cache memory, and read-only memory (ROM). All are direct-access memory; only ROM is nonvolatile. Secondary storage includes magnetic media (tapes, hard drives, and diskettes) and optical media (CD-ROM, DVD, FMD-ROM, and optical jukeboxes).

5. **Distinguish between primary and secondary storage along the dimensions of speed, cost, and capacity.** Primary storage has much less capacity than secondary storage, and it is faster and more expensive per byte stored. Primary storage is located much closer to the CPU than is secondary storage. Sequential-access secondary storage media such as magnetic tape is much slower and less expensive than direct-access media (e.g., hard drives, optical media).

6. **Define enterprise storage and describe the various types of enterprise storage.** An enterprise storage system is an independent, external system with intelligence that includes two or more storage devices. There are three major types of enterprise storage subsystems: redundant arrays of independent disks (RAIDs), storage area networks (SANs), and network-attached storage (NAS). RAID links groups of standard hard drives to a specialized microcontroller. SAN is an architecture for building special, dedicated networks that allow access to storage devices by multiple servers. A NAS device is a special-purpose server that provides file storage to users who access the device over a network.

7. **Describe the evolution of computer hardware.** Computers have evolved from first generation machines (using vacuum tubes), to second generation (transistors), to third generation (integrated circuits), to fourth generation (very large scale integration, ultra large scale integration, grand scale integration), to fifth generation (massively parallel processing).

8. **Describe the hierarchy of computers according to power and their respective roles.** Supercomputers are the most powerful, designed to handle the maximum computational demands of science and the military. Mainframes are not as powerful as supercomputers, but are powerful enough for use by large organizations for centralized data processing and large databases. Minicomputers are smaller and less powerful versions of mainframes, often devoted to handling specific subsystems. Workstations are in between minicomputers and personal computers in speed, capacity, and graphics capability. Desktop personal computers (PCs) are the most common personal and business computers. Network computers have less computing power and storage, relying on connection to a network for communication, data, processing, and storage resources.

Laptop or notebook computers are small, easily transportable PCs. Personal digital assistants and Internet-enabled cell phones are examples of handheld microcomputers, usually configured for specific applications and limited in the number of ways they can accept user input and provide output. Wearable computers free their users' movements. Embedded computers are placed inside other products to add features and capabilities. Employees may wear active badges as ID cards. Memory buttons store a small database relating to whatever they are attached to. Smart cards contain a small processor, memory, and an input/output device that allows them to be used for personal identification and financial transactions. RFID tags can send or receive large quantities of information without a line of sight to an item.

9. **Differentiate the various types of input and output technologies and their uses.** Principal human data-entry input technologies include the keyboard, mouse, optical mouse, trackball, touchpad, joystick, touchscreen, stylus, and voice-recognition systems. Principal source-data automation input devices are ATMs, POS terminals, barcode scanners, optical mark readers, magnetic ink character readers, optical character readers, sensors, cameras, and retinal scanning displays. Common output technologies include various types of monitors, impact and nonimpact printers, plotters, and voice output.

10. **Describe what multimedia systems are and what technologies they use.** Multimedia computer systems integrate two or more types of media, such as text, graphics, sound, voice, full-motion video, images, and animation. They use a variety of input and output technologies, often including microphones, musical instruments, digitizers, CD-ROM, magnetic tape, and speakers. Multimedia systems typically require additional processing and storage capacity.

11. **Discuss the general trends in hardware technology.** In about 10 years, the cost-performance ratio of computers versus manual work will improve by a factor of 100. This means that computers will have increasingly greater comparative advantage over people in performing certain types of work. In terms of storage, devices are becoming much smaller and storing increasing amounts of information. Self-healing computers have the ability to repair themselves and keep running without human intervention. A sensor web consists of a group of pods (small metal boxes) set up to collect various kinds of information, communicate with nearby pods, and in some cases, communicate wirelessly with outside devices. Nanotechnology refers to the creation of materials, devices, and systems at a scale of 1 to 100 nanometers (billionths of a meter). Finally, researchers are looking into using the basic quantum states of matter as a fundamental unit of computing.

12. **Discuss strategic issues that link hardware design to business strategy.** Strategic issues linking hardware design to business strategy include: How do organizations keep up with the rapid price/performance advancements in hardware? How often should an organization upgrade its computers and storage systems? How can organizations measure benefits gained from price/performance improvements in hardware?

INTERACTIVE / LEARNING

Instructions for accessing the Interactivities on the Student Web Site:

1. Go to
   wiley.com/college/turban
2. Select Turban Rainer Potter's *Introduction to Information Technology, Third Edition*
3. Click on Student Resources Site, in the toolbar on the left
4. Click on Interactivities Web Site
5. Click on Interactivities Web Site and use your password to enter the site (your password card is located in the inside cover of your textbook)

Selecting Hardware Systems
Go to the Interactivities section on the Student Web Site and access Technology Guide 1: Computer Hardware. There you will find some animated, hands-on activities that help you make some decisions about the hardware that will support different businesses ranging from auto parts manufacturing to advertising.

More Resources
More resources and study tools are located on the Student Web Site. You'll find additional chapter materials and links to organizations, people, and technologies for each chapter. In addition, self-quizzes that provide individualized feedback are available for each chapter.

DISCUSSION QUESTIONS

1. What factors affect the speed of a microprocessor?
2. If you were the chief information officer (CIO) of a firm, what factors would you consider when selecting secondary storage media for your company's records (files)?
3. Given that Moore's Law has proven itself over the past two decades, speculate on what chip capabilities will be 10 years in the future. What might your desktop PC be able to do?
4. If you were the chief information officer (CIO) of a firm, how would you explain the workings, benefits, and limitations of a network computer–based system as opposed to using networked PCs (that is, "thin" client vs. "fat" client)?
5. Where might you find embedded computers at home, at school, and/or at work?

INTERNET ACTIVITIES

1. Access the Web sites of the major chip manufacturers, for example Intel (*intel.com*), Motorola (*motorola.com*), and Advanced Micro Devices (*amd.com*), and obtain the latest information regarding new and planned chips. Compare performance and costs across these vendors.
2. Access Intel's Web site (*intel.com*) and visit its museum and the animated microprocessor page. Prepare a presentation of each step in the machine instruction cycle.

TEAM ASSIGNMENTS

Interview your campus CIO and find out on what basis he or she decides to upgrade particular systems. What is the CIO's view of the dynamics of technology advancement, costs of new technologies, costs of in-place systems (sunk costs), and anticipated gains in productivity?

HARDWARE AT CLUB IT

1. What personal computer features are important for Club IT? Consider the major components of a personal computer, and describe what configuration you would recommend for Lisa and Ruben's office.

2. What features would you want in a handheld device for waitstaff? Research the various PDA's available today and make a recommendation.

Go to wiley.com/college/turban to access the CLUB IT Web Site on the Student Web Site

Computer Software

Outline

Learning Objectives

1. Differentiate between the two major types of software.
2. Describe the general functions of the operating system.
3. Differentiate among types of operating systems and describe each type.
4. Identify three methods for developing application software.
5. Describe the major types of application software.
6. Describe the major software issues that organizations face today.
7. Explain how software has evolved and trends for the future.
8. Describe middleware and enterprise software.

TG2.1 SIGNIFICANCE OF SOFTWARE

Computer hardware is only as effective as the instructions we give it, and those instructions are contained in *software*. The importance of computer software cannot be overestimated. The first software applications of computers in business were in the early 1950s. Software was less important (and less costly) in computer systems then, because early hardware was literally hardwired by hand for each application. Today, software comprises a much larger percentage of the cost of modern computer systems. The price of hardware has dramatically decreased, while the complexity, and consequently the price, of software has dramatically increased.

The increasing complexity of software also leads to the increased potential for errors or bugs. Large applications today may contain millions of lines of computer code, written by hundreds of people over the course of several years. The potential for errors is huge, and testing and *debugging* software is expensive and time-consuming.

Regardless of the overall trends in software (increased complexity, increased cost, increasing numbers of defects, increased usage of open source software), software is ubiquitous in our business and personal lives. Keep in mind that, regardless of your major, you will be involved with the various types of software from the beginning and throughout your career.

Software Fundamentals

computer programs *The sequences of instructions for the computer, which comprise software.*

stored program concept *Modern hardware architecture in which stored software programs are accessed and their instructions are executed (followed) in the computer's CPU, one after another.*

documentation *Written description of the functions of a software program.*

Software consists of **computer programs**, which are sequences of instructions for the computer. The process of writing (or *coding*) programs is called *programming*, and individuals who perform this task are called *programmers*.

Unlike the hardwired computers of the 1950s, modern software uses the **stored program concept**, in which stored software programs are accessed and their instructions are executed (followed) in the computer's CPU. Once the program has finished executing, a new program is loaded into the main memory and the computer hardware addresses another task.

Computer programs include **documentation**, which is a written description of the functions of the program. Documentation helps the user operate the computer system and helps other programmers understand what the program does and how it accomplishes its purpose. Documentation is vital to the business organization. Without it, if a key programmer or user leaves, the knowledge of how to use the program or how it is designed may be lost.

The computer is able to do nothing until it is instructed by software. Although computer hardware is, by design, general purpose, software enables the user to instruct a computer system to perform specific functions that provide business value. There are two major types of software: systems software and application software. The relationship among hardware, systems software, and application software is illustrated in Figure TG2.1.

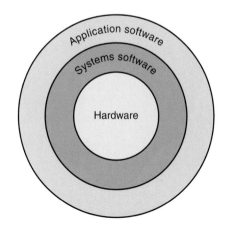

Figure TG2.1 *Systems software services as intermediary between hardware and functional applications.*

Systems software is a set of instructions that serves primarily as an intermediary between computer hardware and application programs, and may also be directly manipulated by knowledgeable users. Systems software provides important self-regulatory functions for computer systems, such as loading itself when the computer is first turned on, managing hardware resources such as secondary storage for all applications, and providing commonly used sets of instructions for all applications to use. *Systems programming* is either the creation or maintenance of systems software.

Application software is a set of computer instructions that provide more specific functionality to a user. That functionality may be broad, such as general word processing, or narrow, such as an organization's payroll program. An application program applies a computer to a certain need. *Application programming* is either the creation or the modification and improvement of application software. Application software may be proprietary or off-the-shelf. There are many different software applications in organizations today, as this chapter will discuss.

> **systems software** *The class of computer instructions that serve primarily as an intermediary between computer hardware and application programs; provides important self-regulatory functions for computer systems.*

> **application software** *The class of computer instructions that direct a computer system to perform specific processing activities and provide functionality for users.*

Before you go on . . .

1. What does this statement mean: "Hardware is useless without software"?
2. What are differences between systems software and application software?

TG2.2 SYSTEMS SOFTWARE

Systems software is the class of programs that control and support the computer system and its information-processing activities. Systems software also facilitates the programming, testing, and debugging of computer programs. Systems software programs support application software by directing the basic functions of the computer. For example, when the computer is turned on, the initialization program (a systems program) prepares and readies all devices for processing.

Systems software can be grouped into two major functional categories: system control programs and system support programs.

System Control Programs

System control programs control the use of the hardware, software, and data resources of a computer system. The main system control program is the operating system. The **operating system** supervises the overall operation of the computer, including monitoring the computer's status and scheduling operations, which include the input and output processes. In addition, the operating system allocates CPU time and main memory to programs running on the computer, and it also provides an interface between the user and the hardware. This interface hides the complexity of the hardware from the user. That is, you do not have to know how the hardware actually operates, just what the hardware will do and what you need to do to obtain desired results.

The operating system manages the program or programs (also called jobs) running on the processor at a given time. In the simplest case (a desktop operating system), the operating system loads a program into main memory and executes it. The program utilizes the computer's resources until it relinquishes control. Some operating systems offer more sophisticated forms of program management, such as *multitasking*, *multithreading*, and *multiprocessing*.

The management of two or more tasks, or programs, running on the computer system at the same time is called **multitasking**, or **multiprogramming**. The first program is executed until an interruption occurs, such as a request for input. While the input request is handled, the execution of a second program begins. Because switching among these programs occurs so rapidly, they appear to be executing at the same time. However, because there is only one processor, only one program is actually executing at

> **system control programs** *Software programs that controls the use of the hardware, software, and data resources of a computer system.*

> **operating system** *The main system control program, which supervises the overall operations of the computer, allocates CPU time and main memory to programs, and provides an interface between the user and the hardware.*

> **multitasking/multiprogramming** *The management of two or more tasks, or programs, running concurrently on the computer system (one CPU).*

multithreading *A form of multitasking that runs multiple tasks within a single application simultaneously.*

multiprocessing *Simultaneous processing of more than one program by assigning them to different processors (multiple CPUs).*

virtual memory *A feature that simulates more main memory than actually exists in the computer system by extending primary storage into secondary storage.*

graphical user interface (GUI) *System software that allows users to have direct control of visible objects (such as icons) and actions, which replace command syntax.*

social interface *A user interface that guides the user through computer applications by using cartoonlike characters, graphics, animation, and voice commands.*

operating environment *A set of computer programs that add features that enable developers to create applications without directly accessing the operating system; function only* with *an operating system.*

plug-and-play *Feature that enables the operating system to recognize new hardware and install the necessary software (called device drivers) automatically.*

any one time. Multithreading is a form of multitasking that focuses on running multiple tasks within a single application simultaneously. For example, a word processor application may edit one document while another document is being spell-checked.

Multiprocessing occurs when a computer system with two or more processors can run more than one program, or thread, at a given time by assigning them to different processors. Multiprocessing uses simultaneous processing with multiple CPUs, whereas multiprogramming involves concurrent processing with one CPU.

Virtual memory simulates more main memory than actually exists in the computer system. It allows a program to behave as if it had access to the full storage capacity of a computer, rather than just access to the amount of primary storage installed on the computer. Virtual memory divides an application program or module into fixed-length portions called *pages*. The system executes some pages of instructions while pulling others from secondary storage. In effect, virtual memory allows users to write programs as if primary storage were larger than it actually is.

The ease or difficulty of the interaction between the user and the computer is to a large extent determined by the *interface design*. Older text-based interfaces like DOS (*d*isk *o*perating *s*ystem) required typing in cryptic commands. In an effort to make computers more user-friendly, the graphical user interface was developed.

The graphical user interface (GUI) allows users to have direct control of visible objects (such as icons) and actions that replace complex command syntax. The GUI was developed by researchers at Xerox PARC (Palo Alto Research Center), and then popularized by the Apple MacIntosh computer. Microsoft soon introduced its GUI-based Windows operating system for IBM-style PCs.

The next generation of GUI technology will incorporate features such as virtual reality, head-mounted displays, sound and speech, pen and gesture recognition, animation, multimedia, artificial intelligence, and cellular/wireless communication capabilities. Future GUIs also will provide social interfaces. A social interface is a user interface that guides the user through computer applications by using cartoonlike characters, graphics, animation, and voice commands. The cartoonlike characters can be cast as puppets, narrators, guides, inhabitants, or avatars (computer-generated humanlike figures).

Types of Operating Systems.   As previously discussed, operating systems are necessary in order for computer hardware to function. Operating environments are sets of computer programs that add features that enable system developers to create applications without directly accessing the operating system; they function only *with* an operating system. That is, operating environments are not operating systems, but work only with an operating system. For example, the early versions of Windows were operating environments that provided a graphical user interface and worked only with MS-DOS.

Operating systems (OSs) are classified into different types depending on the number of users they support as well as their level of sophistication. *Operating systems for mobile devices* are designed to support a single person using a mobile, handheld device, or information appliance. Small computer operating systems (*desktop operating systems* and *workstation operating systems*) are designed to support a single user or a small workgroup of users. Large computer operating systems (*midrange computer operating systems* and *mainframe operating systems*) typically support from a few dozen to thousands of users. Large computer operating systems offer greater functionality than the other types of OS. These functions include reliability, backup, security, fault tolerance, and rapid processing speeds. However, the user interface is an important exception, as it is most sophisticated on desktop operating systems and least sophisticated on large computer operating systems.

The Windows family of operating systems is the dominant small computer operating system. It runs on laptops, notebooks, desktops, and servers. The current version, *Windows XP*, provides a GUI with icons to provide instant access to common tasks and plug-and-play capabilities. Plug-and-play is a feature that can automate the installation of new hardware by enabling the operating system to recognize new hardware and install the necessary software (called device drivers) automatically. Other common operating systems include UNIX, the Macintosh operating system X (ten) (*Mac OS X*) for Apple Macintosh computers, IBM's OS/2, Linux, and Java.

Linux is a powerful version of the UNIX operating system that is open source software. Open source software means that the Linux source code is publicly and freely available. Therefore, programmers around the world work on Linux and write software for it. The result is that, like UNIX, Linux now runs on multiple hardware platforms, can support many different hardware devices, and has numerous applications written to run on it. Linux is becoming widely used by Internet service providers (ISPs), the companies that provide Internet connections and is gaining in market share in enterprise servers. The Linux information clearinghouse is *linuxhq.com*.

Sun's **Java operating system (JavaOS)** executes programs written in the Java language (described later in this chapter) without the need for a traditional operating system. It is designed for Internet and intranet applications, embedded devices, handheld products, and thin-client computing. (For a more technical discussion of the various desktop and notebook computer operating systems—MS-DOS and Windows, Linux, and Apple Macintosh—see Online File W-TG2.1.)

Linux *A powerful version of the UNIX operating system that is open source software (publicly and freely available).*

Java operating system (JavaOS) *Operating system designed to execute programs written in Java, for Internet and intranet applications, embedded devices, handheld products, and thin-client computing.*

wiley.com/college/turban

System Support Programs

The second major category of systems software, **system support programs**, supports the operations, management, and users of a computer system by providing a variety of support services. Examples of system support programs are system utility programs, performance monitors, and security monitors.

System utilities are programs that have been written to accomplish common tasks such as sorting records, checking the integrity of diskettes (i.e., amount of storage available and existence of any damage), and creating directories and subdirectories. They also restore accidentally erased files, locate files within the directory structure, and manage memory usage. **System performance monitors** are programs that monitor the processing of jobs on a computer system. They monitor computer system performance, in areas such as processor time, memory space, input/output devices, and system and application programs. **System security monitors** are programs that monitor the use of a computer system to protect it and its resources from unauthorized use, fraud, or destruction.

system support programs *Software that supports the operations, management, and users of a computer system by providing a variety of support services (e.g., system utility programs, performance monitors, and security monitors).*

system utilities *Programs that accomplish common tasks such as sorting records, creating directories and subdirectories, locating files, and managing memory usage.*

system performance monitors *Programs that monitor the processing of jobs on a computer system and monitor system performance in areas such as processor time, memory space, and application programs.*

system security monitors *Programs that monitor a computer system to protect it and its resources from unauthorized use, fraud, or destruction.*

Before you go on . . .

1. What are the two main types of systems software?
2. What are differences among mobile device, desktop, departmental server, enterprise, and supercomputer operating systems?

TG2.3 APPLICATION SOFTWARE

As defined earlier, application software consists of instructions that direct a computer system to perform specific information processing activities and that provide functionality for users. Because there are so many different uses for computers, there are a correspondingly large number of different application software programs available.

proprietary application software *Software that addresses a specific or unique business need for a company; may be developed in-house or may be commissioned from a software vendor.*

Types of Application Software

Application software includes proprietary application software and off-the-shelf application software. **Proprietary application software** addresses a specific or unique business need for a company. This type of software may be developed in-house by the organization's information systems personnel or may be commissioned from a software vendor. Such specific software programs developed for a particular company by a vendor are called **contract software**.

Alternatively, **off-the-shelf application software** can be purchased, leased, or rented from a vendor that develops programs and sells them to many organizations.

contract software *Specific software programs developed for a particular company by a vendor.*

off-the-shelf application software *Software purchased, leased, or rented from a vendor that develops programs and sells them to many organizations; can be standard or customizable.*

Off-the-shelf software may be a standard package or it may be customizable. Special-purpose programs or "packages" can be tailored for a specific purpose, such as inventory control or payroll. The word package is a commonly used term for a computer program (or group of programs) that has been developed by a vendor and is available for purchase in a prepackaged form. We will further discuss the methodology involved in acquiring application software, whether proprietary or off-the-shelf, in Chapter 11.

package *Common term for a computer program developed by a vendor and is available for purchase in prepackaged form.*

Types of Personal Application Software

General-purpose, off-the-shelf application programs that support general types of processing, rather than being linked to any specific business function, are referred to as personal application software. This type of software consists of nine widely used packages: spreadsheet, data management, word processing, desktop publishing, graphics, multimedia, communications, speech-recognition software, and groupware. *Software suites* combine some of these packages and integrate their functions.

personal application software *General-purpose, off-the-shelf application programs that support general types of processing, rather than being linked to any specific business function.*

Personal application software is designed to help individual users increase their productivity. Below is a description of the nine main types.

Spreadsheets.
Computer spreadsheet software transforms a computer screen into a ledger sheet, or grid, of coded rows and columns. Users can enter numeric or textual data into each grid location, called a *cell*. In addition, a formula can be entered into a cell to obtain a calculated answer displayed in that cell's location. With spreadsheets, users can also develop and use macros, which are sequences of commands that can be executed with just one simple instruction.

spreadsheet software *Software that uses a grid of coded rows and columns to display numeric or textual data in cells.*

macros *Sequences of commands used in spreadsheet software that can be executed with just one simple instruction.*

Computer spreadsheet packages can be used for financial information, such as income statements or cash flow analysis. They are also used for forecasting sales, analyzing insurance programs, summarizing income tax data, and analyzing investments. They are relevant for many other types of data that can be organized into rows and columns. Although spreadsheet packages such as Microsoft's Excel and Lotus 1-2-3 are thought of primarily as spreadsheets, they also offer data management and graphical capabilities. Therefore, they may be called integrated packages. Figure TG2.2 shows an example of a spreadsheet format.

integrated packages *Spreadsheet packages that offer data management and graphical capabilities in addition to regular spreadsheet functionality.*

Spreadsheets are valuable for applications that require modeling and what-if analysis. After a set of mathematical relationships has been specified by the user, the spreadsheet can be recalculated instantly using a different set of assumptions (i.e., a different set of mathematical relationships).

Data Management.
Data management software supports the storage, retrieval, and manipulation of related data. There are two basic types of data management software: *Simple filing programs* are patterned after traditional, manual data-filing techniques. *Database management programs* take advantage of a computer's extremely fast and accurate ability to store and retrieve data in primary and secondary storage. File-based management software is typically very simple to use and is often very fast, but it offers limited flexibility in how the data can be searched. Database management software has the opposite strengths and weaknesses. Microsoft's Access is an example of popular database management software. In Chapter 3, we discuss data management in much more detail.

data management software *Software that supports the storage, retrieval, and manipulation of related data.*

Word Processing.
Word processing software allows the user to manipulate text rather than just numbers. Modern word processors contain many productive writing and editing features. A typical word processing software package consists of an integrated set

word processing software *Software that allows the user to manipulate text using many writing and editing features.*

Student Name	Exam 1	Exam 2	Exam 3	Total Points	Grade
Carr, Harold	73	95	90	258	B
Ford, Nelson	92	90	81	263	B
Lewis, Bruce	86	88	98	272	A
Snyder, Charles	63	71	76	210	C
Average	78.5	86.0	86.25	250.75	

Figure TG2.2 *Sample calculation of student grades in a spreadsheet.*

of programs including an editor program, a formatting program, a print program, a dictionary, a thesaurus, a grammar checker, a mailing list program, and integrated graphics, charting, and drawing programs. WYSIWYG (an acronym for "what you see is what you get," pronounced "wiz-e-wig") word processors have the added advantage of displaying the text material on the screen exactly—or almost exactly—as it will look on the final printed page (based on the type of printer connected to the computer). Word processing software enables users to be much more productive because the software makes it possible to create and modify the document electronically in memory.

WYSIWYG   *Acronym for "what you see is what you get" (pronounced "wiz-e-wig"), indicating that text material is displayed on the computer screen just as it will look on the final printed page.*

Desktop Publishing.   **Desktop publishing software** represents a level of sophistication beyond regular word processing. In the past, newsletters, announcements, advertising copy, and other specialized documents had to be laid out by hand and then typeset. Desktop software allows microcomputers to perform these tasks directly. Photographs, diagrams, and other images can be combined with text, including several different fonts, to produce a finished, camera-ready document.

desktop publishing software   *Software that enables microcomputers to combine photographs and graphic images with text, to produce a finished, camera-ready document.*

Graphics.   **Graphics software** enables the user to create, store, and display or print charts, graphs, maps, and drawings. Graphics software enables users to absorb more information more quickly and to spot relationships and trends in data more easily. There are three basic categories of graphics software packages: presentation graphics, analysis graphics, and computer-aided design software.

graphics software   *Software that enables the user to create, store, and display or print charts, graphs, maps, and drawings.*

Presentation graphics software enables users to create graphically rich presentations. Many packages have extensive libraries of clip art—pictures that can be electronically "clipped out" and "pasted" into the finished image. Figure TG2.3 demonstrates some of the capabilities of presentation graphics. One of the most widely used presentation graphics programs is Microsoft's PowerPoint.

presentation graphics software   *Software that enables users to create graphically rich presentations by "pasting" graphic images into a textual presentation.*

Analysis graphics software additionally provides the ability to convert previously analyzed data—such as statistical data—into graphic formats like bar charts, line charts, pie charts, and scatter diagrams. Both presentation graphics and analysis graphics are useful in preparing graphic displays for business presentations, from sales results to marketing research data.

analysis graphics software   *Software that provides the ability to convert previously analyzed data into graphic formats (e.g., bar charts, pie charts).*

Computer-aided design (CAD) software, used for designing items for manufacturing, allows designers to design and "build" production prototypes in software, test them as a computer object under given parameters (sometimes called *computer-aided engineering*, or *CAE*), compile parts and quantity lists, outline production and assembly procedures, and then transmit the final design directly to machines. The prototype in Figure TG2.4 was produced via computer-aided design.

Manufacturers of all sorts are finding uses for CAD software. *Computer-aided manufacturing (CAM)* software uses digital design output, such as that from a CAD system, to

computer-aided design (CAD) software   *Software that allows designers to design and "build" production prototypes in software, test them, compile parts lists, outline assembly procedures, and then transmit the final design directly to machines.*

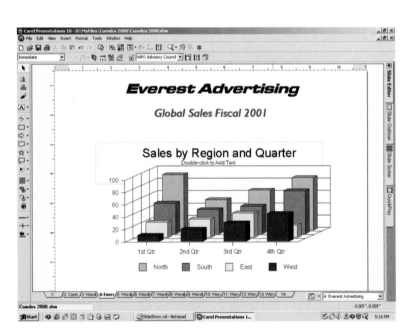

Figure TG2.3   *Presentation graphics software.*

Figure TG2.4   *Computer-aided design (CAD).*

directly control production machinery. *Computer-integrated manufacturing (CIM)* software is embedded within each automated production machine to produce a product. Overall, a design from CAD software is used by CAM software to control individual CIM programs in individual machines. Used effectively, CAD/CAM/CIM software can dramatically shorten development time and give firms the advantage of economies of scope.

Multimedia.   Multimedia software combines at least two media for input or output of data. These media include audio (sound), voice, animation, video, text, graphics, and images. Multimedia can also be thought of as the combination of *spatially* based media (text and images) with *time*-based media (sound and video).

multimedia software *Software that combines spatially based media (text and images) with time-based media (sound and video) for input or output of data.*

Communications.   Computers are often interconnected in order to share or relate information. To exchange information, computers utilize communications software. This software allows computers, whether they are located close together or far apart, to exchange data over dedicated or public cables, telephone lines, satellite relay systems, or microwave circuits.

When communications software exists in both the sending and receiving computers, they are able to establish and relinquish electronic links, code and decode data transmissions, verify transmission errors (and correct them automatically), and check for and handle transmission interruptions or conflicting transmission priorities. E-mail and desktop videoconferencing rely on communications software.

communications software *Software that allows computers, wherever they are located, to exchange data via cables, telephone lines, satellite relay systems, or microwave circuits.*

Speech-Recognition Software.   Two categories of speech-recognition software are available today: discrete speech and continuous speech. *Discrete speech recognition* can interpret only one word at a time, so users must place distinct pauses between words. This type of voice recognition can be used to control PC software (by using words such as "execute" or "print"). But it is inadequate for dictating a memo, because users find it difficult to speak with measurable pauses between every word and still maintain trains of thought.

Software for *continuous speech recognition* can interpret a continuing stream of words. The software must understand the context of a word to determine its correct spelling, and be able to overcome accents and interpret words very quickly. These requirements mean that continuous speech-recognition software must have a computer with significantly more speed and memory than discrete speech software.

Many firms and people use speech-recognition software when use of a mouse and a keyboard is impractical. For example, such software can provide an excellent alternative for users with disabilities, repetitive strain injuries, or severe arthritis.

speech-recognition software *Software that recognizes and interprets human speech, either one word at a time (discrete speech) or in a stream (continuous speech).*

Groupware.   Groupware is a class of software products that facilitates communication, coordination, and collaboration among people. Groupware is important because it allows workgroups—people who need to interact with one another within an organization—to communicate and share information, even when they are working together at a distance. As discussed in Chapter 4, groupware can provide many benefits to businesses, including more efficient and effective project management, location independence, increased communications capability, increased information availability, and improved workflow.

groupware *Software that facilitates communication, coordination, and collaboration among people.*

Groupware comes in many varieties. The most elaborate system, IBM's Lotus Notes/Domino, is a document-management system, a distributed client/server database, and a basis for intranet and electronic commerce systems, as well as a communication support tool. This class of groupware supplements real-time communications with asynchronous electronic connections (e.g., electronic mail and other forms of messaging). Thanks to electronic networks, e-mail, and shared discussion databases, group members can communicate, access data, and exchange or update data at any time and from any place. Group members might store all their official memos, formal reports, and informal conversations related to particular projects in a shared, online data store, such as a database. Then, as individual members need to check on the contents, they can access the shared database to find the information they need.

Other groupware approaches focus on workflow, enhanced electronic mail (e.g., listserve), calendaring and scheduling, electronic meeting support, and videoconferencing. Microsoft's Exchange is primarily an electronic messaging server that incorporates groupware functionality for sharing information. It provides e-mail and supports workgroup activities with additional features such as interactive scheduling, built-in access to shared bulletin boards, forms design, and access to publicly shared folders on computer networks. It also offers built-in connectivity to the Internet or corporate intranets. Other leading groupware products provide functionality similar to Microsoft Exchange. These products include Netscape's SuiteSpot Servers, Novell's GroupWise, and Oracle's InterOffice. (For common groupware features, see Online File W-TG2.2.)

wiley.com/college/turban

Before you go on . . .

1. What classes of personal application software are essential for the productivity of a business or other organization with which you are familiar? Which are nonessential?

2. How can groupware add strategic advantage in that business/organization?

TG2.4 SOFTWARE ISSUES

The importance of software in computer systems has brought new issues to the forefront for organizational managers. These issues include software defects (bugs), "alien" software, software evaluation and selection, licensing, upgrades, open systems, and open source software.

Software Defects

All too often, computer program code is inefficient, poorly designed, and riddled with errors. Carnegie Mellon University's Software Engineering Institute (SEI) says that good software is usable, reliable, defect free, cost effective, and maintainable. In the last 15 years alone, software defects have wrecked a European satellite launch, delayed the opening of Denver International Airport for a year, and destroyed a NASA Mars mission. In another example, on the same day that Microsoft first released Windows XP, the company posted 18 megabytes of patches on its Web site: bug fixes, compatibility updates, and enhancements. With our dependence on computers and networks, the risks are getting worse.

On average, SEI says that professional programmers make 100 to 150 errors in every thousand lines of code they write. Using SEI's figures, Windows XP, with its 41 million lines of code, would have over 4 million bugs. The industry recognizes the problem, but it is so enormous that only initial steps are being taken. One step is better design and planning at the beginning of the development process (discussed in Chapter 11).

Alien Software

Many personal computers have alien software running on them that the owners do not know about. There are different types of alien software.

pestware *Clandestine software that becomes installed on your PC through duplicitous channels; also called* malware *or* scumware.

adware *Software that is designed to facilitate the propagation of pop-up advertisements on your screen.*

spyware *Software that records your keystrokes and/or your passwords.*

spamware *Software designed to use your computer as a launch pad for spammers.*

Pestware, also called *malware* or *scumware*, is clandestine software that becomes installed on your PC through duplicitous channels, often by the vendor or perpetrator tricking you to install it under the guise of so-called advantages to you. Pestware typically is not as malicious as a virus, but it does use up valuable system resources, and it can report on your Web surfing habits and other personal behavior. Analysts estimate that up to 90 percent of all PCs are affected by pestware. One clear indication that software is pestware is if it does not come with an uninstaller program. An *uninstaller* is an automated program that systematically and efficiently removes a particular software package in its entirety.

The vast majority of pestware is **adware**—software that is designed to facilitate the propagation of pop-up advertisements on your screen. Most adware works by trying to display targeted ads to your machine. Adware producers often require you to consent to the installation of the adware, by duping you into thinking you are downloading freeware such as an atomic clock program, a local weather forecasting program, or other innocuous sounding tools.

Well-known adware packages include: BroadcastPC, CasinoOnNet, Comet Cursor, Download Receiver, ExactSearch, GAIN, GeoWhere, Moe Money Maker, Netsonic, Network Essentials, Offer Companion, RespondMiter, SuperBar, and WildTangent.

Some pestware is **spyware**. Spyware programs include keylogger programs that record your keystrokes, password capture programs that record your passwords, and **spamware** designed to use your computer as a launch pad for spammers. *Trojan horse* programs are another type of spyware designed to open your system so that it can be remotely administered by unauthorized users.

Unfortunately, most antivirus programs do not remove or block pestware. However, there are *antipestware* products that actively prevent pestware from running in memory. These pestware-elimination products include:

- Ad-aware (*lavasoft.element5.com/default.shtml.en*)
- Anti-Trojan5.5 (*anti-trojan.net*)
- PestPatrol (*pestpatrol.com*)
- SpyBot Search & Destroy (*safer-networking.org*)
- SpySweeper (*webroot.com*)
- Xcleaner (*xblock.com*)

Software Evaluation and Selection

The software evaluation and selection decision is a difficult one because it is affected by many factors. Manager's Checklist TG2.1 summarizes these selection factors. The first part of the selection process involves understanding the organization's software needs and identifying the criteria that will be used in making the eventual decision. Once the software requirements are established, specific software should be evaluated. An evaluation team composed of representatives from every group that will have a role in using the software should be chosen for the evaluation process. The team will study the proposed alternatives and find the software that promises the best match between the organization's needs and the software capabilities.

Software Licensing

Although many people do so routinely, copying software is illegal. The Software Publishers Association has stated that software piracy amounts to approximately $15 billion annually.

To protect their investment, software vendors must protect their software from being copied and distributed by individuals and other software companies. A company can copyright its software, which means that the U.S. Copyright Office grants the company the exclusive legal right to reproduce, publish, and sell that software. The Software Publisher's Association (SPA) enforces software copyright laws in corporations by auditing companies to see that the software used is properly licensed.

MANAGER'S CHECKLIST TG2.1

Software Selection Factors

Factor	Considerations
Size and location of user base	❑ Does the proposed software support a few users in a single location? ❑ Can it accommodate large numbers of geographically dispersed users?
Availability of system administration tools	❑ Does the software offer tools that monitor system usage? ❑ Does it maintain a list of authorized users and provide the level of security needed?
Costs—initial and subsequent	❑ Is the software affordable, taking into account all costs, including installation, training, and maintenance?
System capabilities	❑ Does the software meet both current and anticipated future needs?
Existing computing environment	❑ Is the software compatible with existing hardware, software, and communications networks?
In-house technical skills	❑ Should the organization develop software applications in-house ❑ Should the organization purchase applications off the shelf or contract software out of house?

As the number of desktop computers continues to increase and businesses continue to decentralize, it becomes more and more difficult for IS managers to manage their software assets. As a result, new firms have sprouted up to specialize in tracking software licenses for a fee. Firms such as ASAP Software, Software Spectrum, and others will track and manage a company's software licenses, to ensure that company's compliance with U.S. copyright laws.

Software Upgrades

Another issue of interest to IS management is software upgrades. Software vendors frequently revise their programs and sell new versions. The revised software may offer valuable enhancements. Or it may offer little in terms of additional capabilities, and may even contain bugs. Deciding whether to purchase the newest software can be a problem for IS managers. It is also difficult to decide whether to be one of the first companies to buy and take strategic advantage of new software before competitors do, but risk falling prey to previously undiscovered bugs.

Open Systems

The concept of **open systems** refers to a model of computing products that work together. Achieving this goal is possible through the use of the same operating system with compatible software on all the different computers that would interact with one another in an organization. A complementary approach is to produce application software that will run across all computer platforms. If hardware, operating systems, and application software are designed as open systems, the user would be able to purchase the best software for the job without worrying whether it will run on particular hardware. Recent advances toward the open-systems goal involve using the Java language, which can be run on many types of computers, in place of a traditional operating system. Programs written in Java can then be executed by any machine (as will be explained in a later section).

open systems *A model of computing products that work together, by use of the same operating system with compatible software on all the different computers that would interact with one another in an organization.*

Open Source Software

Open systems should not be confused with open source software. As discussed in the chapter opening case, **open source software** is software made available in source code

open source software *Software made available in source code form at no cost to developers.*

form at no cost to developers. There are many examples of open-source software, including the GNU (GNU's Not UNIX) suite of software (*gnu.org*) developed by the Free Software Foundation (*fsf.org*); the Linux operating system; Apache Web server (*apache.org*); sendmail SMTP (Send Mail Transport Protocol) e-mail server (*sendmail.org*); the Perl programming language (*perl.com*), the Netscape Mozilla browser (*mozilla.org*); and Sun's StarOffice applications suite (*sun.com*).

Open source software is, in many cases, more reliable than commercial software. Because the code is available to many developers, more bugs are discovered, are discovered early and quickly, and are fixed immediately. Support for open source software is also available from companies that provide products derived from the software, for example, Red Hat for Linux (*redhat.com*). These firms provide education, training, and technical support for the software for a fee.

Before you go on . . .

1. What are some of the legal issues involved in acquiring and using software in most business organizations?

2. What are some of the criteria used for evaluating software when planning a purchase?

3. What is open source software and what are its advantages?

TG2.5 PROGRAMMING LANGUAGES

Programming languages provide the basic building blocks for all systems and application software. Programming languages allow people to tell computers what to do and are the means by which software systems are developed. This section will describe the five generations of programming languages. Table TG2.1 provides an overview of the basic features of the generations of programming languages.

Machine Language

machine language *The lowest-level programming language, composed of binary digits.*

Machine language is the lowest-level computer language, consisting of the internal representation of instructions and data. This machine code—the actual instructions understood and directly executable by the central processing unit—is composed of binary digits. Machine language is the only programming language that the machine ac-

Table TG2.1 Language Generations Table

Features	Generations			
	First Machine	Second Assembly	Third Procedural	Fourth Nonprocedural
Portable (machine independent)	No	No	Yes	Yes
Concise (1:many)	No	No	Yes	Yes
Use of mnemonics and labels	No	Yes	Yes	Yes
Procedural	Yes	Yes	Yes	No
Structured	Yes	Yes	Yes	No
User friendly	No	No	Somewhat	Yes
Machine intensive (processor time)	No	No	Somewhat	Much
Programmer time	Extreme	Much	Somewhat	Little

tually understands. Therefore, machine language is considered the **first-generation language**. All other languages must be translated into machine language before the computer can run the instructions.

Machine language is extremely difficult to understand and use by programmers. As a result, increasingly more user-friendly languages have been developed, making it easier and less time-consuming for people to program using them. However, additional processor time is required to translate the program before it can be executed.

Assembly Language

Assembly language is still considered a lower-level language but is more user-friendly because it represents machine-language instructions with *mnemonics*, or memory aids, which people can more easily use. Assembly languages are considered second-generation languages. Translating an assembly language program into machine language is accomplished by a systems software program called an assembler.

Procedural Languages

Procedural languages are the next step in the evolution of user-oriented programming languages. They are also called third-generation languages, or 3GLs. Procedural languages are considered the first level of *higher-level languages*.

Procedural languages require the programmer to specify, step by step, exactly how the computer must accomplish a task. A procedural language is oriented toward how a result is to be produced. Language translators convert the high-level program, called *source code*, into machine language code, called *object code*. There are two types of language translators—interpreters and compilers.

The translation of a high-level language program to object code is accomplished by a software program called a compiler, which translates the entire program at once. In contrast, an interpreter is a compiler that translates and executes one source program statement at a time. Because this translation is done one statement at a time, interpreters tend to be simpler than compilers. This simplicity allows for more extensive debugging and diagnostic aids to be available on interpreters. For examples of FORTRAN, COBOL, and C, see Online File W-TG2.3.

Nonprocedural Languages

Another type of high-level language, called nonprocedural languages, allows the user to specify the desired result without having to specify the detailed procedures needed for achieving the result. These languages are fourth-generation languages (4GLs). An advantage of nonprocedural languages is that they can be used by nontechnical users to carry out specific functional tasks. These languages greatly simplify and accelerate the programming process, as well as reduce the number of coding errors. The 4GLs are common in database applications as query languages, report generators, and data-manipulation languages. They allow users and programmers to interrogate and access computer databases using statements that resemble natural language.

Visual Programming Languages

Programming languages that are used within a graphical environment are often referred to as visual programming languages. These languages use a mouse, icons, symbols on the screen, or pull-down menus to make programming easier and more intuitive. Visual Basic and Visual C++ are examples of visual programming languages. Their ease of use makes them popular with nontechnical users, but the languages often lack the specificity and power of their nonvisual counterparts. Although programming in visual languages is popular in some organizations, the more complex and mission-critical applications are usually not written in visual languages.

---

first-generation language *Machine language; the level of programming languages actually understood by a CPU.*

assembly language *A lower-level programming language that is slightly more user-friendly than machine language.*

second-generation language *Assembly language; requires that each statement be translated into machine language through use of an assembler.*

assembler *A systems software program that translates an assembly language program into machine language.*

procedural languages *User-oriented programming languages, which require programmers to specify step by step how the computer must accomplish a task.*

third-generation languages *The first level of higher-level programming languages, which are closer to natural language and therefore easier for programmers to use.*

compiler *Software program that translates an entire high-level language program into object code at once.*

wiley.com/college/turban

interpreter *A compiler that translates and executes one source program statement at a time.*

nonprocedural languages *A type of high-level language that enables users to specify the desired result without having to specify the detailed procedures needed for achieving the result.*

fourth-generation languages (4GLs) *A type of high-level programming languages, which can be used by nontechnical users to carry out specific functional tasks.*

visual programming languages *Programming languages that use a mouse, icons, symbols on the screen, or pull-down menus to make programming easier and more intuitive.*

Hypertext Markup Language

hypertext *An approach to data management in which data are stored in a network of nodes connected by links and are accessed through interactive browsing.*

hyperlinks *The links that connect data nodes in hypertext.*

hypertext document *The combination of nodes, links, and supporting indexes for any particular topic in hypertext.*

Hypertext Markup Language (HTML) *The standard programming language used on the Web to create and recognize hypertext documents.*

dynamic HTML *The next step beyond HTML, which lets users interact with the content of richly formatted pages without having to download additional content from the server.*

cascading style sheet (CSS) *An enhancement to HTML that adds page layout features to Web documents.*

Extensible Markup Language (XML) *A programming language designed to improve the functionality of Web documents by providing more flexible and adaptable data identification.*

Hypertext is an approach to data management in which data are stored in a network of nodes connected by links (called **hyperlinks**). Users access data through an interactive browsing system. The combination of nodes, links, and supporting indexes for any particular topic is a **hypertext document**. A hypertext document may contain text, images, and other types of information such as data files, audio, video, and executable computer programs.

The standard language the World Wide Web uses for creating and recognizing hypertext documents is the **Hypertext Markup Language (HTML)**. HTML gives users the option of controlling visual elements such as fonts, font size, and paragraph spacing without changing the original information. HTML is very easy to use, and some modern word processing applications will automatically convert and store a conventional document in HTML. Dynamic HTML is the next step beyond HTML. **Dynamic HTML** presents richly formatted pages and lets the user interact with the content of those pages without having to download additional content from the server. This functionality means that Web pages using Dynamic HTML provide more exciting and useful information.

Enhancements and variations of HTML make possible new layout and design features on Web pages. For example, **cascading style sheets (CSSs)** are an enhancement to HTML that act as a template defining the appearance or style (such as size, color, and font) of an element of a Web page, such as a box.

Extensible Markup Language

Extensible Markup Language (XML) is designed to improve the functionality of Web documents by providing more flexible and adaptable information identification. XML describes what the data in documents actually mean. XML documents can be moved to any format on any platform without the elements losing their meaning. That means the same information can be published to a Web browser, a PDA, or a smartphone, and each device would use the information appropriately. Figure TG2.5 compares HTML and XML. Notice that HTML only describes where an item appears on a page, whereas XML describes what the item is. For example, HTML shows only that "Introduction to MIS" appears on line 1, where XML shows that "Introduction to MIS" is the Course Title.

Componentware

componentware *A term used to describe component-based software applications.*

software components *The "building blocks" of applications, which can be used again and again by the applications.*

Componentware is a term used to describe component-based software applications. **Software components** are the "building blocks" of applications. They provide the operations that can be used again and again by the application (or other applications). Any given application may contain hundreds of components, each providing specific business logic or user-interface functionality.

Consider a database application as an example: The data-entry screen may contain several user-interface components for providing buttons, menus, list boxes, and so forth. There may also be business logic components to perform validation or calculations on the data, as well as components to write the data to the database. Finally,

English Text	HTML	XML
MNGT 3070	`<TITLE>Course Number</TITLE>`	`<Department and course="MNGT 3070">`
Introduction to MIS	`<BODY>`	`<COURSE TITLE>Introduction to MIS<COURSE TITLE>`
3 semester hours	`<UL>`	`<HOURS UNIT="Semester">3</NUMBER OF HOURS>`
Professor Smith	`<LI>Introduction to MIS`	`<INSTRUCTOR>Professor Smith<INSTRUCTOR>`
	`<LI>3 semester hours`	
	`<LI>Professor Smith`	
	`</UL></BODY>`	

Figure TG2.5 *Comparison of HTML and XML.*

there can be components to create reports from the data, either for viewing in an on-screen chart or for printing. Component-based applications enable software developers to "snap together" applications by mixing and matching prefabricated plug-and-play software components.

Virtual Reality Modeling Language

The **Virtual Reality Modeling Language (VRML)** is a programming language that specifies a file format for describing three-dimensional interactive worlds and objects. It can be used with the World Wide Web to create three-dimensional representations of complex scenes such as illustrations, product definitions, and virtual reality presentations. VRML can represent static and animated objects, and it can have hyperlinks to other media such as sound, video, and image.

Virtual Reality Modeling Language (VRML) *Programming language that describes three-dimensional interactive worlds and objects; used on the Web to create three-dimensional representations of complex scenes.*

Object-Oriented Programming Languages

Object-oriented programming (OOP) languages are based on the idea of taking a small amount of data and the instructions about what to do with that data (these instructions are called **methods** in object-oriented programming) and putting both of them together into what is called an **object**. This process is called **encapsulation**. When the object is selected or activated, the computer has the desired data and takes the desired action. This is what happens when you select an icon on your GUI-equipped computer screen and click on it. For example, windows on your GUI screens do not need to be drawn through a series of instructions. Instead, a window object could be sent a message to open at a certain place on your screen, and the window will appear at that place. The window object contains the program code for opening and placing itself.

The **reusability feature** of object-oriented languages means that classes created for one purpose can be used in a different object-oriented program if desired. Popular object-oriented programming languages include Smalltalk, C++, and Java. Because Java is a powerful and popular language, we will look at it here in more detail.

object-oriented programming (OOP) languages *Programming languages that encapsulate a small amount of data with instructions about what to do with the data.*

methods *In object-oriented programming, the instructions about what to do with encapsulated data objects.*

object *In object-oriented programming, the combination of a small amount of data with instructions about what to do with the data.*

encapsulation *In object-oriented programming, the process of creating an object.*

reusability feature *Feature of object-oriented languages that allows classes created for one purpose to be used in a different object-oriented program if desired.*

Java. **Java** is an object-oriented programming language developed by Sun Microsystems. The language gives programmers the ability to develop applications that work across the Internet. Java can handle text, data, graphics, sound, and video, all within one program. Java is used to develop small applications, called **applets**, which can be included in an HTML page on the Internet. When the user uses a Java-compatible browser to view a page that contains a Java applet, the applet's code is transferred to the user's system and executed by the browser.

Java becomes even more interesting when one considers that many organizations are converting their internal networks to use the Internet's TCP/IP protocol. This means that with a computer network that runs the Internet protocol, applications written in Java can be stored on the network, downloaded as needed, and then erased from the local computer when the processing is completed. Users simply download the Java applets as needed, and no longer need to store copies of the application on their PC's hard drive.

Java can benefit organizations in many ways. Companies will not need to purchase numerous copies of commercial software to run on individual computers. Instead, they will purchase one network copy of the software package, made of Java applets. Rather than pay for multiple copies of software, companies may be billed for usage of their single network copy, similar to photocopying. Companies also will find it easier to set information technology standards for hardware, software, and communications; with Java, all applications processing will be independent of the type of computer platform. Companies will have better control over data and applications because they can be controlled centrally from the network servers. Finally, software management (e.g., distribution and upgrades) will be much easier and faster.

Java *Object-oriented programming language, developed by Sun Microsystems, that gives programmers the ability to develop applications that work across the Internet.*

applets *Small Java applications that can be included in an HTML page on the Internet.*

Unified Modeling Language (UML). Developing a model for complex software systems is as essential as having a blueprint for a large building. The **Unified Modeling Language (UML)** is a language for specifying, visualizing, constructing, and

Unified Modeling Language (UML) *A programming language that provides a common set of notations for object-oriented software systems.*

documenting object-oriented software systems. The UML makes reuse easier because the language provides a common set of notations that can be used for all types of software projects.

Before you go on . . .

1. What generation of languages is popular for interacting with databases?
2. What language does a CPU actually respond to?
3. What is the difference between applications and components?
4. What are the strategic advantages of using object-oriented languages?
5. What is the Unified Modeling Language?

TG2.6 ENTERPRISE SOFTWARE

To respond to competitive challenges and opportunities, companies must frequently streamline their organizational processes. This kind of reorganization frequently means changing the IT infrastructure to better support the new processes. A serious difficulty that confronts most organizations in the throes of such change is the sheer complexity that arises from the variety of hardware and software in use. A large firm may have thousands of software programs to run its various systems, dozens of types of hardware, and varying operating systems. Some applications may have been custom-made in-house, some specially made by vendors, and some generic off-the-shelf. Many of these applications are legacy applications, older systems that are typically mainframe-based. The situation is compounded when an organization seeks to communicate and collaborate electronically with its business partners.

Trying to get all these elements to work in harmony in the first place is difficult enough. Trying to reconfigure them is often a nightmare. Firms and their IT management have to approach this new challenge differently. Two approaches to this problem are middleware and enterprise software, which we discuss next.

Middleware

middleware *Software designed to link application modules developed in different computer languages and running on heterogeneous platforms.*

wiley.com/college/turban

Middleware is software designed to link application modules developed in different computer languages and running on heterogeneous platforms, whether on a single machine or over a network. Middleware keeps track of the locations of the software modules that need to link to each other across a distributed system and manages the actual exchange of information. (For a technical discussion of middleware, see Online File W-TG2.4.)

Organization-Wide Applications

enterprise software *Software programs that manage the vital operations of an organization (enterprise).*

wiley.com/college/turban

As discussed at length in Chapter 8, **enterprise software** consists of programs that manage the vital operations of an organization (enterprise), such as supply chain management (movement of raw materials from suppliers through shipment of finished goods to customers), inventory replenishment, ordering, logistics coordination, human resources management, manufacturing, operations, accounting, and financial management. Some common modules of enterprise applications software are payroll, sales order processing, accounts payable/receivable, and tax accounting. For other common enterprise modules, see Online File W-TG2.5.

Enterprise software vendors are producing software that is less expensive, based on industry standards, compatible with other vendors' products, and easier to configure and install. The largest vendors—Systeme Anwendung Produkte (SAP) AG, Oracle Corporation, PeopleSoft Inc., Baan Co., Computer Associates, and J.D. Edwards—are developing software programs that make the jobs of business users and IT personnel easier. Because of the cost, complexity, and time needed to implement enterprisewide corporate applications, many companies are purchasing only the specific application (or module) required, such as manufacturing, financial, or sales force automation.

Before you go on . . .

1. What are the strategic advantages of the enterprise software approach?
2. Why is adoption of enterprise software an inherently difficult process?

WHAT'S IN IT FOR ME?

ACC

FOR THE ACCOUNTING MAJOR

Accounting application software performs the organization's accounting functions, which are repetitive and high volume. Each business transaction (e.g., a person hired, a paycheck produced, an item sold) produces data that must be captured. After capture, accounting applications manipulate the data as necessary. Accounting applications adhere to relatively standardized procedures, handle detailed data, and have a historical focus (i.e., what happened in the past).

FIN

FOR THE FINANCE MAJOR

Financial application software provides information to persons and groups both inside and outside the firm about the firm's financial status. Financial applications include forecasting, funds management, and control applications. Forecasting applications predict and project the firm's future activity in the economic environment. Funds management applications use cash flow models to analyze expected cash flows. Control applications enable managers to monitor their financial performance, typically by providing information about the budgeting process and performance ratios.

MKT

FOR THE MARKETING MAJOR

Marketing application software helps management solve problems that involve marketing the firm's products. Marketing software includes marketing research and marketing intelligence applications. Marketing applications provide information about the firm's products and competitors, its distribution system, its advertising and personal selling activities, and its pricing strategies. Overall, marketing applications help managers develop strategies that combine the four major elements of marketing: product, promotion, place, and price.

POM

FOR THE PRODUCTION/ OPERATIONS MANAGEMENT MAJOR

Managers use production/operations management applications software for production planning and as part of the physical production system. POM applications include production, inventory, quality, and cost software. These applications help management operate manufacturing facilities and logistics. Materials requirements planning (MRP) software is also widely used in manufacturing. It identifies the materials that will be needed, their quantities, and the dates on which they will be needed, thus enabling managers to be proactive.

HRM

FOR THE HUMAN RESOURCES MANAGEMENT MAJOR

Human resources management application software provides information concerning recruiting and hiring, education and training, maintaining the employee database, and termination and benefits administration. HRM applications include workforce planning, recruiting, workforce management, compensation, benefits, and environmental reporting subsystems (e.g., equal employment opportunity records and analysis, union enrollment, toxic substances, and grievances).

SUMMARY

1. **Differentiate between the two major types of software.** Software consists of computer programs (coded instructions) that control the functions of computer hardware. There are two main categories of software: systems software and application software. Systems software manages the hardware resources of the computer system and functions between the hardware and the application software. Systems software includes the system control programs (operating systems) and system support programs. Application software enables users to perform specific tasks and information-processing activities. Application software may be proprietary or off-the-shelf.

2. **Describe the general functions of the operating system.** Operating systems manage the actual computer resources (i.e., the hardware). Operating systems schedule and process applications (jobs), manage and protect memory, manage the input and output functions and hardware, manage data and files, and provide clustering support, security, fault tolerance, graphical user interfaces, and windowing.

3. **Differentiate among types of operating systems and describe each type.** There are five types of operating systems: mobile, desktop, departmental, enterprise, and supercomputer. Mobile device operating systems are designed to support a single person using a mobile, handheld device or information appliance. Desktop operating systems have the least functionality, and enterprise operating systems have the most, with departmental operating systems in the middle. Desktop operating systems are typically designed for one user, departmental operating systems for up to several hundred users, and enterprise operating systems can handle thousands of users and millions of transactions simultaneously. Supercomputer operating systems are designed for the particular processing needs of supercomputers.

4. **Identify three methods for developing application software.** Proprietary software can be developed in-house to address the specific needs of an organization. Existing software programs can be purchased off the shelf from vendors that sell programs to many organizations and individuals. Or a combination of these two methods can be used, by purchasing off-the-shelf programs and customizing them for an organization's specific needs.

5. **Describe the major types of application software.** The major types of application software are spreadsheet, data management, word processing, desktop publishing, graphics, multimedia, communications, speech recognition, and groupware. Software suites combine several types of application software (e.g., word processing, spreadsheet, and data management) into an integrated package.

6. **Describe the major software issues that organizations face today.** Computer program code often contains errors. The industry recognizes the problem of software defects, but it is so enormous that only initial steps are being taken. Another issue is alien software: Pestware is clandestine software that becomes installed on your PC through duplicitous channels. Pestware includes adware, spyware, and spamware. The software evaluation and selection decision is a difficult one because it is affected by many factors. Manager's Checklist TG2.1 summarizes these selection factors. Software licensing is yet another issue for organizations and individuals. Copying software is illegal. Software vendors copyright their software to protect it from being copied. As a result, companies must license vendor-developed software to use it. Organizations also must decide what to do about upgrades. Software vendors frequently revise their programs and sell new versions. Deciding whether to purchase the newest software can be a problem for organizations and IS managers.

7. **Explain how software has evolved and trends for the future.** Software and programming languages continue to become more user oriented. Programming languages have evolved from the first generation of machine languages, which is directly understandable to the CPU, to higher levels which use more natural language and do not require users to specify the detailed procedures for achieving desired results. This trend ensures that end users and the IS staff will become more productive. In addition, software is becoming much more complex, expensive, and time-consuming to develop. As a result, the trend is toward purchasing off-the-shelf software, often in the form of components, rather than developing it in-house. In the future, organizations will tend to buy component-based software modules to reduce costs and development time.

8. **Describe middleware and enterprise software.** Middleware is software designed to link application modules developed in different computer languages and running on heterogeneous platforms, whether on a single machine or over a network. Organizations want packaged applications that support integration between functional modules, that can be quickly changed or enhanced, and that present a common graphical look and feel. In addition, organizations want individual components—software modules—that can be combined as necessary to meet changing business needs. Enterprise software typically consists of modules that manage a company's vital operations, such as supply chain management, logistics coordination, human resources management, and accounting and financial management.

INTERACTIVE / LEARNING

Choosing the Right Software Components

Go to the Interactivities section on the Student Web Site and access Technology Guide 2: Computer Software. There you will find some animated, hands-on activities that help you make some decisions about the operating system, enterprise application, languages, and database software that will support businesses in different industries.

More Resources

More resources and study tools are located on the Student Web Site. You'll find additional chapter materials and links to organizations, people, and technologies for each chapter. In addition, self-quizzes that provide individualized feedback are available for each chapter.

DISCUSSION QUESTIONS

1. You are the CIO of your company and have to develop an application of strategic importance to your firm. Do you buy an off-the-shelf application or develop it in-house? Support your answer with pros and cons of each choice.

2. You are the CIO of your company. Which computing paradigm will you support in your strategic information technology plan: the *standard desktop computing model*, with all the necessary functionality on the local machine, or the *network computing model*, where functionality is downloaded from the network as needed? Support your answer with pros and cons of each choice.

3. You have to take a programming course, or maybe more than one, in your MIS program. Which programming language(s) would you choose to study? Why? Should you even have to learn a programming language?

4. What is the relationship between network computers and Java?

5. If Java and network computing become the dominant paradigm in the industry, will there be any need for in-house information systems staff? What would the staff still have to do?

INTERNET ACTIVITIES

1. A great deal of software is available free over the Internet. Go to *shareware.com* and observe all the software available for free. Choose one and download it to your computer. Prepare a brief discussion about the software for your class.

2. Enter the IBM Web site (*ibm.com*) and search on "software." Click on the drop box for Products, and notice how many software products IBM produces. Is IBM only a hardware company?

TEAM ASSIGNMENTS

Discuss with your university's CIO the issue of software licensing. How does your university maintain compliance? How does your college and your department maintain compliance?

SOFTWARE AT CLUB IT

1. Identify a commercial off-the-shelf software package designed for clubs and restaurants, and describe its system requirements.

2. Make a recomendation to Lisa and Ruben on how to reduce or eliminate spyware and adware from their workstations.

Go to wiley.com/college/turban **to access the CLUB IT Web Site on the Student Web Site**

Managing Organizational Data and Information

Learning Objectives

1. Discuss traditional data file organization and its problems.
2. Explain how a database approach overcomes the problems associated with the traditional file environment.
3. Describe how the three most common data models organize data, and the advantages of each model.

TG3.1 BASICS OF DATA ARRANGEMENT AND ACCESS

Data, when properly managed, become the information upon which business decisions are based. Few business professionals are comfortable making or justifying a business decision that is not based on solid information, especially when modern data management techniques, coupled with modern hardware, software, and trained IS staff, can make access to that information rapid and easy. Organizations must be able to collect, organize, analyze, and interpret data in order to survive in hypercompetitive global markets. And data management is vital to all business functions.

The Data Hierarchy

A computer system organizes data in a hierarchy that begins with bits and proceeds to bytes, fields, records, files, and databases (see Figure TG3.1). A *bit* (*b*inary dig*it*) represents the smallest unit of data a computer can process (a 0 or a 1), and a group of eight bits, a *byte*, represents a single character, which can be a letter, a number, or a symbol. A logical grouping of characters into a word, a small group of words, or a complete number is called a field. For example, a student's name in a university's computer files would appear in the "name" field. A logical grouping of related fields, such as the student's name, the courses taken, the date, and the grade, comprise a record. A logical grouping of related records is called a file. For example, the student records in a single course would constitute a data file for that course. A logical grouping of related files would constitute a database. The student course file could be grouped with files on students' personal histories and financial backgrounds to create a student database.

A record describes an entity. An entity is a person, place, thing, or event about which information is maintained (such as a customer, employee, or product). Each characteristic or quality describing a particular entity is called an attribute (for example, customer name, employee number, product color).

Every record in a file should contain at least one field that uniquely identifies that record so that the record can be retrieved, updated, and sorted. This identifier field is called the primary key. For example, a student record in a U.S. college would probably use the Social Security number as its primary key. In addition, locating a particular record may require the use of secondary keys. Secondary keys are other fields that have some identifying information, but typically do not identify the file with complete accuracy. For example, the student's last name might be a secondary key. It should not be the primary key, as more than one student can have the same last name.

field *A logical grouping of characters into a word, a small group of words, or a complete number.*

record *A logical grouping of related fields.*

file *A logical grouping of related records.*

database *A logical grouping of related files.*

entity *A person, place, thing, or event about which information is maintained in a record.*

attribute *Each characteristic or quality describing a particular.*

primary key *The identifier field that uniquely identifies a record.*

secondary key *An identifier field that has some identifying information, but typically does not identify the file with complete accuracy.*

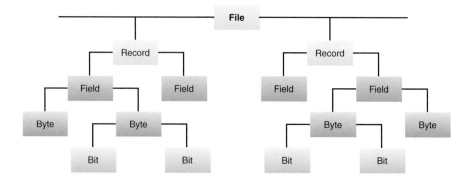

Figure TG3.1 *Hierarchy of data for a computer-based file.*

Before you go on . . .

1. What are the smallest and largest units of the data hierarchy?
2. What is a primary key? A secondary key?

TG3.2 THE TRADITIONAL FILE ENVIRONMENT

From the time of the first computer applications in business (mid-1950s) until the early 1970s, organizations managed their data in a *file environment*. This environment began because organizations typically began automating one application at a time. These systems grew independently, without overall planning. Each application required its own data, which were organized in a data file. A *data file* is a collection of logically related records. Therefore, in a *file management environment*, each application has a specific data file related to it, containing all the data records needed by the application.

Over time, organizations developed numerous applications, each with an associated, application-specific data file. For example, a university has many computer-based applications involving students. These applications include course registration, fee payment, and grades, among others. In a file management environment, each of these applications would have its own student data file (see Figure TG3.2). This approach to data management, where the organization has multiple applications with related data files, is considered the *traditional approach*.

Problems with the Data File Approach

The traditional data file approach led to many problems. The first problem is **data redundancy**. As applications and their data files were created by different programmers over a period of time, the same piece of information could be duplicated in several places. Data redundancy leads to the potential for **data inconsistency**. Data inconsistency means that the various copies of the data no longer agree. File organization also leads to difficulty in accessing data from different applications, a problem called **data isolation**. In addition, **data security**—the control of access to data—is difficult to enforce in the file environment, because new applications may be added to the system on an ad-hoc basis and with more applications, more people have access to data. The file environment may also cause **data integrity** problems. For example, the students' Social

data redundancy *A duplication of the same data in several places in an information system.*

data inconsistency *Lack of agreement among various copies of a supposedly same piece of data in an information system.*

data isolation *Difficulty in accessing data from different applications in an information system.*

data security *The control of access to data held in IS applications.*

data integrity *Preservation of the accuracy, completeness, and reliability of data for its intended use.*

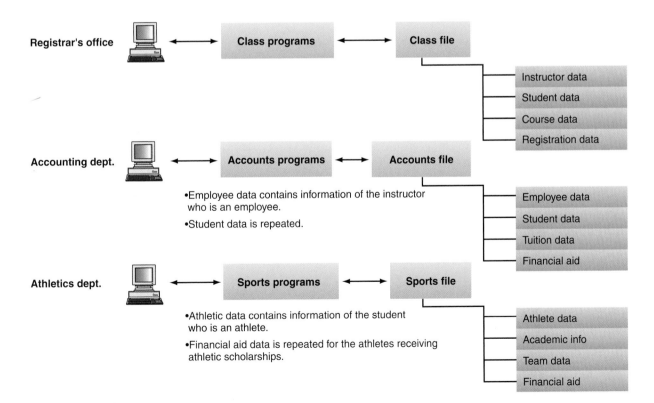

Figure TG3.2 *Computer-based files in the traditional file environment cause problems such as redundancy due to partial or full duplication, inconsistencies across files, and data isolation.*

Security data field should contain no alphabetic characters. It is difficult to place across multiple files data integrity constraints on the accuracy, completeness, and reliability of data for its intended use.

Finally, applications should not have to be developed with regard to how the data are stored. That is, the applications and data in computer systems should be independent—a characteristic called **application/data independence**. In the file environment, the applications and their associated data files are dependent on each other.

Storing data in data files that were tightly linked to their applications eventually led to organizations having hundreds of applications and data files, with no one knowing what the applications did or what data they required. There was no central listing of data files, data elements, or definitions of the data. The numerous problems arising from the file environment approach led to the development of databases.

application/data independence *The storage of data apart from the applications in which the data will be used.*

Before you go on . . .

1. What other problem is often found with the problem of data redundancy?
2. How does data isolation prevent different departments, for example, from using the same data file?

TG3.3 DATABASES: THE MODERN APPROACH

database *A logical group of related files that stores data and the associations among them.*

A **database**, which is a logical group of related files that stores data and the associations among them, can eliminate many of the problems associated with a traditional file environment. Databases are arranged so that one set of software programs—the *database management system*—provides access to all the data. Therefore, data redundancy, data isolation, and data inconsistency are minimized, and data can be shared among all users of the data. In addition, data security and data integrity are increased, and applications and data are independent of one another (see Figure TG3.3).

Creating the Database

conceptual design *An abstract model of a database from the user or business perspective.*

physical design *Layout that shows how a database is actually arranged on storage devices.*

To create a database, designers must develop a conceptual design and a physical design. The **conceptual design** of a database is an abstract model of the database from the user or business perspective. The **physical design** shows how the database is actually arranged on storage devices.

The conceptual database design describes how the data elements in the database are to be grouped. The design process identifies relationships among data elements

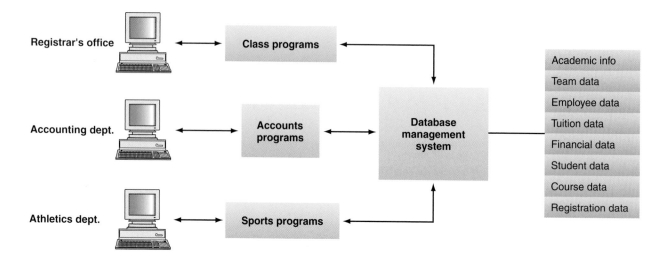

Figure TG3.3 *A database management system (DBMS) provides access to all data in the database.*

and the most efficient way of grouping data elements together to meet information requirements. Entity-relationship modeling and normalization are employed to produce optimal database designs.

Entity-Relationship Modeling.   Database designers plan the database design in a process called **entity-relationship modeling**. They often document the conceptual data model with an **entity-relationship (ER) diagram**. ER diagrams consist of entities, attributes, and relationships; each is represented on the diagram. Entities are pictured in boxes, and relationships are shown in diamonds. The attributes for each entity are listed next to the entity, and the keyfield is underlined. Figure TG3.4 shows an entity-relationship diagram.

As defined earlier, an *entity* is something that can be identified in the users' work environment. For example, consider student registration at a university. Students register for courses and register their cars for parking permits. In this example, STUDENT, PARKING PERMIT, COURSE, and PROFESSOR are examples of entities as shown in Figure TG3.4.

Entities of a given type are grouped in **entity classes**. In our example, STUDENT, PARKING PERMIT, COURSE, and PROFESSOR are examples of entity classes. An **instance** of an entity class is the representation of a particular entity. Therefore, a

entity-relationship modeling *The process of designing a database by organizing data entities to be used and identifying the relationships among them.*

entity-relationship (ER) diagram *Document that shows data entities and attributes and relationships among them.*

entity classes *A grouping of entities of a given type.*

instance *A particular entity within an entity class.*

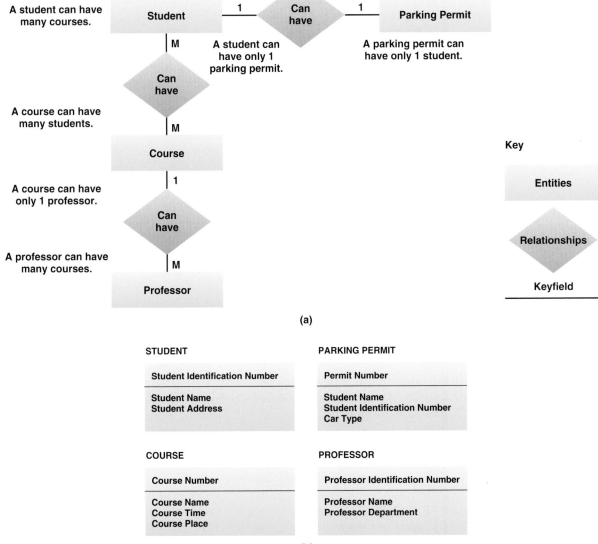

Figure TG3.4 *Entity-relationship diagram model.*

particular STUDENT (James Smythe, 145-89-7123) is an instance of the STUDENT entity class; a particular parking permit (91778) is an instance of the PARKING PERMIT entity class; a particular course (76890) is an instance of the COURSE entity class; and a particular professor (Ted Wilson, 115-65-7632) is an instance of the PROFESSOR entity class.

identifier *An attribute that identifies an entity instance.*

Entity instances have **identifiers**, which are attributes that identify entity instances. For example, STUDENT instances can be identified with StudentIdentificationNumber; PARKING PERMIT instances can be identified with PermitNumber; COURSE instances can be identified with CourseNumber; and PROFESSOR instances can be identified with ProfessorIdentificationNumber. These identifiers are underlined on ER diagrams (see Figure TG3.4).

Entities have attributes, or properties, that describe the entity's characteristics. In our example, examples of attributes for STUDENT would be StudentIdentificationNumber, StudentName, and StudentAddress. Examples of attributes for PARKING PERMIT would be PermitNumber, StudentName, StudentIdentificationNumber, and CarType. Examples of attributes for COURSE would be CourseNumber, CourseName, and CoursePlace. Examples of attributes for PROFESSOR would be ProfessorIdentificationNumber, ProfessorName, and ProfessorDepartment. (Note that each course at this university has one professor—no team teaching.)

Why are StudentName and StudentIdentificationNumber attributes of both the STUDENT and PARKING PERMIT entity classes? That is, why do we need the PARKING PERMIT entity class? If you consider all interlinked university systems, the PARKING PERMIT entity class is needed for other applications (fee payment, parking tickets, and external links) to the State Department of Motor Vehicles.

relationships *The conceptual linking of entities in a database.*

Entities are associated with one another in **relationships**, which can include many entities. (Remember that relationships are noted by diamonds on ER diagrams.) The number of entities in a relationship is the degree of the relationship. Relationships between two items are common and are called *binary relationships*. There are three types of binary relationships:

1. In a *1:1* (*one-to-one*) relationship, a single-entity instance of one type is related to a single-entity instance of another type. Figure TG3.4 shows STUDENT-PARKING PERMIT as a 1:1 relationship that relates a single STUDENT with a single PARKING PERMIT. That is, no student has more than one parking permit, and no parking permit is for more than one student. See Figure TG3.4.

2. The second type of relationship, *1:M* (*one-to-many*), is represented by the COURSE-PROFESSOR relationship in our example. This relationship means that a professor can have many courses, but each course can have only one professor. See Figure TG3.4. (Remember that we have no team-teaching in our university example.)

3. The third type of relationship, *M:M* (*many-to-many*), is represented by the STUDENT-COURSE and SCHEDULE-COURSE relationships in our example. The first relationship means that a student can have many courses, and a course can have many students. The second relationship means that a schedule can have many courses and a course can appear on many schedules (see Figure TG3.4).

normalization *A method for analyzing and reducing a relational database to its most streamlined form for minimum redundancy, maximum data integrity, and best processing performance.*

Normalization.   In order to use a relational database model (discussed below) effectively, the data must be analyzed to eliminate redundant data elements. **Normalization** is a method for analyzing and reducing a relational database to its most streamlined form for minimum redundancy, maximum data integrity, and best processing performance. When data are *normalized*, attributes in the table depend only on the primary key.

As an example, consider an automotive repair garage. This business takes orders from customers who want to have their cars repaired. In this example, ORDER, PART, SUPPLIER, and CUSTOMER would be examples of entities. In this example, there are many PARTS in an ORDER, but each PART can come from only one SUPPLIER. In a nonnormalized relation called ORDER (see Figure TG3.5), each ORDER would have to repeat the name, description, and price of each

Order	Order Number	Number of Parts	Part Number	Part Description	Unit Price	Supplier Number	Supplier Name	Supplier Address	Order Date	Delivery Date	Order Total	Customer Number	Customer Name	Customer Address

Figure TG3.5   *Non-normalized relation.*

PART needed to complete the ORDER, as well as the name and address of each SUPPLIER. This relation contains repeating groups and describes multiple entities.

The normalization process breaks down the relation, ORDER, into smaller relations, each describing a single entity. This process is conceptually simpler and eliminates repeating groups (see Figure TG3.6). For example, consider an order at the automobile repair shop. The normalized relations can produce the order in the following manner.

1. The ORDER relation provides the OrderNumber (the key), OrderDate, Delivery-Date, OrderTotal, and CustomerNumber.

2. The key of the ORDER relation (OrderNumber) provides a link to the ORDERED-PARTS relation (the link numbered 1 in Figure TG3.6).

3. The ORDERED-PARTS relation supplies the NumberofParts information to ORDER.

4. The key of the ORDERED-PARTS relation (PartNumber) provides a link to the PART relation (the link numbered 2 in Figure TG3.6).

5. The PART relation supplies the PartDescription, UnitPrice, and SupplierNumber to ORDER.

6. The SupplierNumber in the PART relation provides a link to the SUPPLIER relation (the link numbered 3 in Figure TG3.6).

7. The SUPPLIER relation provides the SupplierName and SupplierAddress to ORDER.

8. The CustomerNumber in ORDER provides a link to the CUSTOMER relation (the link numbered 4 in Figure TG3.6).

9. The CUSTOMER relation supplies the CustomerName and CustomerAddress to ORDER. The automotive repair shop order now has all the necessary information.

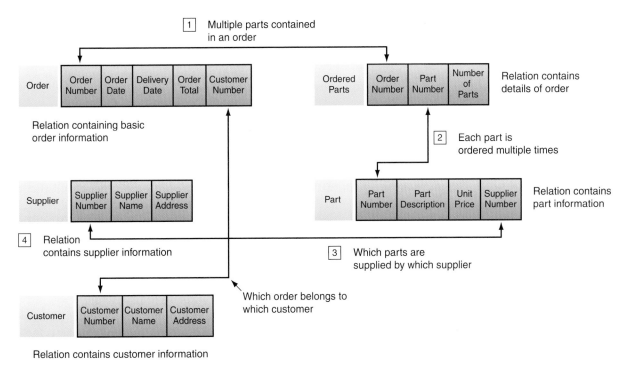

Figure TG3.6   *Normalized relation.*

Before you go on . . .

1. What are the common options for locating data in databases?
2. What tools and techniques are used to produce optimal database designs?

TG3.4 DATABASE MANAGEMENT SYSTEMS

database management system (DBMS) *The software program (or group of programs) that provides access to a database.*

The software program (or group of programs) that provides access to a database is known as a **database management system (DBMS)**. The DBMS permits an organization to store data in one location from which it can be updated and retrieved, and it provides access to the stored data by various application programs. DBMSs also provide mechanisms for maintaining the integrity of stored information, managing security and user access, and recovering information when the system fails. Various database functions can be accessed from within an application written in a third-generation, fourth-generation, or object-oriented language. The DBMS provides users with tools to add, delete, maintain, display, print, search, select, sort, and upgrade data. These tools range from easy-to-use natural-language interfaces to complex programming languages used for developing sophisticated database applications. As essential as databases and DBMSs are to all areas of business, they must be carefully managed.

Logical versus Physical View

A database management system provides the ability for many different users to share data and process resources. But as there can be many different users, there are many different database needs. How can a single, unified database meet the differing requirements of so many users? For example, how can a single database be structured so that sales personnel can see customer, inventory, and production maintenance data while the human resources department maintains restricted access to private personnel data?

physical view *The plan for the actual, physical arrangement and location of data in the direct access storage devices (DASDs) of a database management system.*

logical view *The user's view of the data and the software programs that process that data in a database management system.*

A DBMS minimizes these problems by providing two views of the database data: a physical view and a logical view. The **physical view** deals with the actual, physical arrangement and location of data in the *direct access storage devices (DASDs)*. The **logical view**, or user's view, of a database program represents data in a format that is meaningful to a user and to the software programs that process that data. That is, the logical view tells the user, in user terms, what is in the database. The advantage here is that while there is only one physical view of the data, there can be an endless number of different logical views—one specifically tailored to each individual user, if necessary.

DBMS Components

There are four main components in a database management system: the data model, the data definition language, the data manipulation language, and the data dictionary.

data model *Definition of the way data in a DBMS are conceptually structured.*

Data Model. The **data model** defines the way data are conceptually structured. Examples include the hierarchical, network, relational, object-relational, hypermedia, and multidimensional models. We will present a more detailed discussion of these models in Section TG3.5.

data definition language (DDL) *Set of statements that describe a database structure (all record types and data set types).*

schema *The logical description of the entire database and the listing of all the data items and the relationships among them.*

subschema *The specific set of data from the database that is required by each application.*

Data Definition Language. The **data definition language (DDL)** is a set of statements that defines what types of information are in the database and how they will be structured. The DDL is essentially the link between the logical and physical views of the database.

A DBMS user defines views, or *schemas*, using the DDL. The **schema** is the logical description of the entire database and the listing of all the data items and the relationships among them. A **subschema** is the specific set of data from the database that is required by each application.

Data Manipulation Language.   The data manipulation language (DML) is used with third-generation, fourth-generation, or object-oriented languages to query the contents of the database, store or update information in the database, and develop database applications. The DML allows users to retrieve, sort, display, and delete the contents of a database.

Requesting information from a database is the most commonly performed operation. Because users cannot generally request information in a natural-language form, *query languages* form an important component of a DBMS. Structured query language (SQL) is the most popular relational database language, combining both DML and DDL features. SQL offers the ability to perform complicated searches with relatively simple statements. Key words such as SELECT (to specify a desired attribute), FROM (to specify the table to be used), and WHERE (to specify conditions to apply in the query) are typically used for the purpose of data manipulation. For example, a state legislator wants to send congratulatory letters to all students from her district graduating with honors from the state university. The university information systems staff would query the student relational database with an SQL statement such as SELECT (Student Name), FROM (Student Database), WHERE (Congressional District = 7 and Grade Point Average ⇒ 3.4).

Another way of interfacing with a database is to use query by example (QBE). QBE enables the user to fill out a grid or template (also known as a form) to construct a sample or description of the data wanted. Users can construct a query quickly and easily by using drag-and-drop features in a DBMS such as Microsoft Access. Conducting queries in this manner is simpler than keying in SQL commands.

Data Dictionary.   The data dictionary stores definitions of data elements and data characteristics such as individuals, business functions, programs, and reports that use the data elements. A *data element* represents a field. Besides listing the standard data name and aliases for the element, the dictionary lists the names that reference this element in specific systems and identifies the individuals, business functions, applications, and reports that use this data element.

Data dictionaries provide many advantages to the organization. Because the data dictionary provides standard definitions for all data elements, the potential for data inconsistency is reduced. That is, the probability that the same data element will be used in different applications, but with a different name, is reduced. In addition, data dictionaries provide for faster program development because programmers do not have to create new data names. Data dictionaries also make it easier to modify data and information because programmers do not need to know where the data element is stored or what applications use the data element in order to make use of it in a program.

data manipulation language (DML)   *Instructions used with higher-level programming languages to query the contents of the database, store or update information, and develop database applications.*

structured query language (SQL)   *Popular relational database language that enables users to perform complicated searches with relatively simple instructions.*

query by example (QBE)   *Database language that enables the user to fill out a grid (form) to construct a sample or description of the data wanted.*

data dictionary   *Collection of definitions of data elements, data characteristics that use the data elements, and the individuals, business functions, applications, and reports that use this data element.*

> ## Before you go on . . .
>
> **1.** What is the difference between the logical and the physical views of the data in a database?
>
> **2.** What are the main components of a DBMS?

TG3.5 LOGICAL DATA MODELS

The three most common data models are *hierarchical, network,* and *relational.* Other types of data models include multidimensional, object-relational, hypermedia, embedded, and virtual. Using these models, database designers can build logical or conceptual views of data that can then be physically implemented into virtually any database with any DBMS. Hierarchical and network DBMSs usually tie related data together through linked lists. Relational and multidimensional DBMSs relate data through information contained in the data. We'll look at most of these models in this section.

Hierarchical Database Model

The **hierarchical database model** rigidly structures data into an inverted "tree" in which each record contains two elements. The first is a single root or *master field*, often called a *key*, which identifies the type, location, or ordering of the records. The second is a variable number of *subordinate fields*, which define the rest of the data within a record. As a rule, while all fields have only one "parent," each parent may have many "children." An example of a hierarchical database is shown in Figure TG3.7.

The hierarchical structure was developed simply because hierarchical relationships are commonly found in many traditional business organizations and processes. For example, organization charts most often describe a hierarchical relationship—top management at the highest level, middle management at lower levels, and so on. Within each hierarchy, each level of management may have many employees or levels of employees beneath it, but each employee generally has only one manager. The hierarchical structure is characterized by this one-to-many relationship among data.

The strongest advantage of the hierarchical database approach is the speed and efficiency with which it can be searched for data. This speed is possible because so much of the database is eliminated in the search with each "turn" going down the tree. As shown in Figure TG3.7, half the records in the database (East Coast Sales) are eliminated once the search turns toward West Coast sales, and two-thirds of the West Coast Sales are eliminated once the search turns toward stemware. Organizational transaction processing systems (e.g., airline reservation systems) typically use the hierarchical approach for the speed and efficiency it offers.

But the hierarchical model does have problems. Access to data in this model is predefined by the database administrator before the programs that access the data are written. Programmers must follow the hierarchy established by the data structure.

Network Database Model

The **network database model** creates relationships among data in which subordinate records (called *members*, not children) can be linked to more than one data element (called an *owner*). In this way, many-to-many relationships are possible with a network database model. See Figure TG3.8 for an illustration of the network database model.

The network model essentially places no restrictions on the number of relationships or sets in which a field can be involved. This model, then, is more consistent with real-world business relationships where, for example, vendors have many customers and cus-

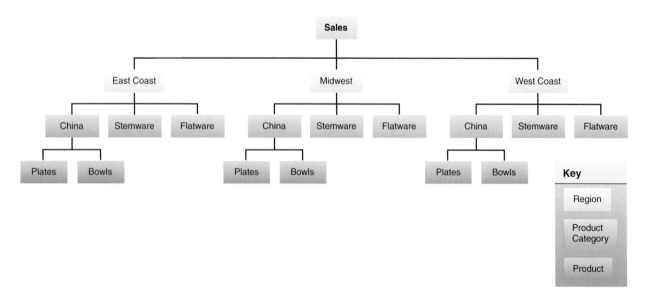

Figure TG3.7 *Hierarchical database model.*

tomers have many vendors. However, network databases are very complex. The network model is by far the most complicated type of database to design and implement.

Relational Database Model

Although most business organizations have been organized in a hierarchical fashion, most business data—especially accounting and financial data—have been traditionally organized into simple tables of columns and rows. Tables allow quick comparisons by row or column, and items are easy to retrieve by finding the point of intersection of a particular row and column. The **relational database model** is based on the simple concept of tables in order to capitalize on characteristics of rows and columns of data.

In a relational database, these tables are called **relations**, and the model is based on the mathematical theory of sets and relations. In this model, each row of data is equivalent to a record, and each column of data is equivalent to a field. In the relational model terminology, a row is called a **tuple**, and a column is called an **attribute**. A relational database is not always, however, one big table (usually called a *flat file*) consisting of all attributes and all tuples. That design would likely entail far too much data redundancy. Instead, a database is usually designed as many related tables.

There are some basic principles involved in creating a relational database. First, the order of tuples or attributes in a table is irrelevant, because their position relative to other tuples and attributes is irrelevant in finding data based on specific tuples and attributes. Second, each tuple must be uniquely identifiable by the data within the tuple—some sort of primary key data (for example, a Social Security number or employee number). Third, each table must have a unique identifier—the name of the relation. Fourth, there can be no duplicate attributes or tuples. Finally, there can be only one value in each row-column "cell" in a table.

In a relational database, three basic operations are used to develop useful sets of data: select, join, and project. The **"select" operation** creates a subset consisting of all records in the file that meet stated criteria. "Select" creates, in other words, a subset of rows that meet certain criteria. The **"join" operation** combines relational tables to provide the user with more information than is available in individual tables. The **"project" operation** creates a subset consisting of columns in a table, permitting the user to create new tables that contain only the information required.

One of the greatest advantages of the relational model is its conceptual simplicity and the ability to link records in a way that is not predefined (as is the case with hierarchical and network models). This ability provides great flexibility, particularly for end users. The relational or tabular model of data can be used in a variety of applications. Most people can easily visualize the relational model as a table, although the model does use some unfamiliar terminology.

Consider the relational database example on East Coast managers shown in Figure TG3.9 (page 454). The table contains data about the entity called East Coast managers. Attributes or characteristics about the entity are name, title, age, and division. The tuples, or occurrences of the entity, are the four records on A. Smith, W. Jones, J. Lee, and K. Durham. The links among the data, and among tables, are implicit, as they are not necessarily physically linked in a storage device but are implicitly linked by the design of the tables into rows and columns.

This property of implicit links provides perhaps the strongest benefit of the relational model—flexibility in relating data. Unlike the hierarchical and network models, where the only links are those rigidly built into the design, in the relational model all

relational database model *Data model based on the simple concept of tables in order to capitalize on characteristics of rows and columns of data.*

relations *The tables of rows and columns used in a relational database.*

tuple *A row of data in the relational database model.*

attribute *A column of data in the relational database model.*

"select" operation *Basic operation in a relational database that creates a subset consisting of all file records that meet stated criteria.*

"join" operation *Basic operation in a relational database that combines relational tables.*

"project" operation *Basic operation in a relational database that creates a subset consisting of columns in a table, permitting the user to create new tables that contain only the information required.*

Name	Title	Age	Division
Smith, A.	Dir., Accounting	43	China
Jones, W.	Dir., Total Quality Management	32	Stemware
Lee, J.	Dir., Information Technology	46	China
Durham, K.	Manager, Production	35	Stemware

Figure TG3.9 *Table from relational database model.*

the data in a table and between tables can be linked, related, and compared. This ability gives the relational model much more data independence than do the other two models. That is, the logical design of data into tables can be more independent of the physical implementation. This independence allows more flexibility in implementing and modifying the logical design. Of course, as with all tables, an end user needs to know only two things: the identifier(s) of the tuple(s) to be searched, and the desired attribute(s).

The relational model is currently the most popular of the three most common database structures because it provides the most flexibility and ease of use. But this model has some disadvantages. Because large-scale databases may be composed of many interrelated tables, the overall design may be complex and therefore may have slower search and access times (as compared to the hierarchical and network models). The slower search and access times may result in processing inefficiencies that lead to an initial lack of acceptance of the relational model.

Advantages and Disadvantages of the Three Database Models

The main advantage of the hierarchical and network database models is processing efficiency. The hierarchical and network structures are relatively easy for users to understand because they reflect the pattern of real-world business relationships. In addition, the hierarchical structure allows for data integrity to be easily maintained.

Hierarchical and network structures have several disadvantages, though. All the access paths, directories, and indices must be specified in advance. Once specified, they are not easily changed without a major programming effort. Therefore, these designs have low flexibility. Hierarchical and network structures are programming intensive, time-consuming, difficult to install, and difficult to remedy if design errors occur. The two structures do not support ad-hoc, English-language-like inquiries for information.

The advantages of relational DBMSs include high flexibility in regard to ad-hoc queries, power to combine information from different sources, simplicity of design and maintenance, and the ability to add new data and records without disturbing existing applications.

The disadvantages of relational DBMSs include their relatively low processing efficiency. These systems are somewhat slower because they typically require many accesses to the stored data to carry out the select, join, and project commands. Relational systems do not have the large number of pointers carried by hierarchical systems, which speed search and retrieval. Further, large relational databases may be designed to have some data redundancy in order to make retrieval of data more efficient. The same data element may be stored in multiple tables. Special arrangements are necessary to ensure data integrity. Therefore, this model must be enforced with good design principles. Manager's Checklist TG3.1 summarizes the advantages and disadvantages of the three common database models.

Emerging Data Models

Two emerging data models are the *object-relational* and *hypermedia* models, which we discuss here.

object-relational database model
Data model that adds new object storage capabilities to relational databases.

Object-Relational Database Model. The **object-relational database model** adds new object storage capabilities to relational database management systems. Systems based on this model integrate management of traditional fielded data, complex objects such as time-series and geospatial data (e.g., maps and photos derived from satellite transmissions), and diverse binary media such as audio, video, images, applets, and formatted and unformatted text. Object-relational database management systems include both data and processes—that is, what information the users have and what they are going to do with it.

MANAGER'S
CHECKLIST
TG3.1

Advantages and
Disadvantages of Logical
Data Models

Model	Advantages	Disadvantages
Hierarchical database	❑ Searching is fast and efficient.	❑ Access to data is predefined by exclusively hierarchical relationships, predetermined by administrator. ❑ Limited search/query flexibility. ❑ Not all data are naturally hierarchical.
Network database	❑ Many more relationships can be defined. ❑ There is greater speed and efficiency than with relational database models.	❑ This is the most complicated database model to design, implement, and maintain. ❑ Greater query flexibility than with hierarchical model, but less than with relational model.
Relational database	❑ Conceptual simplicity; there are no predefined relationships among data. ❑ High flexibility in ad-hoc querying. ❑ New data and records can be added easily.	❑ Processing efficiency and speed are lower. ❑ Data redundancy is common, requiring additional maintenance.

Object-relational databases can be particularly helpful in multimedia environments, such as in manufacturing sites. Data from design blueprints, photographic images of parts, operational acoustic signatures, and test or quality-control data all can be combined into one object, itself consisting of structures and operations. In general, object-relational databases allow organizations to structure their data and use them in ways that would be impossible, or at least very difficult, with other database models.

Hypermedia Database Model. The **hypermedia database model** stores chunks of information in the form of *nodes* connected by links established by the user. The nodes can contain text, graphics, sound, full-motion video, or executable computer programs. Searching for information does not have to follow a predetermined organizational scheme. Instead, users can branch to related information in any kind of relationship. The relationship between nodes is less structured than in a traditional DBMS. In most systems, each node can be displayed on a screen. The screen also displays the links between the node depicted and other nodes in the database.

hypermedia database model *Data model that stores chunks of information in* nodes *that can contain data in a variety of media; users can branch to related data in any kind of relationship.*

Specialized Database Models

Because a database management system need not be confined to storing just words and numbers, firms use them to store graphics, sounds, and video as well. These capabilities have led to specialized databases, depending on the type or format of data stored. For example, a **geographical information database** may contain locational data for overlaying on maps or images. Using this type of data, users are able to spatially view customer and vendor locations instead of simply reading the actual addresses. A **knowledge database** can store decision rules used to evaluate situations and help users make decisions like an expert. A **multimedia database** can store data on many media—sounds, video, images, graphic animation, and text.

geographical information database *Data model that contains locational data for overlaying on maps or images.*

knowledge database *Data model that can store decision rules that can be used for expert decision making.*

multimedia database *Data model that can store data on many media.*

Small-Footprint Databases

Small-footprint databases enable organizations to give workers in the field certain types of data. These databases offer more information, more readily available, in a form that is accessible. Whereas once laptops were the only portable machines capable of running a database, advances in technology such as more powerful CPUs and increased memory at lower cost are enabling handheld devices and Internet-enabled

small-footprint database *The subset of a larger database provided for field workers.*

cell phones to run some form of an SQL database and to synchronize that mobile database with a central database at headquarters. A common application of these databases is for salespeople who need information to carry with them, eliminating the need to connect to their organization's database from the field.

Embedded Databases

embedded database *A database built into devices or into applications; designed to be self-sufficient and to require little or no administration.*

Embedded databases (also called built-in databases) cover a broad range of implementations. Some are built into devices ranging from medical-imaging systems to the flight controls of the Boeing 777. Others are used in mobile phones and PDAs. Still others are used by software developers who build them into applications, making the databases invisible to users. Embedded databases are particularly prevalent in accounting software, retail applications, and applications for the health-care industry. The key difference between embedded databases and mainstream databases such as Oracle 9i and IBM DB2 is that mainstream databases are designed for maximum performance and require a great deal of management. Embedded databases are designed to be self-sufficient and require little or no administration, thereby lowering the total cost of ownership.

For example, boating-supplies retailer West Marine (*westmarine.com*) deployed a point-of-sale system throughout its 250 stores. Embedded in the software running on each store's server, and invisible to employees, is an embedded database handling a variety of pricing and inventory-management tasks. The system tracks the stores' 160,000 inventory items and 500,000 price records.

Virtual Databases

virtual database *A database that consists only of software; manages data that can physically reside anywhere on the network and in a variety of formats.*

Virtual databases provide a way of managing many different data sources as though they were all in one place. Instead of being comprised of software that manages data (DBMS) and a physical place to keep that data, virtual databases consist only of software. The data it manages can physically reside anywhere on the network and in a variety of formats. To the user, it all looks like data in one database. The benefits of virtual databases include lower development costs, faster development time, less maintenance, and a single point of entry into a company's data.

Before you go on . . .

1. What are the relative advantages and disadvantages of hierarchical, network, and relational databases?
2. How might a company use a multimedia DBMS for competitive advantage?
3. Why might a company want to use a small-footprint database or a virtual database?

SUMMARY

1. **Discuss traditional data file organization and its problems.** In a file management environment, each application has a specific data file related to it, containing all the data records needed by the application. The traditional data file organization led to problems of data redundancy, data inconsistency, data isolation, data integrity, data security, and application/data dependence. Storing data in data files that are tightly linked to their applications resulted in organizations having hundreds of applications and data files, with little or no coordination among the applications and files, and no overall plan for managing corporate data.

2. **Explain how a database approach overcomes the problems associated with the traditional file environment.** A database, which is a logical group of related files, eliminates the problems associated with a traditional file environment. In a database, data are integrated and related so that one set of software programs provides access to all the data. Therefore, data redundancy, data isolation, and data inconsistency

are minimized, and data can be shared among all users of the data. In addition, data security and data integrity are increased, and applications and data are independent of one another.

3. **Describe how the three most common data models organize data, and the advantages of each model.** The hierarchical model rigidly structures data into an inverted "tree" in which records contain a keyfield and a number of other fields. The hierarchical structure is characterized by one-to-many relationships among data. In the network model, records can be linked to more than one parent, allowing many-to-many relationships among the data. The relational model uses tables to capitalize on character-istics of rows and columns of data that are consistent with real-world business situations.

The main advantage of the hierarchical and network database models is processing efficiency. The hierarchical and network structures are relatively easy for users to understand because they reflect the pattern of many (but not all) real-world business relationships. In addition, the hierarchical structure allows for data integrity to be easily maintained.

The advantages of relational databases include high flexibility in regard to ad-hoc queries, power to combine information from different sources, simplicity of design and maintenance, and the ability to add new data and records without disturbing existing applications.

DISCUSSION QUESTIONS

1. What are the major problems with managing data with traditional file structures?
2. What are the advantages and disadvantages of the database approach to managing data?
3. What are the advantages and disadvantages of the hierarchical database model?
4. What are the advantages and disadvantages of the relational database model?
5. Define small-footprint databases, embedded databases, and virtual databases.

INTERNET ACTIVITIES

1. Access the Web sites of some of the major data management vendors, such as Oracle (*oracle.com*), Sybase (*sybase.com*), and IBM (*ibm.com*). What are the capabilities of their latest products? Compare these capabilities. Pay particular attention to the Web connections offered by each vendor's products.
2. Access the Web site of the Gartner Group (*gartnergroup.com*). Examine its research papers on marketing databases and data management. Prepare a report noting the most current practices in these two areas.

TEAM ASSIGNMENTS

Examine the data that your university keeps on its students. (You will have to go to your university computer center for this project.) List the fields that are included in each student's record. What applications would be supported by the fields in your record? Are you surprised by how much information your university keeps on its students?

DATABASES AT CLUB IT

1. What are some advantages to Club IT to store their club members' information in a database instead of in a spreadsheet?
2. Search the web for multimedia database products. How might a multimedia database be useful to Club IT?

Go to wiley.com/college/turban **to access the CLUB IT Web Site on the Student Web Site**

Network and Telecommunications Basics

Outline

Learning Objectives

1. Describe the components of a telecommunications system.
2. Describe the eight basic types of communications media, including their advantages and disadvantages.
3. Describe the major types of network services.
4. Describe the Ethernet and TCP/IP protocols.
5. Differentiate between client/server computing and peer-to-peer computing.
6. Describe the two major types of networks.

TG4.1 THE TELECOMMUNICATIONS SYSTEM

telecommunications system *Combination of hardware and software that transmits information (text, data, graphics, and voice) from one location to another.*

analog signal *Continuous waves that transmit information by altering the amplitude and frequency of the waves.*

digital signal *A discrete pulse, either on or off, that conveys information in a binary form.*

A **telecommunications system** consists of hardware and software that transmits information from one location to another. These systems can transmit text, data, graphics, voice, documents, or full-motion video information. They transmit this information with two basic types of signals, analog and digital. **Analog signals** are continuous waves that transmit information by altering the characteristics of the waves. Analog signals have two parameters, amplitude and frequency. For example, voice and all sound is analog, traveling to human ears in the form of waves. The higher the waves (or amplitude), the louder the sound; the more closely packed the waves, the higher the frequency or pitch. **Digital signals** are discrete pulses that are either on or off, representing a series of bits (0s and 1s). This quality allows them to convey information in a binary form that can be clearly interpreted by computers. See Figure TG4.1 for a graphic representation of analog and digital signals.

The major components of a telecommunications system include the following:

- *Hardware.* All types of computers (e.g., desktop, server, mainframe) and communications processors (such as a modems or small computers dedicated solely to communications).
- *Communications media.* The physical media through which electronic signals are transmitted, including wireless media (used with satellites and cell phones).
- *Communications networks.* The links among computers and communications devices.
- *Communications software.* Software that controls the telecommunications system and the entire transmission process.
- *Data communications providers.* Regulated utilities or private firms that provide data communications services.
- *Communications protocols.* The rules for transmitting information across the system.
- *Communications applications.* Electronic data interchange, teleconferencing, videoconferencing, e-mail, facsimile, electronic funds transfer, and others.

Figure TG4.2 shows a typical telecommunications system. Note that such systems have two sides, the transmitter of information and the receiver of information.

Communications Processors

communications processors *Hardware devices that support data transmission and reception across a telecommunications system.*

Communications processors are hardware devices that support data transmission and reception across a telecommunications system. These devices include modems, multiplexers, and front-end processors.

modem *Device that converts signals from analog to digital and vice versa.*

Modem. The U.S. public telephone system (called POTS, for "Plain Old Telephone Service") was designed as an analog network to carry voice signals or sounds in an analog wave format. In order for this type of circuit to carry digital information, that information must be converted into an analog wave pattern. The conversion from digital to analog is called *modulation*, and the reverse is *demodulation*. The device that performs these two processes is called a **modem**, a contraction of the terms modulate/demodulate (see Figure TG4.3).

Figure TG4.1 *Analog versus digital signals.*

Analog data transmission
(wave signals)

Digital data transmission
(pulse signals)

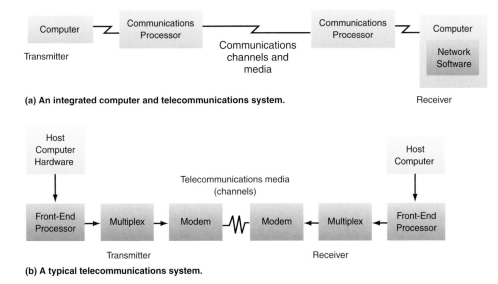

(a) An integrated computer and telecommunications system.

(b) A typical telecommunications system.

Figure TG4.2
Telecommunications system.

Modems are always used in pairs. The unit at the sending end converts a computer's digital information into analog signals for transmission over analog lines. At the receiving end, another modem converts the analog signal back into digital signals for the receiving computer. Like most communications equipment, a modem's transmission speed is measured in bits per second (bps). Modem speeds range up to 56,600 bps.

Multiplexer.   A **multiplexer** is an electronic device that allows a single communications channel to carry data transmissions simultaneously from many sources. Multiplexers lower communication costs by allowing devices to share communications channels. Multiplexing thus makes more efficient use of these channels by merging the transmissions of several computers (e.g., personal computers) at one end of the channel, while a similar unit separates the individual transmissions at the receiving end (e.g., a mainframe).

multiplexer *Electronic device that allows a single communications channel to carry data transmissions simultaneously from many sources.*

Front-End Processor.   With most computers, the central processing unit (CPU) must communicate with multiple computers at the same time. Routine communication tasks can absorb a large proportion of the CPU's processing time, leading to degraded performance on more important jobs. In order not to waste valuable CPU time, many computer systems have a small secondary computer dedicated solely to communication. Known as a **front-end processor**, this specialized computer manages all routing communications with peripheral devices.

front-end processor *A small secondary computer, dedicated solely to communication, that manages all routing communications with peripheral devices.*

Communications Media and Channels

For data to be communicated from one location to another, some form of pathway or medium must be used. These pathways are called **communications channels**.

communications channel *Pathway for communicating data from one location to another.*

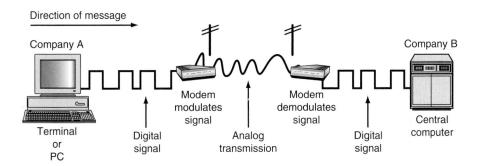

Figure TG4.3   *A modem converts digital to analog signals and vice versa.*
[Source: Stern and Stern, Computing in the Information Age, *1996, p. 334.]*

The communications channels, in two types of media, are shown below.

Cable Media	Broadcast Media	
1. Twisted-pair	4. Microwave	7. Cellular radio
2. Coaxial cable	5. Satellite	8. Infrared
3. Fiber optic	6. Radio	

cable media *Communications channels that use physical wires or cables to transmit data and information.*

broadcast (wireless) media *Communications channels that use electromagnetic media (the "airwaves") to transmit data.*

twisted-pair wire *Strands of copper wire twisted together in pairs; used for most business telephone wiring.*

Cable media use physical wires or cables to transmit data and information. Twisted-pair wire and coaxial cable are made of copper, and fiber-optic cable is made of glass. However, with the exception of fiber-optic cable, cables present several problems, notably the expense of installation and change, as well as a fairly limited capacity. The alternative is communication over **broadcast or wireless media**. The key to mobile communications in today's rapidly moving society is data transmissions over electromagnetic media—the "airwaves." Manager's Checklist TG4.1 summarizes the advantages and disadvantages of the various communications channels. Each of the channels is discussed in this section.

Twisted-Pair Wire.   **Twisted-pair wire** is the most prevalent form of communications wiring; it is used for almost all business telephone wiring. Twisted-pair wire con-

MANAGER'S CHECKLIST TG4.1

Advantages and Disadvantages of Communications Channels

Channel	Advantages	Disadvantages
Twisted-pair	❏ Inexpensive. ❏ Widely available. ❏ Easy to work with. ❏ Unobtrusive.	❏ Slow (low bandwidth). ❏ Subject to interference. ❏ Easily tapped (low security).
Coaxial cable	❏ Higher bandwidth than twisted pair. ❏ Less susceptible to electromagnetic interference.	❏ Relatively expensive and inflexible. ❏ Easily tapped (low-to-medium security). ❏ Somewhat difficult to work with.
Fiber-optic cable	❏ Very high bandwidth. ❏ Relatively inexpensive. ❏ Difficult to tap (good security).	❏ Difficult to work with (difficult to splice).
Microwave	❏ High bandwidth. ❏ Relatively inexpensive.	❏ Must have unobstructed line of sight. ❏ Susceptible to environmental interference.
Satellite	❏ High bandwidth. ❏ Large coverage area.	❏ Expensive. ❏ Must have unobstructed line of sight. ❏ Signals experience propagation delay. ❏ Must use encryption for security.
Radio	❏ High bandwidth. ❏ No wires needed. ❏ Signals pass through walls. ❏ Inexpensive and easy to install.	❏ Creates electrical interference problems. ❏ Susceptible to snooping unless encrypted.
Cellular radio	❏ Low to medium bandwidth. ❏ Signals pass through walls.	❏ Requires construction of towers. ❏ Susceptible to snooping unless encrypted.
Infrared	❏ Low to medium bandwidth.	❏ Must have unobstructed line of sight. ❏ Used only for short distances.

sists of strands of copper wire twisted in pairs. It is relatively inexpensive to purchase, widely available, and easy to work with. It can be made relatively unobtrusive by running it inside walls, floors, and ceilings. However, twisted-pair wire has some significant disadvantages. It is relatively slow for transmitting data, is subject to interference from other electrical sources, and can be easily tapped for gaining unauthorized access to data by unintended receivers.

Coaxial Cable.   **Coaxial cable** consists of insulated copper wire. It is much less susceptible to electrical interference than is twisted-pair wire and can carry much more data. For these reasons, it is commonly used to carry high-speed data traffic as well as television signals (thus the term cable TV). However, coaxial cable is more expensive and more difficult to work with than twisted-pair wire. It is also somewhat inflexible.

Fiber Optics.   **Fiber-optic cables** consist of thousands of very thin filaments of glass fibers that transmit information via light pulses generated by lasers. The fiber-optic cable is surrounded by cladding, a coating that prevents the light from leaking out of the fiber.

Fiber-optic cables offer significant size and weight reductions over traditional cable media. They also provide greater data-carrying capacity and greater security from interference and tapping. Optical fiber has reached data transmission rates of six trillion bits (terabits) per second and, theoretically, can carry up to 25 terabits per second. Fiber-optic cable is typically used as the high-speed trunk line (called the backbone) for a network, while twisted-pair wire and coaxial cable connect the trunk line to individual devices on the network.

Attenuation is the reduction in the strength of a signal. It occurs for both analog and digital signals, and is also a problem for fiber optics. Attenuation requires manufacturers to install equipment to receive the distorted or "dirty" signals and send them out "clean" and amplified. These signal regenerators can cost tens of thousands of dollars to install on land; those under water can cost a million dollars each.

Microwave.   We now turn our attention to broadcast or wireless media, which have greatly expanded telecommunications offerings. **Microwave transmission** systems are widely used for high-volume, long-distance, point-to-point communication. Microwave towers usually cannot be spaced more than 30 miles apart because the earth's curvature would interrupt the line of sight from tower to tower. To minimize line-of-sight problems, microwave antennas are usually placed on top of buildings, towers, and mountain peaks. Long-distance telephone carriers use microwave systems because they generally provide about 10 times the data-carrying capacity of wire without the significant efforts necessary to string or bury wire. Compared to 30 miles of wire, microwave communications can be set up much more quickly (within a day) at much less cost.

The fact that microwave requires line-of-sight transmission severely limits its usefulness as a practical large-scale solution to data communications needs, especially over very long distances. Additionally, microwave transmissions are susceptible to environmental interference during severe weather such as heavy rain or snowstorms. Although still widely used, long-distance microwave data communications systems are being replaced by satellite communications systems.

Satellite.   Communication satellites are used in **satellite transmission** systems. As with microwave transmission, satellites must receive and transmit via line of sight. However, the enormous footprint (the amount of the earth's surface in the line of sight for a specific satellite) of a satellite's coverage area from high altitudes overcomes the limitations of microwave data relay stations. Currently, there are three types of orbits in which satellites are placed.

Geostationary earth orbit (GEO) satellites orbit 22,300 miles directly above the equator and maintain a fixed position above the earth's surface. These satellites are excellent for sending television programs to cable operators and broadcasting directly to homes. However, transmissions from GEO satellites take a quarter of a second to send and return. This brief pause, called **propagation delay**, makes two-way

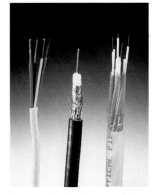

Twisted-pair telephone cable, coaxial cable, and fiber-optic cable.

coaxial cable   *Insulated copper wire; used to carry high-speed data traffic and television signals.*

fiber-optic cable   *Thousands of very thin filaments of glass fibers, surround by cladding, that transmit information via light pulses generated by lasers.*

microwave transmission   *Communications channel that uses towers to send wireless signals; used for high-volume, long-distance, point-to-point communication.*

satellite transmission   *Communications channel that uses orbiting satellites to send digital transmissions point-to-point.*

propagation delay   *Brief pause between the sending and receipt of a satellite transmission.*

telephone conversations difficult. Also, GEO satellites are large and expensive, and the equatorial orbit cannot hold many more GEO satellites than the number that now orbit there.

Medium earth orbit (MEO) satellites are located about 6,000 miles above the earth's surface, in orbits inclined to the equator. While fewer satellites are needed to cover the earth than in LEO orbits, telephones need more power to reach MEO satellites than to reach LEO satellites.

Low earth orbit (LEO) satellites are located 400 to 700 miles above the earth's surface. These satellites are much closer to the earth, reducing or eliminating apparent propagation delay. They can pick up signals from weak transmitters, so handheld telephones need less power and can use smaller batteries. They consume less power and cost less to launch than GEO and MEO satellites. The footprints of LEO satellites are small, requiring many of them to cover the earth. (Multiple LEO satellites from one organization are referred to as LEO *constellations.*) Table TG4.1 shows the differences among the three types of satellites.

Many companies are in the process of building constellations of satellites for commercial service. Teledesic (*teledesic.com*) and its partners are building a global broadband wireless network they call the "Internet in the Sky." It will use a constellation of 288 LEO satellites. Another LEO system, SkyBridge (*skybridgesatellite.com*), will use two constellations of 40 LEO satellites each to cover the entire earth, except for the polar regions.

global positioning system (GPS)
A wireless system that uses satellites to enable users to determine their position anywhere on the earth.

Global Positioning Systems. As discussed in Chapter 6, a **global positioning system (GPS)** is a wireless system that uses satellites to enable users to determine their position anywhere on the earth. GPS is supported by 24 satellites that are shared worldwide. At any point in time, the exact position of each satellite is known, because the satellite broadcasts its position and a time signal. By using the known speed of the signals and the distance from the three satellites, it is possible to find the location of any receiving station, within a range of 10 feet. GPS software can convert the latitude and longitude computed to an electronic map.

Commercial use of GPS has become widespread, including navigation, mapping, and surveying, particularly in remote areas. Cell phones in the United States now must have a GPS embedded in them so that the location of a caller to 911 can be detected immediately. The city of Charleston, South Carolina, has even installed GPS equipment on its garbage trucks to be able to plan their routes more efficiently and avoid any bottlenecks in traffic.

Table TG4.1 Three Basic Types of Telecommunications Satellites

Type	Considerations	Orbit	Number
GEO	• Satellites remain stationary relative to point on Earth. • Few satellites needed for global coverage. • Transmission delay (approximately .25 second). • Most expensive to build and launch. • Longest orbital life (12+ years).	22,300 miles	8
MEO	• Satellites move relative to point on Earth. • Moderate number needed for global coverage. • Require medium-powered transmitters. • Negligible transmission delay. • Less expensive to build and launch. • Moderate orbital life (6–12 years).	6,434 miles	10–12
LEO	• Satellites move rapidly relative to point on Earth. • Large number needed for global coverage. • Require only low-power transmitters. • Negligible transmission delay. • Least expensive to build and launch. • Shortest orbital life (as low as 5 years).	400–700 miles	Many

Radio. **Radio transmission** uses radio-wave frequencies to send data directly between transmitters and receivers. It does not have to depend on microwave or satellite links, especially for short ranges such as within an office setting. Radio is being used increasingly to connect computers and peripheral equipment or computers and local area networks. For data communications, the greatest advantage of radio is that no metallic wires are needed. Radio waves tend to travel easily through normal office walls. Radio devices are fairly inexpensive and easy to install. Radio also allows for high data transmission speeds.

However, radio media can create electrical interference problems—with other office electrical equipment and from that equipment to the radio communication devices. Also, radio transmissions are susceptible to snooping by anyone similarly equipped and on the same frequency.

radio transmission *Communications channel that uses radio wave frequencies to send data directly between transmitters and receivers over short distances.*

Satellite Radio. One problem with radio transmission is that when you travel too far away from the source station, the signal breaks up and fades into static. Most radio signals can only travel about 30 or 40 miles from their source. However, **satellite radio**, also called **digital radio**, overcomes this problem: It offers uninterrupted, near CD-quality music beamed to your radio from space.

XM Satellite Radio (*xmradio.com*) and Sirius Satellite Radio (*sirius.com*) have launched satellite radio services. XM broadcasts its signals from geosynchronous satellites; Sirius broadcasts its signals from middle-earth orbit satellites. Listeners subscribe to either service for a monthly fee. For example, XM offers 70 music channels and 30 channels of news, talk, sports, and entertainment for $9.99 per month.

satellite radio (digital radio) *Form of radio transmission that offers uninterrupted, near CD-quality music beamed to your radio from space.*

Cellular Radio Technology. Telephone users are increasingly employing cellular radio technology for data communications. **Cellular radio technology** works like this: The Federal Communications Commission (FCC) (*fcc.gov*) has defined geographic cellular service areas. Each area is subdivided into hexagonal cells that fit together like a honeycomb to form the backbone of that area's cellular radio system. A radio "transceiver" (transmitter and receiver) and a computerized cell-site controller that handle all cell-site functions are located at the center of each cell. All the cell sites are connected to a mobile telephone switching office that provides the connections from the cellular system to a wired telephone network. As a user travels out of the cell serving one area and into another, the switching office transfers calls from one cell to another.

Cellular service in the United States is primarily analog, like ground-based telephones; in Europe it is digital. Digital transmission offers the potential of much greater traffic capacity within each cell, less susceptibility to interference, greater voice clarity, and fewer data errors. A conversion to digital is underway in the United States.

cellular radio technology *Use of radio transmissions between cells in geographic service areas and a mobile telephone switching office, enabling wireless phone service.*

Personal Communication Services. **Personal communication services (PCS)** technology uses lower-power, higher-frequency radio waves than does cellular technology. The lower power means that PCS cells are smaller and must be more numerous and closer together. The higher frequency means that PCS devices are effective in many places where cellular telephones are not, such as in tunnels and inside office buildings. PCS telephones need less power, are smaller, and are less expensive than cellular telephones. They also operate at higher, less-crowded frequencies than cellular telephones, meaning that they have the bandwidth necessary to provide video and multimedia communication.

personal communication services (PCS) technology *Wireless communication technology that uses lower-power, higher-frequency radio waves than cellular radio technology, making PCS devices effective in places where cellular devices are not.*

Emerging Wireless Applications. A number of wireless applications are emerging, including terrestrial fixed wireless (also called *broadband wireless*), ultrawideband wireless (see *timedomain.com*), wireless local loop, multichannel multipoint distribution service (MMDS), local multipoint distribution service (LMDS), and free space laser. In general, these technologies are quick, easy, and inexpensive to deploy compared with placing wire or fiber. However, with the exception of ultrawideband, these technologies require unobstructed lines-of-sight, and their signals can be degraded by bad weather such as heavy rain or snow.

infrared *Red light not commonly visible to human eyes; can be modulated or pulsed for conveying information.*

Infrared. Infrared light is red light not commonly visible to human eyes. It can be modulated or pulsed for conveying information. The most common application of infrared light is in television or videocassette recorder remote control units. With computers, infrared transceivers are being used for short-distance connections between computers and peripheral equipment or between computers and local area networks. Many portable PCs can be bought with infrared ports, which are handy when cable connections with a peripheral (such as a printer or modem) are not practical.

Transmission Speed

bandwidth *The range of frequencies available in a communications channel, stated in bits per second.*

Bandwidth refers to the range of frequencies available in any communications channel. Bandwidth is a very important concept in communications because the transmission capacity of any channel (stated in bits per second or bps) is largely dependent on its bandwidth. In general, the greater the bandwidth, the greater the channel capacity.

The speeds of particular communications channels are as follows:

- Twisted-pair wire   up to 100 Mbps (million bits per second)
- Microwave   up to 200 Mbps
- Satellite   up to 200 Mbps
- Coaxial cable   up to 200 Mbps
- Fiber-optic cable   up to 6 Tbps (trillion bits per second)

Before you go on . . .

1. Compare and contrast the wireline communications channels.
2. What are the emerging wireless communications channels?

TG4.2 NETWORK SERVICES

computer network *A system connecting communications media, hardware, and software needed of two or more computer systems and/ or devices.*

A computer network is a system that connects communications media, hardware, and software needed of two or more computer systems and/or devices. Computer networks are essential to modern organizations for many reasons. First, networked computer systems enable organizations to be more flexible and adaptable to meet rapidly changing business conditions. Second, networks enable companies to share hardware, computer applications, and databases across the organization. Third, networks make it possible for geographically dispersed employees and workgroups to share documents, ideas, opinions, and creative insights, encouraging teamwork, innovation, and more efficient and effective interactions. Finally, networks are now the link between businesses and between businesses and their customers.

Networks provide a number of services designed to enable rapid, high-volume, accurate data transmission over any type of network.

Switched and Dedicated Lines

switched lines *Telephone lines through which data transmissions can be routed or switched to their destination.*

Switched lines are telephone lines, provided by common carriers (the long-distance telephone companies), that people can access from their computers to transmit data to another computer; the transmission is routed or switched through paths to its destination. A *switch* is a special-purpose circuit that routes messages along specific paths in a telecommunications system.

dedicated lines (leased lines) *Telephone lines that provide a constant connection between two devices and require no switching or dialing.*

Dedicated lines, also called leased lines, provide a constant connection between two devices and require no switching or dialing. These lines are continuously available for transmission. The lines can be leased or purchased from common carriers or private communications media vendors. The lessee typically pays a flat rate for total access to the line. These lines typically operate at higher speed than switched lines and are used for high-volume transactions.

Integrated Services Digital Network

Integrated services digital network (ISDN) is a high-speed data-transmission technology that allows users to transfer voice, video, image, and data simultaneously at high speed. ISDN uses existing telephone lines and provides two levels of service: basic-rate ISDN and primary-rate ISDN. ISDN transmission is a popular upgrade with firms whose transmission requirements exceed standard telephone capacity.

Basic-rate ISDN serves a single device with three channels. Two channels are B (bearer) channels with a capacity to transmit 64 Kbps of digital data. The third or D channel is a 16 Kbps channel for signaling and control information. *Primary-rate ISDN* provides 1.5 Mbps of bandwidth. The bandwidth contains 23 B channels and one D channel. A second generation of ISDN is *broadband ISDN (BISDN)*, which provides transmission channels capable of supporting transmission rates greater than the primary-rate ISDN.

> **integrated services digital network (ISDN)** *A high-speed technology that allows users to transfer voice, video, image, and data simultaneously, over existing telephone lines.*

Digital Subscriber Line

Digital subscriber lines (DSL) provide high-speed, digital data transmission from homes and businesses over existing telephone lines. The existing lines are analog and the transmission is digital, so modems are necessary with DSL technology. Used under similar circumstances, DSL is a popular alternative to ISDN.

> **digital subscriber line (DSL)** *A high-speed, digital data-transmission technology using existing analog telephone lines.*

Cable Modems

Cable modems are modems that operate over coaxial cable (e.g., cable TV). They offer high-speed access to the Internet or corporate intranets at speeds of up to four Mbps. Cable modems use a shared line; large numbers of users can slow down the access speed of cable modems.

> **cable modem** *A modem that operates over coaxial cable and offers high-speed access to the Internet or corporate intranets.*

Packet Switching

Packet switching is a transmission technology that breaks up blocks of text into small, fixed bundles of data called packets. Each packet travels independently through the network. Packets of data originating at one source can be routed through different paths in the network, and then may be reassembled into the original message when they reach their destination.

Packet switching is causing a telecommunications revolution. Telecommunications providers are transforming their infrastructure from the existing, public, circuit-switched networks designed to carry analog voice traffic to packet-switched networks designed and optimized for data that carry voice as just another data type. The main reason for this revolution is the growth of the Internet, which is a packet-switching network.

> **packet switching** *Data transmission technology that breaks up blocks of text into small, fixed bundles of data (packets) that are sent independently through the network.*

Frame Relay

Frame relay is a faster and less expensive version of packet switching. Frame relay is a shared network service that packages data into frames that are similar to packets. Frame relay, however, does not perform error correction, because modern digital lines are less error-prone than older lines, and networks are more effective at error checking. Frame relay typically can communicate at transmission speeds of 1.544 Mbps, although the technology can reach speeds of 45 Mbps.

> **frame relay** *A data transmission technology that is faster and less expensive than packet switching.*

Fiber Distributed Data Interface

Fiber distributed data interface (FDDI) passes data around a ring network with a bandwidth of 100 Mbps. Although the FDDI standard can use any transmission medium, it is based on the high-speed, high-capacity capabilities of fiber optics. FDDI can significantly boost network performance, but this technology is about 10 times more expensive to implement than most LAN networks.

> **fiber distributed data interface (FDDI)** *Data transmission standard based on the high-speed, high-capacity capabilities of fiber optics.*

Asynchronous Transfer Mode

asynchronous transfer mode (ATM) *Data transmission technology that uses packet switching and allows for almost unlimited bandwidth on demand.*

Asynchronous transfer mode (ATM) networks allow for almost unlimited bandwidth on demand. These networks are packet-switched, eliminating the need for protocol conversion. ATM creates a virtual connection for the packet transmission, which disappears on the completion of a successful transmission.

ATM offers several advantages: It makes possible large increases in bandwidth. It provides support for data, video, and voice transmissions on one communications line. It offers virtual networking capabilities, which increase bandwidth utilization and simplify network administration. ATM currently requires fiber-optic cable, but it can transmit up to 2.5 gigabits per second. On the downside, ATM is more expensive than ISDN and DSL.

Switched-Hub Technologies

switched-hub technology *Data transmission technology that boosts local area networks by adding an ATM-like packet-switching capability.*

Switched-hub technologies are often used to boost local area networks. A switched hub can turn many small LANs into one big LAN. A network need not be rewired nor adapter cards replaced when changes are made; all that is needed is the addition of a switching hub. Switched-hub technology can also add an ATM-like packet-switching capability to existing LANs, essentially doubling bandwidth.

Synchronous Optical Network

synchronous optical network (SONET) *An interface standard for transporting digital signals over fiber-optic lines; allows the integration of transmissions from multiple vendors.*

Synchronous optical network (SONET) is an interface standard for transporting digital signals over fiber-optic lines that allows the integration of transmissions from multiple vendors. SONET defines optical line rates, known as optical carrier (OC) signals. The base rate is 51.84 Mbps (OC-1), and higher rates are direct multiples of the base rate. For example, OC-3 runs at 155.52 Mbps, or three times the rate of OC-1.

T-Carrier System

T-carrier system *A digital transmission system that defines circuits that operate at different rates, all of which are multiples of the basic 64 Kbps used to transport a single voice call.*

The **T-carrier system** is a digital transmission system that defines circuits that operate at different rates, all of which are multiples of the basic 64 Kbps used to transport a single voice call. These circuits include T1 (1.544 Mbps, equivalent to 24 channels); T2 (6.312 Mbps, equivalent to 96 channels); T3 (44.736 Mbps, equivalent to 672 channels); and T4 (274.176 Mbps, equivalent to 4,032 channels).

Before you go on . . .

1. What is packet switching and why is it so important?
2. Compare and contrast FDDI, ATM, SONET, and the T-carrier system.

TG4.3 NETWORK PROTOCOLS

Computing devices that are connected to the network access and share the network to transmit and receive data. These components are often referred to as "nodes" of the network. They work together by adhering to a common set of rules that enable them to communicate with each other. This set of rules and procedures governing transmission across a network is a **protocol**.

protocol *The set of rules and procedures governing transmission across a network.*

The principal functions of protocols in a network are line access and collision avoidance. *Line access* concerns how the sending device gains access to the network to send a message. *Collision avoidance* refers to managing message transmission so that two messages do not collide with each other on the network. Other functions of protocols are to identify each device in the communication path, to secure the attention of the other device, to verify correct receipt of the transmitted message, to verify that a message requires retransmission because it cannot be correctly interpreted, and to perform recovery when errors occur.

Ethernet

The most common network protocol is Ethernet. Ethernet 10BaseT means that the network has a speed of 10 Mbps. Fast Ethernet is 100BaseT, meaning that the network has a speed of 100 Mbps. The most common protocol in large corporations is the gigabit Ethernet. That is, the network provides data transmission speeds of one billion bits per second (666 times faster than a T1 line). However, 10-gigabit Ethernet is becoming the standard (10 billion bits per second).

Ethernet *The most common network protocol.*

gigabit Ethernet *The most common network protocol in large corporations, which provides data transmission speeds of one billion bits per second.*

TCP/IP

The Transmission Control Protocol/Internet Protocol (TCP/IP) is a file transfer protocol that can send large files of information across sometimes-unreliable networks with assurance that the data will arrive in uncorrupted form. TCP/IP is the protocol of the Internet. It allows efficient and reasonably error-free transmission between different systems. TCP/IP is becoming very popular with business organizations due to its reliability and the ease with which it can support intranets and related functions.

Transmission Control Protocol/ Internet Protocol (TCP/IP) *A file transfer protocol that can send large files of information across sometimes-unreliable networks with assurance that the data will arrive uncorrupted.*

The International Standards Organization Open Systems Interconnection Protocol

Network devices from different vendors must communicate with each other by following the same protocols. Unfortunately, commercially available data communication devices follow a number of different protocols, causing substantial problems with data communications networks.

Attempts at standardizing data communications have been somewhat successful, but standardization in the United States has lagged behind other countries where the communications industry is more closely regulated. Various organizations, including the Electronic Industries Association (EIA), the Consultative Committee for International Telegraph and Telephone (CCITT), and the International Standards Organization (ISO) have developed electronic interfacing protocols that are widely used within the industry.

Typically, the protocols required to achieve communication on behalf of an application are actually multiple protocols existing at different levels or layers. Each layer defines a set of functions that are provided as services to upper layers, and each layer relies on services provided by lower layers. At each layer, one or more protocols define precisely how software on different systems interacts to accomplish the functions for that layer. This layering notion has been formalized in several architectures. The most widely known is the Open Systems Interconnection (OSI) model of the International Standards Organization (ISO). The *ISO-OSI model* defines how software on different systems communicates at different layers. The model has seven layers, each having its own well-defined function.

Layer 1: Physical layer. Defines the mechanism for communicating with the transmission media and interface hardware.

Layer 2: Data link layer. Validates the integrity of the flow of data.

Layer 3: Network layer. Defines the protocols for data routing to ensure that information arrives at the correct destination.

Layer 4: Transport layer. Defines the protocols for structuring messages.

Layer 5: Session layer. Coordinates communications and maintains the session for as long as needed, including security and log-on functions.

Layer 6: Presentation layer. Defines the way data is formatted, converted, and encoded.

Layer 7: Application layer. Defines the way that applications programs such as e-mail interact with the network.

TG4.4 NETWORK PROCESSING STRATEGIES

distributed processing *Network architecture that divides processing work between two or more computers, linked together in a network.*

Organizations typically use multiple computer systems across the firm. **Distributed processing** divides processing work between two or more computers, enabling computers in different locations to communicate with each other via telecommunications links. A common type of distributed processing is client/server processing. A special type of client/server processing is peer-to-peer processing.

Client/Server Computing

client/server computing *Form of distributed processing in which some machines (servers) perform computing functions for end-user PCs (clients).*

Client/server computing links two or more computers in an arrangement in which some machines (called "servers") perform computing functions for end-user PCs (called "clients"). Sometimes either machine can perform processing and store applications. Usually, however, an organization has the bulk of its processing or application/data storage done on suitably powerful servers that can be accessed by less powerful client machines. The client requests applications, data, or processing from the server, which acts on these requests by "serving" the desired commodity.

In a client/server approach, the three components of an application (presentation, application, and data management) can be distributed over the enterprise rather than being centrally controlled. The presentation component is the application interface (that is, how the application appears to the user). The application logic is the bulk of the software program, created to perform some business function. The data management component consists of the storage and management of the data needed by the application. The exact division of processing tasks depends on the requirements of each application, including its processing needs, the number of users, and the available resources. The processing may be distributed at various sites in a telecommunications network.

Client/server computing leads to the ideas of "fat" clients and "thin" clients. *Fat clients* have large storage and processing power and can handle the three components of an application. *Thin clients* may have no local storage and limited processing power. This means that thin clients can handle only the presentation component. Network computers are popular thin clients.

Peer-to-Peer Processing

peer-to-peer processing *A type of client/server distributed processing that allows two or more computers to pool their resources, making each computer both a client and a server.*

Peer-to-peer processing is a type of client/server distributed processing that allows two or more computers to pool their resources. Individual resources such as disk drives, CD-ROM drives, and printers become shared resources that are accessible from every computer. Unlike standard client/server networks, where network information is stored on a centralized file server and made available to many clients, the information stored across peer-to-peer networks is uniquely decentralized. Because peer-to-peer computers have their own disk drives that are accessible by all computers, each computer acts as *both* a client and a server. Each computer has transparent access (as assigned for security or integrity purposes) to all files on all other computers.

There are three basic types of peer-to-peer processing. The first accesses unused CPU power among networked computers. Well-known applications of this type are Gnutella (*gnutella.wego.com*) and SETI@home (*setiathome.ssl.berkeley.edu*). These applications are from open-source projects and can be downloaded at no cost.

The second form of peer-to-peer is real-time, person-to-person collaboration, such as America Online's Instant Messenger. Companies such as Groove Networks (*groove.net*) have introduced P2P collaborative applications that use buddy lists to establish a connection, then allow real-time collaboration within the application.

The third peer-to-peer category is advanced search and file sharing. This category is characterized by natural-language searches of millions of peer systems and lets users discover other users, not just data and Web pages. One example of this is Madster (*madster.com*), which allows searching of the major Internet file-sharing services, such as AOL and Gnutella. The search is accomplished through Madster's integration with instant messaging tools.

Before you go on . . .

1. What is client/server computing?
2. What is peer-to-peer processing?

TG4.5 TYPES OF COMPUTER NETWORKS

There are various types of computer networks, ranging from small to worldwide. Types of networks include (from smallest to largest) local area networks, wide area networks, and the Internet. Here we look at local area and wide area networks. See Technology Guide 5 for discussion of the Internet.

Local Area Networks

A **local area network (LAN)** connects two or more communicating devices in a limited geographical region (usually within the same building), so that every user device on the network has the potential to communicate with every other device.

LANs come in an assortment of topologies. The **topology** of a network is the physical layout and connectivity of a network. Specific protocols are often used on specific topologies, but the two concepts are different. *Topology* refers to the ways the channels connect the nodes, whereas *protocol* refers to the rules by which data communications take place over these channels. There are five basic LAN topologies: star, bus, ring, hierarchical, and hybrid. Figure TG4.4 (page 472) illustrates these different types.

Each topology has strengths and weaknesses. When systems developers choose a topology, they should consider such performance issues as delay, speed, reliability, and the network's ability to continue through, or recover after, failure in any device or connection to the network. The company should also consider such physical constraints as the maximum transmission speed needed, the distances between nodes, the network's susceptibility to errors, and the overall system costs.

LAN Technology.   A LAN consists of a file server, a number of client machines (called nodes), cabling or wireless technology linking individual devices, network interface cards (special adapters serving as interfaces to the cable), and software to control LAN activities. The LAN **file server** is a repository of various software and data files for the network. The server determines who gets access to what and in what sequence. Servers may be powerful microcomputers with large, fast-access hard drives, or they may be workstations, minicomputers, or mainframes. The server typically houses the LAN's network operating system, which manages the server and routes and manages communications on the network. The LAN **network interface card** specifies the data transmission rate, the size of message units, the addressing information attached to each message, and network topology.

The network gateway connects the LAN to public networks or other corporate networks so that the LAN can exchange information with networks external to it. A **gateway** is a communications processor that can connect dissimilar networks by translating from one set of protocols to another. A **bridge** connects two networks of the same type. A **router** routes messages through several connected LANs or to a wide area network.

---

local area network (LAN) *Network that connects communications devices in a limited geographical region (e.g., a building), so that every user device on the network can communicate with every other device.*

topology *The physical layout and connectivity of a network.*

file server *A repository of various software and data files for the network, which determines who gets access to what and in what sequence.*

network interface card *Hardware that specifies the data transmission rate, the size of message units, the addressing information attached to each message, and network topology.*

gateway *A communications processor that connects dissimilar networks by translating from one set of protocols to another.*

bridge *A communications processor that connects two networks of the same type.*

router *A communications processor that routes messages through several connected LANs or to a wide area network.*

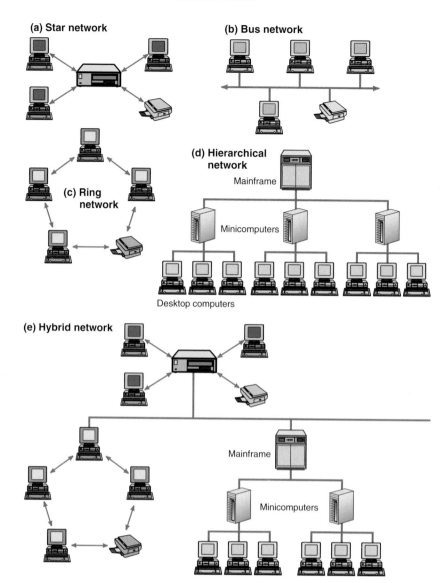

Figure TG4.4 *The five main network topologies.*

wireless local area network (WLAN) technologies *Technologies (e.g., Bluetooth and Wi-Fi) that provide LAN connectivity over short distances, typically limited to less than 150 meters.*

Bluetooth *A wireless technology that enables temporary, short-range connection between wireless devices and enables these devices to communicate with each other via low-power radio frequencies.*

Wi-Fi (Wireless Fidelity) *A wireless technology that can transmit information at a range up to 300 feet; another name for the 802.11b standard on which most WLANs run.*

Wireless Local Area Networks (WLANs). **WLAN technologies** provide LAN connectivity over short distances, typically limited to less than 150 meters. WLAN technologies include Bluetooth and Wi-Fi. Wireless LANs are sometimes referred to as *personal area networks*. Chapter 6 discusses wireless technology in detail.

Bluetooth. **Bluetooth** is a wireless technology that enables temporary, short-range connection (data and voice) between wireless devices and enables these devices to communicate with each other via low-power radio frequencies. Bluetooth can also form a home network by linking devices like lights, televisions, the furnace and air conditioning, and the garage door. Bluetooth does not operate by line-of-sight, thus allowing transmissions to occur around corners, through walls, and through briefcases. Problems with Bluetooth include security, transmission speed (maximum transmission speed is 720 Kbps), and cost.

Wi-Fi. **Wi-Fi (Wireless Fidelity)** is a wireless technology that can transmit information as fast as 11 megabits per second at a range up to 300 feet. As discussed in Chapter 6, Wi-Fi is another name for the 802.11b standard on which most WLANs run. With a Wi-Fi enabled computer, users within range of a Wi-Fi "hot spot" (access point), can log on and take advantage of very fast connection speeds. Even though there are about 30,000 hot spots in the United States in airports, libraries, hotels, and food establishments (e.g., Starbucks stores), it may be difficult to find one (check out *wifinder.com*). Many hot spots offer free, public access, while other hot spots charge for access.

Private Branch Exchanges. A **private branch exchange (PBX)** is a type of LAN that controls telephone switching at a company site. PBXs can carry both voice and data and perform a wide variety of functions to make communications more convenient and effective, such as call waiting, call forwarding, and voice mail. PBXs also reduce the number of outside lines, provide internal extensions, and determine least-cost routings.

private branch exchange (PBX) *A type of LAN that controls telephone switching at a company site.*

Wide Area Networks

Of course, businesses have to transmit and receive data beyond the confines of the local area network. This is accomplished by connecting to one or more wide area networks. As their name indicates, **wide area networks (WANs)** are networks that cover wide geographic areas. They generally are provided by common carriers. WANs include regional networks such as telephone companies or international networks such as global communications services providers. They have large capacity and typically combine switched and dedicated lines, microwave, and satellite communications.

wide area network (WAN) *A network, generally are provided by a common telecommunications carrier, that covers a wide geographic area.*

Some WANs are commercial, regulated networks, while others are privately owned, usually by large businesses that can afford the costs. Some WANs, however, are "public" in terms of their management, resources, and access. One such public WAN is the Internet.

Value-Added Networks. **Value-added networks (VANs)** are types of WANs. They are private, data-only networks that are managed by outside third parties and used by multiple organizations to obtain economies in the cost of service and in network management. VANs add value through the telecommunications and computing services these networks provide. VANs can offer message storage, tracking, and relay services as well as teleconferencing services, thus enabling their users to more closely tailor communications capabilities to specific business needs.

value-added network (VAN) *A private, data-only network that is managed by an outside third party and used by multiple organizations to obtain economies in the cost of network service and network management.*

Companies obtain VAN services through subscription. Customers do not have to invest in network hardware and software or perform their own error checking, editing, routing, and protocol conversion. Subscribers realize savings in line charges and transmission costs because the costs of using the network are shared by many users.

Virtual Private Networks. A **virtual private network (VPN)** is a WAN operated by a common carrier. VPNs provide a gateway between a corporate LAN and the Internet, and they allow access to a corporate network's e-mail, shared files, or intranet, via an Internet connection. VPNs allow an organization to leverage the robust, shared communications infrastructure of the Internet to hook up with remote users, branch offices, and business partners worldwide, without paying the distance-sensitive fees that carriers charge for conventional network links.

virtual private network (VPN) *A WAN operated by a common carrier; provides a gateway between a corporate LAN and the Internet.*

In the connection with the Internet, a VPN server handles the security, such as authentication, permitting access from the Internet to an intranet. The data travel over the Internet in encrypted form, a process called **tunneling**. VPNs are particularly effective for extranets, because they allow the use of the Internet among business partners instead of using a more expensive VAN. VPNs are also especially important for international business, where long-distance calls or VANs remain very expensive.

tunneling *The process of sending data over the Internet in encrypted form.*

Enterprise Networking

Organizations today have multiple LANs and may have multiple WANs, which are interconnected to form an **enterprise network**. Figure TG4.5 (page 474) shows a model of enterprise computing. Note that the enterprise network in the figure has a backbone network composed of fiber-optic cable using the FDDI protocol. The LANs are called *embedded LANs* because they connect to the backbone WAN. These LANs are usually composed of twisted-pair wire.

enterprise network *Interconnected multiple LANs and WANs.*

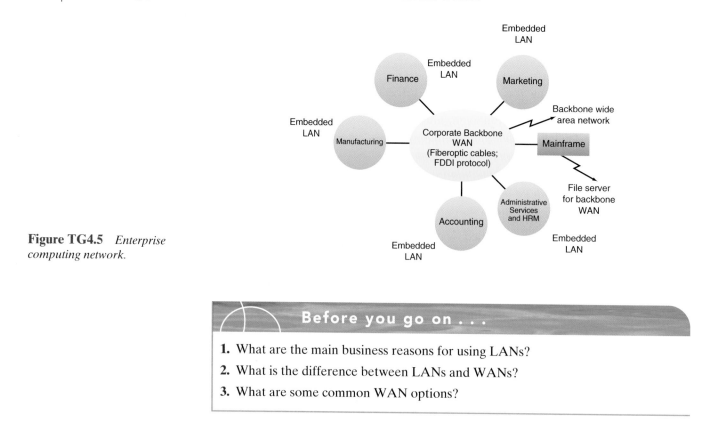

Figure TG4.5 *Enterprise computing network.*

Before you go on . . .

1. What are the main business reasons for using LANs?

2. What is the difference between LANs and WANs?

3. What are some common WAN options?

SUMMARY

1. **Describe the components of a telecommunications system.** Telecommunications systems are composed of computer hardware (both client on the desktop and host computers, such as servers and mainframes), and of communications media, networks, software, providers, protocols, and applications.

2. **Describe the eight basic types of communications media, including their advantages and disadvantages.** The eight basic types of communications media are twisted-pair wire, coaxial cable, fiber-optic cable, microwave, satellite, radio, cellular radio, and infrared transmission. The first three media are cable media, and the remaining five are broadcast (wireless) media. Manager's Checklist TG4.1 describes the advantages and disadvantages of each medium.

3. **Describe the major types of network services.** *Switched lines* are telephone lines that people can access to transmit data to another computer; the transmission is routed or switched through paths to its destination. *Dedicated lines* (leased lines) provide a constant connection between two devices and require no switching or dialing. *Integrated services digital network (ISDN)* technology allows users to transfer voice, video, image, and data simultaneously at high speed, using existing telephone lines. *Digital subscriber lines* provide high-speed, digital data transmission, also over existing telephone lines. *Cable modems* operate over coaxial cable (e.g., cable TV).

Packet-switching technology breaks up blocks of text into small, fixed bundles of data (packets), which travel independently through the network and are reassembled into the original message at their destination. *Frame relay* is a shared network service that packages data into frames that are similar to packets. *Fiber distributed data interface (FDDI)* passes data around a ring network with a bandwidth of 100 Mbps. *Asynchronous transfer mode (ATM)* networks are packet-switched and allow for almost unlimited bandwidth on demand. *Switched-hub technologies* boost local area networks by turning many small LANs into one big LAN. *Synchronous optical network (SONET)* is an interface standard for transporting digital signals over fiber-optic lines, allowing integration of transmissions from multiple vendors. The *T-carrier system* is a digital transmission system, whose circuits operate at different rates, all of which are multiples of 64 Kbps.

4. **Describe the Ethernet and TCP/IP protocols.** The most common network protocol is *Ethernet*. Ethernet 10BaseT means that the network has a speed of 10 Mbps. Fast Ethernet is 100BaseT, meaning that the network has a speed of 100 Mbps. The most common protocol in large corporations is the gigabit Ethernet, which provides data transmission speeds of one billion bits per second. The 10-gigabit Ethernet (10 billion bits per second) is becoming the standard. The *Transmission Control Protocol/Internet Protocol*

(*TCP/IP*) is a file transfer, packet-switching, protocol that can send large files of information with assurance that the data will arrive in uncorrupted form. TCP/IP is the communications protocol of the Internet.

5. **Differentiate between client/server computing and peer-to-peer computing.** Client/server architecture divides processing between clients and servers. Both are on the network, but each processor is assigned functions it is best suited to perform. In a client/server approach, the components of an application (i.e., presentation, application, and data management) are distributed over the enterprise rather than being centrally controlled. Peer-to-peer processing is a type of client/server distributed processing that allows two or more computers to pool their resources, so that each computer acts as both a client and a server.

6. **Describe the two major types of networks.** The two major types of networks are local area networks and wide area networks. LANs encompass a limited geographic area and are usually composed of one communications medium. WANs encompass a broad geographic area and are usually composed of multiple communications media.

DISCUSSION QUESTIONS

1. What are the implications of having fiber-optic cable going to everyone's home?
2. Would you recommend that all organizations employ client/server architectures? Why or why not? Would you recommend that all organizations employ centralized, mainframe architectures? Why or why not?
3. Compare and contrast the three basic types of satellite.
4. Do you feel that satellite telephones will eventually replace today's cell phones? Support your answer.
5. Compare and contrast local area networks, wide area networks, and value-added networks.

INTERNET ACTIVITIES

1. Prepare a report contrasting the regional Bell operating companies (RBOCs) as to location, size, number of employees, market capitalization, strategy, and strategic alliances. You will have to access the Web to find the names of the RBOCs and then access their home pages. (Hint: Start with an Internet search engine such as Google.)
2. Access the Web sites of the companies entering the satellite market and obtain the latest information regarding the status of their satellite constellations. Prepare a report detailing the current status of these constellations.

TEAM ASSIGNMENTS

Your team is in charge of telecommunications and networking at a rapidly expanding manufacturing company. The company has three plants in the United States (South Carolina, Oregon, and Texas) and is building new manufacturing facilities in Ireland, Singapore, and Mexico. The CEO wants a plan to upgrade the corporate networks. Develop a plan for the upgrade, to include the proposed type and topology of the new network. Be sure to address the networks across the enterprise as well as the networks inside the new plants.

CLUB IT wiley.com/college/turban

TELECOMMUNICATIONS AT CLUB IT

1. What equipment does Club IT need to buy to provide wireless Internet access to their customers?
2. Common Layer 7 applications include http, ftp, telnet, and smtp. Describe what each application is used for and if they are useful for Club IT.

Go to wiley.com/college/turban to access the CLUB IT Web Site on the Student Web Site

Internet Basics

Outline

Learning Objectives

1. Describe what the Internet is, how it works (including the role of the TCP/IP protocol), and how users connect to it.
2. Describe the capabilities that the Internet offers to users.
3. Describe the World Wide Web and differentiate it from the Internet.
4. Identify and briefly describe the management challenges caused by the Internet.
5. Define the term intranet and discuss how intranets are used by businesses.

TG5.1 WHAT IS THE INTERNET?

Internet ("the Net") *The massive network that connects computer networks of businesses, organizations, government agencies, and schools around the world, quickly, seamlessly, and inexpensively.*

nodes *Computing devices that are connected to a network, including the Internet.*

The **Internet ("the Net")** is a network that connects approximately one million internal organizational computer networks in over 200 countries on all continents, including Antarctica. Examples of these internal organizational computer networks include a university computer system, the computer system of a corporation such as General Motors or General Electric, or a hospital computer system. Participating computer systems, called **nodes**, include PCs, local area networks, database(s), and mainframes. On the Internet, a node may include several networks of an organization, possibly connected by a wide area network. As a network or networks, the Internet enables people to access data in other organizations and to communicate, collaborate, and exchange information seamlessly around the world, quickly and inexpensively. Thus, the Internet has become a necessity in the conduct of modern business.

Evolution of the Internet

The Internet grew out of an experimental project of the Advanced Research Project Agency (ARPA) of the U.S. Department of Defense. The project began in 1969, as the *ARPAnet*, to test the feasibility of a wide area computer network over which researchers, educators, military personnel, and government agencies could share data, exchange messages, and transfer files.

From four nodes at its beginning, the Internet has grown to millions of nodes today. The major growth occurred after commercial organizations were allowed to join ARPAnet, which was renamed the Internet in 1993. There are over 500 million Internet users today.

backbone *The main fiber-optic network that links the nodes of a network.*

The computers and organizational nodes on the Internet can be of different types and makes and are connected to each other by data communications lines of different speeds. The main network that links the nodes is referred to as the **backbone**. For the Internet, the backbone is a fiber-optic network currently operated mainly by telecommunications companies such as MCI.

No central agency manages the Internet. The cost of its operation is shared among hundreds of thousands of nodes, and therefore the cost for any one organization is small. Organizations must pay a small fee if they wish to register their names, and they need to have their own hardware and software for the operation of their internal networks. The organizations are obliged to move any data or information that enters their organizational network, regardless of its source, to its destination, at no charge to the senders. The senders, of course, pay the telephone bills for using the backbone or regular telephone lines.

Future of the Internet

In some cases, the Internet is too slow for data-intensive applications. In addition, the Internet can be unreliable and insecure. As a result, three initiatives are underway to improve today's Internet.

Internet2 *A new, faster telecommunications network with limited access, devoted exclusively to research purposes.*

Internet2. The academic research community, which the Internet was originally intended to serve, found the Internet too slow for data-intensive applications (such as transmitting supercomputer model data or telemedicine). In 1996, a consortium of 34 universities began establishing a faster network with limited access, devoted exclusively to research purposes. Today, **Internet2** includes over 180 universities working in partnership with industry and government to develop and deploy advanced network applications and technologies. Internet2 is not a separate physical network from the Internet.

The primary goals of Internet2 are to: create a leading edge network capability for the national research community; enable revolutionary Internet applications; and ensure the rapid transfer of new network services and applications to the broader Internet community. For more detail, see *Internet2.edu*.

Next-Generation Internet (NGI).   The Next Generation Internet (NGI) initiative is a multiagency, U.S. federal government research and development program that is developing revolutionary applications that require advanced networking. The broad goals of the NGI initiative are to research and develop advanced end-to-end networking technologies, focusing primarily on reliability, robustness, security, quality of service guarantees for multicasting and video, and bandwidth allocation. That is, the NGI initiative aims to create an Internet that is fast, always on, everywhere, natural, intelligent, easy, and trusted. To this end, NGI is building two test beds, one at speeds at least 100 times faster than today's Internet, and the other 1,000 times faster. For more detail, see *ngi.gov*.

Very-High-Speed Backbone Network Service (vBNS).   The vBNS is a high-speed network designed to support the academic Internet2 and the government-sponsored Next-Generation Internet (NGI) initiative. The vBNS was first implemented as an OC-3 (155 Mbps) backbone but has been upgraded to OC-12 (622 Mbps). The goal is to increase the vBNS backbone to OC-48 (2.4 Gbps).

Next-Generation Internet (NGI)
A multiagency, U.S. federal government research and development program that is developing revolutionary applications that require advanced networking.

vBNS (Very-High-Speed Backbone Network Service)   *A high-speed network designed to support the academic Internet2 and the government-sponsored Next-Generation Internet (NGI) initiative.*

Before you go on . . .

1. Describe the evolution of the Internet.
2. What are two future initiatives for the Internet?

TG5.2 OPERATION OF THE INTERNET

The set of rules used to send and receive packets from one machine to another over the Internet is known as the Internet Protocol (IP), which operates at the network layer of the seven-layer ISO-OSI model (see Technology Guide 4). Other protocols are used in connection with IP, the best known of which is the *Transmission Control Protocol (TCP)*, which operates at the transport layer of the ISO-OSI model. The IP and TCP protocols are so commonly used together that they are referred to as the *TCP/IP protocol*.

The Internet, a packet-switching network, breaks each message into packets (see Figure TG5.1). Each packet contains the addresses of the sending and receiving machines, as well as sequencing information about its location relative to other packets in the message. Each packet can travel independently across various network interconnections. Therefore, packets may utilize different paths across the Internet and arrive out of sequence. When all packets arrive at the receiving computer, they are reassembled into the complete message.

Internet Protocol (IP)   *The set of rules used to send and receive packets from one machine to another over the Internet.*

Accessing the Internet

There are several ways to access the Internet. From your place of work or your university, you can access an Internet-connected file server on your organization's LAN.

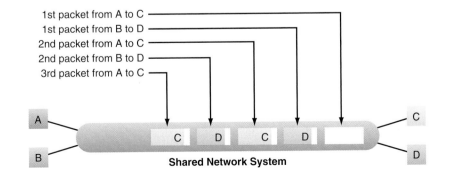

1st packet from A to C
1st packet from B to D
2nd packet from A to C
2nd packet from B to D
3rd packet from A to C

A
B
C
D
Shared Network System

Figure TG5.1   *How packet switching works.
[Source: Douglas E. Cromer,* The Internet Book, *2nd ed. (Upper Saddle River, NJ: Prentice-Hall, 1997). Reprinted by permission.]*

A campus or company backbone connects all the various LANs and servers in the organization to the Internet. Using a modem you can connect to your campus or company network from any place that offers a dial tone. You can also log onto the Internet from your home or on the road, and wireless connections are also possible. Connection to the Internet is also available through commercial providers (e.g., America Online, AOL), for which you pay a fee. Many telephone providers, such as AT&T and MCI, also sell Internet access, as do computer companies such as Microsoft. Companies that provide Internet connections for a fee are called **Internet service providers (ISPs)**.

We now turn our attention to the various ways that you can connect to the Internet.

Connecting via LAN Server. This approach requires the user's computer to have specialized software called a *communications stack*, which provides a set of communications protocols that perform the complete functions of the seven layers of the OSI communications model (see Technology Guide 4).

Connecting via Serial Line Internet Protocol/Point-to-Point Protocol (SLIP/PPP). This approach requires that users have a modem and specialized software that allows them to dial into a SLIP/PPP server through a service provider. This type of connection is advantageous, for example, for employees working at home who need to access the Internet or their own company's intranet.

Connecting via an Online Service. This approach requires a modem, standard communications software, and an online information service account with an Internet service provider. Large ISPs include Juno (*juno.com*), Earthlink (*earthlink.net*), Net-Zero (*netzero.net*), AT&T (*download.att.net*), and thousands of others. To find a local ISP, access *thelist.com*; there, you can search by your telephone area code for an ISP that services your area.

Connecting via the Television. For people who do not own a computer, television can also provide access to the Internet. Using a television set, a special connection device, and a telephone connection, viewers can surf the World Wide Web in their living rooms. The concept was pioneered by Web TV Networks (now a division of Microsoft at *msntv.com*), which manufactures an add-on device for the television.

An alternative is a combined PC and TV, which is a PC with a TV feature. It takes advantage of the convergence of telecommunications, television, and computer to deliver video and other multimedia content over the Internet at low cost. Technologies are now available to enable PCs to decode TV signals and to receive full-motion video over the Internet. TV sets also have the ability to access the Internet through a $100 set-top box.

Connecting via Other Means. There have been several attempts to make access to the Internet cheaper, faster, and/or easier. Special Internet terminals called "Internet Lite" or network computers (see Technology Guide 1) are used by some companies. Also, **Internet kiosks** are terminals placed in public places like libraries and airports (and even in convenience stores in some countries) for use by those who do not have computers of their own. Accessing the Internet from cell phones and pagers is also growing very rapidly.

Addresses on the Internet

Each computer on the Internet has an assigned address, called the **IP** (Internet Protocol) **address**, that uniquely identifies it from the other computers. The IP address consists of numbers, in four parts, separated by dots. For example, the IP address of one computer might be 135.62.128.91.

Most computers also have names, which are easier for people to remember than IP addresses. These names are derived from a naming system called the **domain name system (DNS)**. Currently, 82 companies, called registrars, are accredited to register domain names from the Internet Corporation for Assigned Names (ICANN) (*internic.net*).

Internet service providers (ISPs) *Companies that provide Internet connections for a fee.*

Internet kiosks *Terminals for public use.*

IP address *An assigned address that uniquely identifies a computer on the Internet.*

domain name system (DNS) *The system administered, by the Internet Corporation for Assigned Names (ICANN), that assigns names to each site on the Internet.*

Domain names consist of multiple parts, separated by dots, which are translated from right to left.

For example, consider the domain name *software.ibm.com*. The rightmost part of an Internet name is its **top-level specification**, or the **zone**. It designates the type of organization that owns the site. The letters "com" in *software.ibm.com* indicate that this is a commercial site. There are 18 other top-level specifications, the last six of which are under consideration at this time. The 19 top-level specifications are as follows:

com	commercial sites
edu	educational sites
mil	military sites
gov	government sites
net	networking organizations
org	organizations
firm	businesses and firms
store	businesses offering goods for purchase
info	information service providers
web	entities related to World Wide Web activities
arts	cultural and entertainment activities
rec	recreational activities
nom	individuals
aero	air-transport industry
biz	businesses
coop	cooperatives
museum	museums
name	registration by individuals
pro	accountants, lawyers, physicians

To finish our domain name example, "ibm" is the name of the company (IBM), and "software" is the name of the particular machine (computer) within the company to which the message is being sent.

In some domain names, you will find two letters to the right of the top-level specification. These two letters represent the country of the Web site. For example, "us" stands for the United States, "de" for Germany, "it" for Italy, and "ru" for Russia.

There are some 300,000 registered domain names, and these domain names have commercial value in themselves. As discussed in Chapter 5, this value has led to the practice of *cybersquatting*—buying a potentially coveted domain name and hoping someone wants that name enough to pay for it. The practice of cybersquatting grew out of the early policy of registering domain names on a first-come, first-served basis. This policy resulted in companies or individuals registering a domain name associated with an established firm before the established firm did, which resulted in disputed names and legal actions. Dreams of six-figure payouts all but ended when the U.S. Congress passed the Anti-Cybersquatting Consumer Protection Act in November 2000.

domain name *The name assigned to an Internet site, consisting of multiple parts, separated by dots, which are translated from right to left.*

top-level specification (zone) *The rightmost part of an Internet name, indicating the type of organization that owns the site.*

Before you go on . . .

1. Describe the various ways that you can connect to the Internet.
2. Describe the parts of an Internet address.

TG5.3 SERVICES PROVIDED BY THE INTERNET

The Internet provides a variety of services: discovery, communications, collaboration, Web services, and the World Wide Web (see Chapter 4 for detailed discussions).

Discovery services involve browsing and information retrieval, and provide customers the ability to find, view, download, and process information. Discovery is facilitated by software agents because the amount of information on the Internet and intranets continues to grow rapidly.

The Internet also provides fast and inexpensive *communications services* that range from messages posted on electronic bulletin boards to complex information exchanges among many organizations. Communications services include e-mail, chatting, newsgroups, and Internet telephony (called *voice over IP*, or *VoIP*), among others.

The Internet enables electronic *collaboration* among individuals and groups, as well as collaboration among organizations. Several tools are available for collaboration, ranging from screen sharing and teleconferencing to group support systems.

The next step in software evolution will have software applications provided in the form of services delivered over the Internet. Web Services are self-contained, self-describing business and consumer modular applications, delivered over the Internet, that users can select and combine through almost any device (from personal computers to mobile phones). Web Services allow users to transparently access rich software content from any site on the Web. For further discussion, see Technology Guide 6.

Microsoft's platform for XML Web Services is .NET. The .NET framework allows unrelated Web sites to communicate with each other and with programs that run on personal computers. By using .NET, one click could set off many different applications without requiring the user to open new programs or visit additional Web sites.

The final one of the Internet services listed above is the *World Wide Web*. Because it has such great importance for e-commerce (discussed in Chapter 5), we will discussed it as a separate topic, in Section TG5.4.

Web Services *Self-contained business/consumer modular applications delivered over the Internet.*

Before you go on . . .

1. Describe the services offered by the Internet.

2. What are Web Services?

TG5.4 THE WORLD WIDE WEB

the Web (World Wide Web) *System with universally accepted standards for storing, retrieving, formatting, and displaying information via a client/server architecture; uses the transport functions of the Internet.*

Hypertext Markup Language (HTML) *Programming language used on the Web, which formats documents and incorporates dynamic hypertext links to other documents stored on computers.*

Standard Generalized Markup Language (SGML) *Text-based programming language for describing the content and structure of digital documents; the language from which HTML was developed.*

home page *A text and graphical screen display that welcomes users and explains the organization that has established the page.*

The Internet and the World Wide Web are not the same thing. The Internet functions as a transport mechanism, and the World Wide Web (the Web, WWW, or W3) is an *application that uses those transport functions*. Other applications also run on the Internet, with e-mail being the most widely used.

The Web is a system with universally accepted standards for storing, retrieving, formatting, and displaying information via a client/server architecture. The Web handles all types of digital information, including text, hypermedia, graphics, and sound. It uses graphical user interfaces, so is very easy to use. The technology underlying the World Wide Web was created by Timothy Berners-Lee, who in 1989 proposed a global network of hypertext documents that would allow physics researchers to work together.

The Web is based on a standard hypertext language called Hypertext Markup Language (HTML), which formats documents and incorporates dynamic hypertext links to other documents stored on the same or different computers. HTML was derived from the more complex Standard Generalized Markup Language (SGML), a text-based language for describing the content and structure of digital documents. HTML is a simpler subset of SGML and incorporates tables, applets, text flow around images, superscripts, and subscripts. Using these hypertext links (which are typically blue, bold, and underlined), the user points at a highlighted word, clicks on it, and is transported to another document. Users are able to navigate around the Web freely with no restrictions, following their own logic, needs, or interests.

Offering information through the Web requires establishing a home page, which is a text and graphical screen display that usually welcomes the user and explains the organization that has established the page. In most cases, the home page will lead users to other pages. All the pages of a particular company or individual are known as a Web site. Most Web pages provide a way to contact the organization or the individual. The person in charge of an organization's Web site is its Webmaster.

To access a Web site, the user must specify a uniform resource locator (URL), which points to the address of a specific resource on the Web. For instance, the URL for Microsoft is *http://www.microsoft.com*. HTTP stands for hypertext transport protocol, which is the communications standard used to transfer pages across the WWW portion of the Internet. HTTP defines how messages are formatted and transmitted and what actions Web servers and browsers should take in response to various commands. The remaining letters in this URL—*www.microsoft.com*—indicate the domain name that identifies the Web server storing the Web site.

Browsers

Users primarily access the Web through software applications called browsers. Browsers provide a graphical front end that enable users to point-and-click their way across the Web, a process called surfing. Web browsers became a means of universal access because they deliver the same interface on any operating system under which they run. The two leading browsers are Internet Explorer from Microsoft and Netscape Navigator.

Web site *Collectively, all of the Web pages of a particular company or individual.*

Webmaster *The person in charge of an organization's Web site.*

uniform resource locator (URL) *Set of letters that identify the address of a specific resource on the Web.*

hypertext transport protocol (HTTP) *The communications standard used to transfer pages across the WWW portion of the Internet; defines how messages are formatted and transmitted.*

browsers *Software applications through which users primarily access the Web.*

surfing *The process of navigating around the Web by pointing and clicking a Web browser.*

Before you go on . . .

1. What is a URL? Describe the different parts that make up a URL.
2. What are the roles of browsers?

TG5.5 INTERNET CHALLENGES

Challenges facing the Internet in the next few years include Internet regulation, expansion, and privacy.

Internet Regulation

Technical organizations, such as the Internet Engineering Task Force, the World Wide Web Consortium, and others, are not formally charged in any legal or operational sense with responsibility for the Internet. However, they define the standards that govern the Internet's functionality.

Internet Expansion

The Internet was not designed to provide a mass-market interchange of high-density information. As a result, the massive growth of Internet traffic has strained some elements of the network. The strains manifest themselves as slowdowns in retrieval time, unreliable transmission of streamed data, and denial of service by overloaded servers.

A wide range of factors contributes to congestion or slowdowns. These problems include improperly configured networks, overloaded servers, rapidly changing Internet usage patterns, and too much traffic for available bandwidth. Approaches to solve these problems include installing high-speed transmission media to accommodate large amounts of data; bigger, faster routers and more sophisticated load balancing and management software to handle peak traffic periods; local caching (storing) of frequently requested Web pages to improve response times; and more reliable tiers of service for those willing to pay for them.

Internet Privacy

Web sites collect information with and without consumers' knowledge. One way to collect information at Web sites is through registration (as on such sites as Time Warner Inc.'s Pathfinder or Amazon.com). Visitors to the site enter data about themselves, and obviously know that such information is available for future use by the company that collects the data.

The most common way Web sites collect information, though, is through *clickstream data*—that is, information about where people go within a Web site and the content they see. Clickstream data are most commonly collected by cookies. A cookie is a small data file placed on users' hard drives when they first visit a site. This software can be used to exchange information automatically between a server and a browser without a user seeing what is being transmitted.

cookie *A small data file placed on users' hard drives when they first visit a Web site.*

Cookies are used to track users' actions and preferences. When a user goes back to a site, the site's computer server can read the usage data from the cookies. This background information can then be used to customize the Web content that is given to the user. That information is stored in a database and can be used to target ads or content, based on the preferences tracked. Some users object to the idea of having their online activities tracked by cookies. These users delete cookies from their computers or use anticookie software.

The Federal Trade Commission randomly checks Web sites to see if site operators are posting privacy notices that explain how personal information—such as e-mail addresses, shopping habits, and consumer financial data—is being used and whether it is being protected from unwarranted intrusion. Privacy on the Internet is at this point not a sure thing.

Before you go on . . .

1. What industries should pay close attention to efforts to regulate the Internet?
2. What might be some implications of "cookie" software? How could you or your firm be affected?

TG5.6 INTRANETS

intranet *A private network that uses Internet software and TCP/IP protocols.*

An intranet is a private network that uses Internet software and TCP/IP protocols. Companies increasingly are using intranets—powered by internal Web servers—to give their employees easy access to corporate information. Intranets also are an effective medium for application delivery.

The most common applications on corporate intranets are for human resources policies, procedures, and forms; document sharing; organizational telephone directories; training programs; search engines; customer databases; product catalogs and work manuals; groupware; organizational charts; organizational news and updates; crisis alerts (what IT systems are down and when they will be operational); and data warehouse and decision support access.

Security

public key security *Procedures used to protect intranets from outside intrusion.*

encryption *The process of scrambling outgoing data to make them indecipherable to outsiders.*

digital certificate *Electronic identification card that gives validate access to an intranet.*

With this number and variety of applications, intranet security is critically important. Companies can prevent unwanted intrusion into their intranets in several ways. Public key security is used to protect intranets from outside intrusion. It has two parts: encryption and certificate authorities. Encryption scrambles outgoing data in order to make them indecipherable to outsiders. Digital certificates are like electronic identification cards, which let an organization know that the person trying to access the intranet is a valid user. ValiCert is a leader in the certificate authority market with its database that checks whether a digital certificate it issued has expired. In addition,

ValiCert is the only company that is able to check the validity of any other vendor's certificate.

The industries in which public key security is starting to gain momentum all have external forces driving its adoption: financial securities, where regulations require encryption; legal, where the courts have said unencrypted e-mail is not covered by attorney-client privilege; and health care, where security of electronically transmitted medical records is paramount.

Another important way for companies to protect their intranets is with the use of firewalls. A **firewall** is a device located between a firm's internal network (e.g., its intranets) and external networks (e.g., the Internet). The firewall regulates access into and out of a company's network. Firewalls permit certain external services, such as Internet e-mail, to pass. Also, firewalls allow access to the Internet from internal networks. A firewall can allow access only from specific hosts and networks or to prevent access from specific hosts. Firewalls can also allow different levels of access for different hosts.

firewall *A device located between a firm's internal network and external networks (specifically, the Internet), to regulate access into and out of a company's network.*

For higher security, companies can implement assured pipelines. Whereas a firewall examines only the header information of a packet, an **assured pipeline** examines an entire request for data and then determines whether the request is valid.

assured pipeline *A security device that examines an entire request for data and then determines whether the request is valid.*

Before you go on . . .

1. What are common types of corporate information and services available on intranets?

2. What security techniques are used with intranets?

SUMMARY

1. **Describe what the Internet is, how it works (including the role of the TCP/IP protocol), and how users connect to it.** The Internet is a network of networks, which exchange information seamlessly by using open, nonproprietary standards and protocols. It is a collection of individual computer networks owned by governments, universities, organizations, and companies. The Internet is a packet-switched network that uses the Transmission Control Protocol/Internet Protocol (TCP/IP). Users can connect to the Internet via a LAN server, via SLIP/PPP, or through an Internet service provider.

2. **Describe the capabilities that the Internet offers to users.** The Internet provides a variety of services: discovery, communications, collaboration, Web services, and the World Wide Web. *Discovery services* involve browsing and information retrieval, and provide customers the ability to find, view, download, and process information. *Communications services* range from messages posted on electronic bulletin boards to e-mail to complex information exchanges among many organizations. *Collaboration services* among individuals, groups, and organizations are enabled by tools ranging from screen sharing and teleconferencing to group support systems. *Web Services* provide software applications over the Internet.

3. **Describe the World Wide Web and differentiate it from the Internet.** The Web is a system with universally accepted standards for storing, retrieving, formatting, and displaying information via a client/server architecture. The Internet functions as the transport mechanism, and the Web is an application that uses those transport functions. Other applications also run on the Internet, with e-mail being the most widely used.

4. **Identify and briefly describe the management challenges caused by the Internet.** Internet challenges include regulation, expansion, and privacy. The Internet Engineering Task Force and the World Wide Web Consortium have been instrumental in the development of the Internet, but are not formally charged in any legal or operational sense with responsibility for regulating the Internet. They do, however, define the standards that govern the Internet's functionality. The massive growth of Internet traffic has strained some elements of the network, manifested by slowdowns in retrieval time, unreliable transmission of streamed data, and denial of service by overloaded servers. Web-site registration and "cookie" technology have caused privacy concerns.

5. **Define the term intranet and discuss how intranets are used by businesses.** An intranet is a private network that uses Internet software and

TCP/IP protocols. Intranet applications include human resources policies and procedures, document sharing, telephone directories, training programs, search engines, customer databases, product catalogs and manuals, groupware, customer records, document routing, and data warehouse and decision support access. Public key security, firewalls, and assured pipelines are used to provide intranet security.

DISCUSSION QUESTIONS

1. Should the Internet be regulated? If so, by whom?
2. Is it possible to obtain too much information from the Internet? If so, how would you address this problem?
3. Does the use of cookie technology violate the user's right to privacy? Discuss.
4. Would it be possible to deliver this book over the Internet? Do you think it would be a good idea? Support your answers.
5. Access the Web site of your university. Does the Web site provide high-quality information (right amount, clear, accurate, etc.)? Do you think a high-school student who is thinking of attending your university would feel the same way?

INTERNET ACTIVITIES

1. Access the White House Web site (*whitehouse.gov*). Prepare a report on the most interesting content you find there.
2. Access the Web site of the Recording Industry Association of American (*riaa.com*). Discuss what you find there regarding copyright infringement (i.e., downloading music files). How do you feel about the RIAA's efforts to stop music downloads? Debate this issue from your point of view and from the RIAA's point of view.

TEAM ASSIGNMENTS

Find two companies on the Web that are in the same business. (For example: *edmunds.com* and *autobytel.com*, or *dell.com* and *gateway.com*.) Compare the Web sites of the pairs you have chosen on the basis of ease-of-use and usefulness. Pick the better Web site in each pair and explain your choice.

INTERNET AT CLUB IT

1. Lisa and Ruben want to create and register a domain name for the Club IT Web site. Make a list of the best names available (*clubit.com* is already reserved!), and tell them how to register one of them.
2. Assuming Club IT is located near your university, what are the Internet service options available to them? Which one would you choose, and why?

**Go to wiley.com/college/turban to access the
CLUB IT Web Site on the Student Web Site**

A Technical View of System Analysis and Design

Learning Objectives

1. Describe the hierarchy and steps of IT architecture.
2. Describe the SDLC and its advantages and limitations.
3. Describe the major alternative methods and tools for building information systems.
4. Describe the use of component-based development and Web services.

TG6.1 DEVELOPING AN IT ARCHITECTURE

An IT architecture is a conceptual framework for the organization of the IT infrastructure and applications. It is a plan for the structure and integration of IT resources and applications in the organization.

A Six-Step Process

Once the corporate strategy team or steering committee decides on potential applications, an architecture must be developed. Koontz (2000) suggested a six-step process for developing an IT architecture. These steps, described below, constitute a hierarchy of IT architecture.

> **Step 1: Business goals and vision.** This step, in which the system analyst reviews the relevant business goals and vision, was discussed in Section 11.2. This step is sometimes referred to as "business architecture."

> **Step 2: Information architecture.** In this step a company analyst defines the information necessary to fulfill the objectives of Step 1. Here, one should examine each objective and goal, identify the information currently available, and determine what new information is needed. All potential users need to be involved.

> **Step 3: Data architecture.** Once you know what information must be processed, you need to determine a *data architecture*—that is, exactly what data you have and what you want to get from customers, including Web-generated data. Of special interest is the investigation of all data that flows within the organization and to and from your business partners.
>
> The result of your investigation will probably show that data are everywhere, from data warehouses to mainframe files to Excel files on users' PCs. You need to conduct an analysis of the data, understanding its use, and examine the need for new data. This is when you need to think about how to process this data and what tools to use. If large amounts of data are used, tools such as Microsoft Transaction Server, Tuxedo, or CICS for mainframe data should be considered. Also, think about data mining and other tools. All this analysis needs to be done with an eye toward security and privacy.

> **Step 4: Application architecture.** At this point, you define the components or modules of the applications that will interface with the required data defined in Step 3. In this step you will build the conceptual framework of an application, but not the infrastructure that will support it. An example is shown in Figure TG 6.1.
>
> Many vendors, such as IBM, Oracle, and Microsoft, offer sophisticated IT application platforms that can significantly reduce the amount of code that programmers need to write. These application platforms also explain how the application should be structured. In this step, you can decide on a specific vendor-defined application architecture, such as Microsoft Distributed Network Architecture (DNA).

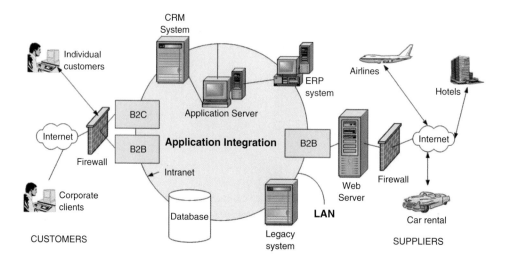

Figure TG6.1 *Architecture of an online travel agency.*

Other factors that must be considered are scalability, security, the number and size of servers, and the networks. The need to interface with legacy systems and with sales, ERP, accounting, and human resources data must be considered. In addition the ability to read real-time data is also important.

The major output of this step is to define the software components that meet the data requirements. For example, to deal with updated, real-time information, one may consider IBM's MQSeries or Microsoft MSMQ.

Step 5: Technical architecture. During the previous steps, designers informally considered the technical requirements. In this step, they must formally examine the specific hardware and software required to support the analysis in the previous steps. An inventory of the existing information resources is made, and an evaluation of the necessary upgrades and acquisitions is performed.

At this stage, designers must also examine the middleware needed for the application. EC applications require a considerable amount of transaction processing software. The more scalability and availability required, the more you need to invest in additional application servers and other hardware and software.

When selecting a programming language, designers may consider Java, Visual Basic, C11, CGI, and even COBOL, depending on the application. Also in this step, the operating systems, transaction processors, and networking devices required to support the applications must be decided upon. Obviously, you want to leverage your existing IT resources, but this may not be the optimal approach.

Step 6: Organizational architecture. An organizational architecture deals with the human resources and procedures required by Steps 1 through 5. At this point, the legal, administrative, and financial constraints should be examined. For example, a lack of certain IT skills on your team may require hiring or retraining. Partial outsourcing may be a useful way to deal with skill deficiencies.

In the worst-case scenario, you outsource the entire job, but you can give the architecture to the vendor as a starting point. Also, vendor selection can be improved if the architectures (business, information, data, application, and technical) are considered.

Conclusion

Creating IT architecture may be a lengthy process, but it is necessary to go through it. You may want to develop metrics to help you to track the effectiveness of your IT architecture, and you certainly need to document the process and output of each step.

Once the IT architecture has been decided upon, a development strategy can be formulated.

Before you go on . . .

1. List the steps in developing IT architecture.

2. Relate business goals to IT architectures.

3. It is said that the information infrastructure is determined by the technical architecture. Explain.

TG6.2 OVERVIEW OF THE TRADITIONAL SYSTEMS DEVELOPMENT LIFE CYCLE

The **systems development life cycle (SDLC)** is the traditional systems development method used by organizations for large IT projects such as IT infrastructure. The SDLC is a structured framework that consists of sequential processes by which information systems are developed. As shown in Figure TG6.2 (page 490), these processes include: investigation, analysis, design, programming, testing, implementation, operation, and maintenance. The processes, in turn, consist of well-defined tasks. Large projects

systems development life cycle (SDLC) *Traditional structured framework, used for large IT projects, that consists of sequential processes by which information systems are developed.*

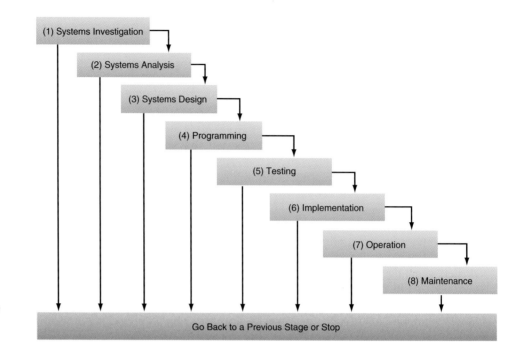

Figure TG6.2 *An eight-stage system development life cycle (SDLC).*

typically require all the tasks, whereas smaller development projects may require only a subset of the tasks.

Other models for the SDLC may contain more or fewer than the eight stages we present here. The flow of tasks, however, remains largely the same, regardless of the number of stages. In the past, developers used the **waterfall approach** to the SDLC, in which tasks in one stage were completed before the work proceeded to the next stage. Today, systems developers go back and forth among the stages as necessary.

Systems development projects produce desired results through team efforts. Development teams typically include users, systems analysts, programmers, and technical specialists. *Users* are employees from all functional areas and levels of the organization who will interact with the system, either directly or indirectly. **Systems analysts** are information systems professionals who specialize in analyzing and designing information systems. **Programmers** are information systems professionals who modify existing computer programs or write new computer programs to satisfy user requirements. **Technical specialists** are experts on a certain type of technology, such as databases or telecommunications. All people who are affected by changes in information systems (users and managers, for example) are known as **systems stakeholders**, and are typically involved by varying degrees and at various times in the systems development.

In the remainder of this section we will look at each of the processes (phases) in the eight-stage SDLC.

Systems Investigation

Systems development professionals agree that the more time invested in understanding the business problem to be solved, in understanding technical options for systems, and in understanding problems that are likely to occur during development, the greater the chance of successfully solving the problem. For these reasons, systems investigation begins with *the business problem* (or business opportunity).

Problems (and opportunities) often require not only understanding them from the internal point of view, but also seeing them as organizational partners (suppliers or customers) would see them. Another useful perspective is that of competitors. (How have they responded to similar situations, and what outcomes and additional opportunities have materialized?) Creativity and out-of-the-box thinking can pay big dividends when isolated problems can be recognized as systemic failures whose causes cross organizational boundaries. Once these perspectives can be gained, those in-

waterfall approach *SDLC approach in which tasks in one stage were completed before the work proceeded to the next stage.*

systems analysts *IS professionals who specialize in analyzing and designing information systems.*

programmers *IS professionals who modify existing computer programs or write new computer programs to satisfy user requirements.*

technical specialists *Experts on a certain type of technology, such as databases or telecommunications.*

systems stakeholders *All people who are affected by changes in information systems.*

volved can also begin to better see the true scope of the project and propose possible solutions. Then, an initial assessment of these proposed system solutions can begin.

Feasibility Studies.   The next task in the systems investigation stage is the feasibility study. The **feasibility study** determines the probability of success of the proposed project and provides a rough assessment of the project's technical, economic, organizational, and behavioral feasibility. The feasibility study is critically important to the systems development process because, done properly, the study can prevent organizations from making costly mistakes (like creating systems that will not work, will not work efficiently, or that people cannot or will not use). The various feasibility analyses also give the stakeholders an opportunity to decide what metrics to use to measure how a proposed system (and later, a completed system) meets their various objectives.

Technical Feasibility.   **Technical feasibility** determines if the hardware, software, and communications components can be developed and/or acquired to solve the business problem. Technical feasibility also determines if the organization's existing technology can be used to achieve the project's performance objectives.

Economic Feasibility.   **Economic feasibility** determines if the project is an acceptable financial risk and if the organization can afford the expense and time needed to complete the project. Economic feasibility addresses two primary questions: Do the benefits outweigh the costs of the project? Can the project be completed as scheduled?

Three commonly used methods to determine economic feasibility are return on investment (ROI), net present value (NPV), and breakeven analysis. The first two were discussed in Chapter 11: **Return on investment** is the ratio of the net income attributable to a project divided by the average assets invested in the project. The **net present value** is the net amount by which project benefits exceed project costs, after allowing for the cost of capital and the time value of money. **Breakeven analysis** determines the point at which the cumulative cash flow from a project equals the investment made in the project.

Determining economic feasibility in IT projects is rarely straightforward, but it often is essential. Part of the difficulty stems from the fact that benefits often are intangible (as discussed in Chapter 11). Another potential difficulty is that the proposed system or technology may be "cutting edge," and there may be no previous evidence of what sort of financial payback is to be expected. For an example of ROI analysis at Sears, see Online File W-TG6.1.

Organizational Feasibility.   Organizational feasibility has to do with an organization's ability to accept the proposed project. Sometimes, for example, organizations cannot accept a financially acceptable project due to legal or other constraints. In checking organizational feasibility, one should consider the organization's policies and politics, including impacts on power distribution, business relationships, and internal resources availability.

Behavioral Feasibility.   **Behavioral feasibility** addresses the human issues of the project. All systems development projects introduce change into the organization, and people generally fear change. Overt resistance from employees may take the form of sabotaging the new system (e.g., entering data incorrectly) or deriding the new system to anyone who will listen. Covert resistance typically occurs when employees simply do their jobs using their old methods.

A more positive and pragmatic concern of behavioral feasibility is assessing the skills and training needs that often accompany a new information system. In some organizations, a proposed system may require mathematical or linguistic skills beyond what the workforce currently possesses. In others, a workforce may simply need additional skill building rather than remedial education. Behavioral feasibility is as much about "can they use it" as it is about "will they use it."

After the feasibility analysis, a "Go/No-Go" decision is reached. The functional area manager for whom the system is to be developed and the project manager sign

feasibility study *Investigation that gauges the probability of success of a proposed project and provides a rough assessment of the project's feasibility.*

technical feasibility *Assessment of whether hardware, software, and communications components can be developed and/or acquired to solve a business problem.*

economic feasibility *Assessment of whether a project is an acceptable financial risk and if the organization can afford the expense and time needed to complete it.*

return on investment *The ratio of the net income attributable to a project divided by the average assets invested in the project.*

net present value *The net amount by which project benefits exceed project costs, after allowing for the cost of capital and the time value of money.*

breakeven analysis *Method that determines the point at which the cumulative cash flow from a project equals the investment made in the project.*

wiley.com/college/turban

behavioral feasibility *Assessment of the human issues involved in a proposed project, including resistance to change and skills and training needs.*

off on the decision. If the decision is "No-Go," the project is put on the shelf until conditions are more favorable, or the project is discarded. If the decision is "Go," then the systems development project proceeds and the systems analysis phase begins.

Systems Analysis

Once a development project has the necessary approvals from all participants, the systems analysis stage begins. *Systems analysis* is the examination of the business problem that the organization plans to solve with an information system. This stage defines the business problem, identifies its causes, specifies the solution, and identifies the information requirements that the solution must satisfy. Understanding the business problem requires understanding the various processes involved. These can often be quite complicated and interdependent. (Note that this stage is similar to Step 1 described in Section TG6.1. The difference is that the steps in that section could apply to any type of system acquisition; here, the process refers specifically to building applications.)

Organizations have three basic solutions to any business problem relating to an information system: (1) Do nothing and continue to use the existing system unchanged. (2) Modify or enhance the existing system. (3) Develop a new system. The main purpose of the systems analysis stage is to gather information about the existing system, in order to determine which of the three basic solutions to pursue and to determine the requirements for an enhanced or new system. The end product (the "deliverable") of this stage is a set of *information requirements*.

Arguably the most difficult task in systems analysis is to identify the specific information requirements that the system must satisfy. Information requirements outline what information, how much information, for whom, when, and in what format. Systems analysts use many different techniques to obtain the information requirements for the new system. These techniques include structured and unstructured interviews with users and direct observation. Structured interviews pose questions written in advance. In unstructured interviews, the analyst does not have predefined questions but uses experience to elicit the problems of the existing system from the user. With direct observation, analysts observe users interacting with the existing system.

In developing information requirements, analysts must be careful not to let any preconceived ideas they have interfere with their objectivity. Further, analysts must be unobtrusive, so that users will interact with the system as they normally would.

There are problems associated with eliciting information requirements, regardless of the method used by the analyst. First, the business problem may be poorly defined. Second, the users may not know exactly what the problem is, what they want, or what they need. Third, users may disagree with each other about business procedures or even about the business problem. Finally, the problem may not be information related, but may require other solutions, such as a change in management or additional training.

The systems analysis stage produces the following information: (1) Strengths and weaknesses of the existing system. (2) Functions that the new system must have to solve the business problem. (3) User information requirements for the new system. Armed with this information, systems developers can proceed to the systems design stage.

Systems Design

Systems analysis describes what a system must do to solve the business problem, and *systems design* describes *how* the system will accomplish this task. The deliverable of the systems design phase is the technical design that specifies the following:

- System outputs, inputs, and user interfaces
- Hardware, software, databases, telecommunications, personnel, and procedures
- How these components are integrated

This output represents the set of *system specifications*.

Systems design encompasses two major aspects of the new system: **Logical system design** states what the system will do, using abstract specifications. **Physical system design** states how the system will perform its functions, with actual physical specifications. Logical design specifications include the design of outputs, inputs, processing, databases, telecommunications, controls, security, and IS jobs. Physical design specifications include the design of hardware, software, database, telecommunications, and procedures. For example, the logical telecommunications design may call for a wide-area network connecting the company's plants. The physical telecommunications design will specify the types of communications hardware (e.g., computers and routers), software (e.g., the network operating system), media (e.g., fiber optics and satellite), and bandwidth (e.g., 100 Mbps).

When both these aspects of system specifications are approved by all participants, they are "frozen." That is, once the specifications are agreed upon, they should not be changed. However, users typically ask for added functionality in the system (called *scope creep*). This occurs for several reasons: First, as users more clearly understand how the system will work and what their information and processing needs are, they see additional functions that they would like the system to have. Also, as time passes after the design specifications are frozen, business conditions often change, and users ask for added functionality. Because scope creep is expensive, project managers place controls on changes requested by users. These controls help to prevent *runaway projects*—systems development projects that are so far over budget and past deadline that they must be abandoned, typically with large monetary loss.

logical system design *Abstract specification of what a computer system will do.*

physical system design *Actual physical specifications that state how a computer system will perform its functions.*

Programming

Systems developers utilize the design specifications to acquire the software needed for the system to meet its functional objectives and solve the business problem. As discussed in Chapter 11, organizations may buy the software or construct it in-house.

Although many organizations tend to purchase packaged software, many other firms continue to develop custom software in-house. For example, Wal-Mart and Eli Lilly build practically all their software in-house. The chief benefit of custom development is systems that are better suited than packaged applications to an organization's new and existing business processes. For many organizations, custom software is more expensive than packaged applications. However, if a package does not closely fit the company's needs, the savings are often diluted when the information systems staff or consultants must extend the functionality of the purchased packages.

If the organization decides to construct the software in-house, then programming begins. **Programming** involves the translation of the design specifications into computer code. This process can be lengthy and time-consuming, because writing computer code remains as much an art as a science. Large systems development projects can require hundreds of thousands of lines of computer code and hundreds of computer programmers. In such projects, programming teams are used. These teams often include functional area users to help the programmers focus on the business problem at hand.

programming *The translation of a system's design specifications into computer code.*

In an attempt to add rigor (and some uniformity) to the programming process, programmers use structured programming techniques. These techniques improve the logical flow of the program by decomposing the computer code into *modules*, which are sections of code (subsets of the entire program). This modular structure allows for more efficient and effective testing, because each module can be tested by itself. The structured programming techniques include the following restrictions:

- Each module has one, and only one, function.
- Each module has only one entrance and one exit. That is, the logic in the computer program enters a module in only one place and exits in only one place.
- GO TO statements are not allowed.

For example, a flowchart for a simple payroll application might look like the one shown in Figure TG6.3 (page 494). The figure shows the only three types of structures

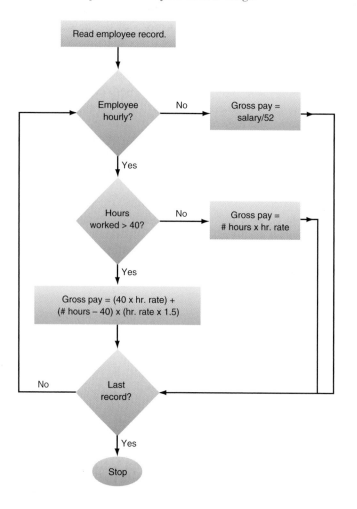

Figure TG6.3 *Flowchart diagram of a payroll application of structured programming.*

that are used in structured programming: sequence, decision, and loop. In the *sequence* structure, program statements are executed one after another until all the statements in the sequence have been executed. The *decision* structure allows the logic flow to branch, depending on certain conditions being met. The *loop* structure enables the software to execute the same program, or parts of a program, until certain conditions are met (e.g., until the end of the file is reached, or until all records have been processed).

As already noted, structured programming enforces some standards about how program code is written. This approach and some others were developed not only to improve programming, but also to standardize how a firm's various programmers do their work. This uniform approach helps ensure that all the code developed by different programmers will work together. Even with these advances, however, programming can be difficult to manage.

Testing

Thorough and continuous testing occurs throughout the programming stage. Testing checks to see if the computer code will produce the expected and desired results under certain conditions. Testing requires a large amount of time, effort, and expense to do properly. However, the costs of improper testing, which could possibly lead to a system that does not meet its objectives, are enormous.

Testing is designed to detect errors ("bugs") in the computer code. These errors are of two types: syntax errors and logic errors. *Syntax errors* (e.g., a misspelled word or a misplaced comma) are easier to find and will not permit the program to run. *Logic errors* permit the program to run but result in incorrect output. Logic errors are more difficult to detect, because the cause is not obvious. The programmer must follow the flow of logic in the program to determine the source of the error in the output.

As software increases in complexity, the number of errors increases, making it almost impossible to find them all. This situation has led to the idea of *"good-enough" software*, software that developers release knowing that errors remain in the code but believing that the software will still meet its functional objectives. That is, they have found all the "show-stopper" bugs, errors that will cause the system to shut down or will cause catastrophic loss of data.

Implementation

Implementation (or deployment) is the process of converting from the old system to the new system. Organizations use four major conversion strategies: parallel, direct, pilot, and phased.

In a **parallel conversion**, the old system and the new system operate simultaneously for a period of time. That is, both systems process the same data at the same time, and the outputs are compared. This type of conversion is the most expensive, but also the least risky. Most large systems have a parallel conversion process to lessen the risk.

In a **direct conversion**, the old system is cut off and the new system is turned on at a certain point in time. This type of conversion is the least expensive, but the most risky if the new system doesn't work as planned. Few systems are implemented using this type of conversion, due to the risk involved.

A **pilot conversion** introduces the new system in one part of the organization, such as in one plant or in one functional area. The new system runs for a period of time and is assessed. After the new system works properly, it is introduced in other parts of the organization.

A **phased conversion** introduces components of the new system, such as individual modules, in stages. Each module is assessed, and, when it works properly, other modules are introduced until the entire new system is operational.

implementation *(deployment) The process of converting from an old computer system to a new one.*

parallel conversion *Implementation process in which the old system and the new system operate simultaneously for a period of time.*

direct conversion *Implementation process in which the old system is cut off and the new system is turned on at a certain point in time.*

pilot conversion *Implementation process that introduces the new system in one part of the organization on a trial basis; when new system is working properly, it is introduced in other parts of the organization.*

phased conversion *Implementation process that introduces components of the new system in stages, until the entire new system is operational.*

Operation and Maintenance

After conversion, the new system will operate for a period of time, until (like the old system it replaced) it no longer meets its objectives. Once the new system's operations are stabilized, *audits* are performed during operation to assess the system's capabilities and determine if it is being used correctly.

Systems need several types of maintenance. The first type is *debugging* the program, a process that continues throughout the life of the system. The second type is *updating* the system to accommodate changes in business conditions. An example would be adjusting to new governmental regulations (such as tax rate changes). These corrections and upgrades usually do not add any new functionality; they are necessary simply in order for the system to continue meeting its objectives. The third type of maintenance *adds new functionality* to the system—adding new features to the existing system without disturbing its operation.

Before you go on . . .

1. What are the basic steps in the traditional systems development life cycle (SDLC)?
2. What is the purpose of structured programming?
3. What are the common strategies for implementing new systems?

TG6.3 ALTERNATIVE METHODS AND TOOLS FOR SYSTEMS DEVELOPMENT

Organizations use the traditional systems development life cycle because it has three major advantages: control, accountability, and error detection. An important issue in systems development is that the later in the development process that errors are detected, the more expensive they are to correct. The structured sequence of tasks and milestones in the SDLC thus makes error detection easier and saves money in the long run.

However, the SDLC does have disadvantages. By its structured nature, it is relatively inflexible. It is also time-consuming, expensive, and discourages changes to user requirements once they have been established. Development managers who must develop large, enterprisewide applications therefore find it useful to mix and match development methods and tools in order to reduce development time, complexity, and costs. These methods and tools include prototyping, rapid application development, component-based development, Web services, integrated computer-assisted software engineering (ICASE) tools, and object-oriented development. Although all these methods and tools can reduce development time, none can consistently deliver in all cases. They are perhaps best considered as options to complement or replace the SDLC or portions of it. This section discusses each of these methods and tools.

Prototyping

prototyping *Approach that defines an initial list of user requirements, builds a prototype system, and then improves the system in several iterations based on users' feedback.*

As described in Chapter 11, the **prototyping** approach defines an initial list of user requirements, builds a prototype system, and then improves the system in several iterations based on users' feedback. Developers do not try to obtain a complete set of user specifications for the system at the outset and do not plan to develop the system all at once. Instead, they quickly develop a prototype, which either contains parts of the new system of most interest to the users or is a small-scale working model of the entire system. Users make suggestions for improving the prototype, based on their experiences with it.

The developers then review the prototype with the users and use the suggestions to refine the prototype. This process continues through several iterations until either the users approve the system or it becomes apparent that the system cannot meet users' needs. If the system is viable, the developers can use the prototype on which to build the full system. Developing screens that a user will see and interact with is a typical use of prototyping. (See Online File W-TG6.2 for a model that shows the prototyping process.)

wiley.com/college/turban

The main advantage of prototyping is that it speeds up the development process. In addition, prototyping gives users the opportunity to clarify their information requirements as they review iterations of the new system. Prototyping is especially useful in the development of decision support systems and executive information systems, where user interaction is particularly important.

Prototyping also has disadvantages. Because it can largely replace the analysis and design stages of the SDLC in some projects, systems analysts may not produce adequate documentation for the programmers. This lack of documentation can lead to problems after the system becomes operational and needs maintenance. In addition, prototyping can result in an excess of iterations, which can consume the time that prototyping should be saving.

Joint Application Design

joint application design (JAD) *A group-based tool for collecting user requirements and creating system designs.*

Joint application design (JAD) is a group-based tool for collecting user requirements and creating system designs. JAD is most often used within the systems analysis and systems design stages of the SDLC.

In the traditional SDLC, systems analysts interview or directly observe potential users of the new information system *individually* to understand each user's needs. The analysts will obtain many similar requests from users, but also many conflicting requests. The analysts must then consolidate all requests and go back to the users to resolve the conflicts, a process that usually requires a great deal of time. In contrast, JAD has a *group meeting* in which all users meet simultaneously with analysts. It is basically a *group decision-making process* (Chapter 10) and can be computerized or done manually. During this meeting, all users jointly define and agree upon systems requirements. This process saves a tremendous amount of time.

The JAD approach to systems development has several advantages. First, the group process involves many users in the development process while still saving time. This involvement leads to greater support for the new system and can produce a system of higher quality. This involvement also may lead to easier implementation of the new system and lower training costs.

The JAD approach also has disadvantages. First, it is very difficult to get all users to the JAD meeting. For example, large organizations may have users literally all over the world. Second, the JAD approach has all the problems caused by any group process (e.g., one person can dominate the meeting, some participants may not contribute in a group setting). To alleviate these problems, JAD sessions usually have a facilitator, who is skilled in systems analysis and design as well as in managing group meetings and processes. Also, the use of groupware (such as GDSS) can help facilitate the meeting.

Rapid Application Development

Rapid application development (RAD) is a systems development method that can combine JAD, prototyping, and integrated CASE tools (described below) to rapidly produce a high-quality system. Initially, JAD sessions are used to collect system requirements, so that users are intensively involved early on. The development process in RAD is iterative, similar to prototyping, in which requirements, designs, and the system itself are developed with sequential refinements. However, RAD and prototyping use different tools. Prototyping typically uses specialized languages, such as fourth-generation languages (4GLs), Web-based development tools, and screen generators; RAD uses ICASE tools (discussed next) to quickly structure requirements and develop prototypes. As the prototypes are developed and refined, users review them in additional JAD sessions. RAD produces functional components of a final system, rather than limited-scale versions. For more details, see Figure TG6.4. The figure also compares RAD to SDLC.

rapid application development (RAD) *A development method that uses special tools and an iterative approach to rapidly produce a high-quality system.*

Rapid application development (RAD) methodologies and tools make it possible to develop systems faster, especially systems where the user interface is an important component. RAD can also improve the process of rewriting legacy applications. An example of how quickly experienced developers can create applications with RAD tools is provided in Online File W-TG6.3.

wiley.com/college/turban

Integrated Computer-Assisted Software Engineering Tools

Computer-aided software engineering (CASE) is a development approach that uses specialized tools to automate many of the tasks in the SDLC. The tools used to automate the early stages of the SDLC (systems investigation, analysis, and design)

computer-aided software engineering (CASE) *Development approach that uses specialized tools to automate many of the tasks in the SDLC; upper CASE tools automate the early stages of the SDLC, and lower CASE tools automate the later stages.*

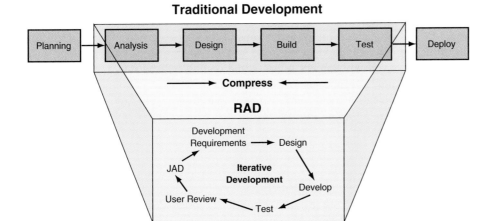

Figure TG6.4 *A rapid prototyping development process versus SDLC.*
[Source: datawarehouse-training.com/Methodologies/rapid-application-development.]

are called upper CASE tools. The tools used to automate later stages in the SDLC (programming, testing, operation, and maintenance) are called lower CASE tools. CASE tools that provide links between upper CASE and lower CASE tools are called integrated CASE (ICASE) tools.

CASE tools provide advantages for systems developers. These tools can produce systems with a longer effective operational life that more closely meet user requirements. CASE tools can speed up the development process and result in systems that are more flexible and adaptable to changing business conditions. Finally, systems produced using CASE tools typically have excellent documentation.

On the other hand, CASE tools can produce initial systems that are more expensive to build and maintain. CASE tools do require more extensive and accurate definition of user needs and requirements. Also, CASE tools are difficult to customize and may be difficult to use with existing systems.

integrated CASE (ICASE) tools
CASE tools that provide links between upper CASE and lower CASE tools.

Object-Oriented Development

object-oriented development *Begins with aspects of the real world that must be modeled to perform a task.*

Object-oriented development is based on a fundamentally different view of computer systems than that found in traditional SDLC development approaches. Traditional approaches provide specific step-by-step instructions in the form of computer programs, in which programmers must specify every procedural detail. These programs usually result in a system that performs the original task but may not be suited for handling other tasks, even when the other tasks involve the same real-world entities. For example, a billing system will handle billing but probably will not be adaptable to handle mailings for the marketing department or generate leads for the sales force, even though the billing, marketing, and sales functions all use similar data (e.g., customer names, addresses, and purchases). An object-oriented (OO) system, on the other hand, begins not with the task to be performed, but with the aspects of the real world that must be modeled to perform that task. Therefore, in the example above, if the firm has a good model of its customers and its interactions with them, this model can be used equally well for billings, mailings, and sales leads. For a list of other advantages of the object-oriented approach (and some disadvantages), see Online File W-TG6.4

wiley.com/college/turban

Object-Oriented Analysis and Design. The development process for an object-oriented system begins with a feasibility study and analysis of the existing system. Systems developers identify the *objects* in the new system—the fundamental elements in OO analysis and design. Each object represents a tangible real-world entity, such as a customer, bank account, student, or course. Objects have *properties*. For example, a customer has an identification number, name, address, account number(s), and so on. Objects also contain the *operations* that can be performed on their properties. For example, customer objects' operations may include obtain-account-balance, open-account, withdraw-funds, and so on.

Therefore, object-oriented analysts define all the relevant objects needed for the new system, including their properties (called *data values*) and their operations (called *behaviors*). They then model how the objects interact to meet the objectives of the new system. In some cases, analysts can reuse existing objects from other applications (or from a library of objects) in the new system, saving time spent coding. In most cases, however, even with object reuse, some coding will be necessary to customize the objects and their interactions for the new system.

Comparison of the various development methods, including those covered in Chapter 11, is given in Online File W-TG6.5.

wiley.com/college/turban

Other Methods

Several other system development methods exist, especially for e-business and Web-based applications. Most notable are component-based development and Web Service, the topics of our next section.

1. What are some common disadvantages of the SDLC approach?

2. What alternative methodologies does RAD typically encompass? What are the advantages of such an approach?

3. What are the advantages of CASE tools? The limitations?

4. How is object-oriented systems development fundamentally different from the SDLC approach?

TG6.4 COMPONENT-BASED DEVELOPMENT AND WEB SERVICES

Component-Based Development

Object-oriented development, discussed in Section TG6.3, has its downside: Business objects, though they represent things in the real world, can become unwieldy when they are combined and recombined in large-scale commercial applications. What is needed, instead, are *suites* of business objects that provide major chunks of application functionality (e.g., preprogrammed workflow, order placing) that can be "snapped together" to create complete business applications.

This approach is embodied in **component-based development (CBD)**, the upcoming evolutionary step beyond object-oriented development. CBD uses preprogrammed components to develop applications. *Components* are self-contained packages of functionalities that have clearly defined, programmed tasks with open interfaces that offer easy integration and fast development time. Components can be distributed dynamically for reuse across multiple applications and heterogeneous computing platforms. Components take the best features of objects to a higher level of abstraction. For description of the key characteristics of components, see Online File W-TG6.6.

Examples of components include user interface icons (small), word processing (a complete software product), a GUI, online ordering (a business component), and inventory reordering (a business component). Search engines, firewalls, Web servers, browsers, page displays, and telecommunication protocols are examples of intranet-based components.

Code reusability, which makes programming faster and more accurate, is the first of several reasons for using component-based development. Others include: support for heterogeneous computing infrastructure and platforms; rapid assembly of new business applications for quick time-to-market; and the ability of an application to scale. And because major software vendors are committed to component architecture, application builders can mix and match best-of-breed solutions. For a methodology of evaluating component-based systems see Dahanayake et al. (2003).

Component-Based Development of E-Commerce Applications. Plug-and-play business application components can be "glued together" rapidly to develop complex distributed applications, such as those needed for e-commerce. Component-based EC development is gaining momentum. It is supported by Microsoft and the Object Management Group (OMG), which have put in place many of the standards needed to make component-based development a reality. There are several methods that developers can use for integrating components (e.g., see Linthicum, 2001). A logical architecture for component-based development of e-commerce applications can be described in layers, as shown in Online File W-TG6.7.

The Role of Component-Based Approach in Software Reuse. The efficient development of software reuse has become a critical aspect in the overall IS strategies of many organizations. An increasing number of companies have reported reuse successes. The traditional reuse paradigm allows changes to the code that is to be reused ("white-box reuse"). Component-based software development advocates

component-based development (CBD) *A method that uses preprogrammed components to develop applications.*

wiley.com/college/turban

wiley.com/college/turban

that components are reused as is ("black-box reuse"). Taking the black-box reuse concept one step further is the idea of leveraging existing software using Web Services (our next topic). Both component-based development and Web Services are receiving growing interest among members of the IS community.

Web Services in System Development

As described in Technology Guide 5, the major application of Web Services is systems integration. Applications need to be integrated with databases and with other applications. Users need to interface with the data warehouse to conduct analysis, and almost any new system needs to be integrated with older ones. Finally, the increase of B2B and e-business activities requires the integration of application and databases of business partners (external integration). Because Web Services can contribute so much to systems integration, their use is growing rapidly.

Web Services *Self-contained, self-describing business and consumer modular applications, delivered over the Internet, that users can select and combine through almost any device.*

Basic Concepts. There are several definitions of Web Services. Here is a typical one: **Web Services** are self-contained, self-describing business and consumer modular applications, delivered over the Internet, that users can select and combine through almost any device (from personal computers to mobile phones). By using a set of shared protocols and standards, these applications permit different systems to "talk" with one another—that is, to share data and Services—without requiring human beings to translate the conversations.

Specifically, a Web Service fits the following three criteria: (1) It is able to expose and describe itself to other applications, allowing those applications to understand what the service does. (2) It can be located by other applications via an online directory, if the service has been registered in a proper directory. (3) It can be invoked by the originating application by using standard protocols.

Web Services have great potential because they can be used in a variety of environments (over the Internet, on an intranet inside a corporate firewall; on an extranet set up by business partners) and can be written using a wide variety of development tools. They can be made to perform a wide variety of tasks, from automating business processes, to integrating components of an enterprisewide system, to streamlining online buying and selling. Key to the promise of Web Services is that, in theory, they can be used by anyone, anywhere, any time, using any hardware and any software, as long as the modular software components of the services are built using a set of key protocols.

The Key Protocols. Web Services are based on a family of key protocols (standards). These protocols are the building blocks of the Web Services platforms. The major protocols are:

- ***XML.*** *Extensible Markup Language* (Chapters 2 and 9) makes it easier to exchange data among a variety of applications and to validate and interpret such data. An XML document describes a Web Service and includes information detailing exactly how the Web Service can be run.

- ***SOAP.*** *Simple Object Access Protocol* is a set of rules that facilitate XML exchange between network applications. SOAP defines a common standard that allows different Web Services to interoperate (i.e., it enables communications, such as allowing Visual Basic clients to access Java server). It is a platform-independent specification that defines how messages can be sent between two software systems through the use of XML. These messages typically follow a Request/Response pattern (computer-to-computer).

- ***WSDL.*** The *Web Services Description Language* is used to create the XML document that describes tasks performed by Web Services. It actually defines the programmatic interface of the Web Services. Tools such as VisualStudio.Net automate the process of accessing the WSDL, read it, and code the application to reference the specific Web Service.

- ***UDDI.*** *Universal Description, Discovery, and Integration* allows for the creation of public or private searchable directories of Web Services. It is the registry of Web Services descriptions.

- *Security protocols.* Several security standards are in development such as *Security Assertion Markup Language (SAML)*, which is a standard for authentication and authorization. Other security standards are XML signature, XML encryption, XKMS, and XACML.

See Cerami (2002) for a list of other protocols that are under development.

The Notion of Web Services as Components.

Traditionally, people view information systems, including the Web, as relating to information (data) processing. Web Services enable the Web to become a platform for applying business services as components in IT applications. For example, user authentication, currency conversion, and shipping arrangement are components of broad business processes or applications, such as e-commerce ordering or e-procurement systems. (For further discussion, see Stal, 2002.)

The idea of taking elementary services and gluing them together to create new applications is not new. As we saw earlier, this is the approach of component-based development. The problem is that earlier approaches were cumbersome and expensive. According to Tabor (2002) existing component-integration technologies exhibit problems with data format, data transmission, interoperability, inflexibility (they are platform specific), and security. Web Services offer a fresh approach to integration. Furthermore, business processes that are comprised of Web Services are much easier to adapt to changing customer needs and business climates than are "homegrown" or purchased applications (Seybold, 2002).

Manager's Checklist TG6.1 lists the advantages and some limitations of Web Services.

A Web Services Example.

As a simple example of how Web Services operate, consider an airline Web site that provides consumers with the opportunity to purchase tickets online. The airline recognizes that customers also might want to rent a car and reserve a hotel as part of their travel plans. The consumer would like the convenience of logging onto only one system rather than three, saving time and effort. Also, the same consumer would like to input personal information only once.

The airline does not have car rental or hotel reservation systems in place. Instead, the airline relies on car rental and hotel partners to provide Web Services access to their systems. The specific services the partners provide are defined by a series of WSDL documents. When a customer makes a reservation for a car or hotel on the airline's Web site, SOAP messages are sent back and forth in the background between the airline's and the partners' servers. In setting up their systems, there is no need for the partners to worry about the hardware or operating systems each is running. Web Services overcome the barriers imposed by these differences. An additional advantage for the hotel and car reservation systems is that their Web Services can be published in a UDDI so that other businesses can take advantage of their services.

Advantages	Disadvantages
❏ Greater interoperability and lower costs, due to universal, open, text-based standards.	❏ Standards still being defined.
❏ Enable software running on different platforms to communicate with each other.	❏ Require programming skill to implement.
❏ Promote modular programming and reuse of existing software.	❏ Security: Applications may be able to bypass security barriers.
❏ Operate on existing Internet infrastructure, so are easy and inexpensive to implement.	
❏ Can be implemented incrementally.	

MANAGER'S CHECKLIST TG6.1

Web Services Advantages and Limitations

Sources: Compiled from E. M. Dietel et al., *Web Services Technical Introduction* (Upper Saddle River, NJ: Prentice-Hall, 2003) and from C. Shirky, *Planning for Web Services* (Cambridge, MA: O'Reilly and Associates, 2002).

Before you go on . . .

1. Why has component-based development become so popular?
2. How does Web Services facilitate system development?

SUMMARY

1. **Describe the hierarchy and steps of IT architecture.** IT architecture is derived from the business goals and objectives that lead to information architecture and then to data (more detailed) architecture. Then comes the specific application architecture, which leads to the technical architecture and infrastructure. Finally, the organizational architecture is defined.

2. **Describe the systems development life cycle and its advantages and limitations.** The systems development life cycle is the traditional method used by most organizations today. The SDLC is a structured framework that consists of distinct sequential processes: systems investigation, systems analysis, systems design, programming, testing, implementation, operation, and maintenance. These processes, in turn, consist of well-defined tasks. Some of these tasks are present in most projects, while others are present in only certain types of projects. That is, smaller development projects may require only a sub-

set of tasks; large projects typically require all tasks. Using the SDLC guarantees quality and security, but it is slow and expensive.

3. **Describe the major alternative methods and tools for building information systems.** A common alternative for the SDLC is quick prototyping, which helps to test systems. Useful prototyping tools for SDLC are JAD (for finding information needs) and RAD (which uses CASE tools). For smaller and rapidly needed applications, designers can use object-oriented development tools, which are popular in Web-based applications.

4. **Describe the use of component-based development and Web Services.** Building computer systems from preprogrammed components saves time and money. Components are usually small application (e.g., an ordering system) that can be "glued" together in different ways. Similarly, using universal standards (protocols), Web Services can help connect different components or complete information systems.

DISCUSSION QUESTIONS

1. Why is it important for everyone in business organizations to have a basic understanding of the systems development process?
2. Should prototyping be used on every systems development project? Why or why not?
3. Discuss the various types of feasibility studies. Why are they all needed?

4. What are the characteristics of structured programming? Why is structured programming so important?
5. Discuss the logic of using components to build systems. What are some possible limitations?

INTERNET ACTIVITIES

1. Use an Internet search engine to obtain information on CASE and ICASE tools. Select several vendors and compare and contrast their offerings.

2. Use the Web to learn about analysis and design of intranets. What sort of sites have the most (and the most useful) information?

TEAM ASSIGNMENTS

As a group, design an information system for a startup business of your choice. Describe your chosen systems development methodologies, and justify your choices of hardware, software, telecommunications support, and other aspects of the proposed system.

PHOTO CREDITS

REFERENCES

CHAPTER 1

Caplan, J. "Applying a Little Business Intelligence." *CFO.com*, July 22, 2003.

Carr, N. G. (ed.). *The Digital Enterprise*. Boston: Harvard Business School Press, 2001.

Choi, S. Y., and A. B. Whinston. *The Internet Economy: Technology and Practice*. Austin, TX: SmartEcon Pub., 2000.

Cohen, A. "Fantasy Football: CBS SportsLine." *PC Magazine*, December 4, 2002.

Cohen, A. "Online Prescriptions." *PC Magazine*, August 19, 2003.

Gage, D., and J. McCormick. "Delta's Last Stand." *Baseline Magazine*, April 1, 2003.

Hafner, K. "A New Kind of Revolution in the Dorms of Dartmouth." *New York Times*, September 23, 2003.

Hamm, S. "Borders Are So 20th Century." *Business Week*, September 22, 2003.

Hammer, M., and J. Champy. *Reengineering the Corporation*. New York: Harper Business, 1993.

"IBM Brings Wi Fi to More Than 600 Boys & Girls Clubs." *ibm.com*, August 13, 2003.

Nash, K. S., and M. Duvall. "PepsiCo: No Deposit, No Return." *Baseline Magazine*, May 1, 2003.

"National Geographic Sells Its Stunning Images Using IBM Technology." *ibm.com*, August 15, 2003.

"New York City Transit Tokens May Take a Hike." Associated Press, January 27, 2003.

Porter, M. E. *Competitive Advantage: Creating and Sustaining Superior Performance*. New York: Free Press, 1985.

Porter, M. E. "Strategy and the Internet." *Harvard Business Review*, March 2001.

Salkever, A. "Soon, a PC May Be the Game's MVP." *Business Week*, May 1, 2003.

Schonfeld, E. "Next Stop: The 21st Century." *Business 2.0*, September 2003.

"Twins Crack Face Recognition Puzzle." *cnn.com*, August 11, 2003.

Williams, M. "Computer Trouble Grounds All Japan Flights." *Computerworld*, March 3, 2003.

Winkler, C. "Thrift Thrives on Low Tech." *Computerworld*, July 21, 2003.

CHAPTER 2

Bass, A. "Cigna's Self-Inflicted Wounds." *CIO Magazine*, March 15, 2003.

Buss, D. "Land O'Lakes Shares the Load." *CIO Insight*, May 9, 2003.

Carr, D. "Small Companies, Big Returns." *Baseline*, October 1, 2003.

Cohen, A. "Inside the Dark Age of Camelot." *PC Magazine*, July 1, 2003.

Cone, E. "Dallas Mavericks." *Baseline Magazine*, October 1, 2003.

Hoffman, T. "Speedy Cures." *Computerworld*, December 23, 2002.

Lundquist, E. "Wal-Mart Gets It Right." *eWeek*, July 14, 2003.

McCormick, J. "Worldspan: Up, Up, and Away." *Baseline*, May 1, 2003.

McDougall, P. "Guinness on Tap: Beer Maker Signs Utility Computing Deal." *Information Week*, August 22, 2003.

Melymuka, K. "Meeting of the Minds." *Computerworld*, July 28, 2003.

Metz, C. "Grid Computing: Case Study—Entelos." *PC Magazine*, January 1, 2003.

Murphy, C. "Market-Leading Wal-Mart Leads the Way with RFID." *InformationWeek.com*, June 11, 2003.

lesaunda.com.hk (last accessed October 24, 2003).

worldspan.com (last accessed September 22, 2003).

www-1.ibm.com/industries/financialservices/doc/content/casestudy/277262103.html (last accessed October 15, 2003).

CHAPTER 3

Amato-McCoy, D. "Victoria's Secret Works to Keep Orders Alive." *Stores*, January 2003.

Amato-McCoy, D. "Commerce Bank Manages Knowledge Profitably." *Bank Systems and Technology*, January 2003.

Apte, C., et al. "Business Application of Data Mining." *Communications of the ACM*, August 2002.

Berry, M. *Survey of Text Mining: Clustering, Classification and Retrieval*. Berlin: Springer-Verlag, 2002.

Buss, D. "Danskin Launches Virtual Showroom for Retail Clients." *Stores*, March 2003.

Edvinsson, L. "The Intellectual Capital of Nations." In *Handbook on Knowledge Management*, vol. 1 (ed. C. W. Holsapple). New York: Springer-Verlag, 2003, pp. 153–163.

Levinson, M. "Jackpot! Harrah's Entertainment." *CIO Magazine*, February 1, 2001.

Loveman, G. "Diamonds in the Data." *Harvard Business Review*, May 2003.

Mearian, L. "Breaking the Paper Habit." *Computerworld*, August 4, 2003.

O'Dell, C. S., et al. "Achieving Knowledge Management Outcomes." In *Handbook on Knowledge Management*, vol. 1 (ed. C. W. Holsapple). New York: Springer-Verlag, 2003, pp. 253–288.

Oguz, M. T. "Strategic Intelligence: Business Intelligence in Competitive Strategy." *DM Review*, May 31, 2003.

Park, Y. T. "Strategic Uses of Data Warehouses." *Journal of Data Warehousing*, April 1997.

Red Herring, March 2003.

Schlosser, J. "Looking for Intelligence in Ice Cream." *Fortune*, March 17, 2003.

Terry, K., and D. Kolb. "Integrated Vehicle Routing and Tracking Using GIS-Based Technology." *Logistics*, March/April, 2003.

Vasilash, G. S. "447,000 Heads Are Better Than One." *Automotive Design & Production*, June 2002.

Ziff-Davis Smart Business. "Inside Information." *Smartbusinessmag.com*, June 2002, pp. 46–54.

CHAPTER 4

Carr, D. "Pediatrix." *Baseline*, October 1, 2003.

Chen, D. "Leaping Forward Online, With Amazon as Her Guide." *New York Times*, October 25, 2003.

Choi, S. Y., and A. B. Whinston. *The Internet Economy: Technology and Practice*. Austin, TX: SmartEcon Publishing, 2000.

Elgin, B. "Web Searches: The Fix Is In." *Business Week*, October 6, 2003.

Green, H. "The Underground Internet." *Business Week*, September 15, 2003.

Grimes, B. "Microsoft .NET Case Study: Allstate Financial Group." *PC Magazine*, March 25, 2003.

McDonald, D. "A Website as Big (and Cheap) as the Great Outdoors." *Business 2.0*, October 2003.

Prince, M. "Easy Doesn't Do It." *Wall Street Journal*, July 17, 2002.

Rifkin, G. "GM's Internet Overhaul." *MIT Technology Review*, October 2002.

St. John, W. "Dating a Blogger, Reading All About It." *New York Times*, May 18, 2003.

Tedeschi, B. "A Fresh Spin on 'Affinity Portals' to the Internet." *New York Times*, April 17, 2000.

Urdan, T., and C. Weggen. "Corporate E-Learning: Exploring a New Frontier." W. R. Hambrecht & Co., March 2000, *http://www.e-learning.nl/publicaties/marktonderzoek/New_Frontier.pdf*.

CHAPTER 5

Athitakis, M. "How to Make Money on the Net." *Business 2.0*, May 2003.

Bayers, C. "The Last Laugh (of Amazon's CEO)." *Business 2.0*, September 2002.

Bayles, D. L. *E-Commerce Logistics and Fulfillment*. Upper Saddle River, NJ: Prentice Hall, 2001.

Chen, H. "Digital Government: Technologies and Practices." *Decision Support Systems* (special issue), February 2003.

Choi, S. Y., et al. *The Economics of Electronic Commerce*. Indianapolis, IN: Macmillan Technical Publications, 1997.

Daisey, M. *21 Dog Years: Doing Time @ amazon.com*. New York: Free Press, 2002.

Deitel, H. M., et al. *e-Business and e-Commerce for Managers*. Upper Saddle River, NJ: Prentice Hall, 2001.

Doll, M. W., et al. *Defending the Digital Frontier*. New York: Wiley, 2003. *eBay.com* (2002–2003).

Gallaugher, J. M. "E-Commerce and the Undulating Distribution Channel." *Communications of the ACM*, July 2002.

Kalakota, R., and A. B. Whinston. *Electronic Commerce: A Manager's Guide*. Reading, MA: Addison-Wesley, 1997, p. 12.

Kambil, A., and E. van Heck. *Making Markets*. Boston: Harvard Business School Press, 2002.

Kaplan, P. J. *F'd Companies: Spectacular Dot.com Flameouts*. New York: Simon & Schuster, 2002.

Kaplan, S., and M. Sawhney. "E-Hubs: The New B2B Marketplaces." *Harvard Business Review*, May 1, 2000.

Reda, S. "Online Check Service Expands Internet Payment Options." *Stores*, February 2002.

Segev, A., and J. Gebauer. "B2B Procurement and Marketplace Transformation." *Information Technology and Management*, July 2001.

Shelter, K. M., and J. D. Procaccino. "Smart Card Evaluation." *Communications of the ACM*, July 2002.

Stead, B. A., and J. Gilbert. "Ethical Issues in Electronic Commerce." *Journal of Business Ethics*, No. 34, 2001.

Strauss, J., et al. *E-Marketing*, 3rd ed. Upper Saddle River, NJ: Prentice Hall, 2003.

Turban, E., et al. *Electronic Commerce 2004*. Upper Saddle River, NJ: Prentice Hall, 2004.

Useem, J. "Dot-Coms: What Have We Learned?" *Fortune*, October 2000.

Wong, W. Y. *At the Dawn of E-Government*. New York: Deloitte Research, Deloitte & Touche, 2000.

Zwass, V. "Electronic Commerce: Structures and Issues." *International Journal of Electronic Commerce*, Fall 1996, p. 6.

CHAPTER 6

91expresslanes.com (accessed May 2002).

Bughin, J., et al. "Mobile Portals Mobilize for Scale." *McKinsey Quarterly*, April–June, 2001.

Chatterjee, A., et al. "A Road Map for Telematics." *McKinsey Quarterly*, April–June, 2002.

Coursaris, C., and H. Hassanein. "Understanding M-Commerce: A Consumer-Centric Model." *Quarterly Journal of Electronic Commerce*, July–September 2002.

cyberatlas.internet.com/markets/wireless/article/0,1323,10094_995801,00.html (accessed June 2003).

Davies, N., and H. W. Gellersen. "Beyond Prototyping: Challenges in Deploying Ubiquitous Systems." *Pervasive Computing*, January–March 2002.

Ecklund, R. "Mobile CRM Comes of Age." *CRM Magazine*, July 15, 2002, *destinationcrm.com/articles/default.asp?ArticleID=2352* (accessed June 2003).

Estrada, M. "Bridging the Wireless Gap." *Knowledgestorm: The Upshot*, October 2002, *knowledgstorm.com/info/user_newsletter/092402/wireless.jsp* (accessed June 2003).

Estrin, D., et al. "Embedding the Internet." *Communications of the ACM*, May 2000.

Hamblen, M. "Get Payback on Wireless." *Computer World*, January 1, 2001.

Henning, T. "Wireless Imaging." *The Future Image Report*, 2002.

Hornberger, M., and C. Kehlenbeck. "Mobile Financial Services on the Rise in Europe." September 19, 2002, *banktech.com/story/wireless/BNK20020919S0005* (accessed June 2003).

Hunter, R. *World without Secrets: Business, Crime, and Privacy in the Age of Ubiquitous Computing.* New York:Wiley, 2002.

Ishida, T. "Digital City Kyoto." *Communications of the ACM*, July 2002.

Islam, N., and M. Fayad. "Toward Ubiquitous Acceptance of Ubiquitous Computing." *Communications of the ACM*, February 2003.

Kontzer, T. "Top Ten Uses for SMS." *Information Week*, June 11, 2003.

Nelson, M. "Kemper Insurance Uses Wireless Digital Imaging to Lower Costs, Streamline Process." *Information Week*, September 25, 2000, *informationweek.com/805/photo/htm* (accessed June 2003).

Pitkow, J., et al. "Personalized Search." *Communications of the ACM*, September 2002.

Raskin, A. "Your Ad Could Be Here! (And Now We Can Tell You Who Will See It)." *Business 2.0*, May 2003.

Republica IT. "Busta Paga en Pensione Lo Stipendio Arriva via SMS." March 20, 2001, *republica.it/online/tecnologie_internet/tim/tim/tim.html* (accessed June 2003).

Sadeh, N. *M-Commerce.* New York: Wiley, 2002.

Sarkar, D. "Lawmakers Form 911 Caucus." *Federal Computer Week*, February 24, 2003, *fcw.com/fcw/articles/2003/0224/web-caucus-02–25–03.asp* (accessed July 2003).

Scanlon, J. "The Way We Work." Special Wired Report, Supplement to *Wired*, May 2003, *wired.com/wired/archive/11.05/unwired* (accessed June 2003).

Sharke, P. "Smart Cars." *Mechanical Engineering*, May 2003.

Stafford, A., and A. Brandt. "The No-Hassle Networking Guide." *PC World* (accessed May 2002).

Standford, J. "Using Technology to Empower Assisted Living Patients." *Healthcare Review*, July 2, 2000).

Weiser, M. "The Computer for the Twenty-First Century." *Pervasive Computing*, January–March 2002; originally published in *Scientific American*, September 1991.

Wired. "Get Wireless." Special Wired Report, Supplement to *Wired*, May 2003 (11 articles), *wired.com/wired/current.html* (accessed November 2003).

CHAPTER 7

Aberdeen.com. "Best Practices in Streamlining the Financial Value Chain: Top Seven FVCM Implementations," *Aberdeen Group*, 2002, *aberdeen.com/ab_company/hottopics/fvcm2002/default.htm* (accessed June 2003).

Baker, W., et al. "Price Smarter on the Net." *Harvard Business Review*, February 2001.

Bernstein, P.A., and Newcomer, E. *The Principles of Transaction Processing.* San Francisco: Morgan Kaufmann, 1997.

Degnan, C. "Best Practices in Expense Management Automation," Special Report. Boston: Aberdeen Group, January 2003, *aberdeen.com/ab_company/hottopics/emabp/default.htm* (accessed June 2003).

Ensher, E. A., et al. "Tales from the Hiring Line." *Organizational Dynamics*, October–December 2002.

Giesen, L. "Stein Mart Implements Check Consolidation and Electronic Re-presentment Service." *Stores.org*, January 2003, *solutran.com/news/SteinMart%20Implements%20RCC%20and%20RCK_Stores%20Jan2003.pdf* (accessed October 2003).

Gentile, G. "Audience Tracking Becomes High-Tech." *Los Angeles Times*, May 6, 2002.

Reda, S. "Word-of Mouth Marketing Enjoys New Life as Potent Online Advertising Strategy." *Stores*, October 2002.

Reed, C., et al. *e-CFO: Sustaining Value in New Corporations.* Chichester, UK: Wiley, 2001.

Sadeh, N. M., *M-Commerce: Technologies, Services, and Business Models.* New York: Wiley, 2002.

Strauss, J., et al. *E-Marketing*, 3rd ed. Upper Saddle River, NJ: Prentice Hall, 2003.

Subrahmanyam, A. "Nuts and Bolts of Transaction Processing: A Comprehensive Tutorial." *subrahmanyam.com. . . articles/ transactions/ NutsAndBoltsOfTP.html* (accessed March 2, 2002).

Surmacz, J. "Payback's a Cinch." *CIO.com*, February 12, 2003, *mcs.be/downloads/fm/payback%20is%20a%20cinch/contractmgt. htm* (accessed October 2003).

Sweeney, T. "Web Kiosks Spur Spending in Stores." *InformationWeek.com*, March 12, 2001, *informationweek.com/828/ kiosk.htm* (accessed June 2003).

Wind, Y. "The Challenge of Customization in Financial Services." *Communications of the ACM*, July 2001.

CHAPTER 8

Davenport, T. H. *Mission Critical: Realizing the Promise of Enterprise Systems.* Cambridge, MA: Harvard Business School Press, 2000.

DeFazio, D. "The Right CRM for the Job." *Technologydecisions. com*, November 2000.

Donovan, R. M. "Supply Chain Management: Cracking the Bullwhip Effect." *Material Handling Management*, Director Issue, 2002/2003.

Greenberg, P. *CRM at the Speed of Light: Capturing and Keeping Customers in Internet Real Time*, 2d ed. New York: McGraw-Hill, 2002.

Hagel, J., III. *Out of the Box.* Boston: Harvard Business School Press, 2002.

Lucas, M. E., and R. Bishop. *ERP for Dummies.* Greensboro, NC: Resource Publication, October 2002.

"Nice Guys Finish First—Customer Relationship Management." *Darwin Magazine,* October 2000.

Palaniswamy, R., and T. G. Frank. "Enhancing Manufacturing Performance with ERP Systems: Five Case Studies." *Information System Management*, summer 2000.

Patricia Seybold Group. *An Executive's Guide to CRM.* Boston, MA: Patricia Seybold Group, 2002, *psgroup.com/ freereport/imedia/resport/asp* (accessed April 15, 2003).

Poirier, C. C., and M. J. Bauer. *E-Supply Chain: Using the Internet to Revolutionize Your Business.* San-Francisco, CA: Berrett-Koehler, 2000.

Ragowsky, A., and T. M. Somers (eds.). "Enterprise Resource Planning," special issue. *Journal of Management Information Systems*, summer 2002.

Reid, D., and N. R. Sanders. *Operations Management.* New York: Wiley, 2002.

Romano, N. C., Jr., and J. Fjermestad (eds.). "Introduction to the Special Section: Electronic Commerce Customer Relationship Management (ECCRM)." *International Journal of Electronic Commerce*, winter 2001/2002.

Sandoe, K., et al. *Enterprise Integration.* New York: Wiley, 2001.

Sheikh, K. *Manufacturing Resource Planning (MRP II).* Boston, MA: McGraw-Hill, 2002.

Simatupang, T. M., and R. Sridharan. "The Collaborative Supply Chain." *International Journal of Logistics Management*, vol. 13, no.1, 2002.

Sullivan, M., et al., "Case Studies: Digital Do-Overs." *Forbes.com*, October 7, 2002.

Turban, E., et al. *Electronic Commerce 2004.* Upper Saddle River, NJ: Prentice-Hall, 2004.

Vakharia, J. (ed.). "E-business and Supply Chain Management," special issue. *Decision Sciences*, fall 2002.

Worthen, B. "Drilling for Every Drop of Value." *CIO Management*, June 1, 2002.

Yao, D. D., et al. "Extended Enterprise Supply-Chain Management at IBM." *Interfaces*, January–February 2000.

CHAPTER 9

Aberdeen Group Inc. "Asite Builds E-Marketplace Using Combined Strength of Commerce One, Microsoft, and Attenda." *Aberdeen Group Profile*, 2001.

asite.com (2002).

Boucher-Ferguson, R. "A New Shipping Rout (Web-EDI)." *eWeek*, September 23, 2002.

Business Wire (2003).

Coupey, P. *Marketing and the Internet.* Upper Saddle River, NJ: Prentice-Hall, 2001.

Dell.com. Press releases (2000–2003).

Grimes, B. "Microsoft.NET Case Study: Allstate Financial Group." *PC Magazine*, March 25, 2003.

Hagel, J., III. *Out of the Box.* Boston: Harvard Business School Press, 2002.

Handfield, R. B., and E. L. Nichols, Jr. *Introduction to Supply Chain Management.* Upper Saddle River, NJ: Prentice-Hall, 1999.

Handfield, R. B., et al. *Supply Chain Redesign: Transforming Supply Chains into Integrated Value Systems.* Upper Saddle River, NJ: Financial Times/ Prentice-Hall, 2002.

Harrison, T. P. "Global Supply Chain Design." *Information Systems Frontiers*, October–December 2001.

Heizer, L., and B. Render. *Principles of Operations Management*, 5th ed. Upper Saddle River, NJ: Prentice-Hall, 2003.

Linthicum, D. *B2B Application Integration: E-Business-Enable Your Enterprise.* Boston, MA: Addison-Wesley, 2000.

McCreary, L. "Toshiba America Information Systems Inc." *CIO Web Business*, July 1999.

Raisinghani, M. (ed.). *Cases on Worldwide E-Commerce.* Hershey, PA: The Idea Group, 2002.

Schecterle, B. "Managing and Extending Supplier Relationships." *People Talk*, April–June 2003, *peoplesoft.com.au/corp/ en/peopletalkonline/april_2003/sidebar2.jsp* (accessed June 2003).

Turban, E., et al. *Electronic Commerce 2004.* Upper Saddle River, NJ: Prentice-Hall, 2004.

CHAPTER 10

Amato-McCoy, D. M. "Speech Recognition System Picks Up the Pace in Kwik Trip DC." *Stores*, May 2003.

Ante, S. "Owens & Minor." *BusinessWeek*, November 24, 2003.

Barrett, L., and S. Gallagher. "New Balance: Shoe Fits." *Baseline Magazine*, November 1, 2003.

Bates, J. "Business in Real Time—Realizing the Vision." *DM Review*, May 2003.

Choy, J. "Growing Interest in Business Performance Management." *Asia Computer Weekly Singapore*, April 28, 2003.

DeSanctis, G., and B. Gallupe. "A Foundation for the Study of Group Decision Support Systems." *Management Science*, vol. 33, no. 5, 1987.

Dignan, L. "Lowe's Big Plan." *Baseline Magazine*, June 16, 2003.

Edwards, C. "Charles Schwab." *BusinessWeek*, November 24, 2003.

Gorry, G. A., and M. S. Scott-Morton. "A Framework for Management Information Systems." *Sloan Management Review*, vol. 13, no. 1, Fall 1971.

Green, H. "Northern Group Retail." *BusinessWeek*, November 24, 2003.

Hackathorn, R. D., and P. G. W. Keen. "Organizational Strategies for Personal Computing in Decision Support Systems." *MIS Quarterly*, September 1981.

Haddad, C. "UPS." *BusinessWeek*, November 24, 2003.

Hovanesian, M. D. "Wells Fargo." *BusinessWeek*, November 24, 2003.

Kahn, J. "It's Alive." *Wired*, March 2002.

Kumagai, J. "Talk to the Machine." *IEEE Spectrum*, September 2002.

Mintzberg, H. *The Nature of Managerial Work*. New York: Harper & Row, 1973.

Pastore, R. "Cruise Control." *CIO Magazine*, February 1, 2003.

Simon, H. *The New Science of Management Decisions*, rev. ed. Englewood Cliffs, NJ: Prentice-Hall, 1977.

Sorenson, D. "Emerging Technology Innovation and Products in the Vanguard." *CIO Magazine*, February 2003.

CHAPTER 11

Benaroch, M. "Managing Information Technology Investment Risk: A Real Options Perspective. *Journal of MIS*, vol. 19, no. 2, fall 2002.

Broadbent, M., and Weill, P. "Management by Maxim: How Business and IT Managers Can Create IT Infrastructures." *Sloan Management Review*, spring 1997.

Database. "5-Minute Briefing: Data Integration." *Database: Trends and Application*, dbta.com/5_minute_briefing/3–10–03. html (accessed December 2003).

Devaraj, S., and Kohli, R. *The IT Payoff: Measuring Business Value of Information Technology Investments*. Upper Saddle River, NJ: Financial Times Prentice-Hall, 2002.

El Sawy, O. *The BPR Workbook*. New York: McGraw-Hill, 1999.

Gerlach, R., et al. "Determining the Cost of IT Services." *Communications of the ACM*, vol. 45, no. 9, September 2002.

Gunasekaran, A., et al. "A Model for Investment Justification in Information Technology Products." *International Journal of Information Management*, March 2001.

Kaplan, R. S., and D. P. Norton. *The Balanced Scorecard: Translating Strategy into Action*. Boston: Harvard Business School Press, 1996.

Kendall, K. E., and J. E. Kendall. *Systems Analysis and Design*, 5th ed. Upper Saddle River, NJ: Prentice-Hall, 2002.

Kern, T., and T. Kreijger. "An Exploration of Application Service Provision Outsourcing Option." *Proceedings of 34th HICSS*, Maui, January 2001.

Martin, E. W., et al. *Managing Information Technology*. Upper Saddle River, NJ: Prentice-Hall, 2000.

Overby, S. "Bringing I.T. Back Home," *CIO Magazine*, March 1, 2003, cio.com/archive/030103/home.html (accessed January 2004).

Sachdeva S. "Outsourcing Strategy Helps Ansett Australia Streamline Its Business." *IBM Success Story*, 2000, ibm.com/ services/successes/ansett.html (accessed January 2004).

Sarkis, J., and R. P. Sundarraj. "Evaluating Componentized Enterprise Information Technologies: A Multiattribute Modeling Approach." *Information Systems Frontiers*, vol. 5, no. 3, 2003.

Sterlicchi, J., and E. Wales. "Custom Chaos: How Nike Just Did It Wrong." *Business Online* (*BolWeb.com*), June 2001.

Ward, J., and J. Peppard. *Strategic Planning for Information Systems, 3/e*. New York: Wiley, 2002.

Whitten, J., et al. *Systems Analysis and Design Methods*, 6th ed. New York: Irwin/McGraw-Hill, 2003.

CHAPTER 12

Associated Press. "Makers of Kazaa Are Suing Record Labels." *eWeek*, September 24, 2003.

Associated Press. "Reborn Napster Unveils Test Version." *msnbc.com*, October 9, 2003.

Black, J. "The High Price of Spam." *BusinessWeek Online*, March 1, 2002.

Boonnoon, J. "Phone Technology Is Boon for the Visually Impaired." *The Nation* (Thailand), March 28, 2000.

Broad, W. "Salvagers Say a Shipwreck Trove Is Worth Millions." *New York Times*, November 30, 2003.

Bruno, L. "Out, Out Damned Hacker!" *Red Herring*, January 2002.

"Bugbear Worm Steals Credit Card and Password Details." *Information Management and Computer Security*, June 2003.

Burrows, P. "Napster Lives Again—Sort Of." *Business Week*, October 20, 2003.

Davidson, P. "29 Nations Team Up vs. Cross-border Scams." *USA Today* (International issue), June 17, 2003.

Greene, J. "Music Magic." *Business Week*, November 10, 2003.

Hellweg, E. "The Skype Is Calling." *MIT Technology Review*, November 19, 2003.

Kushner, D. "Digital Entertainment Post-Napster." *MIT Technology Review*, November 2002.

Lee, J. "Web Firms Strive to Get Around Governments' Internet Bans." *Herald International Tribune*, April 27, 2001.

Lee, M. K. O. "Internet Retailing in Hong Kong, China." *Electronic Commerce B2C Strategies and Models*. Singapore: Wiley, 2002.

Levin, C. "The Insurance Plan That Came to the Rescue." *PC Magazine*, January 29, 2002.

Loundy, D. L. *Computer Crime, Information Warfare, and Economic Espionage*. Durham, NC: Carolina Academic Press, 2003.

Lubbe, S., and J. M. Van Heerden (eds.). *The Economic and Social Impacts of E-Commerce*. Hershey, PA: The Idea Group, 2003.

Lubell, S. "Campuses Move to Block Music Sharing." *New York Times*, October 2, 2003.

Metz, C. "The Changing Face of Online Music." *PC Magazine*, September 24, 2003.

Olsen, S. "Charter Files Suit Against RIAA." *msnbc.com*, October 6, 2003.

Phillips, D. "JetBlue Apologizes for Use of Passenger Records." *Washington Post*, September 20, 2003.

Richardson, R. *2003 CSI/FBI Computer Crime and Security Survey*. San Francisco: Computer Security Institute (*gocsi.com*), 2003.

Scalet, S. D. "Saving Money, Saving Lives." *CIO Magazine*, August 1, 2003.

Scheeres, J. "Tracking Junior with a Microchip." *Wired*, October 10, 2003.

Schwartz, J. "Music's Struggle with Technology." *New York Times*, September 22, 2003.

Shenk, D. "Watching You." *National Geographic*, November 2003.

Spaulding, M. "The ABC's of MP3: A Crash Course in the Digital Music Phenomenon." In *Signal or Noise? The Future of Music on the Net*. Berkman Center for Internet & Society at Harvard Law School and the Electronic Frontier Foundation, August 23, 2000, *cyber.law.harvard.edu/events/netmusic_brbook.html#_Toc475699191* (accessed May 2003).

Stanford, D., and J. Ledford. "2 More States Back Off Matrix." *Atlanta Journal-Constitution*, October 17, 2003.

Sullivan, A. "U.S. Arrests 135 in Nationwide Cybercrime Sweep." *Yahoo!News*, provided by Reuters, May 16, 2003.

Verton, E., and J. Brownlow. *Black Ice: The Invisible Threat of Cyberterrorism*. New York: McGraw-Hill, 2003.

Walsh, N. P. "Stolen Details of 6 Million Phone Users Hawked on Moscow Streets." *The Guardian*, January 27, 2003.

Zetter, K. "BlackBerry Reveals Bank's Secrets." *Wired*, August 25, 2003.

Zetter, K., and S. Miastkowski. "Viruses: The Next Generation." *PC World*, December 2000.

TECHNOLOGY GUIDE 6

Cerami, E. *Web Services Essentials*. Cambridge, MA: O'Reilly and Associates, 2002.

Dahanayake, A., et al. "Methodology Evaluation Framework for Component-Based System Development." *Journal of Database Management*, March 2003.

Dietel, E. M., et al. *Web Services Technical Introduction*. Upper Saddle River, NJ: Prentice-Hall, 2003.

Koontz, C. "Develop a Solid E-Commerce Architecture." *e-Business Advisor*, January 2000.

Linthicum, D. S. *B2B Application Integration: e-Business-Enable Your Enterprise*. Boston: Addison Wesley, 2001.

Seybold, P. *An Executive Guide to Web Services*. Boston, MA: Patricia Seybold Group (*psgroup.com*), 2002.

Shirky, C. *Planning for Web Services*. Cambridge, MA: O'Reilly and Associates, 2002.

Stal, M. "Web Services: Beyond Component-Based Computing." *Communications of the ACM*, October 2002.

Tabor R. *Microsoft.Net XML Web Services*. Indianapolis, IN: SAMS, 2002.